THE
TORONTO MAPLE LEAF
HOCKEY CLUB

THE
TORONTO MAPLE LEAF HOCKEY CLUB
OFFICIAL CENTENNIAL PUBLICATION

KEVIN SHEA
AND JASON WILSON

McClelland & Stewart

CONTENTS

John Tory

Mayor

I never knew my great-grandfather with whom I share a name, but I do know he was a lucky man! He was on the board of Maple Leaf Gardens when it opened in November 1931. He must have been a loyal fan, but no more so than his great-grandson.

Whether it was trying to get the Frank Mahovlich hockey coin from the Jell-O box or hiding the transistor radio under my pillow to listen to Foster Hewitt call a Sunday night away game, the Leafs were part of my growing up as they have been for boys and girls of all ages for 100 years.

They are our pride and our joy. They inspire, and yes, sometimes disappoint. But they are ours, and we are theirs—loyal, passionate fans who love hockey, who love the Leafs, and who are lucky enough to live in the hockey capital of the world.

Happy 100th anniversary, Toronto Maple Leafs. You are a huge part of a globally admired city, and on behalf of the people of Toronto, I wish you every success in your second century.

Toronto Mayor John Tory

TORONTO MAPLE LEAF HOCKEY CLUB

Growing up in Toronto, you inherit a love for the Toronto Maple Leafs and an obsession with the game of hockey. Watching *Hockey Night in Canada* every Saturday night, and your heroes in blue and white, was not only an important family tradition, it made you feel like you lived in the centre of the hockey universe.

No matter where I have gone in my National Hockey League career, my earliest memories of the game, and my connection to it, began with the Toronto Maple Leafs. I always knew that I was just one of millions of fans around the world who cheered for this team, and the opportunity to join the team as president was beyond a dream come true.

A centennial anniversary for any organization is a monumental milestone. For the Toronto Maple Leaf Hockey Club, its alumni, its legion of fans, and the city of Toronto, the team's centennial marks so much more than just memories of the great wins and 13 Stanley Cup championships over those years. It is a tribute to the great men who have worn the iconic Maple Leaf on their chest. Whoever your Leafs hockey heroes were, now is a time to remember your first time walking into Maple Leaf Gardens, or shaking the hand of your favourite player. Most important, it is a year to celebrate the truly special connection that the Maple Leafs have with their fans, Leafs Nation.

My goal, as I came to lead the hockey team I grew up idolizing, was to restore the pride in the Maple Leaf and for all of Leafs Nation—the organization, its fans, our city, and the players—to write a memorable new chapter in this team's history.

In 1927, Conn Smythe spoke about what the Maple Leaf meant when he renamed the team formerly known as the St. Pats:

> The Maple Leaf, to us, was the badge of courage, the badge that meant home. It was the badge that reminded us all of our exploits and the different difficulties we got into and the different accomplishments we made. It was a badge that meant more to us than any other badge we could think of . . . so we chose it . . . hoping that the possession of this badge would mean something to the team that wore it and when they skated out on the ice with this badge on their chest . . . they would wear it with honour and pride and courage, the way it had been worn by the soldiers of the first Great War, in the Canadian Army.

Honour, pride, and courage. That is what the Maple Leaf on the team's sweater has meant for so many years, and that is what we strive every day to continue to represent.

Enjoy this book commemorating 100 years of your favourite sports team, and mine. Thank you for wearing the Maple Leaf sweater proudly and for being an important part of Leafs Nation. We look forward to writing the next great chapter in Maple Leaf history together.

Yours truly,

Brendan Shanahan
PRESIDENT AND ALTERNATE GOVERNOR
TORONTO MAPLE LEAF HOCKEY CLUB

DEFEAT DID NOT REST LIGHTLY
ON THEIR SHOULDERS!

MAJOR CONN SMYTHE
FOUNDER TORONTO MAPLE LEAFS

INTRODUCTION
OUR STORY, YOUR STORY

Our story is about a professional hockey team. It is a story that will review those watershed moments in the history of the franchise: the big goals, the star players, the curious characters, those painfully low ebbs, those extraordinary highs, the Stanley Cup victories and the joyful parades that followed. Yet, it isn't just about *what*, it is about *where*. Our story is every bit about Mutual, Carlton, and Bay Streets, and the avenues, neighbourhoods, and communities that surround them, as it is about what happened on the ice.

It is more, still. Sometimes our story is about those spaces where we faithfully re-enact "the game" – perhaps on a Cabbagetown cul-de-sac, or maybe on an outdoor rink in Downsview, or perhaps farther afield on an icy prairie pond or the frozen inlet of a Maritime village. Then again, sometimes our story is about a place that lives only in our minds, where fanciful dreams of hockey past and future are dreamt. This particular "place" belongs to children – of every age – who count themselves among that passionate collective known as Leafs Nation. Our story is about the people who live on these streets, who skate on these ponds, who dream in royal blue and winter white, and who live and die with this blessed team. Our story, then, is your story.

. . .

The first chapter of our story was bound *to* and *by* a place known as the city of Toronto. When it first began play in 1917, the Toronto Hockey Club scarcely caught the attention of sporting enthusiasts within the city's core. Interest, however, soon grew, especially after the team claimed the Stanley Cup during its very first season and changed its name to the Arenas. In the years following the First World War, the franchise, now called the St. Patricks, had built on its base of fans and tried to engage the city's significant Irish population. Despite a Stanley Cup championship in 1922, the results were mixed.

When Conn Smythe took over management of the team and changed its name to the Maple Leafs, however, interest in the franchise grew exponentially. Soon, Smythe's team lined up with the sentiments and tastes of the majority of Toronto's populace. It was a brand that honoured the city's British roots, Protestant ideals, and military past. As such, the Maple Leafs had established a "place" – actual and abstract – in the hearts and imagination of the citizenry. This place made room for the King, for God, and, perhaps most importantly, for the mothers, fathers, wives, sons, and daughters of the thousands of Torontonians who had perished during the First World War. With the Leafs, the city's glory and grief had been united and adorned with a blue and white robe.

Technology would transmit the Maple Leafs' deep allegory well past the Queen City's limits. Radio allowed Foster Hewitt's voice to carry Maple Leafs broadcasts across the nation and into the living rooms of Canadians during the Great Depression and yet another miserable world war. The Maple Leaf message – once bound by the rivers Don and Humber – now heartened millions of souls living between the Atlantic and Pacific Oceans during the country's darkest hours.

Television would pick up this message and likewise manufacture generations of supporters in the process of broadcasting the franchise's most glorious era. Increasingly, the bulk of Leafs Nation lived outside of Toronto. Maritime fishers, B.C. loggers, prairie farmers, and miners toiling in Canada's north were now earnestly calling the Maple Leafs *their* team.

In the relatively recent past, support for the Maple Leafs has managed to transcend Canada's borders. Newer technology, emigration, an influx of foreign players and an overwhelming rise in the global interest in hockey have all helped to make Leafs Nation a truly worldwide community. Leafs fans can be spotted in thousands of other places. It seems that in the 21st century, this nation of ours has no borders.

Top:
In 1955, the first seven players to serve as captain of the Toronto Maple Leafs met to pose with a picture with their "boss" in front of Maple Leaf Gardens. Left to right: Hap Day (1927–37), Charlie Conacher (1937–38), Red Horner (1938–40), team president Conn Smythe, Syl Apps (1940–43; 1945–48), Bob Davidson (1943–45), Ted Kennedy (1948–55; 1957), and Sid Smith (1955–56).

Bottom:
In 2005, nine of the men who wore the C on their blue and white sweater gathered to trade stories. Left to right: Ted Kennedy (1948–55; 1957), George Armstrong (1958–69), Dave Keon (1969–75), Darryl Sittler (1975–79; 1980–82), Rick Vaive (1982–86), Rob Ramage (1989–91), Wendel Clark (1991–94), Doug Gilmour (1994–97), and Mats Sundin (1997–2008).

This is important when we consider what "place" really means and how it works. On February 7, 1976, for example, Darryl Sittler managed a record-setting ten points in a single game against the Bruins in Maple Leaf Gardens. That's *what* happened. But *where* it happened is just as important to the story: the sounds, the sights, and even the smells can all figure into our memories of an event. And *where* isn't necessarily just one place.

You might have actually been at that famous game. Maybe you were way up in the greys. You will no doubt remember the palpable buzz when everyone in the building began to realize that Darryl was on to something special. Or maybe you were watching the game on that old, enormous, and temperamental black-and-white television you had when you used to live on such-and-such a street. Or perhaps you were driving down a lonely southwestern Ontario road, fist-pumping, to no one in particular, every time you heard Sittler figure in the scoring on the radio. Or maybe you were a Canadian signaller, serving with the Second United Nations Emergency Force in the Sinai Peninsula, who only got to read about Sittler's feat in a week-old newspaper during your break from keeping the peace. You may remember the general gist of the event, but you will always remember exactly where you were when it happened.

In years to come, there will be someone, perhaps not yet born, who will recall his or her first game at Air Canada Centre. While, in time, they may not be able to tell you what the final score was, or who was in net for the visiting team, or who the three stars were, they will almost always be able to tell you how excited they felt in the ritualistic carnival that occurs outside Union Station prior to every Leafs home game. They will be able to lucidly recall the fantastical world they had just stepped into: how vaguely dangerous the scalpers shilling their tickets appeared to be and how Mom tightened her grip as they passed; how loud the voices of the hawkers who sold the programs; how irresistible the smell of pizza that wafted past as they entered their gate; how bright the white rink was made by the television lights; how striking the blue uniforms of the home team; and how perfect a first Maple Leafs game really is.

In our story, then, *where* really is as important as *what*. And the wonderful thing about loving the Maple Leafs is that it doesn't matter *where* we are in this big beautiful world; we can all still belong, we can all still claim residency within that wonderful legion called Leafs Nation.

Through this journey of a hundred years of ups and downs, triumphs and tears, laughter and laments, the Toronto Maple Leafs will forever remain: our team, your team.

Through the extraordinary 100-year history of the Toronto Maple Leaf Hockey Club, Leafs Nation has witnessed the highest of highs. Arguably the greatest goal in the franchise's history was scored by Bill Barilko, the 24-year-old defenceman, who got the dramatic Stanley Cup–winning goal in 1951.

OFFICIAL

Hockey Programme . . .

ARENA GARDENS

TORONTO

Season 1917-18

THE NOBLE CAUSE
1917–18 TO 1918–19

MUDDY LITTLE YORK

Twelve log homes lined the Don River when John Graves Simcoe, the first lieutenant-governor of Upper Canada, arrived in the area in 1793. While the lodgings may have been humble, they were filled with proud colonial spirits that developed a place that would one day become known as Toronto, a city in which, there can be no doubt, hockey has been a central part of life for the past century.

Today, the Greater Toronto Area is home to over six million people and is the most populous metropolitan area in the country. In 1917, though, Toronto was the *second*-largest city in Canada (behind Montreal), with only about half a million people. Today, Toronto can genuinely be considered one of the most culturally diverse and cosmopolitan cities in the world. In 1917, however, the city had a clear majority of people who were either British-born or of British heritage. Through the years, we have had Leafs with surnames like Borschevsky, Crha, Franceschetti, and Mahovlich. The 1917 team, though, was made up of players with thoroughly British surnames such as Adams, Cameron, and Noble.

As for hockey, the fledgling professional game had only just won the Athletic War (1906–09) against those who wanted to preserve the old amateur code. There were plenty of teething issues. The National Hockey Association (NHA), for instance, chose to cease its operations in 1917. This was mainly because the league wanted to rid itself of the unwanted owner and much-maligned coach of the Toronto Blueshirts, Eddie Livingstone. In its place, the four-team – and very soon afterwards, three-team – National Hockey League (NHL) emerged.

Yet in December 1917, hockey was hardly foremost on the minds of Torontonians. People were less interested in any new professional hockey league than in helping the city's young men and women who were serving overseas. Toronto was a city wholly committed to winning the war. And Torontonians gave to the war effort in every conceivable way. Businesses donated great sums of money

and freed their men for the fight. Physicians offered free services to the families of soldiers. The Imperial Order Daughters of the Empire raised $100,000 to furnish a hospital ship for the Admiralty. Prominent citizens such as John Craig Eaton offered $100,000 to purchase a battery of Vickers machine guns that would be mounted on armoured trucks. Everyone, it seemed, was doing their bit.

It was, however, the soldiers themselves who gave the most. Stunningly, three out of every four eligible men in Toronto had, by war's end, offered to serve. Approximately 70,000 young Torontonians enlisted. By November 1918, nearly 5,000 of these would be dead, along with another 55,000 other Canadians.

Even with these sobering numbers, the city would vote overwhelmingly in favour of Sir Robert Borden's Unionist Party and its mandate to bring in compulsory military service. On December 17, 1917, Borden received the support of approximately 90 per cent of Toronto's voters and won the federal election with the largest share of the popular vote in the history of Canada. Two nights later, Toronto played its first game against the Wanderers in Montreal.

LIVINGSTONE, I PRESUME

Toronto had had a lively hockey scene since before the turn of the 20th century. The problem was that the city lacked a suitable arena for the country's highest level of hockey. There had been plans to include two Toronto teams in the National Hockey Association as early as 1911. Both teams were slated to play at a newly built arena on Mutual Street between Dundas and Gerrard, but construction of the rink was delayed when the refrigeration pipes for the artificial ice surface were installed incorrectly, and that meant another year without a suitable rink.

Finally, by October 1912, the Arena Gardens was completed. The arena was owned by the Toronto Arena

A programme from the inaugural season of the NHL's Toronto Arena Hockey Club. The first game took place on December 19, 1917, a 10–9 loss to the Wanderers in Montreal.

finished the season with a losing record. Meanwhile, the NHA was about to get a lot more complicated.

In November 1915, Eddie Livingstone also purchased the Toronto Professional Hockey Club, a team known as the Blueshirts. The acquisition gave Livingstone two professional hockey clubs in Toronto, infuriating the owners of the other NHA franchises.

One of Livingstone's main detractors was Sam Lichtenhein, the Montreal Wanderers' owner, who tried to pressure the other clubs into having Livingstone removed from the league. Lichtenhein offered $3,000 for Livingstone's franchise, simply to be rid of him. Livingstone countered with an offer of $5,000 if Lichtenhein would sell his Wanderers. The two men's bitter feud would eventually spell the end of the NHA.

Meanwhile, the NHA was trying to fend off head-hunting raids from the Pacific Coast Hockey Association (PCHA). Frank Patrick of the PCHA's Vancouver Millionaires targeted the NHA – in particular, Livingstone's Blueshirts. By offering substantial salaries, Patrick succeeded in stripping the team of its significant players. As a result, Livingstone had only enough players to ice one competitive team, so he took several players from the Shamrocks lineup to rebuild the Blueshirts.

The rest of the league's franchise owners then called a meeting in Montreal on November 9, 1915. There, they agreed that no owner could own more than one franchise. Livingstone was ordered to divest himself of one team by November 20. When he missed their deadline, the league seized the Shamrocks and removed the team from the schedule. That season, the NHA operated with just five franchises.

At the same time, the NHA owners were trying to mitigate the effect that the First World War was having on its stock of players. Many hockey players had enlisted in the Canadian Expeditionary Force. Military teams were beginning to appear in other senior leagues. The NHA's response, in an attempt to remedy the situation, was to award one unit, the 228th Battalion, the defunct Shamrocks franchise.

The NHA had been toying with the idea of suspending its operations for the duration of the war, because it was becoming harder and harder for the league to justify able-bodied men playing professional hockey during the conflict. At the same time, NHA officials witnessed the credibility that teams of soldiers had brought to the amateur Ontario Hockey Association (OHA). Admitting the 228th was a small price to pay, and a proactive way to protect against the league's collapse.

Eddie Livingstone's unpopularity among the other members of the National Hockey Association effectively led to the formation of the NHL. He would make several attempts to launch rival leagues over the years.

Company under Sir Henry Pellatt (of Casa Loma fame) and was the largest indoor rink in Canada. It was certainly the most modern one, too, although the seats – long, painted planks – left a little to be desired. The rink was built at a cost of $500,000 and held 7,500 spectators for hockey, although it was also used for curling and public ice skating. Toronto was now able to ice big-time teams in the country's big-time league.

Just prior to the 1914–15 season, Eddie Livingstone purchased the Ontarios Hockey Club, one of two Toronto-based teams in the National Hockey Association. Livingstone was an avid Toronto sportsman who had enjoyed success in coaching and managing hockey teams and was also the assistant sports editor at the *Mail and Empire*. Midway through his first season as owner of the Ontarios, Livingstone changed the team's name to the Shamrocks. Despite the lucky-sounding name, the team

Not all NHA owners were on side with the idea, however. For one, the 228th Battalion, tagged the "Northern Fusiliers," would receive additional monies on top of their service pay. And protests grew louder in response to the unexpected success the army team enjoyed in the first half of the 1916–17 season. There was a question as to whether some military decisions were being influenced by on-ice matters. Certainly, the battalion had quietly and deliberately recruited some of the nation's best hockey stars. As enlisted soldiers, these players could continue playing hockey at the highest level, provided that the battalion remained based in Canada. But on March 4, 1917, the Northern Fusiliers were summoned to France.

When the 228th Battalion team was posted overseas, the NHA was once again rendered an odd-numbered league. The owners met to discuss how to execute the remaining schedule. Livingstone was not at the meeting, but he sent a telegram indicating his desire to have the NHA continue as a five-team circuit for the remainder of the schedule. The other owners, however, disagreed. An odd-numbered league had not done well in the past. In addition, the war effort had drained the clubs of talent, and they were anxious to reduce the number of teams by one so as to strengthen the others. The team they chose to remove was the Toronto Blueshirts. The owners suspended the operation of the Blueshirts for the remainder of the season and dispersed the players by lottery among the other teams. NHA president Frank Robinson stipulated that the players would be returned when the club was reinstated, but he would not guarantee that the Toronto club would be allowed to return, stating that that decision would be made at the NHA's annual meeting. Incensed, Livingstone issued writs against the NHA and its member clubs for damages resulting from dropping his franchise.

At its annual meeting prior to the 1917–18 season, the NHA announced that it would continue as a four-team league because "it was unfeasible to operate as a five-team league" and because the war had made hockey talent scarce. There was something of an element of conspiracy to the decision, given that it was no secret that Livingstone was intensely disliked by the others because of his often-quarrelsome demeanour.

The other club owners met privately to discuss how they could rid themselves of the Toronto owner. However, they learned that the NHA's constitution did not allow them to vote Livingstone and his team out of the league. Instead, they decided to abandon the NHA and simply reorganize as a new league without Livingstone. The owners voted to suspend the NHA's operations, which meant that Livingstone would still have his franchise, but it would be the only one in the NHA. Lichtenhein could not veil his sarcasm: "We didn't throw Livingstone out. He's still got his franchise in the old National Hockey Association. The only problem is, he's playing in a one-team league!"

THE NHL

The new league, the National Hockey League, was formed on November 26, 1917. The inaugural NHL teams were the Montreal Canadiens, Montreal Wanderers, Ottawa Senators, and Quebec Bulldogs, although the latter chose to suspend operations for financial reasons. Very quickly, though, the NHL owners realized the importance of including a Toronto franchise. As such, the directors agreed to give a temporary franchise to the Toronto Arena Company on the condition that Livingstone not be involved in any way.

The Toronto Arena Company, owners of the Arena Gardens, leased players who had been members of Livingstone's Blueshirts. The players were paid in cash on a game-to-game basis, and most played without a contract. Charlie Querrie, a prominent lacrosse player from Markham, Ontario, and the manager of the arena, served as the new team's manager. Dick Carroll was hired to coach the team.

To no one's surprise, Livingstone disputed all of the actions that had transpired. Frank Calder, the first president of the National Hockey League, implored the Toronto Arena Company and Livingstone to come to some resolution. For several years, Livingstone battled the owners and the NHL, trying unsuccessfully to launch rival leagues. His lawsuit made it to the Supreme Court of Canada, but his claims were unsuccessful. Livingstone was on the outside looking in, and that's where he would remain.

Meanwhile, the Toronto Arena Company's team had no official name. The club was referred to as the "Arenas," but because the roster comprised many former Blueshirts, journalists continued to call the team by that name. Not helping the situation was the fact that the players wore the same uniform they had worn during the previous season in the NHA: a blue sweater with a large white *T* on the front.

At this point, those players who had been dispersed among the other NHA teams in early 1917 were returned to the Toronto club, giving the Torontos – or Arenas, or Blueshirts, or whatever other nickname they might have been given – a full complement of players to begin the first-ever season for the new franchise. It had been a long and muddled road, and the events leading to the emergence of the Toronto Arena Company's new team have confused and confounded hockey historians for a century. What is certain, however, is that December 19, 1917, was the zero hour for a franchise that would later become the Toronto Maple Leafs.

Toronto started its first NHL season with two goalies in its camp: Art Brooks, who played the first four games of the season and then never again, and the only slightly more seasoned Sammy Hebert, who had played the previous season with the Quebec Bulldogs after serving a year in the military. Defensively, Toronto had Harry Cameron, who had been with the Stanley Cup–winning Blueshirts in 1914, on point. They also boasted Ken Randall, who had been with the Blueshirts for the 1912–13 season and then again from 1915 through 1917, at cover-point. He had missed out on the Cup-winning year, as he was playing with the Montreal Wanderers at the time.

And then there were two players who were already – or at the very least would soon be – stars: Corbett Denneny and Reg Noble. The former's brother, Cy Denneny, was already very much a professional hockey star, and the latter was the first player from the St. Michael's College School team to graduate to the city's NHL team. It was a process that would happen several times over the coming decades. Rounding out the lineup was forward and local boy Alf Skinner, and the team's reserve players: Jack (a.k.a. Jerry) Coughlin and rookie Harry Meeking. Later, when Quebec decided not to participate, its players were dispersed and Toronto picked up the talented American-born point Harry Mummery. Stacked as it was with future Hall of Famers Cameron, Denneny, and Noble, the Toronto team was in very good stead before the first puck was dropped.

Charlie Querrie instituted strict rules for the team, warning players that indifferent play would result in fines and that, if they wanted to fight, they should go over to France. It was clear to all from the outset that Querrie would be calling the shots.

The schedule, as it happened, was divided into two halves: the first with 14 games, the second with 8. The opening game of the NHL season for the Toronto club took place on December 19. Toronto was in Montreal to face the Wanderers. Only 700 fans – mostly soldiers – were on hand to watch the affair, which Montreal won 10–9.

Toronto, however, rebounded nicely in its home opener. "Hockey fans were agreeably surprised by the work of the reorganized Toronto team," the *Globe*

reported. "Displaying speed and stamina which was of midseason calibre, they swept the Easterners before them in the 60 minutes of play, and were not at any time seriously threatened by defeat."

Toronto trounced Ottawa 11–4.

The team's third game was a 7–5 defeat of the Montreal Canadiens. Rushing defenceman Harry Cameron scored a goal, collected an assist, and got into a fight. Although it was 11 years before "Mr. Hockey" was even born, Cameron had effectively registered the NHL's first Gordie Howe hat trick.

The *Toronto World* reported that manager Querrie had not travelled with the team to Montreal for its game on December 29. There was some speculation as to whether he had handed in his resignation. The fact of the matter was that Querrie had tired of Eddie Livingstone's constant campaign against the league and the new Toronto franchise, but while he had considered walking, he returned to his duties later that week.

Livingstone was not the league's only issue. On January 2, 1918, the Montreal Arena – or Westmount Arena, as it was also known – burned to the ground. The fire left both the Canadiens and Wanderers without a home. The Canadiens were able to move to the Jubilee Rink, but the Wanderers suspended play for the season and subsequently folded.

The loss of the Wanderers reduced the league to an odd-numbered circuit, but the NHL continued as best it could. Some of the Wanderers wandered over to other teams, including Jack Marks, who joined the Torontos. But the most important acquisition came on January 4, when Charlie Querrie signed a veteran goaltender and another future Hall of Famer. Harry "Hap" Holmes had been with the Seattle Metropolitans in the PCHA the previous season and was a much stronger force in goal than either Hebert or Brooks had been.

With Holmes now playing the lion's share of games in goal, the Torontos finished the first half of the season in second place with eight wins and six losses. The Canadiens sat atop the league with ten wins and four losses. The Ottawa Senators were third, and the unfortunate Wanderers were no more, having played just four of their scheduled fourteen games and forfeited two others.

The second half of the Torontos' season began against the Canadiens in Montreal on February 9. Earlier that day, both Jack Adams and Rusty Crawford were signed by Toronto as free agents. Adams had been playing senior hockey with the Sarnia Sailors. Crawford was picked up

Reg Noble had been a member of the Toronto Blueshirts of the NHA, but joined the Arenas when the team debuted in the NHL in 1917–18. He'd make the transition to the St. Patricks in 1919–20.

after being released by the Ottawa Senators. But because the league rules prohibited players signed after February 1 from taking part in the Stanley Cup final, the two free agents played the second half of the NHL season and the league championship, but were, bizarrely, not allowed to compete for the Stanley Cup.

There was another move: the first trade in NHL history took place on February 11, 1918, when Toronto sent its spare goaltender, Ottawa native Sammy Hebert, to the Senators for cash. To that point in the season, Hebert had only played one full game and part of a second in relief of Art Brooks, allowing ten goals.

Certainly, the young league had not yet ironed out all of its administrative wrinkles. And the NHL at this time was full of larger-than-life characters. Toronto's Ken Randall, for instance, had been suspended by the league for non-payment of $35 in fines he had accrued during the season. Prior to the Torontos' game against Ottawa on February 23, Randall brought $32 in bills as well as 300 pennies. The league refused the coins. Incensed, Randall tossed the bag of pennies onto the ice. One of the Ottawa players swiped at the bag and it burst open, scattering the pennies around the ice surface. The game was delayed while the pennies were picked up.

As a team, though, Toronto had picked up its game and managed to finish first in the second half of the NHL season, winning five and losing three. Reg Noble led the team in scoring with 30 goals and 40 points, placing third in the league in both categories.

The NHL playoff format in 1918 called for the winner of the first half of the season to face the winner of the second half, with the victor of the series to go on to play the PCHA champion for the Stanley Cup. This meant the Torontos would face the Canadiens for the inaugural championship of the National Hockey League.

In the opening contest of the two-game, total-goals playoff series, the Torontos dumped the heavily penalized Canadiens 7–3 in the Arena Gardens. The second game, played in Montreal, was described as a "brutal" affair in the press. At one point, Montreal's Newsy Lalonde knocked out Harry Meeking. In the end, however, Toronto knocked out Montreal. While the Canadiens won the second game 4–3, Toronto won the series and the NHL championship by outscoring Montreal 10–7 over the two games.

Now the Torontos awaited the Vancouver Millionaires, champions of the PCHA. The best-of-five series was held at Toronto's Arena Gardens. The first game, using the NHL's six-player rules, saw the Torontos skate away with

a 5–3 victory. Game Two, though, was played under the PCHA's rules. While the NHA had dropped the position of rover in 1911, the West Coast league, founded the same year, still included it. The Millionaires were obviously far more comfortable when playing, as the *Globe* termed it, "their own peculiar style of play": the Torontos fell to Vancouver, 6–4.

Fortunately for Toronto, Game Three reverted to eastern rules, and the Blueshirts restored their series lead with a 6–3 victory. Vancouver, with their rover intact in Game Four, came back with a vengeance, shredding the Torontos, 8–1. The *Globe* confirmed: "Torontos were simply lost at the seven-man game. Vancouver ran all over them with speed and had a bag of tricks that left the Blue Shirts gasping. Torontos tried the three-man defence play, but it didn't bother the Westerners. They streaked in two, three and four at a time, and Holmes was simply helpless before the onslaught."

Game Five seemed to start out the same way, as Vancouver dominated early. But Holmes was brilliant in goal and the teams were back playing the six-man game that suited the Torontos. And then there was the breakout performance of Corb Denneny. As the *Globe* observed, "The surprise of the game, however, was the stellar work of little Corbett Deneny [*sic*]. Displaying speed that was only eclipsed by [Mickey] McKay [*sic*], and stick-handling ability that almost equalled that of the veteran [Cyclone] Taylor."

Denneny scored the Cup-winning goal on a spectacular rush in the third period. Toronto took the game, 2–1, and won the series, three games to two. The new franchise had delivered a somewhat unexpected Cup victory for Toronto.

Still, the Torontos and the league in which they played were still trying to cultivate a steady fan base. With no immediate end to the Great War in sight, there was some question as to whether or not there would even be a season or a Stanley Cup final the next year.

MUDDY LITTLE FRANCE

Hockey leagues everywhere proved to be effective instruments of recruitment for the military. The martial spirit and the emphasis on one's loyalty to teammates made hockey players ideal candidates for the Canadian Expeditionary Force (CEF). There was also the question of patriotism. While there were certainly many different ideas about what being "Canadian" meant at this time, many players, compelled by some sense of Canadian and/or British imperial patriotism, felt a duty to enlist and serve.

> To wear a Maple Leafs sweater, to be part of the team, was something I had dreamed about for years and years.
>
> **Red Horner**
> PLAYER
> 1928–40

More often than not, young men from the same street, community, club, or team would sign up together. This resulted in the so-called pals' battalions, a practice that was outlawed following the war, after whole communities lost scores – and sometimes all – of their young men. But for now, these pals' battalions were popular – especially among hockey players, who knew well the tenets of loyalty and avenging any wrong done to your teammates.

Many ice warriors saw a jump from the ice to the mud of Flanders as something of a natural progression. As Captain James T. Sutherland, one of the great hockey minds of the day, assured, "with every man doing his bit, Canada will raise an army of brains and brawn from our hockey enthusiasts the likes of which the world has never seen."

There was one man whose effect on Toronto's hockey landscape would, even today, be regarded as without parallel. Constantine Falkland Cary Smythe was born in Toronto on February 1, 1895. Smythe captained the University of Toronto's Varsity Blues hockey team, which played in the OHA's junior division. Four days after Varsity won the Ontario junior championship in March 1915, the entire team, including Smythe, enlisted in the CEF in the spirit of the pals' battalion. With the stroke of a pen, team captain Conn Smythe became Gunner Conn Smythe of the 25th Battalion of the Canadian Field Artillery.

Before heading overseas, Gunner Smythe joined Gordon Southam's 40th Battery of the Royal Canadian Artillery. The battery was able to ice a hockey team in the OHA's senior division, which just happened to include ten of the province's finest hockey players. After Smythe played one game with the team, he replaced himself with another player and settled in as the team's manager. When word came that the battery would be heading to England, Smythe and Southam wagered the entire season's gate receipts on what would be the final game of their season. The two men put down $2,800 on themselves to win. And then they told the rest of the team what they had done.

A mood that oscillated between seething anger and fear spurred the 40th to a comfortable victory. The $7,000 in winnings furnished a lavish Christmas dinner for the battery before it was deployed overseas. For many at the table, including Gordon Southam, it was the last Christmas dinner they would ever enjoy. Every senior officer in Smythe's battery was either killed or badly wounded.

When he finally got to Europe, Smythe would figure in no fewer than four major battles in which the Canadians were involved. As far as Smythe was concerned, hockey had provided him with the fortitude to cope in the direst of circumstances.

On February 12, 1917, Lieutenant Smythe charged a German trench with a revolver, shot three Germans, and brought two prisoners back to the Canadian lines:

> I was right in the middle of a battle between the two front lines, until I jumped down into the German trench with my revolver and fired a few shots, hitting two Germans, and then came around a corner, and saw a big German with his rifle up on the parapet. He just had time to look at me when I jammed my revolver in his stomach and pulled the trigger. He slid down into the trench, cursing in German all the way. I don't know German but I know what he thought of me.

For his effort, Smythe was awarded the Military Cross. A couple of months later, he would take part in the single most important Canadian battle of the First World War: the capture of Vimy Ridge.

By the spring of 1917, Conn Smythe was an artillery observer in the Royal Flying Corps. He spent the summer of 1917 training in England under the supervision of the Canadian flying ace, Lieutenant-Colonel W.G. "Billy" Barker. The ace would later play a role in his pupil's future hockey franchise. For now, though, Barker tried to arm Smythe with the necessary knowledge to survive.

When Smythe was sent to France, he was teamed up with pilot Andrew Ward. The duo was sent to the unspeakable horror that was the Battle of Passchendaele. On October 14, 1917, Smythe and Ward's RE8 single-propeller biplane crashed into a shell hole behind enemy lines. As the artillery observer recalled:

> We were alive, but we were in No Man's Land. A couple of guns were firing at us. Not far away also there was a man waving at us. I said, "We'll make it." For the next hour and a half or so we went from shellhole to shellhole. We came to this position where the man had been waving – and he was a German!

Smythe was furious. "I just stood on the parapet and cursed him for every kind of rotten bastard. He pulled out his revolver and shot twice from point-blank range. Another German dove at him and told him to stop, prisoners were better than dead men." There were holes in Smythe's flying coat on both sides of his chest. Somehow, Conn was still alive. But now he was a prisoner of war,

I vividly remember joining the Leafs. They were looking for some sandpaper at that time. I was pretty boisterous with my personality, so for me, it was a good situation to walk into. As much as I loved playing the game, I loved the entertainment of it, too. I liked to be on the ice in front of 20,000 people and have them as loud as possible. The feeling that Leafs fans give you as a former player is like no other place that you can play . . . Anybody that gave it their all here and was that hard-working, lunch-bucket sort of guy, is certainly remembered by the fans.

Darcy Tucker
PLAYER
2000–08

THE ARENA HOCKEY CLUB OF TORONTO

·1918· ·1919·

CHAMPIONS OF THE WORLD

THE O'BRIEN CUP.

THE STANLEY CUP.

The Toronto Arena Hockey Club, tagged the Arenas and the Blueshirts by the press, beat the PCHA Vancouver Millionaires to win the Stanley Cup in the NHL's inaugural season.

and would remain so for the duration of the hostilities.

Back in Toronto, the papers first reported Conn Smythe as missing in action. His father had been told that his son was presumed dead. Conn's dad would have to tell his son's betrothed, Irene Sands, that her beau had been killed in action.

Then, on November 19, the *Globe* reported the happy news that Smythe wasn't dead, but was instead a POW – alive, but in prison. After he got out of a German hospital, Smythe was moved from one prison to another behind enemy lines. Although he tried to escape along with another prisoner in April 1918, he would not set foot in Toronto until February 1919. His wartime experience would shape the trajectory of his life and spark the evolution of what would become Toronto's most beloved team. In an effort to honour all of those "pals" who would not

come home, Conn Smythe built a veritable institution, one that captured the hearts and imaginations of a nation, and one that would be revered like no other in professional hockey.

PANDEMIC

On November 11, 1918, the long, miserable war that had cost the world 17 million dead and 20 million wounded was finally and mercifully over. To the exasperation of almost everyone involved with the NHL, however, the war with Eddie Livingstone was not. The Toronto Arena Company had agreed to pay Livingstone what amounted to approximately 60 per cent of the team's profits for the lease of the team's players. Therefore, when the Toronto Arena Company reported revenue of $53,000,

Livingstone insisted on his rightful share. Despite the profit-sharing agreement, the management of the Arena Gardens refused to pay out the $9,000 that was due to Livingstone. Instead, the company offered Livingstone $5,958 if he would relinquish any future claims on the team. Livingstone declined the offer. The former owner demanded full payment and sued the Toronto Arena Company for $20,400 in damages, and even cited the gate receipts from the Stanley Cup games, which had not been included in the initial tally. While it took him eight years and several appeals, Eddie Livingstone would eventually win his suit.

Back in 1918, however, the Toronto Arena Company had made a complicated situation even more challenging. Refusing to pay Livingstone or return the leased players to him, the company chose instead to return their "temporary" franchise to the National Hockey League and form a new club: the Toronto Arena Hockey Club. The owners were listed as Charlie Querrie and Hubert Vearncombe, the treasurer of the franchise.

On October 19, 1918, the Toronto Arena Hockey Club officially requested franchise rights in the NHL, which were duly granted by league president Frank Calder. Now the Torontos/Blueshirts/Blue Shirts had legitimately become the Toronto Arenas.

The club had ingeniously, if somewhat clandestinely, limited Livingstone's hand as far as it came to the future of the hockey team. By returning the Torontos to the NHL and opening up a new team, the Toronto Arena Company had cut Livingstone out of its operations. The company then announced that its arena would only be used for professional hockey that involved the National Hockey League. This move completely precluded Livingstone from using the Arena Gardens.

Livingstone insisted that he still owned the contracts of Jack Adams, Corb Denneny, Harry Meeking, Reg Noble, Ken Randall, Dave Ritchie, and Alf Skinner. Technically, these players were the property of Livingstone and his (National Hockey Association) Toronto Blueshirts. All of the players, however, agreed to defy Livingstone and play for the Toronto Arenas without contracts while being paid in cash. Prior to the season opener on December 23, 1918, Livingstone warned, "There is but one in a hundred that tonight's game will be played." The game, however, went off without a hitch, excepting that the visiting Montreal Canadiens outscored the Arenas, 4–3.

As for the actual play of the new team, the *Toronto Daily Star* reported, "Torontos looked the better team and then tossed it away by gross carelessness, the result of

over-confidence." Arenas coach Dick Carroll admitted that "being the best skaters and puck carriers doesn't count alongside of placing that little old puck in the net."

After a Boxing Day game against the Senators, the Leafs lost Hap Holmes to his old team, the Seattle Metropolitans of the PCHA. Desperate for a goaltender, the Arenas signed free agent Bert Lindsay, father of future Detroit Red Wings legend Ted Lindsay. Bert had played four games for the Montreal Wanderers during that team's ill-fated 1917–18 season.

The signing was not an unqualified success. Toronto lost, 3–0, to the Canadiens in Lindsay's debut on December 28. Not long afterwards, on January 11, 1919, the Canadiens embarrassed Lindsay and the Arenas by a humiliating 13–4 score. Following the game, the *Montreal Herald* hypothesized, "Either the players are not trying to win or they are in no condition to play, possibly a combination of both." The *Star*, in a mood that was no more charitable, remarked, "The Toronto forwards and defence played far below their standard, and left the greater portion of the work to be done by goalkeeper Lindsay. He was unequal to the whole job, and the blue-shirted players were given a sound trouncing."

The Toronto Arena Hockey Club finished the first half of the season with three wins in ten tries for 6 points, well behind Montreal's 14 points and Ottawa's 10 in the three-team NHL.

The second half of the season was no more kind to the woeful Arenas. Following a 4–3 overtime loss to Ottawa on February 18, Harry Meeking and Ken Randall were given permission to leave the Arenas to sign with the Glace Bay Miners of the Cape Breton Hockey League. In his finale as a member of the Arenas, Randall, according to the *Star*, "put on a high-class performance just to show the public what a good boy Manager Querrie has consented to let go." Two nights later, after another loss to Ottawa, the Arenas were officially eliminated from play-off contention.

To expedite the playoffs, and because there was no real need to play out the remainder of the schedule, Toronto, with permission from the league, forfeited its remaining two games. As a result, the second half of the 1918–19 season consisted of just eight games. Ottawa finished with 14 points, Montreal with 6, and Toronto, with just two wins, finished with 4 points. Alf Skinner led the Arenas with 12 goals and 16 points.

THE BELFAST OF CANADA
1919-20 TO 1925-26

GREEN AND WHITE

A great sense of pan-Canadian nationalism began to emerge across the country in the years immediately following the First World War. Canada began to flower as a nation unto itself: separate from the mother country and different, at least a little, from its next-door neighbour.

The nation underwent a cultural awakening, and Toronto was central to these movements. Canadian artists such as the Group of Seven, and writers such as Stephen Leacock, would soon be crafting distinctly Canadian works of art and gaining international recognition. Hockey, too, played a role. While American radio programs were finding large audiences with Canadian listeners, hockey would help to alter the landscape of the airwaves.

But in the fall of 1919, Toronto hockey fans were still reeling from the poor season the Arenas had turned in during the previous campaign. The *Star*, for example, observed that "everybody was disgusted at the in and out performances of the team last year, and it became patent early in the year that if any attempt was made to carry on with the same old crew, that the pro game would not receive the support of the newspapers or the public."

The truth of the matter was that there would be, in effect, no "old crew" to worry about. The persistent Eddie Livingstone won a judgment against the Toronto Arena Company, which declared bankruptcy in order to avoid paying Livingstone his $20,000. The Arena Company wanted to sell the franchise, and the team's manager, Charlie Querrie, wanted to be a part of a new ownership group. He wasn't the only one.

Potential suitors kicked the tires of the franchise all through the summer. In the end, they all backed away from consummating a final sale. War veteran Art Duncan of the PCHA's Vancouver Millionaires tried to obtain control of the team. When negotiations fell through, Duncan returned to the West Coast.

With no one willing to step in, Querrie announced on December 7, 1919, that a new organization would take over the franchise in the short term and operate under the name of the Tecumseh Hockey Club. The principals of the club were Querrie and Fred Hambly. Three days later, the St. Patricks Hockey Club, which had a team in the senior division of the OHA, purchased the franchise. The deal, brokered by Querrie himself, allowed the former Arenas manager to hold an ownership stake in the franchise.

The St. Patricks (alternatively spelled with an apostrophe) had existed since the early 1900s and were well regarded in Toronto's hockey circles. While the city, with its huge Protestant majority, epitomized Old Orange Ontario, there were many fledgling immigrant communities within Toronto that encompassed a significant number of minorities. Most notably, of course, was the city's Irish Catholic population.

The Great Famine that began in the late 1840s and lasted until 1852 had killed a million Irish and caused another million to seek refuge around the world. In 1847, Toronto had a population of approximately 20,000. That same year, 38,000 Irish immigrants arrived in the city. They did not, of course, all remain in Toronto. And, unfortunately, 1,100 immigrants – and many Torontonians who tried to help – would perish in the so-called fever sheds at the corner of King and John Streets, from the typhus epidemic of that same miserable year. But many did stay, and by 1851, one-quarter of Toronto's population was Irish.

While many Torontonians welcomed the Irish immigrants, the city was still fervently Protestant. Although the First World War had, at least to a certain degree, interrupted the usual antipathy that existed between Catholics and Protestants in Toronto, there was a resumption of ill feelings following the armistice. It was during this time, when the troubles of the old world were being played out in the new, that Toronto became known as "the Belfast of Canada."

Still, the sectarian divide made for good hockey rivalries, and NHL owners were not oblivious to this fact. At a meeting held at the Prince George Hotel in Toronto

For seven seasons, Babe Dye starred for the St. Patricks, leading the league in scoring in 1922–23 and 1924–25, and leading the team to the Stanley Cup championship in 1922.

on December 13, 1919, the NHL officially transferred the Toronto franchise to the St. Patricks for a fee of $5,000. Listed as principals were Dr. John Noble (honorary president), Dr. Hugh Cooke (honorary vice-president), Fred Hambly (president, and owner of one-fifth of the team), Paul Ciceri (first vice-president, and owner of one-fifth of the team), Harvey Sproule (secretary-treasurer, and owner of one-fifth of the team), Charlie Querrie (manager, and owner of one-fifth of the team), and Frank Heffernan, who was named playing coach and also owned one-fifth of the team. The sweater colours were changed from the blue and white of the Arena Hockey Club to green and white, in honour of the Emerald Isle.

The uniform colours would not be the only change for the Toronto squad. The roster's turnover would be substantial. The 1919–20 NHL season saw a return of big-time hockey to Quebec City. As such, many players who had been with the Quebec Bulldogs before they suspended operations had to be returned to the team, which was now called the Athletics. The St. Pats lost Rusty Crawford, Harry Mummery, and Dave Ritchie. At the same time, the PCHA had raided the Toronto roster in the off-season. Vancouver scooped Jack Adams and Alf Skinner, while Victoria was able to lure Harry Meeking away from Ontario. On top of these losses, netminder Bert Lindsay retired. Only Harry Cameron, Corb Denneny, Reg Noble, and Ken Randall would be holdovers from the Arenas. The St. Pats signed several new players, including goaltenders Howard Lockhart and Ivan Mitchell, centre Mickey Roach, and wingers Cecil "Babe" Dye and Cully Wilson. It seemed that the St. Pats really would be a brand-new team.

The season began in Ottawa on December 23, 1919, in front of Governor General Victor Cavendish. Before the game, player-coach Frank Heffernan was presented with a floral horseshoe. It was not, as it turned out, the lucky kind – the St. Pats lost, 3–0. The *Toronto Daily Star*, however, was optimistic: "This St. Patrick pro hockey team is going to be popular with the fans if they only stick to their knitting and win a few games."

To add to the team's attack, Querrie and company sought to bring Goldie Prodger into the St. Pats camp. The talented Prodger was playing for the Montreal Canadiens but desperately wanted to play in Toronto to be closer to his family in London, Ontario. On January 10, 1920, Toronto sent Harry Cameron to Montreal for Prodger. In the *Star*'s opinion, "The departure of Cameron will be a sore blow to many of the Toronto fans who have grown to admire his spirited work

in the big arena . . . In Prodgers [*sic*], the Toronto team is getting a player of sterling calibre."

It did not seem to help much, at least not at first. That same night, Toronto ventured into Montreal for the Canadiens' home opener in the newly built Mount Royal Arena. There, Montreal butchered Toronto, 14–7. The combined total of 21 goals set an NHL record.

The team did not fare much better for the remainder of the first half of the season, which ended with Toronto in third place, well behind first-place Ottawa and second-place Montreal.

A particularly noteworthy change occurred prior to the season's second half. Frank Heffernan surrendered his coaching role and was replaced by Harry Sproule, one of the team's owners and a fine hockey player himself. With Sproule, the St. Patricks hoped that they could take the second half and force a playoff with Ottawa to decide the NHL championship.

Toronto started the second half of the season on the wrong side of a 6–5 score against Montreal on February 4, 1920. After this, though, the St. Patricks went on a tear and won their next four games. The *Montreal Herald* exclaimed, "The Saints have improved 100 per cent over their form of the first-half . . . [they] have speed galore, stick-handling ability and they are playing hockey like a team."

With many soldiers returned from duty, more and more people were coming out to see NHL hockey. On February 21, for instance, the Arena Gardens experienced a record night: 8,500 people came out to see the St. Pats take on the Senators. The home crowd, however, would be disappointed. Toronto lost to Ottawa, 5–3.

Still, the St. Pats were making a run for it and were playing much better. The team was also not done adding to the roster. They signed Jake Forbes, an outstanding goal-tender for Aura Lee in the junior division of the OHA. On February 28, Forbes made his debut against the Senators. While Ottawa defeated Toronto, 1–0, the goaltender drew admiration from the *Toronto Star*, who reported that "Forbes played his position like a veteran, and undoubtedly saved St. Patrick's from far worse beating. Forbes was a veritable stone wall. After getting a goal to the good, [Ottawa] played a strictly defensive game and managed to hold the Irishmen out for the balance of the contest."

Unfortunately, the loss meant that the Toronto St. Patricks could not catch the leading Senators.

In the end, the St. Patricks finished the second half in second place, but Ottawa finished first, as they had done in the earlier half. As a result, there was no need for a playoff to determine the NHL champion. The Senators hosted the PCHA champions, the Seattle Metropolitans, and went on to win the Stanley Cup.

The "Irish" had played much better in the second half and finished with 12 wins and 12 losses for 24 points. Corb Denneny led the St. Pats with 24 goals and 36 points, which was good for fourth overall in the league. Reg Noble was sixth, with 24 goals and 33 points. It was certainly an improvement on the Arenas' campaign a year previous, and the new players and their green-and-white jerseys seemed to be winning Torontonians over.

A TALE OF TWO HALVES

Eddie Livingstone continued to be a thorn in the side of the National Hockey League. When the controversial character threatened to create a rival league that included Hamilton as one of its cities, the NHL headed Livingstone off at the pass. NHL president Frank Calder convinced team owners to admit a Hamilton franchise to the league.

At the time, Hamilton was the fifth-largest city in Canada, and it had a brand new arena owned by the Abso-Pure Ice Company. As far as the NHL was concerned, it made good business sense to move the struggling Quebec franchise to Hamilton. While Quebec owner Mike Quinn was hesitant about the proposal, he eventually conceded and sold the team to Hamilton. The team was now called the Hamilton Tigers.

Quebec's players were transferred to Hamilton, and Calder asked the other three franchises to supply additional players to help shore up the Tigers' weak roster. The Toronto St. Patricks sold goaltender Howard Lockhart to the Tigers and loaned them Babe Dye. When Dye scored twice for Hamilton in a 5–0 win over the Canadiens, the St. Pats quickly recalled the forward and gave the Tigers Mickey Roach in his place.

Meanwhile, Toronto lost its 1920–21 season opener in Ottawa by a score of 6–3. St. Pats goalie Ivan Mitchell had played well, but was injured and would only appear in the Irish's first four games. Mitchell was replaced in goal by Jake Forbes, who played the remainder of the season.

Toronto's home opener came on Christmas Day against Montreal. Harry Cameron scored a goal and "a rap in the mouth that shook up all his dentistry, but he wouldn't quit." The Canadiens' Georges Vézina was sensational in goal, but the St. Pats still won, 5–4.

While Toronto was still trying to figure out what sort of team it actually had, the NHL was fighting to stay alive against the amateur game, which was still, in many respects, more popular. Many fans struggled with the

An original member of the Toronto Arena Hockey Club, Jack Adams returned to Toronto to join the St. Pats in 1922–23 and was a prolific goal scorer through four seasons.

concept of professionalism, which was infiltrating all sports at this time. It was a task made harder by larger-than-life hockey mercenaries, who often proved hard to herd. Frankly, Sprague Cleghorn – and players like him – sold tickets. In early 1921, Cleghorn and Punch Broadbent were sent to the Hamilton Tigers from the Ottawa Senators, but both refused to report. In desperation, President Calder ordered Cleghorn to join the St. Pats instead on January 25, 1921. As Cleghorn told author Brian McFarlane:

I only agreed to the move when the Toronto club met my salary demands – $3,000 for the balance of the season. There was a further understanding that should Ottawa win the league championship, I would be returned to the Senators for the Stanley Cup battles. The whole cockeyed scheme was just another of those desperate measures brought into play when the professional game was fighting for its life against powerful amateur opposition.

Cleghorn scored three goals and added 31 minutes in penalties in 13 regular-season games with the St. Pats.

The Ottawa Senators won the first half of the season with 16 points in the ten-game schedule. The St. Pats snuck into second with a 5–5 record. Toronto was much stronger in the second half of the season, opening with a 10–3 shellacking of the Hamilton Tigers on January 26, in which Corb Denneny scored six times. Toronto went on to win the second half with a 10–4 record, giving the St. Pats a chance at the O'Brien Cup as NHL champions. The Cup, which had previously been presented to NHA champions, had not been awarded since Montreal won it in 1917, after that league's final season. Now the O'Brien Cup was dusted off and given a similar purpose in the NHL.

The NHL's playoff format at the time meant the winners of the two halves would meet in a two-game, total-goals series. Having claimed the NHL and O'Brien Cup championships, the series winner would move on to play the PCHA champion for the Stanley Cup.

Babe Dye had led the St. Pats in scoring, with 33 goals and 38 points – the two goals he scored in his lone game with Hamilton gave him a league-leading 35, while his 40 total points was good for second place.

The opening game of the league championship was held in Ottawa. Unfortunately for Toronto, Babe Dye was out with an injured knee, and Corb Denneny and Reg Noble were both suffering from colds. Clint Benedict was sensational in goal for Ottawa, who earned a 5–0 victory.

The teams travelled to Toronto's Arena Gardens for Game Two. On the day of the game, Toronto released Sprague Cleghorn for indifferent play. Then the opening faceoff was delayed by 15 minutes as the St. Patricks players, in a dispute over a week's wages, refused to take the ice. They finally agreed to play, accepting half the amount they'd demanded. After two scoreless periods, Ottawa scored twice in the third to win the game, 2–0. This gave the Senators a 7–0 aggregate victory in the two-game series. As a result, Ottawa went on to face, and beat, the Vancouver Millionaires for the Stanley Cup, but the St. Pats' improved season led fans to believe that the team was trending in the right direction.

DYED IN THE WOOL

Big-time hockey continued to evolve. In 1921 a third major professional league, the Western Canada Hockey League (WCHL), was introduced into the equation. The following spring, the champion of the WCHL would play the winner of the PCHA to see who would meet the winner of the NHL for the Stanley Cup.

There were also changes in store for the NHL. The season would no longer be divided into two halves. Instead, the top two teams would face off to determine the NHL/O'Brien Cup champion, with the winner advancing to the Stanley Cup final.

Meanwhile, the St. Patricks had to solve a few roster riddles before the 1921–22 season began. Babe Dye, for one, returned his contract unsigned. The forward was enjoying a promising professional baseball career, and the hockey contract called for service from December to March. But Dye was required to report for spring training with the Buffalo Bisons in March. *The Sporting News* described Dye as "a nifty baseball player, a good hitter, reliable outfielder, and speedy on the base paths." Dye had begun his baseball career with the Toronto Maple Leafs of the International League in 1920, and although the Boston Red Sox owned his rights, the major-league team never exercised them. In September 1921, Dye was sold to the Bisons. Fortunately for the St. Pats, Dye finally signed his contract at the end of November.

There was also an issue in net. Jake Forbes had made some extraordinary demands of the St. Patricks. As Toronto's manager Charlie Querrie acknowledged:

> Forbes is a mighty good goalkeeper and we know it, but he is awfully hard to get along with. We had trouble with him last season. He wanted the earth, and as we could not replace him, we had to eat crow and kowtow to him. This season, after a bit of dickering, he signed his contract. Then he wanted the reserve clause eliminated. We did that, and right on top of that, he wanted the right to go to Ottawa for our games there on the noon train instead of with the team. And then he objected to practicing on Monday . . . It had to come to a stop somewhere.

Rather than compromise, Forbes became the first NHL player to sit out an entire season due to a contract dispute. At the conclusion of the 1921–22 season, he would be sold to the Hamilton Tigers.

To replace Forbes in goal, the St. Patricks signed John Ross Roach. The team paid more for Roach than they would have spent on Forbes, but it seemed worth it. The St. Pats had obtained an outstanding goaltender who, the *Toronto Daily Star* suggested, "looks to be even better a net guardian than the famous Vézina, the wizard of the Canadiens." Roach, just five feet, five inches, and 130 pounds, had starred in goal for the Toronto Granites of the OHA's senior loop in 1920–21.

It was special to be a Leaf, and I remember telling all of my former teammates, especially from Philly and Calgary, that before they retired, they HAD to play for the Toronto Maple Leafs because it is awesome to be a member of the National Hockey League, but it is special to be a Toronto Maple Leaf. That's just how I felt. To hear the long time PA announcers in both buildings [Maple Leaf Gardens and Air Canada Centre] say your name, whether it was for a goal, assist, penalty or starting lineup, was something that I will never forget.

Brad Marsh
PLAYER
1988–91

Meanwhile, Frank Carroll, who had guided the St. Patricks in 1920–21, moved on to coach the Granites and was replaced by rookie coach George O'Donoghue. The *Star* suggested that Toronto-born O'Donoghue appeared to be "smooth as vaseline handling high-strung athletes." It was with these "high-strung athletes" that O'Donoghue opened the St. Pats' camp in early December.

Toronto started the 1921–22 season with a 5–2 victory over the Montreal Canadiens. While Ivan Mitchell started the season in goal, he was injured during the third game, and Roach took over for the rest of the season. Roach turned in a sound performance throughout the campaign, finishing with a decent 11–10–1 record.

The St. Pats enjoyed a fairly strong season and finished with a record of 13 wins, 10 losses, and a tie. Their 27 points placed them second only to Ottawa, who finished 14–8–2 for 30 points.

After almost losing him, the Irish were very fortunate to have held on to Babe Dye, who again led the team in scoring. Dye's 31 goals were second only to Punch Broadbent of the Senators, and his 38 points were good for third in the league.

The St. Pats met the Ottawa Senators in the two-game, total-goals O'Brien Cup final. It was a rematch of the previous year's final, when Ottawa had rolled over Toronto. Game One, played in Toronto, was something of a nail-biter. As the *Star* reported, "the Paddies started with plenty of snap and dash, and mauled the champions for two goals in exactly three minutes and five seconds." The Senators, however, battled back. By the end of the first period, Ottawa was up 3–2.

Roach was sublime in goal and, according to the *Star*, "seemed to be slipping them out with his toes, nose and fingertips at times, but he kept them out." It looked as though the teams were headed for overtime tied at four, but during a scrum in front of Ottawa netminder Clint Benedict, Corb Denneny spotted the loose puck and pushed it under the goalie. The disc, as the *Star*'s sportswriter observed, "wobbled on the line and the goal umpire waved his hand." Benedict had to be dragged away as the referee upheld the decision and counted the goal. Toronto had taken the first game by a 5–4 score.

Game Two was played at Dey's Arena in Ottawa. The governor general, Lord Byng of Vimy, was also on hand for the game. The *Star* prophesized that "any team that beats Ottawa in Ottawa with a championship and a $10,000 Stanley Cup series at stake is a real team." The pressure was on.

The St. Pats played a strong defensive game and proved that they were, indeed, a real team. Roach was once again marvellous in goal, and the *Globe* described his performance as "the most masterful exhibition of goaltending ever shown locally. The wee lad blocked with stick, feet, body, hands, head, pads, and in every conceivable manner. He turned down effort after effort that was ticketed through and his great display alone saved the Irish."

While Roach may indeed have been "masterful," the St. Pats also employed the curious strategy of icing the puck whenever possible to keep Ottawa out of their zone. While it made for less than spectacular hockey, the strategy worked: Toronto shut down several legends of the game, including Frank Boucher, Punch Broadbent, Cy Denneny, Frank Nighbor, and a 19-year-old rookie named Francis "King" Clancy. The game ended in a 0–0 deadlock, which meant that the Toronto St. Patricks had won the NHL championship five goals to four, and now moved on to face the Vancouver Millionaires for the Stanley Cup.

It seemed only appropriate that the Stanley Cup final would commence on March 17: St. Patrick's Day. While the series was to be played in its entirety at the Arena Gardens, games would again alternate between NHL and PCHA rules. The Millionaires, featuring some ex-Toronto players and the sensational Hugh Lehman in goal, were heavily favoured by all accounts.

Toronto nevertheless began well. Babe Dye opened the scoring and finished with two on the night. Vancouver, however, featured former Toronto Arena Jack Adams. The speedy skater, who was, according to the *Star*, "as prominent as a carbuncle on a fat man's neck," scored three times to lead the Millionaires to a 4–3 win.

Game Two was played under PCHA rules and was so physical that referee Cooper Smeaton visited both teams in their dressing rooms after the first period to read them the riot act. The game was tied at one at the end of 60 minutes, with Adams scoring for Vancouver and Denneny for Toronto.

In the overtime period, Corb Denneny led a rush up the ice. After he was knocked off the puck, Dye picked it up and, as the *Globe* exclaimed, settled the issue with a "rifle-like shot." Dye's winning goal at 4:50 of extra time tied the best-of-five final at one game apiece.

Game Three of the 1922 Stanley Cup final was likely the first Stanley Cup playoff game to be featured on radio. Though the medium was certainly in its embryonic stage, many enterprising Canadians were building their own crystal sets in order to listen in to American stations flooding across the border. Not wanting to miss out on

The first game I played with Toronto was probably the most nervous I've ever been in my life. There I was in Toronto, on the ice at Maple Leaf Gardens, one of hockey's biggest stages. I had been watching this team play since 1960. It was always my favourite team, and now I was on it. A chance to play for the Toronto Maple Leafs is something that Canadian kids dream about their whole lives.

Barry Melrose
PLAYER
1980–83

St PATRICK'S PROFESSIONAL HOCKEY CLUB • LIMITED •

PRESIDENT FRED HAMBLY

VICE PRES. PAUL CICERI

SECRETARY CHAS. QUERRIE

TREASURER PERCY HAMBLY

The Toronto Arenas were sold to a new ownership group, and the Toronto St. Patricks debuted on December 23, 1919, in a 3–0 loss to the Senators in Ottawa.

an opportunity, Canadian newspapers began to launch their own radio stations. Vancouver was on the leading edge of the new technology. The March 24 edition of the *Vancouver Sun* reported that "a comprehensive story of the hockey game at Toronto was broadcasted last night and given to the public hours before it appeared in print. Radio fans reported that the broadcast of the hockey game was exceptionally clear and loud. 'It was just like being at the game,' exclaimed one amateur."

While it wasn't exactly play-by-play, the station read telegraphed reports sent to them from Toronto and provided occasional details on the action as they were received in real time on the night of March 23. In a little over ten years, radio would profoundly affect every aspect of the game, and millions of hockey fans would tune in to hear the match on Saturday nights. In 1922, though, radio played a limited but fascinating role in the Stanley Cup final, reserved for a small fragment of the country's populace.

Whoever was tuning in that night, however, would have heard reports of a very aggressive game. Despite Smeaton's warning during Game Two, the third contest proved to be even rougher. Harry Cameron, for instance, injured his shoulder, while Ken Randall broke a thumb. Vancouver's Lehman was once again sensational, and the Millionaires blanked the St. Pats, 3–0, to retake the series lead.

Vancouver looked to capture the Stanley Cup with a win in Game Four. The St. Pats were hampered by the loss of Randall, and were therefore forced to dress the little-used Shrimp Andrews, whom Toronto had signed midway through the season. It was a fortuitous replacement, and

Andrews scored twice for the Irish. In fact, Toronto completely dominated Vancouver, with Denneny, Dye, and Noble playing their best games of the entire season. Roach was perfect in blanking Vancouver, 6–0.

In the fifth and deciding game, Toronto came out with a vengeance, eager to wrestle the Stanley Cup away from Vancouver. The St. Pats smothered the Millionaires from the opening whistle. There was, however, cause for concern early on when Roach was caught in the face by a shot fired by Ernie Parkes. Although his left eye was half-closed, Roach remained in the game for the duration.

The St. Pats needed their stars to step up if they were going to have any chance of beating the favoured Millionaires. Perhaps unsurprisingly, the hero of the night was Babe Dye. The sharpshooting wizard scored four times in the 5–1 Stanley Cup–clinching victory. "Babe Dye was in the limelight most of the time," the *Globe* observed. "The baseball-hockey star was never better. It was his masterpiece in hockey, and it was Dye and his bullet shot as much as anything else, which enabled the locals to carry off the highest honours professional hockey can give."

Toronto mayor Charles "Alf" Maguire committed to a celebratory reception for the victorious St. Patricks, held on March 29 at the Hotel Carls-Rite, located at the corner of Wellington and Simcoe Streets. There, Mayor Maguire commended the hockey team and stated, "Toronto is proud to honour a team of great athletes who battled their way against tremendous odds to the pinnacle of fame." Maguire then presented St. Patricks president Fred Hambly with "the battered and scratched old silver *jardinière*" – the

Stanley Cup. NHL president Frank Calder followed with the presentation of the O'Brien Cup to captain Reg Noble to commemorate the St. Patricks winning the NHL championship. Additionally, the players and management were presented with silver-mounted rabbit's feet.

Hambly thanked Mayor Maguire and President Calder and humbly offered: "When I and my associates took hold of the pro team in Toronto, we determined to do our utmost to elevate professional hockey and make it a game at which no one would point a finger. That we have, to a certain measure, succeeded is evidenced by this reception to our team by the city council."

After the celebrations, Babe Dye headed south to Buffalo. In 134 games and 468 at-bats with the Bisons that year, the Stanley Cup hero hit .312.

DEFENDING

Not surprisingly, the reigning Stanley Cup champions saw little need to alter their lineup. Shrimp Andrews earned a regular spot on the team after his performance in the 1922 playoffs. Management felt that the core of John Ross Roach, Harry Cameron, Babe Dye, and Ken Randall could, with the support of a cast of substitutes, carry the team.

It looked as though the management was spot on. The St. Patricks opened the 1922–23 season with a healthy 7–2 trouncing of the Montreal Canadiens. While Montreal rookie Aurèle Joliat scored both goals for the Canadiens, his admirable performance was dwarfed by that of Babe Dye, who seemed to pick up where he had left off and scored five goals in the rout.

Even with the victory, the St. Pats chose to make a stunning move after the game, sending Corb Denneny to the Vancouver Millionaires in return for flashy forward Jack Adams. Adams had led the Pacific Coast Hockey Association in scoring in 1921–22, with 26 goals and 30 points, but his business enterprises in eastern Canada now kept him from playing on the West Coast.

While Adams fit into the fold nicely, the St. Patricks' play was somewhat mediocre. By the turn of the calendar, Toronto had a 2–3 record. While the Hamilton Tigers were a soft team, the Irish were certainly in tough if they hoped to get past either Ottawa or Montreal.

Meanwhile, radio continued to capture more and more of the nation's imagination. And while it was a perfect vehicle for news, dramas, and music, broadcasters began to see the opportunity that the medium presented to the sporting world. On February 8, 1923, Norman Albert "described" an OHA intermediate game at the Arena

Gardens, played between North Toronto and Midland on the *Toronto Daily Star*'s own radio station, CFCA. As the *Star* explained, Albert "was right by the side of the rink, and as he spoke, his voice was shot into space."

Six nights later, the idea was translated to National Hockey League action. On February 14, Albert was once again on hand to describe the action, this time for the third period of the St. Patricks' 6–4 victory over the Ottawa Senators. According to hockey historian Eric Zweig, this was the first radio broadcast of an NHL game. CFCA broadcast the third periods of the St. Pats' remaining home games: a 4–3 win over Montreal on February 24, a 4–3 victory against the Hamilton Tigers on March 3, and the 2–0 blanking of the Senators in the final game of the regular season on March 5.

The announcer on each of the latter three games was an upstart named Foster Hewitt. Hewitt had been born into sports when he arrived in this world on November 21, 1902. His father, William, was sports editor of the *Star*, manager of the Toronto Rugby Football Club, and secretary of the Ontario Hockey Association. Throughout the school year, Foster and his family lived in the posh Rosedale neighbourhood. From May until September, the Hewitts lived on the Toronto Islands, where father and son enjoyed watching all manner of sporting events.

The Hewitts were an entrepreneurial family. William, for instance, had been promoting the Paragon Score Board as early as 1901. This device allowed people in one city to follow the play-by-play of a baseball game from another city via a specially constructed board that was constantly updated by telegraph. The machine was operated during World Series baseball games at various Toronto theatres. As Foster explained:

> The arrangement was that a telegrapher at the ball game wired his play-by-play description directly to the theatre where it was received on a ticker machine. Then, an announcer dramatized the action by giving the batter's name and whether each pitch was a ball or strike. On the huge board, lights indicated runners on the basepaths. Other lights showed where the ball was hit and whether the batter was safe or out. The combination of board, lights and announcer was so effective that capacity crowds rooted with all the volume and enthusiasm of fans at the actual game.

The Paragon Score Board was, in some ways, a precursor to the live play-by-play reporting that would one day make Foster famous.

When Joseph Atkinson, publisher of the *Star*, announced his paper's intention to use radio to improve its circulation, Foster Hewitt quit both his job *and* his arts course at the University of Toronto. The young Canadian was now on the fast track to becoming one of the nation's most famous voices.

After months of successful experimenting, the *Star*'s radio station officially signed on the air on June 22, 1922. CFCA occupied two rooms in the *Star*'s building at 18 King Street West. Foster was hired as a staff announcer, often setting up equipment for remote broadcasts at local churches as well. For its part, the *Star* actually drove a truck through the streets, parks, and beaches of the city to prove to locals that its radio station was real and worth tuning in to. Foster was often the driver.

In short order, the *Star*'s radio station had garnered widespread appeal and was constantly searching for added programming. Foster spoke to this quest:

> One morning, Mr. Johnson said to my dad, who was then the *Star*'s sports editor, "Mr. Hewitt, we want to extend the interest in radio. We think a broadcast of a hockey game would be good for us and good for the listeners. What do you think of the idea?" Dad later reported that his associates discouraged the idea. Some thought radio was a passing fad. Others believed hockey was too fast for anybody's eyes and tongue.

Although the date has been vigorously debated through the years, and was even incorrectly recalled in his own autobiography, Foster Hewitt's first hockey broadcast took place on February 16, 1923, at the Arena Gardens. That night, Foster recapped periods one and two of an intermediate contest between Kitchener and the Toronto Argonauts, then proceeded to do a live play-by-play of the third period. The following day's paper reported that "last night, a staff reporter of the *Toronto Star* sat in a soundproof box right at the side of the rink, and told to the many thousands of his listeners what was happening." As it happens, the teams were tied at three at the end of regulation time, and the game took four five-minute overtime periods to conclude, with the Argonauts emerging as 5–3 winners. Foster was back at it for the St. Pats' last three games of the season. Hewitt's nation-altering story, however, was still about 11 years off.

As far as the team on the ice was concerned, the St. Patricks had turned in a decent performance throughout the season, but were unable to catch the Canadiens or the Senators. Toronto finished with 27 points, one

behind second-place Montreal, and only two agonizing points behind first-place Ottawa. Babe Dye led the team and the league with 26 goals and 37 points, becoming the first Toronto player to lead the NHL in scoring. The reacquired Jack Adams added 19 goals, while Reg Noble netted 12. Fans of the Irish had reason to be hopeful. The question remained whether that hope would prove misplaced.

DIAMOND DREAMS

While there had only been minor tweaks a year prior, the St. Pats opted to turn over much of their roster before the puck dropped on the 1923–24 season. Harry Cameron, for example, signed with the Saskatoon Crescents of the WCHL.

Then, on the eve of the season opener, Charlie Querrie packaged Ken Randall and the NHL rights to Corb Denneny and sent them to the Hamilton Tigers for Amos "Butch" Arbour, George Carey, and Bert Corbeau. Arbour had been a slick-skating forward for the Montreal Canadiens before he joined Hamilton. There was also great hope for the veteran Carey, who was "as wide as a steam pipe and as hefty as a flea," but who was also considered a "skating wizard." (Regardless, Carey lasted just four games in Toronto.) And then there was "Pig Iron" Corbeau. The 30-year-old veteran had spent most of his career with the Canadiens and was one of the most feared players in the league. For example, in a game between Hamilton and Toronto, Corbeau had taken umbrage with Babe Dye during a skirmish and knocked out two of Dye's bottom teeth, split his nose, and injured his wrist. Now the two were teammates.

Still, there were some questions surrounding the team's star. It seemed as though Babe Dye's heart was on the baseball diamond. Coming off another solid year with the Buffalo Bisons in 1923, in which he managed a terrific .318 batting average, it looked as though Dye was a small step away from the major leagues. On September 6, 1923, he announced he was leaving hockey to pursue baseball full time. The St. Patricks would have to prepare for life without one of the best snipers in the NHL.

The Dye-less Irish began the new campaign on December 15. Bert Corbeau scored the first goal of Toronto's season in the 2–1 opener against Montreal. Billy "Red" Stuart scored the winner that night when his shot from centre ice bounced off Georges Mantha and eluded goaltender Georges Vézina.

When Toronto played the Hamilton Tigers in a home-and-home on December 22 and 26, it almost seemed like an intra-squad contest. Looking across the faceoff circle from the St. Pats were former teammates Corb Denneny, Goldie Prodger, Ken Randall, and Mickey Roach, as well as netminder Jake Forbes. Toronto won both games, 5–2 and 2–1.

While the St. Pats were a respectable 3–3 at the end of the calendar year, they were buoyed by the news that Babe Dye had decided to return to the ice. He was back in the lineup as of January 2, and there was hope that Toronto would now soar. It didn't turn out that way. In fact, the Irish lost the first three games after Dye's return. The St. Pats had, as the *Toronto Daily Star* suggested, "faded like snow on a hot stove."

The team finally broke out of its slump on January 12 against Montreal at the Arena Gardens. Dye scored a goal in the 5–3 win after Georges Mantha bizarrely stopped to tie his skate during the play. There were more bizarre moments for the Irish later that month. Manager Charlie Querrie was so incensed during a 7–2 loss in Ottawa that he protested the game to NHL president Frank Calder. Referee Art Ross had sent off Reg Noble, Jack Adams, and Bert Corbeau, which forced the St. Pats to play with three men against six Senators. While the score stuck, the protest was accepted and Ross was not allowed to referee in any further games that the St. Patricks played that season.

It didn't much matter. The season ended when the Senators squashed the St. Pats, 8–4. In the end, it was a repeat of the previous season: Ottawa finished first, Montreal second, and Toronto third. The main difference was that this time, the St. Patricks had finished a *distant* third. Toronto had 10 wins and 14 losses for a 20-point season, only two points better than last-place Hamilton. The outcome was a disappointment, though there were some impressive individual performances: despite missing five games at the start of the season, Babe Dye led the team in scoring with 16 goals and 19 points, which were good enough for second- and fourth-best in the league, respectively; Adams finished seventh in the league with 18 points, and his 14 goals ranked fourth in the NHL; and Noble was tenth with 15 points, including 12 goals. On balance, however, the St. Patricks were trending the wrong way. Changes were almost certainly coming.

DAWNING OF THE DAY

With general interest in the professional game on the rise, the NHL grew from four to six teams for the 1924–25 season. New to the league were the Boston Bruins – the first U.S.-based franchise in the NHL – and the Montreal Maroons. The Maroons would play their home games in a newly built ice palace, the Montreal Forum, but oddly enough it was the Canadiens who hosted the first game in the new rink, on November 29, 1924. The natural ice surface in their usual home, the Mount Royal Arena, wasn't ready for opening night, so the game moved the Forum, where the Canadiens trounced the St. Patricks, 7–1, in front of 9,000 fans – the largest crowd to have watched a hockey match in Montreal to that date.

Despite having missed the playoffs the previous year, and despite the general consensus that changes were likely coming for the franchise, the St. Pats had made very few adjustments to their roster. There were, however, some minor moves. Goalkeeper John Ross Roach, for instance, was named team captain. And Charlie Querrie decided to relinquish his role as coach and promote assistant coach Eddie Powers to replace him. Powers had been an outstanding lacrosse player and had come to hockey in a most unusual fashion. While working at Eaton's department store in Toronto, Powers had been recruited to coach the store's hockey team. His leadership skills were noticed by the hockey community, and after coaching various amateur teams, Powers was asked to join the St. Patricks.

The St. Pats did make one key acquisition prior to training camp when they signed Bert McCaffrey. The free agent had been a key member of the Toronto Granites, who won the Allan Cup championship in 1922 and 1923. As the reigning senior champions, the Granites represented Canada at the 1924 Olympic Winter Games in Chamonix, France, where they dominated the tournament. McCaffrey scored 20 goals in five games on the way to the gold medal.

After the drubbing at the hands of the Canadiens in Montreal, the St. Pats responded well in their home opener with a 5–3 win over the Boston Bruins. The game was not, however, without its share of controversy. The contest, according to the *Toronto Daily Star*, "was as full of incident as a sunfish is of bones." The St. Pats were up 2–1 in the second period on a pair of goals by Jack Adams when Babe Dye was called offside on a particular play. Dye disagreed and got into a heated argument with the official. He was quickly joined by Adams, then Noble, and finally the fans. When the dust cleared, Adams and Dye were assessed five-minute penalties, and Dye was handed a misconduct penalty, but the Irish did hold on for the win.

St. Pats forwards Corb Denneny
(left) and Bert McCaffrey
(right) flank netminder
John Ross Roach.

Two nights later, the St. Pats entertained the Hamilton Tigers. The latter, as it turned out, were not hospitable guests. Red Green scored five times to lead Hamilton to a 10–3 debacle. Although it was only three games into the season, Toronto had been outscored 20–9. The newspapers were already calling for change. "St. Pats simply must have some new blood," the *Star* demanded, adding, "Convinced, at last, that some of their veterans will not do, the Irish management is combing the province for likely boys."

Changes happened quickly, but they didn't occur on the ice as expected. On December 10, 1924, Fred and Percy Hambly, who each held 99 of the 400 shares in the Toronto St. Patricks, sold their interests in the team to John Paris Bickell and Nathan Nathanson. The two entrepreneurs were among the wealthiest men in Canada: Bickell was president of McIntyre Porcupine Mines, while Nathanson was president of Famous Players Canadian Corporation, which operated a chain of movie theatres. The two men also sought to secure Paul Ciceri's 99 shares in the team, but the horse-racing magnate chose to stay on, saying, "You never saw me desert a ship because I thought it was sinking. St. Pats looked terrible last Friday, but they are not quite that bad. I'm sticking to my shares in the old club whether it's a winner or a loser." Nevertheless, the St. Pats' cheques would now be signed by men who dealt in gold bars and silver screens.

At first, J.P. Bickell played only a peripheral role when it came to the team's affairs. The mining magnate, whose real impact on the city's hockey landscape was still a few years off, invested $25,000 in the St. Pats and served mostly as a silent partner. Bickell only got involved, as hockey legend Frank Selke recalled, "as a matter of civic pride and because of his friendship for Charles Querrie." Querrie was the team's fourth major stakeholder, and he was now appointed the St. Pats' new managing director.

Querrie, in his new position, did not hesitate to shuffle the St. Pats deck. First, he sold Reg Noble to the Montreal Maroons for $6,000. The Toronto fans had grown disenchanted with Noble. As the *Star* explained, for five or six years Noble "was a mighty useful player. Then, he commenced to look upon himself as a fixture with the St. Pats, and once he got that idea in his head, his value to the club depreciated rapidly." Noble would, however, enjoy another nine seasons in the NHL.

At the same time, Querrie signed one of the more outstanding prospects in amateur hockey in Ontario.

Clarence "Hap" Day had starred for two seasons with the OHA's Hamilton Tigers, and when he moved to Toronto to enrol in the Faculty of Pharmacy at the University of Toronto, he joined the Toronto Varsity team in the OHA's senior division. Although Day dreamed of becoming a pharmacist, Conn Smythe, who coached the Varsity squad at U of T, implored him to accept Querrie's offer of a career in professional hockey.

On December 10, the date of the sale to Bickell and Nathanson, the rejuvenated St. Pats travelled to Ottawa and doubled the Senators 6–3. One *Star* writer was quick to offer praise: "I always said that the St. Pats gang could play real hockey, but that some of them were not giving 100 per cent of their ability to the boys who were paying the 'shot.' It certainly looks as if the shadow of the axe made the boys in green and white turn on all the juice."

For his part, Day impressed his many judges. While his debut was in a 3–1 loss to the Maroons on December 13, onlookers could see that Day was going to be a big part of the franchise moving forward.

With two games remaining in the now-extended 30-game regular season, the Hamilton Tigers led the second-place St. Pats by three points. This meant that two losses by the Tigers, combined with two wins by Toronto, would give the St. Pats first place and a bye into the NHL final. It was not to be, as Ottawa shut out the St. Pats, 3–0, in the final game of the season.

Toronto finished with a record of 19 wins and 11 losses to finish a single point behind the league-leading Tigers. Babe Dye collected a league-best 38 goals and was the league's scoring leader with 46 points. The team was vulnerable, however, in goal. Roach allowed 84 goals, the most of any goaltender in the league. Only the expansion Bruins, who used four different netminders, gave up more goals (119) than Toronto.

In the playoffs, second-place Toronto was scheduled to face the third-place Canadiens in a semifinal to decide who would compete against first-place Hamilton for the NHL championship. The two-game, total-goals series began in Montreal. The Canadiens won, 3–2, led by a pair of goals from sophomore centre Howie Morenz. Babe Dye fired a shot in the waning minutes of the game that he insisted had entered the net and quickly rebounded out. But the goal judge did not raise his hand to indicate a goal. Dye and his teammates argued their point for several minutes, to no avail.

Two nights later, the St. Pats hosted the Canadiens at the Arena Gardens. While the St. Pats might have been the better team in the first game, the second contest was all Montreal's, as they scored a goal early and then fell into an impenetrable defensive shell that shut down the St. Pats' attack. The Canadiens took the series, five goals to two.

While Toronto and Montreal were fighting it out on the ice, the players for the Tigers had gone on strike. They informed team manager Percy Thompson that, unless each player received $200 for participating in the final, they would refuse to play. The Tigers claimed that their contracts expired with the final regular-season game and that they were entitled to extra money for the playoffs. The NHL had extended the season from 24 to 30 games, but the owners of the Tigers insisted that the players' contracts ran from December 1 to March 30, regardless of the number of games played during that period of time. Frank Calder informed the team that they would be suspended if they did not play the winner of the Toronto–Montreal series. The Tigers players stuck to their guns and did not play in the NHL final.

The NHL then declared that Hamilton had defaulted on the series, which made the Canadiens the 1924–25 league champions. It was, according to Calder, "an inglorious ending to an otherwise brilliant season."

THE WANING OF THE GREEN

Eddie Livingstone reappeared in 1925, with designs on resurrecting the idea of a second professional hockey league. His league would theoretically involve eastern Canada and the Atlantic seaboard. And it would rival the NHL. When it became clear that Livingstone was intent on including Pittsburgh in his plans, the NHL quickly awarded a franchise to that same city. The Pittsburgh Pirates became the third American team in what was now a league of seven, joining the Bruins and another expansion franchise, the New York Americans. The latter was effectively stocked with the suspended Hamilton Tigers players when Big Bill Dwyer, a noted New York City bootlegger, bought the rights to the players and the NHL quietly lifted the players' suspensions.

Meanwhile, the prognosticators fingered the Toronto St. Patricks as one of three real Stanley Cup contenders. With several veterans returning, including Jack Adams, Bert Corbeau, John Ross Roach, and Babe Dye – who had just been appointed captain – the Irish appeared to be up to the task. In September, the team added another key piece in the form of the talented young winger

Pete Bellefeuille. The St. Pats, it seemed, were heading in the right direction.

Unfortunately, the team got off on the wrong foot. On the very first day of training camp, Roach's goalie stick accidentally jabbed Dye in the eye, which forced the captain off the ice and into a doctor's office. Fortunately, it turned out to be a bruise, but it was an ominous beginning to the new campaign.

In the season opener at the Arena Gardens on November 28, the Boston Bruins edged the St. Pats, 3–2. By the end of December, the Toronto St. Patricks had tumbled to last place in the NHL.

Fans wondered what was wrong with the team's top two forwards. Neither Babe Dye nor Jack Adams had been playing their usual fast, rugged style. The duo had been labelled "ineffective" by the dailies. There was, as it turned out, good reason for their less than stellar play. Adams, for one, was suffering from intestinal flu while an ear, nose, and throat specialist removed a tumour from Dye's inner ear, and he missed five games while he recuperated. Dye would never really recover during that season, and the St. Pats suffered accordingly.

Part of the problem for Toronto was that the expansion teams were all performing well above expectations. The Pittsburgh Pirates had actually played together as the Pittsburgh Yellow Jackets, which had won the U.S. Amateur Hockey Association championship in 1924 and 1925. The team was coached by the innovative Odie Cleghorn, who was likely the first coach to use three forward lines throughout the game. Previously, teams had used one forward line, adding substitutes occasionally through the course of a game.

The St. Pats were unable to turn the season around. The team struggled out of the gate and never made up any ground, finishing well out of the playoff running with a disappointing record of 12 wins, 21 losses, and 3 ties that ranked sixth in the seven-team league. While the team could score (they were tied for the league lead in goals scored with 92), defensively – with 114 goals against – they were the worst in the NHL. Jack Adams led the team with 21 goals and 26 points, for sixth-best in the NHL that season. Despite his operation, Babe Dye still managed 18 goals and 23 points. With the St. Patricks out of the playoff race early, interest seemed to be fading in the Irish. And many, including its owners, began to question the team's relevance.

When I was drafted by the Leafs in 1979, it was a culmination of something I had hoped and dreamed would someday become a reality. To be able to play with some character individuals like Ron Ellis, Darryl Sittler, Lanny McDonald, and Tiger Williams was an incredible experience. It was a time I fondly look back on as being a life-changing experience both as a hockey player and as a person.

Laurie Boschman
PLAYER
1979–82

BLUE AND WHITE
1926–27 TO 1930–31

OUR CIVIC DUTY

After missing the playoffs, Charlie Querrie intended to reverse the fortunes of his team. The wheeling and dealing began. Babe Dye was sold to the newly introduced Chicago Black Hawks for $15,000 on October 18, 1926. In five of his seven seasons with the St. Patricks, Dye had led his team in goals and points, and he had also led the NHL in scoring twice. The St. Pats also said goodbye to their other big gun, Jack Adams, sold to the Ottawa Senators on November 4. In the space of a week, the St. Pats lost the two players who were responsible for 39 of the team's 92 goals in 1925–26.

To replenish the roster, Querrie signed Bill Carson. While earning his medical degree, Carson had played on the University of Toronto's Varsity team that won the Allan Cup in 1921. Querrie also signed Irvine Bailey from Peterborough of the OHA senior league and picked up Butch Keeling, Bill Brydge, and Danny Cox from other senior clubs. Toronto then acquired the rights to Corb Denneny after the Saskatoon Sheiks – the team he was playing with in the Western Hockey League (as the WCHL was now known) – folded. Although Denneny would later be returned to Saskatoon due to complications surrounding the original transaction, the St. Pats found good use for the veteran during his second time around in Toronto.

These additions joined the returning members of the St. Patricks in training camp, including netminder John Ross Roach, captain Bert Corbeau on defence, Hap Day, who moved between forward and defence, and forwards Pete Bellefeuille and Bert McCaffrey.

Meanwhile, another NHL franchise had begun its training camp in Toronto. The newly minted New York Rangers gathered at Toronto's Ravina Gardens in October 1926 to train under their manager, Conn Smythe. Smythe had been busy since the war. He owned and operated C. Smythe 4 Sand, a sand and gravel business located in Toronto's west end. In the evenings, Smythe coached the University of Toronto Varsity team with some success. The war veteran was soon regarded as an astute hockey man in the highest circles of the game. Colonel John Hammond, president of Madison Square Garden Corporation, which owned the Rangers hockey club, offered Smythe $10,000 to build the Rangers for him. Smythe agreed, on the condition that he could remain in Toronto.

Using his vast knowledge of the best available players, Smythe secured an outstanding cast that included Taffy Abel, Frank Boucher, brothers Bill and Bun Cook, Ching Johnson, and Murray Murdoch. But after assembling an impressive team (the Rangers would win the Stanley Cup in 1928), Colonel Hammond decided that the franchise needed a general manager who would devote the entire year to overseeing the team while based in New York. Hammond offered Smythe a substantial raise to leave his aggregate business in Toronto, but Smythe declined. On October 27, Smythe was dismissed by the Rangers. Lester Patrick was hired in his place.

Smythe hoped to return to coach Varsity in the OHA senior league, but his request was denied by the Amateur Athletic Union of Canada. The AAU ruled that once Smythe had accepted the salary from the Rangers, he had turned professional. Instead, he was elected president of the OHA's junior league, where he served alongside William A. Hewitt and Frank Selke. But after arguing his position and saying that he would be willing to return the money he was paid by the Rangers, he was allowed to coach the Varsity Grads.

Defenceman Francis "King" Clancy (left) proved to be one of the most popular players in the history of the Blue and White. The acquisition cost Toronto $35,000 (including the $20,000 down payment shown below) and two players, but in his second season as a Maple Leaf, he helped lead the team to a Stanley Cup championship.

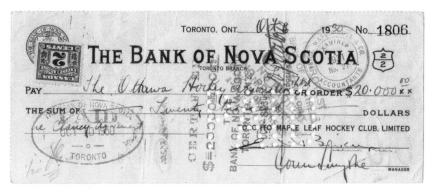

The Rangers invited Smythe to attend their inaugural game at Madison Square Garden. At his wife Irene's insistence, Smythe reluctantly agreed. There, he met team owner Tex Rickard. Smythe explained to Rickard that he believed that his contract had entitled him to $10,000, while Smythe had only received $7,500. Rickard paid him the additional $2,500. That money would change the history of hockey in Toronto.

As the Smythes returned to Canada, they drove through Montreal. There, Conn bet the entire $2,500 on a football game between the University of Toronto and McGill University. He doubled his money. With the winnings, he placed another bet, this time that the New York Rangers would defeat the St. Patricks in Toronto's home opener at the Arena Gardens on November 20. The Rangers won, 5–1. Over the course of three days, Smythe had turned $2,500 into approximately $10,000, and he knew exactly what he wanted to do with it.

Meanwhile, with the loss against the Rangers, the St. Pats were now 0–2 to start the season. Through the first two months, Toronto simply couldn't score and was shut out in six of its first 15 games. By New Year's Day 1927, the St. Patricks were a woeful 4–10. To make matters worse, the team was effectively without a coach. Charlie Querrie had been behind the bench while the team considered a more permanent solution, and not surprisingly, the media questioned his ability as a coach. On February 7, the *Toronto Daily Star*, with tongue placed firmly in cheek, offered, "Charlie Querrie may not know all the inside hockey in the world, but he has wonderful harmony among the players."

The fact of the matter was that the Toronto St. Patricks were a bad hockey team, and not only had interest in the squad continued to decline steadily, but the Irish were up for sale, and everyone knew it.

The St. Pats ownership group was, understandably, tired of losing money. They wanted out. C.C. Pyle, an American theatre owner and sports agent, offered a solution. Pyle inquired about the asking price of the St. Pats and was informed that the team could be his for $200,000. The entrepreneur, without so much as blinking, made plans to purchase the team. Pyle was no stranger to team ownership, having already co-owned the Boston Bulldogs, Chicago Bulls, and New York Yankees of an early incarnation of the American Football League. The writing for the Toronto St. Patricks, it seemed, was on the wall.

Meanwhile, J.P. Bickell and Conn Smythe were having some very interesting conversations. When Querrie no longer wanted to be behind the bench, Bickell had hired Mike Rodden to coach the St. Pats. Rodden had had some success coaching Canadian football, but he'd never coached big-time hockey before. Upon hearing of Bickell's decision, Smythe warned that Rodden would prove to be a failure. Smythe was right, and when Bickell contacted him to see if he was up for the St. Pats job, Smythe, ever the opportunist, recognized an opening. But he wasn't just interested in coaching the St. Pats; he now insisted on a share of the club. Perhaps Smythe's nerve impressed Bickell, because he got his way.

At the same time, the city's hockey fans were alerted to the potential consequences of Pyle purchasing the St. Pats. The *Toronto Telegram* reported, "What is most important about the deal, if it goes through, is that Mr. Pyle will transfer the club, intact, to Philadelphia." The Queen City was going to lose its team to the City of Brotherly Love. It didn't feel right. In the years leading up to the Depression, Toronto was certainly a city on the rise. Since the First World War, the city had truly flourished and had finally surpassed Montreal as the nation's most important business hub. As far as Smythe was concerned, it was Bickell's duty to keep the team in Toronto. Bickell was sufficiently swayed, and Toronto looked as though it would get to keep its team. There was only one small matter: How?

For his part, Bickell agreed to hold on to his existing $40,000 stake in the club, leaving it to Smythe to somehow raise the remaining $160,000 with other investors. Smythe, energized, was also able to persuade Charlie Querrie, who still owned a substantial share of the team, that civic pride was infinitely more important than money. Smythe walked the walk: he put his $10,000 gambling winnings into the team and then put together a consortium that included several other investors besides Bickell. On February 14, 1927, Smythe's group met with the owners. The backers, who included stockbroker Ed Bickle, were – with Bickell's crucial assistance – able to put down $75,000, and they undertook to pay the remaining $75,000 in 30 days. Smythe, with the help of some very powerful friends, had kept big-time hockey in Toronto.

The *Star* broke the story on February 14, reporting, "The Toronto Maple Leaf Hockey Club has been incorporated and is taking over today the assets and franchise in the National Hockey League of the St. Patricks Hockey Club Ltd. A meeting of the NHL is being held in Toronto to ratify the transfer."

The next day, the newspapers confirmed that the sale had been ratified. Perhaps the *Toronto Globe* provided

John Paris Bickell, an investor in the St. Patricks franchise, was a significant member of the consortium that purchased the hockey club, renaming it the Maple Leafs.

the most memorable headline: GOOD-BYE ST. PATS! HOWDY MAPLE LEAFS!

> With the sale of the St. Patrick's Hockey Club of the pro league to the Toronto Maple Leaf Hockey Club yesterday, the Irish cognomen passes out. The Toronto team will wear a brilliant hued jersey with maple leaves and the name "Toronto" across the chest in bold letter. Much desirable publicity for the Queen City is bound to accrue.

It was the sort of publicity that Smythe dearly desired for his team. And he knew he wasn't going to get it with the team's existing name. The St. Patricks nickname had been an unabashed attempt to charm the significant Irish population in Toronto, a ploy that had enjoyed only mixed results. Many Irish Torontonians remained loyal to the city's more traditional Irish squad, the St. Michael's junior hockey team. Toronto was still very much an outpost of Protestant Britain, and an enduring love affair with an English King and British iconography persisted. The critical mass in Toronto had not responded favourably to the St. Patricks' Irish green and vague Catholicism.

Apart from demographics, the Great War – to which Toronto had lost 5,000 sons and daughters – remained very much in the consciousness of the Queen City. It seems obvious, at least from a business perspective, that "marketing" efforts should have been aimed at the British majority and not the Irish population.

Soon after the takeover, the group focused its energy on building a new brand with corresponding iconography more in harmony with the predominant sentiments of Toronto: Union Flags, "God Save the King," portraits of the King, and odes to the Canadian effort in the First World War. These were the symbols that embodied the stuff of old Toronto. It was this brand that would open up the hearts of the local population.

Canada had a long history with the Maple Leaf well before the nation's resplendent red and white flag was officially inaugurated in 1965. By the late 1840s, Toronto's pre-Confederation *literati* could boast a journal entitled *The Maple Leaf Annual*. It is hardly surprising that the journal referred to the Maple Leaf as the chosen "emblem of Canada" in 1848. Soon afterwards, the Maple Leaf became a symbol of Confederation.

Perhaps the most famous celebration of the Maple Leaf came when Alexander Muir penned "The Maple Leaf Forever." Muir wrote the song – inspired by a large maple tree that stood at Memory Lane and Laing Street in Toronto, where the composer lived – in October 1867 to celebrate the new country. The song served as English Canada's unofficial national anthem between Confederation and the Second World War.

Predictably, the Maple Leaf found solid representation within sporting spheres. From the middle of the 19th century onwards, the Maple Leaf had appeared in various sporting contexts throughout Toronto. In the 1860s, there were baseball teams called the Maple Leafs in Guelph and Hamilton. The Maple Leaf Cricket Club and Yorkville Maple Leaf lacrosse club competed as early as the 1870s. The Maple Leaf Club of Parkdale and the Maple Leaf Curling Club in Scarborough were in operation by the late 19th century, and the Maple Leaf Stakes has been a feature of the horse-racing calendar since its inauguration in 1892. The maple tree and its leaves were clearly entrenched elements of Canadiana and the nation's sporting teams many years before the hockey Leafs ever took to the ice.

Crucial to the story, though, was the Toronto Maple Leafs baseball team, a successful fixture in the city since 1896. In fact, the two teams were indirectly linked. By the time Bickell and Smythe began their partnership in 1927, the baseball Leafs were enjoying great success, winning the International League pennant in 1926. They had long been filling various venues adorned in blue and white, including Sunlight Park (Queen Street East and Broadview Avenue), Hanlan's Point Stadium (on the Toronto Islands), Diamond Park, and by 1926, the brand new Maple Leaf Stadium (at Bathurst and Fleet Streets – the latter would become Lake Shore Boulevard).

Timing suggests that the hockey Leafs may have been inspired by the already winning and popular baseball Leafs. But the connections run even deeper. The baseball Leafs were owned by Lol Solman, a prominent Toronto businessman who was also the managing director of the Arena Gardens, home of the St. Pats.

Of course, the emblem shared greater currency among Torontonians than the baseball Leafs' success on the diamond. It was heavily employed by Canadian soldiers, creating a cultural touchstone for the city. The Maple Leaf represented military success for the nation, and in particular, victory at Vimy Ridge. In terms of reverence *for* and attachment *to* that "war to end all wars," Toronto was unlike any other city in Canada. Smythe, Bickell, and the rest of the new ownership team knew this. Here was an opportunity, as Smythe explained:

The Maple Leaf, to us, was the badge of courage, the badge that meant home. It was the badge that reminded us of all our exploits and the different difficulties we got into, and the different accomplishments that we made. It was a badge that meant more to us than any other badge that we could think of, so we chose it, hoping that the possession of this badge would mean something to the team that wore it, and when they skated out on the ice with this badge on their chest, they would wear it with honour and pride and courage, the way it would have been worn by the soldiers of the first Great War in the Canadian Army.

Rooted in the Canadian war experience, Smythe recommended the legendary Victoria Cross recipient Lieutenant-Colonel William "Billy" Barker to serve as the Maple Leafs' first president.

The Britishness of Old Orange Ontario would be the life force driving Smythe's Maple Leaf brand. The seemingly ancient Anglo-Protestant tenets of propriety, thrift, and self-restraint would find expression through the Leafs. Visually, the club would reflect this vision. The team would wear royal blue and white, and Smythe envisioned the day when a grand palace, accessorized by a large portrait of the King and multiple Union Flags, would flank the arena. Smythe also imagined the 48th Highlanders piping "God Save the King" to serve as an aural reminder of Toronto's ties to Britain, while the band's rendition of "The Maple Leaf Forever" would reconnect the spectator with the team's military roots and iconography. The most obvious link, however, would be the audience itself. Over 80 per cent of Torontonians were of British ancestry in the late 1920s. Moreover, two-thirds of non-native residents had been born in the United Kingdom.

In this way, the majority of Torontonians would see their own reflection staring back from the Gardens ice. The team and its new home would be already somehow "familiar." The discourse that ensued between player and spectator would be a conversation in which only those truly in the know could participate. The Leafs would forge an unbreakable bond, first on Mutual Street and later at Carlton and Church – one that harmonized player and spectator. The Maple Leafs brand articulated that deep sense of self that was surging through the veins of Toronto's people.

It was also very good business. The 1927 board of Toronto Maple Leaf Hockey Club Limited read like a who's who of the Canadian business world. One name, however, was conspicuous by its absence: Conn Smythe.

Smythe did not, of course, have the deep pockets that his colleagues had. At least for now, his stake was far more modest than those of the rest of the ownership group. Still, it was Conn Smythe who became the face of the franchise. And in 20 years, he would become the owner of the Toronto Maple Leafs. But before Smythe rolled his sleeves up to work on the Leafs, he honoured his commitment and completed the season coaching the University of Toronto's Varsity Grads to the Allan Cup championship in 1927. It was a busy time for the man who saved Toronto's NHL team.

Meanwhile, Mike Rodden's tenure behind the bench lasted just two games, both losses. The second, played on February 16, was also the final game played under the Toronto St. Patricks name. At the time, the game meant little in the overall scheme of things, and it would have been largely forgettable had it not taken on somewhat historic proportions.

The team faced the Detroit Cougars, who, during their inaugural season, played their home games across the river in Windsor, Ontario, at the Border Cities Arena while their new arena, the Olympia, was being built. That night, Detroit beat Toronto, 5–1, in front of a crowd of only 150 people.

Fittingly, Corb Denneny – the only player to play with the Blueshirts, the Torontos, the Arenas, the St. Patricks, and, in due course, the Maple Leafs – scored the final goal for the Irish. The St. Patricks – name, jersey, and entity – were officially retired after the game with a record of 8 wins, 19 losses, and 4 ties to that point in the season. In 24 hours, the team would be at the Arena Gardens and facing off against the New York Americans as the Toronto Maple Leafs.

The team looked to Alex Romeril, who had travelled with Charlie Querrie and the team to Windsor to see the St. Pats' final game, to replace Rodden behind the bench. As a player, Romeril had won the OHA junior championship with the Toronto Canoe Club in 1912 and had been an Allan Cup champion with the Winnipeg 61st Battalion in 1916 and the Toronto Granites in 1922 and 1923. Although he had enjoyed great success as a player, he was new to the management side of hockey. Romeril was nevertheless hired to coach the team for the remainder of the season.

The Toronto Maple Leafs made their debut at home against the New York Americans on February 17, 1927. Original discussions suggested that the team would change the colour of its sweaters from green and white to red and white, but when they took to the ice for their first game as the Maple Leafs, the team wore new white sweaters with a green Maple Leaf crest and the word

I was born, bred, and raised in Toronto, and breathed blue and white since I was in my crib. My dad died back in '98–'99, but he was just on top of the world knowing that I was the organist for the Maple Leafs. He loved hockey. My family has always been Leafs fans. There's never been anybody else.

Jimmy Holmstrom
ORGANIST
1987–PRESENT

TORONTO on the chest. The *Star* thought the new uniforms made the players look like "a lot of galloping ghosts in white." While it would be a temporary look, the newly minted Maple Leafs were successful in their first game, defeating the Americans, 4–1. Midway through the second period, rookie George "Paddy" Patterson got the first goal scored in a Toronto Maple Leafs uniform, which just happened to be his first NHL goal. Irvine Bailey scored twice, and Bert Corbeau added the fourth goal for Toronto.

The Maple Leafs improved slightly on the St. Patricks' performance, going 7–5–1, and with a 2–1 win over the Montreal Canadiens the eventful season came to an end. The team concluded the 44-game season with 15 wins, 24 losses, and 5 ties. The 35-point total was good for last place in the NHL's Canadian Division. More happily, rookies Irvine Bailey and Bill Carson led the team in scoring; Bailey had 15 goals and 28 points, good for sixth-place in NHL scoring, and Carson had 16 goals and 22 points. There was reason to be hopeful. Soon, the city would awaken to the Maple Leafs' brand of play and spirit.

GALLOPING GHOSTS

On September 27, 1927, the *Toronto Daily Star* reported:

> Pro hockey fans will be re-introduced to the Toronto team this fall. Peter G. Campbell and his associates have arranged to doll the team out in new colours. The jersey will be banded blue and white with a large Maple Leaf on the breast. The words 'Toronto Maple Leafs' appear in blue letters on the Maple Leaf.

Smythe once claimed to have changed the team's colours from green and white to blue and white because "the blue represents the Canadian skies, while white represents snow." This was revisionist history. In truth, blue and white also happened to be the same colours used on the trucks of Smythe's sand and gravel business. In the end, though, the blue and white suited – even if it by accident – the mythology that Smythe and company were trying to cultivate around the team. Incidentally, that season the pioneering Maple Leafs became the first NHL team to feature two different sweaters as part of their on-ice ensemble. They introduced a white sweater with a blue Maple Leaf to accompany their blue sweater with the white leaf. Part of the rationale was to avoid confusion when playing teams like the New York Rangers and New York Americans, both of whom wore sweaters that featured blue prominently.

Training camp opened on October 22, and players participated in softball and soccer games at the Don Flats, followed by relay races and then a four-kilometre run back to the Arena Gardens. It was heavy going. Under Smythe, the rules were simple, as the *Star* explained:

> Aside from what you wear, what you say, what you eat, what you drink, who you're with, where you're going, how much you weigh and what you think, the club has little, if any, interest in the hired help, outside working hours. There's one thing about it: the pay is good and it's always on time. There's more civil liberty in digging a ditch. But most of these guys are in a rut. They still seem to prefer hockey.

Joe Primeau and Carl Voss, two of the first players Smythe had signed for the New York Rangers, had both been invited to the Maple Leafs' training camp. Curiously, Smythe had purchased Primeau's contract when he left the Rangers' employ. "I bought it with my own money, and for one summer, Joe Primeau and I constituted an organization with no franchise, no place to play, a manager and one player."

Smythe, looking for players with character, traded to get the 36-year-old Art Duncan from Detroit, who was also a First World War fighting ace. With veteran Bert Corbeau gone to the Leaf-affiliated Toronto Ravinas of the Canadian Professional league, Smythe named Hap Day as the team's new captain. Charlie Querrie said that Day was "just about the most useful player in the National Hockey League. He goes 60 minutes at top speed and is a prime favourite with the fans." Day was given a $500 bonus to serve as captain of the Toronto Maple Leafs, which he would do for the next ten seasons.

True to his vision, on November 15, 1927, Smythe had the 48th Highlanders perform before the opening faceoff on the first-ever opening night for the Toronto Maple Leafs. The band performed "The Maple Leaf Forever," and Ontario's lieutenant-governor, William Donald Ross, dropped the ceremonial first puck. Unseasonably warm weather, combined with the frigid ice, created a fog that enveloped the ice surface and made play difficult for the Leafs and the visiting New York Rangers. In fact, it was so bad that both teams circled the ice in a futile attempt to dissipate the fog between periods. The Leafs played as though lost in the haze as the Rangers claimed a 4–2 victory.

After a month of hockey, the Leafs were, at best, a mediocre team. Smythe made some moves, adding

The Maple Leafs swapped goalies with the New York Rangers in October 1928, sending John Ross Roach to New York and receiving Lorne Chabot (pictured) in return. That season, Chabot backstopped the team to their first playoff appearance as the Maple Leafs.

Eddie Rodden from Chicago and Jimmy "Sailor" Herbert from Boston. It was hoped that the latter would add some scoring, but after an inauspicious start – on his first shift, Herbert fell onto the ice, and then proceeded to stand on the wrong blueline, shoulder to shoulder with the opposing Chicago Black Hawks – Herbert failed to deliver the expected production and was gone after the season.

More worrisome, on February 2, a skate blade slashed the Achilles tendon of captain Hap Day. It was a colossal loss for the Blue and White, and it would be eight months before Day began skating again.

The team's fortunes hardly improved. On March 3, goaltender John Ross Roach suffered a gallstone attack and was hospitalized. Without a netminder, Conn Smythe borrowed Joe Ironstone from the Toronto Falcons (formerly the Ravinas) of the Can-Pro League. Ironstone had only one game of NHL experience, and that was as an emergency fill-in for the New York Americans in 1925–26. Through "70 minutes of guerrilla-like hockey," as the *Montreal Gazette* described it, Ironstone led the Leafs to a scoreless draw. Despite the shutout, Ironstone's second NHL game would also be his last.

For six seasons, beginning with 1930–31, the NHL allowed up to three assists to be awarded on a goal, but in a 1–1 tie with Ottawa on March 13, 1928, Toronto's sole tally registered *four* assists. Danny Cox scored with assists awarded to Eddie Rodden, Art Smith, and Gerry Lowrey.

The team plodded along, but the loss of players such as Day, Roach, and Bill Carson, who was also injured, greatly impacted the Maple Leafs. Toronto was officially eliminated from playoff contention on March 14, 1928. The team had missed the playoffs for a third straight season.

In 1927–28, their first full season as the Maple Leafs, and under the tutelage of Conn Smythe, the team finished fourth in the Canadian Division with a record of 18–18–8, six points back of the Ottawa Senators. Despite missing 12 games, Bill Carson led the team in scoring with 20 goals and 26 points, which was good for eighth in the league's scoring race. Likewise, although he missed half of the season, Hap Day had the Leafs' second-best scoring record with 9 goals and 17 points. More impressively, however, the team as an entity had generated $83,000 in revenue. There was, it appeared, more interest in a mediocre team that better represented the majority of Toronto's citizens than there had been in the Leafs' Irish predecessors. But mediocrity did not sit well with Conn Smythe.

BETWEEN THE DON AND THE HUMBER

While Smythe had some key pieces in Day, Carson, and Bailey, he knew he needed more. In October 1928, Andy Blair was signed as a free agent, and Lorne Chabot was added in goal when Smythe sent John Ross Roach and $10,000 to the New York Rangers. Roach had tended goal for Toronto for eight seasons, backstopped the Stanley Cup champion St. Patricks in 1922, and captained the team during the 1925–26 campaign. But the "Port Perry Woodpecker" was holding out for more money, so when the Rangers suggested a trade involving Chabot, Toronto was eager to make the exchange. After all, Chabot had been a key member of the Rangers, and had shut out opposing teams 21 times in his first two NHL seasons. Years later, on February 11, 1935, a *Time* magazine article described Lorne Chabot as a:

> bulky, silent, languid French Canadian . . . Chabot almost never leaves his net. Slow at regaining his feet when he falls down, he indulges in few of the acrobatic tricks that make the work of smaller goaltenders more spectacular. These qualities give his style of play a peculiar indolence which he exaggerates as much as possible. Instead of chattering encouragement to his teammates, he munches slowly on a huge wad of chewing gum, rarely speaks a word during a game. Instead of waving his arms, he lounges against his cage as if it were a mantel-piece. All this helps mask his real capabilities: preternaturally quick eyes, phenomenal ability to spread his bulky frame across the goal.

It would be Chabot's "bulky frame" that would help lift the Leafs into the playoffs for the first time.

Still, there were more changes in the offing. In fact, by the time Smythe was done at season's end, only four regulars would remain from the team he had taken over in 1927.

The Leafs began the new season on a positive note. George "Shorty" Horne, another new signing, and Andy Blair each scored to give Toronto a 2–0 victory over the Chicago Black Hawks on November 15 in the season and home opener.

But while Smythe's Maple Leafs may have been winning over Torontonians, his team was not nearly as strong as he had hoped, and neither were they the only game in town. In fact, Frank Selke's junior OHA Toronto Marlboros, who also played at the Arena Gardens, were attracting as much and sometimes more attention in the city. Ironically, it was Selke and his discriminating taste in

Once you start playing for the Leafs and start travelling through the league, you understand the legacy of the Maple Leafs and how many Leafs fans there are everywhere. That's what makes it really fun playing for the Leafs. It's a huge honour to play for an Original Six team, and especially the Toronto Maple Leafs.

Wendel Clark
PLAYER
1985–94; 1996–98; 2000

hockey players that would prove pivotal in manufacturing the future Stanley Cup–winning Maple Leafs.

Selke had been intimately linked with Toronto hockey since the First World War era and had taken his University of Toronto Schools hockey team to a Memorial Cup championship in 1919. Selke had also coached the St. Mary's junior team to an OHA championship in 1925. This team effectively became the Toronto Marlboros and would be forever linked with the professional Maple Leafs franchise. The Marlboros were victorious again in 1927, and Selke's mentoring prepared several players for an eventual jump to NHL stardom. Selke later remembered Smythe's desperation:

Conn was in a mood more despondent than usual, he asked me what I thought he should do about it. "How in the world am I ever going to get a team good enough to whip those Maroons?" he groaned. "I'll tell you how," I said. "Just fire the old men you have playing on your team now. Replace them with these young bucks I have with me on the Marlboros. Do that and you'll never look back."

Smythe heeded Selke's sound advice and slowly began to introduce a variety of young Marlboros veterans to the Leafs roster. These key pieces would one day form the heart and soul of the city's team. This was no abstract notion; many of these future stars had honed their craft as boys on ice pads throughout Toronto. Moreover, these hometown boys were good players and would, in short order, become among the most popular athletes the city had ever known.

Toronto in the late 1920s was parcelled into various and widely divergent neighbourhoods, but the growing appeal of the Leafs transcended Toronto's significant religious and racial divides. Very soon, the Depression would play the role of equalizer, but in 1928 several of these neighbourhoods, including Cabbagetown, the Beach, Moss Park, and the Junction, were notable for their slums. The residents of these neighbourhoods were accustomed to seeing grey-faced men haunt their streets, walking door to door in hopes of selling their modest wares and rags – or, more often than not, receiving handouts from good-hearted souls who could scarcely afford to part with anything themselves.

The Junction struggled with widespread gambling, including the infamous "poolroom" that only added to the heartbreak of many families. It was from this seemingly helpless environment that two of the most important figures of the 1930s Maple Leafs emerged.

The Jacksons lived in a three-storey home on Quebec Avenue. Their son, Harvey, was a rink rat and learned to skate on the aptly named "Poverty Pond" at Keele Street and Humberside Avenue using his sister's skates – skates later claimed by a thief when Harvey's head was turned. The Jackson family was not immune to the ravages of the economic tumult. As Jackson remembered, "There wasn't a job around, but somehow people had to eat." They had to skate, too. The rink rat worked his way around various rinks, including Grenadier Pond and the Ravina Gardens. As a teenager in 1925, Jackson negotiated with the Ravina Gardens' manager for ice time by shovelling the rink. It was here that his graceful strides eventually caught the eye of Frank Selke, who soon talked Jackson into signing on with the Marlboros.

Less than a ten-minute walk from Harvey Jackson's house lived the Primeau family. Joe Primeau had been born in Lindsay, Ontario, but moved to Toronto at an early age. When he and his family settled in the Junction, they lived by Town Park, at Oakmount Road and Glenlake Avenue. Primeau, five years Jackson's senior, had played for St. Michael's College in a four-team prep league before joining Toronto St. Mary's. Selke spotted the playmaking Primeau and promptly recruited him for his Marlboros. From this one gritty neighbourhood, then, Selke had found two rough diamonds that would one day shine for Smythe's NHL team.

A short streetcar ride from the Junction, east along Bloor Street, would bring you to Yorkville. In the late 19th century, Yorkville had been a prestigious country town. The neighbourhood, however, underwent a transition from residential to commercial during the 1920s, and parts of the neighbourhood were left to waste. It was during this period of transition, on a decaying Davenport Road, that one of Canada's most famous sporting families would emerge.

If ever a single hockey star evolved from this radio-centric era, it was Charlie Conacher. Standing over six feet and weighing close to 200 pounds, Conacher stood head and shoulders over most of his opponents and teammates. But it was his story of growing up in Toronto that made him the larger-than-life hero of thousands. On December 10, 1909, Charlie was born to a family considered so poor that they "couldn't afford a tube of toothpaste." Benjamin Conacher drove his horse and wagon around the city doing odd jobs, including hauling sod from the Don Valley and cutting ice in the lagoons off of the Toronto Islands. There, he made only $7.50 a week for his troubles.

The Toronto Maple Leafs are the only team I wanted to play for . . . Once I got here, I hoped to one day be able to raise the Cup, and I was fortunate enough to have that happen. After that, my mind went to, "Boy, I'd like to play my whole career here. That'd be something to be proud of." I was very fortunate that it turned out that way. To get over a thousand games with the Leafs – that's tying up your skates a good number of times! And to pull on the blue and white jersey was always something special. I look back at my years with the Leafs very fondly. I've been very blessed . . . They were very special years and very special times.

Ron Ellis
PLAYER
1964–81

The Conachers' Davenport Road address was in a neighbourhood that Charlie called "one of Toronto's higher-class slums." Here, toughness was a matter of survival. The Conachers had a large brood of ten kids: five boys and five girls. Although the family was "poor as church mice," it was sports that led Charlie and his siblings out of a cycle of poverty.

The Conacher boys played shinny year round, and all ten of the Conacher kids thrived in the humble schoolyard playground. Charlie's older brother Lionel excelled in football, boxing, wrestling, lacrosse, baseball, and hockey, and in 1950 was named Canada's best athlete of the first half of the 20th century. During Lionel's excellent hockey career, he starred with the Pittsburgh Pirates, New York Americans, Montreal Maroons, and Chicago Black Hawks, and won a Grey Cup with football's Toronto Argonauts in 1921. Charlie's younger brother Roy starred with Boston, Detroit, and Chicago during a hockey career that also led to the Hockey Hall of Fame. Roy's twin, Bert, was an exceptional hockey prospect until a road hockey accident cost him the sight in one eye. Twin girls, Nora and Kay, were outstanding baseball players and track and field stars in their own right.

And then there was Charlie. A poor skater as a youngster, he began his hockey life as a goaltender. Charlie worked diligently on his skating by the hour and was eventually recruited to play junior with Selke's Marlboros alongside future Leafs linemate Harvey Jackson. Conacher's torrid scoring pace over a couple of seasons led the Marlboros to a Memorial Cup victory in 1929. There was no doubt in the minds of anyone who saw the young man play that Charlie was destined for the National Hockey League.

A 20-minute walk southwest from the Conachers' home in Yorkville would take you to the grounds of the University of Toronto. It was in this part of the city that the Leafs' first bona fide "enforcer" emerged. George Reginald Horner was born in Lynden, Ontario, but moved with his family to Toronto when he was eight years old. In his early teens, Red Horner moved in with his half-brother, who ran a grocery store at the corner of Spadina and Sussex Avenues. Red delivered groceries to the Selkes. He aspired to play big-time hockey and knew how important Frank Selke was to Toronto's hockey world. In 1926, Red approached Mrs. Selke and asked her if she thought her husband would mind if he went to try out for the Marlboro juniors.

Frank Selke welcomed the youngster, and despite formidable competition, Red Horner made the team.

Starting as a substitute, he soon became a regular and later served as team captain.

While still a member of the Marlboros, Red debuted as a Toronto Maple Leaf on December 22, 1928, in a 3–2 loss to the Pittsburgh Pirates. Horner remembered the scenario:

On Friday night, I played with the Marlboro Juniors. I played Saturday afternoon with Solway Mills [in Toronto's Mercantile Hockey League]. Smythe was at the game and he came to me and said, "Red, you've had enough of this amateur hockey. We want you to come with us!" This was just before Christmas in 1928. I said, "Thank you very much, Mr. Smythe. When do you want me?" He said, "Tonight!" I said, "But I played last night and this afternoon!" He said, "Well, that's nothing for you." He said, "I'll tell you what I'm going to do. I'll pay you $2,500 for the balance of the season."

At the time, the former grocery boy was making $25 a week as a clerk at the Standard Stock Exchange. But Horner didn't own a car. He informed Smythe that "if you'd like to pick me up and take me down tonight, I'll take you and introduce you to my mother and father and I'm pretty sure it'll be all right." Smythe agreed and the deal was sealed with a handshake.

Smythe recognized the brawn that Horner could provide. Red himself knew his role: "I was just naturally a heavy hitter. I always was. I wasn't a graceful skater but when I joined the Leafs, Frank Selke told me, 'Red, if you can learn to break fast from the blueline, you'll make this team.' I worked at it. Hard." Horner would lead the NHL in penalty minutes for eight consecutive seasons. Opponents were given fair warning that, if called upon, the handsome grocery boy would deliver.

By early January 1929, Horner and his team had eleven wins against eight losses. But then the Leafs went into a tailspin, going winless in their next seven games. In order to stem the bleeding, Toronto acquired Eric Pettinger and the rights to Hugh Plaxton from Boston on January 10 in exchange for the rights to George Owen, whose claim to fame was being the first NHL player to regularly wear a helmet.

During the season's final stretch, Smythe installed a policy that gave all of the Leafs' substitutes the chance to play during the final week of the campaign. Goaltender Chabot and backup Benny Grant combined to share a shutout in a 5–0 rout of the New York Americans on March 14. Toronto closed out the season with a 2–0 loss to Ottawa two days later.

Irvine Bailey, who was now being called "Ace," finished as the NHL's top scorer with 32 points on 22 goals and 10 assists. More importantly, the Maple Leafs finished the season in third place with 47 points on the strength of 21 wins, 18 losses, and 5 ties. It was the first time the team had made the playoffs as the Toronto Maple Leafs.

The opening series was a two-game, total-goals series against the Detroit Cougars. The Leafs took Game One, 3–1, and it was clear that the Cougars–Leafs rivalry had intensified over the course of the season. As the *Toronto Daily Star* reported, "There were 14,000 fans at the game and every time that any decision was made against a Detroit player, there was a shower of newspapers, programs and coins on the ice."

Two nights later, the puck dropped for Game Two. Ace Bailey – who had been knocked unconscious in the first period – cemented a 4–1 Toronto win, scoring with less than two minutes to play. The Leafs had easily won the series, seven goals to two.

The semifinal was a best-of-three affair against the defending Stanley Cup champions, the New York Rangers. Before the opening game in New York, Ace Bailey was

presented with the Paul Whiteman Trophy, an award donated by the famous bandleader for leading the NHL in goals. The short-lived trophy was the equivalent of the Maurice "Rocket" Richard Trophy issued today.

The Rangers took Game One, 1–0. Former Maple Leaf Butch Keeling scored the Rangers' lone goal, while John Ross Roach earned the shutout against his former team. Toronto played hard and fast game in Game Two at the Arena Gardens. It was, according to the *Star*, "a thriller right from the opening." The teams traded goals early in the game, but at the end of 60 minutes, the score remained tied at one. Then the Maple Leafs put themselves in a hole from which they couldn't climb out. Eric Pettinger was called for high-sticking. During a scrum in front of the Leafs goal, Hap Day threw the puck to safety but was penalized for his efforts. With Toronto two men short, Frank Boucher scored at 1:52 of overtime to end the game, the series, and the Leafs' much-improved season.

Now that he had tasted playoff hockey, Conn Smythe was determined to capture hockey's big prize. And to get it, he knew that he would have to add some more Marlboros into the mix.

The brash and bruising Red Horner (left) led the league in penalty minutes eight straight seasons, and retired as the NHL's all-time penalty leader, with 1,264 minutes.

Centre Joe Primeau (middle) was just 23 and wingers Charlie Conacher (left) and Harvey "Busher" Jackson (right) just 18 when they were united as the Kid Line. They dominated the NHL through the 1930s, forming part of the Stanley Cup–winning Toronto team in 1932 and making four more appearances in the finals through the next six seasons.

CRASH

The Great Depression crashed down on October 29, 1929. It was on that infamous day that the world's stock markets were set into a free fall. Toronto would be hit hard by the Depression. Fortunately, the Maple Leafs would serve as an escape.

The Leafs played their first game of the season against the Chicago Black Hawks, just a little over two weeks after the stock market crash. Lieutenant-Governor William Donald Ross was joined at centre ice by Maple Leafs president Ed Bickle to drop the ceremonial puck. First, they requested a moment's silence for George "Shorty" Horne, a five-foot, six-inch forward who had died on a canoeing

trip on a lake just north of Gogama in northern Ontario three months earlier, and a bugler played "The Last Post."

As of that night, the game would be played differently. To encourage higher scoring in games, the National Hockey League had rewritten the rules to allow forward passing in the offensive zone. Previously, forward passes had been relegated to the neutral and defensive zones only. Bizarrely, players were also now allowed to enter the offensive zone before the puck. In fact, the only offside rule was that passes were not allowed from one zone to another. Players found the new rules confusing, and so too did the fans, who protested loudly. Naturally, players found ways to abuse the new rule by positioning themselves in front of the opponents' net, waiting for a pass. The rule was discarded partway through the season and players were no longer allowed to enter the offensive zone before the puck.

Meanwhile, the Maple Leafs introduced a handful of new players to full-time NHL employment. Red Horner had played 20 games for the Leafs the previous season, but had earned a spot on a terrific blueline that included Hap Day, Art Duncan, and Art Smith. Joe Primeau had been given a taste of the NHL with six games the previous season and was now earning regular play at centre. But the most exciting discovery was Charlie Conacher, the muscular right winger who, like Horner, had graduated from the Toronto Marlboro juniors.

In the second period of the home opener, Smythe gave Conacher his first NHL shift. The *Toronto Daily Star* described Charlie's entry: "Conny Smythe tossed young Conacher out with his relief line and the kid gave the congregation its first real chance to warm up when he sailed down his right wing, took a pass from [Eric] Pettinger, walked in around his check and smoked a sizzler by [Charlie] Gardiner for the first goal of the season." Although the game ended in a two-all tie, Conacher's impact had been immediate.

The Leafs went six games before recording their first win. That victory finally came on November 26, when the Leafs beat the Rangers, 4–3. Lorne Chabot followed this win with consecutive shutouts: 1–0 over the Detroit Falcons and 6–0 against the New York Americans.

After this decent stretch, however, the Leafs lost their way. In an attempt to remedy the situation, Smythe summoned another Marlboro to the big team. Harvey Jackson was inserted into the lineup on December 7 for a game against the Montreal Canadiens. This marked the first appearance of the soon-to-be famous Kid Line. Jackson replaced Baldy Cotton at left wing alongside centre Joe Primeau and right winger Charlie Conacher. While Jackson didn't get much chance to prove himself that night, the line would soon be something of a permanent feature for the team.

Despite some inconsistencies, the Maple Leafs had become a far more competitive club. Toronto could rely on Ace Bailey to provide some scoring, and the team now had strong leadership from captain Hap Day and decent goaltending from Chabot. And then there were the youngbloods. By December 29, the Kid Line began to produce pure hockey magic. Central to their success was Conacher, who had earned the nickname "The Big Bomber" for his booming shot. Harvey Jackson picked

up his nickname, "Busher," from Toronto's trainer, Tim Daly. Jackson was asked by Daly to carry some sticks, but the player refused. Jackson informed Daly that he wasn't a stick boy, he was a hockey player. Daly replied that he "was nothing but a fresh 'busher,'" a term used to describe someone who had just arrived from the "bush leagues," or minors. The name stuck. Finally, Joe Primeau, the eldest member of the line, was likewise coming into his own and proved to be a tremendous playmaking centre. Primeau was a perfect foil to Conacher and Jackson.

While the Kid Line would be the most important feature of the Leafs' near future – and one of the greatest lines in hockey history – the team was still looking to the past to help it through the 1929–30 season. Frank Nighbor, "The Pembroke Peach," had been playing with the Toronto Blueshirts in the NHA when Conacher was three years old, and Harvey Jackson just one. Smythe and the Leafs hoped that Nighbor, who had been starring with the Ottawa Senators for 15 seasons, would like to spend the twilight of his career back in Toronto. Working in the Leafs' favour was the fact that Ottawa was struggling financially. In the end, the Senators agreed to send Nighbor to the Leafs for Danny Cox and an undisclosed sum of money.

But while Nighbor may have added a veteran presence, he didn't add much more, scoring only two goals in 22 games. Toronto had fallen short and was out of the playoffs. With 17 wins, 24 losses, and 6 ties, the Leafs finished the season with 40 points, placing them fourth in the Canadian Division, ten points behind the third-place Senators, who held the last playoff spot.

Ace Bailey led the team in scoring with 22 goals and 43 points, and while his debut season would be abbreviated by an infected hand and tonsillitis, rookie Charlie Conacher still managed 20 goals and 9 assists in 38 games. Red Horner led the Leafs in penalty minutes with 96. Still, with the young guns, the Leafs promised to be a fast and exciting team in the following season. The ever-growing numbers of Toronto fans began to wonder if their team was just one player away from something very special.

RARE JEWEL

While Smythe had made some great acquisitions, he realized that he would need to further upgrade his lineup if his Leafs were to win the Stanley Cup. The trouble was that teams, amidst a scarcity of high-impact players, were now paying what were considered exorbitant amounts of money to retain star players. Eddie Shore demanded an annual salary of $25,000 from the Bruins and got it. The New York Americans spent $20,000 to purchase goaltender Roy Worters from the Pittsburgh Pirates. The New York Rangers offered $50,000 to the Montreal Canadiens for Howie Morenz, but the offer was declined.

One team, however, was vulnerable and therefore possibly open to some reasonable deals. After years of prosperity, the Ottawa Senators had fallen on hard times, and at the NHL's annual meeting in 1927, Redmond Quain, a member of the club's board of directors, reported on the team's challenges, proposing changes to the league's revenue-sharing agreement that would buoy the franchises that were struggling. The proposal was rejected.

It was in this hostile climate that the Senators needed to offload some of their assets in order to make payroll. Smythe had already exploited the situation to bring Nighbor to Toronto for a season, but now he saw another, potentially more fruitful opportunity, and targeted a colourful, rushing defenceman. Francis "King" Clancy, Ottawa's captain, was coming off the most productive season of his career with 17 goals and 40 points in 44 games. Yet, when Smythe inquired the price to secure Clancy, he was quoted the astronomical price tag of $35,000. While the Senators were poor, they weren't naive. Nevertheless, Smythe asked the Senators for a five-day window to secure the financing to purchase Clancy, and was granted that privilege. He then went to his board of directors and pleaded his case that, by securing Clancy, the Maple Leafs would be that much closer to a championship. The board approved the amount of $20,000 for the purchase of the star defenceman, but Ottawa's board stuck to its guns and wanted the full $35,000.

As the story goes, Smythe financed the trade through a fortuitous day at Woodbine Racetrack in Toronto. Conn had purchased a filly named Rare Jewel for $250. She had never won a race. That day, however, the 106–1 longshot would do the unthinkable. While Smythe was busy placing a large wager on his new horse, her trainer slipped a flask of brandy into Rare Jewel's feed. Well fuelled with high-octane feed in an era when no saliva or urine tests were issued to measure stimulants in the animal's body, Rare Jewel ran the race of her life. She won and paid $214.40 on a $2 bet. As a result, Smythe won $9,372 on the actual bet and another $4,000 on the purse. With his winnings and the $20,000 offered by the board, Smythe sent the money, along with Eric Pettinger and Art Smith, to Ottawa and received King Clancy in return.

In a clever bit of marketing, Smythe decided to ask fans of the Toronto Maple Leafs to vote on whether or not the team should acquire Clancy. He ran ads in the local papers on October 9, 1930, that read:

> Fans – The Directors of the
> Toronto Maple Leaf Hockey Club
> will make their decision on Friday regarding the
> purchase of
> FRANK KING CLANCY
> from the Ottawa Senators.
> What Do You Think of the Deal?
> Write the Hockey Club's Office.
>
> C. Smythe
> Managing Director

Thousands of positive responses came back, which helped fuel the excitement about the acquisition of the new Leaf. In truth, Smythe and the Ottawa Senators had already consummated their deal, but they held off on the announcement until October 11.

Smythe was certain that his lucky acquisition was going to pay off handsomely. And, like so many times before, Smythe was right. King Clancy would star on the blueline for the Toronto Maple Leafs for several years. Clancy would not only help the Leafs capture the big prize, but would prove to be one of the most popular players of any era in Toronto.

Though Clancy was on the small side, his size did not detract from his speed or feistiness. As author Brian McFarlane claimed, Clancy started a thousand fights but never won one. Fortunately for King, he would be blessed with backup from some Toronto boys who knew how to handle themselves.

The 1930–31 season opened at home against the New York Americans on November 13. The ceremonial faceoff was conducted by Toronto mayor Bert Wemp, a war veteran and the first Canadian to be awarded the Distinguished Flying Cross. While there was great hope for the new team, the game was rather unremarkable and ended in a 0–0 tie. Still, it was in some manner indicative of the Leafs' superb goaltending in the early going. Incredibly, Toronto earned five consecutive shutouts to start the season. Lorne Chabot blanked the Americans in the season opener, followed by shutouts over the Philadelphia Quakers (4–0) and Montreal Maroons (3–0). Benny Grant was in goal for Toronto when they battled to another scoreless tie with the Americans, before Chabot returned to the net for a 2–0 win over the Chicago Black Hawks. With two games going into ten-minute overtimes, the Maple Leafs had held their opponents to an astonishing 320 minutes of scoreless hockey.

The season was not, however, without its share of disappointments. On December 2, the Leafs were beaten by the Bruins, 3–2. Toronto, though, lost more than the game. While the Big Bomber scored both of the Leafs' goals, he also broke his wrist. Conacher was out of action until the new year. To complicate matters, Joe Primeau broke his left hand in the Leafs' very next game, a 4–2 win over the Rangers.

Toronto limped its way into its game on December 13 against Boston. Joining Conacher, Primeau, and now Baldy Cotton in the Leafs' sick bay was Hap Day, who that night injured his hip. The Leafs borrowed Rolly Huard from the Buffalo Bisons of the International Hockey League (IHL) to fill the lineup. Ace Bailey, Andy Blair, and Busher Jackson made up one line, with the ragtag trio of Huard, Hap Hamel, and Roger Jenkins as the other. Huard scored in what would be his only game in the NHL, on a dribbler from the point, but the shorthanded Leafs went down to defeat, 7–3.

On balance, though, the Leafs were far more competitive in 1930–31. Smythe and company also saw the benefit of promoting junior players when needed. On March 2, 1931, the Maple Leafs called up forward Bob Gracie and defenceman Alex Levinsky from the Toronto Marlboros. The two young men played the following night against the Montreal Maroons. Gracie played on the Kid Line, replacing Busher Jackson, who had been suspended after incurring three major penalties.

Shortly afterwards, the Leafs met the Bruins in Boston. The Leafs were leading, 3–1, in the third period, but Boston tied the game with two quick goals to send the contest into overtime. During a furious goalmouth battle, Lorne Chabot froze the puck, which forced a faceoff directly in front of the Toronto goal. Cooney Weiland won the draw against Joe Primeau and slammed the puck past Chabot into the net. King Clancy, however, reported himself offside on the scoring play. Remarkably, the referee ordered another faceoff. This time, Primeau won the draw and the game ended in a tie. It had been, as the *Toronto Daily Star* perhaps exaggerated, "the most spectacular pro contest staged in seven years on Boston ice."

Not surprisingly, Boston GM Art Ross was so incensed that he rushed to Conn Smythe after the game and, during a verbal exchange, took a swing at Smythe. The Leafs' managing director ducked, while onlookers restrained Ross. It was the beginning of a bitter, decades-spanning feud. While the result of Clancy's quick-wittedness was all a bit fantastical, the Bruins stopped short of protesting the game when the point they earned in the tie secured their fourth consecutive American Division championship.

The Maple Leafs, meanwhile, finished a solid second behind the Canadiens in the Canadian Division. In his first season in blue and white, King Clancy helped Toronto catapult 13 points in the final standings and was named to the NHL's First All-Star Team, as the league named its best for the first time. Clancy was also an all-star comedian – or at least, a source of comedy. As he explained years later:

> I was the butt of many jokes on that Toronto hockey club. During a game in New York, I had some of my teeth knocked out and my tongue split open, but the doctor there couldn't do anything at the time. The day after, we were back in Toronto, and Hap [Day] took me to the office of Dr. Johnny Rush, who had to stitch up my tongue. Dr. Rush said, "Hap, I think we might do mankind a great service if I cut this right off."

Clancy had a strong supporting cast. In his sophomore year, Charlie Conacher led the NHL in scoring with 31 goals and finished third in points with 43. Ace Bailey had 42 points, including 23 goals, and Joe Primeau finished sixth in scoring with 41 points, including a league-best 32 assists.

In the playoffs, the Leafs faced the Chicago Black Hawks, who finished second in the American Division. Toronto had owned Chicago during the regular season, winning all four games and outscoring the Hawks, 16–6. The Black Hawks, however, adopted a new strategy for the postseason: close checking, to contain the high-flying Leafs in the two-game, total-goals series.

In Game One, the teams skated to a 2–2 tie. Toronto simply couldn't escape the tight-checking Hawks. In Game Two, the score was 1–1 at the end of 60 minutes. After nearly a full overtime period of cautious play, Chicago's Stew Adams banged in a rebound past Chabot at 19:20 of the extra frame to win the game and the series.

Despite adding Clancy, who played superbly in his first season with Toronto, an outstanding defence corps that would serve the team well for seasons to come, and the flourishing of the exciting Kid Line, the Toronto Maple Leafs weren't able to advance in 1930–31. Still, the future looked very bright indeed. Now, the rest of the teams in the NHL recognized that they were in for a tough go every time they visited the rink on Mutual Street.

And the following season, visiting teams would have to call in to a new address, less than a kilometre north of the Arena Gardens.

I always knew I was going to play for the Leafs. It was in my mind when I was "Busher" Jackson as an eight-year-old playing road hockey in the streets. I was going to play for the Toronto Maple Leafs – that's all there was to it.

George Armstrong
PLAYER
1949–71

HOPE IN THE GREAT DEPRESSION
1931-32

Each year before winter, Toronto passes through an "in-between" period. Here, Heaven has yet to throw its blanket of snow; only flurries tease the streets. Here, the deep auburns and golds of the city's sumacs and maples have blazed out, fallen. The strips of greenery that edge the roads and byways have matted, brown, in preparation for winter slumber. Nature's resignation is in the air and the city's humanity tacitly surrenders to the granite cool, grey and ugly.

Perhaps Toronto was never greyer, never uglier than it was during the years of the Great Depression. Certainly, it was never greyer and uglier for so long. Improbably, it was during this pallid purgatory that a cathedral to rival all of the city's many spiritual spires was built. It was a cathedral built on hope and imagination: hope for the defeated, the weary, and the accidentally idle; an imaginative distraction for the poor. This church on Church promised to rupture the dull dross and grey trance with royal blue and brilliant winter-white dreams. And from it, Toronto was delivered.

GOING TO CHURCH

By 1931, close to 20 per cent of Torontonians were unemployed. The following year, that number grew to 30 per cent. In many ways – given the virtual moratorium on the city's construction endeavours after 1932 – Maple Leaf Gardens was built just in time. Yet the human suffering in the city was evident everywhere.

Veterans of the First World War were hit particularly hard in the years leading up to and during the Depression. In some of the more desperate cases, medal-wearing heroes who had served Canada proudly were forced to take to the street to sell five-cent apples from boxes, just to subsist. Many men believed they had received a raw deal from their country after what they had sacrificed. It was truly difficult to see it in any other way.

As a veteran himself, Smythe did his level best to find places for veterans within the business operations of

the Maple Leafs. Fighting ace Billy Barker, the Victoria Cross recipient and the most decorated serviceman in the history of the country, was given an honorary position as the first president of the newly named Maple Leafs in 1927. Captain Art Duncan, who had shot down 11 German planes and was awarded the Military Cross with Bar for his efforts, was made player-coach of the Leafs in 1930. Smythe also found places for the less famous, too. Many vets who were down on their luck were taken on as ushers or general labourers at the Gardens. Instilled with a sobering sense of duty, Smythe never lost sight of the importance of that Great War in his writing of the Maple Leafs narrative.

By 1931, the economic catastrophe had ground construction in the city to a halt. Yet Toronto's population increased by nearly 200,000 between the beginning of the Depression and the end of the Second World War. With a dearth of affordable housing and the average Canadian's income stuck at just under $2,000 a year, people simply couldn't fathom how they were going to get by. Against this bleak backdrop, the city needed something to dream about. As a professional dreamer, Conn Smythe was the man for the job. And with Conacher, Jackson, Primeau, and Horner, Smythe's growing group of former Marlboros would all be in the starting lineup when Maple Leaf Gardens opened in November 1931. These local boys would help transform the sporting landscape in the city in which they lived.

THE RAISING

The Arena Gardens had opened in 1912 and was then only the third hockey rink in the country that could boast artificial ice. Yet by the mid–1920s, the arena could not compete, in terms of capacity, with some of the newer rinks sprouting up around the NHL. The Arena Gardens also lacked in comfort. There was no heat in the building, and even the best seats were simply wooden benches. The experience for viewing big-time hockey left a lot to be desired.

While hundreds of players have worn the Leafs' blue and white through 100 years, the franchise has called but three rinks home through that same period: Arena Gardens (top), Maple Leaf Gardens (bottom), and Air Canada Centre.

Built in 1912, the Arena Gardens, often called the Mutual Street Arena, boasted artificial ice and was the largest indoor arena in Canada at the time, hosting about 7,500 hockey fans. Deemed too small for the growing game, the final regular-season game played there by the Maple Leafs took place on March 19, 1931, a 9–2 win over Chicago.

In the carefree years leading up to the crash of 1929, the NHL put on a veritable "high hat." Many of the league's teams had outgrown their old barns, and owners wanted to attract a broader and more refined clientele. To be sure, simply watching hockey at this time could be a rowdy affair. Smythe and company – at least publicly – wanted to get away from this proverbial "bear pit" atmosphere and take the hockey-watching experience to a new level of comfort. Smythe envisioned a place for which people would dress up, "a place that people can be proud to take their wives or girlfriends to." Other cities had shown what a new building could do for business. With the success and grandeur of the Montreal Forum (1924) and New York's Madison Square Garden (1925), Smythe and the Leafs' board of directors knew that their franchise needed to part ways with their comparatively ramshackle Mutual Street home. But getting a new building constructed was no easy task. It would take all of Smythe's will and his good connections, mostly secured via J.P. Bickell, to bring a new rink to town.

Hockey commentator Foster Hewitt was also enlisted to help during his broadcasts from the Arena Gardens. Foster's plugs caught the attention of many hockey fans and journalists, and *Toronto Telegram* sports columnist Ted Reeve picked up on Hewitt's cue:

> Have we not in this grand and glorious hamlet the Canadian National Exhibition, the tallest skyscrapers in the British Empire, the most beautiful race track in North America (Woodbine, not Dufferin), government control, the University of Toronto, and the Balmy Beach Canoe Club? The answer is, Yes, we have all these and many more remarkable and prepossessing public institutions, and why, then, should we be curtailed to a theatre of thump that will only hold eight thousand people with one foot in the aisle?

Smythe's plan had paid off, and what had been a healthy buzz soon turned into a full-scale fervour. Toronto demanded a new hockey arena.

The building of Maple Leaf Gardens in less than six months in the heart of the Great Depression was a remarkable feat. It required an extraordinary effort from many different people, and its very existence spoke to the spirit of those living through the worst economic period in Toronto's history.

Not everyone, however, was on side with the Maple Leafs' plans. The T. Eaton Co., which operated a department store at Yonge and College Streets, wielded a large influence in the city and wanted the block surrounding its emporium to remain within the existing aesthetic of a retail district. Eaton's owners were not sure whether they wanted a huge hockey rink so close to their store. The company had to be convinced several times that the proposed Maple Leaf Gardens would add value to the street, not detract from it. Eaton's explained that it was trying to attract the civilized bourgeois customer. Yet this harmonized with Smythe and Bickell's hopes of bringing a broader clientele through the Gardens' turnstiles.

Still, Eaton's continued to raise objections, hoping that the Leafs would take an inside lot on either Wood Street or Alexander Street. This did not suit, as the Maple Leafs board knew how important the corner of Church and Carlton would be to the success of the franchise, and the business team that Bickell and Smythe had put together would not be denied. In the end, there were simply too many important financial players who had bought into the dream and joined Smythe's group: the coal and cement baron Alfred Rogers, for example, as well as his influential colleagues Larkin Maloney and stockbroker Ed Bickle. The Leafs' powerhouse front-office team likewise included the Sun Life insurance company, the Montreal-based Ross and Macdonald architectural firm (which had built the Royal York Hotel and Union Station), as well as several of J.P. Bickell's connections at the Bank of Commerce, the William Wrigley Co., the Bank of Nova Scotia, the British-American Oil Co., the Canadian National Railway, Algoma Steel, Canada Life, and the Simpson's department-store chain. Eaton's had no choice but to play hockey.

While the business details were constantly being ironed out in the boardroom, workers furiously rushed through the summer to complete Maple Leaf Gardens in time for the home opener. Remarkably, the job was completed in the impossibly short period of only five and a half months. On September 21, 1931, several hundred people gathered on Carlton Street near Church as the building's cornerstone was placed. The day was a command performance for the executives of the Toronto Maple Leaf Hockey Club, who had been operating out of offices at 11 King Street West, near Yonge, while they awaited the completion of the new arena.

J.P. Bickell presided over the ceremony, joined by vice-presidents Ed Bickle and Harry MacGee, managing director Conn Smythe, board members J. Earl Birks, Alfred Rogers, and Victor Ross, and investor John A. Tory. These men were joined by several other movers and shakers in Canadian hockey, as well as Alderman Fred Hamilton and Lieutenant-Governor William Donald Ross.

On that auspicious day, Bickell addressed his introductory remarks to Lieutenant-Governor Ross:

> This building perhaps might be regarded as a civic institution rather than a commercial venture because its object is to foster and promote the healthy recreation of the people of the British and sports-loving city. It represents the combined efforts of all sections of the community. Capital for its erection has come very largely from those who are actuated by a spirit of civic patriotism, rather than a desire to reap financial benefit.

The lieutenant-governor responded in kind:

> Toronto is, and has been for years, a sports centre. Our position on Lake Ontario; our national exhibition, our general enthusiasm for sports of all kinds, amateur and professional, make this city the logical location for a building worthy of our record, of our need and for our ambition . . . Man is not separable into physical, intellectual and spiritual parts. Each contributes to the whole. The work of an arena, a university and a church are different, but all are necessary. In the hope and expectation that Maple Leaf Gardens will play well its part in the development of good and clean athletic sports, I hereby declare its cornerstone to be well and truly laid.

Included within the cornerstone was a time capsule. Placed inside a copper box were four newspapers – the *Evening Telegram*; *Globe*; *Mail and Empire*; and *Toronto Daily Star* – from September 21, 1931, as well as a Toronto municipal handbook, a stock prospectus from Maple Leaf Gardens, a Red Ensign flag, three hockey rule books, a four-page letter from the directors of Maple Leaf Gardens Ltd., and, bizarrely, a small ivory elephant. The time capsule remained untouched for 80 years within a block that displayed the legend "AD 1931" to passers-by on Carlton Street. With the cornerstone laid, Reverend Dr. John Inkster then offered a dedication prayer: "Grant, O Lord, that [Maple Leaf Gardens] may contribute to wholesome entertainment, healthful recreation and good fellowship. Keep everything connected with this arena clean, pure and honest."

Toronto the Good had received its arena. The city's big-time hockey team could now eschew the confines of the Arena Gardens on Mutual Street. Now, the good hockey-loving people of the city had a proper place of worship.

OPENING NIGHT

For months now, many Torontonians had watched busy workers twine their beams, mould their mortar, and assemble their bricks into what would become the city's hockey cathedral. The site of this new coliseum certainly stood out. How could it not? Construction projects had been on the wane in the early Depression days, and this undertaking was one of the most important developments in the city since the Royal York Hotel went up in 1929. So grand was the Gardens that it towered over every building that was near it and transformed the look of the downtown core. Before the new season began, the excitement within the city continued to build. While the outside was spectacular enough, people simply could not wait to see the stunning insides of Maple Leaf Gardens.

On November 12, 1931, the Gardens officially opened its doors. Parking was available for 25 cents at the new "Ann Street Parking Station," which could handle 160 cars. The *Toronto Daily Star* observed that the Gardens only seated "12,471, but with every fan in town and half of those in Ontario just yearning to get in and assist in the dedication ceremonies, it will be strange if the boys cannot pack in more than 13,000." More than a thousand workers had begun their labours on June 1 to build the magnificent new arena at a cost of over $1.5 million. Now, it was ready for hockey.

While season tickets had been gobbled up when they went on sale on October 14, the club had reserved some general admission tickets, and when the box office opened that evening, a long procession of excited fans lined up to snag the opportunity to witness history. With an event of such historical import as this, security was tight. Earlier in the evening, Conn Smythe proudly walked amongst the crowds waiting to enter the building, but when a police officer suspected that he was butting into line, Smythe was angrily escorted from the premises until his identity could be established.

Smythe could hardly have been too put out when he learned that a record crowd of 13,233 – the largest number of fans to attend a hockey game in the city to that point – shoehorned themselves into the new arena. Spectators paid anywhere from 95 cents for general admission to $2.75 for the best seats to watch the team's inaugural contest against the visiting Chicago Black Hawks. In the end, the financial take for this first game was a staggering $19,677.50.

The city was joyous. To be sure, not everyone could afford to get in to see the Leafs play, but the excitement surrounding the opening of the Gardens was infectious. Though it had largely been a time of despair, it was a song of hope – "Happy Days Are Here Again" – that carried the day. It was with this song that Pipe Major James Fraser and the 48th Highlanders of Canada Pipes and Drums commenced the opening ceremonies at precisely 8:30 P.M.

Speeches followed. President Bickell proceeded with a lengthy speech that drew catcalls from the crowd. Ontario premier George Henry kept his comments brief, but still earned the wrath of the fans who, according to the *Toronto Telegram*, "made it pretty clear that they had come to see a hockey game and didn't care much about speeches." Then Toronto mayor William J. Stewart spoke briefly and presented the members of the Maple Leafs with floral horseshoes on behalf of the city. Black Hawks captain Cy Wentworth wished the fans well on behalf of his teammates. He was followed by Toronto's captain, Hap Day, whose Happy Day Pharmacy would open concurrently with Maple Leaf Gardens, one door west of the main entrance on Carlton Street. Day, much to the delight of those in attendance, boldly predicted that the Leafs would win the Stanley Cup.

Mayor Stewart dropped the ceremonial faceoff that saw Toronto's Red Horner line up opposite Chicago's Harold "Mush" March. Some 65 years later, Horner and March would repeat the feat for the ceremonial faceoff that preceded the final NHL game played at the Gardens. For now, though, having dispensed with the pomp and circumstance, it was time for the teams to get down to business.

Those who couldn't get or afford a ticket could listen in on the game on radio. CFCA had been airing Leafs games regularly since the 1929–30 season. The broadcasts usually featured music during the intermissions, which was provided live from the Palais Royale courtesy of J. Wilson Jardine and his orchestra. CFCA broadcast the first game at the Gardens in its entirety, including

the opening ceremonies, while CKGW, broadcasting out of the King Edward Hotel on behalf of Gooderham and Worts Distillery, picked up the game at 9:00 P.M. Foster Hewitt provided the play-by-play.

While the Gardens was being built, Foster had been consulted on where he felt the broadcast booth should be located. At first, as he revealed,

> it was the intention to work close to ice level, but that would have involved blocking the view of many spectators and also occupying space that could produce much-desired revenue . . . [The architect] suggested we go downtown to the fifth floor of Eaton's on Bay Street and take a look. We went, and as I stood at the window, I was amazed at how clearly I could observe folks crossing the street. It didn't take long to convince me that there would be no visual problem while working from an elevation.

As a result, the "gondola" was constructed on steel beams 54 feet above the ice surface. It was from this vantage point that the city – and later the entire nation – would hear Foster's famous call: "He shoots, he scores!"

As the apparatus inside the Gardens was being established for radio, Smythe and company were working out the means and sources for paying for the broadcasts. Foster Hewitt had exclusive broadcast rights to Toronto Maple Leafs games at the Gardens, and, fortunately for all parties, General Motors was looking to sponsor a feature, and its advertising agency suggested hockey. With a sponsor's fee of $500 per game, General Motors Hockey Broadcasts commenced with the Gardens' opening night. Although they hardly could have known at the time, this agreement would change the way the game was disseminated and enjoyed throughout the country, and it certainly sowed the seeds of Leafs Nation from shore to shore.

Construction began on the new arena on June 1, 1931, and in an astonishing five months and two weeks, Maple Leaf Gardens was opened on November 12, 1931, with the Maple Leafs losing 2–1 to the Chicago Black Hawks.

The Toronto Maple Leafs, playing their first season in the new building, swept the New York Rangers in a best-of-five series that has become known as the "tennis series" because the Maple Leafs scored six goals in each game: 6–4, 6–2, and 6–4.

While the unveiling of the brand-new arena – complete with gondola – might have been something to behold, the game itself was not. According to the *Star*, the Leafs' defence "looked terrible. Levinsky was the only defenceman to show anything. Clancy tried too hard. He tried to crash everybody, but he missed as often as he hit." Not even Hap Day was spared. The *Star* found the captain to be "overanxious." It didn't take long for the first Chicago goal to be scored. The *Telegram* described the tally at 2:30 of the first period: "March got in fast and was Johnny-On-The-Spot for a pass from Cook to flip the puck over the bending Chabot." Although the Leafs worked hard offensively, they were denied by the sensational goaltending of the Scottish-born Charlie Gardiner. Toronto's only goal, and the first Leafs goal ever scored at the Gardens, came courtesy of Charlie Conacher. The Big Bomber took a pass from Joe Primeau and, as the *Globe* related, "drilled a beautiful shot into the corner of the net" at 18:42 of the second period. The Hawks' Vic Ripley, however, put a puck past Lorne Chabot in the third. The game ended: Chicago 2, Toronto 1.

While the Leafs lost the game, the unveiling was victorious. The majesty of the building and its hopeful promise had counted a massive triumph in the hearts and minds of the people of Toronto. Maple Leaf Gardens had elevated Toronto's position in the North American sports market. It also elevated the imagination of those who called Toronto home.

DELIVERANCE

After losing on opening night, the Maple Leafs went winless through the next four games, and Conn Smythe decided that he had to make a change in the coaching position. War veteran Art Duncan had joined Toronto as a player in 1927, played three seasons on the Maple Leaf blueline, and been named coach for the 1930–31 season, but would still dress occasionally when circumstances demanded. After Toronto lost to the Montreal Canadiens on November 26, Smythe fired Duncan, offering him a position as a scout and advisor. Duncan took the high road and quietly accepted the decision, but most believed that he had struggled with Conn Smythe, who was guilty of pulling the strings behind the scenes; it was something the latter would continue to do for many years to come.

Dick Irvin was hired to take over Duncan's job. Irvin had been an outstanding forward with the Portland Rosebuds. That team had effectively become the Chicago Black Hawks in 1926, and Irvin had been named the Hawks' first captain, but he suffered a fractured skull in a game against

the Montreal Maroons in December 1927. He was never the same player again. Irvin served as Chicago's playing coach in 1928–29 and was hired as the team's head coach for the 1930–31 season. During this campaign, Irvin took the Black Hawks to the Stanley Cup final, where they lost to the Montreal Canadiens, but was fired after the playoffs following a disagreement with team owner Major Frederic McLaughlin. Irvin had found work coaching in Regina when Smythe called on him to lead his Maple Leafs.

Smythe's hiring of Irvin paid off immediately. In Irvin's first month, the Leafs won eight, tied two, and lost only three. Part of the success was owed to Irvin's ingenuity. The innovative coach brought some very interesting tactics to the Leafs. When the Leafs were trailing, 2–1, in a game against the Canadiens on January 21, 1932, for example, Irvin pulled goalie Lorne Chabot late in the game and inserted an extra attacker. Although Aurèle Joliat scored to give Montreal a 3–1 win, this was one of the earliest instances of an NHL team pulling the goalie.

The savvy Irvin also knew how to fully utilize the rule book to his advantage. In this era, any player stepping onto the ice while his team was at full strength was automatically assessed a major penalty. Three majors earned a one-game suspension. At one point during the season, Charlie Conacher and Red Horner were both sitting on two major penalties for the season. Both men were also injured. In one particular game, with only five seconds remaining, the calculating Irvin sent them out during play. Both were immediately assessed major penalties. As it was the third major penalty of the year for each man, Conacher and Horner were suspended for the next game. It was, of course, a stroke of genius: Conacher and Horner were injured and unlikely to play the next game anyway, but the suspension wiped their penalty slate clean while the players convalesced.

Under Irvin's stewardship, the Maple Leafs finished the 48-game regular season with 53 points and a franchise record of 23 wins. This put them in second place in the NHL's Canadian Division. Busher Jackson led the league with 53 points and Joe Primeau finished second with 50, including an NHL-best 37 assists. Primeau was awarded the Lady Byng Trophy as the league's most gentlemanly player. The other member of the Kid Line, Charlie Conacher, fired an NHL-leading 34 goals and finished with 48 points. Yet, a broken hand cost the Big Bomber three weeks and likely deprived Charlie of a scoring title. Had he been healthy, the NHL's scoring race might have finished with Maple Leafs players in first, second, and third place. As it was, Howie Morenz of the Canadiens snuck into third place with 49 points. Red Horner collected 97 penalty minutes, which was the most in the league. The NHL selected Jackson to the First All-Star Team and Conacher was named to the Second Team.

Toronto faced Chicago in the first round of the playoffs. Despite being shut out in the opening game, the Leafs won the two-game, total-goals series, 6–2. The Montreal Maroons served as the Leafs' opponents in the semifinal. Toronto once again emerged victorious, outscoring the third-place Maroons, 4–3, in the two-game series. With a little good fortune, the Leafs had made it to the Stanley Cup final against the American Division victors: the New York Rangers.

The best-of-five Cup challenge began in New York. Here, the Maple Leafs outscored the Rangers, 6–4, with Busher Jackson getting three goals during the second period alone.

Game Two was scheduled for two days later at Madison Square Garden, but the Rangers ran into what would be a perennial problem during April in New York: the arena had been booked in advance for the Ringling Brothers and Barnum & Bailey Circus. It was simple: the circus made more money than hockey. There was also the matter of removing eight inches of dirt from the floor to convert the Garden from circus to hockey. That process would take a day, and then another day to replace it – an impossible task, and so Game Two was played at the neutral site of Boston Garden. That night, Toronto again managed an even half-dozen goals and defeated the Rangers, 6–2.

With Game Three, the final moved to Toronto. Torontonians had already witnessed the miraculous raising of Maple Leaf Gardens in the span of only five and a half months. Now, the Leafs were poised to add another fairy tale to the year.

On April 9, 1932, the Toronto Maple Leafs triumphed over the New York Rangers, 6–4, to win the Stanley Cup. The line of Ace Bailey, Andy Blair, and Harold Cotton led the way with four goals, with Bailey firing the Cup-winning tally at 15:07 of the third period. Hap Day had made good on his opening-night prediction that his Leafs would win the Stanley Cup. With scores of 6–4, 6–2, and 6–4, the final became known as the "tennis series." The *Star* trumpeted:

> 14,366 paying guests packed the Carlton Street 'Palais de Glace' and went into a general and sustained mob hysteria as the Leafs won the Stanley Cup in the grand finale of the greatest hockey season Toronto ever experienced . . . No team received a greater or more spontaneous ovation from a Toronto crowd than the Leafs did at the conclusion

of the game . . . No team you ever saw would have beaten those Leafs on Saturday night!

The team received a ten-minute ovation from the Maple Leafs faithful.

NHL president Frank Calder presented the Stanley Cup to Conn Smythe and Dick Irvin. A microphone was prepared at ice level near the penalty box, and in turn, Smythe, Irvin, Hap Day, and Mayor Stewart addressed the spectators, many of whom later made their way to the dressing room for autographs. Conacher, who led playoff scorers with six goals, crashed through the mob of fans, knocking autograph books and pens aside, in order to embrace his wife. Eleven-year-old Stafford Smythe, Conn's son and the team mascot, happily mingled amongst fans and players. Joe Primeau remarked, "You have the sense of accomplishment after reaching what you have been driving for for so long, and you have this feeling of relief."

Relief was felt everywhere, even well outside the confines of the Gardens. The Leafs had helped their Depression-fatigued fans – not just those who could afford a ticket, but also those who listened in on radio or followed along in the newspapers – feel a little less weary. Spring was here; the grey was shifting. Perhaps happy days – or at the very least, happier days – *were* here again.

Despite its resistance to the building of the Gardens, Eaton's celebrated the Leafs victory and displayed the Stanley Cup in the window of its College Street store. Meanwhile, the team held a banquet on April 30 at the Royal York Hotel. Each member of the Stanley Cup championship team was presented with a gold medallion by J.P. Bickell, which allowed players admission to any event at Maple Leaf Gardens for the rest of their lives. They also received illuminated scrolls from the City of Toronto, travelling sets from the Ontario Athletic Commission, and belts and braces from a local menswear shop. The players presented Conn Smythe with a stopwatch.

It was, in hindsight, an appropriate gift. Had he known what the rest of the decade held for his team, Smythe may well have wanted to stop time. He had realized the seemingly impossible dream of putting up his ice palace in a city that was struggling to find hope amidst economic disaster. His team had brought home the shiny silver Stanley Cup, the reflection of which brightened up the prevailing gloom. And the Maple Leafs brand was now pushing past the boundaries of the city. Soon, it would ride the radio wavelengths across the nation in a bid to invite all of English Canada into its blue and white dreams.

Playing for the Toronto Maple Leafs was probably the biggest dream that I've ever had. I used to watch the Maple Leafs on Saturday nights in Sarnia. It was a big night in the Neely household. The Leafs were my team, watching [Johnny] Bower and [Eddie] Shack and [Bob] Pulford and all those guys. Wearing the Leafs uniform and playing in Maple Leaf Gardens, seeing the seats full, was an unbelievable feeling. Like any other Canadian kid, it was a childhood goal to become a Leaf. And there I was – I'm with the Toronto Maple Leafs!

Bob Neely
PLAYER
1973–78

"HELLO CANADA"
1932–33 TO 1938–39

Radio started a conversation across Canada. It liberated imagination; it eliminated distance, taking something that was happening many miles away and delivering it directly into the living rooms of the country. Its dial promised adventure; its speaker, an escape from Depression drudgery. Radio's relay towers united the Maritimes fisherman with the logger of British Columbia. Each Saturday night, a staggering number of souls would tune in to hear a young man from Toronto introduce a program that became one of a few truly national rituals: "Hello Canada, and hockey fans in the United States and Newfoundland, and to Canadian servicemen overseas." His enthusiasm made the game more exciting than it actually was, and his earnestness won him a legion of faithful listeners. It was more than just hockey; for two carefree hours or so, the Kid Line would take the nation's collective mind off of the breadlines that seemed to haunt every Main Street in the country.

DEFENDING THE CUP

Following the Maple Leafs' Stanley Cup championship, it fell to other distractions to help assuage some of the Depression gloom in the city during hockey's off-season. Wrestling was immensely popular in the 1930s, and competing Toronto wrestling promoters Ivan Mickailoff and Jack Corcoran worked together to create a fundraising event that would benefit the 50,000 Club Unemployment Relief Fund, putting together a terrific wrestling card. But the bout that attracted the greatest interest was between Maple Leafs captain Hap Day and NHL penalty leader Red Horner. The promoters billed the match as one "which will settle the wrestling supremacy of the Maple Leafs club."

The exhibition took place on April 25, 1932, just two weeks after the Leafs' Stanley Cup victory. Surprisingly, the event drew only 4,500 people – about half of what had been expected. The match nevertheless went ahead. And there was plenty of theatre. Red Horner climbed into the

ring wearing, appropriately, a crimson-coloured kimono over top of his tights. Hap Day's tights were shrouded in a soft-blue robe. The *Globe* spoke to the sincerity of the two combatants, as many felt that "this would be a farcical bout, but the athletes crossed the guessers and made it an honest-to-goodness struggle, with nearly all the modern tactics on display."

Due to his "bad boy" reputation, the popular consensus was that Red Horner would have a decided advantage over Hap Day. This wasn't the case, as Day knew too much wrestling for Horner. They called the match a draw, as per arrangement, but there was no doubt that Day had defeated Horner in the contest. However, Conn Smythe put an end to any thoughts of similar events taking place in the future by insisting that he would never again allow his players to risk injury like that. The team, of course, had a Stanley Cup to defend.

The Maple Leafs began their Cup defence at the season opener on November 10, 1932. Ontario's new lieutenant-governor, Herbert Alexander Bruce, performed the ceremonial faceoff between the Leafs and visiting Boston Bruins. The game ended in a 1–1 tie.

Leafs management introduced Young Canada Night for the game against the Chicago Black Hawks on Christmas Eve 1932. Every premium ticket holder received a second ticket for a child 14 years of age or younger, and the event became a long-standing tradition that would take place at the last home game before Christmas.

At season's end, Toronto finished first in the Canadian Division, earning 54 points on 24 wins, 18 losses, and 6 ties. Busher Jackson finished second in goals, with 27, and points, with 44. For a second consecutive season, Red Horner was the league's penalty leader, with 144 minutes. Jackson, Conacher, and Clancy were all selected to the NHL's Second All-Star Team.

The Leafs squared off against the Boston Bruins in the playoff semifinal. The Bruins had finished first in the American Division, and the best-of-five series seesawed back and forth. The Bruins won the opening game, 2–1,

The importance of Foster Hewitt's radio broadcasts to the formation of Leafs Nation cannot be overstated. For four decades, Hewitt was the voice of the Maple Leafs from his gondola overlooking the ice surface of Maple Leaf Gardens.

50,000 CLUB UNEMPLOYMENT RELIEF FUND

The Season's Biggest Wrestling Show

Under the Auspices of the Sportsmen's Patriotic Association and Ontario Athletic Commission

Maple Leaf Gardens, TONIGHT at 8.30

MICKAILOFF PROGRAM	SPECIAL ATTRACTION	CORCORAN PROGRAM
Main Bout		**Main Bout**
Count Zarinoff	**"Red" Horner**	**Ray Steele**
vs.	vs.	vs.
Pat McGill	**"Happy" Day**	**Joe Cox**
Preliminary Bout	A finish bout which will settle the wrestling	Preliminary Bout
AL. HASSAN vs. TONY CATALINA	supremacy of the Maple Leaf Hockey Club.	GINO GARIBALDI vs. JOHN KATAN

MASSED BANDS—100 MUSICIANS under the direction of Captain John Slatter. By special permission of the T. M. P. A. **TICKETS:** 50c to $2 plus tax. Ladies with escorts 25c. **AT MOODY'S, KING EDWARD, SCHOLES** and **MAPLE LEAF GARDENS.**

In an exhibition match never to be repeated by two active NHL players from the same team, Hap Day and Red Horner met in the wrestling ring, with Leafs captain Day defeating penalty leader Horner.

in overtime in Boston, but Toronto rebounded with a 1–0 win in Game Two. Again, overtime decided the winner, with Jackson potting the deciding goal.

The series then moved to Maple Leaf Gardens. Eddie Shore scored an overtime goal in Game Three to give Boston a 2–1 win and a lead in the series. Toronto broke out in Game Four, tying the series with a 5–3 victory. Badly bruised and battered, some of the Maple Leafs should not have been playing at all. Red Horner, for instance, was playing with a broken hand, Baldy Cotton had a badly sprained hand, and Ace Bailey, a broken collarbone. Joe Primeau insisted on dressing in spite of suffering from blood poisoning. The *Toronto Star* observed:

All Toronto – yes, the entire hockey world – pays tribute to the gallant Leafs, who, with their backs to the wall, one game short of losing their world's championship title, crippled by injuries, out-fought, out-gamed and out-battled their doughty rivals in what will go down in hockey history as one of the most gruelling and breathtaking contests ever staged.

As gruelling as the series had been so far, it was the deciding contest that would be best remembered.

Game Five began at 8:30 P.M. on April 3, 1933. It did not conclude until 1:55 the next morning. The game was scoreless after 60 minutes. In fact, it remained scoreless after a first overtime. And then another. And then another. Lorne Chabot was terrific in the Maple Leafs net, but Boston's Tiny Thompson was equally sensational. After a fifth overtime ended without a goal, Conn Smythe and Art Ross met and discussed the possibility of deciding a winner through the flip of a coin – provided, of course, that their respective teams would agree. When the idea was presented to the players, both teams took

great offence. As far as the players were concerned, a coin flip was *not* going to decide the winner. A phone call was made to NHL president Frank Calder, who likewise insisted that the game be played until a conclusion resulted, no matter how long it took.

Early in the sixth overtime period, that conclusion arrived. The *Star* detailed the final play:

Shore, weak and weary from a terrific effort, gets the puck down at his own end on a despairing Leaf shot from mid-ice . . . Shore weaves to and fro behind his own blueline, trying to dodge that long-armed checking limpet, Andy Blair. Suddenly, Blair reaches out with a stick that seems as long as a fishing pole and hooks the puck away just inside the [Boston] blueline. Down the right boards comes the smallest man on the ice, skittering and hopping along like a little bowlegged terrier. Wheeling on the back of his skates, Andy relayed the puck to Ken Doraty. The little right winger with his short and choppy stride was through for the shot that meant the victory to his team.

Officially, it was 4:46 of the sixth overtime when Kenny Doraty beat Tiny Thompson for the game's only goal. It was one that propelled his Toronto Maple Leafs back into the Stanley Cup final for a second straight season. The Leafs' victory came after nine unbelievable periods of hockey, in which Toronto had outshot Boston, 119–93. Delirious fans tossed anything within reach onto the ice, and a momentous cheer resounded through the young Gardens. The marathon was the longest game in NHL history at the time and, at the time of writing, still ranks as the second-longest game played, just eight minutes shorter than the March 24, 1936, match between the Detroit Red Wings and Montreal Maroons.

The goal scorer himself was a reclamation project of sorts who, after a short stint with Chicago in the 1926–27 season, had spent six seasons in the minors. Ostensibly, Doraty had been brought back to fill a hole in the Leafs' roster. Improbably, the diminutive Doraty – at only five feet seven tall and 135 pounds – played the role of hero and was carried off the ice on the shoulders of his teammates after scoring one of the most famous goals in franchise history.

The problem with the Game Five marathon, however, was that Game One of the Stanley Cup final was set to start in less than 24 hours. The Leafs left Toronto by train at 3:30 A.M., only an hour and a half after Doraty's goal. The team arrived in New York at 4:30 in the afternoon for what would be a Stanley Cup rematch. Just four hours later, the exhausted team took to the ice. Predictably, the Rangers dumped the Leafs, 5–1, in the first game of the best-of-five series.

While Game Two was closer, the Rangers nevertheless took a two-game lead with a 3–1 victory. Then the series moved to Maple Leaf Gardens and Toronto edged New York 3–2 in Game Three, with the semifinal hero Doraty scoring two goals.

In Game Four, Toronto played its best game of the series. In fact, the Leafs held the edge in play all through regulation time, but couldn't put the puck past Rangers netminder Andy Aitkenhead, who flopped to the ice to smother the puck any time it went near him. In overtime, the Rangers found a new gear and continued to buzz around Chabot in the Leafs goal. And then, misfortune: Alex Levinsky was penalized for tripping, and less than a minute later, Leafs rookie Bill Thoms tried to clear the puck and sent it into the stands, earning a penalty for doing so. The shorthanded Leafs were no match for New York. Just as Levinsky was about to get back into the play, Bill Cook ripped a shot past Chabot at 7:33 of overtime to win the game and the Stanley Cup. It remains the only time in NHL history that the Cup champion has been decided on a power play in overtime. Still, even in defeat, the popularity of the Maple Leaf players grew exponentially. Soon, national radio broadcasts of Toronto games would baptize a multitude of Leafs Nation converts.

WAVELENGTH

As the Depression crept along, companies were forced to lay off employees – or, at the very least, greatly reduce wages. Unsurprisingly, not everyone in Toronto at that time could afford a radio. Just as owning a piano or a gramophone had been, radio ownership was a distinguishing marker of one's class. A "superheterodyne radio" in a gothic cabinet could be the centrepiece of a family's main living space. But while every family wanted one, radios were not cheap.

In 1929, the Royal Commission on Radio Broadcasting highlighted the need for the medium and its potential to unite the nation. More than just entertainment and amusement, radio was a public-service tool, something that could educate and inform. It is unclear whether or not the various social agents and politicians of the day anticipated the role hockey would play in radio's campaign to promote national unity. Regardless, sport – and hockey in particular – quickly proved popular with early listeners.

In terms of home radios, Ted Rogers's "batteryless" radio receivers had been unveiled to much acclaim at the Canadian National Exhibition in 1925. At this time, there were approximately 92,000 receiving sets in Canada. In the space of only five years, there would be 500,000.

Rogers helped to kick-start one of the city's more popular and enduring stations, CFRB (Canada's First Rogers Batteryless), but Canadian stations were, at least in their infancies, heavily reliant on programming from the United States. In fact, most Canadian stations in the late 1920s only broadcast between two and twenty hours a week. As a result, American stations were able to penetrate the Canadian consciousness with American themes. This was a bit of a nightmare for those Canadians whose wish was to "educate and inform" through radio.

American stations were acutely aware of how popular their sports broadcasts had become and had no qualms about increasing their sports coverage. This philosophy ran contrary to the prevailing ideology of the Canadian Radio Broadcasting Commission, which had been established in 1932 and was the predecessor to the Canadian Broadcasting Corporation (CBC). Still, listeners voted with their ears: American shows were wildly popular, and sporting events almost always trumped educational lectures or informative broadcasts. Charlie Conacher and his teammates would soon prove that hockey was something that could excite the listener. The quickness of the play simply made for a thrilling radio show. And no one could thrill hockey fans better than Foster Hewitt.

Foster's play-by-play shrunk the space. One did not actually need to be at the game to feel its excitement. If you could tune in, Hewitt's call washed over you and took you away from what was, for many people living in the 1930s, a drab reality. More than this, he helped people cultivate their own imaginations by allowing them to

picture a game that didn't actually exist. It was hockey's own "theatre of the mind."

History was made on January 7, 1933. That night, the Leafs' game was picked up by a network of radio stations across Canada. While the Leafs lost, 6–1, to the visiting Detroit Falcons, the club's appeal, once regional, was now finding frequency across Canada. Hewitt's broadcasts had opened up a truly national conversation.

At the heart of this were the stars of the 1930s Maple Leafs lineup and, of course, Hewitt himself. Foster received thousands of good-luck talismans during the 1933 playoffs from people who hoped that their trinket would bring the team a second Stanley Cup championship. Around this same time, the makers of Bee Hive Corn Syrup offered fans photographs of their favourite players in exchange for a cardboard "collar" from their syrup containers. The response was stunning, and the company was swamped with thousands of requests for various Leafs. The most requested players were King Clancy, Charlie Conacher, Hap Day, Busher Jackson, and, perhaps not surprisingly, Foster Hewitt. It was, after all, his magical call from his perch in the gondola that had made Toronto's hockey stars household names in Canada. All the while, more and more people invested in and converted to the magic of radio.

FAITH

The steaming summer of 1933 boiled over on August 16 during a baseball game at Willowvale Park, an incident now better known as the Christie Pits riot. On that day, approximately 10,000 fans were assembled to watch a non-Jewish baseball team take on a Jewish team. The tension was already palpable, but the scene turned violent when a young man yelled out "Heil Hitler." Then, another group of young men managed to unveil a giant swastika flag in the park. What ensued was six hours of fighting that included fists, baseball bats, and pipes. Recruits of Jews and Italians (who also felt racialized as "dirty foreigners") were sent for from Toronto's Kensington district. Many young men ended up in hospital, while others, avoiding attention, hobbled home as best they could.

It was during this racially charged summer that Alex Levinsky was preparing for his fourth season with the Toronto Maple Leafs. Levinsky, who was Jewish, was born in Syracuse, New York, but grew up in Toronto and was familiar with the racialized difficulties that members of his own community had to face at times. Before fully turning to pro hockey, Alex regularly played baseball

with St. George's at the very same park that would later host the unfortunate Christie Pits riot. Levinsky had been a Memorial Cup winner with Frank Selke's Toronto Marlboros before being called up to the Leafs. His nickname, "Mine Boy," was born when a sportswriter shared the story of Alex's father, who ran a pool hall at the corner of Queen and Duncan Streets, yelling his approval from the stands: "That's mine boy!" The solid stay-at-home defenceman was one of the first Jewish players in the National Hockey League.

Meanwhile, goaltender Lorne Chabot was in a contract dispute with Conn Smythe. When the terms weren't suitable, Chabot considered retirement. Léo Dandurand, the general manager of the Montreal Canadiens, saw an opportunity. His goaltender, George Hainsworth, had fallen out of favour with Montreal's French-speaking fans and wanted out; Dandurand wanted to secure a strong netminder who was also a francophone, and Chabot fit the bill. On the other hand, Hainsworth had been born in Toronto and seemed to be a perfect fit for the Blue and White. The teams swapped goalies, one for one.

Hainsworth had starred in goal for the Canadiens for seven seasons. The 1928–29 season in particular had been an extraordinary one for Hainsworth: with a goals-against average of 0.92, he recorded 22 shutouts during the 44-game campaign. In his time with the Canadiens, Hainsworth twice led the league in wins, twice in goals-against average, and twice in shutouts. Smythe hoped the goalie could render similar results for Toronto.

The 1933–34 season began with the Bruins visiting Maple Leaf Gardens. The ceremonial faceoff was once again performed by Lieutenant-Governor Bruce, but this time the Leafs beat Boston, 6–1. And it was another game with the Bruins this same year that would challenge existing attitudes about the very way hockey was played. On December 12, 1933, Toronto would be involved in one of its most franchise-defining moments when Irvine "Ace" Bailey's career came to an end.

During the second period, with the Leafs two men short, coach Dick Irvin sent out King Clancy, Red Horner, and Ace Bailey to kill the penalty. As Horner explained, "Bailey was a very expert stickhandler, and he ragged the puck for a while. Eventually, Shore got his stick on the puck and made a nice rush deep into our end. Shore came down my side and I gave him a very good hip check."

As the play moved back into the Boston end, Shore, dazed by the hit and looking for revenge, skated towards Bailey, likely thinking that he was charging Horner. Red surmised that Shore "thought Bailey was me. He charged

Kenny Doraty, whose goal at 104:46 of overtime on April 3, 1933 gave Toronto a 1–0 win over Boston and ended what was, at the time, the longest game in NHL history.

into Bailey on an angle from the side. He hit Bailey and flipped him in the air, just like a rag doll." Shore's left hip struck Bailey with some force. Bailey fell to the ice, hitting the right side of his forehead. Immediately, the Leafs forward went into convulsions. Everyone in Boston Garden knew instantly that Ace was in major trouble.

The incident unfolded right in front of Horner. "I thought to myself, 'That's the end of Ace!'" Bailey lost consciousness and was bleeding from the head wound. Horner, sickened by the sight of his injured teammate, coldcocked Shore, knocking him to the ice. "Shore skated away in a very nonchalant fashion," Horner recalled. "I wasn't going to let him get away with that, so I went after him." Both Bailey and Shore had to be carried off the ice by teammates. Shore suffered a three-inch gash to the head, but Bailey's injury was far more serious. He was being attended to by Boston doctors in the Bruins dressing room when Shore, having regained consciousness, went over to apologize. "It's all part of the game," Bailey said before lapsing into unconsciousness again.

Bailey was rushed to Audubon Hospital with a cerebral hemorrhage. By the next morning, his condition was so poor that his death seemed imminent. While Bailey's concerned teammates had to board the train for a game in Montreal two days later, Conn Smythe stayed behind with Ace. Bailey's wife and two-year-old daughter hurried to Boston from Toronto. Likewise, when word of his son's injuries reached Bailey's father, he immediately bought a train ticket to Boston.

Dr. Donald Munro, a brain specialist, had Bailey transferred to Boston City Hospital. Here, the doctor performed two operations to alleviate pressure on Bailey's brain. The doctor also revealed that there was an intraventricular hemorrhage, which often proved fatal within hours – it was a miracle that he had lived even that long. Dr. Munro felt Bailey's chances of survival were very slim. A priest was called to administer last rites. With a pulse of 160 and a temperature over 106 degrees Fahrenheit, doctors were measuring Ace's life expectancy in minutes. Remarkably, Bailey had, by the following morning, shown sufficient recovery to give the medical staff some hope.

Verna Hallowell, a nurse at the hospital, was credited with saving Ace's life. Hallowell acted immediately when Bailey suffered a relapse. Seated by his side, she continued to prompt him: "Fight, Ace. Fight! You're doing fine." At that moment, he opened his eyes and squeezed her finger. On December 16, Bailey came out of his four-day coma. The blood clot had been removed.

In the meantime, Boston detectives interviewed Shore. The defenceman was initially thought to have a skull fracture, but x-rays dispelled that fear. He did, however, suffer a seven-stitch facial gash from being hit by Horner.

The league conducted its own investigation. NHL managing director Frank Patrick interviewed several Bruins and Leafs players, team trainers, and the Boston sportswriters, while NHL president Frank Calder interviewed Conn Smythe, Bruins coach Art Ross, Eddie Shore, and the two referees who worked the game, Odie Cleghorn and Eusebe Daigneault. Predictably, there were distinct differences in the recollections of those interviewed. All, however, agreed that Shore had struck Bailey with considerable force. Patrick surmised that the league "must assume that whatever did occur was of a spontaneous nature, with no malice behind it . . . Shore is in pretty bad shape mentally. It has him all broken up."

Ross stood firm with his assertion that "we think it was an absolute accident." In accordance with hockey's unwritten covenant, Conn Smythe told the *Boston Record*, "Shore is one of the finest sportsmen I ever met. I do not blame him for the accident."

President Calder suspended Eddie Shore indefinitely, and also suspended Red Horner until the new year. Shore had not been permitted to visit Bailey in the hospital, but when Boston manager Art Ross visited the Leafs star, Ace absolved Shore of any wilful wrongdoing once again.

Despite the league's reprimand and Bailey's willingness to absolve Shore, tensions continued to rise. Several journalists suggested that Shore should voluntarily retire. Smythe threatened that his Leafs would not play the Bruins if Shore was in the lineup.

Many predicted that there would be a bloodbath the next time the Bruins and Leafs met. That game came in Boston on December 26, and was, according to the *Star*, "mild as pigeon's milk." At the same time, Bailey was growing stronger. "This is most gratifying to everyone associated with hockey and to the countless thousands who have earnestly prayed for his recovery," Frank Patrick rejoiced. But while Ace was going to survive, it was just as evident that he would never be able to play hockey again.

President Calder announced that Shore would be allowed to return to the NHL on January 28, ending what was a 16-game suspension. Before Shore returned, Bailey spoke publicly on January 3, 1934. Propped up in his hospital bed, he said, "I didn't see Eddie and he didn't see me and we crashed. That's all." Shore later concurred: "There was no bad feeling between us. It was purely accidental." By January 18, Bailey was well enough to leave Boston and

Ace Bailey (left) and Eddie Shore shake hands in Boston in March 1934, only a few months after Bailey's playing career tragically ended when a hit by Shore sent him crashing to the ice. On February 14, 1934, an all-star game was held to benefit Bailey and his family. Prior to the game, the two players shook hands at centre ice, eliciting a monstrous ovation from the crowd at Maple Leaf Gardens.

The Toronto Maple Leafs honoured beloved defenceman King Clancy with a special night prior to the game on March 17, 1934. Floats were pushed onto the ice at Maple Leaf Gardens, ending with "The King" – in robes, beard, and crown – pulled out on a throne.

return to his home in Toronto. Beyond a sizeable scar on his closely shaved head, the only noticeable difference in Ace's health was a slight slowness to his speech.

While his health had improved somewhat, there was the question of what Bailey was going to do for money now that his career had been cruelly cut short. The Bruins had set aside $6,741 in gate receipts from a contest with the Montreal Maroons, and the money was sent to Bailey's family. While this was certainly welcome, more would be needed. In this knowledge, the NHL's Board of Governors announced that a special benefit game featuring the Toronto Maple Leafs against the best from the rest of the league would be staged at Maple Leaf Gardens on February 14, 1934, with the proceeds going to Bailey and his family.

The idea for the benefit game had originally been proposed by Walter Gilhooly of the *Ottawa Journal*. The Leafs' opposition would be selected by a committee consisting of Frank Calder, Frank Patrick, and league director Thomas Arnold. Two players were chosen from each of the NHL teams excluding Toronto, so that the Leafs roster could remain intact for the game. It was a titillating proposition. Foster Hewitt, for one, wondered what would happen if Shore were included in the All-Star team: "How would the crowd react to his presence? Would hisses, boos and even physical abuse be heaped upon the great

Boston defenceman? Would it be appropriate for Shore and Bailey even to meet? I was personally quite concerned about the project, for I was well aware that crowds can be easily swayed and that the event could become quite ugly."

The very idea that Shore might be added to the lineup attached an element of intrigue to a game that now promised to be more classical tragedy than hockey game.

And then came the clarion call. Lester Patrick, as coach of the NHL All-Stars, named his starting lineup: Chicago's Charlie Gardiner in goal; Howie Morenz of the Canadiens at centre; Aurèle Joliat, also of the Canadiens, and Bill Cook of the Rangers were the wingers; and, on defence, the Rangers' Ching Johnson . . . and Eddie Shore.

All of the Bruins in the All-Star lineup that evening wore leather helmets.

Bailey had recovered sufficiently to attend the benefit game being held in his honour. He insisted that he did not want to be simply a spectator, so he was written into the script for the pregame ceremony. The players assembled at centre ice to have photographs taken in their team sweaters. It was left to Foster Hewitt to introduce each player, who then advanced to receive a couple of specially made tokens of appreciation from Bailey. One by one, in order of their sweater numbers, each of the players approached centre ice to receive his gifts. After introducing goalie Charlie Gardiner, the crucial moment had arrived. Hewitt announced: "Eddie Shore, Boston Bruins." An apprehensive hush fell over the crowd as Shore slowly skated, unsmiling, eyes fixed straight ahead, towards Bailey. Shore extended his ungloved hand to Bailey, who was sporting a fedora that covered his scars. In an act of tremendous sportsmanship and forgiveness, Bailey took Shore's hand. The Gardens faithful roared its approval. As Hewitt declared, "Throughout the entire introduction, not a single disapproving voice was heard in a capacity crowd that exceeded fourteen thousand."

The game raised $20,909.40 for Bailey and his family. The Leafs, wearing specially made jerseys with the word ACE in the usual place of the Maple Leaf crest (which was shifted to the left chest), won the game, 7–3.

One of the happier, if unexpected outcomes of the Bailey–Shore incident and subsequent benefit matches was the birth of the annual NHL All-Star Game. Another outcome was Conn Smythe's decision to retire the number 6 from the Maple Leafs lineup, which he announced on the evening of the benefit match. No sweater number had yet been retired in the NHL's history. And no one ever wore Bailey's number 6 again, until Ace himself implored Maple Leafs management to allow Ron Ellis to wear it in the late 1960s. It would be, for Ellis, his "greatest honour as a Maple Leaf."

Ace's special night was followed by something more lighthearted on St. Patrick's Day. King Clancy was immensely popular with the fans, and he was also fiercely proud of his Irish heritage. Smythe and the Leafs chose to honour their tenacious defenceman with a King Clancy Night before a game against the New York Rangers on March 17.

That night, the centre-ice faceoff dot was surrounded by a green shamrock, with the name KING etched above it and CLANCY below. Conn Smythe acted as emcee for the evening, but each time he began to introduce Clancy, a giant float entered the ice and interrupted his introduction. Fans expected to see their hero Clancy emerge from within each float that appeared. The first, a giant potato, was pulled to centre ice by Rangers defenceman Ching Johnson. The float didn't contain Clancy, but rather several members of the St. Michael's Majors junior team. A huge shamrock arrived next, but instead of Clancy, it was the Rangers' Bill Cook who had been concealed within. Next, a float dressed to look like a bottle of ginger ale contained Leafs trainer Tim Daly. The floats kept coming. Baldy Cotton was inside a gigantic top hat. Ken Doraty was inside a pipe-shaped float. There was a float that looked like a boot with goalie George Hainsworth inside,

and another that looked like a boxing glove in which Red Horner was appropriately placed. Joe Primeau emerged from a giant harp.

Finally, the moment arrived. As Leafs fan Tommy Gaston remembered:

[T]he lights dimmed and Hap Day pulled a throne out onto the ice. It was a big sleigh. Sitting on the throne was our King . . . Clancy. He had on a long robe and a crown and beard. He resembled Old King Cole. When Hap pulled the throne to centre ice, Clancy stepped down and the crowd went nuts.

King later recalled the night in his memoirs: "As the float reached the middle of the rink, I got hit in the face with a handful of soot from Day and Conacher. When the lights came on, I looked like Santa Claus but my face was pitch black. It took me two or three days to get that stuff off!"

Clancy took off the robe to reveal he was wearing a green Maple Leaf sweater with a shamrock on the back where his number, 7, should have been. He was then presented with a number of gifts, including a grandfather clock and a sterling-silver tea service for his wife. Clancy played the first period wearing his green jersey, but Rangers coach Lester Patrick insisted that the sweater was confusing his players, so King was forced to return to his familiar blue and white Leafs sweater. Toronto nevertheless defeated the Rangers, 3–2, on what remains a one-of-a-kind night in Leafs history.

Toronto matched King Clancy Night's flair for drama by finishing atop the Canadian Division – and the overall NHL standings – with 61 points. The Kid Line continued to shine: Charlie Conacher led the league in goals, with 32, and won the scoring crown with 52 points, while Joe Primeau earned more assists than any other NHLer, with 32. His 46 points ranked second in the league. Red Horner once again led the NHL in penalty minutes. The Maple Leafs also dominated the All-Star selections. Conacher, Jackson, and Clancy were named to the First Team, while Primeau was a Second Team choice at centre. Apart from the Bailey incident, this had been a dream season.

Unfortunately for Leafs fans, the playoffs were far less dreamy. In the opening series, Toronto faced the Detroit Red Wings, as the Falcons (formerly Cougars) were now known. While the best-of-five series went the distance, the Red Wings emerged victorious, shutting out the Leafs in the fifth and deciding game. It was an incredibly anti-climactic end to the postseason.

George Hainsworth (pictured) joined the Leafs in 1933–34 in a one-for-one swap that sent Lorne Chabot, who was in a contract dispute with Conn Smythe, to Montreal.

THE GASHOUSE GANG

While the Maple Leafs players of the early 1930s were, at least usually, all business on the ice, they also enjoyed themselves off the ice. The "Gashouse Gang of Hockey," as they were called by sportswriter Ed Fitkin, were led by King Clancy, Charlie Conacher, and Hap Day: the "Three Musketeers" of mirthful mayhem when it came to practical jokes. As the Maple Leafs' top scorer and most popular player, Charlie Conacher was leader of the gang. This self-issued licence meant trouble for the rest of the Leafs.

The woebegone Harold "Baldy" Cotton was the Big Bomber's favourite target. Cotton's aversion to heights was well known, so it became a button that Conacher pushed whenever opportunity allowed. Adding to Cotton's dread was the fact that he and Conacher were often roommates. One day, King Clancy and Hap Day had gathered in Cotton and Conacher's New York hotel room. The roommates got into a disagreement about a hockey matter. Charlie grabbed Baldy in a bear hug and carried him over to the window, demanding, "Admit I'm right, or I'll drop you out the window." Cotton refused. Conacher replied, "Okay, you asked for it." Before Baldy knew what had hit him, he was hanging out the window by his ankles, seven storeys above the busy New York City street.

Cotton's terrified screams alerted Joe Primeau and Busher Jackson in the hotel room below. Opening the window to see what was going on, Primeau and Jackson glanced up to see their petrified teammate, white as a ghost. Conacher continued to hold Cotton by his ankles until he agreed that Conacher's point of view was correct. Charlie then pulled him back into the room and, with a devilish chuckle, deposited him on the floor. It would not be the last time that devilish chuckle would haunt Cotton.

While Cotton might have been shaking after Conacher's prank, Conn Smythe was shaking up the Leafs roster in advance of the 1934–35 season. To begin, Smythe sold defenceman Alex Levinsky to the New York Rangers and Charlie Sands to the Boston Bruins, and loaned Jack Shill to Boston. Smythe inserted Bill "Flash" Hollett, who had already played a handful of games with the Leafs before being loaned to the Ottawa Senators the previous season. The moves proved successful.

For a second straight season, the Maple Leafs finished first overall, 11 points above the second-place Montreal Maroons. Conacher finished the season as the NHL scoring leader with 57 points, including a league-best 36 goals, and was named to the NHL's First All-Star Team. Bill Thoms, in his third season with the Leafs, was a Second Team selection. Once again, Red Horner spent more time in the penalty box than any other NHL player, with 125 penalty minutes. George Hainsworth became the first Maple Leaf goaltender to win 30 games in a season, earning the milestone win on the last night of the regular season against the visiting St. Louis Eagles (the former Ottawa Senators).

In the playoffs, the Leafs met the Boston Bruins. The best-of-five semifinal was an exhausting affair that took its toll on the Leafs. Toronto nevertheless dispensed with the Bruins in only four games. The Leafs clinched the series with a 2–1 win in Game Four when Pep Kelly scored the overtime winner.

The Maple Leafs had made the Stanley Cup final for the third time in four seasons and would now face the Montreal Maroons. Although the Maroons had finished below the Leafs in the standings, they proved to be a surprising challenge. Montreal goaltender Alec Connell was the star of the Stanley Cup final. Connell, aided by a defence corps that featured Charlie Conacher's older brother Lionel, as well as Stewart Evans, Allan Shields, and Cy Wentworth, shut the Leafs down. Toronto appeared lethargic in the series opener, and the Maroons edged the home team, 3–2, in overtime.

While the Leafs were much more energetic in Game Two, they still could not solve the Maroons' defence corps. Montreal won, 3–1. During the game, Conn Smythe grew so frustrated that he raced up the stairs and clocked a fan who was giving the team unsolicited advice. Later, Smythe and the fan met privately, and the latter, although sporting a shiner, accepted Conn's apology.

Although the Leafs worked hard in Game Three, they simply could not compete with the better Montreal side. The Kid Line, which had been so strong during the regular season, was virtually silenced during the series, scoring only once. Montreal won, 4–1, and had swept the Leafs in the best-of-five series to take the Stanley Cup.

The Maroons were undefeated during the playoffs. Even Conn Smythe agreed that Montreal was the better team: "The team that beat us is the greatest professional team I ever saw . . . they were distinctly the better team out there tonight. There are no alibis or excuses. We were just beaten by a wonder team."

While the Leafs' appearance in the finals three times in four years should have been cause for joy, another stumble at the last hurdle had, for many, articulated a worrisome pattern that was beginning to develop. While Toronto's regular-season play had been matchless during the first half of the 1930s, its playoff performance since the Cup win of 1932 remained underwhelming.

It was a pattern that had not yet run its course.

BRIDESMAIDS IN BLUE

Throughout the decade, the Maple Leafs organized charity baseball games, fundraisers, and exhibition hockey matches. The proceeds of these events went to various organizations throughout the city whose mission it was to relieve the human suffering caused by Depression-induced poverty in Toronto. Meanwhile, on the ice, Smythe was searching for relief from losing Stanley Cup finals. Smythe again tinkered with the lineup by dealing Hec Kilrea and prospect Norm Schultz to Detroit, and signing a few free agents, including Jimmy Fowler, Normie Mann, and George Parsons. The biggest change, however, was the sale of veteran Baldy Cotton to the New York Americans. The *Toronto Daily Star* lamented his loss: "Any time a game was going flat or sour, all Dick Irvin had to do was dump the veteran gamester over the boards. Cotton was a battler who waded in regardless of consequences. He hurled himself into the fray like a human bombshell, regardless alike of personal injury or the welfare of his opponents."

It was against Cotton's new team, the Americans, that the Maple Leafs opened their 1935–36 season at Maple Leaf Gardens. Colonel Sam McLaughlin, president of General Motors of Canada, dropped the puck for the ceremonial opening faceoff in a game that finished in a 5–5 draw. The Leafs, while not the dominant side they had been in previous seasons, could still score in bunches and soon proved that they remained a force to reckon with.

While the Leafs continued to win the hearts of Toronto's populace, their on-ice successes rarely strayed too far from the prevailing narrative that Smythe and company had envisioned back in 1927. It was, after all, *royal* blue and white sweaters that the Leafs wore. And the team still represented what J.P. Bickell had termed a "British and sports-loving city." On January 20, 1936, King George V, who had reigned for a quarter of a century, died. Out of respect for the monarch, the Maple Leafs postponed the game against the Canadiens that had been scheduled for the following night. To have played it would have been, as far as Smythe and the majority of Leafs fans were concerned, unthinkable in the Queen City.

At this same time, seeds of enmity between these two teams with very different narratives were being sown. The Maple Leafs–Canadiens rivalry quickly intensified in a game on March 12, 1936. On this night, Montreal's player-coach Sylvio Mantha became embroiled in an argument with Conn Smythe. The disagreement escalated, and soon Smythe had Mantha in a headlock on the bench. Several others got involved, including Leaf coach Dick Irvin, who explained, "I thought Smythe was being mobbed, so I stepped in, and as I did, Mantha's face came up out of the struggle so I let go with both hands." NHL president Frank Calder, who was in attendance, fined Smythe and Irvin $50 each for their involvement. While the height of acrimony between the Maple Leafs' Anglo-Protestant fan base and the Canadiens' Franco-Catholic following was still a few years off, it was clear that these two naturally antagonistic rivals felt little love for one another.

By season's end, Toronto had finished second in the Canadian Division, two points behind the Montreal Maroons. The Leafs' Charlie Conacher and Bill Thoms had tied for the league lead in goals, with 23. Their equally identical 38 points also tied them for fourth in the NHL. To no one's surprise, Red Horner led the NHL in penalty minutes with 167.

The opening playoff series saw Toronto face Boston in a two-game, total-goals series. In the first game, Bruins goalie Tiny Thompson led Boston to a 3–0 shutout victory. Game Two was a different story altogether. After scoring early in the first, it looked to many as though Boston might end Toronto's season prematurely. But then, during a minor penalty to Eddie Shore, the Leafs scored twice to take the lead. Later, Shore came unglued while protesting a goal by Red Horner. Shore threw a punch at referee Odie Cleghorn and earned a ten-minute misconduct. On a six-on-four advantage, the Leafs scored again. Toronto capitalized on the Bruins' errors, and when the dust settled, the Leafs had won the game, 8–3, and the series, 8–6. Smythe was effusive in praising the home-town fans: "It was the greatest crowd reception we ever received. It was greater than we were given after winning the Stanley Cup!"

Next, the Leafs met the New York Americans. This was the furthest the Americans had ever progressed in the postseason. Their game plan was simple: clean, defensive hockey. Former Leaf Baldy Cotton was assigned the task of shadowing his former roommate, Charlie Conacher. The *Star* commented gleefully on the intriguing matchup: "There was Cotton, yippy and eager and persistent, high-tailing it after the big fellow. There was Conacher, pushing Baldy aside, rubbing him with stick and elbow, grinning at his pursuit."

Maple Leaf Gardens was surprisingly warm for the opening match. This made the ice slow and the puck bounced erratically. While New York had scored first, the Leafs replied with three goals in the third to take Game One.

The second game was held at Madison Square Garden. Americans goaltender Roy Worters was the star of the show, holding the Leafs off of the scoreboard in a 1–0 New York win. Game Three had a better result for the Leafs, who managed to close out the series with a 3–1 victory at Maple Leaf Gardens.

Toronto was once again off to the Stanley Cup final to face the Detroit Red Wings. The Wings took early command of the series by winning Game One, 3–1. For Smythe, speed had cost them the opener. "You know what beat us? We forgot, playing those slower Americans, how fast this Detroit bunch can break." Two days later, Detroit set an NHL record for goals in a playoff game by crushing the Leafs, 9–4.

The series moved to Maple Leaf Gardens for Game Three. Down three goals, the Maple Leafs utilized a four-man offence and changed lines every minute, a tactic that paid dividends. They tied the game late in the third, and then Buzz Boll scored in overtime to give Toronto a 4–3 win. But the playoffs ended for the Maple Leafs in Game Four. On this night, the Red Wings won, 3–2, and earned the first Stanley Cup in franchise history. James Norris, who had purchased the team in 1932, beamed. "I achieved the ambition of my life – to win a Stanley Cup." The Red Wings staged a celebration at Toronto's Royal York Hotel before returning to the Motor City. The Maple Leafs and their fans, on the other hand, were growing tired of the perennial spring fever that seemed to afflict the team every April.

SHIFT AND FADE

In 1936, Imperial Oil took over the Leaf hockey broadcasts. Radio listeners' interest in the game had sky-rocketed, and Maple Leafs hockey was soon ubiquitous on the airwaves in Toronto and across Canada. Six million listeners, for instance, tuned in to hear a single game between the Leafs and Detroit in 1937, at a time when the Canadian population numbered only 11½ million. *Hush* magazine criticized radio for pandering to the hockey-crazed city: "Last Saturday, CFCA, CKCL and CFRB were all on a hook-up from the Maple Leaf Gardens, when one station carrying that feature would have been ample." Fan mail flooded in, and in one year alone, Foster Hewitt received 90,000 fan letters. He was thrilled to know that his broadcasts had brought comfort "to so many people, young and old, deaf and blind, healthy or bed-ridden."

As the principal sponsor of what would become *Hockey Night in Canada*, Imperial Oil promoted its Three Star gasoline by selecting the best three players of the game at the conclusion of each hockey broadcast. The stars would be announced via the public-address system, and the selected players would skate out individually to be recognized by the crowd. While Three Star gasoline was phased out in 1949, to be replaced by the Esso brand, the naming of three stars at the end of each game soon became a leaguewide practice and is a tradition that has endured to the present day.

Featured as they were on national broadcasts, all of the Leafs had become national stars. Yet, though the team habitually made it to the final, the Leafs had only one championship to show for their Depression-era efforts.

At the conclusion of the 1935–36 season, Joe Primeau, who had centred the Kid Line so wonderfully, announced that he wouldn't be returning. Primeau had a very successful concrete-block business, and would devote his time to overseeing the operation, but he vowed to continue with hockey in some capacity as the years unfolded. (He would prove to be as good as his word; his role in Leafs history was hardly over.) He was just the first of several dominoes to fall. The Maple Leafs' roster was on the verge of substantial change in 1936–37.

It was during this period that a future Leafs leader was making a name for himself in the hockey ether. Conn Smythe had been alerted to a terrific athletic specimen attending McMaster University in Hamilton, Ontario. Sylvanus Apps starred in several sports, including hockey, while earning a degree in economics. After graduating, Apps joined the Hamilton Tigers of the OHA senior loop and led that league in scoring. In August 1936, Apps also competed at the Olympic Games in Berlin, Germany, and finished sixth in pole-vaulting. Two years earlier, he had captured the gold medal in the sport at the British Empire Games. In the absence of Primeau, Smythe pencilled Apps in to centre a line between the remaining Kid Line forwards, Conacher and Jackson.

The Maple Leafs signed another youngster during the off-season. Gordie Drillon had appeared on Toronto's radar while he was a junior with the Toronto Young Rangers, who practised and played out of Maple Leaf Gardens. In 1935, Drillon joined the Pittsburgh Yellow Jackets of the Eastern Amateur Hockey League. Smythe was livid when he discovered that the New York Rangers were pursuing Drillon, and swore that Drillon was already on the Leafs' protected list. To this end, the Maple Leafs signed Drillon to a contract in April 1936. The signing came just in time for the youngster to join the Maple Leafs as they embarked on a barnstorming tour of western Canada, where the team played exhibition games against the Chicago Black Hawks for the Totem Cup.

Around this same time, a young Toronto boy was starring in goal for the Detroit Olympics of the International Hockey League. As the Leafs' regular goalie, 43-year-old George Hainsworth, was getting on in terms of hockey years, Smythe knew he had to find a netminder for the future. When Smythe saw Walter "Turk" Broda backstop the Olympics to an 8–1 win over the Windsor Bulldogs, the Leafs' chief knew he had found his man.

Broda's rights belonged to the Detroit Red Wings, from whom Smythe purchased them on May 6, 1936, for the exorbitant price of $7,500. The hockey world was stunned. The Red Wings had a surplus of goaltenders that included Normie Smith, John Ross Roach, and Earl Robertson, so many hockey-savvy people believed they had cheated the Leafs. Smythe remained resolute: "Broda could tend goal in a tornado and never blink an eye. And you can blame any carelessness on youth. He'll outgrow that in a hurry."

The Maple Leafs opened the 1936–37 season against the Detroit Red Wings at Maple Leaf Gardens. Lieutenant-Governor Bruce dropped the ceremonial puck. Surprisingly, the Leafs management must have believed that the young Broda had already outgrown any "carelessness" when they started him instead of Hainsworth on opening night. Frustrated, Hainsworth lamented, "I've got one more good year in me, at least." The Red Wings took the opener, 3–1.

The Maple Leafs would struggle throughout the season. Charlie Conacher, for instance, endured several injuries and played just 15 games. Yet the big news came only six games in: after a 4–2 loss to Detroit, the battle-scarred fan favourite King Clancy announced his retirement.

With all my heart, I want to thank the hockey fans of every city in the National Hockey League, the newspapermen and others who gave my clubs and myself the grandest of support . . . I've had 16 years of hockey, and I think I'm doing the right thing to lay down my stick before somebody tells me to. I think the smart guy is the one who senses it before being officially nudged.

Clancy, as it happens, had in fact received a little nudge. During a train journey from Detroit to New York City, Clancy had been summoned into Smythe's compartment, where he was greeted by the unsmiling faces of the Leafs' top brass. There, Smythe, assistant general manager Frank Selke, and coach Dick Irvin advised Clancy that he should retire. The men offered King his full salary for the season as well as a position as team ambassador. As Ed Fitkin observed, "Hurt and defiant, the King reluctantly gave in.

He came out of the conference with tears streaming unashamedly down his cheeks, and the men he left behind in the compartment were almost near tears, too."

The 33-year-old Clancy retired as the top-scoring defenceman in NHL history, having collected 136 goals and 283 points in 592 regular-season games. He did indeed serve as an ambassador for the Maple Leafs for the rest of the campaign, but joined the Montreal Maroons as head coach the next season. That stint was short-lived, and King would spend the next 11 seasons as an NHL referee.

With Primeau and Clancy gone, Smythe decided that he was going to roll the dice and move forward with Turk Broda as his goaltender. In November, after dropping a 5–1 decision to the New York Rangers, George Hainsworth was given his outright release. The little net-minder was signed by the Canadiens in December 1936 and finished his NHL career in the city where it had begun.

The Leafs, it seemed, were in full rebuild mode and finished third in the Canadian Division with a record of 22 wins, 21 losses, and 5 ties. There were, however, several bright spots amidst the gloom. Harvey Jackson's career, for instance, experienced something of a renaissance. Playing on a line with Syl Apps at centre and Gordie Drillon at right wing, Busher scored 21 goals, fourth best in the NHL, and his 40 points ranked fifth in the league. Jackson was selected to the NHL's First All-Star Team. Gordie Drillon shone in his rookie campaign, collecting 16 goals and 17 assists. As impressive as this debut was, it was Apps who proved to be the greatest surprise of all. He scored 16 goals and added 29 assists, a league-best, for 45 points. This put Syl second in NHL scoring in his first season. He was awarded the Calder Trophy as the NHL's finest rookie.

Gordie Drillon (centre) battles for space in front of the Chicago net, with Earl Seibert (left) and goaltender Mike Karakas watching the play. Drillon made a massive impact on the Maple Leafs during his six seasons in blue and white. He was so widely known through radio broadcasts that one fan sent a letter with just his name and image on the envelope (shown above) – and the post office knew where to deliver the mail.

Despite these promising developments, the Leafs' playoffs appearance would be a short one. The quarter-final pitted the Leafs against the New York Rangers, who opened the series with a 3–0 blanking of the host Maple Leafs in Game One. New York then slipped past Toronto with a 2–1 overtime win in Game Two at Madison Square Garden. The Maple Leafs simply could not get uncoiled against the Rangers, and the loss sent them speedily into the off-season.

Members of the old guard had, one by one, begun to shift and fade. Captain Hap Day – the longest-tenured member of the franchise, having joined the Toronto St. Patricks in 1924–25 – was next to leave. The defence-man, who had so successfully partnered with Red Horner for several seasons, had increasingly become the scape-goat for fans at the Gardens and was released so that he could negotiate a deal with the New York Americans. Smythe acknowledged that the move might have been a welcome one for Day: "I guess the old boy will be happier away from his rinkside critics." With the release of Day and the retirements of Primeau and Clancy, the Leafs were now in a process of trying to define their team's new look. In a variety of deals in advance of the 1937–38 season, the Leafs lost Jack Shill and Art Jackson, but added free agents Pete Langelle and Murph Chamberlain. Still, whatever the new Maple Leafs team was going to become, it was clear to all that it was going to be built around a core of Apps, Drillon, and Broda. But the completion of the overhaul was still a wee ways off.

With Day gone, Smythe created ballots and asked each member of the Leafs to choose between Charlie Conacher, Red Horner, and Busher Jackson as the next captain of the Maple Leafs. In the end, it was Conacher who was selected as the new on-ice leader of the Blue and White.

On opening night, Ontario's attorney-general, Gordon Conant, dropped the puck between the Leafs and Detroit Red Wings to signal the beginning of the new season. The game ended in a 2–2 draw. Captain Conacher was on fire to start the season. On November 13, he poured in three goals and an assist in a 7–3 whipping of the Black Hawks. But Conacher remained a leaguewide target. As such, the Big Bomber was habitually sidelined with new and old injuries. By January 19, the broken right winger had had enough. On that day, Charlie stunned the hockey world with the announcement that he was retiring from hockey. The shoulder injury he sustained in December had not fully healed, and other, older injuries still plagued him.

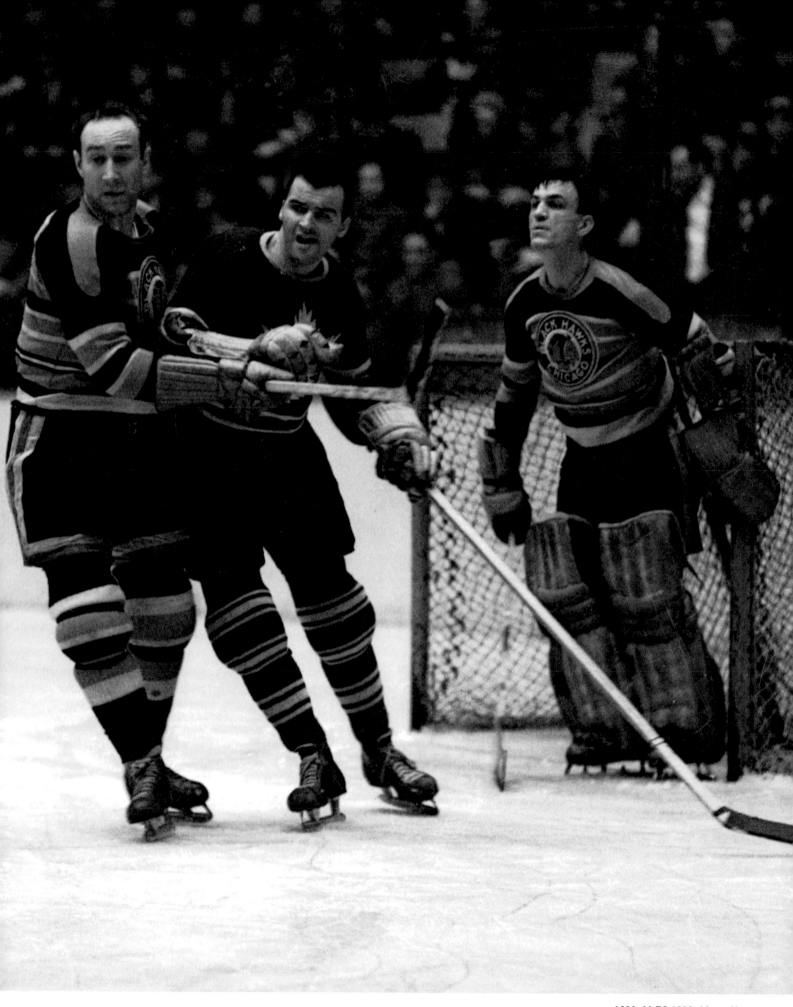

Conacher had come under considerable criticism for his poor play, but sportswriters and Leafs fans were likely unaware of the extent of his injuries. In fact, Conacher had been told by Dr. Rush, the team's physician, that he was in no condition to play hockey and that he was inviting more serious consequences if he continued. Conacher decided to leave the game and informed Smythe of his decision.

The next day, all of the Toronto dailies eulogized Conacher's outstanding, if ephemeral career. The *Star*, for instance, declared that Conacher "was a leader and was never satisfied unless he was in the top row of whatever he might be doing at the moment. Conacher is an example of what hard work, the desire to accomplish things and the will to win will do for one. He was a champion of champions; the Babe Ruth of the ice lanes." The next day, hockey's Babe Ruth sailed to Bermuda to rest.

With Conacher's limited play and eventual retirement, the Leafs became increasingly reliant on the young guns, among them Gordie Drillon. Through radio's long reach, the profile of players such as Drillon continued to rise across the nation. Leafs fans outside of the Queen City now began to embark on special pilgrimages to Maple Leaf Gardens. On one such occasion, nearly 300 Maritimers made the trip to Toronto to watch Moncton, New Brunswick's own Drillon in action. And prior to a contest against the Montreal Maroons on January 8, 1938, Moncton's mayor presented Drillon with a gold watch. As far as Smythe was concerned, Drillon was the "first really smart hockey player we have ever had on our club. He knows instinctively what to do. He accomplishes it without getting hurt. That alone is almost as great an asset to a club as scoring ability." This was, of course, also a not-so-veiled criticism of the on-ice approach of the Big Bomber, who would, according to Smythe, "get smashed up fulfilling his thought."

The Leafs' fortunes were up and down in the new year. One of the downs included a game played on January 22, 1938, when the Bruins butchered Toronto 9–1. Despite this embarrassment, the Leafs still managed to finish first in the Canadian Division with 57 points. The big line of Apps, Drillon, and Bob Davidson continued to be a dominant force. Drillon and Apps finished one-two in the league scoring race. The former led the league in goals, with 26, and points, with 52, while the latter finished first in assists, with 29, and amassed 50 points. Drillon was named to the NHL's First All-Star Team while Apps was selected to the Second Team. Red Horner did not disappoint, once again leading the NHL in penalty minutes, with 92.

The playoffs opened with the Leafs facing the Boston Bruins, who were heavily favoured to capture the Cup. They had finished first overall, ten points ahead of Toronto. The Bruins had great goaltending from Tiny Thompson, and could score with snipers Bill Cowley, Bobby Bauer, Milt Schmidt, and Woody Dumart, but most of all, they were big and tough. Eddie Shore was still the league's pre-eminent defenceman on a blueline that included former right winger Dit Clapper, ex-Leaf Flash Hollett, and Jack Portland. Smythe warned that Boston was "a thundering good club, well-trained, disciplined and coached to undertake certain actions under certain circumstances and carry it out."

The first contest was a knockdown, drag-'em-out fight. The game was scoreless at the end of regulation, and remained so after the first overtime. The Leafs' George Parsons fired the winning goal at 1:32 of the second overtime. The Toronto fans, who refused to leave until the end, littered the ice with anything not nailed down as they whooped and hollered in victory. The second game, also played in Toronto, was equally close. It too ended positively for the Leafs, who won 2–1.

The bitterly fought series continued in Boston for Game Three. Shore, Clapper, and company were hitting the Leafs at every opportunity, but the Toronto team refused to back down. Shore, who seldom came off the ice, had earned a reputation as one of the toughest players in the NHL. He proved it in the third game. All night, he tried to slow down the Apps-Drillon-Davidson line. Twice, Shore and Davidson were sent off with matching penalties.

With the game knotted at one in the third, the Bruins scored what was a highly contested goal. There was some question as to whether or not the puck had actually crossed the goal line. The goal light went on, but the Maple Leafs, as one newspaper reported, "bombarded the goal umpire and chased the referees to the timers' bench. Broda rushed half the length of the ice, wildly protesting the goal." It was to no avail. The goal stood and the Bruins were up, 2–1.

Less than a minute later, however, Gordie Drillon came to the rescue and tied the game with a sensational solo effort. Then, midway through the first overtime period, Syl Apps burst out of the Leafs end and slipped a pass to Drillon, who cut in and scored again to give Toronto a 3–2 win in the best-of-five series. The Leafs were once again heading to the Stanley Cup final, for the fifth time in seven springs.

Providing the opposition were the Chicago Black Hawks, who had won the Stanley Cup in 1934, but given their regular-season record of 14 wins, 25 losses, and

On March 4, 1939, Toronto winger George Parsons was clipped with a high stick in a game against Chicago and lost his left eye. The NHL insisted that the 25-year-old retire. He took a job with CCM and lobbied for decades to make the wearing of helmets mandatory for minor hockey players. In 1976, the Canadian Amateur Hockey Association finally agreed.

9 ties, no one pegged them as a serious contender in 1938, even after playoff victories against the Canadiens and Americans. Surely it was Toronto's time for another Cup.

The Leafs gained an immediate advantage against the Black Hawks before the series even began. Chicago goaltender Mike Karakas had suffered a broken toe and was unable to play in the opening game. The Black Hawks and their fans worried that Karakas might miss the entire final series; for the short term, at least, Chicago had to find another goalie. Paul Goodman, the Hawks' spare goaltender, was playing with the Wichita Skyhawks of the American Hockey Association and would not arrive in time for the game. A few other names were bandied about, but Alfie Moore, netminder with the Pittsburgh Hornets of the International-American Hockey League (IAHL), was a choice that suited everyone, including the Leafs, who had to approve the Hawks' selection. In fact, Frank Selke himself had contacted Moore and told him to arrive at Maple Leaf Gardens ready to play for the visiting Hawks.

"It was nearly 8:00 before we told Moore we'd play him," Black Hawks coach Bill Stewart explained. "Up to then, he was sitting by himself somewhere else. He hadn't been in our dressing room. Moore wasn't sure of the situation, either. When we talked to him, he said he had not expected to be called on."

Pinch-hitting goalie Alfie Moore backstopped the Black Hawks to a 3–1 win in the opener.

Goodman arrived from Wichita and took the crease for Game Two at Maple Leaf Gardens. It was a dogfight from start to finish. Both teams stood their ground and the referees allowed the rough stuff to continue. On the score sheet, however, Toronto had evened the series with a 5–1 win. Game Three in Chicago was a much tamer affair. With new referees, both teams were far better behaved. Karakas had returned to play goal for Chicago, and, buoyed by his presence, the Hawks came out on top, 2–1.

The Leafs and Hawks traded goals in the first period of Game Four at Chicago Stadium. But late in the second, George Parsons tried to carry the puck out of the Leafs zone and lost control, turning it over to Carl Voss, who stepped in and fired the puck past Broda to give Chicago a 2–1 lead. In the third period, Jack Shill lofted a high shot from centre ice towards the Maple Leaf goal. As the *Star* explained, "It twisted straight for Broda . . . Turk came out about eight feet and dropped to smother it. His timing was bad. The puck went through his legs and fell softly into the net. The Leafs gathered around Turk and tried to comfort him."

With these two gaffes, the game was over. Mush March added an exclamation mark with a power-play goal late in the third for a 4–1 Chicago victory. The Black Hawks had, inexplicably, won the Stanley Cup. In fact, the 1938 Black Hawks remain the team with the poorest regular-season record to win the Cup in NHL history.

Despite the disappointing outcome in the final, the *Star* lauded the 1937–38 Toronto Maple Leafs: "And so we come to the end of a long, long drive with your Leafs bloodied but unbowed. They fought the good fight. They kept the faith and they did better over the long race for glory than their most optimistic supporters ever believed they could."

Still, the Maple Leafs had grown impatient with this all-too familiar narrative of *losing* Stanley Cups.

RUMOURS OF WAR

The Montreal Maroons suspended operations prior to the 1938–39 campaign. Reduced to seven teams, the National Hockey League eliminated its Canadian and American Divisions and placed all of the teams in one group. With the coming war, the league would soon be tested to its absolute limits. The Maroons would not be the last team to fold.

Having enjoyed a few months away from the game, Charlie Conacher was beginning to reconsider his retirement. He had begun to tell friends that he was feeling healthy, and he wanted back in the game. Be that as it may, the Big Bomber would not be returning to Toronto – the Maple Leafs had moved on. Toronto agreed to a deal that would send Conacher's rights to Detroit for $16,000. And so began short stints with the Red Wings and New York Americans, before Conacher finally did retire for good at the end of the 1940–41 season. Through 459 regular-season games, he scored 225 goals and added 173 assists for 398 points. During his most productive years, Conacher had led the NHL's scoring race five times in the space of only six years. He was named to the NHL's First All-Star Team in 1934, 1935, and 1936, and to the Second Team in 1932 and 1933.

With Conacher's departure, Red Horner was named captain of the Toronto Maple Leafs. Red was one of the few holdovers from the 1932 Cup-winning team. The average age of the team was now 23, and its core players were all in their prime: Syl Apps was 23, Gordie Drillon 25, and Bob Davidson 26. Even Busher Jackson was still only 27. Captain Horner was the Leafs' oldest player, at 29 years old.

I have great memories of my first NHL game wearing the blue and white. It was in Philadelphia during the second round of the Stanley Cup playoffs in 1976. I was so ready for this game, and then it happened: Kate Smith started singing "God Bless America" with 15,000 fans singing with her, and staring across at me from the other blueline were the likes of Schultz, Holmgren, Kelly . . . I can honestly say I do not remember what I was thinking at that moment, but being there on the ice in Philadelphia it was a combination of fear and excitement, realizing that it does not get any better than this.

Bob Warner
PLAYER
1976–77

Prior to the first game of the new campaign, Albert Matthews, Ontario's 16th lieutenant-governor, dropped the puck for the ceremonial faceoff. Drillon was presented with the Lady Byng Trophy after being recognized as the most gentlemanly player of the prior season. Boston took the season-opening game, 3–2.

In the season's second contest, Drillon was slashed across the hand and suffered a broken thumb in a game against the Stanley Cup champion Chicago Black Hawks. With Drillon out, the Maple Leafs plodded along through November. While Turk Broda was exceptional in goal, earning three shutouts that month alone, the team missed Drillon's scoring prowess, and Apps struggled without his regular linemate.

For his part, Smythe was still tweaking his roster. Conn pulled the trigger on a deal with the Black Hawks in December that sent former All-Star Bill Thoms to Chicago for Doc Romnes. Perhaps remembering the experience of having his nose broken by Red Horner the previous spring, Romnes refused to report to Toronto at first, although he agreed after a day of deliberation. The first of his new teammates to greet him was Horner.

To help shore up the Leafs blueline, Smythe sent a prospect and $10,000 to the Red Wings for defenceman Bucko McDonald, who made his presence felt early and often. McDonald used a potent hip check to stop opponents in their tracks.

Disaster, however, struck in a game between Chicago and Toronto on March 4, 1939. While tussling near centre ice, the Hawks' Earl Robinson tried to lift the stick of George Parsons and caught him in the left eye. The *Star* observed that Parsons "fell like a man stricken with a mortal wound." Parsons beat the ice with his gloves while his legs flailed about. The young Leaf had been seriously injured. According to Dr. Rush, Parsons's vision would be permanently impaired. Though he regained partial vision in his eye, the 23-year-old would never play hockey again. Out of this unfortunate incident, the National Hockey League decided that 5 per cent of all playoff gate receipts would go to a players' fund. Parsons was the first to receive assistance from this pool of money.

Down a man, Toronto finished the season in third place with 47 points, well back of the first-place Bruins (74 points) and behind the New York Rangers (58). Syl Apps led the team with 40 points, sixth best in the NHL that season. Both Apps and Gord Drillon were named to the NHL's First All-Star Team. Red Horner continued his bad-boy streak, finishing with a league-leading 85 penalty minutes.

By the opening round of the playoffs, the Maple Leafs lineup was depleted by injuries – Buzz Boll and Busher Jackson had both been hurt in the final game of the regular season. Despite the holes in their lineup, however, the Leafs dominated their best-of-three quarter-final series, shutting out the New York Americans, 4–0 and 2–0.

Next up were the Detroit Red Wings. The Leafs had been undefeated at home against Detroit during the season and had shut out the Wings three times. They therefore entered the series with a certain degree of confidence. Toronto took Game One of the best-of-three series, 4–1. The *Star* reported that "the Detroiters were outclassed by a team that struck with all the power and destructiveness of a locomotive." Then the Wings came back to take Game Two, 3–1. It took overtime in the third and deciding game at Maple Leaf Gardens for a series victor to emerge. At 5:42 of the extra frame, Gordie Drillon fired a bullet past Tiny Thompson for the winner.

For a remarkable sixth time in eight seasons, the Toronto Maple Leafs had reached the Stanley Cup final. Conversely, the Boston Bruins, Toronto's opponents, had last been to the final in 1930, and had not won the Stanley Cup since 1929. Boston, however, had run away with first place during the regular season, with a 36–10–2 record. Bruins rookie Roy Conacher, Charlie's younger brother, scored an NHL-best 26 goals. His teammate Bill Cowley managed 34 assists, which was also tops in the league. The famous "Kraut Line" of Bobby Bauer, Woody Dumart, and Milt Schmidt was emerging as one of the best in the league. Added to this formidable group was the Bruins defence corps of Eddie Shore, Johnny Crawford, Jack Portland, and Flash Hollett.

The first two games of the series were played at Boston Garden, where the city was experiencing an early-April warm spell. This made the ice poor and sticky. In Game One, with the score knotted at one late in the third period, the Bruins' Bauer stole the puck from Bucko McDonald, eluded a couple of checks, and fired the winning goal past Turk Broda to give Boston the 2–1 victory. Game Two was equally tight. A minor penalty to Mel Hill afforded Toronto the opportunity to score goals within 34 seconds of each other. The game went into overtime, and midway through the extra frame, Doc Romnes scored to give the Leafs a 3–2 win.

The action moved to Toronto for the third and fourth games. The Leafs fans' hatred for Eddie Shore had remained steadfast throughout the better part of the decade. Each time he was on the ice in Toronto, he was soundly booed. This reception only fired up the Bruins defenceman.

> The biggest thrill for me, as a local boy growing up in North York, was making the Leafs, especially after joining competitive hockey at 19 years old. The Leafs were also my dad's favourite team, and I know how proud he was of me.
>
> **Kevin Maguire**
> PLAYER
> 1986–87; 1990–92

In Game Three, Shore belted Busher Jackson and sent him off with a dislocated shoulder. With Shore leading the charge, the Bruins had rattled the Leafs. The death knell for the series was sounded early in the third period, when Bobby Bauer sent the puck towards the net from the far boards, catching Broda with his legs apart. Boston dumped Toronto, 3–1, to take a 2–1 lead in the series.

In Game Four, the Bruins completely stifled the Leafs attack. Apps and Drillon had been frustrated by the blanket being thrown over them by the close-checking Bruins. Frankie Brimsek earned a shutout and Roy Conacher scored both of Boston's goals in the 2–0 victory.

The series returned to Boston for Game Five. Toronto matched the Bruins with a goal apiece until late in the second, when Conacher scored what proved to be the Stanley Cup–winning tally. Boston had defeated Toronto 3–1 to take the championship. As the Bruins celebrated, firecrackers were let off and the Boston Garden organist played "Ça c'est Paris," which remained a staple at Bruins games until the mid-1980s. The Maple Leafs had simply been unable to puncture

The happy-go-lucky Maple Leafs were tagged the "Gashouse Gang" by the press in the 1930s. Here, the team is posed in civilian clothes outside the new Maple Leaf Gardens.

the Bruins defence and, once again, had to endure the championship celebrations of their opponents.

The Leafs' spectacular futility in the finals was agonizing for the team's supporters. The Blue and White had been to the big dance six times during this Great (and miserable) Depression, yet they had managed only one Stanley Cup win. When fans gazed backwards from the end of the decade, the 1932 victory seemed so distant. Clancy, Day, Primeau, Conacher, and the majority of that winning team had either retired or moved on to other pastures. Only Horner and Jackson remained.

There was some hope. Through the magic of radio, the Maple Leafs' popularity had reached unprecedented heights for hockey during the 1930s. Certainly, the local-boys-turned-heroes of '32 and the raising of Maple Leaf Gardens in five and a half months were pretty hard acts to follow. But another generation of youngsters was poised to restore Toronto's place at the top of the hockey world. Apps, Davidson, Drillon, Langelle, McDonald, Metz, and Broda formed a nucleus that would soon bring the Stanley Cup back to Toronto.

WORLD AT WAR
1939–40 TO 1944–45

By the end of the 1930s, Adolf Hitler had successfully brought an end to world peace. In the years leading up to war, Germany's actions had raised concern among the world's leaders. Not long after German troops invaded Poland on September 1, 1939, Britain and France declared war on Germany. On September 10, Canada also declared war.

There was one immediate positive effect on the nation: production demands increased exponentially, serving as an antidote to Canada's decade-long depression. Unemployment rates dropped rapidly, and soon everyone, it seemed, was involved in the war effort. Thousands of Canadian men enlisted in one of the branches of the military, and women stepped up to take the place of men in various industries, especially in munitions factories. Every strata of society, hockey included, was affected by the war.

Conn Smythe, for example, would re-enlist in the Canadian Army and one day run his own battery before getting wounded in France. Several Maple Leaf players earnestly enlisted in various branches of the military. Even the Leafs executives were rolling up their sleeves and joining the fight. J.P. Bickell, for instance, made significant contributions to the war effort. He sent food parcels to Britain, donated planes and money to the Royal Canadian Air Force (RCAF), and was one of the main forces behind stopping Hitler's Operation Sea Lion, the planned invasion of Britain. Bickell arrived in England in time for the Battle of Britain in 1940. The Leafs executive had been recruited by Lord Beaverbrook of the British ministry of aircraft production, and he soon became a member of the all-Canadian foursome the "Four Busy Bs," along with Beaverbrook, former Canadian prime minister R.B. Bennett, and Toronto-born British MP Beverley Baxter. By 1941, the Busy Bs were providing the Allies with the bombers and fighter planes that effectively kept the Nazis out of Britain – which was, at the time, the last country in Europe standing against Hitler.

END OF AN ERA

In May 1939, Conn Smythe pulled the trigger on a big trade, acquiring Sweeney Schriner from the New York Americans for Murray Armstrong, Buzz Boll, Jimmy Fowler, Doc Romnes, and Busher Jackson. Schriner was a great score for Smythe. The forward was a top scorer who had finished atop the league in 1935–36 and 1936–37, placing in the top ten in 1934–35, 1937–38, and 1938–39. He was the NHL's rookie of the year in 1935, and a two-time All-Star, in 1935–36 and 1936-37.

Jackson's departure truly represented the end of an era. Smythe believed that a change of scenery might be beneficial to Busher, whose play had been sliding for the past two years. In 1938–39, Jackson had managed only 10 goals and 17 assists.

Jackson was going to a New York Americans team that favoured veterans, many of whose best years were well behind them. Among the better-known stars on the Americans' 1939–40 roster were Hooley Smith, Nels Stewart, and Eddie Shore. Busher's brother Art Jackson was also with the team, as was Charlie Conacher. The Americans were, in essence, a lineup of yesterday's heroes.

As for Toronto, the departure of a brace of veterans cleared the path for several rookies to step into the lineup. Lex Chisholm, Jack Church, Red Heron, Pete Langelle, and Wally Stanowski were summoned from the Leafs' top farm team, the Syracuse Stars of the International-American Hockey League. Hank Goldup and Don Metz likewise joined the big team from the Senior A Toronto Goodyears. Billy Taylor made the greatest leap, joining the Maple Leafs from junior, where he had starred with the Oshawa Generals.

The Leafs' training camp was spent, as it had been for many years, in what is today Cambridge, Ontario. The team stayed at the luxurious Preston Springs Hotel and played at Galt Arena Gardens. That all changed in the fall of 1939, when the hotel closed. Smythe then moved the team's training camp to St. Catharines, with on-ice work taking place at the newly built Garden City Arena.

Syl Apps (centre) was in the prime of his career when he joined the Canadian Army in 1943. The captain returned in uniform to visit his team, and is here pictured with back-to-back Calder Trophy winners Frank McCool (left), who was the recipient in 1944–45, and Gus Bodnar (right), who won the rookie of the year honour in 1943–44.

On opening night, the Leafs hosted the Stanley Cup champion Boston Bruins at Maple Leaf Gardens and won convincingly, 5–0. "Bewildered by Leafs' speed, bewitched by a wily defence and an impeccable Broda in nets," the *Star* reported, "the battement proceedings began in less than two minutes when Apps swept around the tank corp and whanged the first goal into port."

Broda's clean sheet was the first opening-night shutout the Leafs had had in 11 years. In fact, Broda earned shutouts in three of the season's first four games, and through the first month of the season he surrendered just 13 goals in eight games. Six of these goals came in a single loss to the Bruins on November 28.

The Leafs led the league through the first half of the season, but then injuries took their toll. In a 4–1 Christmas Day win over the New York Rangers, Syl Apps fractured his collarbone and missed 21 games. Likewise, Gord Drillon, who was leading the NHL in scoring, suffered a badly cut foot in a 3–1 win over the Montreal Canadiens in early January. Losing their top two scorers crippled the Leafs. Then, Nick Metz, who had been providing some strong secondary scoring for the Leafs, also took to the sidelines with an injury. While the youngsters stepped into the void, they could not compensate for the loss of the key starters.

To complicate matters, Turk Broda's knee was badly cut in a loss to Boston on January 11, 1940. Smythe summoned Phil Stein to replace Broda. Stein, who had spent five seasons vying for the number one job with Broda, was with the Omaha Knights in the American Hockey Association. In a game against the Detroit Red Wings on January 18, Stein got his first big break in the NHL. Though he surrendered two goals, Stein played well and the game ended in a 2–2 tie.

Smythe had decided to start Stein against the New York Americans in the next game, but this time fate intervened. During the pregame warm-up, Billy Taylor's shot caught Stein on the chin, cutting him for six stitches. Broda, who was still on the mend and sitting in the stands in his civilian clothes, quickly dressed and replaced his replacement. Toronto won the game, 5–1. Stein never again played in the NHL.

Nearing the end of the season, the Maple Leafs went on a tear, blasting Montreal, 8–4, and the Americans, 8–6. The reunited DAD Line of Drillon, Apps, and Davidson was healthy once again. In these two games alone, the line combined for 22 points.

Toronto finished third, well back of first-place Boston and the second-place New York Rangers. Still, with a lineup rife with rookies and injuries plaguing the roster – only Bob Davidson appeared in all 48 games that season – the Leafs were fortunate to finish as well as they did. Gord Drillon finished fourth in goals, with 21, and points, with 40. Red Horner again eclipsed all others in penalty minutes with 87.

The opening round of the playoffs had Toronto facing fourth-place Chicago. Smythe was optimistic about the Leafs' chances. "I am satisfied about the moxie in the Leafs this spring. They are just a bunch of kids. They'll come out fighting." It was the Hawks, however, who came out battling.

Early in the first period of Game One, Chicago's Art Wiebe drifted a shot from the boards that eluded Broda to open the scoring. The Leaf faithful booed the netminder, and the *Toronto Star* reminded readers that "it's not the first lapse of that nature committed by Broda. He kicked away a nice Stanley Cup chance two years ago." While the Leafs hit the Hawks at every opportunity, Mush March scored to give Chicago a 2–0 lead. The kids, however, fought back and managed to tie the game. In overtime, an energized Syl Apps was able to hammer home the winner and give the Leafs the edge in the series opener.

Game Two of the best-of-three quarter-final was played in Chicago, and this time the Hawks beat themselves. With the score tied at one, Hank Goldup fired a shot that was blocked by blueliner Jack Portland. Portland tried to sweep the puck away but knocked it into his own net with about eight minutes to go. Toronto hung on for the 2–1 win and a place in the semifinals against Detroit.

Previous series between Smythe's Leafs and Jack Adams's Red Wings had proven to be heated affairs. This time was no different. After the Leafs edged Detroit, 2–1, at Maple Leaf Gardens in the opener, the series moved to the Olympia. The intensity of the game was apparent to all. It was a veritable powder-keg scenario, and an explosion was becoming more inevitable over the course of the game.

In the second period, Red Horner and Alex Motter received matching roughing minors. While seated in the penalty box, the two men wrestled each other to the ground. This, however, was only a prelude to what was to come. Hank Goldup scored two goals, giving Toronto a 3–0 lead with less than a minute to play. With the game already decided, Detroit's Syd Howe scored a power-play goal at 19:20. This put the match to the powder keg. With the speed and fury of a summer storm, a donnybrook ensued. Players from both benches tumbled over the boards to get involved. Included in the "all-comers" was

Wings goaltender Tiny Thompson, who managed to get a few belts in on Red Horner. From here, other Wings began to pile on the Leafs captain. The whole mess continued for 15 minutes before the police got involved and calmed the situation.

The Red Wings, according to the *Star*, "went out like a bunch of petulant children . . . licked on the ice by a superior force, they couldn't take it like real sportsmen but instead, elected to slug it out with their opposition." It seemed that the Leafs, top-heavy with rookies, were punching above their collective weight.

The sweep of Detroit led Toronto to the Stanley Cup final once again. This time, it was against the powerful New York Rangers. The Rangers took Game One through an overtime goal by Alf Pike, who was making restitution for having accidentally scored on his own goal midway through the first period.

For Game Two, Smythe shuffled his deck. Nick Metz was dropped from the lineup in favour of Billy Taylor. While Taylor had played 29 games for Toronto, he had spent much of his time in the IAHL with the Pittsburgh Hornets. "Billy the Kid," however, scored the opening goal of the second game, followed in short order by Goldup. But it was all Rangers after that. The Broadway Blues struck back with six unanswered goals for a 6–2 final score. Bryan Hextall recorded a hat trick, marking the first time in eight years that a player had managed three goals in a Cup final game. Rangers coach Frank Boucher had been the last player to accomplish the feat when he did so against the Leafs' Lorne Chabot back in 1932.

Back in Toronto, the Leafs took Game Three, 2–1, and were able to tie the series at two with a 3–0 shutout win in Game Four. The Cup was there for the taking.

While the playoff format would have seen Game Five played in New York, the Ringling Brothers and Barnum & Bailey Circus had taken up its usual April residency at Madison Square Garden. The contest was therefore played at Maple Leaf Gardens instead. Mac Colville and Syl Apps traded goals to send the game into overtime in what the *Star* called "the most desperately fought thrill-provoking game of what is a terrific series." No one scored in the first overtime, but at 11:43 of the second extra frame, Muzz Patrick scored to give the Rangers the win and a stranglehold on the Stanley Cup.

Game Six was also a high-energy contest. Apps and Nick Metz scored in the first and second periods, respectively, but the Rangers' Colville and Pike answered in the third. New York clearly had the momentum going into overtime. At 2:07 of extra time, Bryan Hextall rifled a backhand past Turk Broda to win the game and the Stanley Cup for the Rangers.

That night, the Rangers took the Stanley Cup to a Toronto restaurant to celebrate their victory. While there, a Leafs fan tried, unsuccessfully, to steal it. For their part, the dejected Leafs took their time undressing after the game. Syl Apps sat quietly with his head in his hands. With seven appearances in the final in the space of a decade, the Leafs had to endure yet another summer of asking: What if?

The loss also marked the last NHL game in the career of Red Horner. With Horner gone, there was nobody left from the old guard who had brought the Stanley Cup to Toronto in 1932. It was now up to new hands to carry the torch.

MARCHING OFF TO WAR

As concerned as Smythe was about Canada's role in the war – and clearly he was – he was also very interested in building up and maintaining the mythology of the Leafs. With the team's narrative so entwined with the First World War and the British public-school sensibilities of gentlemanly conduct, discipline, courage, and "doing one's duty," Smythe recognized both the responsibility *and* the opportunity that the Second World War brought to the franchise.

Smythe got right behind the war effort. The man who had single-handedly charged a German trench, armed only with a revolver, in the Great War would actively and aggressively campaign for conscription in a very public way during this new war. Smythe also knew that the iconography of Canada's soldiers was already a firm part of the Leafs mythology. Continuing the tradition of the franchise's association with Canada's war effort was crucial to the team's success.

Conn Smythe was eager to serve his country once again. Much to the exasperation of his wife, Irene, Smythe re-enlisted. Many questioned why Smythe, now almost 45 years of age with a family and significant business interests, would insist on joining up again. "I felt it was a shame that we had to go back to Europe and win the war again that we thought we'd won for all time back in 1918. But if we had to, I wanted to be there," he explained. At first, Smythe served as a captain at the Canadian Officers Training Corps, which was based at the University of Toronto. Later, in 1941, Smythe formed the 30th Battery, a sportsmen's unit within the 7th Toronto Regiment of the Royal Canadian Artillery.

Major Conn Smythe became the unit's commanding officer. The battery was later stationed on Vancouver Island to guard against the Japanese threat before being shipped off to England in 1942.

Back in 1940, however, real action for Smythe remained a couple of years away. In the interim, he arranged for his Maple Leaf players and staff to take army training with the Toronto Scottish Regiment in the mornings. Over the course of the season, Smythe personally wrote to every player on the team and in the system, urging them to join Non-Permanent Active Militia (NPAM) units. "In case you are honoured with a call to the Canadian Forces, you will be ready," he wrote. "If you are not called, you will have complied with the military training regulations and be free to play hockey until called upon."

The National Resources Mobilization Act (NRMA), which had passed on June 21, 1940, required hockey players to undergo 30 days of training (the period of training was later extended to four months), and by April 1941, men in nonessential employment were attached to their NRMA units for as long as the war lasted. In the summer of 1940, NHL players were signing up to do their essential NPAM training. By joining, players were committing to training and, theoretically, the possibility of being called up to active service. But ostensibly, signing up allowed many players to continue their professional hockey careers.

Still, the Maple Leafs were proud to announce that a large portion of the roster had enlisted – including Syl Apps, Turk Broda, Jack Church, Bob Davidson, Hap Day, Gord Drillon, Hank Goldup, Reg Hamilton, Red Heron, Phil Stein, and Billy Taylor, all of whom joined the Toronto Scottish. Don and Nick Metz joined the Regina Rifles, while Pete Langelle and Wally Stanowski joined the Winnipeg Rifles. Bucko McDonald joined the Grey and Simcoe Foresters. Bingo Kampman joined a regiment in Kitchener and Lex Chisholm joined up in Oshawa. While the majority of these players, especially those who had been starters for the Leafs, would not see service overseas, there can be no question of the willingness to serve that was apparent up and down the Maple Leafs roster.

At the outset of the 1941–42 season, most pundits believed that the campaign would be a two-horse race between the New York Rangers and the defending Stanley Cup champion Boston Bruins. What lay in store, however, was the most dramatic conclusion to an NHL season yet. Fortunately for Torontonians, the Maple Leafs would be on the right side of what remains the greatest comeback in hockey history.

The Leafs' season began against the Rangers. North Winship, the U.S. consul general, dropped the puck at Toronto's opening game of the season, which saw the visiting New York Rangers take a 4–3 win.

The first half of the Leafs' campaign was generally favourable, but Torontonians were more interested in the ever-evolving world war. On December 7, 1941, the Japanese bombed Pearl Harbor, which brought the United States into the war. That same month, Canada's fighting men saw their first real action in Hong Kong. On Christmas Day 1941, the British colony fell to the Japanese. A total of 550 Canadians lost their lives either on Christmas Day itself or in the hellish slave-labour camps run by the Japanese.

It was far jollier back in Toronto. Santa Claus arrived with a present for Turk Broda on Christmas Day: his third shutout in four games, and his fifth of the season, in a 2–0 victory over the Boston Bruins. In the Montreal–Toronto tilt on January 15, the Leafs took home two points after Nick Metz scored the overtime winner to give them a 3–2 win. Several Leafs, however, left Montreal with injuries from what had been a vicious game. Bob Davidson, for instance, suffered a seven-stitch cut over his left ankle after a hit by Jack Portland. Don Metz lost several teeth from a cross-check, while his brother Nick received a cut on the neck after a Ray Getliffe cross-check. The wounded were given some comfort by a chance encounter on their journey home. The team was paid a special visit by Cyclone Taylor, who was travelling on the same Toronto-bound train. Taylor had been hockey's first "superstar" during the first two decades of the 20th century. Now 57 years of age, Taylor recognized his centrality to early hockey mythology – which, to the delight of the Leafs on board the train, he wore like a comfy sweater.

Coach Hap Day was less comfy with the Leafs defence corps, and he conferred with Conn Smythe about the need to shore up the team's porous blueline. The team was, after all, down to three healthy defencemen. The Leafs summoned Bob Goldham, a terrific shot blocker, from the Toronto Marlboros in late January. The *Toronto Daily Star* called Goldham "the big, tough guy Leafs have lacked since Horner went away." Then, a week later, the Leafs sent Jack Church to the Brooklyn Americans for cash, and replaced him on the blueline with Ernie Dickens, who had also been toiling with the Toronto Marlboros.

Offensively, Toronto had little worry. Several times throughout the season, the Leafs racked up large-margin victories. Pete Langelle recorded his only career hat trick in a 7–3 win over the Montreal Canadiens on January 29;

In 1942, with the Second World War escalating, Conn Smythe asked his players to prepare to serve their country, and they responded. After winning the Stanley Cup in the spring of 1942, a vastly different team hit the ice for the 1942–43 season. The dressing room motto, "Defeat Does Not Rest Lightly On Their Shoulders," suddenly took on additional meaning.

Nick Metz achieved his only hat trick on February 28 in an 8–2 win over the Black Hawks. Yet, while the team could put the puck in the net, the Leafs were as prone to lose by large scores. On the final two nights of the season, a 6–3 loss to last-place Brooklyn was followed by a 7–3 loss to an equally poor Canadiens team. These two games cost the Leafs first place. As it was, Toronto finished the regular season in second, with 57 points, three behind the New York Rangers and just one in front of third-place Boston. The Leafs might well have finished first had they not been plagued by injuries. Don Metz, for example, missed 20 games with a broken ankle. Wally Stanowski was out for 14 games, Syl Apps 10, and Nick Metz 9.

Gordie Drillon and Syl Apps were tied with a team-best 41 points. Drillon scored 23 goals and added 18 assists. Apps had 18 goals and 23 assists, but had appeared in ten fewer games than his linemate. The captain was awarded the Lady Byng Trophy as the NHL's most gentlemanly player. Incredibly, Apps went through the entire 1941–42 season without earning a single penalty. Apps was also named to the NHL's First All-Star Team. Turk Broda, Bucko McDonald, and Gord Drillon were Second Team All-Stars.

Toronto faced the Rangers in the first round of the playoffs. The Leafs took Game One in Toronto by a score of 3–1. Game Two, played at Madison Square Garden, saw the Maple Leafs almost hand over a win to the Rangers when New York scored twice on Nick Metz's third-period penalty. Thankfully for Toronto, Johnny McCreedy's two-goal game helped give the Leafs a 4–2 win and a 2–0 lead in the semifinal series.

Rangers coach Frank Boucher was concerned that his netminder, Sugar Jim Henry, was too distracted to play in Game Three. Henry had learned that his brother, serving in the Canadian Navy, was missing. The netminder nevertheless showed his pluck by blanking Toronto, 3–0.

Game Four was back in Toronto, where the Maple Leafs edged the Rangers, 2–1. A day later, in New York, the Rangers won Game Five, 3–1. Despite the closeness of the series, Hap Day was convinced that his Leafs would see it through. "We'll finish the job tonight," he promised. "We have the tools." He was spot on, but the game was much tighter than Day would have preferred. The Rangers, down 2–0, staged what the *Star* called "the most gallant uphill third period fight of their careers." The Rangers managed to tie the game, but with just six seconds remaining in regulation time, Nick Metz scored a goal to eliminate the powerful New York team.

The spectacular finish propelled the Maple Leafs into the final against the Detroit Red Wings. Although

Two Calgary boys, Lorne Carr (left) and Sweeney Schriner (right), were among the most productive forwards with the Maple Leafs in the early 1940s. They combined for 36 goals in 1941–42 and 46 in 1942–43.

Toronto had finished 15 points higher than the fifth-place Red Wings during the regular season, Detroit was never going to be a pushover. There was also the psychological battle. In the decade leading up to the 1942 final, Toronto had made it to the big dance seven times, but had only one Cup to show for it. Detroit, on the other hand, had appeared in the final just four times during that same period, but had won the Stanley Cup twice. "This series will be decided on a basis, from Detroit's standpoint, of no quarter asked, no holds barred," Smythe warned, adding, "Detroit will come out roaring. Unless we can out-thump them, we'll be behind the eight-ball."

It was the Wings, however, who did the "out-thumping." There would be several wounded Leafs after Game One at Maple Leaf Gardens. Nick Metz suffered a slashed cheek; Bob Goldham, a slice over his eye; Bob Davidson, a bloody nose; and Wally Stanowski, a shiner. Worst of all, the Leafs suffered a 3–2 loss. "We deserved to win," Detroit coach

Ebbie Goodfellow said. "We played them exactly to the plan. That's our game – forechecking and everybody hustling." The key to Detroit's success was their ability to shut down the line of Drillon, Apps, and Davidson. Game Two was much the same and the Red Wings, on the strength of Don Grosso's second straight two-goal game, beat the Leafs, 4–2.

The teams moved to Detroit for the next two contests. While the Maple Leafs led 2–0 on goals by Lorne Carr early in Game Three, the Wings tied the score before the end of the first period. They proceeded to tally twice more in the second and added another in the third to grasp a stranglehold on the Stanley Cup with a 5–2 win. The Wings now enjoyed a seemingly insurmountable three-games-to-none lead in the final. No team had ever rebounded from such a deficit to win a playoff series. Very few believed it was even a remote possibility.

The desperate Leafs were prepared to take some desperate measures. Hap Day phoned Conn Smythe, who was in Petawawa finishing a course to qualify as a major. Day's idea was to bench Gordie Drillon and Bucko McDonald. Drillon, Toronto's leading scorer, was mired in a scoring slump, and McDonald, the team's toughest defenceman, was playing injured with a bruised chest he had received during the series with the Rangers. Surprisingly, Smythe agreed. Don Metz was inserted in place of Drillon, while Ernie Dickens replaced McDonald. Metz had missed much of the regular season with a broken ankle, while Dickens had played only ten games with Toronto, spending most of the season with the American Hockey League's Providence Reds. The coach also added Hank Goldup to the lineup. Goldup had been a regular through the 1941–42 season, but had not yet played a game in the postseason. It was a bold move. Wally Stanowski, the Leafs' "Whirling Dervish" on defence, spoke on behalf of the majority of Toronto's players: "It took a lot of guts . . . Everybody thought Smythe had lost his mind!"

Beyond the lineup changes, the Leafs still had to solve Detroit. The Wings' strategy was unique for the time: Detroit would simply dump the puck into the Leafs zone and then chase it with a fierce forecheck. To counter, Coach Day decided to employ the very same tactic. Bob Goldham later explained: "When Detroit fired the puck into our end from centre, which was a new wrinkle, we'd simply fire it straight back out, which was also a new wrinkle."

The fourth game began very much like the previous three. Toronto fell behind by two goals before the midway point of the second period. Then, Bob Davidson scored. This was soon followed by a goal from Lorne Carr. During the intermission, Day read aloud a letter that he had received prior to the game that night from a young girl:

Dear Mr. Day,

I am 14 years old and have been a fan of the Toronto Maple Leafs my entire life. I live in Detroit and the kids in my school tease me because I like the Maple Leafs. They are all Detroit Red Wings fans. Please, Mr. Day, don't let your team give up. Please beat the Detroit Red Wings. I will be embarrassed to go to school and face my friends if Toronto loses four in a row. Please beat the Red Wings and win the Stanley Cup so I can go back to school with my head held high.

Doris Klein

The team's captain, Syl Apps, decided to echo Doris's plea. He stood up and spoke of the pride he felt in wearing the Maple Leaf on his chest, and how the city – and the country, for that matter – was depending on the Toronto Maple Leafs. Years later, Apps would insist that "we were thinking we couldn't lose four straight and face the people back home." After Apps's speech, Sweeney Schriner let out a whoop and the team gritted their teeth, resolving not to bow to the Red Wings.

During the third period, Detroit's Carl Liscombe scored on a 35-foot shot that eluded Broda to put the Wings up by a goal, but captain Apps scored to tie the game. The tiebreaker came from the hero of Game Four, Nick Metz, who took a pass from Apps as he streaked across the crease. It would prove to be the game winner. Though it was virtually decided, the remainder of the game was filled with much theatre. With just over a minute remaining in the period, a spectator grabbed the stick of the Leafs' Bob Davidson as he leaned against the boards after a whistle. Davidson wrenched the stick back and swung at the fan, and then motioned to the police officers seated in the penalty box. The constables ignored the summons from Davidson, who grew even more livid as he dodged a woman's shoe and a hot-water bottle aimed his way.

On the other side, Jack Adams called referee Mel Harwood over to the Wings bench, but the official refused. Instead, Harwood tried to get the teams to line up for the faceoff. On Adams's instruction, the Detroit players refused to take their places. Eddie Wares picked up the hot-water bottle and handed it to Harwood, who promptly threw him out of the game. After several uncomfortable seconds, the Wings finally did take the faceoff, but they had seven players on the ice. Harwood pointed to the Detroit bench to get a player into the penalty box, and Don Grosso was instructed to serve the bench-minor penalty for too many men on the ice. Grosso, however, at first refused to go to the box. When he finally did, he took his time approaching it, and laid his stick and gloves at the referee's feet in surrender. Grosso's act of defiance earned him a misconduct and a $25 fine.

Back at Maple Leaf Gardens for Game Five, Hap Day replaced Goldup with Gaye Stewart, a promising youngster who had spent much of the regular season playing junior with the Toronto Marlboros and then had joined the Marlboro seniors for their playoff run before spending time with Hershey of the American Hockey League (AHL) for that team's playoff series. As young as he was, Stewart had recently been through quite a few high-stakes games.

Perhaps as a carry-over of the theatrics at the end of the previous game, the Red Wings began to come further unglued. By the end of the second period, they were down 7–0 to the Maple Leafs, who had been feasting on Johnny Mowers in the Detroit goal. In the end, it was a 9–3 spanking. Don Metz led the way with three goals and two assists. Toronto had closed the gap and now only trailed in the series by a margin of three games to two.

Two nights later at the Olympia in Detroit, it was Turk Broda's turn to shine. Broda blanked the Wings, 3–0. Miraculously, the Leafs, who had been a hair's breadth away from being swept, had come back to tie the series. It was the stuff of fantasy.

Conn Smythe was given leave from military duty to head down to Toronto for the deciding game of the Stanley Cup final. Smythe arrived in full army regalia. Sweeney Schriner looked over at the anxious major and casually asked, "What are you worried about, Boss? We'll get you some goals."

Smythe's counterpart, Jack Adams, was equally anxious, but was still serving his suspension. While he made the trip to Toronto on his own, he was prohibited from dealing with his team. A sly photographer, however, snagged a picture of him in the lobby of Maple Leaf Gardens using a pay phone to contact Ebbie Goodfellow with strategic instructions. Caught red-handed, he retired to the dressing room and, through gritted teeth, was forced to listen to the game on the radio.

The first period was scoreless, with both teams playing it safe so as not to commit any costly errors. Syd Howe opened the scoring for the Red Wings, and that single goal stood through 40 minutes. The Leafs had come all the way back, but were now just 20 minutes away from losing yet another Stanley Cup.

Just before the third period, Conn Smythe entered the dressing room and delivered a grand speech. Then, in the third frame, Schriner potted a goal to tie the game just as a minor to Jimmy Orlando expired. Then, Pete Langelle scored at 9:48 to put Toronto ahead. It was a lead the Leafs would never relinquish. Schriner added his second of the night, a shorthanded tally, as insurance, cementing the victory and completing the most astonishing and improbable comeback in hockey history. The 1942 final marked the first – and, nearly three-quarters of a century later, still the only – time a team had come back from three games down to win the Stanley Cup.

As the seconds evaporated, Coach Day leapt over the boards and skidded over to Schriner to congratulate the game's star. NHL president Frank Calder presented the Stanley Cup to Hap Day and team captain Syl Apps. The Leafs captain looked for Smythe and summoned him to join them on the ice: "Come on out, Conn, you've waited long enough for this Cup. Come and get it!" Smythe, standing to one side during the presentation, stole Calder's fedora from the president's head and waved it jubilantly to the Maple Leaf Gardens faithful.

Some 2.6 million war-weary Canadians listened to Game Seven on the radio. This meant that nearly one in four Canadians had tuned in to hear Foster Hewitt deliver the play-by-play. And as the players celebrated inside the dressing room, the largest crowd ever assembled for a hockey game at Maple Leaf Gardens waited close to an hour for the victors to emerge and be saluted. A general hysteria filled Carlton Street. The Stanley Cup had returned to Toronto.

THE END OF THE BEGINNING

Despite its low labour priority, professional hockey was considered something of an essential service during the Second World War. It was argued by some proponents that high-level hockey was culturally important, that it contributed to civilian morale, offered a good diversion from the war, and even contributed to troops' morale through game reels, specially broadcast on Sunday afternoons to Canadian soldiers stationed overseas, in which Foster Hewitt would distill the weekly Imperial Oil hockey broadcast down to a 30-minute recording. Toronto mayor Thomas Church called Maple Leaf Gardens a "patriotic enterprise." This was the exact perception that Smythe and the Maple Leaf Gardens board members had been hoping to get across.

In advance of the 1942–43 season, the face of the NHL had undergone a drastic overhaul. Certainly, the quality of hockey suffered with the absence of some of the league's best. The Maple Leafs lost a number of players. Gone from the previous season were Jack Church, Ernie Dickens, Bob Goldham, Bingo Kampman, Pete Langelle, Johnny McCreedy, Don and Nick Metz, and Wally Stanowski, all to military service and military hockey.

The Brooklyn Americans, meanwhile, suspended operations with the intent of commencing play after the Second World War. That never happened. A special dispersal draft took place, and while Toronto very much wanted Harry Watson, who eventually did join the Leafs, a bid was unsuccessful. The Leafs did, however, pick up Rhys Thomson and Mel "Sudden Death" Hill. Both players proved to be valuable components.

It was the most unlikely conclusion to an NHL season ever experienced. Down three games to none against the Red Wings, Toronto benched some regulars and substituted youngsters, and in doing so, stormed back to win the next four games . . . and the 1942 Stanley Cup. From left to right: Nick Metz, coach Hap Day, and Wally Stanowski.

Hockey continued while the Second World War was being fought across the ocean. With depleted rosters, youngsters stepped into the lineups of NHL teams while hockey veterans added much-needed leadership. Here, veterans and rookies mingle during Maple Leafs training camp in September 1944. Left to right: Gaye Stewart, Frank McCool, Babe Pratt, Sweeney Schriner, Gus Bodnar, and Tommy Anderson.

Wartime NHL teams were filled with older, married men, or very young players who were not yet eligible for service. With a need to fill the holes created by war and the military hockey teams, the Leafs were forced to recruit replacements, and Squib Walker, the Leafs' head scout, delivered George Boothman and Bobby Copp for the blueline and Shep Mayer, Bud Poile, and Gaye Stewart at forward.

It was clear, however, that the end had arrived for Gord Drillon. In spite of having led the team in scoring in four of the previous six seasons, management had had enough. Drillon had been benched during the Stanley Cup final, a sure indicator that his days in blue and white were numbered. The hometown fans, in a practice that occasionally occurs to this day, expected more from their star player and had begun to boo him. Drillon was shopped around the league, and finally, in October, Toronto sold Drillon to the Montreal Canadiens for $30,000.

With the New York/Brooklyn Americans gone, the NHL was now a six-team league: the so-called Original Six. The new-look, defending champion Maple Leafs began their new season at home to the New York Rangers,

who were without the powerful line of Neil and Mac Colville and Alex Shibicky. Also gone were Art Coulter and Bill Juzda. To make matters worse, Rangers goaltender Sugar Jim Henry had enlisted only a week before training camp, and the team had not found a replacement. Someone suggested a goaltender playing intermediate hockey in Swift Current, Saskatchewan, named Steve Buzinski. The five-foot, seven-inch, 140-pound netminder arrived, presumably to save the day. "Buzinski was the most bowlegged goalie I ever saw in my life," Rangers coach Frank Boucher recalled. "He wore a pair of old, tattered goalie pads that curved with his limbs like a pair of rawhide cowboy chaps."

Major Conn Smythe arranged for any former Leaf now serving in the military to be fetched by plane from wherever they were in Canada and brought to the opening game of the season. Private Lex Chisholm, who had been a member of the Maple Leafs for two seasons before the war, dropped the ceremonial first puck between the defending Stanley Cup champions and the previous season's first-place squad.

Toronto easily bested the Rangers, 7–2. The New York goaltender was given the unfortunate, if memorable nickname, "The Puck Goes-Inski" Buzinski. "He adopted the falling system," the *New York World-Telegram* exclaimed. "Buzinski spent more time on the ice than a mackerel in cold storage." Buzinski played only nine NHL games before the Rangers sent him packing. "We were sorry to see him go," Boucher admitted. "He was a lovely little fellow, and we all liked him tremendously, but that simply doesn't stop pucks. Granted, he was one of the worst goalies in NHL history, but he was also one of the funniest."

The second game of the season featured the previous season's finalists, Toronto and Detroit. While it ended in a 5–2 Leaf victory, spectators left the game dazed and disturbed after seeing a vicious display of stickwork between Toronto rookie Gaye Stewart and Detroit veteran Jimmy Orlando. Stewart checked Orlando into the boards, and referee King Clancy called a penalty on the Leaf forward. Orlando then caught up with Stewart, and the two exchanged words. Orlando punched Stewart, knocking him down. Groggy, Stewart got up and made his way to the penalty box. No penalty was called on Orlando, and Stewart was left fuming in the penalty box. When he was allowed back on the ice, the Leaf player raced immediately towards Orlando. In *The Red Wings: Brian McFarlane's Original Six*, Orlando described the ensuing moments:

> I saw him coming so I dropped my gloves and nailed him a good one, sending him sprawling to the ice. Clancy didn't see this because he was way up the ice with everybody else. Then Stewart jumps up, takes his stick and smashes me right across the skull – a vicious blow that cut me for 23 stitches. Clancy gave us both match penalties and the league fined us each $100.

Orlando was suspended from playing in Toronto the rest of the season, and Stewart was likewise banned from playing in Detroit for the remainder of the season.

Toronto was compelled to infuse its lineup with young talent. For example, the Leafs reached into the university ranks for a speedy teenager named Jack McLean. A member of the junior Toronto Young Rangers, McLean was attending the University of Toronto, majoring in engineering, and was enrolled in the Canadian Officer Training Corps.

This was at a time when crossing the Canada–U.S. border was made more difficult by the ongoing war in Europe. The military board refused to grant passports to 19-year-olds to cross the border in order to play hockey.

This had already been an impediment for Bobby Copp, who was studying dentistry, and while Copp had earned a spot on the Leaf blueline, he was only able to play games in Toronto and Montreal. The situation was dire for Toronto in November, when they were shorthanded and forced to visit American teams with just 13 players, including only three defencemen: Reg Hamilton, Bucko McDonald, and Rhys Thomson. The Maple Leafs brass were aware of this challenge when they signed McLean. Without benefit of a single practice with his teammates, he stepped into the lineup on November 12 for a game against the Boston Bruins. It was an auspicious entry into big-time hockey for McLean, who was placed on a line with Bud Poile and Gaye Stewart. The *Star* exalted: "The 19-year-old broke into the dream realm of all kid puck-chasers by firing one goal and assisting on two others as the Leafs spanked the Boston 'Ruins' 3–1 . . . It was McLean, skating as if equipped with rocket blades, who ignited the winning spark." McLean was awarded a silver spoon, which was given to each of the Three Stars of every Leaf home game.

Toronto also feasted on the Montreal Canadiens, 8–0, early in the season. The November 21 game marked the return to Maple Leaf Gardens of ex-Leaf Gord Drillon, who was held scoreless. The *Star* reported cheekily that Montreal "'bleu' completely, were 'blanced' by Broda and their faces were 'rouge' with embarrassment at the finish."

Two weeks later, the Leafs once again bombed Montreal, 9–1. Later still, Toronto went on to shellac *les Canadiens*, 8–1, on December 17; 6–3 on January 2; and 8–4 on January 16.

It would seem that the Leafs owned the Habs during the 1942–43 season. But the Maple Leafs still felt they had to tweak their lineup, and decided to make a significant deal on November 27, acquiring veteran defenceman Babe Pratt from the Rangers in return for Hank Goldup and prospect Dudley "Red" Garrett. Pratt had been an integral part of the 1940 Stanley Cup champion Rangers, but his carefree ways made him expendable to Lester Patrick in New York. Pratt had been sidelined with a shoulder injury since early November, but the Leafs needed a big, veteran defence presence, and management decided to roll the dice.

Such a veteran presence was going to be required after captain Syl Apps broke his leg in a 5–3 loss to Boston on January 30. Apps collided with the goal post on a scoring attempt and got his skate caught in the twine of the net, fracturing his tibia above the ankle. Team doctor Robert Galloway announced to a hushed dressing room, "He's out for the balance of the season, including the playoffs."

While the Leafs were adjusting their roster, the NHL was adjusting its travel schedule, which had been sent into disarray by the war. At a meeting on January 25, led by President Frank Calder, the league was forced to address problems with train travel. Trains had traditionally been held for extended periods at the various stations in league cities to allow for overtime hockey. As train travel had become far more limited and regimented during the war, the NHL was forced to cease overtime play for its regular season. The league also had to consider the issue of the Brooklyn Americans. It was decided – much to the chagrin of general manager Red Dutton – that as Madison Square Garden had turned down the Americans' lease agreement, the franchise was to be dropped for good. Though this might have been bad news for the league, another, far more shocking event occurred that night. During the meeting, Calder suffered a heart attack; he would die on February 4. The league governors now had to find a replacement for the late president. Red Dutton, with no team left to manage, was the interim choice. He would become the full-time president the following season.

The Leafs made another significant trade on February 28, the magnitude of which would be felt within the organization and the city of Toronto for decades to follow. Montreal traded Ted Kennedy for the rights to Frank Eddolls, who was serving in the air force at the time. Kennedy was just 17 years old, but was regarded as "a coming great" by Nels Stewart, Hall of Famer and Kennedy's coach with the junior Port Colborne Sailors.

Hap Day did not completely relish the idea of giving up Eddolls: "We know we are giving up a strong defence player for Kennedy . . . but we won't be shy of defence material after the war, and we do need attack strength now." And they got it – the Maple Leafs' goal production of 198 was best in the six-team league. Lorne Carr scored 27, Gaye Stewart 24, and despite playing in just 29 games, Syl Apps contributed 23. Carr and Billy Taylor tied with a team-best 60 points, good for fifth and sixth respectively in the NHL. Carr was named to the NHL's First All-Star Team and Apps to the Second Team. Gaye Stewart was recipient of the Calder Trophy as the league's rookie of the year.

In the standings, Detroit finished on top, with 61 points; Boston was second, with 57; Toronto third, with 53; and Montreal fourth, with 50. The New York Rangers had the ignominious distinction of going from first to worst in one season. After finishing atop the league with 60 points in 1941–42, the team finished last, collecting just 30 points and, along with Chicago, missing the playoffs.

The postseason began with the Leafs facing the powerful Red Wings. Detroit took Game One at the Olympia, 4–2. Game Two was a marathon. The match was tied at two until 10:18 of the fourth overtime, when Jack McLean took a pass from Bud Poile. As the *Star* reported, McLean "whisked it home for the goal that tied the series, and wrote a story of sustained triumph for a Leaf team wrongly estimated to be considerably weaker by the experts than it really is." While the Leafs had won, 3–2, there was some confusion at the end of the game. Referee King Clancy knew that the puck had clearly entered the net behind Detroit goaltender Johnny Mowers, but there was a question about who scored the goal. Bud Poile shot the puck and believed he had scored, and many of the Wings agreed. But Clancy was certain that Poile's linemate, McLean, had tipped the puck past Mowers. For his part, McLean concurred. As the teams skated off the ice, no official goal scorer had been announced. Two of the three daily newspapers in Detroit credited Poile with the winning tally. All three agreed that the marathon had concluded at 130:18 – at the time, the third-longest NHL game in history.

Finally, almost four days after the goal was actually scored, acting NHL president Red Dutton announced that McLean was, indeed, the official goal scorer. As Dutton affirmed:

The situation is now closed, and I'm glad of it, particularly for the sake of the young McLean. I saw McLean on Saturday and the boy seemed greatly disturbed over all the publicity that had developed out of his goal. He told me he felt badly about the whole thing, and told me he preferred having the goal credited to Poile so the whole matter would be dispensed with. He told me, however, that he honestly believed he had tipped the puck after Poile's shot. Clancy insisted that's how he saw the play. And I'm closing the whole incident by declaring McLean the goal-getter.

"It doesn't matter who scored it so long as we won," Poile insisted.

The series moved to Toronto for Game Three. Though the Leafs were riding an emotional high from the previous game and playing at home, they could not contain the Wings, who won, 4–2. Toronto rebounded with a 6–3 victory in Game Four to tie the series at two games apiece. Back in Detroit, Vézina Trophy winner Johnny Mowers led Detroit to a 4–2 victory in Game Five. While he may have won the game, Mowers ended up losing two front teeth during the affair after Bud Poile's stick caught him in the mouth.

Border crossings were becoming trickier as the war dragged on. On his way to Game Six at Maple Leaf Gardens, the Wings' Jimmy Orlando was stopped by the FBI at the border. Orlando had violated the Selective Service Act by failing to notify his draft board of a change in occupational status and falsifying information provided later to the board. He was released on a $2,000 bond. Orlando was hardly given a warm welcome in Toronto. Fans there remembered his stick fight with Gaye Stewart, and booed him every time he was on the ice.

Unfortunately for the fans, their booing did little to slow the Wings down. Up 2–0 in the third, the Red Wings looked like they were going to take the win and move on to the Stanley Cup final, but even though they had been badly outplayed all game, the Leafs refused to surrender. After the Leafs scored midway through the third, Sweeney Schriner tied the game with just 13 seconds to go in regulation. The two teams jousted back and forth, but at 9:21 of the extra frame, Detroit's Adam Brown scored to end any hope of Toronto repeating as Stanley Cup champions. The *Star* captured the prevailing mood inside Maple Leaf Gardens: "You could slice the gloom like an apple pie."

CONQUEST

The Canadian war effort was extensive and diverse. There was the pilot in the single-seat Hurricane fighter whose wings gave cover to the various Allied ships packed with supplies and soldiers; the pioneer companies that built up the vital infrastructure; the lonely Spitfire pilot who flew predawn patrols in the inky-coal blackness over the English Channel; the tunnellers who were cracking through the Rock of Gibraltar; the crews of the submarine-hunting destroyers; the Wrens of the Women's Royal Naval Service who feverishly decoded the Nazis' every move; the nurses and medical corps; the infantry; and so many others who did their duty during that dark time.

Soldiers craved a variety of creature comforts from home. Cigarettes were highly valued, but not as much as parcels from home. Keeping up with the NHL season through newsreels and radio replays of Saturday night games on the BBC was also popular with the soldiers overseas.

Meanwhile, the war was continuing to exact a toll on every NHL roster. Art Ross of the Boston Bruins suggested that "today's top lines couldn't even have played on our third line a couple of years ago." For their part at the beginning of 1943–44, the Leafs had lost Syl Apps, Sweeney Schriner, Billy Taylor, and netminder Turk Broda.

With Broda playing military hockey, the Leafs filled the crease with Benny Grant, who had first played for the team in 1928, but had spent most of his 16-year pro career in the minors. Grant outplayed both Murray Dowey, a Mercantile League goaltender, and future Toronto mayor Donald Summerville to earn the right to replace Broda. Up front, Ted Kennedy – who wouldn't turn 18 until that December – had earned himself a full-time slot. Kennedy was expected to contribute meaningfully to the attack, as was newcomer August Bodnarchuk (who altered his name to Gus Bodnar). The rest of the roster was littered with youngsters like Ross Johnstone, Don Webster, and Tom "Windy" O'Neill, who, like Jack McLean, was prevented from crossing the border due to wartime restrictions while he studied law at the University of Toronto.

The new-look Leafs opened the season with a 5–2 win over the New York Rangers at Maple Leaf Gardens. Bodnar scored 15 seconds into his first NHL game. The beleaguered Rangers were profoundly affected by the war – so much so that Frank Boucher, their 42-year-old coach, who had been retired for five seasons, was added to the active roster for the season.

There were several bizarre wartime quirks that added further tension to border crossings. American customs, for instance, demanded a duty on hockey sweaters entering the United States. While the Maple Leafs paid duty on their blue sweaters, the team declined to pay a similar tariff on their white sweaters. So, in a game on November 7 at Madison Square Garden, the hometown Rangers, who traditionally wore blue sweaters, were forced to don bright yellow pinnies to differentiate the teams. The next time the Leafs visited New York, Rangers GM Lester Patrick insisted that it was the Leafs' turn to wear the pinnies. Coach Day refused. Consequently, and much to the dismay of the officials and fans, both teams wore their blue jerseys.

While he wouldn't allow his lads to wear the pinnies, Hap Day was willing to send the hard-hitting Bucko McDonald to New York at the end of November. The Leafs received Red Garrett and the option to purchase either Gordie Bell or Charlie Rayner, both goaltenders, at the end of the war. Toronto believed it could spare McDonald because it had Reg Hamilton, Ross Johnstone, Elwyn Morris, and Babe Pratt on the blueline. Ultimately, Day was considering his future goaltending needs: "Broda is touching thirty and is in the Army. He will have to prove himself when it's over."

Garrett had already been a part of Toronto's system. The Leafs had dealt him to New York in 1942 and received Babe Pratt in return. Coach Day was delighted with the prospect of getting Garrett's rights back: "We are looking forward to the future . . . We wanted Garrett because he looks to us like a natural ticket-seller."

Tragically, Red Garrett would not be suiting up for the Leafs or any other NHL team. On November 24, 1944, during a destroyer escort off the coast of Newfoundland, Garrett was killed when the corvette he was on was torpedoed by a German U-boat. His death reminded everyone, including those in the hockey world, just how close this world war really was.

Meanwhile, back in 1943, the Leafs were only a mediocre team through the first half of the season, with a 10–10–2 record. This was not good enough for team management, who went in search of a new netminder to replace the 35-year-old Grant.

Day's attempt to pry Lionel Bouvrette from the Quebec Aces of the Quebec Senior Hockey League was unsuccessful. The coach was, however, able to secure the loan of Paul Bibeault, who had been the Montreal Canadiens' goaltender for three seasons but had lost his job to Bill Durnan. When Bibeault was discharged from the military, several teams vied for his services, but just before Christmas he was signed by the Leafs for the duration of the season for $3,000. Although Day played Benny Grant in goal on Christmas Day (a 5–3 loss to the Rangers), Bibeault stepped into the crease for the next game and shut out those same Rangers, 4–0, on New Year's Eve. It was the first of five shutouts he earned that season.

If the war-altered Leafs had an identity, it was down to the players' feistiness. Windy O'Neill, for example, was much appreciated by Day: "He's just a little guy, but he steps into everybody and doesn't back up." O'Neill and Jack McLean were tagged the "toy bulldogs," and they wore the mantle proudly. Hockey writers noticed the duo's tenacity. In a game against the Canadiens on January 4, the *Star* observed that "McLean and O'Neill took on those twin toughies Chamberlain and Watson in joyous rough and tumble . . . [the Leafs] haven't had willing mixers like McLean and O'Neill on the club since Clancy and Horner retired."

That same toughness also got the Leafs into hot water when, on January 9, Toronto ran all over the Boston Bruins in every way imaginable. The game ended in a 12–3 win for the Leafs, but also put Bruins star Bill Cowley on the injured list. He was taken into the boards aggressively by McLean and suffered a separated shoulder.

Cowley was leading the league in scoring at the time, and Boston coach Art Ross was irate: "Cowley was the central figure in a mass attack craftily designed to put him out of business in a year of hockey that everyone knows is the most critical from a material standpoint in the league's history!"

Ross warned that he would take out three Leaf players the next time the two teams tangled. That date came on January 18. In front of a capacity crowd that was expecting fireworks, Toronto instead handed the Bruins a 7–2 beating. The final game of the season was against those same Bruins, but in an odd twist of circumstance, Boston arrived with only nine players and no goaltender. Their netminder, Maurice Courteau, had been suspended the previous game. The Leafs loaned the Bruins Benny Grant for the game, which ended in a 10–2 Leaf win.

At season's end, the Canadiens finished first with 83 points. Well back were Detroit (58), Toronto (50), and Chicago (49). The Rangers continued to struggle for a second straight season, winning just six games.

Individually, Lorne Carr led the Leafs' scoring with 74 points, third best in the NHL. His 36 goals placed him second to Doug Bentley of the Black Hawks, who scored 38. Carr was voted onto the NHL's First All-Star Team. Babe Pratt was awarded the Hart Trophy as the league's most valuable player. Pratt managed 17 goals from his blueline position and had 57 points. Gus Bodnar, who scored 22 goals and finished with 62 points, earned the Calder Trophy. Paul Bibeault and coach Hap Day were selected for the Second Team. And young Ted Kennedy had proven his worth by adding 26 goals to the Leafs offence.

The Leafs faced the Canadiens in the semifinals, but surprised everyone – particularly Montreal – by taking the first game by a score of 3–1. Hap Day had prepared his troops well. Bibeault was great in net, but it was fierce checking and dogged shot blocking that secured Toronto the well-earned victory.

Game Two, also played in Montreal, was a different story, and Maurice Richard scored all five goals in the Canadiens' 5–1 win. To honour his remarkable night, Richard was awarded all three stars at the conclusion of the game.

Although the series moved back to Toronto for Game Three, momentum had dramatically swung in the Canadiens' favour. It would not swing back again. Montreal took the third game, 2–1, and followed up with a 4–1 victory in Game Four. The worst, however, was yet to come. On March 30, the Canadiens concluded the series with an emphatic 11–0 whipping of the Leafs.

Jack McLean (left) found a roster spot on the Maple Leafs during the war years, when many members of the team were serving their country. McLean, a university student at the time, was only allowed to play in Canada during the school year. He is best remembered for scoring the game-winning goal at the 10:18 mark of the fourth overtime period against Detroit on March 23, 1943 – one of the longest games in NHL playoff history.

If there was any consolation to be found for Leafs fans, it might have been the fact that the Canadiens went on to easily sweep Chicago to win the Stanley Cup.

D-DAY

By 1944, the stage was set for liberation. The Allies – with the Americans now part of the roster – sought to take back Europe from Hitler and his weakening Nazi regime. The Normandy invasion took place on June 6: D-Day. Fourteen thousand members of the 3rd Canadian Division were given the objective of a beachfront, codenamed "Juno." Canadian paratroopers were dropped just east of the beach. The Royal Canadian Navy also contributed 10,000 sailors across 110 ships to support the Juno Beach landings, while the RCAF bombed inland targets, which went some way towards softening the Nazis' formidable fortifications. On the day, 359 Canadians were killed, while over 700 were wounded. The D-Day invasion was the largest amphibious operation in history. With the invasion underway, many began to consider victory in a more concrete sense. But victory in Europe remained months away; in fact, the Maple Leafs would have time to play an entire regular season and playoffs before Germany was forced to surrender.

In the summer of 1944, the Canadian army moved slowly across Normandy, running into heavy fighting along the way. Major Conn Smythe was sent to Caen along with his unit in July, to continue keeping the heat on the Nazis. On July 25, the Luftwaffe bombed an ammunition depot and Smythe was badly wounded. Outside and under attack from enemy planes, Smythe was hit in the back by a bomb fragment. It might well have proved fatal, had it not been for the heavy fabric of his coat. As he later said, "I always thanked some higher power for sending me back to get that trenchcoat." For the rest of his life, Smythe would walk with a limp and be plagued with gastrointestinal issues.

While Smythe was recovering, the conscription crisis was heating up. Several social agents of the day, the opposition Conservatives, and Canadian officers serving in Europe, including Smythe, were calling for reinforcements. Prime Minister William Lyon Mackenzie King, however, was trying to ride out the war without invoking conscription. Although badly wounded, Major Smythe continued to take King and his policy to task. In an article that Smythe dictated from Toronto's Chorley Park Hospital, the Major outlined the importance of sending reinforcements to help Canadian soldiers already at the front. The article made waves, but Smythe's words did articulate a prevailing sentiment among many Canadians: the army needed more men.

By late 1944, King was forced into a corner, and on November 22 he relented and brought in conscription. This meant that those who had been training as part of the NRMA would now be sent overseas. As it happened, the war was coming to a close; only 2,500 of the 13,000 conscripts were sent to Europe.

Meanwhile, back in Toronto, Hap Day realized that he needed to reinvent his team during the off-season. The Leafs simply could not compete with teams like the Montreal Canadiens. While small and fast, the Leafs were easily pushed around. Frank Selke, who assumed the role of general manager in Major Smythe's absence, explained that the Leafs had "lacked colour. In the past, we got the stuffing knocked out of us on the road, and we had nothing to retaliate with. With Mr. Smythe and Mr. Bickle urging us to get in there and fight, we're not going to be the league's whipping boy any longer."

One of the team's more important moves was to trade for Bill Ezinicki, a tough winger with the Buffalo Bisons. In return, the Leafs sent George Boothman and Don Webster to the AHL team just prior to the season opener. At least one sportswriter liked the trade and believed that, with the acquisition, the team would be a little less gentlemanly: "Our Leafs are going after the 'bang' instead of the Byng."

There was, however, another problem that loomed even larger than the team's lack of toughness: the Leafs needed to find a netminder. Although Paul Bibeault had been terrific for Toronto in 1943–44, his rights were owned by Montreal. The Canadiens' main goalie, Bill Durnan, was a war worker and his job had been deemed essential to the war effort. It was unclear whether or not Durnan would be allowed to play hockey. As much as Toronto wanted Bibeault again, Montreal was holding on to his rights while they waited to learn Durnan's status. At one point, the Habs did offer Bibeault to Toronto in exchange for Bob Goldham and Gaye Stewart, but Selke and Day were not interested in parting with those two players.

Montreal was goalie-wealthy. Once it was established that Durnan was indeed going to be with the Habs for the season, the Canadiens loaned Bibeault to the Boston Bruins. Connie Dion, yet another Canadiens goalie, was traded to Detroit. The Leafs, though, were still stuck. Desperate, Toronto turned to Frank McCool, a goaltender who had been recommended by Lorne Carr.

The Calgary-born McCool had attended the New York Rangers' training camp in 1943 and made the team, but he had been forced to leave the club due to stomach ulcers. The goalie returned home to Calgary and continued his position as a sportswriter for the *Calgary Albertan* newspaper. It was there that the Maple Leafs came calling on their new goalie.

Another Calgarian made his mark on opening night of the 1944–45 campaign. Sweeney Schriner had been away from the NHL for a year, serving in the military and playing hockey for the navy in Calgary. Schriner scored both goals for Toronto in their 2–1 season opener against the New York Rangers, and picked up a hat trick one night later in an 11–5 drubbing of the Chicago Black Hawks. Goal scoring proved to be no problem for the Leafs early in the schedule: they outscored their opponents, 33–13, in the first six games.

Yet, the war was still raging, and it continued to wreak havoc on the Leafs' plans. While Bill Ezinicki had been considered one of the team's key elements in 1944–45, his season was cut short. Only eight games into the new campaign, Ezinicki reported to the army for his physical. Wild Bill was handed his documents, but said that he'd like to read the papers before signing. He was told that was not

an option. The fiery Ezinicki then tore up the documents and was arrested on the spot. He went before the officer-in-command and related the sequence of events. He was dismissed, and the corporal was reprimanded for his role in the event. Ezinicki would not return to the Leafs until the war was over.

Meanwhile, Schriner, who was on a torrid goal-scoring pace, added two in a 5–4 Leaf win over Chicago on November 8, giving him 11 goals in nine games. But during that win, Mush March of the Black Hawks pushed Schriner into the goal post of the Leaf net, badly injuring the forward's knee. Sweeney missed 24 games while he recuperated back home in Calgary.

With a shortened bench, Day was at least thankful that his goaltending woes had been seemingly assuaged. After McCool earned his first NHL shutout in a 2–0 win over the Canadiens on November 25, the Leafs coach lauded his netminder's play: "McCool is playing the best goal of any custodian in the league. He was positively sensational against Montreal. He's high-strung and nervously alert, but maybe that's what makes him so good!" McCool went on to contribute back-to-back shutouts against the Rangers on January 27 and 28, his third and fourth of the season.

"Wild Bill" Ezinicki (centre) delivered bone-crunching bodychecks, keeping opponents wary when he was on the ice. Adored by Leafs Nation, Ezinicki was a member of the Stanley Cup championship teams of 1947, 1948, and 1949.

At the end of the regular season, Toronto finished a solid third, with 52 points. The Leafs, however, were outdistanced by the astonishing first-place Montreal Canadiens (80 points) and Detroit (67). The final playoff berth went to Boston, who finished with a paltry 36 points. The Canadiens were paced by the sensational Punch Line of Elmer Lach, Maurice Richard, and Toe Blake, who finished first, second, and third in scoring. Richard stunned the hockey world by scoring 50 goals in 50 games.

In Toronto, Ted Kennedy led the Leafs in scoring and placed fifth in the league with a respectable 54 points, including 29 goals. Babe Pratt was selected to the NHL's Second All-Star Team and 26-year-old rookie netminder Frank McCool was the recipient of the Calder Trophy.

In the first round of the playoffs, Toronto met the powerful Canadiens. Game One was a listless affair that saw the Maple Leafs edge Montreal, 1–0. Ted Kennedy scored on a backhand with just 22 seconds left in regulation. Game Two was yet another upset victory for the Leafs, who earned a 3–2 victory. The third game at Maple Leaf Gardens, however, was an altogether different affair. Montreal took early command of the game and never relented, winning 4–1.

Heading into Game Four, the Leafs faced nagging injuries to Kennedy, who played with his ankle frozen, and Sweeney Schriner, whose wrist was frozen. Despite this disadvantage, the Leafs pulled off a 4–3 overtime victory. From the faceoff, Gus Bodnar put the puck past Bill Durnan at 12:36 of extra time.

Now up three games to one, Toronto was eager to end the series in Montreal in Game Five. The Canadiens were not, however, on the same page. The Habs pumped ten goals past McCool, while the Leafs could only answer with three. Still, the Maple Leafs eliminated the heavily favoured Canadiens in Game Six by a score of 3–2. There was an electric atmosphere in Toronto, as one sportswriter described: "At the conclusion of the match, there was a crowd demonstration of delight which could scarcely have been more voluminous or more prolonged had the Leafs just won the Stanley Cup."

Frank McCool had been terrific for Toronto, but it was Ted Kennedy's moxie that drove the Maple Leafs to victory. The *Toronto Daily Star* confirmed that "Kennedy kept calling on that extra ounce of energy until he thought his legs were gone and his body afire."

The 1945 Stanley Cup final saw Toronto face off against the Red Wings. The Leafs were able to win a tight-checking Game One in Detroit. McCool earned a shutout and Schriner scored the only goal the Leafs needed in the 1–0 victory. While Coach Day had only 11 players at his disposal, the depleted group managed to block shots and frustrate the Wings all night.

Toronto also took Game Two with a 2–0 shutout win. Shockingly, the Red Wings had not earned a single penalty through the first two games of the series. "The thing that astonished everybody," the *Star* observed, "was the lack of desire, the lack of fight, the lackadaisical way the Wings flew."

McCool earned his third consecutive shutout in Game Three, and with it, the Leafs took a commanding series lead. Gus Bodnar scored the sole goal in the 1–0 win. Hap Day's strategy continued: playing a six-man defence at all times and shortening his bench to only 11 players. It had worked so far, as the Wings had yet to score in three games against the Leafs.

Game Four proved to be somewhat different. In a fast-paced and rugged game, the Red Wings struck back and topped Toronto, 5–3, with Kennedy scoring all three goals for the Leafs in the losing cause. The teams returned to Detroit for Game Five. Eighteen-year-old Wings goaltender Harry Lumley blanked Toronto with a 2–0 win. And although the Leafs had the Stanley Cup in their sights, the Red Wings were able yet again to postpone the celebration by earning a 1–0 victory on a goal by Ed Bruneteau at 14:16 of overtime in Game Six. It was the fifth shutout of the Stanley Cup final that year. Leafs fans began to get nervous, wondering if Detroit was out to avenge their part in the greatest comeback in hockey history of three seasons earlier.

The worry was for naught. The Leafs claimed the Stanley Cup with a 2–1 win over the Wings at Detroit's Olympia Stadium. The winning goal came midway through the third period on a power play. Babe Pratt sent a long pass to Nick Metz at the left of Harry Lumley, who made the save, but Pratt rushed in from the blueline and tucked the puck into the back of the net.

Red Dutton presented the Stanley Cup to captain Bob Davidson, coach Hap Day, and Major Conn Smythe. Then, Lieutenant-Commander Barry O'Brien presented the O'Brien Cup to the Detroit Red Wings as runners-up.

Even in victory, many of the jubilant Leafs knew that the team would ice a substantially different lineup the following season. With war coming to an end, the NHL's makeshift rosters would soon be restocked with returning soldiers/hockey players.

VICTORY

Eight days after the Leafs won the Stanley Cup, Adolf Hitler put a bullet through his own head. On May 7, 1945, Germany signed an unconditional surrender in France. The Maple Leafs' Cup win had been trumped – happily – by victory in Europe. Yet Canadians, soldiers and otherwise, were physically and emotionally exhausted when that expected victory finally arrived.

In early August, the United States dropped atomic bombs on Hiroshima and Nagasaki. Japan surrendered on August 15, 1945. The Second World War was officially over.

The war had changed Canada. It had strengthened the country's economy and put it on the map as a true middle power. But it was not without its costs: 1.1 million Canadian men and women served in the three branches of the military. Of these, 45,000 lost their lives while another 54,000 were wounded.

Certainly, a few NHL prospects perished during the war. Detroit's Joe Turner, who had enlisted

in the U.S. Marine Corps, was killed in action in January 1945. So too were one-time Maple Leafs prospects Red Garrett, killed off the coast of Newfoundland, and Red Tilson, who was killed in October 1944 during an early chapter of the liberation of the Netherlands. In contrast to the First World War, though, not one bona fide NHL starter was killed during the Second World War.

Still, hockey – and specifically Maple Leafs hockey – had played an important role in helping Canadians survive the darkness of the time. Just as they had listened to the Leafs to forget about the Depression, so too did Canadians listen to the Leafs to forget about the war. Foster Hewitt's call had been a place to retreat to, a place where troubles were, at least for a moment, forgotten. And the Leafs' Cup win only added to the elation that came with the end of war. Canada had earned a dignified and deserved position in the world's conversation. Now, the country's favourite team was poised to do something very special itself.

Considered the quintessential Maple Leaf by many, Ted "Teeder" Kennedy (sitting on net) joined the team in March 1943 and retired as a Leaf at the conclusion of the 1956–57 season. Kennedy was the heart and soul of the first Leafs dynasty, serving as captain of the Blue and White from 1948–49 to the end of his career, which saw him contribute to five Stanley Cup championships.

THE FIRST DYNASTY
1945–46 TO 1950–51

Canada had, in peace, graduated to what Prime Minister Louis St. Laurent coined "a power of the middle rank." And while the sparsely populated dominion was now a formidable force for good in the world, the Toronto Maple Leafs remained guardians of an older, British tradition. At Maple Leaf Gardens, the ritual endured. When the teams lined up on their respective bluelines for "God Save the King," the incandescent lights were dimmed and the spotlights shone on two small flags that flanked a portrait of King George VI. Maple Leafs fans themselves demonstrated that traditional British tenet of self-restraint and moral probity. "Toronto the Good" was actualized in the Gardens, as storyteller Lorne Brown remembered:

> During the actual game [the fans] were silent. This silence was important. The noise of the spectators followed the rhythm of the game, and was natural and supportive. During dull moments, you could practically hear a pin drop, and this silence occasionally resulted in ironic rhythmic clapping to goad the teams into action. When exciting plays were occurring, the crowd noise was loud, very much adding to the on-ice excitement. A well-played shift earned a round of applause. When a goal was scored there was cheering, even if the goal was scored by the opposition.

Red Barber, the PA announcer, delivered a dry, nonpartisan style that his successors would emulate. Barber even provided some real-time commercials for the fans, imploring his listeners to "start the day the Quaker way with a steaming hot bowl of Quaker Oats." The environment was framed by a perceptible blue haze of smoke, which billowed high above the brownish ice surface. It was in this decidedly static ritual of the Old World that a new dynasty – the best that pro hockey had yet seen – would emerge.

HOMECOMING

Leafs fans were – and remain – among the most hockey-savvy in the world. They were knowledgeable about the rules, the dynamics of the various visiting teams, and, of course, their own favourite individual players. On rare occasions, fans were able to transcend behavioural norms at hockey games and contribute – sometimes meaningfully – to the game itself.

One of the best examples of this can be found in the case of John Arnott. The Scottish-born Arnott saw his first Leafs game in the early 1940s. It was then that he fell in love with hockey and, in particular, the play of Pete Langelle. The very next day, Arnott purchased season tickets.

During one stoppage in play, when Langelle skated out to take his shift, the leather-lunged Arnott hollered from his seat in the greens, "C'mooooooonnnnn, Peeeeeee-terrrrrrr!" Some of the crowd clapped and laughed; a few actually tried to have Arnott removed from the arena. But with every subsequent game, Arnott found an appropriate opportunity to let out his call of encouragement to Langelle, and soon, fans looked forward to his war cry, cheering wildly when they heard the familiar voice.

By 1943, Langelle had enlisted in the Royal Canadian Air Force, after which Arnott turned his affection towards a new favourite: Ted "Teeder" Kennedy. Soon, the Gardens' faithful looked forward to Arnott's booming voice: "C'mooooooooon, Teeeeee-derrrrr." The cheer became almost as well known as the player he was rooting for.

Arnott became an honorary member of the Toronto Maple Leafs, a reward he enjoyed for the rest of his life. When the Leafs won four Stanley Cup championships in five years, Arnott was one of the very few non-playing guests to celebrate with the team, and he sipped champagne from the Stanley Cup on each of the four occasions, the only times alcohol touched his lips

It took six games, but on April 19, 1947, the Maple Leafs captured what would be the first of four Stanley Cup championships in five seasons. As hard as it is to believe, the spring of 1947 was the first time Toronto met the Canadiens in a Stanley Cup final.

through his life. The man with the foghorn voice died on November 12, 1980. Fittingly, Teeder Kennedy served as one of Arnott's pallbearers.

The Toronto Maple Leafs of 1945–46 bore a completely different look than the Stanley Cup–championship roster of the previous spring. In fact, this year's model more closely resembled the 1942 Stanley Cup team. With the war over, several of the lads who had served their country began to filter back into the roster. Bill Ezinicki, Bob Goldham, Bud Poile, Gaye Stewart, Billy Taylor, and team captain Syl Apps all returned to the team. The latter declared optimistically, "There was a feeling among us that with all the veterans returned, we were going to be home-free in the league."

It wasn't so easy. The returning veterans, almost to a player, struggled to return to form after their military

service, although most of them had played a fairly high level of hockey during their time away from the National Hockey League.

One of the most obvious concerns was in net. While Turk Broda had yet to return from his military duty, the Maple Leafs nevertheless had a champion goaltender in Frank McCool. The Calder Trophy winner asked for a raise, seeking $5,000 after earning $4,500 in 1944–45. When Conn Smythe and Hap Day declined, McCool decided to go back home to Calgary. His departure left a gaping hole in the Toronto crease. The Leafs turned to Baz Bastien, a man who was just out of the military himself and who had played senior hockey in Toronto prior to the war.

The Leafs assembled six veterans of the Second World War who had won the Victoria Cross for the opening-night festivities on October 26, 1945. The group included Lieutenant-Colonel David Currie, Major John Mahony, Major Fred Tilston, Corporal Fred Topham, Lieutenant-Colonel Paul Triquet, and Private Ernie "Smokey" Smith, the only private to receive the medal during the Second World War.

That night, the Leafs began their season with a 1–1 tie with the Boston Bruins. As for Bastien, it was the only game the goaltender did *not* lose during his five-game NHL career. After his stint with the big club, the goaltender was sent to the AHL's Pittsburgh Hornets, where he remained for four seasons before an accident ended his playing career.

The Leafs replaced Bastien with Gordie Bell, who had been purchased from the Buffalo Bisons of the AHL. The new goalie fared only modestly better than Bastien and faced an uncharitable chant from the fans: "Bring Back McCool." Bell was in goal for a 6–1 loss to Montreal on November 14, which Hap Day called "an all-time low."

In desperation, the Leafs ended Bell's tenure after only eight games. Remarkably, the Leafs answered the catcalls and brought back McCool. Unfortunately, it made little difference. By New Year's Day 1946, Toronto had won only seven of their first 25 games, against 15 losses and 3 ties. Coach Day admitted, "It is growing more obvious each week that the team hasn't got what is necessary." And the season grew ever more difficult for Toronto. Ted Kennedy was injured, severing a tendon. Shortly afterwards, Syl Apps suffered a dislocated rib.

The Leafs' goaltending outlook improved in February, when Turk Broda returned to the team. He played the final 15 games of the season, of which the Maple Leafs won six, lost six, and tied three, but his arrival was too late to salvage the season. Toronto became only the second defending Stanley Cup champion to miss the playoffs the following year, finishing fifth with 45 points, well back of the Canadiens (61), Bruins (56), Hawks (53), and Wings (50).

In the midst of a dreary season, there were a few highlights. Gaye Stewart emerged as the top goal scorer in the NHL, with 37. He finished with 52 points, second only to Max Bentley of Chicago, and was selected to the NHL's First All-Star Team. Syl Apps reminded Leafs fans that "it took the players coming out of the service half a season to get their bearings again." The Toronto faithful hardly needed reminding of that fact. But as the saying goes, the darkest hour is just before dawn. And a string of remarkable seasons was on the horizon.

RETURN TO FORM

While Conn Smythe was serving his country, a committee headed by Ed Bickle, W.A.H. MacBrien, and Frank Selke was instructed to run Maple Leaf Gardens Ltd., with assistance from coach Hap Day. During that period, the team made what would prove to be a tremendously fortuitous acquisition, trading for Ted Kennedy, who went on to have one of the most important careers in the history of the franchise. Still, Selke would recall that Smythe struggled to forgive him for making the move in his absence, going as far as to make him the scapegoat for the disappointing 1945–46 season:

> Without question, Conn Smythe was the boss at Maple Leaf Gardens. No one wanted it otherwise, least of all Day or myself. When the Maple Leafs were having their long run of success, no one bothered to credit me with any great part in the triumphs. But now, when we failed to make the playoffs for the first time (in 1945–46), I was naturally selected to be the goat.

Smythe was not only upset by the power Selke seemed to be exercising on the ice, but by the amount of time he was spending on other events taking place at Maple Leaf Gardens. Profits at the Gardens during Smythe's absence had never been better – thanks, in part, to ice shows, rodeos, and other non-hockey events. In January 1946, the surplus was large enough that $80,000 was sent to Sun Life to pay off the mortgage at Maple Leaf Gardens. In spite of this auspicious news, Smythe believed that Selke wasn't spending enough time on the hockey team.

Smythe returned from the war with a suspicion that plans were afoot to reduce his control over Maple Leaf Gardens. There were rumours that MacBrien, who served as vice-president of the company, had designs on taking over the presidency from Ed Bickle and that he planned to replace Smythe with Selke. By this point, Smythe and Selke's relationship had completely deteriorated. In May 1946, Selke left his Gardens office for lunch, and when he returned, he found a note from Smythe on his desk: "Any time I am in the building, you are not to leave for lunch or any other purpose without my permission in case I need you." Already disgruntled, Selke left Smythe a note of his own: "Lincoln freed the slaves 80 years ago." Ultimately, Selke resigned on May 31, 1946. Smythe was completely caught off guard when, six weeks later, Selke was hired as the general manager of the Montreal Canadiens.

Through the support of J.P. Bickell and a $300,000 loan, Smythe was able to become Maple Leaf Gardens Ltd.'s largest shareholder. The loan, which allowed Smythe to purchase 30,000 shares at $10 each, was through stockbroker Percy Gardiner. Perhaps unsurprisingly, Smythe called Gardiner and Bickell "the best friends I ever had."

On November 19, Smythe installed himself as president of Maple Leaf Gardens Ltd., which officially gave him full control of the Toronto Maple Leafs and the Gardens. He retained his titles of managing director of the arena and general manager of the team. The *Toronto Daily Star* wrote that the appointment "simply makes official what he has been for years in actuality."

After the dismal campaign of the previous year, Smythe prepared a full overhaul of his club. Smythe felt that the Leafs could be a contender by shedding some of the older veterans and inserting youngsters in their place.

Of the 21 players who had been on the roster the previous season, seven were traded, released, or retired, and four more were sent to the minors before the first puck was dropped on the new season.

Veterans Lorne Carr, Bob Davidson, and Sweeney Schriner were asked to retire. In September, the Leafs picked up Harry Watson from the Detroit Red Wings for Billy Taylor and future prospects. Taylor had played on a highly effective line with Carr and Schriner, but several years before he joined the roster as a player, Billy had served as the team mascot. During the first intermission of Maple Leaf home games, fans would cheer as Billy skated around the ice, wearing a small Maple Leafs sweater and stickhandling a puck.

Babe Pratt was traded to the Boston Bruins for a prospect and cash. During the four seasons he spent in blue and white, he was a huge presence. He set an NHL record for assists by a defenceman in 1942–43, and in 1943–44 broke his own record and set a new league record for total points by a blueliner. That season, he was selected to the NHL's First All-Star Team and was the recipient of the Hart Trophy as the NHL's most valuable player. Pratt was also a key member of the Leafs' 1945 Stanley Cup championship.

The Leafs weren't done tinkering. Toronto traded for Vic Lynn from the Montreal Canadiens. Toronto was Lynn's fourth NHL team; by the end of his career, Lynn would have played for all of the Original Six clubs. Garth Boesch, Joe Klukay, Gus Mortson, and Jimmy Thomson were all promoted from the minor leagues. The biggest surprise, however, was Howie Meeker, who made the leap from junior, where he had played with Stratford in 1945–46. This influx of youth made the Toronto Maple Leafs of 1946–47 the youngest team ever

to play in the NHL to that date. Only four players – Broda, Apps, and the Metz brothers – were over 30, while at the other end of the spectrum, Thomson was only 19 years of age.

Smythe, whose personal motto was "If you can't beat them in the alley, you can't beat them on the ice," insisted on a tougher, more exuberant team. "If they start shoving you around, I expect you to shove them right back, harder," was his philosophy. "If one of our players should get injured by illegal tactics, I expect the players on our team to see that the man responsible doesn't get away with it."

The new-look Leafs were, according to Smythe, "the best team we've had in over ten years."

The season started with a 3–3 tie in Detroit. That night, a young Gordie Howe scored his first of 801 regular-season NHL goals. The Leafs' first home game took place three nights later against those same Red Wings. This time, Toronto doubled Detroit, 6–3.

Toronto quickly found a formula that worked well. Syl Apps centred Bill Ezinicki and Harry Watson on the first line. A second potent combination, the KLM Line, was made up of Ted Kennedy, Vic Lynn, and Howie Meeker. Both trios outworked the opposition and had a flair for scoring. The penalty-killing pair of Nick Metz and Joe Klukay was likewise sensational. On defence, Gus Mortson and Jimmy Thomson made for a formidable pair, and Garth Boesch and Bob Goldham proved to be similarly impenetrable. Veteran Wally Stanowski was rendered a fifth defenceman as a result. And Turk Broda continued to command his rightful place among the top tier of NHL goaltenders.

Beginning this season, Sunday-evening away games were broadcast by Toronto radio station CKEY. The play-by-play was reconstructed in an ingenious manner: regular updates were sent by telegraph throughout the game from the out-of-town city to the station. The information was decoded and forwarded to a sports reporter, who rewrote the copy with flourishes and delivered it to Joe Chrysdale, who used the details provided to create a running commentary. A technician added crowd noise to make the broadcast sound as though Chrysdale was broadcasting live from the arena. Early in the 1951–52 season, however, NHL president Clarence Campbell would intervene, prohibiting these reconstructed games, citing the fact that one radio station had paid $40,000 for the radio rights to Toronto Maple Leafs games.

By the time the calendar flipped over to 1947, Toronto had won eighteen, lost just six, and had tied four. A 10–4 win over the hapless Hawks on January 8 provided a

highlight early in the near year. According to the *Star*, the Leafs goals in that game came "so thick and fast that even the official scorer didn't know where they were coming from." Rookie Howie Meeker was credited with scoring five goals, although whether he actually scored all five remained a subject for debate for decades.

"I scored two of them," Wally Stanowski avowed emphatically. "On the first goal, the puck went in and I came back and sat on the bench. Hap Day, our coach, tapped me on the shoulder and said, 'We are going to give that goal to Meeker.' I said, 'All right. I'm only a defence-man. It's okay with me.'"

On the second of the suspect goals, Stanowski took a shot from the point that took a funny hop before bouncing in. This goal was also credited to Meeker. "One deflected off my stick and the other one bounced in off my ass,"

the rookie forward would later recall. "The only reason I was standing in front of the net was because Wally's shot couldn't break a pane of glass. If he had any spit on his shot, he would have scored a million goals."

The goals had been initially credited to Stanowski, but after Coach Day conferred with the official scorer between periods, both were awarded to Meeker.

In a conversation not long before his 2015 passing, Stanowski pulled no punches: "They were lying. Conny Smythe was just trying to promote Meeker for the rookie-of-the-year award, so talked the referee into giving him the goals." Stanowski never warmed to Meeker and believed that the rookie should have admitted that he hadn't scored the goals. Regardless of the dubious nature of how they were scored, the five goals set a single-game record for NHL rookies. At the time of writing, the

Howie Meeker (right) enjoyed quite a rookie campaign, On January 8, 1947, he scored five goals in a 10–4 win over the Black Hawks. He was awarded the Calder Trophy as top rookie of 1946–47, and was a member of the Stanley Cup–winning team that spring, his first of four Stanley Cup championships with the Maple Leafs.

Wally Stanowski (centre) was a "whirling dervish" on the blueline for the Maple Leafs, and played on four Cup-winning teams in Toronto: 1942, 1945, 1947, and 1948.

record still stands, matched only by Don Murdoch of the New York Rangers, who scored five during a game in October 1976.

Later in January, the Leafs fell victim to injuries and struggled to engineer victories. The team's defence was particularly affected. Bob Goldham, for instance, would play only 11 games throughout the season, while Garth Boesch's year was abbreviated by a groin injury. After a 5–4 loss to Chicago on the first of February, the depleted Leafs were winless in five games.

It was at this point that the team summoned two new players. One was Sid Smith, who had been the leading scorer for the Pittsburgh Hornets of the AHL and was a logical choice to step into the lineup. The Leafs also needed to shore up the defence, however, and finding a blueliner to replace the injured Goldham and Boesch proved to be more of a challenge. The Leafs could have gone with Pete Backor, Ernie Dickens, or Moe Morris of the Pittsburgh Hornets. All three had NHL experience. The Tulsa Oilers of the United States Hockey League, the next rung down on the Toronto Maple Leafs' minor-league

depth chart, had Nick Knott, a sturdy blueliner who likewise had some big-league experience. Despite these options, the Leafs made the surprising decision to reach down even further, to their semi-pro affiliate, the Hollywood Wolves of the Pacific Coast Hockey League. The Wolves' coach, former Leaf Bob Gracie, and Tommy Anderson, a former Hart Trophy winner who had been in the Leafs system, recommended a kid named Bill Barilko. Anderson said of Barilko that "he's pretty green but he's a big boy, not afraid of anyone, bangs 'em around good and he learns fast . . . He'll make plenty of mistakes, but he won't back down from anyone." As far as Smythe was concerned, the Leafs had done fairly well with their youth movement and he was willing to take a gamble.

In Barilko's debut, in Montreal on February 6, the Leafs were crushed, 8–2, but the defenceman raised some eyebrows after he sent Maurice Richard flying with a heavy bodycheck. Two nights later, in his first home game, Barilko scored a goal and hit everything in sight in a 5–2 win over Boston. The Maple Leafs program observed that "Bashin' Bill" was "green as the hills of Killarney but eager as any beaver." It didn't take long for Barilko to establish himself as a fan favourite. Pencilled in to play a handful of games as a fifth defenceman, Barilko had – in story-book fashion – found a permanent spot on the Toronto blueline. Coach Day marvelled that the Leafs had reached "into the bottom of our farm system barrel for a defence-man and we come up with a great, major league prospect who has certainly proved himself so far." Barilko's solid play kept Wally Stanowski on the sidelines.

The young native of Timmins, Ontario, was paired with Garth Boesch, who returned from injury just around the time Barilko debuted with the Leafs. The two formed an airtight seal in front of Broda that the press dubbed the "Maginot Line," borrowing the name of the mas-sive concrete-and-steel fortification that had stretched along France's border with Germany, Luxembourg, and Switzerland prior to the Second World War.

The Maginot Line certainly helped the Leafs in the latter part of the campaign; Toronto ended the season in second place, collecting 72 points, six behind first-place Montreal, and leading the NHL in scoring with 209 goals. Ted Kennedy finished fifth in individual scoring with 60 points, 28 of which had been goals. Howie Meeker, who won the Calder Trophy as the NHL's best rookie, tallied 27 goals, and Syl Apps had 25.

Toronto met fourth-place Detroit in the opening series of the playoffs. The Red Wings were hampered going into the postseason. Goaltender Harry Lumley was replaced by Red Almas, whose resumé included only one NHL game to that point. Still, the first game required an overtime goal by Howie Meeker to decide the 3–2 contest. Game Two ended in embarrassment for Toronto in front of their hometown fans as Detroit blasted the Leafs 9–1. Six of the goals were scored in the third period alone, and three of these in the last three minutes of the game. "We were outskated, outplayed, outpushed, outfought and out anything else you can think of," Conn Smythe fumed. "We have to lose games, but we don't have to let anybody push us around. It will not happen again."

Smythe was correct. It didn't.

An awakened Leafs team now realized that it was capa-ble of losing to the Red Wings. Toronto played substantially better in the subsequent games, beating the Wings twice in Detroit by identical scores of 4–1 before closing the series out with a resounding 6–1 victory at Maple Leaf Gardens.

The Maple Leafs then faced the Montreal Canadiens in the Stanley Cup final for the first time. The opening game was played in Montreal, where the Canadiens made easy work of the Leafs, winning 6–0. One newspaper called

the Habs' win "letter-perfect." Game Two, however, was a different story, and the Maple Leafs responded with a solid 4–0 win in a penalty-filled affair. Early in the second period, the fiery Maurice Richard slashed Vic Lynn, slicing him over the left eye. The blow knocked Lynn unconscious, and as he was carried off the ice, the Rocket received a five-minute major. Later in that period, frustrated by the tireless checking of Bill Ezinicki, Richard cracked his adversary over the head, leaving a seven-stitch cut in his scalp. The incident earned Richard a match penalty, a one-game suspension, and a $250 fine. The match penalty required the Canadiens to play shorthanded for 20 min-utes. "Everything went wrong with us," Habs coach Dick Irvin lamented. "We have no one to blame but ourselves."

The Leafs doubled Montreal, 4–2, in Game Three in Toronto, and then followed that with a thrilling 2–1 overtime victory in Game Four. Both goaltenders were spectacular in the contest. So, too, was defenceman Garth Boesch, who served as a second goaltender, blocking shots in front of Broda. Finally, at 16:36, Leaf captain Syl Apps cradled the puck behind the Montreal goal and, on a wraparound, tucked it between the legs of Bill Durnan.

Down three games to one, the Canadiens won, 3–1, on their return to Montreal for Game Five. After the contest, the victors were visited by Jack Laviolette, who had starred with the Canadiens in their first NHL season (1917–18) before losing a foot in a car accident that ended his career. Laviolette had raised the $250 Richard needed to pay his fine to the NHL. This gesture spoke to the growing cultural importance of Richard – and the Canadiens – to French Canada.

When the teams returned to Toronto for Game Six, the Canadiens shocked Leafs fans by scoring 25 seconds into the game. It was, however, the only goal the Habs would get on the night. The Leafs tied the game, and then, at 14:39 of the third, Ted Kennedy scored the goal that would prove to be the Stanley Cup winner. With only seconds to go before the final bell, Maple Leafs photographer Nat Turofsky jumped onto the ice in front of the Leafs bench in order to capture the celebration. The result (seen on p. 96) is one of the most famous and jubilant photographs ever taken of the Leafs.

The dressing room was crammed with well-wishers following the game. These included Toronto mayor Robert Saunders and Ontario premier George Drew. In the stands, an impatient crowd shouted for the Stanley Cup. As it happened, though, the Cup was not in the building – in fact, the Cup wasn't even in Toronto. As the New York Times explained, "the 'mug' was not forthcoming, being locked in a safe at the Montreal Forum." Some people close to the team believed that Conn Smythe didn't want his team to get overconfident, and had insisted that the Cup remain in Montreal. Officially, the NHL announced that the Stanley Cup "shall be presented at a time and a place to be designated by the winner."

The Stanley Cup arrived the next day in time for one final team photograph. A celebration followed at the Gardens, with speeches from captain Syl Apps, Ted Kennedy, trainer Tim Daly, and, of course, Conn Smythe. The latter lauded his team, saying, "First, there was the coaching of Happy Day, who ran the team and made the decisions. Second, there was the play of the old champions. By that, I mean the veterans of our other great championship teams. Third, there was the play of the kids who wanted to be champions."

The sun was shining in the hearts of Leafs Nation. And the immediate forecast called for clear skies.

STRENGTH DOWN THE MIDDLE

On October 18, following a 4–2 road win against Chicago, the reigning Stanley Cup champions took the Maple Leaf Gardens ice for the first time in 1947–48, facing the Detroit Red Wings. The evening began, as always, with the 48th Highlanders piping "The Maple Leaf Forever." This was followed by the ceremonial puck drop by the governor general, Viscount Alexander of Tunis. As for the game, the teams skated to a 2–2 tie.

In spite of the recent success, Conn Smythe knew that the key to his team's future was to have strength down the middle. He already had two of the best centres in the National Hockey League in Syl Apps and Ted Kennedy, but Apps had given indications that he planned to retire at the conclusion of the 1947–48 season. Smythe was convinced that he needed one more piece, especially if Apps was indeed on the way out.

The Leafs boss set his sights on Max Bentley, the Chicago Black Hawks' star centre. Bentley had been the NHL's scoring leader in 1945–46, a performance that earned him the Hart Trophy as the league's most valuable player. He won the scoring title again in 1946–47. Max played on a line with his brother Doug and Bill Mosienko. The "Pony Line" was small, but exceptionally fast and adept at handling the puck. There was, of course, one small matter for Smythe to consider: Why would Chicago trade one of its very best players? The answer was that in 1946–47, the Hawks had finished last. During the All-Star Game – which took place just prior to the 1947–48

season – Mosienko injured his ankle, after which the Hawks began the campaign by losing their first six games. Smythe smelled vulnerability in Chicago.

So, Smythe called the Hawks' general manager, Bill Tobin, and inquired about the possibility of acquiring Max Bentley. Tobin said he was listening, so Smythe offered defence prospect Ernie Dickens and forwards Gus Bodnar, Bud Poile, and Gaye Stewart. The latter three, all from Fort William, Ontario, played together on a line called the Flying Forts. Stewart had won the Calder Trophy as rookie of the year in 1943, and Gus Bodnar won it the following season.

Despite the promising players Smythe was offering, the acquisition of Max Bentley was still a big ask. Tobin hemmed and hawed before demanding an experienced defenceman to sweeten the deal. Smythe grudgingly agreed to include Bob Goldham, but said he needed another player in return. Tobin told his counterpart that he would include forward prospect Cy Thomas. With that, Smythe had, remarkably, secured the deal.

The trade would have been a blockbuster in any era, and when it was finalized on November 2, 1947, it rocked the hockey world. NHL president Clarence Campbell observed, "It is the biggest deal in NHL hockey in a long, long time and only goes to emphasize the worth of such a player as Bentley and puts him on a very high plane."

Bentley was saddened to leave his brother and his Chicago teammates, but he was quickly embraced in Toronto. His new teammate Sid Smith liked Bentley's creativity with the puck: "Max would go dipsy-doodling. He'd head out of our end, then all of a sudden, he'd whip to one side of the ice." The Leafs made great use of the player known as the Dipsy-Doodle Dandy from Delisle.

Bentley faced his former team in a pair of 5–4 games in November – one a win and the other a loss – before the Leafs blasted Chicago, 12–5, on December 6. Max scored his first and only hat trick as a Leaf in that lopsided contest. The *Star* pointed out that it was doubtful that "ever a crowd has taken to a player as they have to Bentley . . . he only has to move towards the puck and the entire gathering blows straight through the roof."

Yet while the team could certainly score, Coach Day employed a conservative defensive system. In particular, he tried to rein in blueliner Wally Stanowski's offensive forays, without much success. While Stanowski was incredibly popular with the fans, who would chant, "We want Wally!" he simply didn't fit Day's system and saw little ice time. The defenceman recalled one particularly memorable game in March 1948:

Two of the greatest Leafs of all time: Syl Apps (left) was the captain of the Stanley Cup–winning Leaf teams of 1942, 1947, and 1948 before being followed by Ted Kennedy (right), who wore the C for the Stanley Cup wins in 1949 and 1951.

I was still sitting on the sidelines and we were playing in Boston. We only had one goaltender in those days. Frankie Brimsek was the goaltender for Boston and got cut on the head with the puck. He had to skate off and get stitched up. All the players went and sat down on the bench and waited for Frank to come back. There was nobody on the ice, and Hap said to me, "Wally, get out and get warmed up." I was embarrassed. I was the only guy out on the ice. So, I skated towards the middle [of the ice] and I just made a little turn. The organist picked up on it, so I went into a figure skating routine. *La-de-da-de-da*. I made a twirl. And then I was out of breath, so I was skating backwards, and I raised one leg. I was gliding back towards the bench and my foot touched the boards, so I turned around and I looked for Hap. I couldn't see him. He was bent over behind the bench, laughing like hell. I said to him, "Do you think I'm warmed up enough now?" You had to have some fun.

All kidding aside, the Leafs had a terrific season, steamrolling their way to a first-place finish – the first time they had accomplished that feat since 1934–35. The three Toronto centres led their team in scoring: Apps with 26 goals and 53 points, Bentley with 23 goals and 48 points, and Kennedy with 25 goals and 46 points. Turk Broda won the Vézina Trophy for playing the most games for the team with the lowest goals-against average, and was named to the First All-Star Team.

Toronto opened the semifinal at home against the third-place Boston Bruins. Pitting strength against strength, Day put the Kennedy-Lynn-Meeker line out against Boston's Kraut Line of Bobby Bauer, Woody Dumart, and Milt Schmidt. The Leafs won Game One, 5–4. It was a seesaw battle in which Toronto came from behind three times before Nick Metz scored the winning goal in overtime. Game Two saw Toronto outscore Boston again, this time by a 5–3 count, with Ted Kennedy recording four of the five goals.

Despite the scoring output, journalists were surprised by the absence of physical play in the series. That all changed, however, when the series moved to Boston for Game Three. This was a vicious affair, marred by fights both on and off the ice. Despite several scraps through the game, the worst was saved for last. At the final buzzer of the 5–1 Toronto win, spectators swarmed onto the ice and lunged at the Leaf players. One fan in particular had been hurling abuse at the Maple Leaf bench all through the game, and as Hap Day was exiting for the dressing room, the same fan accosted him. The Leaf players surrounded

their coach and escorted him to safety while several other spectators tried to get a punch in. In the hubbub, a fan lunged at Garth Boesch and punched him in the face. Smythe declared the proceedings to be a "positive disgrace that could never happen in Toronto."

For his part, Boston owner Walter Brown committed to adding protection in the form of 21 extra policemen prior to Game Four. The Bruins won the far more subdued contest, 3–2. It would, however, be Boston's only victory, as the Maple Leafs clinched a berth in the Stanley Cup final with a 3–2 win in Game Five.

The Leafs faced the Detroit Red Wings in the final. The series began at Maple Leaf Gardens, where Toronto pulled out a 5–3 win. The victory was costly: late in the second period, having just scored the Leafs' fourth goal, Gus Mortson broke his leg in a collision with Black Jack Stewart. Mortson had played a significant role on the Leafs blueline, and now Wally Stanowski was sent in as his replacement.

Despite the loss of a key defenceman, the Leafs got on with the task at hand. In Game Two, they doubled Detroit, 4–2. The series then shifted to Detroit for the third game, where the Leafs managed a third straight victory, blanking the Red Wings, 2–0.

Toronto mayor Hiram McCallum addressed a telegram to Conn Smythe prior to Game Four. In it, he wrote: "Please convey best wishes to Maple Leafs for success in game for Stanley Cup tonight. If they win this game and are returning during day on Thursday, we shall be glad to extend a civic welcome at City Hall." The ever-superstitious Smythe refused to jinx his team by reading them the telegram.

There would, in the end, be nothing to worry about. The Maple Leafs blasted Detroit, 7–2, to sweep the series and win the Stanley Cup, becoming the first team to claim back-to-back championships since Detroit had done it in 1936 and '37. And once again, the Stanley Cup was not presented after the game – Smythe, not wishing to press his or his team's luck, had again insisted that the trophy remain in the NHL's Montreal head office.

The next day, the train carrying the champions home was greeted by thousands of fans at Union Station. From the train, the players climbed into convertibles that drove north on Bay Street through Toronto's business district, amidst a cascade of multicoloured paper and ticker tape. The parade was led by the Queen's Own Rifles band, playing "For He's a Jolly Good Fellow." The Leafs arrived at the promised civic reception at City Hall. There, the team was greeted by Mayor McCallum and 10,000 well-wishers. After the mayor spoke, Conn Smythe and Hap Day addressed the throng, followed by Syl Apps, who publicly announced his retirement and thanked the Toronto fans for their unwavering support through his brilliant career.

It might be argued that Syl Apps personified the ideal Toronto Maple Leaf better than any other player in the history of the franchise. The captain was athletic, educated, and a natural leader on the ice. More meaningfully, he had connected Leafs Nation to those old, cherished British sensibilities upon which the team was imagined, such as propriety, fair play, and doing one's duty. As the *Hamilton Spectator* contended:

> There is only one Apps; there never was another; there never could be, and while Sylvanus Apps, the idol of Toronto Maple Leaf supporters, has definitely retired from the active sports scene, he will never be displaced from that special sports nook in the hearts of his admirers reserved for one who has already become an almost legendary character. There have been many remarkable athletes in Canadian sport, but few have been more outstanding.

By the end of his career, Apps had been an NHL First Team All-Star twice and a Second Team All-Star three times. In the entirety of his ten-season career, Apps served only 56 minutes in penalties. The captain had performed extraordinarily on an extraordinary Maple Leafs team.

Meanwhile, back at City Hall, after Apps's gracious speech, Ted Kennedy spoke a few words of appreciation, and the team members signed the City Hall guest book. The boys then left for Maple Leaf Gardens, where wives, family, and friends waited to greet them.

The next day, the team returned and dressed for their official Stanley Cup portrait. Gus Mortson, still nursing a broken leg, was transported to the arena by ambulance from Wellesley Hospital. Mortson was helped into his uniform and was able to stand delicately in the back row for the team photo.

The trade for Max Bentley had accomplished what Smythe had intended: a second straight Stanley Cup. No other Toronto hockey team had won both the league title and the Stanley Cup in the same season. To parallel their performance during the regular season, the three centres also led the Leafs' playoff scoring: Kennedy with 14 points, Bentley with 11, and Apps with 8. "No club in the history of hockey ever had four centres like that team," Howie Meeker boasted. "We had Apps and Kennedy, and

Max Bentley was the third-line centre. Nick Metz was the backup. We were the best hockey team that year by a country mile."

DYNASTY

Syl Apps's retirement created a void that would be impossible to fill. He was, after all, only 33 years of age, and had just enjoyed the finest season of his NHL career. Still, the captain had had enough. And as the team's new captain, Ted Kennedy was ready to continue his own legendary career. The young centre felt honoured by how his captaincy had come about:

> We were in the dressing room after practice in the fall of '48 when Hap said, "Since Syl is no longer with us, we have to choose a new captain." Then he put it out to the floor to take nominations verbally and put it to a vote. Turk Broda said, "I think Teeder should be our captain." Day asked if there were any other nominations and no one else was put forward, so they were all satisfied that I became their captain and that's the way it happened . . . To share that honour with Syl Apps, a superb player and perfect gentleman, was a great moment. It was the proudest moment of my life.

There were, however, changes in the roster. Not surprisingly, Wally Stanowski was finally dealt, along with Moe Morris, to the New York Rangers. In return, the Leafs received Cal Gardner, Bill Juzda, Frank Mathers, and René Trudel.

Toronto had been fortunate in filling vacancies in recent times, and Leafs head scout Squib Walker played a crucial role in this process. He had turned up four Calder Trophy recipients in just five years: Gaye Stewart, Gus Bodnar, Frank McCool, and Howie Meeker. For the new season, the Leafs promoted Les Costello and Tod Sloan from the St. Michael's Majors. Likewise, Ray Timgren made the team from the junior Toronto Marlboros. During the summer, Toronto also acquired the much-coveted Danny Lewicki from the Providence Reds of the AHL.

At the 1948–49 home opener, the ceremonial faceoff was performed by Brigadier-General Harry Crerar, Canada's chief of the general staff and leading field commander during the Second World War. The general presented the Stanley Cup to Toronto's retired captain, Syl Apps, who was attending in civilian clothes. NHL president Clarence Campbell then presented the

Prince of Wales Trophy to captain Ted Kennedy and the Vézina Trophy to Turk Broda. The Leafs did not spoil the celebration, beating the visiting Boston Bruins, 4–1.

A long-running feud erupted on New Year's Day 1949, when Kenny Reardon and Cal Gardner went at each other with their sticks. Reardon suffered a 14-stitch gash to his scalp and lost several teeth. The *Hockey News* said that the incident was "nothing short of barbaric." Campbell summoned both to his office, where he remonstrated: "Hockey is the toughest, most rugged game of them all. There's no need for anyone to swing a stick just to prove he's a tough guy." Campbell fined Gardner $250 and Reardon $200 for the incident and suspended both players for the next game between Toronto and Montreal.

Meanwhile, by mid-January, the Leafs' KLM line had been sidelined with injuries. Kennedy was out with a bruised back; Lynn, a separated shoulder; and Meeker missed 30 games with a broken collarbone. As such, Toronto had to struggle through the dog days of the season.

But dogs were not the only quadrupeds on the Leafs' minds in early 1949. Max Bentley heard a voice from the stands holler his name during a game between the Leafs and Red Wings on February 12: "Hey Maxie, score on this shift and I'll give you a horse!" Bentley looked back and saw that the promise had been made by Charlie Hemstead, whom Max knew from the racetrack. Bentley loved a challenge as much as he loved the ponies. Twenty seconds into that second-period shift, he fired the puck past Harry Lumley, then skated over to Hemstead, shook his hand, and thanked him for the horse. Bentley later revealed that George McCullagh, who had just purchased the *Toronto Telegram* and sat on the board of Maple Leaf Gardens, had also promised him a horse. The Leafs centre named the Hemstead horse Royal Hem, and the horse he received from McCullagh, he called Filalo.

Although they lost the final three games of the regular season, surrendering 15 goals in the process, Toronto was able to secure fourth place – and with it, a spot in the postseason. Harry Watson led the team in scoring with 26 goals and 45 points, which was good for seventh-best in the league.

The opening round of the playoffs pitted the Maple Leafs against the second-place Bruins. Boston coach Dit Clapper predicted that it would be a tough series: "You don't knock two-time champions off the throne without a struggle." Clapper's prediction was a sound one. Toronto won the first two games in Boston, 3–0 and 3–2.

Harry Watson scored twice in each game. Back in Toronto, the Bruins edged the Leafs, 5–4, in overtime.

Toronto won Game Four by a 3–1 score, with two goals from AHL call-up Sid Smith. Author Ed Fitkin called Smith "lightning on skates; a darting, devilish will o' the wisp." It would not be the last time Smith contributed in a big game for the Leafs. Back in Boston, the Maple Leafs took the deciding game, 3–2, with the winning goal coming from horse owner Max Bentley.

The first-place Detroit Red Wings, who had polished off Montreal, served as the Leafs' opposition in the 1949 Stanley Cup final. The series opened in Detroit, and required an overtime marker by the Leafs' Joe Klukay at 17:31 to yield a 3–2 decision. In Game Two, Sid Smith collected a hat trick in a 3–1 Toronto victory.

Desperate to reverse the momentum in Game Three, Detroit played the Production Line – Sid Abel, Gordie Howe, and Ted Lindsay – for more than 40 minutes in total. While the line managed one goal, it wasn't enough, as the Leafs managed three and took a 3–0 stranglehold on the series.

During Game Four at Maple Leaf Gardens, the Detroit players used canisters of oxygen on their bench to give players a quick lift. The tactic did not, however, breathe new life into the Red Wings' performance. As the *Star* reported, "The Leafs just skated and hammered their rivals into the pipes." Toronto skated away with a 3–1 victory, with Cal Gardner scoring the Cup-winning goal at 19:45 of the second period. With the victory, the Toronto Maple Leafs became the first team in the history of the National Hockey League to win three successive Stanley Cup championships.

As the third period ended, the band began playing "Happy Days Are Here Again." A table was carried out to centre ice and the Stanley Cup placed on it, a notable difference from the two previous years. NHL president Clarence Campbell congratulated Conn Smythe, Hap Day, and the Toronto Maple Leafs on their accomplishment. As is customary, the winning captain stepped forward to receive the Stanley Cup. The rest of the Leafs then surrounded Kennedy, patting him on the back as they ran their hands over the Stanley Cup. "I don't know why you guys are so excited at winning the Stanley Cup," trainer Tim Daly quipped. "We do it every year!" The fans then began to chant, "We want Meeker!" The still-recovering forward hobbled out onto the ice and waved to the crowd, garnering thunderous applause.

Of the players who were part of all three championships, most still had many good years ahead of them.

Garth Boesch was 27; Joe Klukay was 26; Bill Ezinicki and Harry Watson were 25; and Ted Kennedy was only 24. Jimmy Thomson and Bill Barilko were younger still, at just 22. The elder statesman was Turk Broda, who was 35 and still, by all accounts, the best "money goalie" in hockey.

Interestingly, the Maple Leafs won the 1949 Stanley Cup with a losing regular-season record (22–25–13), becoming only the second NHL team to accomplish that feat, and the first since Chicago in 1938. Despite this quirk, when Conn Smythe was asked many years later to name the greatest team with which he had ever been involved, he did not hesitate to say, "The 1948–49 squad. That was the greatest Maple Leaf team ever."

The Red Wings had now lost three consecutive playoff series to Toronto, winning just one game. Speaking many years later about the 1949 final, Gordie Howe complained: "Those damn Leafs managed to turn it on in the playoffs, they swept us in four straight games again. It was their third Stanley Cup in a row and we were sick of it. Getting swept once was bad enough, but having it happen in back-to-back years was like a punch in the gut."

In the forthcoming season, Howe was determined not to take another punch from the Leafs.

THE BATTLE OF THE BULGE REVISITED

On the heels of three consecutive Cup wins, the Leafs looked unstoppable. And yet more success seemed to be in the cards for the franchise. With the farm system producing outstanding prospects, there was no telling how long the string of championships could extend. But reality often tends to get in the way of dreams.

Several new faces tried to crack the Maple Leafs' already-youthful roster during training camp, including George Armstrong, Bobby Dawes, Danny Lewicki, Fleming Mackell, and Ray Timgren. Smythe was particularly enamoured of Armstrong and Lewicki, calling them "the best pair I've seen together since Conacher and Jackson, and that was 20 years ago."

Several goalkeepers were also in camp, with hopes of one day replacing Turk Broda. The list included Howie Harvey (younger brother of Hall of Fame defenceman Doug), Don Lockhart, and the one considered to be the

Although the Maple Leafs regular-season record was sub-.500, the team persevered and captured their third consecutive Stanley Cup championship in 1949, becoming the first NHL team to accomplish this feat.

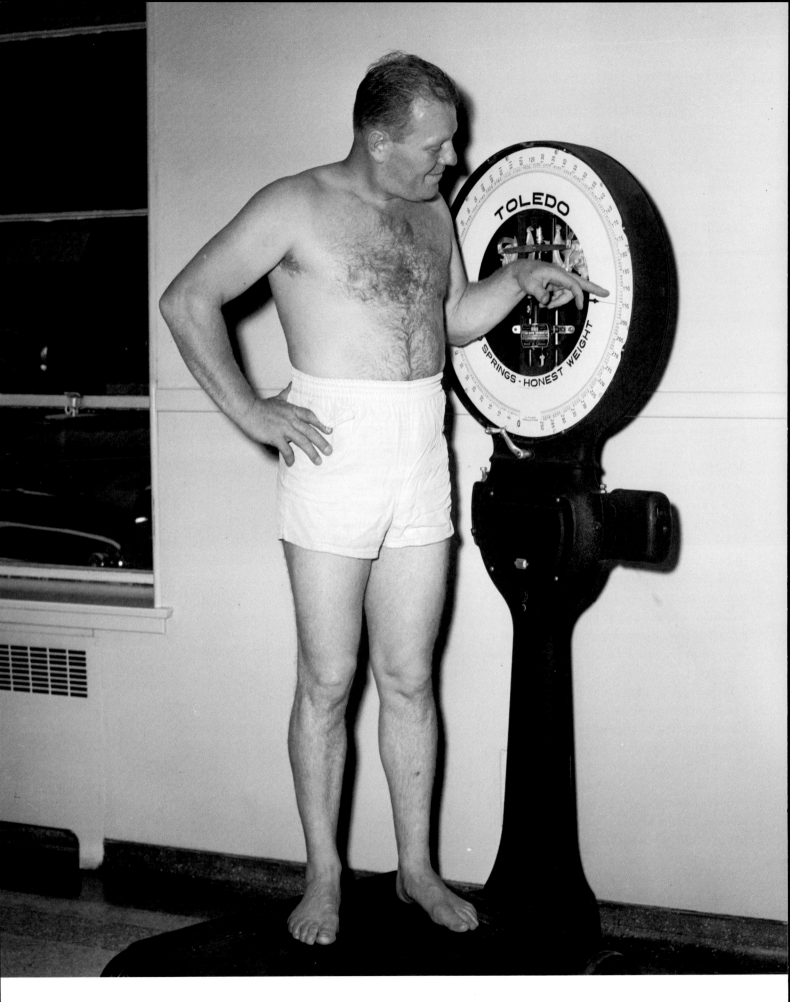

frontrunner, Baz Bastien. This notion, however, was shattered when Don Clark's shot struck Bastien in the eye during a preseason game in Welland. Regrettably, Bastien's eye was damaged so badly that it had to be removed.

The 1949–50 season opened when Ontario premier Leslie Frost officially presented the Stanley Cup to captain Ted Kennedy on behalf of his teammates. The ensuing ceremonial faceoff preceded a game against the Chicago Black Hawks, which ended in a 4–4 tie.

The final instalment of Gardner v. Reardon occurred during a 4–2 Leafs loss to the Canadiens on November 10. This time, the Montreal defender caught Gardner with an elbow at centre ice that shattered his jaw. NHL president Clarence Campbell forced the Canadien to post a $1,000 peace bond against future violence; the money would be returned at the end of his career provided he didn't indulge in any further such acts. In addition, both players were suspended from playing against each other for the remainder of the season, although Gardner's injury forced him to miss most of the remaining season. The feud ended at the conclusion of the season, when the 29-year-old Reardon retired. The two men never forgave one another, and remained bitter enemies for the rest of their lives.

In late November, the Maple Leafs went into a winless skid. Around the same time, Toronto was preparing to host the annual Grey Cup game, in which the Montreal Alouettes and Calgary Stampeders were set to battle for the championship of Canadian football. Long before interest in the Maple Leafs dwarfed any of the city's other professional sports teams, the club had to fight for its share of space in the sports sections of Toronto's dailies. Football enjoyed particular interest among Toronto's sportswriters, and it sometimes took ink away from the Blue and White. With this in mind, and perhaps in an attempt to divert attention from the team's woes, Conn Smythe hatched a scheme to get his team some positive press.

The Leafs boss announced that he had given an ultimatum to six members of his Toronto Maple Leafs. Garth Boesch, Vic Lynn, Howie Meeker, Sid Smith, Harry Watson, and, most astonishingly, Turk Broda were commanded to drop several pounds before Smythe would allow them to dress again for the Leafs. While Broda had recorded three shutouts by mid-November, Smythe realized that his netminder's "best-before" date was steadily approaching, and it was perhaps time to find a replacement.

Broda was informed that he would have to lose seven pounds before he would be able to return. To be sure, Broda enjoyed his food and beer. Turk's wife, Betty, was enlisted to help the process, in what became affectionately known in the media as her husband's "Battle of the Bulge."

"I don't know what I can cut off Turk," Betty said. "He has only a light lunch and then a good steak with non-fattening vegetables at dinner. Turk never gets dessert here and for that reason, we seldom have cakes except for a special treat for the girls. I don't know what to do! I think Walter is just one of those persons who is naturally inclined to be stout."

The papers seized on the challenge set before Broda and even offered suggestions on how the goaltender might drop weight.

While the Battle of the Bulge continued, the Leafs looked to Gil Mayer to take Broda's place in the crease on December 1. Outside of the war years, Mayer had been the first new netminder for the Leafs since Broda replaced George Hainsworth on November 5, 1936. Mayer, known as "The Needle" because of his five-foot, six-inch, 130-pound frame, played well in his debut but surrendered two goals in a 2–0 loss to the Red Wings. The Leafs had now gone seven games without a win.

Two nights later, and nine pounds lighter, Turk Broda returned to tend goal for Toronto in a home game against the Rangers. As he skated to his customary position, the band uncharitably played the "Too Fat Polka." Broda had the last laugh, though, blanking the Rangers and earning his fourth shutout of the season. Turk added yet another shutout on December 18 against those same Rangers.

The goalie's fortunes, however, turned on December 21, when the Red Wings lit up the Leafs, 7–1. A few nights later, Broda was beaten four times in the first period alone by the Boston Bruins. For the rest of the period, the fans cynically cheered every time Broda made an easy save. Smythe stormed down from his seat and ordered Coach Day to pull Broda at the end of the first, yelling, "I don't want to see Turkey humiliated any longer by a club that seems to figure it is working for the Ice Capades!"

When the second period began, Al Rollins made his NHL debut for Toronto. Desperate for a reserve, Smythe in November had dealt Bobby Dawes, $40,000, and future considerations to the Cleveland Barons of the AHL, where Rollins had been serving as the backup to future Leaf Johnny Bower. The Globe reported that Rollins was "one of the brightest prospects ever to come out of Western Canada." The fans greeted him with a rousing ovation. The game nevertheless ended with Boston on top of an 8–4 score.

The new year started more positively. The Maple Leafs reeled off six consecutive wins in January, including

In December 1950, Leafs owner Conn Smythe insisted that Turk Broda (pictured) lose weight or lose his job. The netminder went on a well-publicized diet while minor-league goalie Gil Mayer took his spot in the crease, but Broda won the "Battle of the Bulge" and was back in goal for Toronto after dropping seven pounds.

two more shutouts for Broda, followed by a seven-game unbeaten streak in February. Toronto finished the season in third place, with a record of 31–27–12. Sid Smith led the team in scoring with 45 points, including 22 goals – one fewer than Max Bentley. Turk Broda earned nine shutouts, more than any other NHL goalie that season. Gus Mortson was named to the NHL's First All-Star Team and Ted Kennedy made the Second Team.

Their opponents in the opening round of the playoffs would, once again, be Detroit. The first-place Red Wings were dynamic, and the Production Line of Ted Lindsay, Sid Abel, and Gordie Howe was at its peak, finishing first, second, and third, respectively, in scoring during the regular season. The Leafs had confidence, but Detroit had won eight of the fourteen games between the teams during the season.

The series began in front of a hostile crowd in Detroit. While Game One ended in a 5–0 Maple Leaf victory, it is better remembered for a serious injury suffered by Gordie Howe. At 8:36 of the third period, Howe tried to check Ted Kennedy. He bounced off of the Leafs' captain and went headfirst into the boards before rebounding off of the ice. As the *Toronto Daily Star* reported, Howe "was carried off on a stretcher with blood running from his eye, nose and forehead. He is through for the season and may never play again." Fortunately, the Hall of Famer would return to action the following season.

Meanwhile, Kennedy and the rest of the Leafs instantly became Public Enemy #1 in the Motor City. As for the Leafs' captain, he stated several times throughout his career that he had shown no malice in the play:

> I saw Howe lying on the ice with his face covered with blood and I couldn't help thinking what a great player he was and how I hoped he wasn't badly hurt. Then the Detroit players started saying I did it with my stick. I knew I hadn't. I went over to the Detroit bench and told [coach Tommy Ivan] I was sorry Howe was hurt, but that I wasn't responsible.

Kennedy, who had earlier hurt his leg crashing into the goal post, was wisely pulled from the remainder of the game by Coach Day.

Unsurprisingly, the Detroit papers saw the incident differently and were convinced that Kennedy had butt-ended the Red Wings star, although that account differed from the version submitted by referee George Gravel:

> As Kennedy crossed the Toronto blueline, I saw Howe cut across towards Kennedy, skating very fast. Just before

Howe got to Kennedy, Kennedy passed backhanded and stopped suddenly. Howe just brushed him slightly and crashed into the fence and fell to the ice. Play carried on for a few seconds as Toronto had possession.

The Red Wings' players were far less forgiving, though, and sought payback in Game Two. Just seconds before the end of the second period, the Wings' Lee Fogolin drew a penalty for tripping Kennedy. About what happened next, the *Star* proclaimed, "We have never seen as dirty a hockey brawl. It was a fiasco after the first 39:48 of hockey. At that point, Ted Lindsay touched off one of the wildest free-for-alls in the history of the sport."

While the Leaf captain stood watching Sid Abel argue with the referee, Lindsay kicked Kennedy's legs out from under him from behind. Gus Mortson immediately went after Lindsay. In the meantime, Leo Reise clubbed the Leafs' Jimmy Thomson, slicing him open with a five-stitch gash on the forehead. Reise then went after Kennedy, but Kennedy caught him with a punch as he approached. Reise swung his stick and connected with Kennedy, knocking him to the ice. While he was down, Lindsay slashed Kennedy with his stick. When the Leaf captain regained his feet, Abel lashed into him and the two exchanged punches.

As the furor died down, referee Butch Keeling assessed majors to Reise and Thomson, and minors to Lindsay, Fogolin, and Kennedy. Despite the official report and Kennedy's plea of innocence, those who cheered for the team in red and white saw the Leafs captain as the one responsible for felling their leader.

In the final minute of the 3–1 Red Wing win, Bill Ezinicki paired off with Lindsay. As they tangled, Bill Juzda waded in and tackled Lindsay. According to one newspaper account, Lindsay, seeking to avenge his fallen king, spent the better part of the game racing around the ice "like a bull who'd backed into a pitchfork."

The series shifted to Toronto for Game Three, and the hometown fans booed Lindsay and Reise every time they were on the ice. Juzda and Lindsay, as well as Reise and Thomson, collided on a few occasions, but nothing ignited on the plays. The Maple Leafs won, 2–0. This was, according to Conn Smythe, "hockey as it should be played."

Game Four required overtime before a single goal was scored. The first extra period was scoreless. Then, early in the second overtime, with Bill Barilko serving a penalty, Leo Reise's shot from inside the blueline glanced off Gus Mortson's leg and found its way past a bewildered Broda. The Red Wings' 2–1 victory had tied the series at two games apiece.

The Maple Leafs took enough penalties in Game Five to give Detroit the man advantage for 19 of the 60 minutes. Still, the Blue and White managed to squeak out a 2–0 win and Broda recorded his third shutout of the series.

The sixth game, hosted by Toronto, saw the Leafs face penalty problems once again. This time, the Wings were able to capitalize with two early power-play goals. Detroit never looked back and Harry Lumley earned the shutout in a 4–0 win. The series was knotted at three games each.

Game Seven of the semifinal was played in Detroit. Again, the game required overtime after 60 minutes of scoreless hockey. And once again, defenceman Leo Reise – who had scored just four times during the entire 1949–50 season – became the Red Wings' unlikely hero. At 8:39 of overtime, Reise took a shot that struck Leafs defenceman Bill Barilko and ricocheted past Broda to crush the dreams of a fourth straight Stanley Cup for Toronto. Broda shook his head: "I never saw Reise's goal until it hit the net and bounced back out between my feet. In fact, I didn't know it until the light went on."

Many years later, Ted Kennedy lamented:

We lost that series in seven games on a couple of very fluky goals from the point. That series with the Red Wings was only the semifinal, but the Rangers, who made it to the finals that year, were a very mediocre team. If we had won that series, we probably would have been the first team to win five in a row.

It was not to be. The string of Cups had come to an end. As most of the world was joyfully moving to accept the positive change that the new decade promised, Conn Smythe knew that he too would have to make some changes on his beloved team.

THE LAST GOAL HE EVER SCORED

The disappointment of the previous season was still very much in the minds of the Maple Leafs and their fans when Conn Smythe announced on May 26, 1950, that Hap Day had been promoted to assistant general manager and would be replaced as coach by former Kid Line centre

Joe Primeau (left) and Hap Day (right) had been teammates on the 1932 Stanley Cup–winning Maple Leafs. Day coached the Leafs through the 1940s, but when he was promoted to assistant general manager in 1950, Primeau was hired to coach and led Toronto to a Stanley Cup victory.

Joe Primeau. While Primeau's concrete-block business had been enormously successful, hockey's lure was too strong.

Joe was only 30 years old when he retired in 1936, and he had returned to the game as coach of the junior St. Michael's Majors, whom he led to Memorial Cup championships in 1945 and 1947. Primeau was also behind the bench when the senior Toronto Marlboros won the Allan Cup in 1950. He seemed to have a magic touch for getting the best out of his players.

It was nevertheless a striking move, as Hap Day had become something of a permanent feature behind the Leafs bench. In ten years as coach, Day had won five Stanley Cup championships with Toronto. Now, with Smythe spending most winters in Florida, Day would serve in a role that would today be considered director of player personnel.

The new coach and his team faced a few challenges in advance of the 1950–51 season. At 36 years of age, Turk Broda was considered comparatively ancient for an NHL goalie. He was, however, coming off the best season of his career – one that included nine shutouts. Leafs management chose to platoon Broda with Al Rollins. The two men looked radically different from one another – Broda, at five feet, nine inches, was nudging 200 pounds, while Rollins stood six foot two and weighed 175 – prompting sportswriters to call them "The Fat Man" and "The Thin Man."

On defence, Garth Boesch retired after the 1949–50 season, so the Leafs pencilled in Hugh Bolton as his replacement. Bill Barilko, for one, spoke with confidence on the subject of the Leafs blueline: "Despite the loss of Garth Boesch, I think our defence will be as good as last year. Bill Juzda and I proved we could play well together, and Hugh Bolton will help considerably." Unfortunately, Bolton injured his knee in training camp.

At this same time, Tim Horton was continuing to make a name for himself on the Leafs' AHL farm club, the Pittsburgh Hornets. While a move to the big team was still a couple of years off, the Leafs began to consider Horton – among other options – to fill in the blanks on the blueline.

Up front, Danny Lewicki cracked the veteran-laden lineup while Tod Sloan rejoined Toronto after spending a season with the AHL's Cleveland Barons. While none of these changes could be considered earth-shattering, the Maple Leafs had certainly updated their look for the new campaign in hopes of recapturing the successes of two years previous.

Brigadier-General John Rockingham, the commanding officer of the 25th Canadian Infantry Brigade – which would, in a few months' time, be deep in the Korean War – dropped the ceremonial first puck on the new Maple Leafs season. While Toronto fell 2–1 to Chicago, the Leafs went the next 11 games without losing. During that stretch, Toronto compiled eight wins and three ties, and Turk Broda recorded three shutouts. After Detroit ended the streak on November 11, Turk bounced back the next night with yet another shutout in a 7–0 hammering of Boston.

Despite the strong start, the Leafs were still struggling to ice a solid defence corps. The situation was exacerbated when Bill Barilko suffered a knee injury early in the season. Curiously, Smythe and Day chose not to call on any of their players in Pittsburgh, such as Horton, Frank Mathers, or John Ashley. Instead, the Leafs brought in Bobby Copp, a 31-year-old who had last seen action with the Leafs back in 1943. Since then, Copp had moved to Ottawa, where he had a dental practice and was playing for the Ottawa Senators of the Quebec Senior Hockey League. While it may have been an unusual move, Copp held his own. The London Free Press, for example, believed Copp was "looking right at home in the NHL again." But it was, in the end, a short run: paired with Bill Juzda, Copp played two games – both of them Leaf wins – before he returned to Ottawa.

Reinforcements of a more permanent nature arrived on November 16, when Toronto shipped Bill Ezinicki and Vic Lynn (both of whom were playing in Pittsburgh at the time) to Boston for Fern Flaman, Phil Maloney, Kenny Smith, and junior prospect Léo Boivin. In Flaman, the Leafs got a tough, stay-at-home defenceman. The Toronto Telegram called the blueliner "rough and unpolished," but believed him to be a good policeman and cautioned that he "could hit like a pile driver." The only trouble was that Flaman was devastated by the swap.

"The trade was the lowest point in my life," he would say later. "I had felt a part of Boston. I had played nearly three years with the Bruins, and on top of that, it had been written in the papers that I was an 'untouchable.' Next thing I know, I'm with the Maple Leafs."

As events unfolded, the trade would prove to be mutually beneficial to Flaman and the Leafs.

The Leafs were equally boosted by the play of Barilko after his return from the injured list. Bill had been using his body as effectively as ever, as the Black Hawks' Bill Gadsby would grudgingly attest. In a game against Chicago on November 22, Barilko sent Gadsby to the ice with what the Toronto Daily Star described as "the most terrific check this reporter ever has seen." Gadsby remembered the occasion:

By the 1950–51 season, the Toronto Maple Leafs realized that Turk Broda (right) was nearing the end of his career. Al Rollins (left) was secured and the two split goaltending duties throughout the season, with Rollins winning the Vézina Trophy. Broda and Rollins also split responsibilities in the 1951 Stanley Cup final against the Canadiens.

The toughest injury I ever had came when I had my head down and ran into Bill Barilko of the Maple Leafs . . . When I got to the dressing room, I couldn't raise my arm. The trainer had to cut off my uniform and my undershirt to see what was wrong. A bone was sticking through my skin up by the shoulder!

While Gadsby laid sprawled out on the ice after the check, his teammates pleaded with referee Bill Chadwick, who let the Black Hawks know that there was no penalty on the play and that it had simply been the best check *he* had ever seen.

Another noteworthy incident occurred the next time those same Black Hawks visited Maple Leaf Gardens. While a scoreless tie would suggest a dull affair, the real story of the game was the play of the goaltenders: all three of them. At 6:50 of the second period, Al Rollins was drilled over the left eye by an Ernie Dickens shot. The Leafs netminder was removed on a stretcher and received 12 stitches above and below the eye. The game was delayed 15 minutes while Turk Broda pulled on his equipment. Then, at 16:03 of that same period, the Leafs' Harry Watson fired a puck that broke Chicago goalie Harry Lumley's nose. As the visiting team, Chicago did not have the luxury of a backup goaltender like Broda sitting in the wings. Instead, the balance of the period was tacked onto the third period while doctors repaired Lumley's broken nose so that he could return to the game. All three goaltenders had been exceptional, and in an extremely rare occurrence, were named the game's three stars.

RETURN TO GLORY

The Leafs had been growing together since 1947 and the first of those three consecutive Stanley Cup wins. The players were close both on and off the ice. They rallied behind each other and were profoundly affected when individuals were moved to another team or sent down to the AHL. This was certainly the case with centre Johnny McCormack, who, although having a fine season, was assigned to Pittsburgh immediately after he got married.

In those days, when NHL owners and managers exercised a somewhat autocratic rule over players and their personal lives, some of the Leafs believed that McCormack had been sent down because he got married without running it by team management first. As Howie Meeker explained, McCormack's demotion "sort of rocked us all a bit, but it didn't shock us. It just shows

you that you can think you're all set one day and be on the way to Pittsburgh the next." Still, these events and the routine of the season rather galvanized the squad. As Gus Mortson explained:

Saturday nights we played at home in Toronto, and Sunday on the road. On Wednesdays, we played in Toronto, and Thursday, out of town again. We would all get together on Monday nights and brought our wives. Generally speaking, we went to the Old Mill. We were always able to go there and not be bothered. We had dinner there and there was always music there, so we'd have a dance. We enjoyed ourselves there.

This strong fraternal spirit would bode well for the Leafs, who sailed comfortably into the 1950–51 playoffs. Toronto collected 95 points in the regular season, with 41 wins, 16 losses, and 13 ties. In most years, that would have given Toronto first place, but the Gordie Howe–led Detroit Red Wings finished with a record-setting 101 points to claim the top spot. Max Bentley was the most productive Leaf, with 62 points (third in the league), and Ted Kennedy was one point back, with 61. Tod Sloan and Sid Smith managed 31 and 30 goals respectively, ranking them third and fourth in the NHL. Perhaps more remarkably, after a year in Pittsburgh, rookie Al Rollins had managed to capture the Vézina Trophy. At the time, goaltending tandems were still a novelty, so the trophy went to the principal goaltender on the team that allowed the fewest goals. During 1950–51, the Leafs surrendered 138 goals, one fewer than Montreal. Rollins had a 1.77 goals-against average playing in 40 games, while the veteran Broda made 31 appearances and had an average of 2.23. Unfortunately, Turk's name was not included as a co-recipient. Voters selected Ted Kennedy, Sid Smith, and Jimmy Thomson to the Second All-Star Team.

The Maple Leafs faced off against the Bruins in the semifinal. Boston had not won a game at Maple Leaf Gardens all season, but the Bruins, with Jack Gelineau in goal, shocked the hometown team by shutting them out, 2–0, in the opening game. Al Rollins started in goal, but while chasing a loose puck during the first period, he collided with the Bruins' Pete Horeck. Rollins tore his pads *and* knee ligaments in the process. Turk Broda stepped in and played the rest of the series.

If Game One had been a shocker, Game Two was simply odd: it ended in a 1–1 tie. This was, after all, a Saturday night in Toronto the Good, and although residents had voted in January 1950 to allow team sports to be played on Sunday, there was still a bylaw in effect requiring games started on Saturday night to be finished by 11:45 P.M. At the end of regulation time, it was determined that there was only time enough to play one overtime period – which turned out to be scoreless. The match went into the books as the first playoff tie in the NHL since 1927.

The teams travelled to Boston for Game Three, where Broda and his Leafs won, 3–0. While the Bruins opened the scoring in Game Four, Toronto responded with three unanswered goals to win and take the lead in the series. In a bid to reverse the Leafs' momentum, the Bruins replaced goaltender Gelineau with veteran Red Henry for Game Five in Toronto. It did not achieve the desired result, as the Leafs skated away with a 4–1 win. The Maple Leafs smelled blood in Game Six and whipped Boston, 6–0, to advance to the Stanley Cup final.

In the other semifinal, the Montreal Canadiens defeated the first-place Detroit Red Wings, setting up an all-Canadian championship final. This marked only the second time that Montreal and Toronto had faced each other for the Stanley Cup – the Leafs, of course, had previously triumphed over the Canadiens in 1947.

The 1951 Stanley Cup, by all accounts, remains one of the greatest playoff series of all time. First, despite having met only once before in the final, Toronto and Montreal shared an intense enmity for one another. "We hated them, especially Maurice Richard," Harry Watson said. "There were other teams we wouldn't get as up for, like the Chicago Black Hawks and the Boston Bruins, but Richard's Canadiens . . . we were always ready for them." Naturally, the country could also enact its own sense of self vicariously through the NHL's only two Canadian-based teams. This was mostly French, mainly Catholic Montreal facing off against completely English, mainly Protestant Toronto for the big prize.

Another reason this final was so special was that, for the first time in NHL history, every single game in the Stanley Cup final was decided in overtime. The tandem of Broda and Rollins was outstanding for Toronto, as was Gerry McNeil for the Canadiens. McNeil had performed so brilliantly in upsetting Detroit that Red Wings manager Jack Adams said he had provided "the greatest goaltending this team has ever faced." McNeil would be equally magnificent in the series against the Leafs.

Yet, perhaps the single most important reason that this final is considered one of the most memorable of all time is how it ended – in overtime – and what happened a few short months afterwards. That final, fairy-tale goal, however – a watershed moment for the Toronto Maple Leafs franchise – was still five overtime games away.

Sid Smith fired up the Maple Leaf Gardens crowd in Game One by scoring just 15 seconds after the opening faceoff. The teams battled in seesaw fashion, and after 60 minutes, they were deadlocked at two goals apiece. Early in overtime, Bill Barilko dove across an open goal-mouth to thwart Maurice Richard and deprive Montreal of the win. "If the diving Barilko hadn't reached that scorcher, it was home," the *Toronto Daily Star* marvelled. It fell to Sid Smith to produce some magic. At 5:51 of the extra frame, he skated in from the corner and flipped a backhand over McNeil to give Toronto the victory.

Three nights later, Montreal sought to reverse the decision of the opening game. The score was again tied at two at the end of the third period. As Toronto was changing lines in overtime, Maurice Richard took a pass from Doug Harvey, stepped around the Leaf defence, and beat Broda at 2:55 to make it 3–2, Canadiens. The Habs celebrated in the visitors' dressing room, whooping and hollering as they sang "Alouette."

Game Three was played on Gerry McNeil's 25th birthday. The Maple Leafs, however, were intent on ruining the party. Coach Primeau played a hunch by inserting Al Rollins in goal for the game. The hunch paid off.

In the fourth period, the Habs' Calum MacKay tried to clear the puck from the Montreal end, but it was intercepted by Tod Sloan. Sloan passed it to Ted Kennedy, who fired the puck past the birthday boy at 4:47 for the 2–1 win.

Game Four was the third of the series to be deadlocked at two after 60 minutes. This time, the Leafs' Harry Watson put a low, hard shot past McNeil at 5:15 of the extra period for the 3–2 win. The Leafs returned home with a 3–1 lead in the series and the possibility of winning the Stanley Cup in front of their loyal fans.

Game Five, however, got off to an ominous beginning when Ted Kennedy collided with Montreal's Paul Meger and crashed into the boards. The crowd held its breath, waiting to learn the extent of the captain's injury. Yet, after leaving the ice in incredible pain, Kennedy returned a few minutes later and was greeted by John Arnott's familiar and boisterous bellow: "C'monnnnn, Teeee-derrrr!"

The teams traded goals in the first period. Rocket Richard opened the scoring, while Tod Sloan tied the game at one. After a scoreless second, Meger put the Habs in the lead early in the third period. With 1:33 to play, the Leafs opted to pull Al Rollins for an extra skater. Toronto pressured the Habs in the Montreal end, but the Canadiens were able to clear the zone. Then, Montreal's

Any kid growing up in Canada wanted to put the Maple Leaf on, as a member of the Toronto Maple Leafs and then to represent our country. They are two great sweaters.

Paul Henderson
PLAYER
1968–74

Bill Barilko (centre) holds back Montreal's Maurice Richard as Turk Broda (left) and Howie Meeker (right) look on. The 1951 Stanley Cup final was extraordinary, with each of the five games concluding in overtime.

Kenny Mosdell took off after the puck, corralled it, and was in the clear and staring at an empty net. Out of nowhere, though, Harry Watson cut across the Leafs blueline and stole the puck from Mosdell, denying what would have been a certain goal.

Now, with 61 seconds remaining in the third period and the faceoff just outside the Canadiens blueline, Rollins was forced to return to the net. As soon as Kennedy won the draw, however, the Leafs goalie darted to the bench once again for the extra attacker. The puck was jammed against the boards and the play whistled dead for a faceoff in the Habs' end with just 39 seconds remaining.

Ted Kennedy explained the high drama that was building up to the all-important draw:

> The fellow who is coming in to face off with me for the Canadiens is Billy Reay. He's one guy I'd had a lot of trouble getting the draw from. I'll be a son of a gun, but [Montreal coach] Dick Irvin pulls Reay out and puts Elmer Lach in. I hadn't had all that much trouble with Elmer Lach. I thought, "I've got a chance!"

As one of the best faceoff men in the league, Kennedy had more than a chance. Referee Bill Chadwick dropped the puck, and Kennedy got it back cleanly to Max Bentley on the point. As Kennedy remembered, "Lach disentangled himself with me and rushed right out to Bentley. Max gave him the double shuffle, walked in about three strides, and let fly." The shot hit a leg in the sea of bodies that was screening Gerry McNeil.

Sid Smith recalled the chaos that ensued: "The puck popped down beside me and I shot it through. I could see it hit the post and I thought, 'Oh my God, it didn't go in!' And then all of a sudden, the light went on. It deflected across to Sloanie, who was on the right side, and he batted it in. That saved our bacon right there!"

Tod Sloan's goal, with 32 seconds left, tied the game at two. The Gardens faithful went wild. Programs were launched onto the ice in a spontaneous show of appreciation, and it took several minutes to clear the ice of the debris. As the maintenance crew swept the ice surface, the band began to play. Then a chant began, slowly at first, but growing stronger each time: "We want the Cup! We want the Cup!" Only moments earlier, the Toronto fans had resigned themselves to the reality of a Game Six in Montreal. Now, everyone realized that the Leafs could very well claim the Cup at home that very night.

For an impossible fifth straight game, Toronto and Montreal were heading to extra time. Yet this was Saturday night, and that 11:45 P.M. curfew once again loomed.

The Leafs took command early in overtime. The ever-dangerous Rocket Richard, however, captured the puck, shook away his defenders, and broke in all alone on Rollins. Deking the Leaf netminder out of position, he was about to tuck the puck into the empty net when Bill Barilko once again dove across and deflected the puck away. For the second time in the series, Barilko had robbed Richard, and in so doing, had resurrected the hopes of the city.

Later, after the Maple Leafs had worked the puck over Montreal's blueline, Harry Watson collected the rolling puck and passed it across the front of the net to Howie Meeker. Meeker initially couldn't handle the pass, but corralled it and went in behind the Canadiens goal. He tried to tuck the puck past Gerry McNeil on a wraparound, and McNeil seemed to slip as he went to guard the right post. Meeker pulled the puck back and was chased behind the net by Montreal defenceman Tom Johnson. In front of the net, Harry Watson was perched, watched closely by Butch Bouchard. Meeker tried to get the puck to Watson, who swung at the pass, but it glanced off Bouchard's skate and bounced out to the faceoff circle to the right of McNeil.

What happened next would become one of the most legendary plays in Maple Leafs history. This was the moment that Bill Barilko chose to gamble. He had been warned by Coach Primeau on more than one occasion for being too much of a free spirit. As Ted Kennedy recalled:

> He could be coached, and for the most part, he did what he was supposed to do, but there were times when he'd break rank and do things on his own. Primeau was having a great deal of difficulty keeping him back in his defence position. It got to the point where he was saying, "Bill, when the puck is in their end, you've got to make sure you take up your position!" Shortly before that overtime goal, he said, "Bill, I'm going to get a big hook and I'm going to throw it out there when you're out of position."

Here, in overtime of Game Five, Barilko darted in from the blueline. As McNeil attempted to regain his feet, Barilko drilled the puck on his backhand as he sailed through the air and into Leaf mythology. The puck flew over the right shoulder of the helpless McNeil and crossed the line at 2:53 of the extra frame. It was 11:07 P.M. local time. Barilko had delivered the Stanley Cup to Toronto the Good with 38 minutes to spare.

Maple Leaf Gardens joyfully exploded. The team emptied the bench to celebrate, and Joe Primeau slid out onto the ice to join his players. Barilko ribbed his instructor: "You didn't want a hook on me that time, did you, Coach?" Primeau and the scorer of the Stanley Cup–winning goal then shared a hearty laugh.

It could, however, have ended in tears. "If you look at the famous photograph of the goal," Cal Gardner explained years later, "you'll see me skating in the direction of a Montreal player. It was the Rocket. Barilko had left his defence spot open. If he hadn't scored, the puck could easily have come out to Richard. I was just doing my job, putting a guard on Rocket Richard."

But the Rocket didn't get the puck, Barilko did score, and the Leafs had won their fourth Cup in the space of only five years to become the NHL's first bona fide dynasty.

The Stanley Cup was carried out and NHL president Clarence Campbell presented the trophy to Ted Kennedy. The Leafs captain said:

> First off, I want you all to show your appreciation to captain Butch Bouchard and his Canadiens, who went down fighting all the way. If any one person deserves credit more than any other, it's our coach, Joe Primeau! If you think it was tough for me to succeed Syl Apps as captain, think what a tough job it was for Joe to succeed a man like Hap Day as coach!

The crowd furiously roared its approval.

Primeau then took his turn addressing the fans: "It has been a wonderful season, and winning the Cup is a thrill I never dared to dream of. I've never had a finer bunch of fellows to work with." The Leafs coach had accomplished an incomparable feat as a coach. In addition to the two Memorial Cup championships and the Allan Cup, he had now coached a team to a Stanley Cup championship.

It had been, in truth, more than just a Stanley Cup win. The series had already begun to take on mythical status. "The cash customers couldn't have asked for any more in the way of thrills and drama than they got in these five evenly contested games," the *Hockey News* concluded. The most compelling chapter of the 1951 Stanley Cup championship, however, would be written a few weeks after that last fairy-tale goal.

STORM WARNING
1951–52 TO 1956–57

As the team and its city continued to revel in the recent Stanley Cup victory in the summer of 1951, few saw the storm that was fast approaching. Water would be a recurring theme for the good people of Toronto through the 1950s: a fateful fishing trip and a monstrous hurricane would, over the course of the decade, spawn profound consequences for Torontonians. At the same time, the Toronto Maple Leafs would, more often than not, struggle to negotiate the frozen waters of the NHL's rink pads.

MISSING

The tiny Fairchild 24, a four-seat plane, climbed skyward from the lake in Timmins on August 24, 1951. Its passengers – Dr. Henry Hudson, a Timmins dentist, and the Leafs' Stanley Cup hero, Bill Barilko – were setting off for one final fishing trip before the latter had to return for training camp. Despite his mother's cautions, Barilko and the dentist flew to Seal River, a desolate spot on the James Bay shoreline in northern Quebec, where they would reel in a large quantity of Arctic char. The trip was as fruitful as they had hoped, and the pair stopped in Waskaganish (formerly Fort Rupert) to refuel on their journey home. It was the last time the two men were seen alive.

The plane was expected back in Timmins on the night of Sunday, August 26. There, a group of friends waited for Bill at a going-away party in his honour until two in the morning before deciding that he had likely tried to get in another day of fishing. Likewise, Dr. Hudson's nurse cancelled Monday's appointments when the dentist didn't show up. By Tuesday, though, the story had broken wide open. The *Toronto Star's* front-page headline on August 28 read: BARILKO VANISHES IN NORTH.

The following day, RCAF crews and private planes scoured the area Hudson and Barilko's plane would likely have covered. By September 1, the flying armada had increased to 19 planes and 125 men. Despite the herculean effort, the search proved futile. There were no leads, no clues

to the disappearance. Weeks later, at the end of October, Conn Smythe posted a $10,000 reward for what most people believed would be a recovery, not a rescue mission.

Smythe's world had already been rocked that summer. Squib Walker, the Leafs' head scout, had died at his home in Fort William, Ontario. Then, on August 22, J.P. Bickell died. Bickell had been one of Smythe's closest friends and business partners. Smythe knew well that neither the Toronto Maple Leafs nor Maple Leaf Gardens would have existed without him. Yet, while the deaths of Walker and Bickell were hard on the Leafs' top boss, the disappearance of the likeable Barilko was particularly painful. Smythe held a fondness for the young lad whose improbable leap from hockey's netherworld to the big league had been so recently punctuated with a Stanley Cup–winning goal. There was now, it seemed, a grim addendum to that fairy tale.

Howie Meeker spoke candidly about the impact of Barilko's disappearance: "I can't begin to express how that accident affected our team. Billy was a great guy, a good friend, and a tremendously talented young player. He'd have been an all-star for sure."

Barilko's number 5 sweater hung in his empty stall in the Toronto dressing room. It symbolized the team's hope that he would soon be found. When training camp ended and there was still no word on Barilko, his equipment and sweater were quietly stored away. No Toronto Maple Leaf ever wore number 5 again.

ROYAL BLUE

The Leafs were set to open the 1951–52 season on October 13 against the Chicago Black Hawks. As it happened, Princess Elizabeth and her husband, Prince Philip Mountbatten, were in Toronto. There simply hadn't been enough time in the royals' itinerary to allow them to attend the home opener that evening, so in order to accommodate their schedule, a 15-minute exhibition game between the same two teams was played that afternoon.

In the fall of 1951, Princess Elizabeth, the future Queen of England, visited Toronto and attended a 15-minute exhibition contest between the Maple Leafs and the visiting Chicago Black Hawks. Here, Toronto captain Ted Kennedy welcomes the special guests as Conn Smythe looks on.

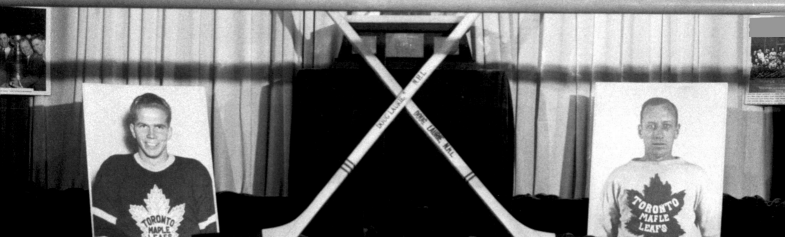

RETIRED SWEATER NUMBERS
TORONTO MAPLE LEAF
HOCKEY CLUB

The visit afforded the royals an opportunity to witness their first ice hockey game.

Princess Elizabeth and Prince Philip arrived at Maple Leaf Gardens and were escorted by Smythe and Ontario premier Leslie Frost through the main entrance of the arena to a box on the west side of the rink. The usual seats had been replaced with chairs more suited to royalty and the box itself was decorated with a giant Union Flag. The proceeds from the contest benefited the Crippled Children's Fund.

Once the game was underway, Princess Elizabeth asked Smythe for explanations on what was taking place. Smythe later relayed his impressions of the royal couple and their observations: "They both enjoyed the game tremendously. Prince Philip roared with laughter at the upsetting bodychecks and the way the eyes of Princess Elizabeth glowed as the players shot by her at full speed." The game ended in a scoreless tie, but Ted Kennedy called the game "the most intense 15 minutes of hockey ever played at Maple Leaf Gardens." Kennedy, who was called upon to meet the princess and the Duke of Edinburgh, might have been feeling the additional intensity. The captain had been instructed on proper protocol in greeting the royal consort and remembered his directives: "Don't speak unless they speak to me. I call them each 'Your Royal Highness.' I don't bow, just shake hands and bow my head slightly." Few, including the captain, could have imagined that the princess would become Queen Elizabeth II in the space of only a few months.

That same evening, the Hawks dumped the reigning Stanley Cup champions, 3–1, in the first real game of the new campaign. In a nice touch that stubbornly defied the facts at hand, the Leafs' official program for the evening listed Bill Barilko as number 5.

With the loss of Barilko hanging over Leafs Nation, fans needed something to hope for. One such hope was invested in a junior sensation named George Armstrong. Although he had played only a couple of games with the Leafs during the 1949–50 season, Armstrong was already being regarded as a future franchise player. The *Toronto Telegram*, for example, trumpeted that he was "hockey's answer to baseball's Mickey Mantle." Still, it was months before Armstrong saw his first game of the season.

In a game against Montreal on February 8, he lived up to the advanced billing. Playing on a line with Max Bentley, Armstrong fired a shot past Gerry McNeil for his first NHL goal, which happened to be the winner in a 3–2 Leafs victory. The hometown crowd gave him a huge ovation, and he earned the game's first star. While

it was an auspicious season debut, the rookie would manage only three goals in the 20 games he took part in that season.

The Leafs would have to wait for Armstrong to fully flower. At the same time, their netminder's faded bloom had begun to wither. Turk Broda had effectively retired at the conclusion of the previous season, and the Maple Leafs planned a Turk Broda Night for a December 22 game against the Bruins. The *Toronto Star* attested, "No other athlete of the present generation has managed to get quite the same grip on the affections of Canadian sports fans as the Turk." It may also be argued that no other athlete was quite as susceptible to the pranks and practical jokes of his teammates and the Toronto media.

Prior to the game against the Bruins, members of the media hosted a dinner to honour Turk. CJBC Radio's Dave Price was doing a gag broadcast when he was interrupted with an "urgent message." Price was supposedly informed that a six-day-old infant had been found abandoned. A collection plate went around the room, stuffed with many dollars. Price then asked, "Is there anyone in the room who has it in their heart to take this abandoned infant into their home? If so, please stand up." The unsuspecting Broda had been seated in a chair that had been wired with batteries. With the flip of a switch, Broda received an electric shock that forced him to leap to his feet. He was, of course, the only one in the room standing, so the infant was rushed into the room and placed in his arms. It was a piglet! Once again, the goaltender was able to provide Torontonians with much amusement.

As Broda made his way out on the ice on December 22, the Maple Leaf Gardens organist played "Turkey in the Straw." Broda was showered with gifts from admirers. He received a dining-room suite from Maple Leaf Gardens, a chesterfield suite from his teammates, a reclining chair from the Toronto sportswriters, a grandfather clock from the Turk Broda Fan Club, cash gifts from the Detroit Red Wings and Montreal Canadiens, a silver pitcher from the Boston Bruins, and various other items. Then, a gold-coloured car was driven out onto the ice surface, a gift from a local brewery. Inside were Turk's wife, Betty, and his daughters, Bonny, Betty, and Barbara. Lost in the excitement was the fact that the Leafs edged Boston, 3–2. Yet Leafs fans had not seen the last of their beloved keeper.

In the new year, the Leafs would be part of a new experiment. The Chicago Black Hawks, who had not been

The Toronto Maple Leafs have honoured several sweater numbers but have retired just two: number 5 for Bill Barilko and number 6 for Ace Bailey. Both had their careers prematurely cut short through tragedy.

drawing well, elected to schedule a few afternoon games. It proved to be a successful experiment. The largest crowd of the season showed up for the first-ever NHL afternoon game, played on January 20, 1952. The Leafs toppled Chicago, 3–1.

Later, a game between the Rangers and Leafs scheduled for February 6 was postponed due to the death of King George VI. The King had died in his sleep that morning, at the age of 56. In honour of Toronto's British links, the Leafs rescheduled the game.

The final game of the regular season was played on March 23 against Boston. Remarkably, Turk Broda came out of retirement to tend goal. It was Broda's first game of the season, and he played the first 30 minutes before Al Rollins took his place to finish the contest. The Bruins doubled Toronto, 4–2, in a game that had no impact on the standings for the Maple Leafs, who finished third with 74 points. The Detroit Red Wings were the elite of the league after collecting 100 points. Montreal was second, with 78 points.

Al Rollins had filled the Toronto goal admirably, finishing second to Terry Sawchuk for the Vézina with a 2.22 goals-against average. Sid Smith finished fifth in league scoring with 57 points, including 27 goals. Smith was named to the NHL's Second All-Star Team, along with teammate Jimmy Thomson, and was awarded the Lady Byng Trophy as the most gentlemanly player in the NHL that season. Ted Kennedy also finished in the top ten NHL scorers, with 52 points.

The playoffs opened with Toronto facing the Red Wings. Pundits were already predicting that the Maple Leafs' dynasty was about to come to a crashing end, while a new one in Detroit was about to begin.

The first game was a rowdy affair that set a record for penalties. Twenty-nine infractions were called against the two teams for a total of 112 minutes, and the game ended with the Red Wings shutting out Toronto, 3–0.

If the rough play of Game One was perhaps predictable, Game Two was full of surprises. Toronto shocked the hockey world by installing Turk Broda in goal. The *Star's* headline that day asked, CAN THE TURKEY GIVE OUR LEAFS THAT EXTRA ZIP? As it turned out, Broda very nearly stole a game for the Leafs, holding Detroit to just one goal. But that one goal was all the Red Wings needed as Terry Sawchuk blanked the Leafs.

Undaunted by the loss, the Maple Leafs came back with Broda in goal for Game Three. Unfortunately, the Red Wings exposed the aging netminder, and the rest of the Leafs, in a 6–2 thrashing. "If I'd had four or

five games under my belt, it might have been different," a perspiring Broda protested. Game Three marked the real end of the road for Broda. The *Toronto Star* hailed the longtime hero: "They should retire Turkey's sweater because, for our money, he's the number one Leaf of all time." The Red Wings completed the series sweep in Game Four with a 3–1 win.

Conn Smythe surmised that the Leafs missed Barilko. "With him gone, we just didn't have the punch last year. We were just a very ordinary hockey club. It's going to be a long time before we find someone to take his place. The old Barilko bounce is missing."

It certainly would be a long time before the Leafs got their missing "bounce" back. In fact, the Leafs' return to Stanley Cup glory would not occur until May 2, 1962. And just over a month after that championship, on June 6, the bodies of Dr. Henry Hudson and Bill Barilko were finally found. The fact that the Leafs were not able to win a Cup until roughly the same time as Barilko was found was – at least for Leafs Nation – proof positive that the two events were linked. The deeply mythologized nature of Barilko's disappearance and recovery remains central to the grand narrative of the Toronto Maple Leafs.

IN BLACK AND WHITE

Following the quick elimination from the playoffs in the spring of 1952, Conn Smythe and Hap Day conferred with coach Joe Primeau to discuss the state of the Maple Leafs. After four championships in five seasons, the Leafs had most recently been summarily dismissed by a far more powerful Detroit Red Wings team. Wholesale changes had to take place; the Maple Leafs were about to embark on a youth movement.

There were also changes coming to the team's veteran core. The Leafs obtained goaltender Harry Lumley, as well as Cal Gardner, Ray Hannigan, and Gus Mortson, from the Chicago Black Hawks in return for goaltender Al Rollins in September 1952. Rollins's time in Toronto had been difficult. In an interview with the *Hockey News,* Rollins admitted, "I was constantly reminded of the fact that I was replacing a fellow who'd been the favourite of the fans for 15 years. It wasn't easy, believe me!" Still, Smythe and the rest of the Leafs management agreed that Lumley was the kind of goalie who won games and sold tickets.

Toronto also wanted to introduce some of the young defensive talent that was chomping at the bit to get into the game. The Leafs made room for both Léo Boivin

and Tim Horton. The Leafs had long been in a quandary about what to do with Horton, who had seen some action with the team in March 1950. There was no doubt that he possessed great ability, but there were still some question marks. As early as 1947, a Leafs scout reported that Horton "seems to have something the matter with one of his eyes. Wears glasses. Seemed to have trouble taking passes on the ice." The Maple Leafs had nevertheless signed Horton and brought him to Toronto to play junior with St. Michael's College School in 1948. Two years later, he turned pro with the Leafs' AHL farm team, the Pittsburgh Hornets, where he honed his talent. The Leafs had faith that Joe Primeau, who had coached Horton in junior, could extract greatness out of the promising youngster.

At the same time, Toronto introduced several other players from whom they expected great things.

Gord Hannigan, Bob Hassard, and Ron Stewart all found spots on the roster, as did George Armstrong.

With such promising players in his stable, Smythe was very confident about the future of his team, saying, "I used to figure it took five years to build a championship team. I'll cut that down to three and say we might be there in two. Our future looks bright because we have the young players in our organization needed to put us back on top of the heap." His confidence was, as it happened, slightly misplaced.

Still, Conn Smythe was celebrating his 25th year with the franchise. To commemorate the milestone, the team feted him before the opening-night contest on October 11, 1952, and had him drop the ceremonial puck before the visiting Chicago Black Hawks faced off against the Leafs. In what was perhaps a sign of things to come, Toronto lost, 6–2.

Both Hall of Fame defencemen who wore the number 7, Tim Horton (left) and King Clancy (right) left indelible legacies through their fierce competitiveness.

Meanwhile, television was making great inroads. Several teams south of the border were already televising hockey games. In Canada, the Canadian Broadcasting Corporation began broadcasting in September 1952 with just two stations: CBFT in Montreal and CBLT in Toronto. Prime Minister Louis St. Laurent made a commitment to the Canadian people that the CBC would continue to expand television's reach throughout the country.

Hockey Night in Canada – the television show – made its English-language debut on November 1, 1952, airing a game between the hometown Toronto Maple Leafs and the visiting Boston Bruins. Foster Hewitt, who had been hockey's radio broadcaster, signed on at 9:30 P.M. This was well after the game had got underway, as there was concern – from Conn Smythe, for one – that if full games were shown, it would eliminate the need for fans to attend games in person. When hockey first debuted on Toronto television sets, it was 6:22 of the second period, and viewers looked on as Maple Leaf teammates congratulated Bob Hassard for having just scored a goal on Boston's Sugar Jim Henry. Eight minutes later, fans watched their fuzzy screens as Max Bentley scored to give Toronto a 2–0 lead. The Leafs went on to win in their Canadian television debut, 3–2.

In short order, *Hockey Night in Canada* became a national phenomenon. During the intermissions, live music was soon replaced with player interviews and primitive highlight reels. Incredibly, the television rights for these quasi-experimental games went for just $100 apiece.

In terms of the Leafs' performance, the youth movement had introduced some exciting new players to Toronto, but the team struggled badly. The *Star* suggested that goaltender Harry Lumley "could have sued a few of his mates for non-support the way they were messing around with the puck in their own end." Near season's end, Boston, Chicago, and Toronto were all within a point of one another for the final two playoff spots. The Maple Leafs had to rely on their enemies to get them into the postseason.

In the penultimate game of the regular season, the Leafs throttled the New York Rangers, 5–0. Detroit was up 3–1 on Chicago, which looked good for the Leafs, but the Hawks rebounded and took the game, 4–3. So for the Leafs to make the playoffs, they would have to beat Boston in their final game of the regular season and hope that the Rangers beat Chicago. While the Leafs held up their end of the bargain by beating the Bruins, 3–1, Chicago defeated the Rangers. Toronto was out of the postseason. The Leafs finished fifth, just two points shy of fourth-place Chicago. The *Star* eulogized derisively that the Leafs were

"the most prosperous club in the league with the most money in the till for the regular season, and a record four Stanley Cups in the last six Aprils. And they've missed the profitable playoffs only twice since the Gardens were opened. That's why any tears which are shed outside Toronto are likely to be crocodile tears." It was an apt, if cynical sentiment that would be revisited many, many times by the Toronto media.

GOING UNDERGROUND

Immediately following the disappointment of missing the 1953 playoffs, Joe Primeau resigned as coach of the Maple Leafs in order to focus on his building block company. The next day, Conn Smythe announced that Primeau's former teammate, King Clancy, had been hired to coach the Leafs. He had led the Pittsburgh Hornets, Toronto's AHL affiliate, to the Calder Cup championship in 1951–52 and had almost reprised that victory the following season, but the Hornets lost in Game Seven of the final.

The Leafs were still hopeful that the youth movement would pay off. Despite the promise of stardom bestowed upon him as a junior, it had taken George Armstrong two seasons to establish himself as an NHL player. Armstrong was nevertheless presented with the celebrated number 10 by Syl Apps, the man who had made it famous for the Maple Leafs. While there may have been some naysayers, Armstrong – at least in the eyes of the Leafs' top brass – had arrived.

On October 10, 1953, opening night of the season for the Maple Leafs, a pregame ceremony was held to honour Ted Kennedy, the inaugural recipient of the J.P. Bickell Memorial Award. The trophy, which honoured the late Gardens chairman, was awarded at the discretion of the Maple Leafs board of directors to someone who demonstrated a tremendous feat, a season of spectacular play, or remarkable service over a number of years. Kennedy was summoned to centre ice, where the $10,000 Bickell trophy was on display. As a keepsake, Kennedy received a miniature 14-karat gold replica valued at $500. That evening, the Leafs outscored Chicago, 6–2. It was the first opening night win for Toronto since 1944–45.

In what would be another transition year, the Leafs had to make more changes. Some of these moves, though, were not necessarily by design. Late in the previous season, Howie Meeker had taken a hard hit into the boards in a game against the Bruins in Boston and badly injured his back. "When I took off my skates at the end of that season, I had a feeling I was pretty well done playing

the game for a living," Meeker recalled. He played the last game of his eight-season NHL career on November 29, a 2–1 loss to Boston.

Still, the Leafs finished third with 78 points, well behind league-leading Detroit, which had 88. And with 13 shut-outs and a goals-against average of 1.86, Harry Lumley was awarded the Vézina Trophy. Lumley was also named to the NHL's First All-Star Team. As for Toronto's skaters, Tim Horton and Ted Kennedy were selected to the Second All-Star Team. Sid Smith and Harry Watson were the team's only 20-goal scorers, with 22 and 21, respectively, while Tod Sloan led the team in scoring with 43 points.

While the Leafs prepared for the playoffs, thousands of Torontonians awaited their chance to climb down into the city's new subterranean rapid-transit line. On March 30, 1954, Canada's first subway line, stretching 7.4 kilometres from Yonge Street and Eglinton Avenue to Union Station, was officially opened by Premier Leslie Frost and Toronto mayor Allan Lamport. The subway changed forever the way Torontonians got around the city. It also affected the way thousands of Leafs fans made their

way to the game. Throngs of hockey enthusiasts could now choose to ride the subway to College Station and walk east on Carlton Street to Maple Leaf Gardens.

Just days before the subway opened, the Leafs were poised to once again square off against the Red Wings in the semifinals. In what was perhaps an example of games-manship, Smythe told reporters, "We haven't got much chance. They've got too many guns for us." Detroit jour-nalists were also quick to point out that Toronto hadn't won a game at the Olympia since November 2, 1952. Unfortunately for the Leafs, that pattern didn't change with the opening game, in which Terry Sawchuk and the Red Wings blanked Toronto, 5–0. But the Leafs sprang back in Game Two with a 3–2 win.

Detroit took Games Three and Four in Toronto by 3–1 and 2–1 scores. The *Globe and Mail* spoke to a fluke goal in Game Four that effectively killed off any hope the Blue and White might have had: "A misguided missile, fired in the waning minutes of a torrid battle, buried Maple Leafs' Stanley Cup chances lower than the new subway." The series returned to the Motor City for Game Five.

Three of the franchise's greatest captains: (from left to right) Syl Apps, Ted Kennedy, and George Armstrong. Kennedy is pointing to the number 10 that, having been worn by Apps, was presented to Armstrong in 1953.

Among the many strengths of the Maple Leafs during their first dynasty years was their defence. Pictured from left to right: Bill Barilko, Jimmy Thomson, Gus Mortson, and Wally Stanowski listen to coach Hap Day, once a terrific defenceman himself.

Harry Watson had been assigned the role of shadowing Gordie Howe and had done a fine job in the first four games, but Howe stepped out in the fifth game by scoring two goals, the first just nine seconds in. At the end of regulation, the teams were locked at three apiece. The same was true at the end of the first overtime. Then, at 1:01 of the second overtime, Ted Lindsay scored the goal that ended Toronto's hopes.

A disheartened Kennedy threatened to retire in order to devote his attention to Canada Building Materials, where he had worked during the previous five summers. Still, time is the great healer, and the captain was back in uniform to start the 1954–55 season.

LIKE A HURRICANE

Hurricane Hazel had taken over 1,000 lives in Haiti before the Category 4 hurricane hit the Carolinas. From there, and after killing 95 Americans, Hazel made its way to Toronto, where it would claim another 81 souls. Hazel was expected to dissipate when it crossed the border; it didn't. Instead, Toronto's skyline on October 15, 1954, portended only a storm that was still to rage. Hazel linked arms with a cold front, and winds gusted at 110 kilometres per hour. In the space of only 48 hours, 285 millimetres of rain fell, and the banks of the rivers and streams surrounding the Greater Toronto Area were overwhelmed. Byways, streets, and highways were washed out and rendered unpassable. Over 1,800 Toronto residents were left homeless.

There was also an enormous financial cost: $135 million in damage, or well over $1 billion in today's currency. The army was brought in to help with the relief effort, and a special relief fund collected over $5 million for the cause. Many of the Leafs players personally contributed to the fund, including captain Ted Kennedy, who, in an impromptu effort in the Leafs dressing room, passed the hat around to players, coaches, and locker-room staff. The hurricane had rattled the emotions of the city.

Meanwhile, Conn Smythe, feeling a little rattled himself, resigned as general manager. It was a role Smythe had held since the team became the Maple Leafs in 1927. "You're under a constant nervous strain in this hockey business. It's too much for me," Smythe acknowledged. "What really made up my mind was that my powers as a hockey man were failing."

While Smythe stayed on as team president – and would, in truth, remain very much involved in the day-to-day operation of the team – the general manager's portfolio was ostensibly handed over to Hap Day.

There had been changes in the roster, too. Fern Flaman was traded to Boston, while Danny Lewicki was dealt to New York. Smythe predicted that the Leafs would finish fourth in 1954–55, but he warned that players such as George Armstrong, Léo Boivin, Gord Hannigan, Tim Horton, Jim Morrison, and Ron Stewart had better get going or "they'll flunk out."

The season started in Detroit, where the Red Wings, who had been unbeaten in 17 home openers, kept their string alive by edging Toronto, 2–1. The home opener, against the Chicago Black Hawks, ended in a 3–3 tie. Marilyn Bell, who had swum across Lake Ontario from Niagara-on-the-Lake to Toronto in September 1954, was on hand to drop the ceremonial first puck.

On November 14, the Leafs were in Boston when they bore witness to the introduction of "a machine which cleans, shaves and resurfaces the ice between periods. It looks like a small locomotive and costs $5,000." It was the first NHL appearance of the Zamboni. Toronto beat Boston, 3–1, on the highly manicured ice sheet.

The Maple Leafs were the hottest team in the league at that point, having gone without a loss in nine games. That stretch, however, ended on November 18, when Jean Béliveau scored with just 14 seconds left in the game to give Montreal a 5–4 win. But after the Leafs started the season red hot, their fortunes withered after the turn of the calendar. Through January, Toronto won four, lost six, and tied five. In March, the Leafs set a NHL record for ties in a season, with 22.

That same month, on March 12, the Maple Leafs lost one of their key players – and with him, any real hope of a meaningful playoff run. As he was making a dash up the ice, defenceman Tim Horton crossed the Rangers blueline at full speed with his head down. There, Bill Gadsby delivered a devastating bodycheck that instantly ended Horton's season. Gadsby's shoulder shattered Horton's jaw, and as he crumpled to the ice his leg buckled beneath him

and snapped just above the ankle. While he regretted that his check had caused an injury, Gadsby blithely called it the best check he had ever thrown.

There was doubt as to whether Horton would ever be able to come back from such an extensive injury. Yet he displayed what would become his trademark stoicism. Dr. Hugh Smythe, team doctor and son of Conn, remarked that "he must have been suffering terrible pain, but there wasn't a peep out of him."

Horton's jaw was wired shut for a month, and doctors had to extract a tooth so he could insert a straw to drink his meals. His leg was in a cast for almost four months. It would take the defenceman two seasons to recover fully.

As the season wound down, a battle for the Vézina Trophy was underway. Toronto's Harry Lumley had a two-goal lead over Detroit's Terry Sawchuk going into the final game of the season. Toronto lost the game to the Rangers, 3–2. Meanwhile, the Red Wings blasted Montreal, 6–0. In the end, Sawchuk secured the trophy over Lumley by a single goal.

Despite being beaten out for the Vézina, Lumley was named to the NHL's First All-Star Team. He was joined by Sid Smith, who finished eighth in scoring, with 33 goals and 54 points. Smith also claimed the Lady Byng Trophy as the league's most gentlemanly player. Ted Kennedy, playing in what he claimed to be his final season, finished second in scoring on the Leafs, with 52 points, and was awarded the Hart Trophy as the league's most valuable player. The team finished third and had to face the first-place Detroit Red Wings in the semifinal.

The series opened in Detroit, where the Red Wings crushed the Leafs, 7–4. Game Two was tighter, although Detroit still won, 2–1. Jim Thomson and Ted Lindsay, who had been teammates in junior, feuded throughout the game. At one point, the Leaf defenceman earned a double minor by grabbing Lindsay's stick and throwing it down an exit passageway.

The semifinal shifted to Maple Leaf Gardens, but unfortunately for Toronto, the Red Wings edged the Leafs, 2–1, to take a commanding 3–0 grip on the series. Detroit then blanked Toronto, 3–0, in Game Four to sweep the Leafs and move on to meet Montreal in the Stanley Cup final. It was the 13th straight win for the Red Wings. At game's end, Ted Kennedy peeled off his equipment slowly, believing that he had played his final game in the National Hockey League. But the Toronto faithful had not seen the last of Teeder.

YOUTH MOVEMENT

The gloom of Barilko – whose body had not yet been found – still hung over Leafs Nation. The decade had been, after all, dismal to that point. Since winning the Stanley Cup in 1951, the Leafs had not finished higher than third place. And in the three seasons, Toronto had not made it past the semifinal round.

Once again, the Leafs looked to younger players to cure the team's ills. Earl Balfour, Billy Harris, Gerry James, and Marc Reaume were among the young guns that would see some time with the Leafs throughout the year. At the other end of the spectrum were the demotion of Joe Klukay to the Pittsburgh Hornets and, of course, the retirement of captain Ted Kennedy.

Kennedy was just 29 years old, but after pouring heart and soul into the game, he decided that the time had come to hang up his skates. The captain was pragmatic: "I've got a wonderful wife, a wonderful three-year-old son Mark, a horse, a Doberman pinscher, my home and a job that I really like." Kennedy was ready to move into full-time employment with Canada Building Materials.

The Kennedy-less Leafs travelled to Montreal for a 2–0 loss in the 1955–56 season opener. The home opener was against the Red Wings. Prior to the game, Colonel W.A.H. MacBrien, the chairman of the Toronto Maple Leafs board, presented Ted Kennedy with the J.P. Bickell Memorial Award to commemorate his importance to the franchise. Then, NHL president Clarence Campbell presented Kennedy with the Hart Trophy. The Leafs did their former leader proud and beat the Wings, 4–2.

With Kennedy retired, Sid Smith had been named the new captain of the Leafs. Still, after leading the team in scoring the season before, Smith was off his game. In fact, the captain was benched from time to time because of his one-dimensional play. And general manager Hap Day and coach King Clancy wanted an altogether tougher team, so they called up Jack Bionda, Ron Hurst, and Gerry James. Hurst's entry into the NHL in November 1955 was an inauspicious one, as he recalled:

> The first time I wore the Maple Leafs sweater was in New York. I had just joined the club from the Pittsburgh Hornets, I hadn't been on the ice yet. Sitting beside me was George Armstrong. In those days, you didn't have the glass. One of the New York defenceman fired the puck out of the zone. George ducked and the puck hit me in the head and cut me for 12 stitches, so my first time on the ice was with a towel held against my head, skating across the ice to get stitched up.

Gerry James actually starred in two professional sports. He played football with his hometown Winnipeg Blue Bombers of the Canadian Football League (CFL) from 1952 to 1963. The Canadian Football Hall of Famer was twice voted the CFL's Most Outstanding Canadian, and his Blue Bombers went to the Grey Cup game six times, winning four championships. James joined the Leafs in December 1955, and Hap Day said of his role with the Leafs, "Maybe Gerry isn't the smoothest guy in the world, but he doesn't skate away from anybody, either. We can stand some guys like that around here. He makes the prowlers respect Toronto property."

Meanwhile, the Leafs had to temporarily replace their steadfast goaltender, Harry Lumley, who had pulled a thigh muscle while making a save in a game against Detroit. As it turned out, Lumley would miss two weeks. There was still, however, the matter of the final 13 minutes of play in that game with the Wings.

The Leafs' spare keeper, Gil Mayer, was in Pittsburgh and would not be available until Toronto's next game. At this time, it was the responsibility of the home team to have a standby goaltender on hand in case of emergency. Therefore, the Red Wings' assistant trainer, Ross "Lefty" Wilson, was chosen to replace Lumley for the remainder of the game. Having a trainer serve as a practice goaltender was not an unusual situation, and in fact, Wilson had played goal in the Toronto Mercantile Hockey League for a few years, so he knew his way around a net. What was ironic, however, was that Wilson hated the Leafs, and had been fined for excessive heckling just a few years earlier. Still, duty was duty, and Wilson was called upon to don the pads and the jersey of his least favourite NHL team and fend off shots from the team that employed him. And he did so with integrity. While the Red Wings did prevail over the Leafs, 4–1, Lefty Wilson kept Toronto in the game, stopping all nine shots he faced.

Mayer arrived in time to tend goal while Lumley was on the disabled list, but the Leafs struggled and won only one of the next six games. Drastic times called for drastic measures, and Hap Day made some severe moves. First, he benched captain Sid Smith as well as Tim Horton. Then, he replaced Mayer in goal with Ed Chadwick, who was enjoying a great season with the Winnipeg Warriors, Toronto's WHL affiliate. Chadwick came up with a starring performance as the Leafs tied the league-leading Montreal Canadiens, 1–1, on February 8, 1956. Chadwick played five games through February, allowing just three goals and collecting two shutouts before Lumley's return.

Lumley and company had been booed by the Leafs faithful while the team was stuck in last place in December. Yet, by March, Toronto was competing for a playoff berth. After a 1–1 draw with Chicago on March 17, Toronto was tied with Boston for the fourth and final playoff spot with only one game left to play. The Bruins lost, 3–2, at home to Chicago, while the Leafs defeated the Red Wings, 2–0, in Detroit. The victory, however, came at a cost: Tod Sloan, Toronto's leading scorer, was belted with a bodycheck by Detroit rookie Larry Hillman and was carried off the ice on a stretcher. It was unlikely that Sloan would return to the Leafs roster for any playoff games that the team might be involved in. Nevertheless, Toronto secured fourth place and a trip to the postseason with a modest 61 points. Montreal, which had dominated the league, had finished first, with 100 points. Detroit was second, with 76, and New York was third, with 74. The injured Tod Sloan finished fifth in NHL scoring with 66 points and was voted onto the NHL's Second All-Star Team.

The Leafs met Detroit in the first round of the playoffs. The first game, played in Detroit, saw Toronto carry a two-goal lead into the third period after playing an outstanding 40 minutes of hockey. In less than 60 seconds, however, it all went asunder. In that minute, Toronto surrendered goals to Johnny Bucyk and Alex Delvecchio. Shortly afterwards, the Red Wings scored again to win the game, 3–2. Remarkably, a helmet-sporting Tod Sloan played, and maintained that he felt no ill effects of his injury. The Wings also won Game Two, by a 3–1 score. It was an extremely physical game. Sloan was hit hard by Gordie Howe in the third period and fractured his shoulder. Now the seemingly durable centre was definitely out of the playoffs.

The series shifted to Toronto for Game Three. Two local newspapers received a call that day stating that a man with a gun was going to shoot Gordie Howe and Ted Lindsay during the game. The Wings were notified at the hotel in Hamilton, Ontario, where they were staying, and extra protection was added at Maple Leaf Gardens as a precaution. On the ice, Toronto took an early lead, and by the halfway point of the third period led the Wings, 4–2. But then Howe scored at 9:11 and Lindsay tied the game a few minutes later. At 4:22 of overtime, Lindsay potted the winning goal. After being congratulated by his teammates, Lindsay skated to centre ice, bowed to the Toronto fans, and then raised his stick to his shoulder, shotgun-style, and pretended to spray bullets at the crowd. "Terrible Ted," it seemed, was not so easily frightened.

Game Four went much better for Toronto. Tim Horton returned to the lineup to shake things up, and Toronto earned a stay of execution with a 2–0 win. Harry Lumley, the hero of Game Four, was given a standing ovation as he left the ice, but was still seething over the criticism that had been levelled at him throughout the series. Lumley refused to talk to reporters after the game, and there was some speculation that he had played his final game at Maple Leaf Gardens for Toronto.

Regardless of where Lumley's career was headed, Game Five in Detroit was the Leafs' final game of the postseason. While it was close, the Red Wings skated away with a 3–1 victory.

The Leafs had once again been eliminated by Detroit. But there was a sense of hope in Toronto. The *Star* spoke to the promise of the young buds that had yet to flower: "There was more youth than you'd find at a junior prom." It was a question of how long it would take for the future to arrive.

POWER IN A UNION

Following the 1955–56 season, coach King Clancy was promoted to assistant general manager. Replacing him behind the bench was Howie Meeker, who had coached Toronto's AHL affiliate in Pittsburgh to a Calder Cup championship in 1955 after retiring as a player. "Frankly, I wasn't such a hot coach although I did have a good way with my players," Clancy said of his time behind the Leafs' bench. "I enjoyed the work to a certain extent but it wasn't as pleasurable as playing or refereeing. I was too emotional and actually worried myself sick at times. I never did coach a Stanley Cup winner. I wished I could have."

Unsurprisingly, the Maple Leafs sent Harry Lumley – the official scapegoat of the 1955–56 season – and Eric Nesterenko to the Chicago Black Hawks for $40,000.

Hap Day announced that the Leafs would carry just 16 players on the team, including their goaltender. This meant that several prospects would be mired for the entire season with Rochester in the AHL, Winnipeg in the WHL, or the junior Marlboros. Despite Day's policy, several young players still managed to emerge.

Goaltender Ed Chadwick, for example, had been nothing short of spectacular in his five-game stint filling in for Harry Lumley the previous February. As such, Chadwick earned his spot in the Leafs crease. Likewise, Marlboro graduate Bob Baun, with his thundering bodychecks, had caught the attention of management, as did Bob Pulford. The latter recalled his arrival in Toronto:

When you grow up in a city like Toronto, it is a special honour to play here with the wonderful fans. In order to win, you've got to play to win, and that's the only way I knew. It was a special time. My hockey career was exciting, the Stanley Cups were an irreplaceable time, and the team members have also always been my friends. [Playing for the Toronto Maple Leafs] is the greatest thing that will ever happen to a Canadian kid.

Bob Baun
PLAYER
1957–67; 1970–73

Harry Lumley joined the Maple Leafs in 1952–53. During his four seasons in Toronto, he was named to the First All-Star Team twice (1953–54 and 1954–55). In 1953–54, he won the Vézina Trophy with a goals-against average of 1.83. That season, he also collected 13 shutouts.

The night before I left for my first Leafs camp, my brother told me, "Remember, when you go out there, you have no friends." It was probably the best advice I ever had, because the first shift at training camp, we just started to scrimmage and I caught George Armstrong with a good bodycheck. Before the shift was over, I had cut Hugh Bolton for 12 stitches. I wasn't a tough guy, but I went there trying to make the team, and I think I made the hockey team on that first shift.

Pulford played on a line with the Cullen brothers. Brian centred the dynamic trio, while brother Barry played right wing, leaving Pulford on the left side. The Cullens had an incredible rapport. "When Barry gets a cold, Brian does the sneezing," the *Star* joked. And in spite of making the leap directly from junior, Bob Pulford was the best left winger at training camp. Together, the trio made a quick and profound impression on Leafs management.

The 1956–57 season opened in Boston with a 4–4 tie against the Bruins. Prior to the game, teammates elected Jimmy Thomson as the Leafs' new captain, replacing Sid Smith, whose production had diminished considerably from his 33-goal season in 1954–55. Toronto's home opener came two nights later. It was a homecoming for the 1932 Stanley Cup champions, and retired players came from all over North America for the reunion. The players joked and caught up, but lamented that their coach, Dick Irvin, who was battling cancer, was not able to join the fun. Also absent was goaltender Lorne Chabot, who had died in 1946. His son, Lorne Chabot Jr., was on hand and dropped the ceremonial faceoff on behalf of the team. Detroit spoiled the reunion by beating the current Leafs, 4–1.

Despite the stumble in the home opener, the young Leafs were on fire through the first month of the season. Toronto won four, tied four, and lost just once. There were, however, a few cracks in the veneer. Tim Horton was benched for several periods for inconsistent play. The team repeatedly threatened to send former captain Sid Smith to Pittsburgh. And injuries started to pile up. George Armstrong missed 16 games, Tod Sloan was out 17 games, and on October 25, Hugh Bolton broke his leg in a game against the Canadiens. The beleaguered Bolton had already suffered through mononucleosis and a broken jaw in consecutive seasons, before finally earning a permanent role on the blueline in 1954–55. The broken leg ended Bolton's NHL career.

The bottom truly fell out of the season in November. Coach Meeker shuffled the deck as best he could – Ron Stewart was asked to play defence, Tim Horton was moved to the wing, and various wingers took their place at centre – trying to patch the holes and spark something on the team. It was all for naught. In desperation, Hap Day persuaded the retired Ted Kennedy to attempt a comeback. Teeder agreed to risk his reputation if the Leafs felt it would help the team, but first, he had to get in game shape. Bobby Baun recalled how he skated with Kennedy every day at Lakeshore Lions Arena in Etobicoke, calling it "a wonderful learning experience. His work ethic was incredible, and at his age, and having been away for a year, you can believe it was hard work. His determination to come back really inspired me." Still, Kennedy was reticent and wondered what effect he might have on the team: "I still figured I wasn't the answer to the Leafs' problems. I'm not sorry I tried, but I never did feel I was the solution."

Kennedy's return was met with great enthusiasm by most, excepting Stafford Smythe, Conn's son, who was the general manager of the junior Toronto Marlboros. In Stafford's view, Day's decision to bring Kennedy out of retirement meant one less available spot for one of his Marlies.

Nevertheless, on January 6, 1957, Teeder Kennedy skated out with the Maple Leafs to face the Detroit Red Wings. Kennedy had agreed to a three-game tryout, with the caveat that both sides had to agree that it was a worthwhile pursuit for him to continue. While the Red Wings edged Toronto, 2–1, Kennedy had played well, although he blamed himself for allowing Johnny Bucyk to score the winning goal. Later, following a 2–1 game against the Montreal Canadiens in which the Leafs lost with just six seconds remaining, Kennedy agreed to play for the remainder of the season. With a touch of class, Jimmy Thomson surrendered the captaincy, deferring to Kennedy's leadership.

Already eliminated from postseason play, the Toronto Maple Leafs exploded with a 14–1 triumph over the Rangers on March 16, 1957. While the Leafs had missed the playoffs for the first time since 1952–53, the Rangers had already clinched a playoff berth and were never really in the game. Every Maple Leafs player except Thomson and goalie Ed Chadwick earned at least one point. Ted Kennedy collected four assists in the game. The game remains the Leafs' greatest margin of victory and the 14 goals are the most the team has ever scored in a single game.

HURRICONN

One historic day was followed by another: on March 17, Conn Smythe's bizarre public condemnation of his team, general manager, and coach drastically altered the trajectory of the franchise. While the team was arriving in New York for a game against the Rangers, Smythe flew up from Florida to meet them. Toronto newspaper reporters were also brought to New York by the Maple Leafs for what would be a momentous announcement.

Seated anxiously in the conference room of the Commodore Hotel, the assembled group hushed when Smythe limped up to the podium and welcomed them all to the media conference:

> I am making it doubly clear, this, which I consider a year of failure, is my complete responsibility. There are five principal factors, in my opinion, that have influenced the club this year and also in the future: number one is the President; number two is the manager; number three is the Players' Association; number four is the quality of team personnel; and number five is the operation of the club.

Hap Day and Howie Meeker sat grim-faced while their boss spoke. The first volley came when Smythe said he did not know whether Hap Day was available to return to the Maple Leafs the next season. To rub salt into the wound, he publicly questioned his general manager's strategy for the team: "We have stressed defensive and not offensive. Our system may be outdated. We have a Spartan system and we may be out of date."

Smythe was the only person who spoke that day, and he refused to take questions.

After picking their jaws up from the floor, the Toronto reporters ran to write their stories. While Smythe might have owned the blame for the failure of the 1956–57 campaign, one newspaper reporter pragmatically predicted how it might all play out:

Conn Smythe, the little pistol of Maple Leaf Gardens, fired what sounded like lethal shots in the breasts of his crewcut lieutenant, Howie Meeker, and the practically thatchless second-in-command, Hap Day. Smythe may refute the suggestion he has even hinted that the heads of Day and Meeker are on the block. He can point out how he included the President's job among the ones which he placed in jeopardy. But that's not such a startling statement when you examine it closely. You can't quite picture the board of directors putting the "zingo" on Smythe. He and his family are the biggest shareholders in Maple Leaf Gardens. Smythe built the Gardens. He has made it one of the most successful sports projects in North America. So, even if he confesses a season of failure, it's reasonable to expect that he will escape the rope. The fate of Day and Meeker will depend on what Smythe advises the board to do. If you judge by what happened here, you are forced to conclude – no matter how much you admire Day and Meeker – that it's the end of the line.

Hap Day was equal measures flabbergasted and wounded: "I feel like a corpse that has been dismembered in public. Any decision I reach will be given directly to Mr. Smythe." Howie Meeker gave little away: "I've been with the Leafs for 11 years. I'm still with them and will be until they tell me otherwise."

Certainly, Conn Smythe had been pondering a succession plan for the Toronto Maple Leafs for some time. He had been heavily pressured by his son Stafford to relinquish management of the team. Stafford argued that the club's fortunes would turn around if there were a new, more youthful attitude in management. Stafford Smythe had been around hockey all of his life, and Conn respected his son's opinion. It was Stafford who had convinced his father that the Toronto area should be supplying more players to the Maple Leafs and helped set up a highly successful tiered farm system that went from junior all the way down to peewee. The junior Marlboros, with Stafford as manager, had won the Memorial Cup in both 1955 and 1956.

While this move to harvest Toronto's talent was a sound plan, there was still a lot to figure out. If Stafford was indeed going to succeed Conn as top boss, the latter would have to step away from the presidency. Simply put, Stafford couldn't and wouldn't work with his father.

The blueprint for the future of the Blue and White was slowly being revealed, and many were able to roughly anticipate how it might unfold: Conn would soon step away from the presidency; Stafford would step in and release Hap Day, thus relieving Conn of the grim business of having to fire his longtime, faithful employee. Stafford would also likely fire Meeker and bring in his own coach – almost certainly Turk Broda, who had coached the championship Marlboros under Stafford.

There was, however, a lot of water yet to pass under the bridge. And in the meantime, a general sense of doom prevailed in Leafland. On March 20, Sid Smith quit the team. The former All-Star had endured incredible heat over the previous two seasons and his play had been routinely questioned.

That night, the Leafs played the Montreal Canadiens. Rabble-rouser Jimmy Thomson and the aging veteran Ted Kennedy were both healthy scratches for the game, but a young winger named Frank Mahovlich was promoted from the St. Michael's Majors for a three-game amateur tryout. Mahovlich was a breath of fresh air in the stale atmosphere of a team folding up.

The next day, Jim Thomson quit. He freely expressed his own take on the situation:

I would refuse a contract for next season if offered one by the Leafs. It would be impossible for me to play with a club that has questioned my loyalty. At no time have I been disloyal to the team. I have given them my best for 12 seasons. My relationship with the club has always been first class, and I'm sorry to leave under such strained circumstances.

Ted Kennedy realized that he had come to the end of the line, and retired, for good this time. Before the final game of the season, Conn Smythe announced that George Armstrong would be the new captain of the Toronto Maple Leafs. Smythe also claimed that the team would abandon the clutch-and-grab system of Hap Day in favour of a more freewheeling brand of hockey. As if on cue, Frank Mahovlich scored his first NHL goal, the sole tally in a 4–1 loss to Detroit.

Neither Conn nor Stafford Smythe had to fire Hap Day. The latter submitted his resignation to Smythe two days after the Leafs' final game of the season. "It was the first time in my years with the Leafs that I had been asked a question about my so-called availability," Day said, not trying to conceal his disappointment. "The inference I took from that press conference was that I was walking the plank."

It was a sad conclusion to what had otherwise been a mutually agreeable relationship. When Smythe and

his consortium purchased the Toronto St. Patricks in 1927, Day was one of the handful of players that Smythe retained. In fact, Day became captain of the Maple Leafs in 1927–28, and served in that role until the end of the 1936–37 season. Away from the rink, Day was also a partner in Smythe's sand and gravel business. After retiring as a player, Day had returned to the Maple Leafs as coach and led his team to five Stanley Cup championships in ten seasons. After he was promoted to assistant general manager in 1950, his name was engraved on the Stanley Cup once again in 1951.

Still, the Leafs' future would, in actuality, be a throwback to its past. Once again, kids who had grown up on the streets of Toronto, such as Bob Baun, Carl Brewer, and Brian Conacher, or those who had at least honed their skills in the Queen City, such as Bob Nevin, Jim Pappin, and Bob Pulford, would graduate through the Toronto-centric system and form the core around which the franchise's most glorious era would develop. It was the 1930s all over again: the nimbus clouds were slowly shifting and the heavy rains were dissipating. Bill Barilko would not remain unfound for much longer, and several local boys were eager to "make good" and be a credit to their city.

Frank Mahovlich was coveted by several NHL teams as a youngster, but it was the Toronto Maple Leafs who earned the skilled forward's allegiance. He would score 20 goals and 36 points in 1957–58, earning the Calder Trophy as the league's best rookie.

SH-BOOM
1957–58 TO 1959–60

In the 1950s, several players would graduate to big-time Toronto hockey after having played at St. Michael's College School, including Tim Horton, Red Kelly, and Frank Mahovlich. At this same time, St. Michael's Choir School was having an effect on the city's pop culture. A vocal quartet formed within the school had hit the big time in the mid–1950s. The Toronto foursome called themselves the Crew Cuts (paying homage to the haircut of the same name) and topped the hit parade in 1954 with "Sh-Boom," a cover of a song by the American doo-wop group The Chords.

With a roster littered with eager youngsters, the Maple Leafs, picking up on the latest rage, announced the team slogan for the 1956–57 season: "Rock 'n' roll with Howie Meeker and the Crew Cuts." Yet, the team's on-ice performance was not lighting up any charts. Instead, the Leafs clung to the same defensive brand of hockey as they had played throughout much of the decade. The strategy, which had brought the team success in the late 1940s and early 1950s, had begun to break down. Part of the reason was a lack of top-level talent. There was also confusion at the top. While a succession plan might have been formulating in Conn Smythe's mind, it remained fairly nebulous. And no matter who was behind the bench, Smythe had still not fully relinquished his command of the team, as coach Howie Meeker confirmed: "Sure, the coaches ran the practices and made most of the speeches at the pep rallies. We helped put the defence pairs together, the forward lines together and suggested changes when things weren't working. But in those days, it was Conn Smythe who really controlled the team."

Still, Meeker claimed that he was always pleased to accept the advice of the man he considered "the smartest man in hockey."

It seems that Smythe was smart enough to realize that Howie Meeker was not the coach the Leafs needed for the 1957–58 season. After some negotiation, the 32-year-old Meeker relinquished the gig, and on May 13, 1957,

accepted the position of general manager. It was an appointment that would not last long.

Just a few days earlier, on May 9, Conn Smythe had retired. He explained that the duties of his new role would be to "sign the players, the coach and the manager in order to hand over to the committee a complete parcel. Then, they will be free to hire, fire and make whatever changes they see fit."

The committee he referred to, and to which he agreed to turn over the team no later than September 1, was an idea that had been in the works for some time. To prepare Stafford for his eventual role as president, Conn had encouraged his son to form a "hockey committee" that would serve as a sounding board on decisions. Under his chairmanship, Stafford recruited jeweller Jack Amell; John W. Bassett, the publisher of the *Toronto Telegram* and future co-owner of CFTO-TV; stockbroker George Gardiner; Bill Hatch, the vice-president of McLaren's Food Products; wine-and-spirits importer George Mara; and lawyer Ian Johnston. Each of the members was a successful entrepreneur in his 30s or early 40s, though this demographic changed somewhat with the departure of Johnston after only nine months. His replacement was 54-year-old Harold Ballard.

Ballard had been involved in Toronto hockey since the 1930s and had been the business manager of the Toronto National Sea Fleas, an OHA senior team that won the Allan Cup in 1932. When he was appointed manager of the junior West Toronto Nationals in 1934, Ballard hired Hap Day, the Leafs captain at the time, to coach his team. The Nationals won the Memorial Cup in 1936, and Day subsequently recommended Ballard as a potential manager of the Toronto Marlboros senior and junior teams. That recommendation brought him into the Leafs fold.

Ballard soon became president and general manager of the Marlboros and, along with Stafford Smythe, enjoyed several successes, including Memorial Cup championships in 1955 and 1956. At the same time, Ballard also ran

After playing goal for the New York Rangers in 1953–54, Johnny Bower (pictured) was replaced by Gump Worsley and sent to the minors. He had to be convinced to join the Maple Leafs for the 1958–59 season. But he did, and spent 11 seasons as Toronto's premier netminder.

Ballard Machinery Supplies, a company created by his father that manufactured sewing machines and at one time had also made skates. Still, it was as a member of the seven-man committee overseeing the Leafs that the future controversial owner first cut his teeth in hockey's top tier.

The committee Ballard joined would soon acquire a nickname: the "Silver Seven." This reflected the group's privileged upbringing and was a nod to the Ottawa Silver Seven, Stanley Cup champions for four consecutive years beginning in 1903. The Silver Seven met weekly to discuss the team's situation and often travelled with the Leafs on the road. Yet, sportswriters questioned the viability of the committee, given the legendary and not-so-veiled carousing that the group was involved in.

Before he relinquished control to the Silver Seven, however, Conn Smythe continued to make hockey moves. One such decision was to hire Montreal Canadiens star Billy Reay. As a coach, Reay had taken the Rochester Americans from last place to second in the AHL, and then to the Calder Cup final.

It appeared that the Leafs could now boast a coach and a general manager who had some degree of autonomy to steer the team out of the fog in which it had been mired. The *Toronto Daily Star* applauded the decision: "For the first time in the history of the club, the Leafs will be coached by the coach." In the past, runners had carried instructions from Smythe's lofty perch in the greens to whoever was behind the bench.

Appearances could be deceiving, however. Stafford Smythe and Howie Meeker had no use for one another. The new general manager would try to make deals for players, but Stafford stalled or just plain ignored him. It was an untenable situation, as Meeker recalled:

> One day, the little weasel called me into his office and began to dress me down for having done nothing to improve the club. I retrieved my briefcase with copies of all the telegrams, letters and calls I'd made to him and Conn. I read every one to him and then told him he knew damn well why I hadn't done anything. I said, "Stafford, I asked for permission to trade for players on three different occasions and you totally ignored my correspondence." He put both hands on my chest and pushed me. That was dumb. I hauled back and popped him good right between the eyes with probably my best hockey punch.

Meeker was officially fired on October 4, 1957 – four days before the start of the season. The position was temporarily filled by a consortium of Stafford Smythe, assistant general manager King Clancy, coach Billy Reay, and head scout Bob Davidson. This quartet placed an emphasis on youth; the 1957–58 roster boasted no fewer than 12 regulars who were under the age of 25. St. Mike's alum Frank Mahovlich and Marlboros graduate Bob Baun played their first full NHL seasons; Billy Harris, who spent most of his sophomore season in the AHL, earned a permanent place in the lineup; and former Major Noel Price and Marlie products Bob Nevin and Carl Brewer would make their big-league debuts during the season. They joined a largely homegrown club anchored by St. Michael's alumni Tim Horton, Dick Duff, and Ed Chadwick, and former Marlboros George Armstrong and Bob Pulford. The two local affiliates were providing the foundation upon which a dynasty would be built.

ROCK BOTTOM

Chicago hosted and won the 1957–58 season opener against Toronto, 1–0. With some Leafs nursing flu symptoms, Toronto also dropped the home opener against Detroit, 5–3.

After being destroyed, 9–3, by the Montreal Canadiens, the Leafs were winless in three straight. They rebounded two nights later with an emphatic 7–0 win over the Bruins in which Brian Cullen and Billy Harris each had hat tricks, while Chadwick got the shutout.

Pete Conacher, son of Charlie, made his Leafs debut in a 3–3 tie against Chicago on November 2. Playing on the same rink where his father had electrified crowds, he confessed, "I hadn't really proved myself, and then because I was from Toronto, because of my dad and because of his history with the Leafs, I felt a lot of pressure putting a Toronto sweater on. I just wasn't comfortable." In actuality, Conacher never did get comfortable in Toronto, and lasted only five games before being shipped off to the New York Rangers, from whom they'd acquired him in June.

In the background throughout 1957 was the movement, spearheaded by Ted Lindsay of Detroit and Doug Harvey of Montreal, to form a players' association, primarily with an eye towards negotiating better pensions and winning a share of television money. The very idea of collective bargaining earned the rancour of team management across the league. As retribution for serving as the secretary-treasurer of the nascent National Hockey League Players' Association (NHLPA), veteran defenceman Jimmy Thomson was sold to Chicago during the off-season. Taking his place as Toronto team representatives were Tod Sloan, Sid Smith, and Dick Duff.

Like Thomson, Sloan would be sold to the woeful Black Hawks following the 1957–58 season.

Sid Smith got off to a slow start, and after a road win against Boston on November 7, in which he played a single shift, the winger was told he was being sent down to Rochester. Smith refused the demotion, electing to retire instead. Persuaded to regain his amateur status, Smith became player-coach of the OHA senior Whitby Dunlops. As Allan Cup champions, the Dunlops were to represent Canada at the 1958 world championship. After an uncharacteristic bronze-medal finish at the 1956 Olympics and a boycott of the 1957 world championship to protest the Soviet Union's invasion of Hungary, Canada was anxious to return to the international stage. With Smith's help, the "Dunnies" took the championship in Oslo, Norway.

Despite jettisoning some of the perceived ringleaders of the players' association, the Leafs were going nowhere fast, and fans began to voice their frustration. Young Frank Mahovlich became a favourite target. While the "Big M" was largely living up to the hype that surrounded him (he scored a hat trick against the Black Hawks on December 1 and another on Christmas night against the Canadiens), fans began to boo him. It was a curious situation that would, unfortunately, continue throughout his time in Toronto. Mahovlich's long, loping strides gave him the appearance of not skating hard on every shift. Fans were more appreciative of feisty players, such as Tim Horton and Rudy Migay, who seemed to go all-out with every shift. Despite the efforts of these players, however, the team's overall performance was generally poor.

It was perplexing. The Leafs occasionally scored in bunches: they pummelled the Rangers, 7–1, on January 25 and hammered the Red Wings, 9–2, on February 1. Yet, the reverse was just as common: they were shut out, 7–0, at the hands of the Bruins on March 9 and blanked by an identical score by the Rangers on March 22. Billy Reay, whose debut as an NHL coach was anything but auspicious, was positively puzzled throughout the year by an extremely inconsistent team.

Dick Duff led the Leafs in scoring with 26 goals and 49 points. Mahovlich edged Bobby Hull as the NHL's best rookie, but there was little else in the way of good news for the Blue and White. The Toronto Maple Leafs finished sixth in the six-team NHL – the first time since becoming the Leafs in 1927 that they ended the year in last place.

The prevailing sentiment following the 1957–58 season was that the franchise had reached its lowest point. Still, few in Leafs Nation could have known that, amidst this roster, the Leafs actually possessed many of the ingredients necessary for victory.

PUNCHING ABOVE THEIR WEIGHT

The Maple Leafs did not, in the summer of 1958, remotely resemble a team on the brink of a dynasty. Toronto had missed the playoffs the previous two springs and seemed poised to flounder yet again. The Leafs' chief rivals, the Montreal Canadiens, were three Stanley Cup championships into what would be a record-setting run of five straight. The Canadiens had, by any standards, a most imposing roster, full of future Hall of Famers.

By contrast, the Leafs lineup scared no one. And after a dismal rookie season, coach Billy Reay knew that changes were needed. In particular, he believed the Leafs needed to upgrade their netminding: "Goalkeeping in hockey is like pitching in baseball, if you haven't got it, you've got nothing at all."

To this end, the general manager–less Leafs worked through the summer to persuade veteran minor-league goalie Johnny Bower to move to Toronto. Bower had been buried in the New York Rangers' system and, at 33 years of age, seemed unlikely to get an opportunity to return to the NHL. Content to continue playing with the AHL's Cleveland Barons, Bower had declined previous overtures from Toronto and Boston. In June 1958, however, Toronto selected Bower from Cleveland in the Intra-League Draft.

Reluctantly, Bower gave Toronto a shot. He was a standup goaltender who was expert in the "poke check," something he had learned in New York from teammate Charlie Rayner. As Bower recalled:

[Rayner] was on his last legs in New York. He came up to me and told me, "You have got to know how to handle a puck and shoot it up ahead, stickhandle just like a forward and know how to poke check." I didn't know what he was talking about then because nobody ever talked to me about goaltending technique or anything. He would come out to our practices and he showed me how to do the poke check. I worked at it and worked at it and finally got it down.

Bower would make this tactical weapon famous.

This was also a time of flux for the netminding position at large. The single-goalie system was being phased out of the NHL in the late 1950s. During the previous campaign, the Stanley Cup–winning Canadiens had enjoyed success by inserting Charlie Hodge into occasional games to keep

I wish I could have played [in Toronto] longer . . . We had some pretty good teams there early. We had some good guys that could play. Money players. I'm proud of what I did as a Maple Leaf.

Mike Palmateer
PLAYER
1976–80; 1982–84

In November 1961, Conn Smythe sold most of his shares in Maple Leaf Gardens to his son, Stafford Smythe (centre), and partners John Bassett (left) and Harold Ballard (right). The triumvirate controlled the destiny of the Toronto Maple Leafs and Maple Leaf Gardens until 1971.

Jacques Plante fresh. Likewise, the Bruins split their goaltending duties between Harry Lumley and Don Simmons, as did the Rangers with Gump Worsley and Marcel Paillé. This inspired Reay to platoon Bower with the Leafs' current goalie, Ed Chadwick. In effect, a new position had opened up in the NHL: the backup goalie.

That summer, the Leafs also claimed 32-year-old Bert Olmstead from the Canadiens in the Inter-League Draft. Disappointed that the Habs had not protected him in the draft, he reluctantly agreed to give Toronto a try.

Meanwhile, the Silver Seven were still in search of a general manager. Stafford Smythe was impressed with George "Punch" Imlach, a teammate of his on the Toronto Donnell-Mudge club in the Toronto Mercantile Hockey League. As a player, Imlach had also starred as a junior with the Toronto Young Rangers (1935–38) and in the senior ranks with the Toronto Goodyears (1938–40) and Marlboros (1940–41). In a game against Windsor, Imlach was on the receiving end of a fierce bodycheck that left him dazed. The *Toronto Telegram* blithely described

Imlach as appearing "punch drunk." The nickname "Punchy" – later shortened to "Punch" – stuck. For the rest of his life, Imlach was known – to everyone but his wife, Dodo – as Punch.

Imlach wrapped up his playing career with the Quebec Aces, a team he would be associated with as coach or general manager through 1956–57. There, he helped groom Jean Béliveau for his Hall of Fame NHL career. It was an experience that also set Imlach up beautifully for his own future.

Punch was hired by the Toronto Maple Leafs in August 1958, to work in concert with the Silver Seven as an assistant general manager. It would prove to be one of the most important moves in the history of the franchise. When Stafford Smythe introduced the relatively unknown Imlach to a room of reporters, few could anticipate the changes that were in store for the team, let alone the priceless inkworthy quotes the man would provide them with over the next decade.

Punch's impact was almost immediate, as Leafs trainer Bob Haggert confirmed:

When Imlach arrived, we knew very little about him. But, from the moment he arrived, it took him maybe two weeks to assess the team. He saw, on one side, that we had this great pool of terrific players who had played for the Marlboros and St. Mike's, and they were so good. So he started to fill in the blanks.

Imlach chose to temper the perpetual youth movement by introducing a number of veterans to the lineup. It was a trend that would continue throughout his first term with the club.

Just prior to the beginning of the 1958–59 season, defenceman Allan Stanley was picked up from Boston for Jim Morrison and cash. Stanley was the first among many whose careers would enjoy a resurrection in Toronto. What might have seemed an unremarkable transaction in fact completed an era-defining Leafs defensive quartet – alongside Horton, Baun, and Brewer – upon which Toronto would come to rely during its most glorious chapter. "I believe, to this day, that the reason I am in the Hall of Fame is because of that foursome," Johnny Bower remarked many years later.

The Imlach blueprint called for each defensive pairing to have one puck rusher and one who was more defensive-minded. Hard-hitting third-year Leaf Bobby Baun was at first paired with Tim Horton, rookie Carl Brewer with Steve Kraftcheck, and Marc Reaume was a spare defence-man. Later, Punch experimented with combining the adventurous Brewer with the steadying influence of Baun. This combination clicked.

Then, Horton and Stanley were paired, and the duo soon became the mainstay of the Leafs blueline. "We played together for most of ten years," Stanely explained. "We just seemed to fit right in. After a while, we knew every move the other one would make in any situation. It's not often that you play with somebody and are able to have that kind of confidence in him. We were like brothers off the ice, too."

By opening night, the Leafs were prepared to put memories of their previous campaign behind them. The *Hockey News* was less convinced, predicting that Toronto was bound for another sixth-place finish. On October 11, the Maple Leafs sought to prove the *Hockey News* wrong as they started their season against the Chicago Black Hawks at Maple Leaf Gardens.

Hap Day, long-time player, coach, and assistant general manager, dropped the ceremonial first puck of the 1958–59 season. As the televised portion of the game began, Foster Hewitt announced the score and the scorers, and then made a surprising announcement: "This season, the play-by-play for radio and TV, I'm very proud to say, will be handled by my son, Bill Hewitt. After 30 years of network play-by-play broadcasting, my efforts will be to interject highlights and comments during the course of the play."

Hewitt the younger was no stranger to Maple Leaf broadcasts. In fact, he'd done a few minutes of play-by-play as an eight-year-old during his father's Young Canada Night broadcast in 1936. Now the sound-alike son took permanent place behind the mic on Leaf broadcasts, as Chicago spoiled the new-look Leafs' plans with a 3–1 victory.

Later in the month, on October 25, Johnny Bower earned his first shutout as a Maple Leaf in a 3–0 win over the Detroit Red Wings. During the second inter-mission, NHL president Clarence Campbell presented Frank Mahovlich with the Calder Memorial Trophy as the league's best rookie of the previous season. Greater days lay ahead for both of them, but in the short term the team was off to a poor start, with just three wins in ten games. After a 4–1 loss to Detroit on November 15, the Silver Seven hockey committee summoned Imlach and asked him to fine each of the players. Punch talked them out of it, but called each player individually into a room where he and Billy Reay explained that neither the management nor the fans were satisfied. He threatened to fine each player $200 if they didn't collect at least one point in the upcoming road games against Boston and New York.

The Leafs tied Boston, 4–4, but were trounced by the Rangers, 7–4. Dismayed with the performance of the team, the Silver Seven met again with Imlach. They discussed firing Reay and asked Punch for his thoughts. "I told them that the team obviously wasn't playing for Reay," said Imlach. "I thought he wasn't tough enough on them; that he was trusting them to do things and they were letting him down. They asked me what I would do about it. I said I wasn't the general manager; I was only the assistant general manager."

On November 21, with the team mired in last place, the Maple Leafs announced that Punch Imlach was now the team's general manager. It was the free hand that Imlach had sought – but this was not where his responsi-bilities would end.

Toronto earned consecutive ties against the Rangers and the Black Hawks in the next two games, before being booed off of the ice after a loss to Detroit on November 26. By then, the general manager had devised a plan. On November 28, Imlach met Conn Smythe and told him he was going to relieve Billy Reay of the coaching duties. After that, Imlach quickly set about getting assurances from all of the players that they would play for him. Having received affirmative responses, Imlach was now both coach and general manager of the Toronto Maple Leafs.

Imlach immediately loosened the on-ice restrictions that Reay had placed on the players. Tim Horton, for example, was now free to carry the puck out of the zone instead of being expected to make an instant pass. While there were several such tactical changes, there was also, more importantly, a change in the Leafs' state of mind. Imlach declared, boldly yet resolutely, that Toronto was going to compete for the Stanley Cup. As the coach later recalled in his autobiography:

> Right then, I started to say, as often as anybody would listen, that we were going to get off the floor, that we were going to make it into one of the first four places in the league – be one of the teams that would play for the Stanley Cup . . . I talked loud and long. I did it on purpose. Somebody had to give that team the idea that they could win.

The attitude was infectious, as was readily apparent to all who followed the team. The *Toronto Telegram*, for instance, summarized Imlach's zeal for success:

> In a world where everything is crazy and mixed-up and dreadfully serious, there is a constant that keeps us poor Canadians from going out of our minds. It is the eternal confidence of George Imlach. Mr. Imlach, as you know, has the cold effrontery and the IBM brain of a riverboat gambler mixed with a little bit of Billy Graham, the evangelist. He makes you believe.

Slowly, and perhaps without any real empirical reason to do so, the whole city began to believe.

The Maple Leafs proceeded to go unbeaten in six, and the general manager–coach could now add "prophet" to his list of titles. While the winning streak came to an end with two pre-Christmas losses and a tie, Ed Chadwick resumed the Leafs' good play by earning a 2–0 shutout over Detroit on Christmas Day. It was Chadwick's first start in five weeks. Imlach's rationale for going back and forth between Bower and Chadwick anticipated the future prerogative of many NHL coaches:

> My idea is that the fellow who is playing the best at the time will continue to play. If Chadwick wins tonight, Bower will have to win his job back again. As it was, Bower was playing well and it had to wait until he had

an injury to put Chadwick in to see what he could do.

You don't change a winning club. If we're winning, we're going to stick with what we have.

Fortunately for the Leafs, Chadwick continued to have the hot hand as Toronto celebrated New Year's Eve by blanking the first-place Montreal Canadiens, 2–0. It was Chadwick's third shutout of the season and his second of the week.

Despite his coaching savvy and early success, Imlach still considered himself a temporary coach. He was, in truth, looking for the right personality to step in. He had spoken to former New York Ranger Alf Pike, who was doing well coaching the Winnipeg Warriors of the WHL. But Winnipeg asked for players in return for the poaching of their coach; Imlach, with few to spare, declined. "After the Pike deal didn't work, I didn't look any more. Especially when I knew that what the Leaf management really wanted was for me to keep on as coach."

The on-ice results bolstered Imlach's decision. The Leafs were undefeated in the first five games of 1959. Still somewhat skeptical about the current lineup, Punch continued to add some important pieces to the puzzle, trading for Gerry Ehman and claiming Larry Regan on waivers. While these players provided the Leafs with some much-needed depth, the team was still seven points out of a playoff spot with just five games left to play. As it stood, any of the last three teams in the standings – Toronto, Detroit, and New York – was capable of stealing the final playoff spot.

On the weekend of March 14 and 15, 1959, the Leafs played a home-and-home set against the Rangers. New York had been struggling, but in truth, Toronto needed to win both games to stay in contention. Imlach, the master motivator, found superb ammunition in the NHL's playoff schedule, which had curiously been announced the morning of the first game against New York. The schedule included contingency plans and dates, but there was no mention of the Toronto Maple Leafs. Imlach, however, clung to the belief that his team was going to compete for the Stanley Cup. In the dressing room before the game, he slammed the league for its lack of faith and, in the words of King Clancy, told his charges that he wanted them to stick the schedule "where Paddy put the potato." To a man, the Leafs understood.

Imlach's spirited charges beat the Rangers, 5–0, in the first game, which included a third-period bench-clearing brawl. Following the game, broadcaster Wes McKnight predicted, "That should be quite a hockey game in Madison Square Garden tomorrow night. There is no love lost between the Leafs and the Rangers, two teams

battling it out for the fourth and last playoff position." And it certainly was.

That night, down 6–5 late in the game, the Rangers pulled their goaltender but came up empty. Toronto hung on for the narrow victory. The four points that the Leafs gained over the weekend catapulted them over Detroit into fifth place. Toronto was now just three points behind New York with three games left to play.

Still, with the remaining games against Montreal, Chicago, and Detroit, the schedule didn't appear to favour the Leafs. There was also the small matter that Toronto had yet to win more than two games in a row through the entire season.

There was, however, something of a gift awaiting the Leafs in their game against Montreal. Jacques Plante

was given the night off after showing up at the rink with a face swollen with boils. Claude Pronovost, brother of Red Wings defenceman Marcel, was designated to play goal for the Canadiens. The Rangers complained bitterly to NHL president Clarence Campbell, believing that Toronto was getting an unfair advantage, but their protest was to no avail. By the end of the second period, Pronovost had allowed five Toronto goals; he was replaced by Claude Cyr, who had spent the season with the Hull-Ottawa Canadiens of the Eastern Professional Hockey League (EPHL). Cyr made his first and only NHL appearance against the Maple Leafs in that game, and was solid if unspectacular, allowing one goal as Toronto doubled Montreal, 6–3. That same evening, Boston beat the Rangers, 5–3, in New York. Going into

Ed Chadwick (pictured) joined the Toronto Maple Leafs in 1955–56 as an injury replacement for Harry Lumley. He became the team's regular goaltender for the next two seasons, playing 140 consecutive games through the spring of 1958, but soon was replaced by Johnny Bower.

the final weekend of the season, the Maple Leafs were only one point behind New York for the last play-off berth.

In an afternoon contest on March 21, the Rangers faced off against Detroit while the anxious Leafs watched the game on television. New York defeated the Red Wings, 5–2, eliminating Detroit from playoff contention for the first time in 21 years. That same evening, Toronto faced the third-place Chicago Black Hawks. Led by a two-goal effort from Frank Mahovlich, the Leafs won, 5–1. Going into the final day of the regular season, Toronto was still one point behind the Rangers for a play-off spot. With a touch of bravado, Imlach told each player to pack enough clothes for a week, because after they beat Detroit to slip into the playoffs, they'd be heading to Boston for the semifinals.

On March 22, the Rangers faced the Canadiens in a game that started at 7:00 P.M., while the Leafs–Red Wings contest began at 8:00. By the time the puck dropped in the Olympia, Montreal was already ahead of the Rangers, 2–1. But before the Leafs knew it, they were trailing the Wings, 2–0. Then, at 16:58 of the first period, the Detroit public-address announcer gave the fans a final score in the out-of-town game: Montreal had defeated New York, 4–2. A Leaf win would now secure fourth place and a spot in the playoffs.

As the players took the ice for the second period, captain George Armstrong told his coach, "Don't worry Punch, we'll get it for you!" Larry Regan scored to close the gap, and Bob Baun got his first goal of the season with a shot from the point. The score then seesawed. Norm Ullman put Detroit up 3–2, but less than two minutes later, Carl Brewer evened the score. Regan scored his second goal of the night just 21 seconds after Brewer, putting Toronto in front 4–3 late in the second, before Pronovost knotted the game at four.

Early in the third, Regan skated over to Dick Duff in the faceoff circle in the Toronto end and told him, "You're going to get the winner. I'm going to give it to you." At the faceoff, Regan darted through the neutral zone with the puck. Cutting left at the Wings blueline, he beat both defencemen, caught a glimpse of Duff flying into the slot, and fed him the puck. Duff fired a one-timer that beat Terry Sawchuk to give Toronto a 5–4 lead. Billy Harris later added an insurance goal.

Miraculously, they had done it. The 6–4 score assured that the Cinderella Maple Leafs were going to be – as Punch Imlach had predicted – one of four teams competing for the Stanley Cup.

Truthfully, Imlach had brought the Maple Leafs back from the dead, as the *Globe* observed:

> Imlach is not satisfied with one miracle a season. He actually believes he can win the Stanley Cup and, at that precise moment, there isn't anybody who might even timidly suggest he is suffering from delusion. A few months ago, the repeated Imlach incantation that the Leafs would reach the playoffs was accepted sceptically by disrespectful hockey writers. They studiously avoided looking at him during his embarrassing spells, trusting that it was only a temporary seizure and that he would recover.

That final regular-season game was a watershed moment for the Leafs and their fans. As Billy Harris later recalled, "Many of us look back at that game as the night we started to turn things around." The Leafs had won their final five games, scoring 28 goals to their opponents' 13. Conversely, New York had lost six of their final seven games en route to elimination. Imlach had inspired his team to reach beyond their perceived ability.

Six of Imlach's players scored 20 or more goals that season: Dick Duff (29), Bob Pulford (23), Frank Mahovlich and Billy Harris (22), Ron Stewart (21), and George Armstrong (20). Though he never asked for it, Duff was given the jersey number 9 as a just reward for his third 20-goal season. The number 9 had a certain magic to it. It was, as Duff explained,

> a number always designated for a certain type of player. Charlie Conacher wore it, and then the Leafs decided that Teeder Kennedy would wear it. Ted Kennedy was regarded by fans and team ownership as one of the best, if not the best player to have worn the crest of the Maple Leafs. I was truly humbled by the gesture. I admired him greatly, and I wore his number with tremendous pride.

Toronto faced the second-place Boston Bruins in the semifinal. Punch, playing prophet again, predicted that the Leafs would win in six games: "The only reason it will go six games is that we want to end it in Toronto in front of our own fans because they've been so faithful to us. Then we'll take the Canadiens in seven, the last one in overtime. I've always been lucky in playoffs and I'm not changing now." It was unadulterated cheek from a man who possessed, according to the *Boston Globe*, "the guts of a safecracker."

One of the bright spots for the Maple Leafs through the 1950s was Dick Duff (centre), here celebrating his first NHL goal during the 1955–56 season. In 1958–59, he was awarded the number 9, which had last been worn by Leafs legend Ted Kennedy.

Still, the Leafs could not crack the Bruins in Game One, which belonged to former Leaf goaltender Harry Lumley. In the 70th playoff game of his career, Lumley allowed just one goal for a 5–1 Bruins win.

While Lumley would shine once again in Game Two, it was the Bruins' Jean-Guy Gendron who was the star of the game. The winger was suffering from the flu and looked, as far as the *Globe and Mail* was concerned, like "an escapee from a funeral parlour." The ghostly Gendron scored what proved to be the winning goal at 15:59 of the third to give the Bruins a 3–2 win and a 2–0 lead in the semifinal.

Yet, even with the 2–0 lead, Boston general manager Lynn Patrick sounded a cautious tone. "I think it's going to be a long series, and I wouldn't care to say right now who will win," he said. "One thing I'm sure about – even if we're leading the series 3–0, I won't feel confident, not with Imlach behind the Toronto bench."

As if on cue, the Leafs battled back in Game Three and edged the Bruins, 3–2. Gerry Ehman, an unlikely hero, scored late in the third to tie the contest and then scored again at 5:02 of overtime to a thunderous ovation at Maple Leaf Gardens.

Toronto emerged from Game Four with an identical result. This time, it was Frank Mahovlich who wired a 20-foot backhander past Harry Lumley in the extra period.

Led by the supreme goaltending of Johnny Bower, the Leafs kept the pressure on Boston in Game Five and won, 4–1. Toronto now led the series three games to two.

Despite all of the serious hockey that was being played, there were some moments of levity to be found during the intense series. As the players slowly undressed after their victory, Harold Ballard entered the dressing room and asked for the club's attention: "I have an announcement to make. I'd like you to meet your new coach." Astonished, the players spun around to see who would be behind their bench. Punch Imlach walked in, removed his fedora, and stood there, sporting a toupee. The wig had arrived at the hotel, from a fan. The dressing room was soon convulsing with laughter.

Game Six, however, was no laughing matter, as Boston surprised Toronto with a 5–4 win at Maple Leaf Gardens. The teams limped back to Boston for the final game, as both rosters had endured their fair share of injuries. Game Seven was tied, 1–1, at the end of the first period. Toronto's goal had come courtesy of Larry Regan, who was playing with a broken hand. By the end of the second period, though, Boston was ahead by one. Bob Pulford tied the score in the third.

Remarkably, it again came down to the Leafs' 27-year-old rookie, Gerry Ehman, to play hero. At 17:27 of the third period in Game Seven, he scored yet another winning goal. The upstart Leafs had eliminated the Bruins to advance to the Stanley Cup final for the first time since Barilko had scored his famous and final goal.

The clouds over Leafs Nation seemed to be parting. Veteran Bert Olmstead played oracle and envisaged in a postgame interview that "three years from now, this Leafs team will be unbeatable because of the invaluable experience they'll pick up in playoffs. Only a few of these fine young players know what it is to be in the Stanley Cup playoffs and they're learning valuable lessons now." The next lesson, however, was going to be a hard one.

The Montreal Canadiens, who had won the Cup the three previous springs, were heavily favoured in the final. They had finished first during the regular season with 91 points, 26 more than the Leafs. With a roster that included names such as Béliveau, Harvey, Moore, Plante, and Richard, it was a team that is still, to this day, considered one of the best in NHL history.

To win a final series against this Montreal club was, for the underdog Leafs, a big ask.

Game One in Montreal was a dull affair. Marcel Bonin, wearing a pair of Maurice Richard's old gloves for good luck, bounced a blooper past Bower for the winning goal at 11:59 of the third, and then Dickie Moore added an insurance marker later in the period to give the Canadiens a 5–3 victory.

Game Two proved more decisive. From the puck drop onward, it was all Canadiens. Claude Provost scored twice as Montreal beat Toronto, 3–1. But in the *Toronto Daily Star*'s estimation, Doug Harvey was the deciding factor for the Canadiens: "Harvey drove the Leaf attackers frantic with his masterful defensive play. His puck control was the acme of perfection."

The series moved to Toronto for Game Three. After 60 minutes, the game was tied 2–2. At 10:06 of overtime, Dick Duff beat Jacques Plante for the game-winning goal:

> I slapped the puck because I was too tired to use a wrist-shot. It hit [Tom] Johnson's skate and changed direction just enough to fool Plante. I was actually sick from the heat of the building and the pace of the game when I went out for that shift. That was my last spurt and I had to make it good.

It was, in the end, a triumph of desire over finesse.

While the the two teams' skill sets differed, so too did their approaches to the game. Even though the Leafs had come out on the winning end, Imlach ran a gruelling 45-minute practice on the morning of Game Four, while Toe Blake called off Montreal's practice after just ten minutes.

The game was nevertheless a thriller: end-to-end but scoreless hockey for the first two periods, followed by a barrage of offence during the third. The Canadiens scored three times in the space of six minutes and won the game by a 3–2 margin, with the deciding goal scored on a 40-foot bullet by Boom Boom Geoffrion that found the net between Bower and the post. With this goal, the Habs now led the series three games to one.

Although the Maple Leafs' Cinderella story was winding down, the clock had not yet struck midnight. Sixty sportswriters were on hand to cover Game Five in Montreal. What they saw was a dominant Canadiens squad mounting a seemingly insurmountable 5–1 lead in the first 50 minutes of the game. The final ten minutes, however, proved to be, as the *Toronto Daily Star* attested, "the wildest finish in the history of the league." Toronto began a rally behind goals from Mahovlich and Olmstead. At 17:27, Imlach pulled Johnny Bower in favour of a sixth attacker. The Leafs pressed feverishly, but alas, the carriage finally turned into a pumpkin. The Canadiens held on for a 5–3 win and a record-setting fourth consecutive Stanley Cup. Montreal would add another the following year.

The Maple Leafs had intended to take the midnight train back to Toronto, but the players were given a reprieve by Punch Imlach, who recommended that his boys "blow off some steam."

Although his first Stanley Cup was still three years away, Tim Horton identified 1958–59's miracle run to the final as the most fun he ever had playing hockey. Likewise, Punch Imlach confessed that the 1958–59 season was "the greatest thrill of my life." In the space of a few months, the team had been roused from a near-decade-long haze. Led by Imlach, the Leafs had brought both confidence and excitement back to the city. The race to the playoffs and the appearance in the final portended well for fans of the Blue and White.

AN INVITATION TO THE DANCE

With the success of the spring campaign, Imlach was confident about the team he had helped assemble. In particular, Punch was pleased with a defence corps that featured Bobby Baun, Carl Brewer, Tim Horton, and Allan Stanley. The general manager had also improved the team's reserve strength. Garry Edmundson arrived from Springfield of

the AHL, Ted Hampson was claimed on waivers from the Rangers, and NHL iron man Johnny Wilson was picked up from the Red Wings. Imlach was now also prepared to trust Johnny Bower with the principal goaltending duties. The aging Bower would be 35 in November 1959, and most believed he had *one* good season left in him. That would prove to be a massive understatement.

The Maple Leafs opened the 1959–60 season against the Chicago Black Hawks. Prior to the game, Prime Minister John Diefenbaker presented the J.P. Bickell Memorial Award to co-recipients George Armstrong and Bob Pulford and then dropped the puck for the season's first faceoff. The Leafs won their first home opener in four years by defeating the Black Hawks, 6–3.

Late November marked the return of Gerry James, who provided the Leafs with some additional grit. James had been busy starring with the Winnipeg Blue Bombers in the Grey Cup. Following the Canadian Football League team's victory over the Hamilton Tiger-Cats, James returned to the ice. It had been a long hiatus for the winger, who had missed the entire 1958–59 season with a leg injury. Whenever Imlach wanted to stir things up, he would send Edmundson, James, and Wilson over the boards to demonstrate their hard-hitting style to Toronto's opponents.

Yet, the most important addition to the Leafs roster during the season was one that caught everyone by surprise. After four Stanley Cup championships, eight All-Star selections, a Norris Trophy for best defenceman (the first one ever awarded), and three Lady Byng Trophies, Red Kelly was traded by the Detroit Red Wings, along with Billy McNeill, to the New York Rangers for Bill Gadsby and Eddie Shack on February 5, 1960. There was just one hitch: both Kelly and McNeil refused to report to New York. Kelly retired, and as such, the trade was voided.

Undeterred, Punch Imlach asked for permission to talk Kelly into renouncing his retirement. Imlach arranged a somewhat clandestine meeting with Kelly for February 9. King Clancy met Kelly at the airport and drove him to the Westbury Hotel, located just behind Maple Leaf Gardens, where Kelly checked in under the pseudonym Fay Bainter, who was an older American film actress at the time. Imlach, Clancy, and Kelly went to eat at a nearby restaurant. When they entered, though, they were horrified to discover that several members of the Montreal Canadiens were having dinner there. In fact, Maurice Richard said hello but made no particular fuss about seeing the unusual trio. The three men later retreated to Maple Leaf Gardens, where, as the Moscow State Symphony Orchestra performed, Kelly signed a contract with the Toronto Maple Leafs.

The biggest Leafs fan I knew was my French-Canadian grandmother, and she was probably my biggest supporter. We developed a very close bond after she had several strokes and came to live with us. I used to watch *Hockey Night in Canada* with Grandma on Saturday nights. She was paralyzed on one side of her body but she had no problem cheering for the Blue and White with one arm in the air. Grandma had more passion as a fan than I have ever seen before. My only regret was that she was not alive to see me put on the Leafs jersey, but I always felt like she was looking over me. What being a Maple Leaf means to the fans is quite remarkable to me, and I'll always have fond memories of being drafted by and playing for the Toronto Maple Leafs.

Peter Ing
PLAYER
1989–91

Tipped off by Johnny Wilson that Jack Adams liked the play of defenceman Marc Reaume, Imlach phoned Adams in Detroit and told him that he'd be happy to send Reaume to him as compensation for Kelly. Reaume had been serving the Leafs in a primarily auxiliary role. Harbouring a little animosity about how the whole deal had gone down, Adams curtly accepted.

Before Kelly had taken his first shift in blue and white, Imlach asked him if he would consider playing centre. Kelly agreed. As the new forward confirmed, "I didn't care where I played as long as I was playing hockey." Imlach outlined his reasoning: "If we're going to win the Stanley Cup, we're going to have to go through Montreal. I need somebody to check Béliveau."

Red Kelly's impact at centre was profound. Among his many admirers was linemate Frank Mahovlich. Years later, the Big M would say, "I've played with Delvecchio and Béliveau, but Red Kelly, to me, was the greatest centreman that I ever played with. He had a knack for studying the opposition and making the right move at the right time with them." The experiment would be a huge success.

While Montreal finished, rather predictably, in first place with 92 points, Imlach's constant tweaking had paid off, and the Leafs surprised the hockey world with a strong second-place finish. Bob Pulford was the Leafs' top scorer with 52 points, including 24 goals. Carl Brewer led the NHL in penalty minutes with 150. Allan Stanley was named to the Second All-Star Team.

The semifinal saw Toronto face fourth-place Detroit. Imlach felt that stifling Gordie Howe's production was key to winning the series, and he planned to have Bert Olmstead shadow the Red Wings star. Sid Abel found this humorous: "If Olmstead is going to keep track of Howe, he'll have to play an awful lot of positions. I'll use Gordie at both wings, centre and both defence posts to shake him loose."

The Red Wings shocked the Leafs with a 2–1 win in Game One at Maple Leaf Gardens. Howe scored early in the first period and Bert Olmstead, who was nursing a cold, felt somewhat overwhelmed with his assignment: "That guy never gets tired. He's stronger when he should be weary than I am when I'm fresh!"

Imlach decided to try to neutralize Howe by using both Olmstead and Mahovlich against the Wings star. The new plan worked, at least in part, and Toronto rebounded with a 4–2 win in Game Two. Imlach was, however, still tinkering with his energy line of Wilson, James, and Edmundson. The trio, which had played so well in the opening contest, was relegated to the bench in the second game. "This is no time to gamble," Imlach said. "I'm going

with the guys who will put me into the Stanley Cup."

The teams travelled to Detroit for Game Three. At the conclusion of the first period, the Maple Leafs marched into their dressing room, where they discovered a huge mound of money on the floor. A message on the bulletin board read, "Take a good look at the centre of the floor. This is the difference between losing and winning – $1,250." Imlach did not even make an appearance in the room. His message said everything that needed saying.

Playing with something to prove against his old club, Red Kelly led the Leafs' charge with two goals. Still, at the end of regulation time, the teams were tied at four. Mahovlich delivered a dressing-room pronouncement to his teammates: "We're going to get it. We're going to win." Three minutes into the third overtime, the Big M took matters in his own hands, redirecting a shot from Kelly to give Toronto a hard-earned 5–4 victory.

Two nights later in Detroit, the teams needed overtime yet again to decide a winner. This time, it was Red Wings rookie Gerry Melnyk who scored the game-winning goal to tie the semifinal series at two wins apiece.

Back at Maple Leaf Gardens, Toronto took Game Five with a 5–4 win, giving the Leafs a 3–2 series lead as the teams headed back to Detroit for the sixth game. There, the Leafs enjoyed a come-from-behind win. Down 2–1 in the second period, Toronto rebounded with three goals to collect a 4–2 victory and a berth in the Stanley Cup final against the Montreal Canadiens.

Former defenceman Red Kelly led the series in scoring, with nine points on three goals and six assists. In defiance, Detroit general manager Jack Adams spoke to his former player's performance: "Kelly wasn't going full for us and we're not sorry we traded him. Reaume will be around for a long time after Kelly is through." History, as it happened, was not so kind to Adams with respect to this prediction. While Reaume's career would indeed survive Kelly's (the former finished his playing days with the Vancouver Canucks in 1971), he would play less than 50 games with the Red Wings before being dealt to Montreal. On the other hand, Kelly, as a Leaf, would add another four Stanley Cup wins to the four he had won with Detroit.

Meanwhile, it was an all-Canadian Stanley Cup final for the second year in a row. Montreal came out strong and took Game One by a 4–2 count, and Game Two began much the same way when the Canadiens leapt out to a 2–0 lead within the first five minutes. While Larry Regan beat Plante later in the period, the Canadiens held on for a 2–1 win. The teams now shifted to Toronto for Game Three.

Unfortunately for the Leafs, the Habs were once again flying. Johnny Wilson and Bert Olmstead scored for the Leafs, but it was a 5–2 Montreal victory. It was in this game that Maurice "Rocket" Richard scored the final goal of his extraordinary career.

The Habs now looked to sweep the Maple Leafs. Despite the Gardens crowd's massive support for their team, the Canadiens – on two goals by Jean Béliveau and one each from Doug Harvey and Henri Richard – would not be denied in a decisive 4–0 win. One of the greatest teams in history had won a record-breaking five consecutive Stanley Cup championships.

Captain Maurice Richard never raised the Cup, but rather leaned down beside it for photographs with the other Canadiens. When they left, a member of the

Gardens ice crew simply pushed the table off the ice. It was a rather unceremonious finale to what remains one of the greatest accomplishments in hockey history.

For their part, the Leafs had already accomplished much at this early juncture in the Imlach era. The team, however, lacked that little bit of finesse that had been so prevalent in the Canadiens' lineup. Ironically, Toronto would find its missing finesse in a young man from "*la belle province*." A young, gifted centre from Rouyn-Noranda was ready to make the move to the big league and prove that he was the missing piece of the Leafs' puzzle. He would, in the end, prove to be one of the best all-around hockey players ever to wear the blue and white. And he was about to skate the city's beloved team onto the pages of the franchise's most glorious chapter.

On February 9, 1960, the Maple Leafs convinced Red Kelly (left) to continue his career in Toronto. They sent Marc Reaume to the Red Wings in a trade, converted Kelly to a centre from defenceman, and saw him work magic with Frank Mahovlich as the Leafs went on to win the Stanley Cup in 1962, 1963, 1964, and 1967.

THE SECOND DYNASTY
1960–61 TO 1965–66

A CONTENDER AGAIN

The Maple Leafs had astonished the hockey world by rebounding from a last-place finish in 1958 to back-to-back Stanley Cup final appearances. After five consecutive championships, though, the Montreal Canadiens were not about to relinquish the Cup without a battle. And there was also Chicago. The Black Hawks, like Toronto, had endured a horrific decade, but now boasted some of the finest young talent in the game, including forwards Bobby Hull and Stan Mikita. Clearly, the NHL's balance of power had shifted somewhat, and 1960–61 promised to be a different sort of a season.

In June's Intra-League Draft, Larry Hillman joined Toronto from Boston. Johnny Bower had performed in goal even better than had been hoped, which relegated Ed Chadwick to a full-time position on the farm team in Rochester. Meanwhile the Leafs' training camp opened, as usual, in Peterborough, but with one person conspicuous by his absence. After more than three decades working with Toronto, trainer Tim Daly had retired, replaced by Bob Haggert, who had served as trainer of the Toronto Marlboros. The *Globe's* Scott Young – who, like most journalists, loved to banter with Daly – wrote, "Everybody within earshot roared that he might try continuing to do what he had been doing before he retired: nothing!"

Defenceman Carl Brewer was also nowhere to be seen in Peterborough. As it turned out, Brewer was at McMaster University in Hamilton, holding out over $100 he felt the team owed him as compensation for time spent in hospital after an ankle injury. The Leafs sent King Clancy to corral the young blueliner. Brewer explained the matter of the $100, and Clancy unfolded $200 from his wallet, handed the money to Brewer, and implored him to return to the Leafs. Carl refused, and insisted on waiting until a contract had been signed. He confirmed that it was "the principle of the thing. If I let them kick me around this early in my hockey career, it will be that way all through my career."

While many considered Brewer a brilliant player, it was his resolute and principled character that, in many ways, defined his career. He became something of an enigma to his own team. As Sue Foster, Brewer's longtime partner, explained: "He was the outsider, the guy who just didn't seem to fit in. Carl was deeply religious, incredibly sensitive, studious, an intellectual and unrelentingly intense. [His teammates] seemed uncomfortable with him and certainly were at a loss to understand the complexity or intensity of his personality."

While Brewer was demonstrating a maturity well beyond his years, the Leafs remained ever watchful for young players rising through the ranks of their junior affiliates in the city, the Marlboros and St. Michael's College. The two teams were achieving the desired result for the big club, but the Marlies and Majors were also entwined in a fierce rivalry in the OHA's Junior A league. "We got into some pretty heated games with them," Bob Nevin, a product of the Marlies, recalled. "Even though you knew that if you progressed far enough you would eventually play with each other, you weren't thinking about that. When you played against them, you didn't like them."

In some ways, the competition between the Marlies and St. Mike's actually engendered a familiarity among those players lucky enough to one day graduate to the Maple Leafs. At the time it was still extremely rare for rookies to catch a break with the big club, as there were precious few spots. One young gun from Quebec, however, managed to do the unthinkable.

Twenty-year-old Dave Keon had had a tremendous September and actually managed to crack the Maple Leafs lineup out of training camp. The naturally gifted Keon had impressed everyone with his speed and dexterity. The unusual nature of his meteoric ascendancy to the big club was not lost on the young forward:

When I broke in, there wasn't a great deal of turnover in players. I think the year I broke in, there may have been

The Maple Leafs celebrate winning the Stanley Cup in 1963 after defeating the Detroit Red Wings in five games. It was the second straight Cup championship for Toronto. Back row, left to right: Ed Litzenberger, Bobby Baun, Ron Stewart, Bob Nevin, Dick Duff (obscured), and Eddie Shack. Front row, left to right: Johnny Bower, Punch Imlach, George Armstrong, and Kent Douglas.

six new players in the league. Toronto had two – me and Bob Nevin. I didn't think that I was going to stick with the Leafs. I was hoping that it would happen, but you can never tell. When I played in the exhibition games, I was fortunate enough that I scored some goals and got some points. It seemed to keep me with the big team.

Keon quickly felt welcome, as so many other Majors and Marlies were already playing for the Leafs.

The Leafs opened the 1960–61 season on the road against the Canadiens. Maurice Richard had retired, but his brother Henri scored two goals in what would be a 5–0 Montreal victory. Obviously, it wasn't the start that the Leafs had hoped for.

Toronto's home opener took place two days later. John Keiller MacKay, lieutenant-governor of Ontario, performed the ceremonial puck drop between the Leafs and Rangers, and presented Johnny Bower with the J.P. Bickell Memorial Trophy for his outstanding contributions to the Leafs in the previous season. Toronto dropped the home opener, 5–2.

It was an inauspicious beginning, to say the least. By the end of the month, the Leafs were in last place. On October 29, though, the Leafs erupted for an 8–4 pasting of the Rangers. Imlach had placed Red Kelly at centre between wingers Bob Nevin and Frank Mahovlich, and the Big M responded with three goals. Mahovlich, on a tear, scored four goals against those same New York Rangers in a lopsided 7–3 victory on November 5.

New York was getting spanked on a regular basis and began to implement some roster changes. These included sending the rambunctious Eddie Shack to Toronto in exchange for Pat Hannigan and Johnny Wilson. A highly touted junior, Shack had collected just 16 goals in 141 regular-season games with the Rangers and was considered by many – including the *Toronto Telegram* – to be "an NHL flop." As it happened, this so-called flop soon became an integral part of the second dynasty team, providing scoring, intimidation, and much amusement to Leafs fans everywhere.

Leafs fans were more than amused, however, when the team quickly climbed out of last place and, by December, was vying for first place with the Montreal Canadiens and Detroit Red Wings. Not surprisingly, the already heated rivalry between the Leafs and Habs began to intensify. On December 1, a penalty-filled third period erupted into a veritable free-for-all with several players pairing off, including Frank Mahovlich versus Henri Richard. The diminutive Richard high-sticked the Big M, and the

two started swinging. The tiff earned the Pocket Rocket two misconducts. But when he stuck to hockey, Henri was the best player on the ice, scoring two goals in the 6–3 Montreal win. The unlikely feud between these two stars would extend beyond this game. In another match down the road, Mahovlich would be accused of shooting the puck at Richard's head.

Meanwhile, Frank Mahovlich was in a fight for the NHL's scoring title. The Big M had been on fire all season, and he scored two in a 5–3 win over Montreal on January 25, giving him 39 on the season – a Toronto franchise record, previously held by Babe Dye, who managed 38 with the St. Patricks in 1924–25. And yet more individual achievements were coming the Leafs' way. In a 6–3 victory over the Bruins on February 11, Red Kelly set a Leafs record for most assists in a season, passing Ted Kennedy's mark of 43 from 1950–51 (Kelly ended the season with 50).

The team was also enjoying a particularly satisfying run. With a 4–2 win over the Red Wings on February 12, the Leafs had gone 14 games without a loss. That very night, however, Johnny Bower pulled a hamstring following a collision with the Red Wings' Howie Young. After the game, Bower was hospitalized, but he admitted he didn't want to relinquish his spot in goal because it might jeopardize his shot at earning the Vézina Trophy.

Still, Bower needed time to heal. Don Simmons, who had been acquired from the Bruins on January 31 in a swap of goaltenders that sent Ed Chadwick to Boston, had yet to report. This meant that Gerry McNamara of the Eastern Professional Hockey League's (EPHL) Sudbury Wolves was called up to replace Bower. McNamara, longtime chattel in the Leafs system, had bounced around the minors since tending goal at St. Michael's College School. His hockey odyssey had taken him from Pittsburgh to Buffalo, Cleveland, Winnipeg, Hershey, Rochester, and Sudbury before he finally made his NHL debut in a 3–1 loss to Montreal on February 15.

In a 4–2 loss to New York on February 19, however, McNamara injured his knee. Cesare Maniago, a virtual unknown who was toiling with the Spokane Comets in the WHL, was summoned to replace him. Maniago's first game as a Leaf was a 3–1 win over Detroit on February 25. Upon his arrival, the young goaltender was tendered an impossible schedule. He was to play simultaneously for the Leafs and their EPHL affiliate in Sudbury. On March 14 and 15, Maniago was in net for the Wolves, and he managed to shut out the Sault Thunderbirds

Toronto-born Carl Brewer joined his hometown Maple Leafs in 1957–58 and was part of the influx of young talent that led to the franchise's second dynasty. Brewer was a three-time All-Star before leaving the Maple Leafs in 1964–65. Curiously, he returned to the Leafs for one last hurrah in 1979–80.

both times. He then returned to Toronto for a 5–2 Leafs loss to Montreal on March 16. It was back to Sudbury for March 17, for a 2–1 win over Kitchener. Maniago then travelled back to Toronto on March 18 for a 6–2 win over the Bruins. He capped off the run on March 19, this time in the nation's capital, where Sudbury defeated Hull-Ottawa, 5–2. He had played six games in six nights.

After a breather of exactly one night, Maniago was once again in net on March 21 for a 5–2 loss to Montreal. That night, he surrendered Bernie Geoffrion's 50th goal of the season, making Boom Boom only the second player in NHL history to score 50 goals in one season.

But Toronto was in a good place: Mahovlich was nearing the 50-goal plateau himself; Bower, although suffering through several nagging injuries, remained a good bet for the Vézina; and the team was in a legitimate fight for first place overall with their closest rivals, the Montreal Canadiens.

In the end, the Leafs would have to settle for second place, two points behind Montreal. Still, they were now in the conversation for the Stanley Cup. Bower, at 36 the oldest player in the NHL, did indeed win the Vézina by two goals over Chicago's Glenn Hall, earning

a $1,000 bonus for the win. The conscientious goalie gave Cesare Maniago and Gerry McNamara $100 each as thanks for their part in the successful campaign.

While Imlach had Mahovlich on the ice for nearly the entire third period of the final game of the regular season, the winger's quest to reach 50 goals was halted at 48. Mahovlich nevertheless joined Bower on the NHL's First All-Star Team. Allan Stanley made the Second Team.

Red Kelly, who had centred Mahovlich's line throughout the season, also had a sensational year. In his first full campaign as a forward, Kelly scored 20 goals to go with his team-record 50 assists. Red received the Lady Byng Trophy for the fourth time in his career.

The Leafs' haul of silverware continued as rookie Dave Keon edged out teammate Bob Nevin for the Calder Trophy. While Nevin had had a tremendous year and actually had accumulated more points than Keon, the latter's overall finesse was becoming more and more apparent to everyone who saw him play. He was becoming a difference-maker for the Leafs. The pieces, it seemed, were in place: reliable goaltending, a solid defence corps, scoring forwards, and a healthy balance of youth and experience, skill and grit. And at the helm, a coach who had more or less willed the Leafs into the Stanley Cup final in his first two years on the job.

The semifinal lined up Toronto with fourth-place Detroit. The Leafs had finished 24 points ahead of the Red Wings during the regular season. As such, every amateur prognosticator believed the Leafs would take the series in a cakewalk. The underdogs, however, had something else in mind.

With Bower still struggling with a leg injury, Imlach started Maniago in goal for the series opener in Toronto. He surrendered a goal to Alex Delvecchio at the 14-second mark of the first period, but Bob Nevin tied it up early in the second. The Wings' Howie Young scored his first NHL goal early in the third, but the Leafs' Ron Stewart bounced a puck past Terry Sawchuk later in the period to tie the game and force overtime. Captain George Armstrong scored the sudden-death winner at 4:51 of the second overtime period to give the Leafs a narrow 3–2 win.

The Leafs started Game Two in a similarly positive way. Billy Harris was credited with the opening goal of the game after Young banged a clearing attempt into his own net past a stunned Sawchuk. But in the second, Maniago fanned on two long shots, one by Marcel Pronovost and the other a shorthanded marker by Leo Labine. Maniago had not looked sharp throughout the game, which was won by the Wings, 4–2. The series was now even at one game apiece.

The teams shifted to Detroit for Game Three. Feeling moderately better, Johnny Bower replaced Maniago in the Toronto goal. The game was scoreless through two periods until Gordie Howe beat Bower with a backhander early in the third. Just over a minute later, Val Fonteyne scored to put the game away for Detroit. The Wings now had a surprising two-games-to-one lead in the series.

Coach Imlach inserted Bert Olmstead back into the lineup for the fourth game, and the veteran responded with a power-play goal in the first period. Dave Keon scored on a breakaway late in the period, but the goal was wiped out by the referee, who had called an interference penalty on Ron Stewart. Instead of being up 2–0, Toronto now had Stewart in the penalty box beside Olmstead, who had been given a misconduct penalty for throwing his stick in disgust. Detroit's Labine then scored to tie the game, 1–1.

In the second period, Gordie Howe fired a rocket into the top corner past Bower to put Detroit up 2–1. The Wings collected two more goals to win, 4–1, and took a 3–1 lead in the series. It was, without a doubt, a huge loss. There was now little chance of a Toronto comeback in the series. It appeared that what had been a magical return

to form for the Blue and White was about to prematurely fizzle out.

The Red Wings – counted out before they had even stepped onto the ice for the opening faceoff in Game One – were now on the verge of eliminating the Maple Leafs in Game Five. Detroit notched three goals before Red Kelly, hobbled by a leg injury, was able to bang a power-play marker past Sawchuk in the second period. Keon scored in the third to bring the Leafs within one goal. With the score 3–2 and with just one minute left to play, Imlach pulled Bower for an extra skater. Toronto looked dangerous, but Sawchuk stole two sure goals. Then, Mahovlich fired the puck wide with an open net with only eight seconds to play. Toronto fans had already been booing the Big M throughout the game, and this did not help his cause. In the end, the Leafs skated off in defeat. Heavily favoured to win the Stanley Cup, the Toronto Maple Leafs had been outplayed, outskated, and outscored by the hungry Detroit Red Wings.

Coach Imlach later looked back at that spring: "We could have won in 1961. If we had gotten by Detroit, we would certainly have knocked Chicago out." Alas, it was not to be. The Leafs had enjoyed all manner of individual triumphs during the season, but simply ran out of steam in the chase for first place (Montreal was, coincidentally, eliminated in the other semifinal by the eventual Stanley Cup winners, the Chicago Black Hawks).

With a roster now second to none in the NHL, Toronto simply needed to learn how to win the big prize.

RECOVERED

After having been denied the chance to claim the Cup that spring, the Maple Leafs were more determined than ever to go the distance in the 1961–62 season. There was, by all accounts, little that the team needed to change. As such, Punch Imlach tinkered with his lineup the least of all NHL GMs. Don Simmons took Cesare Maniago's place as Bower's backup. Defenceman Al Arbour was a valuable Intra-League Draft addition from the Black Hawks. In spite of a defensive style that included diving to block shots, Arbour wore glasses when he played. Still, these were minor changes; the team's core remained unchanged.

There was, however, a slight change at Maple Leaf Gardens. Fans heard a new voice echo through the arena that season. Red Barber, who had been the Leafs' public-address announcer since the Gardens opened in 1931, was replaced by Paul Morris. While Barber had been the rink's internal voice during the years of the Kid Line and later through the first dynasty and for Barilko's goal, Morris would be the voice of the second dynasty – and, in fact, for all future Maple Leafs hockey played at the Gardens.

The Leafs started the season on a positive note by beating the Red Wings, 4–2, in Detroit. Two nights later, former Canadian prime minister Louis St. Laurent dropped the ceremonial puck at the Leafs' home opener, and that night, Toronto edged Boston, 3–2.

While the Leafs were off to a decent start, historic changes were coming to the franchise's front office. On November 23, 1961, Conn Smythe vacated the president's chair at Maple Leaf Gardens after 34 years. Though he would stay on as chairman of the board, the elder Smythe tendered his resignation as president and managing director in favour of his son Stafford. Conn was rewarded with a retiring salary of $15,000 per year for life, an office, secretary, car, driver, and seats to home games.

Stafford Smythe and his partners, Harold Ballard and John Bassett, purchased Conn's 45,000 shares in Maple Leaf Gardens for a price estimated at $2,000,000 – and gained 65 per cent of the Gardens stock as a result. Stafford had several changes in mind for the Gardens, including adding 2,000 new seats in the north end and expanding the arena's schedule of non-hockey events.

Meanwhile, the Leafs went on a tear, winning three and tying two. On December 2, the Leafs dumped Chicago, 6–4. That night, a young Gerry Cheevers was in goal in place of the injured Bower and Simmons. The future Bruins star recalled his NHL debut:

> I got a call on Friday night and took the train down from the Sault. We played Chicago and it was a great thrill – no mask, Bobby Hull, scared to death. Then we got on the train and played the next night in Detroit. We got beat, 3–1. I'll never forget that night. Gordie Howe came down, shot what I thought was a routine wrist shot, and knocked the stick right out of my hands! I thought, "Ooh. They're a little bit bigger and stronger up here!"

Cheevers was returned to the minors as soon as Johnny Bower was able to step back into the crease.

A rash of other injuries necessitated constant tweaking of the lineup. On December 29, Imlach picked up Eddie Litzenberger off the waiver wire from Detroit and inserted him between Mahovlich and Nevin on the Leafs' top line, with positive results.

In the end, the Leafs finished second in the league with 85 points. Montreal finished with 98. Toronto concluded the regular season in Boston on March 25 in a 5–4 loss to the Bruins. The China Wall faced 55 shots, the most he had seen all season. He was not, however, the only impressive player in the 1961–62 season. Frank Mahovlich was Toronto's top scorer, finishing fifth in the league with 71 points on 33 goals and 38 assists. Sophomore Dave Keon finished 11th in scoring and was named the Lady Byng Trophy winner. Through 64 games, the Leafs' star centre earned 61 points and only two minutes in penalties. The 22-year-old centre, already showing maturity beyond his years, was named to the NHL's Second All-Star Team along with teammate Carl Brewer.

The Stanley Cup semifinal saw the Maple Leafs face off against the New York Rangers. It had been 20 years since the two teams had met in postseason action, and four years since New York had made the playoffs at all. Yet, as enticing as the matchup might have been, Game One was a listless affair. Fortunately for the Leafs, it ended in their favour, 4–2.

Both Punch Imlach and Rangers player-coach Doug Harvey vowed that their teams would improve on their first-game effort in Game Two. While the match may have been more compelling and Rangers goalie Gump Worsley was at his acrobatic best, the Leafs came out on top, 2–1, and took a two-games-to-none series lead.

The Rangers rebounded in Game Three with a 5–4 win, and New York's momentum continued in Game Four. Led by rookie Rod Gilbert, who that night scored the first of his many NHL goals, the Rangers managed a 4–2 win to tie the series at two games each.

Back in Toronto, Game Five would require overtime. With the game knotted at 2–2 in the second overtime period, Frank Mahovlich recovered a wayward pass and fired a shot at Gump Worsley. Gump sprawled to smother the puck, but it slithered out and Red Kelly poked it home at 4:23 to end the contest. Doug Harvey argued that the whistle should have been blown, but referee Eddie Powers maintained that he saw the puck and that "ten thousand angels could swear I was right but it wouldn't change the decision." The Leafs were more than happy to take their devilish three-games-to-two lead back to New York.

Only it wouldn't be in New York. While Game Six should have been played at Madison Square Garden, the Ringling Brothers and Barnum & Bailey Circus was once again in town and took precedence over hockey. The homeless Rangers were therefore forced to play Game Six at Maple Leaf Gardens.

In retrospect, it was probably an act of mercy that Game Six wasn't played in front of the Rangers faithful, as Toronto pounded New York by a 7–1 score. Dick Duff and Dave Keon scored twice each. With the win, the Leafs won the series, four games to two, and booked a spot in the Stanley Cup final against the defending Stanley Cup champion Chicago Black Hawks.

The Leafs and Black Hawks had met in a Stanley Cup final only once before, back in 1938. That year, Chicago took the best-of-five series, three games to one, to win the Cup. The 1962 series was being billed as "The Punch and Rudy Show," a play on the traditional Punch and Judy puppet show as well as a nod to the opposing coaches, Punch Imlach and Rudy Pilous.

Game One proved to be very much analogous to the violent puppet show the series was named for. Midway through the first period, the Hawks' Murray Balfour slammed into Bobby Baun after Johnny Bower had frozen the puck. Baun gave Balfour a glove to the face, which precipitated a minor melee. Hawks star Bobby Hull moved in and grabbed Baun, and the two traded punches.

A linesman grabbed Hull, so Baun took the opportunity to get in a couple of extra licks. Meantime, while Bob Pulford and Balfour wrestled behind the net, Carl Brewer and Chicago's Jack Evans traded blows. As the *Globe and Mail* reported:

> Suddenly, from the throng emerged the large and handsome Jack Evans, dangling Carl Brewer at the end of one arm while attempting to extract something from Brewer's eye, possibly the bridge of Brewer's nose . . . One could see nothing but flying fists for nearly a minute between these two, before finally they gripped one another closely, waltzed a few steps and finally came to a halt.

Unbelievably, referee Eddie Powers assessed only roughing minors to Baun, Brewer, Hull, and Evans. "If those weren't fights, I never saw a fight," said Conn Smythe, unable to veil his incredulity. When the dust – or perhaps the dust-ups – had settled, the Maple Leafs had collected a 4–1 win.

Stafford Smythe (left) found it difficult to live in the shadow of his legendary father, Conn. Yet he created his own legacy, overseeing the franchise's return to glory in the 1960s.

Game Two bore some residue of the ill feelings generated in the previous match. Murray Balfour, for example, watched the end of the game from Toronto East General Hospital after being checked into the boards by Carl Brewer late in first period. Balfour was diagnosed with a concussion. While Brewer swore it was the "cleanest check" he had ever dished out, Balfour vowed payback against Brewer – and would make good on this two years later. In the actual game, the Leafs skated away with a 3–2 victory, and Toronto now led the series, two games to none.

Both teams altered their lineup somewhat for Game Three. Balfour was medically cleared to play for the Hawks, although he was persuaded to wear a leather helmet. At the other end, Bert Olmstead returned to the Leafs after sitting out five weeks with a broken shoulder.

It was the strategy of both Toronto and Chicago to shadow their opponent's top gun during the bruising contest. Toronto's Eddie Shack and Bob Nevin blanketed Bobby Hull, while Eric Nesterenko was employed to cover Frank Mahovlich, who had nearly been hanged in effigy by rowdies in the top balcony of Chicago Stadium. The dummy was soon removed by an usher.

The move home to Chicago and their exuberant fans helped the Black Hawks. Down 2–0 in the second period, Imlach shuffled his lines to get his team going. He dropped Red Kelly back to defence and added Ron Stewart to a line with Keon and Mahovlich. It was, however, all for naught as Chicago took Game Three, 3–0.

Unfortunately for the Leafs, Game Four provided much the same result. Johnny Bower was injured while making a save on Bobby Hull. As Bower explained, "It's one of the fastest shots I've seen since I've been up here in this league . . . I really had to move fast for it; I didn't really know I could move that fast." While the Leafs netminder trapped the puck and saved the goal, he felt a snap in his leg during the process. Imlach was forced to pull Bower from the game and insert Don Simmons in his place. Simmons led the Maple Leafs onto the ice for the start of the second period, but despite the backup's good showing, the Black Hawks were able to even the series with a sound 4–1 win.

Punch Imlach made the choice to stick with Simmons over the injured Bower for Game Five. It was a good call, and Toronto enjoyed an offensive bonanza in the fifth game. Bob Pulford opened the scoring at the 17-second mark when he dribbled a backhand through Glenn Hall's feet. Seventeen minutes later, Pulford scored again, this time putting the puck over Hall's glove on a long shot. While the Hawks roared back and actually led the game at one point in the second, the Leafs could rest easy. Frank Mahovlich picked up two goals and Pulford picked up one more for the hat trick. The final score: Toronto 8, Chicago 4.

Foster Hewitt offered: "They say a team that won't be beaten, can't be beaten, and that was the story of the Toronto Maple Leafs tonight . . . That was the most impressive win and performance of the Maple Leaf team, not only this year, but in many years in a playoff."

The Leafs were now just one win away from the Stanley Cup.

The series returned to Chicago for Game Six. Don Simmons remained in goal for the Leafs, while the injured Johnny Bower, too nervous to watch from the stands, insisted on watching the game on television. A ten-foot shot from Bobby Hull eluded Simmons to open the scoring in the first period, but it was the only goal Simmons surrendered.

Later, with 11:05 remaining in the third period, Black Hawks fans erupted and rained a shower of debris onto the ice surface. With the organist providing a soundtrack to the mayhem, the maintenance crew collected the programs, hats, and boots. This unusual break in the action disrupted the Black Hawks' momentum, a fact later confirmed by several members of the team.

The Leafs fought back. Bobby Baun took a shot from the point and Frank Mahovlich picked up the rebound and passed it to Bob Nevin, who drove a shot easily into the back of the Hawks net. The game was now knotted at one. Three minutes later, with the Hawks shorthanded, Dick Duff twice swung on a rebound, connecting the second time with his backhand to put the Leafs in front, 2–1, with just six minutes to play.

After Tim Horton took a penalty with 90 seconds remaining in the game, Imlach called on the defensive pairing of Baun and Brewer and the penalty-killing prowess of Nevin and Keon to thwart the Hawks' offensive volleys. The seconds dragged like hours, but the foursome and their trusty backup-goaltender-*cum*-unexpected-hero had survived the unrelenting Chicago attack. Both Nevin and Keon later agreed that those 90 seconds would stand out as a personal highlight of the era. Duff's goal stood as the championship winner. Toronto and its team had weathered the storm. For the first time in 11 years, the Maple Leafs were Stanley Cup champions.

In an article for the *Toronto Daily Star*, captain George Armstrong wrote:

> I've been playing organized hockey since I was 10 or 11. That's 20 or 21 years in the sport. In all that time, it's been my one and only aim to play for a Stanley Cup team. Every player feels the same. Outside of four fellows – Red Kelly, Bert Olmstead, Al Arbour and Eddie Litzenberger – none of us had made it before. As a matter of fact, we hadn't even come close. We're very happy and consider ourselves very fortunate.

Olmstead, in particular, was credited by many of his teammates with helping to engender a winning atmosphere in Toronto. Throughout the playoffs, he had been something of a de facto assistant coach to Imlach, often reprimanding players who took their duties less than seriously. The veteran would be picked up by the Rangers in the Intra-League Draft held during the off-season, but chose instead to retire a champion.

Reflecting on the journey to the Cup, Punch Imlach declared: "This club had the ability, guts and desire that go to make up a championship team. I called them to win the Stanley Cup back in September and they didn't let me down. I knew when they skated out for the game that they'd come back winners. You could sense it. We just outplayed them, and we couldn't be denied."

But while his public face may have been joyful and full of pride for his boys, Imlach hardly endeared himself to the team in private. As Eddie Shack recalled, following the Cup win:

> [W]e were in Chicago Stadium wahooin' and having a beer in the downstairs dressing room, and Imlach comes in all cranky, like we just lost. Then he says, "If you aren't on the goddamned bus in 15 minutes, you won't be on this team next year!" No congratulations, no "Nice goin'" or anything. What a crabby bastard. He couldn't even loosen up and have a beer with us!

While the coach might have been less than effusive, some Leafs fans would not let the sun rise before they showed their appreciation. The team's plane touched down at Toronto International Airport at 3:30 A.M. Some 2,000 fans were there to greet the champions, including a kilted bagpiper and two trumpeters who forced their way into the customs area as the team was passing through immigration. The pervasive "Go Leafs Go" chant was heard throughout the airport. Punch Imlach emerged with the Stanley Cup, and it was carried high over the crowd as the fans surged to touch it. The Cup was placed in a police cruiser for safekeeping, and the fans returned to the arrivals area to greet their heroes.

As the players emerged, they were hoisted onto the shoulders of fans. Dick Duff, one of the first to be lifted from his feet, waved the stick with which he scored the Stanley Cup–winning goal. George Armstrong presented the puck that Duff had scored the winning goal with to Dodo Imlach, the coach's wife. As the captain explained, "Mrs. Imlach asked for it two weeks ago. She said she wanted the puck that won the Stanley Cup, and I said I'd see that she got it. I know that goal meant as much to Punch as it did us . . . maybe more." That night, Imlach took the Stanley Cup to his Scarborough home.

The Leafs scheduled a team photo with the Stanley Cup the next day. Bert Olmstead, however, had already returned to his farm in Saskatchewan. To solve the issue of the missing Olmstead, the Leafs employed a little 1960s-style Photoshopping, as Billy Harris recalled:

> What the Leafs did for that particular team picture was get the office boy, that year it happened to be Bill Collins, who played briefly in the NHL, and had him come down and dress up in a Leaf uniform, sit in the front row and have his picture taken. But in the official team picture, they transposed Bert Olmstead's head onto Bill Collins's body, so that in the team picture, you're looking at Bert Olmstead's head but not his body.

The Olmstead incident triggered a change in policy: official team pictures would thenceforth be taken early in the playoffs to avoid the possibility of absent players.

On April 25, 1962, the City of Toronto staged a celebration parade on what was an unusually warm afternoon. The response overwhelmed the organizers and the city's police force – over 50,000 people showed up to take part in the festivities. Led by the Queen's Own Rifles, the ticker-tape parade saw the Leafs players seated in convertibles that were driven up Bay Street from the corner of Wellington to City Hall at Queen Street. The short-staffed police department simply did not anticipate such an enormous crowd, nor the ensuing pandemonium. Only the first four of the 15 convertibles carrying the Stanley Cup champions to City Hall were able to get through the crowd.

"It was craziness," Tim Horton's wife, Lori, remembered. "The players had to get out of their cars and walk through Simpson's department store to get to City Hall. The cars just couldn't make it through the crowd anymore."

Eddie Shack, true to his nickname, "The Entertainer," added to the mayhem. Standing in his convertible, Shack did the Twist, the current dance sensation spawned by Chubby Checker's hit song. Fans mobbed the players, pulling their hair and ties and stealing their handkerchiefs. Several people who lined the parade route actually fainted in the unseasonably hot weather.

On the steps of City Hall, Mayor Nathan Phillips declared Toronto to be "the hockey capital of the world." At the top of the flagpole fluttered a giant Canadian flag, although this time, it was blue and white to honour the hometown heroes. While each player was introduced, the noise level was so high that the introductions were drowned out. In fact, so many fans were on hand that the reception had to be moved from the front steps of City Hall to the second-floor council chamber. The crowd was the largest ever to congregate at Toronto's City Hall to that date. Later, in quiet reflection, Bobby Baun rightfully observed that "no matter what we Leaf players did from the day on, our lives would be changed forever. Torontonians are mad about hockey, and that made us ultimate heroes."

As if on cue, and only six weeks after the wild celebration at City Hall, there was news from the north. On June 6, 1962, the teletype machines in newsrooms across Canada tapped out the eerie bulletin:

> The wreckage of what is believed to be the plane that carried hockey player Bill Barilko and Dr. Henry Hudson to their deaths 11 years ago was found today about 45 miles north of Cochrane. The wreckage was spotted by a Department of Lands and Forests helicopter crew which has been combing desolate bush lands north of Cochrane since smashed metal was seen glinting in the sun last Thursday.

At 8:15 that evening, the plane was positively identified as having belonged to Dr. Hudson. By methodically piecing together parts of the fuselage discovered at the site, they were able to read the letters CF-FXT, the registration marks assigned to Hudson's Fairchild 24 plane. The famous 1951 Cup-winning goal and subsequent fishing trip had already become part of Maple Leafs folklore. Now, the discovery of the plane signalled the closing of one chapter, and the opening of another. Bill Barilko had been recovered. So, too, had the Toronto Maple Leafs' winning touch.

REPEAT

The reigning Stanley Cup champions had every reason to feel confident as they entered the 1962–63 campaign. Their talent-laden lineup boasted a nice mix of youthful exuberance and veteran experience. Having tasted victory once, the Maple Leafs wanted to do it again.

For his part, Punch Imlach set the bar even higher. The GM–coach wanted to finish first in the league *and* win the Stanley Cup. It was, without a doubt, a tall order, a feat the Leafs hadn't accomplished since 1948, when Hap Day was behind the bench. Imlach would nevertheless remain focused on this lofty goal.

This year's incarnation of the Leafs looked almost identical to the previous season's championship team. There were, however, some minor changes. The Leafs picked up 26-year-old defence prospect Kent Douglas in a trade with Springfield of the AHL. Bert Olmstead's departure opened up a spot for one of the team's prospects in Rochester, including Bruce Draper, Larry Keenan, and Jim Pappin.

While the on-ice machinations were minor, there was a curious off-ice development when Red Kelly agreed to run for Parliament as the Liberal candidate in the Toronto-area riding of York West. Perhaps unsurprisingly, given the popularity of the Leafs, Kelly won the seat by a healthy margin over Conservative incumbent John Borden Hamilton, who had held the seat since 1954. As Kelly explained, Liberal leader Lester Pearson had personally asked him to run: "I didn't have any experience in politics but I thought, 'If I can help get Lester Pearson elected, it'll be great for the country.'" The governing Conservatives held on, although they went in with a commanding majority (208 of 265 seats) and emerged with just 116 – a minority Parliament.

The life of a hockey-playing MP wasn't exactly an easy one:

> I'd go to practice in the morning, then I'd catch a plane and go to Ottawa for the afternoon and evening sessions and then come home on the last flight and get home at 1:00 or 1:30 in the morning. Most of the time, we played on Saturdays, Sundays and Wednesday nights. The House didn't sit on Wednesday night and it didn't sit on Saturday or Sunday. The only time I had a real problem is when we played in Montreal on a Thursday night. [The government was] in a minority position, so could be defeated. One night, we had votes on a whole pile [of legislation] and I couldn't get away.

After four years in the American Hockey League, Kent Douglas (left) was traded to Toronto in 1962–63. An aggressive defenceman with a booming shot from the blueline, Douglas went on to win the Calder Trophy as the rookie of the year, the first defenceman to win the award. That same spring, he helped the Maple Leafs win the Stanley Cup.

Red's frantic dual life persisted for some time. In fact, John Diefenbaker's minority government lasted less than a year before Canadians had to go to the polls once again. The multifaceted Kelly ran for re-election in April 1963 and defeated his Conservative opponent (this time, Alan Eagleson, the future executive director of the NHL Players' Association), garnering 51 per cent of the vote and helping Lester Pearson form a minority government. When an election was called for November 1965, Kelly opted not to try for a third term.

Meanwhile, Maple Leaf Gardens began to be known in its own right for multitasking. Through the Conn Smythe years, the arena had been relatively busy with hockey, wrestling, political and religious conventions, and the occasional musical program. The new guard took a different approach. While Stafford Smythe engrossed himself in the hockey operations, vice-president Harold Ballard set about finding ways to increase revenue streams. Ballard reduced the number of dark nights at the venue by adding closed-circuit boxing matches, rodeos, religious revivals, and concerts from big-name touring acts. As Dick Beddoes observed, Ballard "started what has become the biggest operation in Canada for bringing in rock groups . . . I don't think Old Man Smythe knew what a rock group was, unless it was a collection of hard-hitting defencemen!"

The Gardens was also reconfigured in 1962. By reducing the size of existing seats and finding new places to install them, 981 new seats were added, some of which came at the expense of the organ loft and the Queen's portrait. The latter was a touchy subject, although Ballard was unmoved: "If people want to see pictures of the Queen, they can go to an art gallery. Besides, what the hell position can a Queen play?"

Ballard also introduced advertising signage to Maple Leaf Gardens. CCM and Ford, for example, paid to have signs at either end of the rink. Schick razor blades were advertised on the escalator risers and the Zamboni sported advertising for Dominion food stores. As George Mara of the Silver Seven management team confessed, Ballard "sold everything . . . everything he did was a money-maker."

Ballard and Stafford Smythe also decided to open a private, members-only club within Maple Leaf Gardens. After some stores along Church Street were removed, the Hot Stove Lounge was born. Ballard's fiscal foresight, coupled with an outstanding era of Leafs hockey, caused profits of Maple Leaf Gardens Ltd. to soar from $300,000 in 1961 to $900,000 in 1964.

These financial gains and ideological changes signified a clear break with the past, the starkness of which would be calibrated to Ballard's ever-growing influence on – and power over – the franchise.

While Ballard could be ingenious when it came to raising revenues, he was also mercurial. Following the annual All-Star dinner at Toronto's Royal York Hotel in October 1962, some of the league's executives decided to relax over cocktails. Maple Leafs brass bemoaned the fact that they had been unable to sign Frank Mahovlich to a deal for the upcoming season. James Norris, chairman of the board of the Chicago Black Hawks, stated that he would pay any amount to get Mahovlich. When Ballard asked Norris to quantify the amount, Norris replied, "A million dollars." Ballard immediately exclaimed, "Sold!"

Norris and Ballard shook hands on the deal and Norris gave Ballard $1,000 in hundred-dollar bills as a show of good faith. Ballard then wrote on a piece of Royal York stationery, "Excepted [sic] by Maple Leaf Hockey Club." Jack Amell, a member of the Silver Seven, also signed the sheet. Punch Imlach was present, but he refused to shake hands on the deal. Norris then contacted Johnny Gottselig, the Black Hawks' publicity director, and told him to announce the transaction.

The release was sent to media outlets across North America in the wee hours of the following morning. The *Globe and Mail* ran with it in Toronto, but in the interim the story had shifted: "A report that Frank Mahovlich had been sold to the Chicago Black Hawks for $1,000,000 early Saturday morning was denied by Maple Leafs' President Stafford Smythe, who admitted the fantastic offer had been made by Jim Norris, chairman of the Chicago Black Hawks' board."

For his part, Norris freely admitted to the deal: "I have offered the Maple Leafs one million dollars for Mahovlich." And general manager Tommy Ivan likewise confirmed that the offer had been made.

While these negotiations were rapidly unfolding, no one had bothered to tell Frank Mahovlich. The Big M was, in the end, told by his father. Mahovlich was dumb-founded: "I hadn't signed a contract but I didn't figure I was going to be traded. We were only $500 apart. Can you believe that? I think I asked for $25,000 and Punch offered $24,500."

At noon, Stafford Smythe, Harold Ballard, and a roomful of reporters greeted Tommy Ivan, general manager of the Hawks, who, as promised, delivered the cheque on behalf of Jim Norris. But Ivan was rebuffed by Smythe. The latter claimed he had no authority to make such a deal without conferring with the board of directors. Ivan left with his boss's personal cheque. Norris was livid and insisted that the transaction was legal, as he had a slip of paper confirming the sale, signed by two executives of Maple Leaf Gardens. The Hawks chairman forced the issue with NHL president Clarence Campbell, who ruled that the sale was null and void on the grounds that "no responsible member of the Maple Leaf organization had accepted the bid." Norris was reeling and believed that the Leafs had reneged on the deal: "I still regard Mahovlich as my property. We shook hands on it. That's been my way of doing business."

As it happened, the order to cancel the deal had actually come from on high. Though he no longer *owned* the team, Conn Smythe was still – at least for the time being – the franchise's chief counsel. He had advised Stafford to kill the deal. The Leafs' head scout, Bob Davidson, confirmed: "Connie Smythe told me that he cancelled the deal . . . Harold Ballard didn't know a hell of a lot about hockey. He just thought it was a great thing to be offered a million dollars."

Though he had nothing to do with the fiasco, Mahovlich was now about to feel the wrath of a man who believed he had been wronged. "Ballard didn't like me because he was embarrassed by the whole situation," the Big M lamented, adding, "I never really felt comfortable with the team after 1962. My relationship with Imlach had suffered and it never got repaired."

As fate would have it, the Leafs' 1962–63 season opener was against the Black Hawks. The mercury rose above 90 degrees in Chicago Stadium, and the ice was slow and so watery that the rink attendants didn't even bother to flood for the third period. The Maple Leafs, however, didn't mind too much and beat the Black Hawks, 3–1. Three nights later, the Leafs had their home opener. The game ended in a 2–2 tie with the visiting Boston Bruins.

The off-season Mahovlich fiasco had intensified the already-heated rivalry between the Leafs and Black Hawks. Things boiled over in a game on November 22. In the second period, Kent Douglas fenced with Stan Mikita, which immediately drew a crowd. Eddie Shack, making his first appearance of the game at 19:07 of the third, traded punches with Murray Balfour, and that likewise set off a flurry of fights. Allan Stanley duked it out with Elmer Vasko, while Reggie Fleming, who had already served three minor penalties in the third period alone, raced to grab Shack but was intercepted and tackled by Tim Horton. Later, Fleming stood in front of the Leafs bench and taunted the Toronto players. Dick

Duff tried to scramble over the boards to get at Fleming, but was grabbed by his jersey as teammates restrained him. The game, incidentally, ended in a 1–0 win for the Black Hawks.

The season wasn't, however, all about cowboys and pugilists. On January 12, 1963, Dave Keon was presented with the Lady Byng Trophy for being the NHL's most gentlemanly player of the previous season. Keon scored two goals and, in an ironic twist, earned a minor penalty as Toronto edged Detroit, 2–1. Keon's penalty, his first of the season and only his fifth in three seasons, resulted when Wings defenceman Howie Young rode him into the boards and held him up there. "I was trying to break loose and when I did, I hit him on the head," the gallant centreman admitted. "It was sort of a chain reaction. I might have been a little browned off."

Toronto battled Detroit and Chicago for first place throughout the season. The Leafs enjoyed a ten-game unbeaten streak – seven wins and three ties – that began against the Hawks on February 27 and left Toronto only one point behind Chicago.

As such, the Maple Leafs went into a game against Montreal on March 20 needing only a tie to clinch first place. A victory against the Habs was a challenge at the best of times, but the Leafs were also suffering at the moment: Mahovlich was out with the flu and Bobby Baun ended up injuring his knee on the first shift of the game. With only a minute to go in the contest, Montreal was up 3–2. At this point, Imlach pulled Simmons for an extra attacker. The Canadiens controlled the puck, but an attempt at an insurance goal went wide. With only seconds remaining, Bob Nevin was able to dump the puck into the corner to the left of Jacques Plante. Duff stripped Terry Harper of the puck behind the Montreal goal and tapped it to Nevin. Keon cut in front of Plante, picked up the pass from Nevin, and flipped a backhander past Plante for his second goal of the game at 19:52. Toronto's tie with Montreal secured first place for the Leafs.

The team had now achieved the first of the two targets set by the coach in September. "I was a little worried before the game," Imlach said. "Our guys were really nervous. They had all been in the Stanley Cup playoffs before, but this is the first time they have had a chance to finish first. As a result, they were afraid to make mistakes."

Imperfect as they might have been, the ecstatic Leafs were now headed to the semifinals.

If Frank Mahovlich was unnerved by the hoopla surrounding the Chicago deal that wasn't, he didn't show it on the ice. He led the team in scoring and finished fourth in the league with 73 points, including 36 goals. Both Mahovlich and Carl Brewer were named to the NHL's First All-Star Team. Tim Horton was selected to the Second Team. After the playoffs were over, Dave Keon would once again be named as the recipient of the Lady Byng Trophy. Keon scored 28 goals and registered 56 points while spending only two minutes in the penalty box all season. Kent Douglas received the Calder Trophy as rookie of the year.

While the Montreal Canadiens had finished the season in third place, they had collected only three fewer points than Toronto. (Chicago finished only one point behind the Leafs, while only five points separated Toronto from fourth-place Detroit.) In this way, the series was far more evenly matched than the rankings suggested.

Toronto nevertheless orchestrated a tight, defensive game and earned a 3–1 victory over the Canadiens in Game One at Maple Leaf Gardens. It was a strong start for the Blue and White. Montreal came out just as strong in Game Two. The play went back and forth, and then late in the second period, Keon tried to deke around Jacques Plante. The forward lost control of the puck, but the desired result was still achieved as he watched it roll under the Montreal goaltender's stick for the winning goal. The 3–2 win gave the Leafs a two-games-to-none lead.

The series then shifted to Montreal. Punch Imlach, who regularly imposed fines for various team infractions, was forced to swallow a spoonful of his own medicine when traffic tie-ups on Highway 401 forced him, assistant GM King Clancy, Red Kelly, and Tim Horton to miss their flight. Harold Ballard insisted that no one was immune from punishment, and he fined Imlach and Clancy $100 each. The Leafs' Dick Duff cheekily insisted, "Not enough, this is the playoffs. [It] should be $1,000 each."

The smiles continued for Toronto in Game Three. Johnny Bower earned his first-ever playoff shutout in his 38th career postseason contest as the Maple Leafs dumped the Canadiens, 2–0. The win put Toronto clearly in the driver's seat. Anxious to sweep out the series in Game Four, the Leafs maintained the close-checking approach that had characterized their postseason success to that point. The Canadiens, though, were able to rebound. Plante was sound and was afforded outstanding protection from the team in front of him as Montreal avoided elimination with a 3–1 win.

Back in the friendly confines of Maple Leaf Gardens, Toronto ended Montreal's hopes with a Game Five blow-out. Johnny Bower earned his second shutout of the playoffs by stopping all 35 shots in the 5–0 victory.

Bower was, according to the *Toronto Daily Star*, "gifted with the knowledge and wisdom of at least 39 years and the rubber legs and reflexes of a teenager."

With the Canadiens dismissed, the Leafs would now face the Detroit Red Wings in the Stanley Cup final. The Wings had upset Chicago in the other semifinal, and despite their fourth-place finish were not to be taken lightly. In fact, Detroit was the only team to hold an edge over the Leafs through the regular season, winning seven, losing six, and tying one in their fourteen meetings.

On the afternoon of Game One, Imlach received a newspaper clipping from a Detroit source. In it, Sid Abel predicted that the Red Wings would "take Toronto and they'll do it easier than the Chicago series." This was perfect ammunition for the coach. Punch used the clipping to his advantage in the pregame pep talk. It worked.

Dick Duff set an NHL record for the fastest two goals scored from the start of a playoff game: his first at the 49-second mark and his second just 19 seconds later. Bob Nevin made it 3–0 for the Leafs later that period, but Toronto let their visitors up off the canvas in the second period. Larry Jeffrey scored twice for Detroit to make the game far more interesting. Yet, while the Leafs seemingly stopped skating, Nevin added an insurance goal to secure the 4–2 win for Toronto.

Game Two bore a striking resemblance to its predecessor. While Mahovlich was out nursing a deep-bruise knee injury, Ed Litzenberger rose to the occasion with a three-point night. In the first period, Litzenberger banged in his own rebound to open the scoring for the Leafs. Later, Ron Stewart broke into the clear, deked Sawchuk, and tucked a backhander into the back of the net for Toronto's second goal. Early in the second, Nevin scored to put Toronto up 3–0. Gordie Howe scored less than a minute after Nevin to put the Wings on the board, but Ron Stewart's goal on a power play restored the three-goal lead. Toronto now led, 4–1, going into the third period. While Howe managed a second goal in the third, it was too little, too late. The Leafs had earned their second 4–2 victory.

While Toronto was up two–nil in the series, the team could have played better. The *Star* noted that the Leafs "weren't puffing hard enough to extinguish a match." The *Globe* suggested that a Leaf sweep in four games "would be the humane thing" to put the Wings out of their misery. The Wings were, however, heartened by the fact they had been down two games to none in their series against Chicago and had still managed to come back to win the next four. The team was also headed home to the Olympia.

I was drafted in the fifth round of the 2003 NHL Draft by the Toronto Maple Leafs. That was a surreal moment. The team I grew up watching had just chosen me! I remember going to a Leafs game with my dad in the early '90s at Maple Leaf Gardens. Dougie Gilmour was my favourite player, and I wore number 93 when I was a kid playing minor hockey, and even tucked my jersey in on the side like him, so to be drafted by the Leafs was amazing.

John Mitchell
PLAYER
2008–11

The early results suggested Detroit might very well duplicate their semifinal feat. Vic Stasiuk scored the Red Wings' first goal on a screened backhand 33 seconds into Game Three. Dave Keon, though, evened the score late in the period. Midway through the second period, the Red Wings' Alex Faulkner fired a 30-foot rocket that went in off the post past Bower. It was the first of two goals the former Leaf scored that night. Tim Horton replied with Toronto's second goal five minutes later, then Faulkner tipped a shot from the point to give Detroit the lead in the second period of the seesaw battle. With no scoring in the third, Faulkner's goal proved to be the game winner, his third winning goal of the 1963 playoffs. With the 3–2 victory, the Wings were back in the series.

The game was, according to Punch Imlach, the Leafs' "poorest game as a team in a month and a half. We weren't skating, gave the puck away too much, our wings weren't coming back and we didn't knock enough of them down." Fortunately for the coach and his players, the Leafs' effort would be much better in Game Four.

While the Wings likely played their most efficient game of the final in Game Four, Johnny Bower was stunning in the Leafs goal. Howe opened the scoring for Detroit, but George Armstrong replied early in the second period. Eddie Joyal regained the lead for the Wings, but late in the second period, Red Kelly faked a drop pass to Mahovlich, used Wings defenceman Bill Gadsby as a screen, and then fired a missile past Sawchuk. Kelly's goal tied the game at two.

Halfway through the third, Dave Keon scored the winning goal. The nimble centre deked two Wings and then passed to Armstrong in front of the net. The captain went in too quickly, and Keon scooted in to claim the puck. He tried to pull it across in front of Sawchuk, but lost control. The puck hit the sliding Sawchuk in the pads, rebounded out, hit Norm Ullman's skate, and then found the back of the net. Red Kelly later scored his second of the game to ice the victory. With a familiar 4–2 score, Toronto took a three-games-to-one lead in the series back to Canada.

With the Stanley Cup on hand, Dave Keon opened the scoring on a shorthanded breakaway late in the first period. Delvecchio scored for Detroit early in the second to tie the game. Midway through the third, Eddie Shack deflected a Kent Douglas shot past Sawchuk to put the Leafs out in front. As Shack explained, "I was cruising near the goal and the puck hit the stick on the handle and went in. I never even saw it. All I wanted to do was get the hell out of the way." Fortunately for the Entertainer, he *didn't* get out of the way: his goal proved to be the Stanley Cup winner.

With the Leafs up 2–1, Bob Pulford was called for holding at 18:07. Coach Sid Abel summoned Sawchuk to the bench for a sixth skater, and what ensued was a frantic attack. Bower used his skate to make a superlative save on Eddie Joyal. Bruce MacGregor then hit the post. Norm Ullman unleashed a shot that struck Gordie Howe as he tangled with Bower in the crease. A stoppage in play allowed Bower to head to the bench to have his catching glove repaired after it was sliced by Howe's skate. The subsequent faceoff took place in the Leafs end. During the scramble, Keon was pulled down, but quickly regained his legs and golfed a backhand shot that wobbled crazily and somehow slid into the empty Detroit goal with only five seconds remaining in regulation.

The Toronto Maple Leafs had won their second consecutive Stanley Cup. The *Globe and Mail* reported that an "explosion of sound rocked the Gardens and Toronto fans, normally the most decorous in the league, even threw programs and a few hats on the ice."

Clarence Campbell presented the Stanley Cup to Toronto captain George Armstrong, who gathered all of his teammates for a photograph around the table where the Cup sat. Everyone but Carl Brewer was in the photo. The defenceman had had a challenging night. With five minutes left in the third period, he broke the radius bone in his arm while attempting to check André Pronovost in front of the Leafs bench. Brewer missed the speedy winger and used his left hand to cushion his blow as he tumbled into the boards. While the Leafs were revelling on the ice, Brewer was in the hospital.

Meanwhile, it was bedlam in the victors' dressing room. The room was jammed with family members, well-wishers, newspaper reporters, and photographers. Over the din, the Maple Leaf Gardens faithful could be heard calling for Dave Keon to provide a curtain call. The scoring star, who had picked up seven goals and five assists through the postseason, obliged, emerging from the dressing room to wave to the crowd. The building shook with cheering.

As the dressing room crowd thinned, a stoic Imlach sat down with reporters and delivered a compelling soliloquy:

Humility is something I usually don't believe in, being a positive thinker. But at the moment, I'm full of humility because of the 110 per cent cooperation I have received from my players – the world champion Maple Leafs – and the fans. The experts said my old players – Johnny Bower, Red Kelly and Allan Stanley – were over the hill. I knew they were wrong. They're a special

For all the youth in most of Ontario, Toronto was our team and the Maple Leaf players like [Charlie] Conacher, [Joe] Primeau, [Busher] Jackson, [King] Clancy, and Hap Day were our heroes . . . It was a boyhood dream to play for Toronto.

Ted Kennedy
PLAYER
1943–55; 1957

breed of athlete. This is a sound hockey club, real champions with just the right blending of age and youth. I have tried to teach my men that you don't wait for things to happen; you have to go out and make them happen. That is what they did this season and that is why they are league champions and Stanley Cup champions.

The City of Toronto hosted a parade for the new Stanley Cup champions one day after the Cup win. Fans began to gather at 9:00 A.M., and by the time the parade began at noon, more than 40,000 people had jammed Bay Street to salute their victors. In order to get a better look, fans climbed onto the roofs of cars. Police chief James Mackey noted that 600 officers lined the parade route to ensure that mayhem didn't spoil the celebration.

As the clock in City Hall struck 12, the red-coated civic honour guard led the parade. The band struck up "Hail, Hail, the Gang's All Here" as the procession of convertibles made its way from Wellington Street to City Hall. Captain George Armstrong sat with the Stanley Cup in the lead car. The ticker tape streamed lazily down from the windows of buildings that lined the victors' route.

Ed Fitkin served as the master of ceremonies from the top of the stairs at City Hall. There, he introduced Mayor Donald Summerville, then bellowed at the Leafs standing before him: "You are *our* world champions!" Every one of the players was handed a gold tie clasp that bore the insignia of the City of Toronto. The gift matched the cuff links the players had received from the city the previous spring. Once the civic reception concluded, the Maple Leafs headed over to Maple Leaf Gardens with their families, as well as the staff and their families, for a quiet party. That night, Stafford Smythe held a party at his home in Etobicoke.

The Leafs had had a very special year. The team had hit both of the targets that Punch had assigned: finish first in the league standings and repeat as Stanley Cup champions. The whole of Toronto knew that this was a special time. And Imlach and his lads firmly believed that the course was not nearly run just yet. While cynics felt that Father Time would soon catch up with the Leafs' core players, the city's optimists were more inclined to embrace the prevailing spirit.

ON ONE GOOD LEG

In the summer of 1963, Tim Horton began to consider life after hockey and pursued a new business outside the game.

Few could have guessed that his business would one day be seen as an indelible symbol of Canadiana. It must be remembered that this was an age when most NHL players still had to seek summer employment. Horton had spent previous summers working in Conn Smythe's gravel pits, but the veteran Leaf was now looking to break out on his own.

Horton experimented with several businesses, including a used-car dealership and, later, a short-lived chain of hamburger and chicken restaurants. While the market was saturated with burger joints, Horton noticed a dearth in donut shops. The defenceman opened up a Tim Horton Do-Nut shop in metropolitan Toronto in 1963. Encouraged, Horton opened a location in what was formerly a gas station on Ottawa Street in Hamilton. It was an immediate success. The store not only capitalized on the donut craze that was sweeping the province but also hit a niche in the market by virtue of the convenience of its drive-in quotient.

Meanwhile, the Maple Leafs felt little need to tinker with the lineup in advance of the 1963–64 season. The only change of consequence was the addition of rookie Jim Pappin. The Leafs did, however, boldly experiment with some international players. A decade before Swedes such as Anders Hedberg, Ulf Nilsson, Börje Salming, and Inge Hammarström began playing big-time hockey in North America, Toronto invited a couple of Swedish imports to training camp in Peterborough, Ontario. These were netminder Kjell Svensson, who had been selected to Swedish league All-Star teams, and Carl-Göran Öberg, who had scored 25 goals and 43 points in only 21 games in Sweden in 1962–63. Svensson and Öberg were inserted into Toronto's lineup for some exhibition games in western Canada. Although they showed well in game action, the experiment was short-lived and both players were returned to Sweden before the start of the season. Still, the trial opened up the possibility that Swedes and other Europeans might one day crack the Leafs lineup.

The Leafs opened the season at home against the Boston Bruins. Prime Minister Lester Pearson was on hand to drop the puck for the ceremonial faceoff. During the first intermission, Pearson also presented Dave Keon with the J.P. Bickell Award. It was the second straight season Keon was recipient of the honour. In terms of the game itself, Red Kelly, the Liberal member for York West, scored in front of his other boss, Prime Minister Pearson, in a 5–1 Leafs victory.

The Leafs doubled Montreal, 6–3, in a chippy contest on October 30. After an on-ice scrap, the Habs' Terry

Having been drafted by the Leafs and played over 300 games for them, and now, back in the fold here working for Leafs TV, I really feel like I'm part of the fabric of the team. And I feel really privileged to do what I do, because I've got that passion for the game of hockey, but certainly, a passion for the Toronto Maple Leafs. It would be an awesome thing one day to see a Stanley Cup being raised here in Toronto, and it'd be great to be a part of it.

Bob McGill
PLAYER
1981–87; 1992–93

Harper and the Leafs' Bob Pulford continued their battle in the penalty box. After the altercation, Stafford Smythe began lobbying the league to have segregated penalty boxes. "It's ridiculous to ask two guys who've been trying to knock each other's heads off to sit quietly side by side," Smythe explained, going on to say, "We've tried policemen, but that didn't work out too well." Smythe vowed that Maple Leaf Gardens would separate the penalty boxes at some point that season. As it happened, the Canadiens beat Smythe to the punch when the Montreal Forum provided a divided penalty box for a game on November 9 against the Chicago Black Hawks.

Across the Atlantic, a massive landslide caused a tsunami in a lake north of Venice. Nearly 2,000 people lost their lives as a result of the subsequent overflowing of the Vajont Dam. In a city with a burgeoning Italian-Canadian community, there was a public outpouring of support. On November 19, the City Radio and Press Club challenged Toronto City Council to a charity hockey game at George Bell Arena, with proceeds going to the flood victims. Billy Harris and Bob Pulford served as honorary coaches, and Frank Mahovlich and Eddie Shack were the referees. Toronto mayor Donald Summerville, who had been a practice goaltender for the Leafs during the 1930s, was in net against the team of local media members. The mayor had only been in the crease for a few minutes when he made his way towards the dressing room. Al Boliska, the morning announcer at CHUM radio, playfully wrestled with the mayor just before he left the ice surface. Mayor Summerville finally made it to the dressing room, where he reached for his medication, but before he was able to take anything, he slumped to the floor, unconscious. The arena manager started artificial respiration while a doctor hurried to His Worship's side, but was unable to find a pulse. An ambulance rushed Summerville to the hospital, where he was pronounced dead. The mayor had suffered an acute coronary occlusion. Only months earlier, Summerville had presided over the Toronto Maple Leafs' Stanley Cup parade and civic reception.

It was not the only bizarre event to involve the Leafs. On November 30, the Canadian Championship Rodeo was held at Maple Leaf Gardens. Although detractors had advised the Maple Leafs' owners against hosting the lucrative event because of the ramifications for the ice surface, Stafford Smythe dismissed the naysayers. As a result, sawdust and soil were dumped directly onto the Gardens ice. Smythe had been assured that the cleanup after the rodeo would not adversely affect the ice. The unprotected ice surface, however, warmed and bonded with the soil and sawdust, as well as waste from the animals. When the Gardens crew tried to remove the layer of dirt and sawdust after the five-day event, they encountered a near-impossible task. As Harold Ballard explained:

> The earth and sawdust melted into the ice and then it froze again to a cement-like consistency. When we started to lift the surface, it refused to move. We had to bring in 200 extra workers to aid our regular staff of 75, and it was a miracle that we got any kind of surface ready by 8:30. We had two bulldozers, four front-loaders, a grader, two sweepers, 15 trucks and 275 men trying to get the ice in shape. We had to truck 20 tons of snow from Richmond Hill to fill the holes caused by the bulldozers and men using 50 flat picks to dig the earth, sawdust and other things out of the ice.

All the work left the ice terribly pockmarked and the puck bounced uncontrollably.

The Leafs were slated to host the Red Wings that night, and had it not been for radio and television commitments, the game almost certainly would have been cancelled. Detroit coach Sid Abel believed that the playing surface wasn't fit for hockey and lodged a formal complaint with league president Clarence Campbell. The game was an hour and a quarter late in starting, and the eventual 1–1 draw marked the first time a game had ever been delayed at Maple Leaf Gardens.

The following week, the Leafs continued their long-standing battle with the Black Hawks. The intense antipathy that had existed between the two teams had not dissipated, and a donnybrook on December 7 served as a continuation of the March 1961 bench-clearing brawl.

In the preamble to the hostilities, Eddie Shack stated in a pregame radio interview that "[Reggie] Fleming was only dangerous when he was behind a player. Face-to-face, he was a little cat who would run away." That set the stage for the battle to come.

Midway through the third, Shack earned a high-sticking penalty for hacking down Fleming with his stick. Fleming waited until the next time both were on the ice together, and, with just over three minutes to go before the end of the game, exacted his revenge. The Black Hawk speared Shack in the solar plexus, sending him to the ice, gasping for air. Fleming was assessed a five-minute major.

Bob Baun, however, didn't believe that the punishment fit the crime. He rushed to the penalty box and grabbed

Andy Bathgate (left) had led the New York Rangers in scoring for eight seasons when he was dealt to Toronto in February 1964. It was just what coach Punch Imlach envisioned, as Bathgate scored the Stanley Cup–winning goal to triumphantly conclude the Maple Leafs' season.

Fleming. Referee Frank Udvari, who had officiated that previous fight-filled contest in 1961, believed it would be most prudent to send Fleming directly to the dressing room. To get there, however, Fleming would have to cross the ice and pass 16 livid Toronto players. Thirty minutes later, Fleming finally made it to the dressing room. He was challenged, in turn, by Baun, Larry Hillman, and Dick Duff. At the same time, other fights broke out. Even Shack made a miraculous recovery and dashed into combat.

The most intense of the scraps, however, would feature the Hawks' Murray Balfour and the Leafs' Carl Brewer.

Brewer, still nursing an injured arm, had been tangled up with Ab McDonald when Balfour hit him. Balfour then engaged Brewer in an open-ice battle. As they waltzed the length of the ice and along the boards, Balfour pulled Brewer's sweater over his head and pushed him towards the boards by the players' benches. "Murray Balfour put his head down and was running me into the boards," Brewer later recalled. "I didn't realize the [gate leading to the] bench was open, and I fell back through the bench – under the bench – and that was the end of the fight."

For his part, Balfour boasted about the event: "I drove him into the bench and I was on top of him, beating the hell out of him. He started yelling, 'Bobby! Bobby!' Then Haggert and Imlach landed on me. I don't know who hit me, but it wasn't one of them."

Hawks coach Billy Reay accused Leafs trainer Bob Haggert of hitting the unsuspecting Balfour, but Haggert pleaded innocence. He claimed that when Balfour was hammering Brewer, he grabbed the Hawk, but then Bill Hay grabbed him.

In the end, 11 Leafs and an equal number of Hawks were fined for leaving their bench to fight, while Baun received a major, a misconduct, and a game misconduct. Ron Stewart and Larry Hillman each received a major and a misconduct. Fleming received his original five minutes for spearing, as well as five for fighting, a misconduct, and a game misconduct. Balfour received a major and a game misconduct, Stan Mikita earned a major and a misconduct, and Chico Maki was tagged with a misconduct.

Imlach believed that the Leafs needed to reset their collective psychological channel. He had been told that Bobby Rousseau of the Canadiens had scored five goals in one game after reading Norman Vincent Peale's *The Power of Positive Thinking*. As such, the coach decided that the book would make an ideal Christmas gift for his players. On the Christmas Day train trip to Boston for a contest against the Bruins, Punch distributed a copy of Peale's bestseller to every member of his team. The book had the desired effect, as Toronto dumped Boston, 5–1, that night.

Clearly, the players must have suspended their positive thinking in a rematch against those same Bruins in on January 18, 1964. This, the *Globe and Mail* declared, was "the date when the lamb backed the butcher into a corner in Maple Leaf Gardens and carved his initials on him with a meat cleaver."

That night, the last-place Bruins skated to an 11–0 win over Toronto. Beleaguered Don Simmons, once a Bruin and now filling in for the injured Bower, took a pounding against his former team. After the second period, the Leafs were down by ten. Ever the comedian, Eddie Shack couldn't get a rise out of his coach: "I could tell just by looking at him that he was in a rage. With the score 10–0, he sent me and Harris over the boards, so I turned to him and said, 'What do you want us to do, tie it or win it?' I don't think he appreciated my humour!"

The Leafs did, however, rebound the next night with a 2–0 victory over Chicago. The team played solid, sound defensive hockey and Simmons recomposed himself for the shutout win.

But the shellacking from Boston remained fresh in the minds of Leafs fans. And when the team dropped another 4–0 stinker to Montreal on February 12, Leafs Nation looked to the realm of the supernatural for help for their team. While commenting on the loss to the Habs the night before, a news reader at CHUM radio in Toronto wondered whether the Maple Leafs needed "a CHUM witch to put a spell on their opponents." And so, Mabel Leaf, the CHUM Witch, was born. Dressed in black with a pointed hat and gruesome green makeup, she looked very much like the Wicked Witch of the West as she stirred a steaming cauldron of "Imlach punch" on Carlton Street outside the Gardens entrance before the contest on February 15. Just before the opening faceoff, Mabel (played by lounge performer Phyllis Shea) sat in the blues and waved her wand as she spat out hexes on the Chicago Black Hawks. Toronto won, 4–0.

Toronto tied the next home game, and the CHUM switchboard lit up with fans demanding that Mabel Leaf return. Punch Imlach, as superstitious a man as has ever lived, called the radio station and demanded that the CHUM Witch attend the next game. She did, and the Leafs beat the Rangers, 5–2. What had been intended as a silly one-off radio stunt had now become a ritual.

The fans simply loved the CHUM Witch. If the CHUM Witch wasn't at a particular game and the Leafs lost, the radio station heard about it for days from the fans – none of whom was more upset by the absence than Imlach. While she wouldn't feature in as many games as Kate Smith did for the Philadelphia Flyers a few years later, Mabel Leaf nevertheless had a stunning record of eleven wins, two losses, and a tie.

But while the spells may have helped brighten the dark days of winter a little for the Leafs, the team management felt that a trade was necessary to shake things up. On February 22, the Toronto Maple Leafs and New York Rangers – who were set to play that very night – pulled off a massive swap. Toronto picked up Andy Bathgate, the fourth-leading scorer in the NHL to that point, along with Don McKenney in exchange for Dick Duff, Bob Nevin, Arnie Brown, Rod Seiling, and Bill Collins. In many ways, the trade addressed the needs of both teams. Toronto was in a scoring slump and needed production. Conversely, the Rangers had accepted that they were likely to miss the playoffs and received pieces to help build for the future.

Punch Imlach had mixed feelings about the trade. While he found it difficult to part with the popular Duff, Imlach claimed that Bathgate was the final ingredient the Leafs needed to win a third consecutive championship.

For his part, Andy Bathgate was excited to be joining Toronto: "There's a soft spot in my heart for the Leafs. They're a good team and a contender and I think I can help them. I hope I can live up to Punch's expectations." On the other hand, Duff expressed his regret about leaving Toronto and the Leafs: "I came to Toronto when I was 15 years old and was 28 when I left. I'd been familiar with the city and the building and the guys that I played with. It won't look like such a good trade three years from now. I'll get more opportunity to play with the Rangers. They're a young team with a future."

Bob Nevin recalled the unusual way he became aware of the trade: "My phone rang at about a quarter to five and it was King Clancy. The only thing he said to me was, 'Hey Bob, when you come down to the Gardens tonight, go into the other dressing room.' I said, 'Excuse me?' And he said, 'Yeah, we just traded you to the Rangers. Good luck.' And that was it."

It would take some time for the fans and for the rest of the Leafs to digest the noticeable changes that had taken place in their dressing room. Several Leafs believed at the time that it was a bad trade. And the new arrivals bore the brunt of their new teammates' misgivings. Years later, Bathgate spoke to the atmosphere he encountered:

I think it was a little cool. Most of the fellows had played their junior hockey together and had grown up together, being Toronto boys. Dickie Duff was very popular and got a lot of important goals for the Leafs. I don't know why Punch made the trade, but you have to give up something to get something.

Five hours after the trade, the Leafs beat the Rangers, 5–2. The next night, the same two teams played again at Madison Square Garden and Toronto came away with a 4–3 win. While it might have been chilly in the Leafs dressing room, Imlach and company had been warmed by the four points they had collected in two nights.

The Leafs were, nevertheless, still experimenting with and tapping into their hometown feeder system. For a game on March 11 at home against Montreal, the Leafs summoned 18-year-old Ron Ellis from the Marlboros for his first NHL game. As Ellis recalled: "Punch called me in and said, 'We'd like to call you up for a game.' It was pretty special. I didn't let my friends at school know because so often, players were called up and didn't get to see much action. They were just there in case someone got hurt. But I guess the Leafs wanted to test me."

The surroundings were not altogether uncomfortable for Ellis, as several former Marlies had already made the jump to the big team. Surprisingly, though, Ellis didn't just dress for the game, he actually made the starting lineup. The Leafs beat the Habs, 1–0, and Ellis returned to Downsview High School the next day as something of a celebrity. His Marlboros won the Memorial Cup that spring, and Ellis would be a full-time Maple Leaf come September.

The Leafs won nine, lost four, and tied two following the blockbuster trade, ending the regular season comfortably in third place with 78 points. The newest Leafs were on fire: Don McKenney scored 9 goals and had 15 points in the 15 games he played with Toronto; Andy Bathgate scored 3 goals and collected 18 points in the same number of games. In fact, Bathgate tied Jean Béliveau's NHL record of 58 assists in a single season. The forward's combined totals from the Rangers and the Leafs saw him finish fourth in the league, with 77 points. Dave Keon was next, with 60 points, including 23 goals. Frank Mahovlich had a team-best 26 goals and was named to the Second All-Star Team.

Tim Horton could not be accused of being distracted by donuts. The defenceman was selected to NHL's First All-Star Team and was runner-up to Pierre Pilote for the Norris Trophy. Horton's teammates were quite astounded at how good the defenceman was despite his terrible eyesight. Without his glasses, as Bob Haggert teased, "Tim can't tell a comma from a cockroach."

Charlie Hodge and the Canadiens blanked Toronto, 2–0, in the opening contest of the 1964 semifinal in Montreal. The longtime rivals also set an NHL playoff record for most penalties in a game, with 31. Next, the Leafs evened the series with a 2–1 win in what was a far more civil Game Two. Frank Mahovlich was lauded by his coach for "playing his best game in three years."

With the series tied, the teams moved to Maple Leaf Gardens for Game Three. While Toronto outplayed Montreal for 57 minutes, J.C. Tremblay took advantage of sloppy defensive play to tie the score at 17:25 of the third. Then, at 19:35, Henri Richard scored the decisive goal in the Canadiens' 3–2 victory.

After two relatively calm contests, Game Four hastened a return to the rough stuff, as 30 penalties were called during the game. Frank Mahovlich still managed a five-point night, including two goals, in the 5–3 Leafs win. The focus of this game, however, was an incident between Henri Richard and Eddie Shack. During a tussle, Shack lowered his head and butted Richard square in the face. Henri's brother Maurice, the legendary Rocket, added

some levity to the situation when he cautioned, "Hey Shack! Good thing you never hit my brother with your nose, eh? You coulda split him in half!"

With the series tied at two games each, the teams returned to Montreal. While Don McKenney managed two goals for the Leafs, it was the home team that came out on top with a 4–2 win. The Leafs, however, refused to roll over, rebounding in Game Six at Maple Leaf Gardens. Johnny Bower starred for the Blue and White and slammed the door on a potent Canadiens offence. McKenney scored for the second straight game in a 3–0 win.

April 9, 1964, marked the first time a seventh game would be required in a series between the Leafs and Canadiens. Dave Keon scored twice in the first period to jump-start the Leafs, his second goal earned on a short-handed breakaway. Ralph Backstrom cut Toronto's lead to 2–1 in the third, but Keon put the victory away with a goal scored into an empty net with 15 seconds left in regulation time, securing a hat trick. The Leafs were headed to the Stanley Cup final again.

The Red Wings had also taken seven games to polish off the Chicago Black Hawks. Yet, if regular-season, head-to-head competition was to be any guide, the Leafs had the clear advantage, having beaten Detroit in 11 out of the 14 meetings between the teams during the campaign. The Red Wings' recent play, however, suggested that they would not be pushovers.

In fact, the Wings opened the scoring in the first period of Game One, when Bruce MacGregor fired a goalmouth pass past Johnny Bower. Thirteen seconds later, however, Allan Stanley blasted a shot from the point that George Armstrong tipped past Terry Sawchuk to tie the score. During a power play midway through the first, Gordie Howe whistled a shot past a helpless Bower to give Detroit a 2–1 lead.

The middle period was scoreless, but Toronto drew even again when George Armstrong scored the second of his two goals early in the third. Later in that same period, the Red Wings had the Leafs on the ropes. Allan Stanley was serving a penalty late in regulation time when

Bobby Baun (centre) is remembered for his legendary performance in Game Six of the Stanley Cup final against the Detroit Red Wings, on April 23, 1964. He fractured his ankle in the game, but returned in overtime, his leg frozen, and scored the game-winning goal. The Leafs went on to win Game Seven to secure their third consecutive Stanley Cup championship.

Bob Pulford poke-checked the puck away from the Wings' Norm Ullman and then took off down the wing with Gordie Howe in pursuit. When Sawchuk came out to cut down the angle, Pulford lashed a backhand that flew over the goalie's shoulder and gave Toronto a 3–2 lead with just two seconds to spare. According to Stafford Smythe, that lucky shorthanded goal "could win us our third straight Cup." For the time being, it meant that the Leafs, who had certainly been outplayed in the game, had nevertheless taken the early lead in the final.

Meanwhile, Game Two saw Allan Stanley and Norm Ullman trade goals early in the first. Detroit, though, leapt ahead with goals from Eddie Joyal and Floyd Smith late in the period. Then, with nine minutes left in regulation and Toronto trailing 3–1, the fortunes quickly reversed. The Leafs' Red Kelly and Gerry Ehman scored to tie the game and send it to sudden-death overtime.

Just past the seven-minute mark of overtime, Norm Ullman stickhandled beautifully over the Toronto blue-line. He passed to Howe, who then took the puck behind the net and threw the puck out front, where Larry Jeffrey was alone. Jeffrey banged the puck past Bower for the 4–3 Detroit win.

At home in the Olympia for Game Three, the Wings completely dominated the early action and were up 3–0 at the end of the first period. Near the end of the second, though, Andy Bathgate put the Leafs on the board. This seemed to inspire Toronto. In the third, Dave Keon banked a shot from behind the net off Norm Ullman's elbow. Then, for the third time in three games, the Leafs scored a late goal to tie the game. This time, Don McKenney played hero.

While the game was almost assuredly heading for overtime, Gordie Howe spotted an open Alex Delvecchio alone in front of the net. With only 17 seconds left in the game, Delvecchio hammered home the game winner. The Wings now led the series, two games to one.

One of the issues that had been hurting the Leafs was that the team simply wasn't shooting the puck enough. Imlach addressed this issue and gave particular attention to Andy Bathgate, who took the directive to heart. In fact, the Leafs as a whole began to shoot far more often, and Toronto started strong in Game Four. Dave Keon scored the first two goals of the game. Then, Bathgate – grimacing with pulled stomach muscles – scored what proved to be the game winner. Frank Mahovlich collected an insurance marker late in the third, as the Leafs won, 4–2, and evened the series at two games apiece.

Bathgate, the hero of Game Four, articulated the "Canadian dream" that began when Foster Hewitt's broadcasts invaded the living rooms of the nation, including the Bathgates': "You think all your life when you're a kid that it'd be a dream to play in Maple Leaf Gardens and you dream that you might have a chance to be on a Stanley Cup hockey team." Andy was close to seeing his dream realized.

Midway through the first period of Game Five in Toronto, an Alex Delvecchio attempt was stopped by Bower, but as Baun and Delvecchio piled up around the crease, the puck was jarred free from the scrum and popped into the net by Gordie Howe. Eddie Joyal scored the eventual winner for the Wings in the third. While George Armstrong scored when the Wings were two men short, it was too little, too late. Detroit's 2–1 win gave the Red Wings a 3–2 series lead.

With a victory at home in Game Six, the Detroit Red Wings could claim the Stanley Cup for the first time since 1955. But it was Toronto who drew first blood. Bob Pulford scored a shorthanded goal in the first period. It was the second period, however, that will be remembered for its flurry of goals. Detroit tied the game on a goal by Paul Henderson, and then Pit Martin made it 2–1 for the Wings. Pulford's second, a shorthanded tally, tied the game, but exactly one minute later, Gordie Howe put the Wings back on top, 3–2. Still, the Leafs battled back, Billy Harris tying the game with just over two minutes left in the second.

While the Red Wings fought ferociously to collect the Stanley Cup in front of their own fans, the Maple Leafs defended with equal strength. There had been no scoring in the third, but there was plenty of drama. One particular incident set up one of the more colourful threads in the Maple Leafs tapestry. Just over seven minutes into the third, Bobby Baun was killing a Leafs penalty when a Gordie Howe shot was deflected and caught the defenceman on the right leg.

As Baun remembered:

I felt a sharp pain . . . I skated two more shifts and at 12:35, I went into the corner very hard with Detroit's André Pronovost and the injury to my right leg was aggravated further. The puck was frozen for a faceoff in our zone and in those days, defencemen took all the faceoffs in the defensive zone, so I lined up at the circle . . . I won the draw, spun on my right leg and tried to interfere with Gordie's [Howe] progress. That's when I heard something pop and my leg just caved in underneath me.

Baun tried to climb to his feet, but was unable to do so. In fact, even with the assistance of his teammates, Baun couldn't put any weight on his leg. The defenceman was subsequently carried from the ice by stretcher. Two doctors examined Baun and suggested taping and freezing the ankle. When Bobby was assured that he likely couldn't do any further damage, he was desperate to get back on the ice.

After the freezing, Baun found that he now could put weight on the leg without pain. Overtime had already started when Baun returned to the bench. Imlach called for the defensive pair of Carl Brewer and Larry Hillman to take a shift, but Baun told Hillman to hold off, jumping onto the ice in his place.

It was still early in the extra frame when Brewer dumped the puck into the corner just to the left of Sawchuk. The Wings' Junior Langlois collected the puck and shot it around the boards. Baun was there to keep the puck inside the offensive zone, and that's when it happened, as the hearty blueliner recalled:

I just managed to make it to the blueline in time or I would have thrown our guys offside. It came off the boards and it was rolling. I just took a slap at it and the puck was going end over end. Bill Gadsby happened to be stopped in front of the netminder, Terry Sawchuk. It hit the shaft of his stick, changed direction and went by him. I've called it a triple flutter blast, with a follow-up blooper.

The unlikely hero with one gammy leg had forced a seventh game and given Leafs fans a goal of mythological proportions. The full extent of Baun's injury still needed to be ascertained, but first there was the matter of Game Seven. And there was no way Bobby was going to miss that.

Baun spent the night before the series finale with his leg immersed in a bucket of ice. Before the game, he once again had his leg frozen and taped. When he skated out to take the pregame warm-up, the crowd at Maple Leaf Gardens went crazy. Baun was also injected with novocaine during the intermissions and would, as it turned out, play well enough to be named one of the three stars.

The Leafs had won the Stanley Cup in Game Seven on two previous occasions: in 1942 and 1945. The Red Wings had done the same in 1950, 1954, and 1955. It was still considered a rare event. As it happened, Game Seven fell on a Saturday night in Toronto the Good. NHL president Clarence Campbell, however, assured fans that, despite the Lord's Day Act, which prevented sporting events before noon on a Sunday, the game would be played to a conclusion. As it turned out, Toronto had nothing to worry about, as the game would be wrapped up long before the stroke of midnight.

Early in the first period, Andy Bathgate capitalized on a Wings mistake, sailed in on Sawchuk, and fired a 25-foot missile past the Detroit netminder to put Toronto up 1–0. While the second period was scoreless, the Leafs exploded for three goals in the third. Dave Keon scored at 4:26 and, just over a minute later, Red Kelly gave Toronto a 3–0 lead. George Armstrong then put the Red Wings away by adding a fourth with less than five minutes to play in the third. As the fans counted down the remaining seconds, Detroit's Larry Jeffrey wrestled the puck into the net, but the red light had already gone on to indicate that time had expired. Toronto had done it again.

The Maple Leafs had won their third straight Stanley Cup. It was, at the time, a feat bettered only by the Montreal Canadiens' five straight (1955–56 through 1959–60) and equalled in league play only by the Maple Leafs themselves (1946–47 to 1948–49). (In the pre-NHL challenge era, the Ottawa Senators won the Cup on March 10, 1903, and successfully took on all comers until March 17, 1906, when the Montreal Wanderers finally defeated them. In that three-year span, they had put down nine consecutive challengers.)

The players mobbed Bower. Al Arbour, Kent Douglas, and Don Simmons, who weren't dressed for the deciding game, scrambled out onto the ice to join their teammates. So too did Punch Imlach, Harold Ballard, King Clancy, trainer Bob Haggert, and, curiously, Bill Stanley, Allan's father.

After Clarence Campbell presented the captain with the Cup, Armstrong skated out to the blueline, where he told *Hockey Night in Canada* viewers, "Everybody went all out. I have to say that the Detroit club is a club that you just don't beat easily. It took everything we had to beat them and they are a credit to all their fans and to themselves." Detroit's general manager and coach, Sid Abel, strode over to add his praise for the victors. "I want to congratulate Punch and King and, of course, George Armstrong and all the Maple Leafs. It was a terrific series. We gave it everything we had. We wanted to win, I'll tell you that!"

Johnny Bower was then summoned to address the viewers and the many fans remaining in Maple Leaf Gardens:

Coaching the storied Maple Leafs was one of the greatest challenges and thrills of my life. The love and passion of Leafs Nation made it fun and difficult. You wanted to do well for them almost as much as you wanted to win for the organization and the players. I will never forget walking behind the bench at Maple Leaf Gardens as the Leafs coach; the same bench I had so often dreamed about standing behind. The Leafs were my favourite team as a kid growing up in Toronto. I was now in the centre of the hockey universe. The memory still gives me goosebumps and a rush.

Mike Murphy
HEAD COACH
1996–98

Johnny Bower (left) was concerned when Toronto picked up Detroit's All-Star goaltender in the 1964 Intra-League Draft. But together, Bower and Terry Sawchuk (right) made a dynamic pairing. Members of the Over the Hill Gang in Toronto, the two goaltenders would play integral roles in the Stanley Cup championship of 1967.

I'd like to thank the people of Toronto for having so much patience with us. And thanks very much to the CHUM Witch tonight by the way also. It certainly is wonderful to win the Stanley Cup and I certainly give a lot of credit to the Detroit Red Wings, who played so well. The city of Toronto deserves the Stanley Cup more than anybody else!

The Leafs had proven the critics wrong: Frank Mahovlich, who was likely never afforded the respect he deserved in Toronto, led the Leafs in playoff scoring with 15 points. Andy Bathgate had scored the Stanley Cup–winning goal.

The entire veteran roster had likewise defied the naysayers. Certainly, the median age of the Leafs had worried many even before the championship run had begun three springs earlier. It seemed that the pundits were perennially discussing whether this would be the last hurrah for Bower, Kelly, or Stanley.

It didn't help that so many Leafs were preoccupied with simply reducing their pain. While in the shower after the game, for instance, the excruciating pain in Red Kelly's knee caused him to pass out. Horton, Stanley, and Stewart carried him from the shower to a makeshift medical area the team doctors set up in the dressing room, and an ambulance pulled into the Gardens an hour later. Police and Gardens employees cleared the dressing room, and photographers were prohibited from taking shots of Red being loaded onto the stretcher and wheeled into the waiting ambulance. He was taken to Toronto General Hospital, where he spent the night.

And, after finally undergoing an x-ray, it was revealed that Bobby Baun had indeed scored that Game Six winner on a broken leg. It was a heroic tale that captured the attention of even the most casual hockey fan. As Baun explained, it still does:

> I am amazed that this has gotten as much attention as it has through the years . . . writers use it as an example of the bravery of hockey players. I don't think a day goes by that someone doesn't bring it up to me. I've had a lot of highs and lows in my life, but I have to say that Game Six of the 1964 Stanley Cup final is the highlight of my career.

Baun would make the celebration parade, but he actually slipped while getting into one of the convertibles and further injured his leg.

Once again, the City of Toronto feted the champions. On April 27, Philip Givens, the third Toronto mayor to preside over a Leafs Stanley Cup reception in three years, tried to address the thousands of fans, yet most of his comments were drowned out by the crowd chanting, "We want Shack! We want Shack!" While Eddie Shack contributed a total of only 21 points to the team during the regular season, his popularity had reached an all-time high.

As the cheering died down and spring turned to summer, Leafs fans wondered where their team would go from here. What of Bower, Kelly, and Stanley? What of young Jim Pappin – would he find a spot? How about Ellis – could he earn a position on the big team? The questions picked up traction as fall arrived, when the Toronto Maple Leafs were poised to defend their Stanley Cup win for the third straight time.

THE DISSENTING VOICE

The Leafs made very few changes during the off-season, but there were a few additions. Teams were allowed to protect two goaltenders and 18 skaters in the Intra-League Draft held every June. Detroit protected Terry Sawchuk and Roger Crozier, but in the third round of the draft, the Wings gambled, selecting goaltender George Gardner from the Bruins. To do so, they had to expose Sawchuk. The veteran was therefore available to any of the other five teams for a waiver fee of $20,000. It was the Leafs' turn to choose next, and Punch Imlach excitedly plucked Sawchuk from the Wings. Toronto now had a dynamic one-two tandem in goal with Bower and Sawchuk.

At 35, Sawchuk was hardly a rookie. Yet Imlach was never much concerned about adding veterans to the team. Punch even took a flier on 33-year-old forward Dickie Moore. While the former scoring champion and future Hall of Famer would only play 38 games with the Leafs, he would have felt comfortable in the dressing room when he looked around and saw Johnny Bower (40), Allan Stanley (38), Red Kelly (36), Tim Horton (34), George Armstrong (33), and Andy Bathgate (31). Imlach was defiant about his choices and told his players to tear up their birth certificates.

At the other end of the spectrum was Ron Ellis. The youngster had just come off an all-star season with the Memorial Cup champion Toronto Marlboros. Ellis believed that his opportunity came after Marlies coach Jim Gregory convinced him to move to right wing from centre in his final year of junior. As Ellis explained, "There were no vacancies at centre for the Maple Leafs. Dave Keon, Red Kelly, Bob Pulford and Billy Harris were there, but there was some room on the right side, and that was a big break for me."

The 19-year-old rookie was happily surprised at the greeting he received, describing them as "a very close knit bunch of guys. They had to be, to win three Cups in a row. I was really the first change they'd made in three years, so I didn't know what to expect. Bathgate, Pulford, Armstrong, Horton, Stanley . . . they really went out of their way to make me feel welcomed and comfortable."

Johnny Bower – 21 years Ellis's senior – got the call to start the 1964–65 season opener in goal against the Red Wings in Detroit. The elder statesman did not disappoint. The Leafs started the new season with a big 5–3 win over the Wings.

The Leafs' home opener was against the Boston Bruins. That night, Earl Rowe, Ontario's lieutenant-governor, presented Johnny Bower with the J.P. Bickell Trophy before conducting the ceremonial faceoff. The Leafs dominated the game. Red Kelly and Frank Mahovlich both collected two goals and an assist. Dave Keon had a goal and two assists, and the rookie Ellis scored his first NHL goal during a 7–2 Toronto win.

But the Leafs' injury list had become a long one: Mahovlich was out suffering from fatigue, Bower had the flu, Sawchuk had strained leg muscles, Carl Brewer had taken an elbow to the side of the head and was out, Keon had injured his groin, Bathgate had a broken wrist, and Don McKenney's wrist was sprained. Mahovlich mercifully returned to action on December 9 after an 11-game absence. And the Big M's first game back impressed his coach: "I thought Frank was more than adequate, considering he's spent most of the last month in bed in the hospital." While the Leafs lost, 3–2, to the Canadiens that night, Mahovlich scored two goals and assisted on two others in a 6–3 win over Boston three nights later.

By the turn of the calendar, the Leafs had been winless since December 19. To shake things up, Toronto tried Tim Horton at forward. The defenceman responded during his short sojourn up front by scoring two goals in a 3–1 victory over the Wings on January 2. In fact, Horton looked so good that he was kept on the wing for several more games, scoring twice in a 6–0 rout of the Rangers on January 10, and twice more in a 3–1 win over Boston on January 17.

On the final weekend of the season, the fourth-place Maple Leafs faced the Red Wings in an epic home-and-home battle. Detroit had locked up their first regular-season championship since 1957. What remained unsettled, however, was who would win the Vézina Trophy. Led by rookie sensation Roger Crozier, who would play all but 32 minutes of the 1964–65 season, the Red Wings had allowed 170 goals. The Toronto tandem of Terry Sawchuk, who had played 36 games, and Johnny Bower, who had made 32 appearances, had allowed 169.

At the time, the Vézina was awarded to a single goaltender. An NHL rule stated that the trophy and $1,000 went to the goaltender playing the most games for the team permitting the fewest goals. It didn't matter if a team had employed two or more netminders during the season; only the busiest one had his name inscribed on the trophy. In 1951, Al Rollins of the Maple Leafs won the Vézina by virtue of playing 39 games, only eight more than Turk Broda. But by the mid-1960s, goaltending tandems were becoming more commonplace. In fact, the NHL had ruled that teams must now carry two goaltenders. As such, the Vézina criteria seemed badly outdated.

A dilemma arose: even though Bower was scheduled to play the final two contests against Detroit, Sawchuk alone would be awarded the Vézina if the Leafs won it. Sportingly, Sawchuk insisted that "if we should win it, I won't accept the trophy unless both our names are on it." The teammates had already made a pact that, should they win, they'd split the $1,000.

In the first of the back-to-back games, on March 27, Detroit dumped the Leafs by a 4–1 margin. This allowed Crozier to take the lead in the Vézina race. In the rematch, however, the Leafs prevailed, 4–0, on the strength of a Johnny Bower shutout. This meant that, by a two-goal margin, the Vézina was heading to Toronto. Detroit had allowed 175 goals; Toronto had surrendered just 173.

Terry Sawchuk's firm stance on sharing the trophy with his partner had the desired effect on the NHL's board of governors. At their annual meeting in June 1965, the board amended the rule to allow for co-winners of the Vézina Trophy, provided that both netminders appeared in a minimum of 25 games. As such, Terry Sawchuk got his wish: both his and Bower's names were engraved on the trophy.

The Big M was the Leafs' top scorer, with 23 goals and 51 points. Dave Keon, with 21 goals and 29 assists, was a single point behind Mahovlich. Ron Ellis scored 23 goals and had 39 points and was runner-up to Roger Crozier for the Calder Trophy as best first-year player. Without question, Toronto's veteran goalie tandem – with a combined age of 76 – was the brightest spot in what was otherwise an underwhelming season for the Leafs. Still, Toronto was heading to the playoffs, to face second-place Montreal in the semifinals.

The NHL's only Canadian teams opened the series at the Forum with a brawl-filled game. In fact, the teams played five-on-five hockey for less than two minutes in the first period. The Canadiens went on to win by a 3–2 score.

On the day of Game Two, Johnny Bower accidentally rubbed oil of wintergreen into his eye. Terry Sawchuk was therefore summoned to play goal for Toronto, and while he performed admirably, the Habs were victorious, 3–1, and took a two-games-to-none lead in the series.

Bower was back in net for the Maple Leafs as the series shifted to Toronto for Game Three. With the score tied

At the time of the 1964–65 season, the NHL awarded the Vézina Trophy to the netminder who played the most games for the team with the lowest goals-against average in the regular season. But Terry Sawchuk – who had played two more games than Johnny Bower – insisted that he would not accept the trophy unless Bower's name was included, and the NHL agreed, changing their bylaws so that the award could be shared by the two goaltenders.

at two at the end of regulation, Dave Keon brought the hometown crowd to its feet when he scored at 4:17 of overtime to give the Leafs a 3–2 win.

Game Four featured spectacular goaltending from Bower. While Montreal scored twice within the first six minutes of the game, he slammed the door after that, and Toronto went on to a 4–2 victory to tie the series.

In Game Five, however, Gump Worsley was as solid as his counterpart had been in the previous match. Bob Pulford managed to beat Worsley in the second period, but it was Toronto's only goal as the Canadiens secured the 3–1 win. With the victory, Montreal now led the series, three games to two.

Keon, Kelly, and Ellis all scored in the first period of Game Six, but the Canadiens rebounded to tie the game in the third period. The contest required overtime to decide a winner. At 16:33 of that first extra period, Claude Provost's backhand eluded Bower and squashed any hope of a fourth consecutive Cup for the Leafs. The Canadiens took Game Six, 4–3, and the series, four games to two.

While Montreal was ascendant once again – the Canadiens would win four Stanley Cups in the next five seasons – Toronto's dynasty appeared to have reached a natural conclusion. Now, more than ever, the age of the roster was going to be a grave concern for Leafs management. At the same time, Punch Imlach's dictatorial approach was having a significant physical and psychological effect on the team.

The Toronto Maple Leafs of the 1960s presented a curious juxtaposition. The team had experienced its greatest-ever success, and Punch Imlach was a huge part of these successes. On the other hand, Imlach's approach did not suit all of the players in the dressing room, and his methods may have acted as more of an impediment than an instrument for success. Frank Mahovlich would lament the team's situation: "I think of what we could have become, and what we did become, in spite of what we were put through." Yet, many of the players appreciated what Imlach brought to the team, including Johnny Bower: "He wasn't perfect, none of us are, but Punch was great as far as I was concerned."

STING LIKE A BEE

Andy Bathgate was traded early in the off-season. The circumstances, however, were far more interesting: a blockbuster deal between the Leafs and the Detroit Red Wings on May 20, 1965, that saw Bathgate, Billy Harris, and Gary Jarrett join Detroit in exchange for

Marcel Pronovost, Autry Erickson, Larry Jeffrey, Ed Joyal, and Lowell MacDonald. Bathgate had been the key piece the Leafs needed to win their third consecutive Stanley Cup; he even scored the Cup-winning goal. But after publicly criticizing Imlach, Bathgate now wore the red and white of the Detroit Red Wings. Conversely – and after 15 excellent seasons in Detroit – 34-year-old Marcel Pronovost was stunned to be on his way to Toronto.

The Leafs made some other moves. Ron Stewart was sent to Boston for Andy Hebenton, Orland Kurtenbach, and Pat Stapleton. The latter, however, was claimed by Chicago in the Intra-League Draft, in which the Leafs also lost Don McKenney to the Red Wings, goaltender Don Simmons to the Rangers, and Gerry Cheevers, also a netminder, to the Bruins.

Only one rookie made the 1965–66 squad from training camp: Brit Selby, who was given number 11 to wear after Ron Ellis moved to number 8, would have a strong debut season and claim the Calder Trophy as rookie of the year.

Perhaps the biggest change was the void that emerged when Carl Brewer left the Maple Leafs to return to school. Bobby Baun had lost his stalwart blueline partner and articulated his deep concerns about Brewer's departure during an intermission interview on *Hockey Night in Canada*: "It's going to be quite a different season, especially after playing eight years together. I wanted him to wait a little while to think it over a bit longer."

While the defence corps lost one of its regulars, the Maple Leafs' grand narrative gained two hit songs. Bizarrely, Johnny Bower and Eddie Shack were about to enjoy some success – on the pop charts!

CBC producer Chip Young had written a short story about a goose that ate so much that he couldn't fly, but was still able to save Santa Claus. Young turned the story into a song with the help of composer Orville Hoover, then approached Punch Imlach to get permission for one of the Leafs to record the song. Granted permission, Young went out to the Tam O'Shanter rink in Scarborough, where the Leafs practised. As Bower remembered:

He came into the dressing room and wanted to know if anybody on the team would be interested in singing these songs. I've never seen so many guys undress and get into the shower so quickly in my life! I was the only one left sitting there. He said, "I guess you're the only one left," and I said, "Look sir, I can't sing." I thought he was nuts!

Few Leafs can lay claim to the popularity of Eddie Shack (left). "The Entertainer" joined Toronto from the Rangers in November 1961. He scored the Stanley Cup–winning goal in 1963 and enjoyed a career season in 1965–66, scoring 26 goals. That same season, he was the subject of a hit song titled "Clear the Track, Here Comes Shack."

Undeterred, Young thought Bower was perfect for the part. And with tremendous apprehension, the goaltender agreed to give it a try. Johnny recruited his 11-year-old son, John Jr., as well as five neighbourhood children, to join him for the recording session. For two weeks, they rehearsed until they had the melody and lyrics down cold. Johnny Bower with Little John and the Rinky Dinks received $100 for their effort. "Honky the Christmas Goose" was pressed within days and released to the public.

The song reached number 29 on the 1050 CHUM chart, the radio station's weekly survey of the city's most popular songs. In December 1965, "Honky the Christmas Goose" knocked the Beatles' double-sided hit, "Day Tripper" coupled with "We Can Work It Out," out of the most-requested spot.

Meanwhile, fan favourite Eddie Shack was about to receive his own musical treatment.

Broadcaster Brian McFarlane wrote a song about Shack and set about getting it recorded:

I already had the idea when I approached Shackie. I told him I was thinking about writing this little song and asked if he had any problem with that. He said he didn't and that I should go ahead and do it. So my brother-in-law, Bill McCauley, who had a doctorate in music, wrote the music, and I wrote the words, and in about 20 minutes, we had the thing done.

McFarlane engaged a group called Douglas Rankine and the Secrets to record the song. The band was offered $500 for their efforts. "Clear the Track, Here Comes Shack" was released in February 1966 and was launched between periods on *Hockey Night in Canada*, accompanied by film footage of Shack. The national exposure on Canada's most-viewed television program did wonders to promote the record. On February 28, 1966, "Clear the Track, Here Comes Shack" displaced Petula Clark's "My Love" as the number one song on the CHUM chart, where it stayed for two weeks.

Meanwhile, back on the ice, the Maple Leafs could not escape the fact that their team had changed and that past successes could no longer be taken for granted. The Leafs' 1965–66 season opener took place at home against the Black Hawks. Crooner Bing Crosby was in attendance, in the company of his longtime friend, Leafs great Charlie Conacher. Frederick G. Gardiner, the first chairman of Metropolitan Toronto Council, presented the J.P. Bickell Award to Johnny Bower, who was receiving the award for the third time. Gardiner and Smythe then presented

the Vézina Trophy to Bower and Terry Sawchuk, the first time co-winners had ever been named. Finally, Gardiner presided over the ceremonial faceoff between Toronto captain George Armstrong and Chicago captain Pierre Pilote.

The sense of optimism that a new season brings was soundly crushed as Bobby Hull scored three goals in a 4–0 Black Hawks victory. The second game of the season was much the same: Roger Crozier earned the shutout as Detroit dumped the Leafs, 3–0. It was 120 minutes into the new campaign and the Leafs had yet to score. In fact, after eight games, the Leafs had managed only 11 goals. The futility of the early season was punctuated on November 7, when Chicago humiliated Toronto, 9–0.

Everyone began looking for answers. The coach sent Jim Pappin to Rochester and called up fan favourite Eddie Shack. The Leafs' early struggles stood in stark contrast to the state of the Rochester Americans. The combination of veterans and youth was paying huge dividends for the farm club. The Americans won the Calder Cup as AHL champions in both 1965 and 1966, with a roster that included Al Arbour, Don Cherry, Gerry Ehman, Ed Litzenberger, Jim Pappin, and Duane Rupp.

With Shack reinstated, the Leafs beat the Canadiens, 3–1, on November 18. The Entertainer's return from the minors was heralded by the Toronto dailies. The *Star*, for example, hypothesized that being sent to Rochester was the best thing that could have happened to Shack: "Shack went to the Leafs' American Hockey League farm club labelled a 'hockey misfit,' a 'clown prince' they could no longer afford. He came back a serious, aggressive, productive player." Placed on a new line with Bob Pulford and Red Kelly, Shack ended up having a career season in 1965–66, with 26 goals.

As the calendar rolled over to 1966, Toronto went on a scoring frenzy, pumping six goals past the Canadiens for a shutout win on January 13, including a hat trick from Brit Selby. Two nights later, Toronto hammered Boston, 6–1.

Yet the Leafs remained a middling team. Injuries played a role in keeping them from the top tier, particularly at the goaltending position. Both Bower and Sawchuk went down during the campaign, and the Leafs ended up using a total of five netminders throughout the season, including Gary Smith, Bruce Gamble, and Al Smith. And while they made do (Gamble had a particularly impressive run), there was, it seemed, a constant shifting of the sand within the Leafs lineup.

Meanwhile, something more akin to a sandstorm began to rage inside Maple Leaf Gardens. In one corner

When we came over from Sweden, we really didn't know how big hockey was over here. I also learned that it was the dream of all the guys who got traded to Toronto to play with the Toronto Maple Leafs, and then I realized, "Jeez, I was really lucky to play here!" I had a great relationship with the fans and everybody in management. They treated me so well. They still treat me so well when I come over with my family. For me, Toronto is my second hometown and the Mecca of hockey. Always has been, and still is. Playing for the Maple Leafs is one of the highest honours in sports.

Börje Salming
PLAYER
1973–89

stood Conn Smythe, representing the old guard and its claim to those sacrosanct tenets of "doing one's duty" that so defined British Ontario in an earlier age. In the other corner, there was Harold Ballard, who represented a new guard, one that never let high morals get in the way of turning a profit.

The issue was the boxing match between Cassius Clay and Toronto's beloved son, George Chuvalo. Clay (later Muhammad Ali) was the heavyweight champion of the world. Yet, Clay had spoken out against the Vietnam War and refused to report to the United States Army for military service. Clay famously defended his defiance: "I ain't got no quarrel with the Viet Cong." As a result, many boxing commissions refused to approve any defence of his belt. Harold Ballard managed to have the Ontario minister of labour – who controlled boxing in the province – approve the match for Maple Leaf Gardens.

Today, Clay's opposition to the Vietnam War is regarded by many as a brave and noble stance, one that would see him convicted of a felony (overturned in 1971 by a unanimous Supreme Court ruling) and deprived of his livelihood. In 1966, however, the boxer was seen as something of a pariah in certain circles. It is safe to say that Conn Smythe was entrenched in one of those circles.

The man who named the franchise was deeply wounded by Ballard's decision to bring the Clay bout to Maple Leaf Gardens. In Major Smythe's view, Ballard had allowed a "draft dodger" to use the Gardens stage to ply his trade. As a result, Smythe resigned his position as a director of Maple Leaf Gardens and, in disgust, sold the last of his shares in the building and team that he had built. In his autobiography, Smythe reminded readers that "the Gardens was founded by men – sportsmen – who fought for their country. It is no place for those who want to evade conscription."

Regardless, Clay–Chuvalo went ahead as scheduled on March 29, 1966, and 13,919 fans were on hand to watch what turned out to be a classic match. While Cassius Clay retained his heavyweight title by defeating Chuvalo, the latter had done his hometown proud – he became the first boxer to go the distance with Clay. "He's the toughest guy I ever fought," the champion said of Toronto's most famous pugilist.

Back on the ice, the Leafs were in a fight for first place, but went into a serious slump in the final two weeks of the season. In the end, Toronto finished in third place, with 79 points. Frank Mahovlich and Bob Pulford tied for top scorer on the team, with 56 points each. The Big M's

32 goals were best on the Leafs. Brit Selby was the league's rookie of the year. Mahovlich and Allan Stanley were named to the NHL's Second All-Star Team.

Once again, the Maple Leafs met the first-place Canadiens in the semifinals. Game One in Montreal went the home team's way, with a 4–3 win. For Game Two, King Clancy was behind the bench in place of an ailing Punch Imlach. Several of the players were also feeling the effects of a flu that had been going around the Leafs dressing room. Toronto nevertheless came out banging and crashing. A penalty-filled first period took almost an hour to complete as 13 penalties were called. All the scoring took place in the third period, and the Canadiens won, 2–0.

Imlach started Bower in place of Sawchuk for Game Three at Maple Leaf Gardens. That night, the Leafs came out flying and took a 2–0 lead in the first period. In the second, however, Montreal roared back with three goals. Sixteen seconds into the third, John Ferguson fired a laser from 30 feet out that caught the top corner behind Bower. The Habs added an empty-netter to cap a 5–2 win.

The Canadiens now enjoyed a three-games-to-none stranglehold in the series. Game Four was memorable because of the sheer volume of the rough stuff. At 3:37 of the first period, for instance, a 12-minute melee took place. In the end, no fewer than eight penalty records were established in the free-for-all, and the teams were forced to play shorthanded for an astounding 32 minutes. For his part, Imlach was so incensed that the Leafs had received two minutes more in penalties than the Habs that he pulled on a pair of skates with the intent of chasing down referee Art Skov. Imlach stood by the gate to the players' bench, threatening to come out onto the ice, but he wisely stopped short.

After a 25-minute delay, Toronto had a brief glimpse of hope in the form of a goal from Larry Hillman. It was, however, all for naught, as the Canadiens buried Toronto for a 4–1 victory. Once again, the Canadiens had eliminated the Maple Leafs. The Habs went on to defeat the Red Wings in six games for their second straight Stanley Cup.

While the Maple Leafs had certainly been hampered by injuries (especially in net), the truth was that the team was inching further away from the glory of their Stanley Cup run earlier in the decade. The question remained: Did this roster – full of players who most argued were past their "best before" date – have one last burst of magic left in them?

OUR CENTENNIAL PROJECT
1966–67

Before Clay–Chuvalo, before the Queen's portrait was taken down, before the Major had severed ties with the very team he had created, Maple Leaf Gardens had been an unapologetic reflection of the establishment. If the city was indeed Toronto the Good, then the Gardens could have served as its headquarters. Though the times might have been a-changin', the Gardens and its main occupant – even after Smythe's departure – chose to cling to the traditions of a previous generation: when hair was growing ever longer, the Leafs' players still sported crew cuts; when a blaze of tie-dyed shirts and blue jeans were becoming the sartorial norm, the Gardens' patrons still dressed up for the games; when the city's youth subculture began to challenge authority, the Maple Leafs' coach was the strictest disciplinarian the franchise had ever placed behind the bench. Joni Mitchell might very well have been singing about ephemeral lovers at the Penny Farthing, but just a couple of kilometres to the south, Maple Leaf Gardens was prayerfully observing the Lord's Day Act on Sundays.

Former Leafs players such as Syl Apps had their own opinions about what was happening to the city they loved. Apps, who by the mid-1960s was a Progressive Conservative member of the Ontario legislature, believed Yorkville to be a "festering sore in the middle of the city." Yet, while there may well have been revolution in the dank air of Yorkville's dimly lit coffee houses, Maple Leaf Gardens' powerful wash of light – now required for *Hockey Night in Canada*'s colour broadcasts – blocked out any hippie mantra blowing in from the north. The Leafs and the Gardens were, at least for the time being, impenetrable and unmovable.

To be fair, Apps was not entirely off the mark. Yorkville's "peace and love" ethic of the mid-1960s would, by the end of the decade, be replaced by disease, drug dependency, and steady violence. The Leafs brand, too, could expect change. Those initial tenets that had anchored the team as a reflection of British, Protestant Ontario would become systematically unfastened by a new regime willing to undo the traditions of the past.

1967

The 1966–67 season would mark the last year of the so-called Original Six era, which had lasted for 25 seasons. While the country was readying itself for Canada's 100th birthday the following July, Punch Imlach was intent on making changes to his hockey team. In the end, though, few actually transpired. The Leafs lost Wally Boyer and Orland Kurtenbach in the Intra-League Draft, while they picked up John Brenneman from the Rangers. Brian Conacher, who had already enjoyed a cup of coffee with Toronto, was the sole rookie to crack the lineup.

It was hoped that Brian's pedigree would stand the Leafs in good stead. After all, Conacher came from one of hockey's most storied families. His father, three uncles, and two cousins had all enjoyed NHL careers. His dad, Lionel, would one day be inducted into the Hockey Hall of Fame. So too would his uncle, Roy Conacher. And his other uncle, Charlie Conacher, was already in the Hall. Harold Cotton, married to his mother's sister, had been an NHL star. Brian's cousins Pete Conacher (Charlie's son) and Murray Henderson (his aunt Dolly's son) also played in the NHL. Now it was Brian's turn.

While there was little change to the roster, Maple Leaf Gardens went through a dramatic metamorphosis during the summer of 1966. The arena's seating capacity had been increased to 15,481. When the Gardens was built in 1931, Conn Smythe installed the motto DEFEAT DOES NOT REST LIGHTLY ON THEIR SHOULDERS on a wall of the Maple Leafs dressing room. In 1966, with Conn out of the picture, the motto was changed to THE PRICE OF SUCCESS IS HARD WORK.

There were also changes to the way the game was being presented. By opening night, *Hockey Night in Canada* was regularly broadcasting games in colour. While there were only approximately 70,000 colour television sets

With a 3–0 win against Chicago on March 4, 1967, goaltender Terry Sawchuk (bottom) earned his milestone 100th NHL shutout.

in Canada at the time, the lucky ones saw John Robarts, the premier of Ontario, drop the puck for the ceremonial faceoff and then watched Brian Conacher – in striking blue and white attire – score two goals for the Leafs, who tied the Rangers, 4–4, to start the new campaign.

Despite the Leafs' sporting a modest record through the first month of the season, King Clancy predicted that they would go to the Stanley Cup final. Clancy spoke to the "new kind of spirit" he had witnessed among the team. There were many times throughout the season that most people would mock the notion of the Leafs reaching the final, but Clancy remained resolute.

As the season progressed, the Montreal Canadiens began to look more and more like the defending Stanley Cup champions that they were. The Habs doubled the Maple Leafs, 6–3, in Montreal on December 7. Terry Sawchuk, who had struggled in goal that night, actually collapsed after the game. During the summer, Sawchuk had undergone spinal surgery, and this was a recurring effect of that operation – one that profoundly affected the career of one of the all-time great goaltenders.

The Canadiens dominated the Leafs once again on December 21. A first-period brawl, initiated when Eddie Shack speared his nemesis, John Ferguson, involved virtually every player on both teams and took almost an hour to quell.

In terms of the actual hockey, Imlach started Bruce Gamble in goal, but switched to Gary Smith after the brawl. The daring Smith did not disappoint those who had come to expect his apparent need for adventure. At one point, he stickhandled to centre ice before shooting the puck away. As the netminder recalled, "This was the old six-team NHL, and I didn't know if I'd ever play another game. I thought, 'What can I do to make people remember that I played in the NHL?' So, I thought I'd go down the ice and try to score."

After Smith had stickhandled to centre ice, J.C. Tremblay nailed him with a bodycheck. Tremblay was not known for his physical play, but he chose to stop Smith dead in his tracks. The goalie looked up and saw that his adventurous trip up the ice had gone terribly wrong: "I was at the red line and spinning around. I saw Punch Imlach pull his hat down over his head on the first spin." Tremblay had corralled the puck and fired a long shot at Toronto's open net. Fortunately for Smith and the Leafs, Marcel Pronovost had scrambled back to block what otherwise would have been a sure goal.

The season had been modestly successful for the Leafs to that point, and the team began Canada's centennial

year with a 2–1 victory over the Rangers in New York on New Year's Day. The tide, however, was about to take a significant turn for the worst. With Bower and Sawchuk out with injuries, it was left to Bruce Gamble to carry the load for Toronto.

On January 15, the Maple Leafs were shut out, 4–0, by the Black Hawks. This began a dismal ten-game spiral for Toronto. A game against Montreal on February 1 was particularly bad. As the *Toronto Star* reported, "They were so inept in the last few minutes while having a man advantage that the Forum crowd laughed as they foundered to a 7–1 humiliation at the hands of the fired-up Montreal Canadiens." Clancy's call for a Stanley Cup appearance a few months earlier now seemed like a cruel joke.

The slump was affecting the players, but it was also affecting the coach.

"You don't sleep at night," he said. "You are always thinking about it, even when driving a car going along the road, you are thinking about who you should be playing and what is wrong with this player and the next thing you know, you are going through a stoplight. We'll have to bring up some young players to give them a chance or we'll have to make some trades. I think the players realize that the pressure is on. They have to do everything the hard way."

Brian Conacher remembered witnessing his coach's meltdowns: "We used to sit in the dressing room when he would rant and rave and was literally pulling his hair out. He was beside himself because he wasn't able to get the team to react to all this ranting and raving. The team just quit on him. There used to be a lottery in the dressing room about how many times he would use the F-word in his motivational speeches."

By the time the Black Hawks – then in possession of first place – arrived on February 11, the Leafs had lost ten in a row.

That night, there was a glimpse of hope. While the Leafs didn't beat Chicago, they did manage a 4–4 draw. Toronto followed this decent showing with a win against Boston the next night. After Bruce Gamble was injured in the game against the Hawks, the ageless Johnny Bower was now well enough to return to the lineup. Of Bower's play in the 2–1 win, the *Star* said, "The old man wasn't great; rather, out of this world."

Growing in confidence after taking three out of four possible points over the weekend, the Leafs pounded the second-place New York Rangers by a lopsided 6–0 score on February 15. The mood in the Leafs dressing room had changed substantially. The dark cloud that had hung over the team for nearly a month had lifted, and the players began enjoying themselves again.

While better days had finally arrived, Coach Imlach was about to take a leave of absence. On February 18, Imlach held his regular morning practice, but afterwards admitted to King Clancy that he felt ill. Clancy suggested that the coach see a doctor, but Imlach brushed him off, reminding him that the Leafs played the Bruins that night. But while the two were having lunch, Imlach noticed Dr. Tait McPhedran and mentioned his condition. McPhedran ran Imlach through tests and immediately told the coach he was to be admitted to the hospital that afternoon, game or no game. Imlach hadn't suffered a heart attack, but he was kept in the hospital for a few more tests.

In place of Punch, Clancy was called on to handle the bench against Boston. The former Leaf defenceman had coached the team from 1953 to 1956 and had filled in for Imlach on two occasions. As Red Kelly suggested, "King's always been around. It would be different if he were a new man brought in for the job. Then it would be upsetting to the club. We have a lot of experienced players who know what we're supposed to do."

The differences between King and Punch were stark. The *Globe and Mail* described Clancy as "the original Good Humour man with the built-in public relations of a Francis of Assisi." The same paper saw Imlach as "perverse, profane, loyal and demanding, refusing to accept less from any player than his absolute best every day."

With the "original Good Humour man" behind the bench, the Leafs beat the Bruins, 5–3. Imlach was not even allowed to watch the game in the hospital. King did, however, visit him afterwards to report the good news.

Clancy could not be accused of following Imlach's blueprint. King, for instance, played Mahovlich 23 minutes of the game – more ice time than he got in any other game that season; Horton was on the ice for 35 minutes; and Jim McKenny, playing in his first game of the season, replaced Baun. Yet the most successful change came when King placed Peter Stemkowski at centre between wingers Bob Pulford and Jim Pappin. It was a line that seemed to gel immediately.

"Pully and I looked at Clancy like, 'Are you insane?'" Stemkowski later remembered. "But Pappin could skate and he would stay wide. I could give him the puck and he had a great shot. Pulford was a bit of a bulldog. He'd stir up things, get in front of the net and screen the goalkeeper. I was the guy that would go in the corners, knock some people over, and get the puck to Pulford. Those

three different styles complemented each other. That's how our line started."

King's brainchild would pay huge dividends for the Leafs in the weeks ahead.

The Clancy-led Leafs continued to win. On February 23, Terry Sawchuk was back in goal for the first time in over two months, and Toronto beat Detroit, 4–2. With each successive game, the players grew ever more assured. Unshackled from Imlach's rule, Frank Mahovlich found a new lease on life and played with tremendous enthusiasm. Any concerns that Stafford Smythe and company might have had about Clancy's ability to handle the coaching position in Imlach's absence had been soundly put to rest: the Leafs were on fire.

Back in the hospital, Imlach's health was improving, but while Punch was released from hospital on March 4, doctors insisted that he not return to coaching until the 12th. In the interim, Toronto faced Chicago on March 4 in what turned out to be a historic contest. On that evening, Terry Sawchuk earned his 100th regular-season NHL shutout when Toronto blanked the Black Hawks, 3–0. Sawchuk would go on to finish his career with a league-record 103 shutouts – nine more than the next best, George Hainsworth. Sawchuk's record stood for over 40 years until Martin Brodeur surpassed it in 2009.

The first teammate back to congratulate Sawchuk was Marcel Pronovost, who, as a longtime teammate of Sawchuk's in both Detroit and Toronto, had witnessed most of his shutouts. "He's the greatest goalie I've ever seen and certainly the greatest competitor," Pronovost said of his friend. Sawchuk drily quipped, "The first hundred are the hardest." Lost in Terry Sawchuk's massive achievement was the fact that George Armstrong also reached a milestone, scoring his 250th career goal in the third period of that same game.

After having lost ten in a row, the Maple Leafs had now gone undefeated in ten, a streak that ended with a 5–2 loss in Chicago on March 5. Unfortunately, the loss to the Black Hawks was accompanied by a host of injuries. Johnny Bower pulled a hamstring in his left leg while making a spectacular save on Eric Nesterenko. Although Bower stayed in the game at that time, he left after Bobby Hull scored at the 58-second mark of the second period. While Johnny insisted he was fine to finish the game, Clancy noted that his goaltender was hampered in trying to reach the puck and insisted that he leave the game.

There were others. Bobby Baun left the game early in the third when his bum shoulder gave out on him, and

Dave Keon sprained an ankle when he tumbled into the boards in the third period. This was not the news the Leafs were hoping for as they headed into the final stretch of the regular season.

The Leafs rebounded from the loss, beating Montreal and tying the Rangers to close out King Clancy's impressive term behind the bench. With Clancy at the helm, Toronto had accumulated seven wins, two ties, and only one loss. In retrospect, his contribution may very well have saved the season for the Maple Leafs. Perhaps Clancy's tone had brought some much-needed levity to a team still searching for itself. As Larry Hillman explained, "Clancy was the spark plug, the funny guy, where Imlach was serious. Everybody just wanted to play for King. I don't think he coached any better than Imlach. It was just a change, and it was a welcome change."

Though Clancy had helped alter the mood, he did make some significant coaching contributions, which included using Mahovlich on the point during power plays, giving Mike Walton more ice time, therefore boosting the young player's confidence, and, most brilliantly, putting Stemkowski, Pappin, and Pulford together on a formidable line that had begun to haunt the rest of the NHL.

Imlach's return on March 12 did not go as well as he would have liked. That night, the Chicago Black Hawks – for the first time in their history – clinched first place by blanking Toronto, 5–0. In fact, the Leafs also lost on Punch's second night back. They did, however, trounce Chicago, 9–5, in their next meeting, on March 18.

Behind Chicago, which had 94 points, the standings at season's end were incredibly tight. Montreal finished second, with 75 points, and, on the strength of their late-season surge, the Leafs managed third, with 74, followed by the Rangers, who claimed the last playoff spot with 72.

Dave Keon led all Maple Leaf point-getters with 52 points. Ron Ellis was the team's top goal scorer with 22 and Jim Pappin had 21, in spite of playing a handful of games in Rochester. The NHL's Second All-Star team included Tim Horton. As the numbers suggest, the Leafs were a team in the classic sense.

"We had a lot of good individual hockey players. We didn't have that one big guy that could go out and get you that goal," Allan Stanley said. "We had talented goaltenders that worked harder than anybody I ever saw . . . But this was a team effort. Our talent was spread evenly over the team. You've got to get something from everybody. You can't afford to have any weak links. We had a group of players that wouldn't quit."

And a complete team effort would be required if Toronto was to upset the heavily favoured Chicago Black Hawks in the semifinals.

The Leafs had failed to win at Chicago Stadium all season; the best they were able to muster was a November tie. Still, despite a very talented lineup, Chicago had fallen victim to a trend of underachieving in recent years. While the Hawks had won the Cup in 1961, the team was commonly referred to by sportswriters as the "choke-up brigade."

Prior to the series, Punch Imlach summoned Aut Erickson and Milan Marcetta from the Victoria Maple Leafs of the WHL to cover for some of the injured players. Erickson was an NHL veteran who had played with both Boston and Chicago, but had only seen action in six playoff games. By contrast, the 30-year-old Marcetta had yet to play a single game in the NHL. Imlach nevertheless wanted the two players on hand to help out if need be. Both men would see some action – albeit limited – in the playoffs.

The Leafs were sequestered in Peterborough as they prepared for the opening faceoff against the Hawks. Yet all was not peaceful there, as Bobby Baun and Punch Imlach were involved in a very public argument. This open conflict likely contributed to Baun's limited ice time during the spring of 1967, and almost certainly expedited his exit from Toronto via the expansion draft in the summer.

The series began at Chicago Stadium, where the ice was horrific. The Ice Capades had just completed a two-week stand, and a new sheet of ice was required for the semifinal opener. As the *Chicago Tribune* explained, "It normally takes a week for the ice to age properly and reach the right degree of hardness, a fact of which the Hawks' management was aware before it scheduled the ice show." As this was impossible, the ice was filled with ruts and holes and the Zamboni inadvertently dumped a large amount of muddy water in one corner of the rink. While the slushy ice certainly affected both teams, Chicago managed to take Game One by a 5–2 score.

While the first game was hampered by bad ice, Game Two almost never happened: a bomb scare late in the afternoon threatened the start. Chicago police, however, scanned the stands and cleared the Stadium for the game. Terry Sawchuk played brilliantly and allowed only one goal. The Leafs hung on to tie the series with a 3–1 win.

The teams moved to Maple Leaf Gardens for Game Three. Chicago decided to change netminders, opting for veteran Glenn Hall over Denis DeJordy. Terry Sawchuk was once again in goal for Toronto.

The Maple Leafs had suffered through a ten-game losing streak when Punch Imlach (right) was hospitalized with what doctors diagnosed as exhaustion on February 18, 1967. Replacing him behind the bench was King Clancy (left), and his jovial ways seemed to be the elixir that the team needed. In ten games with Clancy coaching, Toronto found themselves back in playoff contention.

Pundits questioned the Leafs aged roster in 1966–67, but the Over the Hill Gang delivered a Stanley Cup to Toronto. Back row: Punch Imlach, Marcel Pronovost (36), George Armstrong (36), Red Kelly (39), and Allan Stanley (41). Kneeling: netminders Johnny Bower (42) and Terry Sawchuk (38). Missing from the photo is 37-year-old Tim Horton.

Toronto went up 3–0 by the end of the second. But for a second straight game, Chicago foiled Sawchuk's quest for a shutout when Bobby Hull scored late in the third. Hull's best shot of the day, however, came before the game, when the winger rifled a shot that cleared the end glass and caught Leafs owner Harold Ballard right between the eyes, breaking his nose and glasses. The *Toronto Daily Star* joked that Ballard was hit so hard "that doctors picked an eyebrow from the back of his neck." The Leafs had, nevertheless, taken a 2–1 series lead with their second consecutive 3–1 win.

Game Four was what the *Star* termed "a bruising, battering cliff-hanger." The Hawks' Kenny Wharram beat Terry Sawchuk just nine seconds after the opening faceoff. By the end of the first, though, the Leafs had rebounded and the score was knotted at two. After a scoreless second, the Hawks scored twice more in the third. Then, at 16:41, Jim Pappin felled Glenn Hall with a blast that removed a tooth and required 25 stitches to close. Denis DeJordy skated out in relief as Hall was patched up.

Punch Imlach pulled his netminder in favour of a sixth attacker at 17:28 of the third – much earlier than tradition dictated. The manoeuvre worked: Mike Walton beat DeJordy just nine seconds later to reduce Chicago's lead to 4–3. At 18:28, Sawchuk again was pulled for the extra skater, but while the Leafs threw everything they had at DeJordy, they were unable to add an equalizer. Chicago had tied the series at two games each.

In advance of Game Five in Chicago, Terry Sawchuk – battered and bruised from the previous four semifinal games – asked Imlach to start Bower instead. Punch complied and Bower was put in goal. It was, however, short-lived. After surrendering two goals, Bower was replaced by Sawchuk during the first intermission. Toronto had managed to tie the game at two during the first period, and from the opening faceoff of the second frame onward, the Leafs, led by the ailing but amazing Sawchuk in goal, were flawless. Toronto took the game, 4–2. Bobby Hull attested to Sawchuk's heroic performance: "I saw him make those saves but I still can't believe it. That was the most frustrating experience of my career."

The series moved back to Toronto for Game Six. Earlier that day, Leaf great Charlie Conacher had undergone surgery for throat cancer. Perhaps taking inspiration from his uncle's plight, Brian Conacher turned out to be the unlikely hero in the game. On the first of his two goals, Conacher made no mistake in firing the puck past Hall. In the third period, on what would be the game-winning goal, Conacher flattened the Hawks' Ed Van Impe, picked up the puck, and found himself in a two-on-one with Dave Keon. The Leaf forwards closed in on Pat Stapleton. As Conacher recalled, "Dave yelled, and this forced Stapleton to hold his ground and allowed me to move in closer for my shot. I didn't aim or try to pick a spot. I just fired and I think it went in off Hall's pad." In the end, the Leafs won, 3–1, and eliminated the much-heralded Black Hawks, four games to two.

"Getting by Chicago made us all believe that maybe we had a chance to win it all," Ron Ellis said. "When you knock off the first-place team, that's big. That was when it started to sink in that we could win the Stanley Cup."

The flames of the fiery Leafs–Habs rivalry hardly needed fanning. Yet this Stanley Cup final, in Canada's centennial year, took on added significance for fans on both sides of the Quebec–Ontario border. The Habs represented the dreams and aspirations of French Canada at the peak of the Quiet Revolution. Add to this the fact that Montreal was hosting Expo 67, a world's fair, and it's easy to recognize the poetic quality that a Stanley Cup win might have held for the Canadiens in 1967. The city had even brazenly announced that a special spot to exhibit the Stanley Cup had been secured in the Quebec Pavilion on the Expo 67 grounds.

Predictably, this raised the ire of Ontarians, who had envisioned a different sort of poetry. This was, it must be remembered, the last stand of an old guard that represented an old idea. For many Torontonians, theirs was still a "British and sports-loving city." It was, of course, changing, and changing fast. Harold Ballard would soon be shredding much of the tradition that had long been associated with the team. Likewise, the city itself would soon shed its long-standing image as a place where a majority were of British heritage; as Canada's immigration policy was reformed, more and more people from diverse parts of the world began to call Toronto home. But for one last time, one last series, the NHL's only two Canadian-based teams could re-enact all of the "battles glorious" – their own, but also those that stretched back through the centuries to Wolfe and Montcalm.

It would be the last hurrah for many of the Leafs, who had now been nicknamed the Over the Hill Gang. It was hard to argue the point. Bower, Stanley, Kelly, Horton, Sawchuk, and Pronovost were all, or seemed to be, at the very end of their careers.

There was also the question of expansion. With six new teams on the verge of joining the NHL, no one was labouring under the impression that this Leafs lineup would look remotely the same come September. Late April 1967 was, even as it was being played, a precious time capsule for anyone who followed the game.

The Canadiens were not, of course, without their own issues. On February 11, Gump Worsley was injured and backup netminder Charlie Hodge took his place. When Hodge faltered, the Habs looked to rookie goaltender Rogatien Vachon to replace the veteran. Vachon found a regular spot in goal. Though Worsley returned, he was reinjured after being struck by an egg thrown from the crowd. Worsley suffered a concussion, and Vachon soon became the Canadiens' principal goalie.

The rookie did not disappoint. Down the stretch, Vachon played 19 games, winning 11, losing only 3, and tying 4. Vachon then played, and won, all four of the Habs' semifinal games against the Rangers. Shortly after the Habs had eliminated the Rangers, Vachon stated that he hoped Toronto would beat Chicago in the semifinal because he thought the Leafs would be an easier opponent to face than the Hawks. With his comments, the young goalie may have put his foot in his mouth. Arguably, he gave the Over the Hill Gang yet another rallying point, while inspiring Punch Imlach's retort: "Tell that cocky Junior B goaltender that he won't be facing New York Ranger peashooters when he plays against the Leafs." Imlach then added, "I just hope [Habs coach Toe Blake] doesn't disappoint me by putting somebody else in besides Vachon."

Despite the trash talk, Game One went very much Montreal's way. The Canadiens' Yvan Cournoyer scored the opening goal of the game when he whipped a power-play backhander past Terry Sawchuk in the first period. Fifteen seconds later, Larry Hillman fired a shot that hit a stick and deflected into the upper corner of the net behind Vachon. Henri Richard put Montreal ahead, 2–1, later in the first period.

Cournoyer scored his second power-play goal of the game in the second period. Then Jean Béliveau flipped a puck past Sawchuk. The Leafs' Jim Pappin, however, fired a power-play rocket into the far corner to bring the score to 4–2 at the close of the second period.

Henri Richard scored his second goal of the game early in the third to make it 5–2 Montreal. After this goal, a tired Sawchuk made his way to the Toronto bench and Johnny Bower skated out to take his place. Sawchuk was certainly banged up: the goalie had a bruised ankle, a bump on the head, and a banged nose. Both Imlach and Sawchuk agreed that it was better to save his energy, as Game One had already really been decided.

With the game out of reach, Imlach sent his auxiliary players over the boards in the third period; Aut Erickson made what would turn out to be his sole appearance with the Maple Leafs. In the end, Vachon backstopped the Canadiens to a definitive 6–2 win to open the series. When Imlach was reminded of his quote about the rookie Montreal goaltender, he replied: "Vachon's still Junior B, but he's the best Junior B in the country."

The opening salvo of the series had shocked the Leafs into action, and it was an entirely different team that showed up for the Game Two matinee. To begin with, Bower started in goal and played sensationally. With Terry Harper in the penalty box, Peter Stemkowski batted home Pulford's goalmouth pass to open the scoring. In the second period, Mike Walton scored on a bullet from 40 feet out to put Toronto up, 2–0. The Leafs added another when Brian Conacher pried the puck loose and slipped it to Stemkowski, who then passed it back to Horton on the blueline. Horton wired a shot past Vachon for the Leafs' third goal late in the second. The Leafs had tied the series with the 3–0 victory, but Imlach had a singular focus: "That 3–0 win over the Canadiens doesn't mean a thing

unless we can add three more victories and regain the Stanley Cup as our Centennial project. There's no champagne for finishing second, just sour grapes!"

Lost in the many subplots of Game Two was the fact that the Leafs had ended the Canadiens' 16-game undefeated streak.

The victory was a turning point for the Leafs. Ron Ellis later observed that the game proved to the Leafs themselves that they had what it takes: "Once we won at the Forum, we found our confidence."

Game Three in Toronto was an epic contest that ended up being the second-longest game ever played at Maple Leaf Gardens to that point. "For 88 minutes and 26 seconds, two of the world's great shinny teams had traded every trick of their skilled profession," the *Toronto Daily Star* enthused. "The result was a standoff, mostly because a pair of weary warriors – Johnny Bower and Rogatien Vachon – were too stubborn to accept defeat."

Indeed, the stars were shining bright for both sides. While Jean Béliveau had endured his worst output in hockey during the regular season, *le Gros Bill* had come alive in the postseason. Béliveau opened the scoring in Game Three with his fourth playoff tally.

At the other end, the Clancy-inspired Pappin-Pulford-Stemkowski line produced all three Leaf goals on the night. With John Ferguson fuming in the penalty box, Stemkowski scored his fifth goal of the playoffs halfway through the first. Jim Pappin also scored his fifth playoff marker, putting the Leafs ahead, 2–1, midway through the second period. Ferguson, however, made restitution for his earlier sin and tied the game with less than a minute to play in the second frame.

The teams were held scoreless in the third, and sudden-death overtime was required to determine a winner. In the first extra period, Johnny Bower used his poke check to rob Yvan Cournoyer. It was a game-changer. "I knew he was going to beat me and there wasn't a thing I could do about it," the Roadrunner lamented.

Early in the second overtime period, Jim Pappin got possession of the puck and slid it across the front of the net, where it eluded several sticks and skates before landing on Bob Pulford's stick. With Vachon still on the other side of the goal, Pulford directed the puck into the net at 8:26 for the Leaf victory. "That's probably the most thrilling goal I've scored," Pulford said, unable to conceal his delight.

While Imlach wasn't particularly fond of the line Clancy had put together, the trio had produced in spectacular fashion and had now put the Leafs up two games to one in the Stanley Cup final. In spite of these heroics, Imlach instead pointed to the Leafs' goaltending as the key to victory. Bower was brilliant in Game Three, stopping 54 shots to Vachon's 62. The 42-year-old veteran, however, was injured in the warm-up prior to Game Four, forcing Terry Sawchuk to return to the crease.

Sawchuk earnestly skated out to take his place in goal for the Leafs, while Al Smith was summoned to Maple Leaf Gardens to serve as his backup. The night did not go so well for Sawchuk.

"I've had better nights and I've had worse nights, but real early, I found out what kind of night I was going to have," the goaltender said. "The first of Backstrom's goals changed direction. The first one by Béliveau hit the back of my leg and squirted into the goal. On the third, by Richard, I got a piece of it with my glove but wasn't fast enough. That's the way it was all night."

The unforgiving Toronto fans jeered Sawchuk every time he touched the puck in the second and third periods. While goals by Walton and Horton gave the home team a glimmer of hope, Montreal added three more for a decisive 6–2 Canadiens win. The series was now tied at two games apiece.

Following the game, King Clancy faced the reporters and made no apologies, defending the Leafs goaltender: "Look, it was Terry who got us here. I won't say he played his best game, but just about everybody we had was bad." Although he waited until game day to announce the starting goalie in Game Five, Imlach came back with Sawchuk. The veteran would fare much better.

While Montreal opened the scoring in the first period, Sawchuk would not be beaten again on the night. Toronto scored its first goal when Jim Pappin fired a long shot past Vachon while Montreal was shorthanded. Early in the second period, Brian Conacher picked up a rebound from a Red Kelly attempt and lifted it over Vachon. Then, with Red Kelly serving a rare penalty, Marcel Pronovost lugged the puck up the left boards and fired a shot from the blueline that seemed to change direction before catching the far side of the net. With Ellis and Duff serving matched minors, Dave Keon scored the Leafs' fourth goal on an outstanding individual effort at 19:27 of the period.

The Forum crowd was stunned as it watched its team skate off the ice on the short end of a 4–1 score. The Leafs now enjoyed a lead of three games to two in the final. Sawchuk's one blemish was obscured by his 37 saves, including many spectacular ones. The rookie Vachon, on the other hand, had finally shown signs of cracking under

the immense pressure. He surrendered four goals on only 19 shots over two periods before being replaced by the veteran Gump Worsley at the beginning of the third. Both Worsley and Sawchuk would be in their respective goals for Game Six in Toronto.

Prime Minister Lester B. Pearson was among the electrified audience that gathered at Maple Leaf Gardens on May 2, 1967. During his pregame talk, Imlach dispensed with the standard hellfire-and-brimstone fare and opted for a more conversational tone:

> Some of you have been with me for nine years. It has been said that I stuck with the old men so long we couldn't possibly win the Stanley Cup. For some of you, it's a farewell. Go out there and put that puck down their throats!

The first period suggested that the Gardens faithful, and the millions tuning in to listen or watch, were in for a classic nailbiter.

The opening goal, scored at 6:25, gave the Leafs much-needed momentum. Red Kelly, playing in what would be his final NHL game, corralled a stray puck and carried it over the Canadiens blueline. Kelly fired a shot that Worsley saved, but Ellis barged in and scored on the rebound. The goal scorer spoke to the lift that his tally had given: "It gave us our start and got the fans behind us. I thought we controlled the game from that point on. The team realized they were a period and a half away from the Cup. Everybody just reached down and played their hearts out." The Leafs were well on their way.

For his part, Sawchuk's miraculous performance continued, while the rest of the lineup played a solid positional game that largely held the Canadiens at bay. Until, that is, former Leaf Dick Duff showed some of his best moves when he danced past Horton and Stanley and then fired a backhand past Sawchuk at 5:28 of the third. The Habs were now back in the game.

With just under a minute remaining in the third period, the Leafs' Larry Hillman added to the tension after he fired the puck the length of the ice. Toronto was called for icing. As the players retreated to the Toronto zone, Montreal coach Toe Blake waved Worsley over to the bench in favour of a sixth attacker.

For this critical faceoff, Imlach sent out his old guard: George Armstrong, Red Kelly, and Bob Pulford up front, and Tim Horton and Allan Stanley on defence. "I think I knew at that moment that that was our swan song," Pulford later recalled. "That was the swan song

I was such a lucky kid then and I'm such a lucky man now to have that Maple Leaf tattoo stamped on my ass. To wear the Maple Leaf is outstanding.

Jim Dorey
PLAYER
1968–72

of this dynasty." Including goaltender Sawchuk, all six Maple Leafs on the ice for that crucial last minute of play would one day be inducted into the Hockey Hall of Fame.

In an era when defencemen regularly took faceoffs in their own end, it fell to Allan Stanley to take the draw. Stanley had, in fact, been the Leafs' best faceoff man on the night, winning five of his eight draws. The veteran Leaf defenceman lined up against Jean Béliveau for what became an era-defining faceoff.

Hockey Night in Canada viewers heard Bill Hewitt set up the action:

> So, it's six attackers for Montreal, trailing the Leafs 2–1. They've got Cournoyer, Béliveau, Roberts, Ferguson, Henri Richard and Jacques Laperrière. Now, then, Backstrom comes out . . . all set for the faceoff now . . . The net is empty, 55 seconds left. Armstrong goes over to the bench, and it's electrifying here at Maple Leaf Gardens at the moment.

Stanley coasted into the faceoff circle to the left of Sawchuk in the Toronto crease and looked across to see Jean Béliveau, Montreal's finest centre.

Stanley later provided a window into the gamesmanship that was transpiring at the time:

> On the way out, I skated out very slowly. You know, Béliveau is an expert. I got out there and Kelly was standing over to the right of the circle. I think everybody has to put on a little show, so I asked Red to move to the right side of the faceoff circle instead of the left. I think I was just trying to waste a little time to figure out what the hell I was going to do . . . I determined that I was going to take one half-swipe at the puck, play his stick, and then run the son of a gun right out of there. I was pretty good at anticipating the drop, which I did. I just took one swipe. I got his stick and then I ran him right out of there. So, the puck came back a little bit, which meant I got the draw.

With Béliveau hollering "faceoff interference" at referee John Ashley, radio listeners hung on Hewitt's every word:

> The puck is dropped. It rolls to Kelly, who tipped it to Pulford. Pulford gets it over to Armstrong. Armstrong gets a shot at the empty net. . . . scores! Armstrong has scored what will be the deciding goal. Armstrong, the captain, scores the third goal for the Maple Leafs and

> that makes it 3–1 . . . the Leafs have just about salted away the Stanley Cup with that shot by Armstrong from Pulford.

The Leafs faithful counted down the evaporating seconds: "seven, six, five, four, three, two, one!" The Blue and White had done it; the Over the Hill Gang had won the Stanley Cup.

While Armstrong's goal was not the Stanley Cup–winning tally – that distinction belongs to Ron Ellis – it is the goal that fans of the Leafs dynasty remember best. The goal, crucial and conclusive as it might have been, was – like its shooter – more solid than spectacular. But that insurance marker enabled the man who shot the puck to bask in the limelight of the most satisfying Stanley Cup triumph of his long, unselfish career.

Johnny Bower was the first off the Leaf bench to congratulate Sawchuk. When Punch Imlach joined the embracing players, Peter Stemkowski grabbed the coach's fedora and flung it in celebration.

The Stanley Cup was carried out, and NHL president Clarence Campbell gripped the microphone and began the presentation. George Armstrong skated over, joined by his son Brian, and accepted hockey's most prestigious trophy. The captain smiled and then held the Cup over his head before waving his teammates over to revel in their victory.

Neither Bobby Baun nor Terry Sawchuk waited for Campbell's Stanley Cup presentation, choosing instead to retire to the dressing room. The two men, however, had distinctly different reasons for their actions. "I just didn't feel part of the team at that particular time," Baun explained. "I think that was probably my competitive spirit or it might have been an immaturity, I'm not sure."

As for Sawchuk, it was the end of a glorious NHL season. "It may sound corny, but this has to be the greatest thrill of my life," he reflected. "I've had a lot of wonderful moments in hockey and other Stanley Cups, but nothing to equal this . . . First, I had that back operation. Then, Punch had to talk me out of walking out of training camp and quitting hockey. Next, there was my physical collapse in the Montreal Forum shower in midseason. I wondered if I'd ever play again. And it wound up in a Stanley Cup win, so I guess it was all worthwhile. It'd be nice to bow out a winner in a Cup-winning game. I have a wife, six kids and another on the way and I miss them very much during the hockey season."

Meanwhile, the Leafs dressing room was bedlam. Jim Pappin and Mike Walton carried their coach, suit and all,

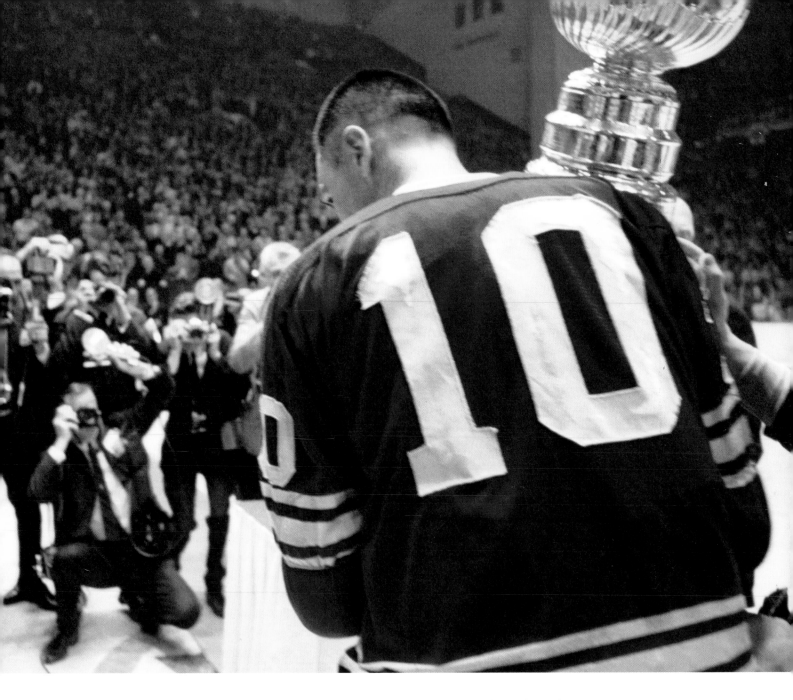

into the shower. Right behind them, Ron Ellis hustled King Clancy in for his soaking. "I think it was one of the happiest moments I can remember in hockey," Tim Horton said, echoing Sawchuk's appraisal. "When Army scored that goal, I actually thought I was going to start crying, there were tears starting to go down my cheeks, and it's never happened that way before."

Punch Imlach would later reflect on the importance of Horton to the Maple Leafs during the 1960s: "I would say that Horton, a little more than any other player, was the key to the success we had. He was always there, always the same, always giving the effort, the best he had, every night."

Although the NHL vowed to keep the identity of the winner of the Conn Smythe Trophy under wraps until the next day, it was learned during the celebration that Dave Keon had been selected. It was, according to Imlach, "certainly a wise choice. He's on our power play, he kills penalties and takes a regular shift. Keon is a competitor who wants to win. He gives 100 per cent all the time. He plays with a bulldog tenacity. That's the only way he knows how to play the game. What more can you ask?"

Keon scored three goals and had five assists during the 12 games of the postseason. Reflecting on that last Leaf championship, the young forward said, "There was a great deal of turmoil during the year. But in the playoffs, for one month, we played very, very well. We had some injuries but everybody contributed. We were the best team for a month. That's what it boiled down to."

The all-Canadian 1967 final pitted the rival Toronto Maple Leafs and Montreal Canadiens against each other. Leading the series three games to two, the Leafs edged Montreal, 3–1, on May 2 to capture the Stanley Cup. It was the 11th Cup celebration by the Maple Leafs and the 13th by the franchise.

Team owner Stafford Smythe hosted a team party at his home in Etobicoke the night after the Cup win. Smythe's Stanley Cup championship parties were legendary: the music was live and loud, the food was excellent, and the beverages flowed freely.

This bash, however, had its share of hijinks, as Eddie Shack recalled:

> Horton and Pully were carrying Stafford, pretending they were going to throw him into the pool, clothes, wallet, watch – the f*%kin' works – so while they're making a big show for everybody, I came running up behind and pushed all three of them in . . . Serves [Smythe] right for sending me to Rochester. But Timmy was a handful. The best thing to do was to stay out of his way.

Thirteen days after the Leafs won the Stanley Cup, Shack was sent to the Boston Bruins for Murray Oliver and $100,000. However, he was still in town on May 5 when the City of Toronto feted its championship hockey team for the fourth time in six years. This time, the parade ended at Toronto's impressive new City Hall. The victory procession was led by a phalanx of mounted police constables, followed by the 48th Highlanders, and Mayor William Dennison welcomed them. Each Maple Leaf player rode in an open convertible with his name affixed to the side of the car. The players wore blue and white carnations on their lapels, and Peter Stemkowski added a yellow lei to his ensemble. Captain George Armstrong, clutching the Stanley Cup, rode in the lead car, along with Stafford Smythe and Harold Ballard. Every Leaf except Bobby Baun, who had chosen to take his sons fishing, was present for the parade.

Once again, there was chaos. "I was a 13-year-old kid in the parade on Bay Street in '67," Jimmy Holmstrom, the longtime organist at Toronto Maple Leaf home games, remembered. "I didn't think I'd ever see my mom again because somebody threw me into the back of one of the convertibles and I went three blocks before I realized I left my six-year-old brother behind on Bay Street with 100,000 people and ticker tape. I jumped out and I found my brother."

Those assembled in the civic square cheered as a slightly altered Canadian flag was hoisted up the flagpole in Nathan Phillips Square. Once again, it was – for this very special occasion – blue and white.

Most of those who gathered in the civic square that day recognized that Toronto's Cup win during Canada's centennial year represented the closing of a chapter in the Leafs narrative. Within a few short months, many Leafs would find themselves filling the rosters – and attending the training camps – of new teams based in Los Angeles, Minnesota, Oakland, Philadelphia, Pittsburgh, and St. Louis.

The year 1967 marked the 50th anniversary not only of the Toronto franchise but of the National Hockey League. During that half-century, Toronto had appeared in 21 Stanley Cup finals (winning 13 championships) – 42 per cent of the final series that had been played.

No fewer than ten members from that 1967 Stanley Cup win have been elected to the Hockey Hall of Fame: Armstrong, Bower, Horton, Kelly, Keon, Mahovlich, Pronovost, Pulford, Sawchuk, and Stanley. Punch Imlach was also elected to the Hall in the Builder category. It is a staggering testament to the quality of the 1960s-era Maple Leafs.

The spring of 1967 is still in the living memory of many people, and many of the players, now in their 70s and 80s, are still with us. The vast majority of current Leafs fans, however, were either not yet born or not old enough to see Armstrong clinch the Cup with his empty-netter. These souls must instead rely on footage – not all of it in colour – of those curious, helmetless heroes who vanquished an ancient French-Canadian adversary. They must search YouTube for digitized 16-millimetre film of the convertibles drawing the champions through the streets of a CN Tower–less Toronto, a place that scarcely resembles the city today. It was a city that had become accustomed to ticker-tape parades: winning, expecting success. How could its citizens have known that nothing, from that moment forth, could be taken for granted when it came to its most beloved team?

The book on the Maple Leafs' second dynasty remained open for a little while after the parade, through that "Summer of Love," long enough to see the Stanley Cup displayed at Expo 67 after all: in the *Ontario Pavilion*. And a postscript was written on December 30, with the passing of the Leafs' Depression-era star Charlie Conacher, who had hung on to see his nephew Brian shine for his old team during that sublime, if fleeting, spring of '67.

Dave Keon (left) is awarded the Conn Smythe Trophy as the most valuable player of the 1967 playoffs. The cerebral centre collected eight points through twelve games, and is the only Maple Leaf to claim the trophy named after the team's former owner, which had been awarded for the first time in 1965.

PUNCH OUT

1967-68 TO 1968-69

EXODUS

From the first puck drop of the 1967–68 campaign, the National Hockey League would be entirely different from seasons past. What had been a six-team league since 1942–43 had now doubled in size. New teams were introduced: the Los Angeles Kings, Minnesota North Stars, Oakland Seals, Philadelphia Flyers, Pittsburgh Penguins, and St. Louis Blues. All six cities had hosted minor-league teams over the years, while Philadelphia, Pittsburgh, and St. Louis had all enjoyed brief flirtations with the NHL with the Quakers, Pirates, and Eagles, respectively.

The newly awarded franchises needed to stock their rosters with players, and so the league organized a draft, with each of the six established franchises "protecting" one goaltender and eleven skaters. Also excluded from the draft were players still of junior age (born on or after June 1, 1946), whether they were still playing junior or had already turned professional. The remaining players were added to a pool from which the new expansion teams could choose in turn. Every time an Original Six team lost a player to the draft, it was entitled to claw back one of its unprotected players and add him to its protected list. Each expansion club could draft a total of eighteen skaters and two goalies.

The Maple Leafs chose to protect Johnny Bower in goal and skaters Brian Conacher, Ron Ellis, Larry Hillman, Tim Horton, Dave Keon, Frank Mahovlich, Jim Pappin, Bob Pulford, Marcel Pronovost, Peter Stemkowski, and Mike Walton.

The expansion draft was very much like a rummage sale. For the most part, the players made available to the new franchises were aging veterans nearing retirement, career minor leaguers, and youngsters whose future in the NHL was, at best, uncertain.

From the Leafs, the Los Angeles Kings plucked Terry Sawchuk plus prospects Mike Corrigan, Bill Flett, Ed Joyal, and Lowell MacDonald. Red Kelly, who had retired, became the Kings' first coach. The Oakland Seals looked as much like the Leafs as Toronto did, with Bobby Baun, Kent Douglas, Aut Erickson, and Gary Smith, who had all played on the 1966–67 Maple Leafs team, joining former Leafs Wally Boyer, Larry Cahan, Terry Clancy, Ted Hampson, Billy Harris, prospect Mike Laughton, and former Marlboro Charlie Burns. And Gerry Ehman, who was starring with Rochester in the AHL, would be traded to the Seals in October 1967.

Don Blackburn and Brit Selby were selected by the Philadelphia Flyers, and Larry Jeffrey went to the Pittsburgh Penguins. The St. Louis Blues selected Al Arbour, John Brenneman, Darryl Edestrand, Fred Hucul, Larry Keenan, and Gary Veneruzzo. In the end, the Minnesota North Stars were the only team not to select a player from Toronto, although at Christmas the Maple Leafs sent Milan Marcetta and Jean-Paul Parisé to Minnesota. The draft had radically altered the champions' roster. In essence, the Leafs roster had been gutted. The Stanley Cup champion team from April had, by September, been dismantled.

Ron Ellis, then only 22, spoke to the difficult transition: "I don't think the Leafs management gave it much thought. Come training camp that fall, it was a different team . . . We ended up more like an expansion team than the expansion teams were."

Certainly, Toronto was not the only team to be hurt by the expansion draft, but the Leafs front office didn't help its own cause. Management compromised the franchise's depth by selling its AHL farm team, the Rochester Americans, to a group made up of local businessmen (though Leaf general manager Punch Imlach was also an investor) for $400,000 in July 1966. The following year, the team sold its WHL affiliate, the Victoria Maple Leafs, to a group from Phoenix. Combined with the phasing-out of NHL clubs sponsoring junior clubs in favour of a "universal" draft of amateur players, the farm system that through the decades had provided a wealth of talent ready to step onto the ice, whether for a game or for the season, was now effectively gone.

In March 1968, the Maple Leafs finalized a blockbuster deal that sent Frank Mahovlich, Peter Stemkowski, Garry Unger, and Carl Brewer to the Red Wings, with Floyd Smith, Norm Ullman, and Paul Henderson (pictured) brought to Toronto.

And the Maple Leafs had long relied on a veteran team, a strategy whose wisdom had been questioned as early as 1962. Journalists had debated whether or not Allan Stanley was through, or whether or not Johnny Bower should retire, or how much hockey George Armstrong still had in him. These players had defied the odds, and Imlach had not only ridden his veterans, but added more – including Kelly, Pronovost, and Sawchuk – along the way. His method, as history has shown, was genius at the time, and Imlach was able to squeeze every bit of pride and talent they had left out of them. There was now, however, little left to squeeze. If Leafs Nation was asking, in the fall of 1967, how long it would be before the Over the Hill Gang finally showed its age, the answer was "now."

While the champions had begun a descent, the National Hockey League Players' Association was gaining a solid foothold. An earlier attempt at forming a union, in 1957–58, had not survived, but in June 1967 the NHLPA was formed. When representatives of the six existing NHL teams met, they elected the Leafs' Bob Pulford as the association's first president, and appointed Alan Eagleson – a lawyer and a former schoolmate of Pulford's – as its first executive director.

Perhaps unsurprisingly, Pulford's position with the PA caused him to clash with coach/general manager Punch Imlach, costing him his leadership role on the team. In a fury, Imlach stripped Pulford of his role as an alternate captain. Pulford believed that "losing that *A* might have been the worst thing that happened to me as a hockey player in Toronto." Imlach's contempt for player agents in general, and Eagleson in particular, never subsided.

Meanwhile, the pundits – and Imlach, for that matter – believed that despite the significant changes, the Maple Leafs were still legitimate contenders in the new NHL. The *Toronto Star* predicted that the Maple Leafs would repeat as Stanley Cup champions in 1968 by playing steady, if unexciting hockey. To help motivate the team, Imlach threatened to fine each player $100 for every home loss to an expansion team. Toronto lost only three home games to the new clubs through the course of the season.

Robert Stanfield, the new leader of the Conservative Party, dropped the puck for the ceremonial faceoff between Toronto and Chicago at the Gardens home opener. The Leafs took the game, 5–1, and then defeated the Hawks in Chicago the very next night by a 5–3 score. It was a promising start.

Two weeks later, the Maple Leafs defeated Montreal, 5–0. Frank Mahovlich was chosen as one of the three

stars of the game. The next morning, he was admitted to hospital on the recommendation of team doctor Hugh Smythe. There was an immediate outpouring of affection from fans. As Harold Ballard suggested, "Frank would have to be sick for ten years to read all his get-well wishes."

While Mahovlich had been suffering, the team was looking good. By January 23, 1968, the defending Stanley Cup champions were in second place in the NHL's East Division with a record of 22 wins, 14 losses, and 8 ties. It took only one month for this strong start to come undone. By February 29, the Leafs had plummeted to fifth, winning just two and tying one in a 16-game span. Toronto scored only 22 goals during that stretch and were shut out three times.

In reaction to the team's dearth of scoring in February, Imlach pulled off a blockbuster trade with Detroit on March 3. Mahovlich was sent to the Red Wings, with Peter Stemkowski, Garry Unger, and the NHL rights to Carl Brewer, for Paul Henderson, Floyd Smith, Norm Ullman, and prospect Doug Barrie (who was sold back to Detroit at the end of the season). In 1968–69, his first full season in Detroit, the Big M scored a career-high 49 goals.

Players reacted differently to the trade. Paul Henderson was initially devastated by the move and the way in which he found out. "I loved playing in Detroit. Bruce MacGregor's wife phoned me at seven o'clock one morning and said, 'Paul, I just heard on the radio that you, Normie, and Floyd have just been traded to the Toronto Maple Leafs.' To learn about a trade from the radio really hurt. But hindsight is 20/20, and going to Toronto was the best thing that ever happened to me."

Ullman was similarly disappointed by the trade at first, but eventually came into his own with the Leafs. "It was a real strange feeling after playing for one team for so long and then, all of a sudden, you're wearing a different uniform. Punch Imlach thought a lot of me and insisted that I be in on the trade with Mahovlich and said he wouldn't make the deal without me."

Unger had just 15 NHL games under his belt when the trade took place. But when the young forward suited up for the Leafs on February 25, 1968, he began a streak of 914 consecutive games played – a record-breaking run that lasted until December 21, 1979. Although his mark was eclipsed by Doug Jarvis in 1986–87, Unger remains at number two on the NHL's list of all-time iron men.

At first blush, the trade seemed to favour the Maple Leafs. In March, Toronto did end up winning

Prior to the 1968–69 season, Ace Bailey (right), by then an off-ice official at Maple Leaf Gardens, requested that his retired number 6 be awarded to young Leafs star Ron Ellis (left).

nine games (including three by shutout), losing just four, and tying one. But it was far too little, too late. Punch Imlach held out hope to the very end, but it was not to be. The Maple Leafs were officially eliminated from the postseason with a 3–2 loss to Montreal on March 20.

New Leaf Norm Ullman finished seventh in the league in scoring with 72 points, although most of those points were earned while playing with Detroit. Tim Horton was voted onto the NHL's First All-Star Team. Johnny Bower and Bruce Gamble, who collectively earned nine shutouts through the season, were runners-up for the Vézina Trophy.

With expansion, the league had been separated into two divisions. The East Division consisted entirely of the established franchises, while the West Division was made up of the new teams. The top four in each division made the playoffs, competing for the championship of their respective division, with the two division champions competing for the Stanley Cup. Although the Leafs finished with a record of 33 wins, 31 losses, and 10 ties, for 76 points, they were fifth in the East Division and missed the playoffs for the first time since 1958. Toronto's record was better than any of the six expansion teams in 1967–68 – including the four that, by virtue of the new format, actually *made* the playoffs.

FEDORA FAREWELL

After a disappointing season, wholesale changes were in order. In particular, the blueline needed to be shored up, and the team needed to get tougher. Toronto lost Larry Hillman to the New York Rangers and Duane Rupp to the Minnesota North Stars in the Intra-League Draft. Allan Stanley was lost to the Quebec Aces (the Philadelphia Flyers' AHL affiliate) in the Reverse Draft, which allowed minor-league teams to claim NHL players. (Stanley would play for Philadelphia in 1968–69.) To fill the gaps, Pat Quinn was picked up from the St. Louis Blues for the rights to Dickie Moore, and the Leafs promoted Jim Dorey and Rick Ley to join Tim Horton, Jim McKenny, Mike Pelyk, and Marcel Pronovost.

To add defensive depth, winger Jim Pappin was sent to Chicago for Hawks captain Pierre Pilote, a three-time Norris Trophy winner as the league's premier defenceman. Pilote had been named to one of the NHL's All-Star Teams in a remarkable eight straight seasons, but after thirteen big-league campaigns he was nearing the end of his career.

Toronto also made deals for forwards later in the season, trading Mike Byers, Gerry Meehan, and Bill Sutherland to Philadelphia for Forbes Kennedy and, back for a second stint, Brit Selby.

There was another, somewhat ceremonial change for the Leafs. Ron Ellis, who had first worn sweater number 11 and then 8, was approached by Leafs legend Ace Bailey to consider wearing *his* old number, 6, which had been retired when Bailey's career ended in the 1930s. Ellis was flattered:

Ace Bailey was working at the Gardens at the time. He was the timekeeper in the penalty box and had watched me play for a few years. He asked me if I would wear his sweater [number 6] if he brought it out of retirement . . . The reason Ace wanted me to wear his number was because he felt our styles were very similar. I was very, very pleased and honoured to be able to wear his sweater.

Toronto's 1968–69 season opener took place in Detroit, where the Leafs edged the Red Wings, 2–1. The home opener was against Pittsburgh, a team the pundits had picked to finish last in the NHL's West Division. Bill Davis, Ontario's minister of education, dropped the puck for the ceremonial faceoff. While the game ended in a two-all tie, it is remembered for Jim Dorey's tumultuous introduction to Toronto.

While his dad watched from the stands, and other family members sat transfixed in front of the television, Dorey would immediately establish himself as one very tough Leaf. At 18:47 of the second period, Pittsburgh's Ken Schinkel suckered Dorey into taking a penalty. While Dorey argued the call, Schinkel laughed at him, which prompted the rookie to drop his gloves. When the Penguins saw Dorey pummelling Schinkel, they emptied their bench, which prompted the Leafs to do the same.

The officials seemed to have things settled when John Arbour challenged Dorey and was knocked to the seat of his pants for his efforts. Referee Art Skov assessed a minor, two fighting majors, a misconduct, and a game misconduct to Dorey.

Combined with two earlier minors, Dorey left his second NHL game with 48 penalty minutes, a new NHL record:

They asked me to leave the game. I was sitting in the dressing room, thinking, "What the hell happened?" I could fight, but this was crazy. King Clancy and Punch

On October 16, 1968, in a game against Pittsburgh, Jim Dorey's (left) noteworthy NHL debut saw him earn 48 minutes in penalties, an NHL record at the time.

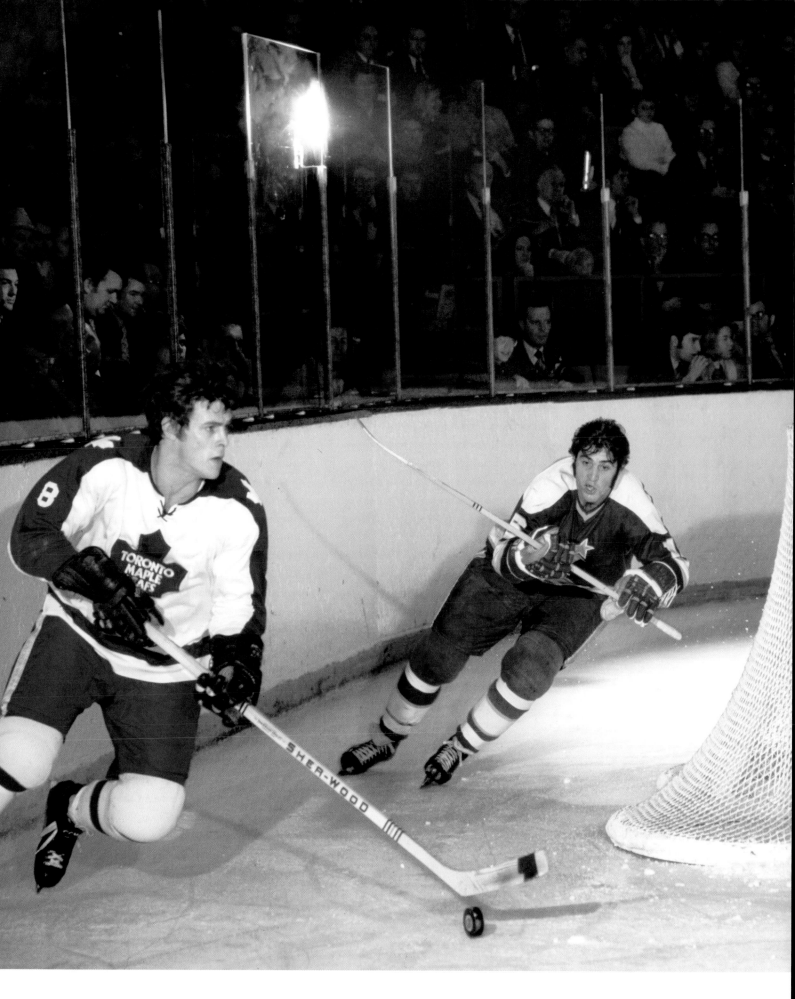

came in, and I was thinking, "They're going to tell me to get out of hockey." King Clancy was hitting the roof in the dressing room. "That's the kind of hockey we want!" I was thinking, "What?!" Punch said, "That was a good showing, kid." He opened his wallet and handed me a hundred dollars and said, "Get lost for the weekend. Don't do any press or anything like that." The game was still on and I went out and there was my dad. He asked, "What happened, Jim?" I said, "Punch gave me a hundred bucks, dad. I guess I'm still around."

Dorey had earned the strong approval of his coaches and the fans; he would prove to be a fighting asset for the team.

Home-and-home series could be particularly incendiary. Such was the case when Boston and Toronto met up for back-to-back games in March. In a 7–4 victory on March 15, the Leafs' Pat Quinn incurred the wrath of the Bruins players, coaches, and fans when he ran Bobby Orr hard into the crossbar of the Toronto net while the latter was trying to dig the puck out from Bruce Gamble's pads. When Orr hit the ice, Quinn kicked him. As the Leaf explained to the *Globe and Mail*, "I gave him a kind of half-hearted kick, but it was in the seat of the pants." The two men tangled and drew fighting majors. It would not, however, be their last encounter.

The next day, with Quinn absent because of a groin pull, the Bruins got their revenge. Although the Maple Leafs took a 2–0 lead in the first period, it was all Boston after that. In fact, the Leafs would endure one of the worst losses in franchise history. The Bruins broke an NHL record with an eight-goal outburst in the second. Al Smith replaced Bruce Gamble in goal for the third period, and the Bruins added three more goals in that period to take the game, 11–3. It was an utter humiliation.

Regardless, the Leafs would secure a playoff spot. The *Toronto Daily Star* suggested that this year's club was "the dullest assortment of misfits to appear in Leaf suits since the days of wartime hockey." But the misfits finished fourth in their division, on the strength of 85 points. Tim Horton, with a career-high 40 points, enjoyed a superb season. He was selected to the First All-Star Team for the third time and was runner-up to Bobby Orr for the Norris Trophy as the top defenceman in the league. Norm Ullman led Toronto scorers with 35 goals and 77 points.

There was, however, some confusion behind the bench. In December, Stafford Smythe actually asked Imlach to relinquish the coaching job to John McLellan and concentrate solely on managing the team. Imlach refused

and told Smythe to either fire him or leave him alone. By the end of the season, though, Smythe was calling Imlach a "coaching genius" for getting the 1968–69 edition of the Maple Leafs into the playoffs.

Toronto faced its current nemesis, the second-place Boston Bruins, in the quarter-finals. Boston still hadn't forgiven Quinn and the Maple Leafs for the earlier incident with Bobby Orr. As such, Game One was a debacle. On April 2, the Bruins, who had set an NHL record with 303 regular-season goals, demolished the Leafs, 10–0.

The Leafs tried to show the Bruins that, while they were being soundly defeated on the scoreboard, there was still pride in the Blue and White and they weren't going to surrender without a fight. With 1:57 remaining in the second period and the score already favouring the Bruins, 6–0, Quinn delivered one of the most famous bodychecks in Maple Leafs history. Orr had picked up the puck behind his own net and barrelled up the boards out of his zone. As he reached the Boston blueline with his head down, Quinn stepped into him with as much force as he could muster.

Orr couldn't believe how fast it all happened: "I was being angled toward the boards and momentarily lost the puck in my skates. I looked down for a split-second to locate the puck and I really wasn't expecting anyone to be pinching inside our blueline." He was unconscious before he even hit the ice.

A hush fell over Boston Garden as Ken Hodge placed his glove under Orr's head. Referee John Ashley sent Quinn to the penalty box with a five-minute major for elbowing, but Orr was finally able to get to his feet and, though dazed, take a few strides. Two teammates supported him as he began to head off to the dressing room, but he pulled away and skated past the penalty box, angrily nattering at Quinn.

On the ensuing power play, Phil Esposito scored his fourth goal of the game with just nine seconds left in the period to make it 7–0. That was it for Bruce Gamble, and 44-year-old Johnny Bower skated out to tend goal in the third. When Quinn stepped out of the penalty box, the Bruins made him a target, running him at every opportunity. But for the rest of his life, Quinn insisted that the hit was clean, maintaining that he hit Orr with his shoulder.

At 6:14 of the third period in a game that was effectively over, referee John Ashley signalled a delayed slashing penalty to Boston. At that point, Bruins goalie Gerry Cheevers slashed Forbes Kennedy across the ankle. Kennedy was no pacifist. Although only five feet, eight inches and 150 pounds, he had racked up over 219 penalty minutes during the regular season. He cross-checked

Both my mother and my father were interested in hockey, and we used to have the Leafs games on, listening to Foster Hewitt. The Leafs were my favourite team, and Ted Kennedy was my favourite player. There was a good reason for that. I was born in Port Colborne, and the place where I was born and where he was born were less than a block apart. He was a key member of the Leafs at the time. When I came to Toronto, he took a special interest in me and made sure I was looked after.

Jim Gregory
GENERAL MANAGER
1969–79

Cheevers in revenge, but Ted Green high-sticked him, cutting him on the nose. Kennedy dropped his gloves and exchanged punches with Green.

Undeterred, Kennedy went after Cheevers again and the two squared off. The teams flooded off their benches. Johnny Bower tried to stop Boston's backup goalie, Eddie Johnston, from joining the fray. This brought Bruce Gamble into the fight. Kennedy recalled, "They were coming from everywhere!"

Linesman George Ashley tried to break up the melee, and Kennedy knocked him to the ice. The fight gravitated towards the boards, and Kennedy, completely out of control, went at Cheevers again. At last, surrounded by teammates, Kennedy seemed to calm himself down, but as he skated past Johnny McKenzie, he started anew against the Bruin. McKenzie cut Kennedy below the left eye and was able to pull Kennedy's jersey over his head.

Finally quelled, Kennedy was banished from the game. His laundry list of penalties set NHL records that night: eight penalties in a playoff game (four minors, two fighting majors, a ten-minute misconduct, and a game misconduct), 38 penalty minutes in a game, six penalties in one period, and 34 penalty minutes in one period. Kennedy was slapped with a four-game suspension and fined $1,000 for knocking an official to the ice. It was the last contest Forbes Kennedy would play in the NHL. It was a memorable exit from the game for Kennedy, who actually was forced to retire due to a knee injury.

Game Two, at least in terms of the score, seemed to pick up where the previous game ended. Once again, Boston humiliated Toronto, this time by a margin of 7–0. In only 120 minutes, the Bruins had outscored the Leafs 17–0.

The next two contests were played in Toronto, and the Gardens faithful lustily booed Bobby Orr every time he touched the puck. While the scores were more presentable, Boston still edged the Leafs 4–3 in Game Three and 3–2 in Game Four to end Toronto's season.

After losing the fourth game to Boston, Imlach stood congratulating the Bruins as they left the ice. As he did so, Stafford Smythe asked Imlach to join him in a private room. Stafford extended his hand and said, "Well, that's it." Imlach, stunned, asked for clarification: "You're telling me that I'm fired?" Smythe confirmed that he was indeed firing the Leafs GM/coach.

Broken, Imlach waited a few minutes and then entered the Maple Leafs dressing room. As he had done at the conclusion of every season, he went around the room, shaking the hands of each Leaf player and thanking them for their work during the season. He never mentioned his firing.

Imlach always knew Smythe would end up edging him out. "The one war I could not win was with Stafford Smythe . . . I could win battles, but not the war," Imlach later confessed. "Stafford and I did not get along. He found it galling that it was my team, not his."

It was, however, Imlach's no more.

There is little doubt that Imlach's own hubris contributed to the premature demise of the dynasty. Riding the miraculous finish in 1958–59, and then a repeat visit to the Stanley Cup final in 1959–60, seemed to confirm his methods. But, as the Maple Leafs were happily in the thrall of multiple Stanley Cup wins, Imlach became bigger than the team. His methods had worked, but at what cost? Imlach's notable battles with several of his players did much to erode the team's spirit.

There was, however, another side to the story and the man. The often-dictatorial Imlach had still managed to cultivate positive relationships with some of the members on the team in his charge.

Imlach had indeed had battles with several players, but not all balked at his methods. Several veterans – including George Armstrong, Johnny Bower, Tim Horton, Dave Keon, and Allan Stanley – had a good rapport with the coach. Indeed, when Imlach was fired, King Clancy vowed to leave the team in support. And Johnny Bower said that Punch "was the reason I stayed around. I thought I could help him in this rebuilding season. I thought he did a great job with the green defencemen. We might have gone further if a few guys had shown a little more desire."

Imlach walked out of Maple Leaf Gardens on April 6, 1969, after 11 seasons and four Stanley Cup championships. Shortly after he arrived at his Scarborough home, friends began to congregate, including King Clancy, *Toronto Telegram* sportswriter George Gross, and former Leaf and longtime friend Windy O'Neill.

Imlach chose to celebrate. "In each of my four Stanley Cups in the 1960s, champagne had flowed, and each time, I had put a bottle aside, taken it home and saved it. It seemed a good time to open the four bottles of champagne and toast not only what had been good about the last ten and a half years, but what was going to happen next, whatever it was."

The first and most glorious Imlach era was over. That year, the last man to coach the Maple Leafs to the Stanley Cup published a memoir entitled *Hockey Is a Battle*. He would one day return to Maple Leaf Gardens, and when he did, he would quickly learn how much truth that title contained.

DOWN IN THE BUNKER
1969–70 TO 1978–79

Not long after Stafford Smythe had dispatched Punch Imlach, he addressed the media. "That's the end of the road," he said. "[Imlach] did a great job here. Jim Gregory will replace him and Johnny McLellan of Tulsa will be the coach . . . I called Jim Gregory and told him to get ready. He would be the new general manager."

Gregory had been a part of the Toronto Maple Leafs organization since arriving at St. Michael's College School in 1953. While he couldn't make the hockey team, Gregory remained close to the hockey program by serving as the trainer of the St. Michael's Majors, the school's Junior A team, which was sponsored by the Leafs.

While Gregory was disappointed with how his playing career had turned out, he had, unknowingly, been set on a path that would ultimately lead him to the National Hockey League. Gregory had learned the intricacies of the game from Bob Goldham, Joe Primeau, and Father David Bauer, all of whom had coached the Majors. And now, just 33 years old, Jim Gregory was the general manager of the Toronto Maple Leafs.

The new coach, McLellan, had been a minor-league centre for the majority of his playing career, although he appeared in two games for the Maple Leafs in 1951–52. Where McLellan found his greatest hockey success, however, was as a coach. He won back-to-back Eastern Hockey League championships with the Nashville Dixie Flyers in 1965–66 and 1966–67, and followed that with a Central league championship with the Tulsa Oilers. McLellan was with Tulsa when he was hired by the parent Maple Leafs.

Smythe was looking for a fresh style and knew that his new coach had "learned his hockey under Primeau, and, like Joe, uses the soft sell with remarkable success." In terms of personality, McLellan was Punch Imlach's polar opposite. That did not necessarily mean that his approach was going to work.

It was, after all, a very different team. First, the Maple Leafs would be without veterans Pierre Pilote and Marcel Pronovost, both of whom wrapped up their Hall of Fame careers at the conclusion of the previous season (although Pronovost would appear briefly in seven more games for the Leafs when the team was struck by a rash of injuries). There was also a transition occurring in goal. The Leafs would rely primarily on Bruce Gamble and 35-year-old Marv Edwards, who had played only one NHL game prior to joining the Leafs. Johnny Bower was still on the team, but the seemingly ageless netminder's playing days were winding down.

George Armstrong, who had served as the captain from October 1957 until the conclusion of the 1968–69 season, had retired and appeared to have hung up his sweater for good. As such, and to no one's surprise, David Keon was named the Leafs' new captain on October 31, 1969. While Armstrong returned to the Leafs fold in November and played for another two seasons, Keon remained captain for the remainder of his years with the Leafs. By the turn of the new decade, only Armstrong, Ellis, Horton, Keon, and Pulford remained as holdovers from the 1967 championship team.

The 1969–70 season started in Detroit. McLellan admitted to experiencing "a few extra butterflies before the game" as he made his NHL coaching debut. Some familiar faces – Bobby Baun, Carl Brewer, Frank Mahovlich, and Peter Stemkowski – were playing for Detroit, who won, 3–2.

Toronto's home opener saw the Leafs host the Montreal Canadiens. Before the game, legendary broadcaster Foster Hewitt presented the J.P. Bickell Award to Tim Horton, and then Hewitt dropped the opening faceoff. The teams skated to a 2–2 draw.

After a 6–3 loss to the Canadiens at the Montreal Forum on November 8, the Maple Leafs learned that their flight to Chicago had been cancelled due to fog. The team boarded a train and travelled 19 hours to face the Black Hawks the next day. The game was delayed 30 minutes pending the Leafs' arrival, but the trip had taken its toll and Toronto was bombed, 9–0.

Darryl Sittler (pictured) replaced Dave Keon as captain to start the 1975–76 season. On February 7, 1976, Sittler set an NHL record by collecting ten points (six goals and four assists) in a contest against the Boston Bruins.

While Gamble had claimed the starting role and Edwards the job of primary backup, the China Wall would get one last start for the Leafs. On December 10, Johnny Bower pulled on his pads for his first game of the season, and the last of his career. The 45-year-old veteran looked good during the first two periods, but surrendered four goals in the third period in a 6–3 loss to the Canadiens in Montreal. Then, during a workout a few weeks later, the legendary goalie suffered knee cartilage and ligament damage that ended his career. The Maple Leafs reassigned the man who helped backstop the Leafs to four Stanley Cup wins as a goalie coach and scout in March. The Hall of Famer stayed with the team until 1990, the year he turned 65 and announced his retirement.

Leafs management was certainly remaking the team by shedding veterans in favour of youth. On March 3, 1970, the Maple Leafs traded 40-year-old Tim Horton to the New York Rangers in a complicated deal that would eventually involve three teams: the Leafs, Rangers, and St. Louis Blues. While the Leafs ended up with an even older player in 41-year-old goaltender Jacques Plante, they also picked up 28-year-old Guy Trottier, as well as promising 21-year-old Denis Dupéré.

Horton had been as important as Bower during the team's second dynasty. The defenceman played his first game with the Leafs in 1949–50 and had been a stalwart on the blueline through 1,185 games with Toronto. He had been a three-time First Team All-Star, most recently in 1968–69, and had been on the Second All-Star Team three times as well. By season's end, two key members of the Over the Hill Gang were gone.

The campaign ended with the Chicago Black Hawks and Boston Bruins tied with 99 points each atop the East Division. As the Hawks had collected more wins, they took first place. Detroit finished third and the Rangers slipped back to fourth. The Montreal Canadiens matched the Rangers' 92 points, but came in fifth because of a tiebreaker. Toronto was last in the division with a distant 71 points. With neither Montreal nor Toronto in the playoffs, it marked the first time in NHL history that no Canadian-based team would take part in the postseason.

The new captain, Dave Keon, led the team in scoring with 62 points. The youth movement had not been an unqualified success. "It would be better for the club if we stuck with these kids, but it might not be good for me," rookie GM Jim Gregory acknowledged. "A general manager can't get away with too many last-place finishes in this league."

KNIGHT IN SHINING ARMOUR

On May 31, goaltender Terry Sawchuk died as the result of a pulmonary embolism suffered in a tragic accident. His formidable legacy included 971 NHL games, 103 shutouts, a 2.52 goals-against average, 4 Vézina Trophies, and 4 Stanley Cup championships – three with the Detroit Red Wings and one, his last, with the Maple Leafs in 1967.

Meanwhile, Leafs management continued down the road of transforming an aged collection of veterans into a young, fast, skilled team. On June 11, only a month after Bobby Orr scored the Stanley Cup–winning goal that became the subject of one of hockey's most famous photographs, ending the Bruins' 29-year Stanley Cup drought, the NHL held its Amateur Draft. With their first-round pick, eighth overall, the Toronto Maple Leafs chose Darryl Sittler of the London Knights. A shy, quiet kid from St. Jacobs, Ontario, Sittler learned that he would wear the blue and white in rather peculiar circumstances.

"I was building swimming pools in the off-season to earn some money, and we were in an old truck with a bunch of gravel and cement in the back," Sittler recalled. "On this crackling radio, I heard this sports broadcaster say, 'Darryl Sittler was drafted by the Toronto Maple Leafs.' That's how I found out. A week or so later, Jim Gregory called me and said, 'Congratulations! We're happy we drafted you.'"

At training camp, Gregory escorted Sittler to the Leafs dressing room.

"He opened the door, pointed, and said, 'You'll be sitting over there,'" Sittler remembered. "The stall had number 27. I was honoured because I knew the significance of Frank Mahovlich. As a first-round pick, to be given that number was special. I wore that number with a lot of pride."

Sittler would nevertheless earn that honour in his own right, becoming one of the most successful Maple Leafs of all time.

The Leafs opened the 1970–71 season with a 5–2 defeat against the expansion Vancouver Canucks. The *Toronto Star* gave a ruthless first-night critique:

Inexperienced defence. Erratic clearing. Effete checking. Slipshod positional play. Remember all those negative features that highlighted the Toronto Maple Leafs' underwhelming last-place 1969–70 season in the National Hockey League? Well, nothing has changed; at least if the Leafs' performance in the '70–71 opener is any indication of what's ahead.

Three nights later, the Leafs had their home opener against the St. Louis Blues. NHL president Clarence Campbell was on hand to drop the first puck as the Leafs blasted the Blues, 7–3. To steady a blueline made up largely of youngsters (it had been nicknamed the Pablum Defence), the Maple Leafs reached back to the dynasty years when they landed Bob Baun, who returned for his second tenure with the Blue and White, in a trade with St. Louis on November 13.

The Maple Leafs enjoyed a terrific December. Toronto won ten games against only four losses. Jacques Plante and Bruce Gamble each earned two shutouts during that month. The Leafs carried that momentum into 1971, trouncing the Red Wings, 13–0, on January 2. It was the worst loss in Detroit's history.

It seemed as though the Leafs were finally firing on all cylinders. Coach McLellan had put centre Norm Ullman with wingers Ron Ellis and Paul Henderson, and it was paying dividends for the Maple Leafs. For his part,

Henderson knew it was a great move: "I've never seen Norm play better hockey. He's doing it all – checking, scoring, and making plays."

Yet, in a commanding 8–1 win over the Los Angeles Kings on January 15, the Leafs suffered a terrible loss. Darryl Sittler broke his wrist when he was cross-checked by Gilles Marotte.

"I shattered my wrist in about fourteen pieces," he recalled. "I was going through a difficult period. I wasn't playing as well as I thought I should. Obviously, the expectations of a first-round pick were there, so Normie [Ullman] took me to lunch and said to me, 'Darryl, when things are going well, remember that they're not always going to go well, and when things aren't going well, keep your feet on the ground and keep your head out of the clouds but come to work every day with a positive attitude and you'll make yourself a better player and a better person, and that's all you can control.' And I've always remembered that."

Dave Keon was named captain of the Maple Leafs on October 31, 1969. He succeeded George Armstrong in the role and served until August 1975, leaving as the franchise's all-time leading goal scorer with 365 tallies.

Ullman's point was perfectly illustrated the following night: the Bruins dumped the Leafs, 9–1. It was Toronto's most humiliating defeat of the season, and Bruce Gamble had been left so alone by his team that the *Star* suggested he "should sue his mates for non-support."

As it turned out, Gamble wasn't long for Toronto. The goaltender was included in a January deal that sent him, Mike Walton, and a draft pick to Philadelphia for Bernie Parent. There was no question that Parent had a real future in the NHL. "I regard him as the finest young goaltender in hockey," Jim Gregory said. "He's a good size, stands up and plays the angles well."

While Parent had been initially dumbfounded by the trade, he soon consoled himself with the fact that he'd be sharing the duties with his boyhood hero. In Toronto, Parent became the protégé of Jacques Plante. "Plante was like a god to me," Parent said. "I had been watching him on TV since I was a kid. Now I was on the same team with him . . . I learned more from him in two years with the Leafs than I did in all my other hockey days . . . That old guy made a good goalie out of me."

With the goaltending shored up, the Leafs finished with 82 points, good for fourth in the East Division.

While the Leafs were determined to overhaul the club with an exciting group of youngsters, it was the veterans who helped lead Toronto to a solid finish in the regular season. Norm Ullman finished sixth in NHL scoring with a franchise-record 85 points, including 34 goals, and Dave Keon was ninth with 76 points, including a team-best 38 goals. The talk of the league, however, was the play of 42-year-old Jacques Plante, who earned the lowest goals-against average in the league, with 1.88, and was runner-up for the Vézina Trophy. Plante was selected to the NHL's Second All-Star Team along with Keon. The *Hockey News* named coach John McLellan as the top coach in professional hockey.

The Leafs met the powerful New York Rangers in the opening round of the 1971 playoffs. The Rangers had managed to rally around the death of Sawchuk in the off-season and finished second in the East, 27 points better than Toronto. Coach McLellan decided to start the more experienced Plante in goal, but the veteran surprisingly turned in a poor performance and the Rangers topped Toronto, 5–4, in the opener. Bernie Parent started Game Two and showed great confidence, throwing his arm over the shoulders of his coach and telling him, "Stop worrying, John. It's in the bag."

With the Leafs having taken the lead, the contest erupted into a brawl in the third period. Jim Dorey

thundered the Rangers' Ted Irvine with a solid bodycheck, after which the game became what the *Toronto Star* called a "riot-scarred mess." Jim Harrison and Vic Hadfield duked it out, which led to Parent and New York goalie Eddie Giacomin leaving their creases to get involved along with the rest of their respective teams. In the ensuing melee, Hadfield reached over and grabbed Parent's mask and tossed it into the Madison Square Garden crowd. King Clancy tried to find the fan who caught it, but had no luck. Reports later suggested that the mask was passed from person to person, up into the upper balcony, until it disappeared. Without a spare, Parent refused to continue barefaced, so Plante stepped in to play the final 4:42, and the game ended in a 4–1 Leafs win.

Jim Gregory offered a reward of return airfare to Toronto, accommodation, and tickets to Game Three, but the mask did not resurface. Emile Francis, coach and general manager of the Rangers, scolded, "If Parent had stayed in his net where he belonged, he wouldn't have lost his mask. As it is, he's lucky that's all he lost."

A strong power play and diligent penalty killing led the Maple Leafs to a 3–1 home win in Game Three of the series. Toronto, however, lost its steam and dropped Game Four to the Rangers by a 4–2 score. Two nights later, after returning to New York, the Rangers managed a 3–1 win, taking the lead in the series. New York's aggressive forechecking rattled the weary Leafs to the point that King Clancy warned, "There is no way we can win playing as we did in this game." He was right.

Hoping his veteran goalie might inspire the Leafs to victory, McLellan started Plante for Game Six. It wasn't to be: the Rangers won, 2–1. Former Leaf Bob Nevin scored the overtime winner with a low, hard shot that eluded Plante at 9:07. The season was over.

Still, the Maple Leafs had made definite strides. After the game, John McLellan offered, "Our fellows gave it everything they had. They lost to a hell of a hockey team. It had too much experience, depth, and strength for us." Jacques Plante was similarly proud of how the Maple Leafs ended the 1970–71 season. "This team has come a million miles since I first skated on the ice with them in training camp," he said. "I rate it as a tremendous year for a club in the first season of a rebuilding program. The players and management deserve a lot of credit and can be proud of their efforts."

SWINDLE AND FRAUD

On October 1, 1968, each member of the Maple Leaf Gardens board of directors was sent a confidential letter

from Price Waterhouse that stated that a provincial court judge in Ottawa had authorized federal authorities to search the offices of Maple Leaf Gardens and the residences of Harold Ballard and Stafford Smythe. Later that day, RCMP officers arrived at the arena and seized documents. The following year, the Department of National Revenue charged Ballard and Smythe under the Income Tax Act. There had been several improprieties, including billing Maple Leaf Gardens for renovations to their personal homes and cottages, and charging back other personal expenses to the company.

"They set up a fictitious bank account under the name S.H. Marlie, and money from the Canadian Amateur Hockey Association, which was intended for the Toronto Marlboros, was deposited into it," Tommy Smythe explained. "The signing officers on the account were my father and Harold, and money was withdrawn for their personal use."

As Maple Leaf Gardens was a publicly traded company, this was against the law.

Fifteen of the 23 members of the board of directors met in June 1969. The discussion revolved around whether or not Smythe should be fired as president of Maple Leaf Gardens and Ballard as executive vice-president. Many hoped that they would simply resign, sparing the organization public embarrassment, but their lawyers instructed the two executives that resigning would be viewed as an admission of guilt. The board voted on

Toronto secured Jacques Plante (left) in a deal with St. Louis during the summer of 1970. In his first season tending goal with the Leafs, Plante led the NHL with a goals-against average of 1.88 and was named to the league's Second All-Star Team.

the issue, and there was a deadlock: seven in favour of firing against seven to allow them to keep their positions.

John Bassett, as the board chair, did not normally have a vote, but it fell to him to break the tie. This put Bassett in a very unenviable position. He had partnered with Ballard and Smythe to purchase the team, but he also had business considerations of his own: as publisher of the *Toronto Telegram*, his newspaper's integrity was at stake, while the broadcasting licence for CFTO-TV depended on his remaining in the government's good graces. He also felt a moral obligation to do what was right. And so, Bassett decided to vote against his partners.

After this difficult decision, George Mara was named president of Maple Leaf Gardens. To save face, the Toronto Maple Leaf Hockey Team was created as a separate entity from Maple Leaf Gardens Ltd. Smythe was named president and Ballard vice-president of the hockey team.

There was discord between the corporate leadership, headed by Bassett and Mara, and Ballard and Smythe. Together, the latter two men owned 40 per cent of the stock in Maple Leaf Gardens and had, despite their transgressions, retained strong friendships with many on the board. Matters were resolved, in a manner of speaking, in the fall of 1970, when the Gardens board of directors was reorganized to include just nine members. The other sixteen directors, including Bassett, were gone. The only remaining members of the old Silver Seven committee from the 1950s were Ballard, Smythe, Mara, and Paul McNamara.

During 1971, Ballard and Smythe fought a fierce battle with John Bassett over control of the Gardens. Bassett tried to buy up as much stock as he could, including the shares owned by the other ousted directors. But by September, stating that the team "was so much a part of Mr. Ballard and Mr. Smythe," he sold his shares to his two former partners. For Ballard, it was a victory he was all too pleased to revel in: "It was the first battle [Bassett] ever lost in his life." As defeats go, it was a profitable one; in ten years, Bassett's original investment of $900,000 had made him approximately $7 million.

A few months earlier, in July, Smythe and Ballard had been arrested on criminal charges involving theft and fraud and had been released on bail of $50,000 each. Their lawyer insisted that he would only take on the case if they agreed to make a deal that would involve a jail sentence of one or two years. Ballard felt they should face the sentence, get it over with, and then proceed with their lives, but Stafford was deeply affected by the charges. He worried about the shame that would be brought to both the Smythe name and to the hockey club. "I will never go to jail," he vowed.

He didn't.

On October 13, 1971, just 12 days before he and Ballard were to stand trial, Stafford Smythe died as a result of complications arising from a perforated ulcer. He was only 50 years old. While his body rested at his Toronto home before the funeral, a distraught Ballard attempted to pull the body out of the casket. It took the efforts of several in attendance to restrain him.

Tommy Smythe wrote the epitaph that graced the large rock marking Stafford Smythe's resting place in Muskoka:

Here lies Conn Stafford Smythe, Lieut. RCNVR 1940–1944. He was dearly beloved of his wife, children and many friends. He was persecuted to death by his enemies. Now he sleeps in the quiet north country that loved him for the person he truly was.

Ballard was the executor of Smythe's will, which contained a provision allowing him to purchase his partner's shares in Maple Leaf Gardens Ltd. Borrowing heavily, he acquired Stafford's 251,545 shares for $7 million. In a bid to keep the corporation in the family, Stafford's brother, Dr. Hugh Smythe, and son Tommy had tried to buy Ballard out, but were unable to raise the funds. Admitting defeat, Hugh even sold his personal lot of 1,200 shares to Ballard. As unfathomable as it must have been to many, the Smythe name was, by February 4, 1972, no longer tied to the Toronto Maple Leafs or Maple Leaf Gardens.

Six months later, Harold Ballard was convicted on 47 of 49 charges of fraud and theft of money, goods, and services totalling $205,000 from Maple Leaf Gardens. Sentencing was scheduled for September 7, but was postponed so that Ballard could attend the Summit Series between Canada and the Soviet Union. He was sent to Kingston Penitentiary in October 1972. Ballard never believed it would actually come to this. "I was totally surprised when the judge convicted me," he said. A little later, he was moved to a minimum-security facility at the then-new Millhaven Institution in nearby Bath, Ontario, and served only one year of two consecutive three-year sentences. He was paroled in October 1973.

The entire situation was incredibly hard on the team.

"It really tainted the image of the Maple Leafs," Ron Ellis said years later. "I was so proud to be a Maple Leaf.

This was my team; Toronto was where I wanted to play. I took a lot less money along the way because I always wanted to be known as a Leaf. So for me to feel that way about the Toronto Maple Leafs and then to have the owner in jail was hard to swallow. It was frustrating to read all the news about Harold, especially his running the Gardens from a jail cell. I respected the Toronto Maple Leaf tradition so much that this bothered me a lot."

Sportswriter Dick Beddoes admitted that he had misread the character of both men:

I thought Smythe with his bloodlines would be the one who would bear up. Ballard is a buccaneer and a pirate who could have sailed with Sir Francis Drake, but I thought he, being the softer man, would be the one to break. But it was Stafford who couldn't stand the heat. Ballard has ridden it out with a kind of dignity and grandeur.

The man with "a kind of dignity and grandeur" would sail his team through the treacherous waters of the NHL for the better part of two decades.

On October 8, 1971, the Leafs began a new campaign in earnest. The season opened with a 3–2 win over Vancouver. The Leafs' home opener against Detroit, scheduled for October 13, was postponed due to the death of Stafford Smythe earlier that day. The Maple Leafs had only ever postponed two games: on January 20, 1936, following the death of King George V, and February 6, 1952, after the passing of George VI. The first home game therefore ended up being the October 16 date with the Rangers. Coach John McLellan and the Leafs players wore black armbands in tribute to Smythe.

While they were commemorating the life of Smythe, who had effectively grown up with the team, the Maple Leafs were also celebrating the 40th anniversary of the Gardens and the first Stanley Cup championship season under the Leaf brand. There was an on-ice reunion of that 1932 team: Conn Smythe and Frank Selke led a parade that included Ace Bailey, Andy Blair, King Clancy, Harold Cotton, Harold Darragh, Hap Day, Frank Finnigan, Alex Levinsky, Joe Primeau, and Fred Robertson. The only surviving team member not present was Red Horner, who had flown in for the scheduled home opener on October 13, but when it was delayed, returned to his villa in Portugal.

The Rangers ruined the celebration by beating the Leafs, 5–3, but centre Norm Ullman collected an assist,

earning him his 1,000th NHL point. Ullman became the first player to reach that plateau in a Maple Leaf uniform, and only the fifth NHL player ever to do so.

When the postponed home opener against Detroit was finally played on November 1, it made for a very rare scheduling quirk: the Leafs were playing their third game in three nights. Toronto, however, battled hard and soundly beat Detroit by a 6–1 score. The team's first line, comprising Ron Ellis, Paul Henderson, and Norm Ullman, scored five of the goals, which included a hat trick for Ellis.

While the Leafs had had a decent start, January 1972 proved to be a bad month for the team. Toronto scored just 18 goals in 14 games and was shut out five times. The young defence corps was often exciting, but regularly left its goaltender without protection. Jim McKenny, as the Toronto Star observed, had "turned into a one-man charity organization. Usually, McKenny's slickness with the puck is his strength, but he's specialized in giveaways."

On February 23, with 16 games remaining in the season, coach John McLellan was hospitalized with a duodenal ulcer and was unable to return for the remainder of the season. King Clancy, the assistant general manager who had last coached during Punch Imlach's hospitalization in 1967, once again took charge behind the bench. And, like the last time Clancy was the acting coach, the Maple Leafs went on a roll – winning nine, losing four, and tying three – and snuck into a playoff spot. The Leafs' 80 points gave them a fourth-place divisional finish.

Norm Ullman was Toronto's leading scorer with 73 points. The team's comparatively modest offensive output included Paul Henderson's team-best 38 goals. Despite a laudable struggle to reach the playoffs, the Leafs couldn't catch a break, drawing Boston in the opening round. Boston had scored 121 goals more than Toronto during the regular season.

The Bruins, led by Gerry Cheevers in goal, comfortably defeated the Leafs, 5–0, in Game One of the quarter-final in Boston. The loss, however, fired up the Leafs team. After 60 minutes of hockey in Game Two, the score was tied at three. At 2:58 of overtime, former Bruin Jim Harrison rifled a shot into the Boston goal to give the Leafs the win. The game was, according to the Star, "one of the finest comebacks and major upsets of Stanley Cup play."

But in Game Three, with Ed Johnston in goal, Boston shut out Toronto, 2–0, at Maple Leaf Gardens to take

For a Toronto kid growing up in what was then the borough of Etobicoke, getting the opportunity to play for the Toronto Maple Leafs was really a dream come true. My parents were, and still are, huge Leafs fans, so there was no choice for me and my two brothers in the Reid house but to be a Leafs fan. I can remember the first time I pulled the sweater over my head and saw the blue Maple Leaf crest on my chest – that was really cool for me.

Dave Reid
PLAYER
1988–91

Red Kelly, who had served the Maple Leafs so admirably during the 1960s, was hired to coach Toronto in August 1973 and led the team to the playoffs in each of his four seasons behind the team's bench.

back the lead in the series. The Leafs bounced back a bit in Game Four and even enjoyed a 4–2 lead at one point in the third period. Then, as if on cue, Bobby Orr went to town and set up three successive Boston goals for a 5–4 Boston win. The Bruins finished off the Leafs in Game Five on home ice with a 3–2 win, and they would eventually claim their second Stanley Cup in three springs. For King and the Leafs, though, the jig was up.

Certainly, the Clancy-led Leafs had shown resiliency. They had been, for the better part of two months, one of the better teams in the NHL. Yet they were still no match for Orr, Esposito, Bucyk, Hodge, and company. Still, Tom Johnson, Boston's coach, graciously paid his respects to his vanquished opponent: "That is the most improved team in the National Hockey League over the past seven weeks. They've been murder since King Clancy took over as coach. I can't recall such a complete reversal of form."

For his part, Clancy was delighted with the mini-run of success: "Those guys gave me a great effort, I was proud of every mother's son. We lost to a great hockey machine." The fans were pleased, too. Three hundred waited at the airport to congratulate their team when they arrived in Toronto just before 1:00 A.M.

A RIVAL LEAGUE

In the summer of 1972, hockey – as an enterprise – was about to experience a seismic shift. At the conclusion of the 1971–72 season, the Maple Leafs had just three players under contract: Bobby Baun, Rick Kehoe, and Jacques Plante. In the meantime, the World Hockey Association (WHA) had begun operations and would forever change the way the game was run. For the first time since the 1920s, the NHL had a rival league to contend with, and the Maple Leafs were completely ill prepared for what would come to pass.

To attract fan interest, the fledgling league needed to lure NHL stars to its fold, offering salaries much higher than their NHL counterparts were willing or able to pay. And those players, who believed they had long been undervalued, were ready to entertain the WHA's offers. Most NHL teams took measures to lock up their stars, but Harold Ballard scoffed at the upstart league. This was a colossal blunder.

One of the first players to be snatched up was Bernie Parent. Toronto's goaltending situation had been tenuous since the days of the Sawchuk–Bower tandem. Parent was pegged to become the Leafs' go-to guy in goal. On the precipice of stardom, Bernie was making $25,000 a year with Toronto. But the Miami Screaming Eagles offered Parent $600,000 over five years. When Parent's agent sent a telegram requesting a meeting with Ballard, the Leafs' owner chose to rip it into pieces in front of several reporters. Ballard refused to believe that an unproven franchise would pay a player that kind of money.

While the Miami team never played a game, the franchise became the Philadelphia Blazers. The young goalie got his big new contract and would, in two years' time, return to the NHL with the Philadelphia Flyers. There, Bernie Parent won back-to-back Vézina and Conn Smythe Trophies and led the Flyers to two Stanley Cup championships.

Parent was far from the only player the Leafs would lose to the WHA: Jim Harrison joined the Alberta Oilers; Rick Ley and Brad Selwood became New England Whalers; and Guy Trottier became a member of the Ottawa Nationals. The Leafs likewise lost several minor-league prospects, lured by the promise of major-league paycheques, to the upstart league.

Thankfully for the Blue and White, Bobby Baun, Ron Ellis, Paul Henderson, Dave Keon, Jim McKenny, Norm Ullman, and the talented Darryl Sittler resisted the temptation. In an effort to stem the exodus and dissuade the WHA from placing teams in several key markets, the NHL quickly granted expansion franchises to Atlanta (the Flames) and Long Island (the New York Islanders). This too took its toll on the Leafs roster: Toronto lost Billy MacMillan to Atlanta, and Brian Marchinko and Brian Spencer to the Islanders.

With an opening-night lineup further depleted by the absence of Summit Series hero Paul Henderson, the Maple Leafs started the 1972–73 season with a home game against the Chicago Black Hawks. Prior to the game, King Clancy was presented with the J.P. Bickell Memorial Award and then dropped the opening faceoff. The Leafs put on a poor showing in a 3–1 loss, with the disgruntled crowd occasionally breaking into chants of "Where's Paul Henderson?"

The Summit Series had captured the imagination of the nation. It saw the best of the Soviet Union face off – for the first time – against the best Canadian players from the NHL. For Canadians, the series was supposed to be a celebration of their global hockey supremacy. On the other hand, the Soviets intended to show the world that, through their immeasurable skill, they had claimed the Canadian game as their own. For the month of September, Canadians were glued to the series.

It was, of course, far more than just a hockey series: it was East versus West, communism against capitalism, and the players were fully swept up in the larger cultural ramifications that the games provided. What was supposed to be a cakewalk for the Canadians actually ended up coming down to the final 34 seconds of the eighth and final game. That's when Foster Hewitt, who had come out of retirement specifically for the series, made the famous call from the Luzhniki Ice Palace in Moscow on September 28, 1972: "Here's a shot. Henderson made a wild stab for it and fell. Here's another shot, right in front, they score! Henderson has scored for Canada!"

Henderson was emotionally spent from the epic tournament. As GM Jim Gregory acknowledged, "Paul's doctor said he needed a rest away from hockey."

There would be other absentees. During his fifth game of the season, Bobby Baun hurt his neck while duelling with Detroit's Mickey Redmond behind the net. Baun was rushed to Wellesley Hospital for x-rays, and while they were negative, a neurosurgeon examined Baun as a precautionary measure. The news, according to Baun, was not good: "The doctors told me that if I got hurt again, there was a 95 per cent chance I would wind up in a wheelchair, so I decided to retire."

The Leafs were in rough shape. With the loss of Parent to the WHA, there was added pressure on the veteran Jacques Plante. By November 25, Toronto had won only three games. Fortunately, the Leafs enjoyed something of a respite that night when they claimed an 11–0 victory at home against the California Golden Seals.

Still, Plante was suffering from recurring asthma attacks, giving rookie Ron Low a chance to step up as the team's starting goalie. Soon afterwards, Toronto added Gord McRae, who made his first start in net on January 31, 1973. In March, Gregory decided to gamble on the two young goalies and dealt Plante to Boston for a first-round pick and future considerations, which turned out to be veteran goalie Ed Johnston, who would play just 26 games with the Leafs during the following season.

As for this season, it basically ended on March 11, when the team was mathematically eliminated from the playoffs. It was the Maple Leafs' earliest exit ever. Toronto finished sixth in the eight-team East Division with a record of 27 wins, 41 losses, and 10 ties. The full scale of just what those migrations to the WHA had meant to the Leafs was becoming clear.

In only his third season with the team, 22-year-old Darryl Sittler led the team with 77 points, including 29 goals. The team also got good production from

Rick Kehoe (33 goals and 75 points) and Dave Keon (a team-best 37 goals and 73 points). Paul Henderson's production, however, dropped precipitously. With no time for mental readjustment, the Canadian hero struggled, finishing with 18 goals – 20 fewer than he had the previous season. Henderson never had the chance to switch out of the Superman cape he wore at the Summit Series to the workman's duds he regularly wore with the Maple Leafs.

FROM SWEDEN WITH LOVE

Johnny McLellan resigned as the head coach of the Maple Leafs shortly after the 1972–73 season had mercifully come to a conclusion. His health had suffered and he was reassigned as assistant general manager to Jim Gregory. Red Kelly took McLellan's place as coach. Since starring with the Leafs in the 1960s, Kelly had coached the Los Angeles Kings and, more recently, the Pittsburgh Penguins, from 1969–70 until midway through the 1972–73 season.

After being fired by Pittsburgh, Kelly did not have to wait long before being courted by a new suitor. The job offer he received was, to say the least, unconventional. "I got a call from Mr. Ballard. He was serving time in Millhaven Penitentiary," Kelly related. "He asked me if I'd be interested in coaching in Toronto. I think I'm the only coach who's been hired by somebody incarcerated!"

While a new coach had been lined up, goaltending was still a question mark. Ed Johnston eventually arrived as a result of the Plante trade, but the Leafs still weren't satisfied with their situation. They received Dunc Wilson in a trade with Vancouver, and then landed Doug Favell and a first-round pick from the Flyers for the NHL rights to Bernie Parent. The latter wanted to return to the NHL but refused to return to the Leafs after being snubbed by Ballard in 1972. Toronto sent Ron Low to its farm team in Tulsa, but the crease was still crowded, with Johnston, Favell, and Wilson competing for playing time.

The Leafs fared very well with the draft choices they had picked up through the trades. With three first-round selections, they chose Lanny McDonald, Bob Neely, and Ian Turnbull. All three would immediately crack the big team's roster. An old face was poised to return to the fold: fan favourite Eddie Shack was purchased from Pittsburgh. And still the front office remained on the hunt for more skill. The search took them to Europe.

On May 12, 1973, the Leafs signed two free agents from Sweden. Toronto scout Gerry McNamara had initially been sent there to evaluate a goaltender in a Christmas tournament. What he uncovered instead was a pair of skaters he thought would fit nicely into his team's plans: forward Inge Hammarström, one of the top scorers in the Swedish league, and defenceman Börje Salming, who had been selected to the all-star team at the 1973 IIHF World Championship. Both were playing for Brynäs IF of the Swedish league. Salming was, in fact, ejected from the game, but McNamara, already suitably impressed, decided to visit the Swedish dressing room. There, he introduced himself to Salming and handed him a business card.

The two Swedes were flown to Toronto. The Leafs hoped to dazzle the young men with their city, facilities, and money, and convince them to wear the blue and white.

"I told myself not to be impressed, that I was dealing with flesh-and-blood people just like me," Salming remembered. "The skyscrapers whizzed by and the gentlemen were very friendly. The Maple Leafs worked hard to win us over. During three days in Toronto, we visited Niagara Falls, saw a Roy Orbison and Chubby Checker concert, ate in fine restaurants, went shopping, and toured the city."

Both Salming and Hammarström were sold, and they became members of the Toronto Maple Leafs. The two new Leafs debuted on opening night of the 1973–74 season. To commemorate the evening, Åke Malmaeus, Sweden's ambassador to Canada, was invited to drop the ceremonial faceoff between Toronto and Buffalo. The Leafs came out on top that night by a 7–4 score.

Both Salming and Hammarström were nervous in their first NHL contest, but getting over the opening-night jitters turned out to be the easy part. Throughout that first season and in several years to follow, both faced a barrage of abuse at the hands of opponents. But Salming stood up to it all.

"There were a lot of taunts of 'Chicken Swede,'" he said. "I heard every bad word there is. In Philadelphia, you would even have to stay away from the boards because they would try to grab you and yell at you. I got the treatment, and so does every rookie. If you fight back, they'll eventually leave you alone and let you play hockey."

The fighting that had become so common in this era, typified by Boston's Big, Bad Bruins and Philadelphia's Broad Street Bullies, was entirely unfamiliar to Hammarström and Salming. The two men were regularly challenged by opponents seeking to test their mettle.

Salming knew there was fighting in North American hockey, but he didn't realize how rough it would be.

Börje Salming (pictured) and Inge Hammarström were scouted and joined the Maple Leafs from Sweden in May 1973, and both made their NHL debuts in the 1973–74 season opener. They faced the taunts of opponents and fans in opposing rinks, but survived to enjoy strong NHL careers.

During his five seasons as a Maple Leaf, Tiger Williams (left) was as feared a player as ever skated in the NHL. He could score as well as fight, and created room for his teammates. Tiger twice led the NHL in penalty minutes while with Toronto: 338 in 1976–77 and 298 in 1978–79.

"We came in when it was the toughest time," he said of his and Hammarström's arrival. "When I asked the guys on my team if it was like that before, they said, 'No! There were some tough guys before, but not like this.'

"But I had to adjust. I was not a fighter. I could handle myself, but luckily, after a few years, I didn't have to because my coach said, 'We want you on the ice. You're not supposed to fight.' But sometimes you didn't have a choice. In the '70s, there were so many brawls. There was nothing you could do when 40 guys are out there on the ice fighting. Then you had to do it."

While the two men would persevere, more and more teams felt the need to stock their teams with players whose *raison d'être* was to fight.

It was into this world that the Swedes had come. In his rookie campaign, the smooth-skating Salming collected 39 points and was chosen as Toronto's winner of the inaugural Molson Cup for accumulating the most three-star selections throughout the course of the season. For his part, Inge Hammarström scored a respectable 20 goals.

Tragedy befell a Maple Leaf hero on February 21, 1974, when Tim Horton died in a horrific single-car accident on the Queen Elizabeth Way near St. Catharines, Ontario. At 44 years of age, Horton was still playing regularly for the Buffalo Sabres, who had lost 4–2 to the Maple Leafs just hours before. While an injury limited his play, Horton had still been selected as one of the game's three stars.

"He was hurting too bad to play a regular shift in the third period," Punch Imlach, who was at that point coaching the Sabres, recounted. "We faded without him and lost the game to the Leafs. After the game, he and I took a little walk up Church Street . . . He was down in the dumps because he didn't like to miss a shift and he felt he had cost us the game. I got on the bus with the team. Tim drove the cursed car back to Buffalo."

At 4:30 in the morning, Horton lost control of his white De Tomaso Pantera sports car. The car rolled several times and Horton was killed instantly. Horton's name would, however, endure like few others – in part because his stellar career meant that he was posthumously inducted into the Hockey Hall of Fame in 1977, but also because his donut enterprise would continue to grow and later become – as it remains today – the number-one restaurant franchise in the country.

On the final night of the regular season, two-time Lady Byng Trophy winner Dave Keon earned the only fighting major of his NHL career. In the second period of a contest against the Bruins, the Toronto captain was high-sticked by Gregg Sheppard and cut near his eye. Exasperated, Keon engaged Sheppard in a tussle. The game ended in a 6–4 Boston win, but set the table for the two teams to face one another yet again in the first round of the playoffs.

The Leafs improved substantially on their dismal finish of the previous season, placing fourth in the East Division with 86 points, up 22 from 1972–73. Darryl Sittler again led Toronto in scoring, finishing eighth in the NHL with 84 points, including 38 goals. While not ideal, the three-goalie system had worked efficiently enough to get the Leafs to the playoffs, and the load had been spread out fairly evenly: Doug Favell appeared in 32 games, Dunc Wilson in 24, and Eddie Johnston in 26.

There was no love lost between the Bruins and Maple Leafs, and Toronto was in tough, as Boston had led the league with 113 points. Most of the Bruins also enjoyed the benefit of having been part of two Stanley Cup championships.

Game One was unusually low-scoring. Coach Red Kelly used a checking line of Ron Ellis, Dave Keon, and Garry Monahan to stifle the Bruins' overpowering line of Wayne Cashman, Phil Esposito, and Ken Hodge. The Bruins were nevertheless able to manage a 1–0 victory.

While Toronto's checking line performed another masterful job on Boston's top line in Game Two, the trio of Johnny Bucyk, Bobby Schmautz, and Gregg Sheppard stepped into the breach and were in on five goals in the Bruins' 6–3 win. Boston had taken a two-games-to-none lead in the series.

In advance of Game Three at Maple Leaf Gardens, Red Kelly, playing a hunch, replaced Favell with Johnston, the former Bruins netminder. The switch did not provide the desired result. Boston recorded another 6–3 win and now had a stranglehold on the series.

In a fiercely contested Game Four, Inge Hammarström managed to tie the game at 3–3 with just 1:17 left in the third, which sent the game into overtime. Unfortunately for Leafs Nation, Ken Hodge deflected Carol Vadnais's blast past Doug Favell at 1:27 of the extra period to end the Leafs' season. Despite yet another early exit, the Maple Leafs had proven to be, as the *Toronto Daily Star*

insisted, "competitive, entertaining, and they're bound to get even better in the years to come." While this may have been so, matters *off* the ice would, as time marched on, be forever impeding progress *on* it.

SPRINGTIME FOR SITTLER

The WHA, which had been a thorn in the side of the NHL for two years, raised the stakes in 1974, adding franchises in Indianapolis and Phoenix. Not to be outdone, the established league continued to expand its own footprint, admitting the Kansas City Scouts and Washington Capitals. The Maple Leafs lost three players to the Capitals in the June Expansion Draft: goaltender Ron Low, defenceman Joe Lundrigan, and defensive forward Denis Dupéré.

The 1974 NHL Amateur Draft was another fruitful one, however. With the team's first pick, Toronto chose centre Jack Valiquette. Tough guy Dave Williams was acquired with their second selection. And in the fifth round, the Leafs picked up a highly entertaining young goaltender named Mike Palmateer.

Williams had been known as Tiger since he was a toddler, and he was extremely excited to be a member of the Maple Leafs. His signing took place in somewhat surreal circumstances.

"A lot of the negotiating was done in Clancy's office, where he had a fish tank filled with piranha," Tiger remembered. "Every so often, Clancy would throw some goldfish into the tank, and as the piranha tore at them, he would say, 'That's how I like my hockey players – hungry.'

"When Clancy said, 'Tiger, we'll pay you $75,000 a year,' I didn't say a word. I just got up from my chair and walked over to the fish tank. I watched the piranha darting around and said, 'When I'm a pro, that's the way I'll be.'"

While Williams was being wooed, Paul Henderson left the Maple Leafs, but not Toronto – he signed with the Toros of the WHA. Defenceman Mike Pelyk was also lured to the rival league. The Leafs sent goaltender Ed Johnston to the St. Louis Blues for Gary Sabourin, and traded with Philadelphia for winger Bill Flett. Just before the season started, Rick Kehoe demanded a trade, suggesting that he'd join the WHA's Toros if he didn't get dealt to one of the NHL cities of his choice. He was sent to the Pittsburgh Penguins for Blaine Stoughton and a first-round draft pick. The Leafs also picked up free-agent defenceman Claire Alexander and goaltender Pierre Hamel.

The season opened with Toronto hosting the newly minted Kansas City Scouts. Broadcaster Gordon Sinclair dropped the puck for the first faceoff of the season, and with four goals in the third period, the Maple Leafs ruined the Scouts' debut with a 6–2 win. This would not, as it turned out, be much of a glowing accomplishment, as Kansas City lost a staggering 110 games (and an alarming amount of money) in two years before the team moved to Denver, Colorado.

To be sure, the Leafs were not off to any great roaring start themselves. By the time they met St. Louis on November 25, their record was 5–11–3. In that game, Toronto lost both of its young defensive stars to injury: Börje Salming cracked his heel bone and Ian Turnbull tore knee ligaments. It was fortunate that the team had picked up Dave Dunn and Rod Seiling to shore up the blueline.

While the slow start had been hard enough to bear for the team and its fans, Harold Ballard made matters worse with one of his many tirades. In this outburst, Ballard told a *Globe and Mail* reporter that Red Kelly was a poor coach and that the players were putting on a "stinking exhibition." Then, Ballard stuck a knife into the heart of the team when he called Dave Keon a weak captain. Humiliated, Keon made up his mind that he could no longer play for the Toronto Maple Leafs, and while he finished the season, he would not be back in the fall.

Smarting from their owner's comments, the Leafs rolled into New York on November 27 for a game against the Rangers. Standing behind the bench, Red Kelly was holding a six-foot bullwhip. "There have been a couple of comments that I'm not cracking the whip enough," Kelly sardonically offered, "so I cracked it a few times behind the bench. It worked well enough in the first period, but after that, it didn't go so well." The Leafs lost 4–1 despite a terrific 48-save effort from goaltender Doug Favell, who commented on Kelly's tactic: "It didn't bother me. He couldn't reach the net with it, so I was safe."

To bolster the injury-depleted blueline, Toronto elevated 29-year-old rookie Claire Alexander from Oklahoma City of the Central Hockey League (CHL). Just two years prior, Alexander had been delivering milk for a living in Orillia, Ontario, where he played Senior A hockey for the Allan Cup champion Terriers. Toronto offered him a five-game minor-league tryout in 1972–73, after which he debated staying in a secure job he loved versus reaching for the brass ring and trying to realize every Canadian boy's dream. After agreeing to give it a shot, he earned rookie-of-the-year honours in the CHL in 1973–74. On November 30, 1974, in a 7–1 win over Washington, "The Milkman" made his debut with the Maple Leafs.

Rough play seemed to be escalating in the NHL, and the Leafs lacked policemen capable of confronting the league's more villainous element. When, for example, Rod Seiling was blatantly speared by the Flyers' Bobby Clarke, none of the Leafs reacted. Fed up, Jim Gregory summoned Tiger Williams from Oklahoma City. In half a season with the Leafs' farm team, Williams had racked up 16 goals and more than 200 penalty minutes. Tiger made his NHL debut in a 5–3 loss to the New York Islanders on January 7, 1975. He was under no illusion about his role: "You had to show Ballard you had balls. If you didn't, he would drive you away from Toronto and maybe even the league."

During a 4–4 tie in the final game of the regular season, the bad blood between Toronto and Boston resulted in yet another brawl. It began when the Bruins' Bobby Schmautz ran Gord McRae in the Toronto goal, and a stick-swinging duel was initiated. When Bob Neely stepped in to help his goalie, both benches emptied, and Tiger Williams and Terry O'Reilly engaged in spirited fisticuffs. Red Kelly, in defending his team, shed a light on how different his team had become since earlier in the season: "The Bruins fired us up by trying to maul our goalie and rough us up. It was a mistake. No team will chase us out of their rink."

With a nice surge in March that included a nine-game unbeaten streak, the Maple Leafs finished third in the newly created Adams Division. For the third straight year, Darryl Sittler was the team's top producer, with 80 points. Börje Salming again received the Molson Cup as the player with the most three-star selections. He was also selected to the NHL's Second All-Star Team. Tiger Williams, in his half-season rookie stint, collected 187 penalty minutes, seventh in the league that season.

The top three teams in each division qualified for the 1975 Stanley Cup playoffs. Toronto's 78 points put them comfortably ahead of the fourth-place California Golden Seals, with 51, but as the lowest-seeded team in the preliminary round of playoffs, the Leafs had to face the Los Angeles Kings, who had earned 105 points. It was a best-of-three series that ended up involving a whole lot more travel than it did actual hockey.

Los Angeles hosted Game One and edged Toronto, 3–2, on an overtime goal by future Leafs coach Mike Murphy. Two nights later in Toronto, the home team bounced back. Blaine Stoughton scored the game winner in overtime for a 3–2 Toronto victory. The very next night, the teams once again crossed the continent for the third and deciding game. Toronto earned a hard-fought – and jet-lagged – 2–1 victory to eliminate the Kings. Inge Hammarström scored the winning goal in the second period.

The victory earned Toronto a spot in the quarter-finals against the defending Stanley Cup champions, the Philadelphia Flyers. Toronto was up by two in the opening game of the series, but the Flyers, who had enjoyed a week's layoff – first-place teams earned a bye into the quarter-final round – roared back with four goals in the third and skated away with a 6–3 decision in Game One.

The Flyers then collected an easy 3–0 win in Game Two. The *Toronto Star* observed that "they out-skated our heroes and outmuscled them in practically every encounter. It was so easy for the Phils that Bernie Parent, the talented goaler for the Flyers, may be asked to refund his night's pay." Parent, the one who had gotten away, faced just 13 Leaf shots.

The series then moved to Toronto. Philadelphia was both skilled and tough. Theirs was a game of intimidation, and they challenged the highly skilled Börje Salming at every opportunity. The Flyers capitalized on a Jim McKenny mistake to score one of their goals, prompting the hometown fans to boo the defenceman whenever he touched the puck. Parent, who collected his second straight shutout against Toronto, said, "Against us, you have to earn everything." The Flyers earned a 2–0 win and took a 3–0 lead in the series.

Game Four was yet another battle. The Leafs twice led the Flyers but saw their leads evaporate. Then, in the third period, Toronto came from behind to send the game into overtime. Dave Schultz picked up an errant pass, carried the puck into the Leafs zone, and froze the defencemen. He then sent a pass to André "Moose" Dupont, who beat Gord McRae at 1:45 for the 4–3 win to end Toronto's season.

While the Flyers had swept the Leafs, Coach Kelly tried to focus on the positive aspects of the 1974–75 season: "We came together and played well late in the season and won a playoff series, which was a step forward. So all in all, I'm not dissatisfied. What I'm trying to do here can't happen overnight. It's got to be done gradually." The question, though, was whether or not the Leafs owner and the team's fans would have the patience Kelly's gradual approach demanded.

The lineup was very much in flux, and several veterans would not be returning. Eddie Shack, for example, played just 26 games and retired after the season concluded. Bill Flett and Gary Sabourin were likewise slated to move on. Norm Ullman had seen both his ice time and production plummet and knew that his days in Toronto were num-bered. Realizing that he was not part of the team's plans moving forward, he signed with the Edmonton Oilers of the WHA during the off-season.

At the top of this outbound group, however, was Dave Keon. After being publicly slighted by Ballard, the captain had vowed – at least to himself – that he would leave the Leafs at the end of the year. As far as the team's owner was concerned, there was no longer any place for Keon on the Leafs. The 35-year-old Keon was invited to make his own deal with any other NHL team – the problem being that whatever team signed him would need to offer compen-sation to Toronto. With his trademark cynicism, Ballard set the compensation bar so high that other teams stayed clear. The owner had, in effect, blocked Dave Keon's path to another NHL team. That summer, Keon signed with the Minnesota Fighting Saints of the WHA.

PYRAMID POWER

With their first pick in the 1975 Amateur Draft, the Leafs chose centre Don Ashby. In the second round, they chose another centre, Doug Jarvis, whom they quickly traded to Montreal for defenceman Greg Hubick. The Leafs also sent their first-round pick in the 1976 draft to the Canadiens for goaltender Wayne Thomas. And to add more toughness to the lineup, Pat Boutette was promoted from their minor-league club in Oklahoma City.

While it seemed that all the veteran players who were on their way out had already left, the Leafs were in for a big surprise during training camp: the early retirement of Ron Ellis. Just 29 years old, Ellis was the last remaining member of the 1967 Stanley Cup–winning team. But he was struggling. "I was really wondering, 'Where does Ron Ellis go from here?' A dark cloud was starting to come over me." Ellis left hockey and opened a sporting goods store in Brampton, Ontario. Without a captain following Keon's departure, Toronto named Darryl Sittler as the new team leader on September 10, 1975. Sittler was honoured but cautious. "They were trying to figure out who should be captain, and logically, it would have been Ronnie Ellis," he said. "He was the senior guy and well respected. He would have been a good captain. They went to Ronnie and he said, 'Darryl should be the captain.'

"Jim Gregory was right up front with me and told me that they went to Ronnie first, but it was a big thrill and an hon-our for me. I said that the day I was named captain. But I also said, 'I've seen how they treated Dave Keon.' I'm 24 years old and I see Dave Keon, this great Leaf, being treated the way he was, and I said, 'Someday, who knows, that could be me.'"

Unfortunately, Sittler would be spot on. For now, though, the new captain settled in and was about to enjoy a string of great seasons with the Leafs.

When I was young, I used to go to Maple Leaf Gardens with my dad. He used to pick me up at school and we'd go right down and get autographs from the guys going into Maple Leaf Gardens. My dad was born in Scotland, but he's one of the biggest Leafs fans you could meet, so those days were pretty special to him, too. I was fortunate to be a fan of the Leafs when I was a boy, and then to be able to put on the Leafs sweater was something special . . . You go anywhere in the world and you see people wearing that Toronto Maple Leafs logo – that's something special. As players, every time you put on that jersey, it's a special moment.

David Clarkson
PLAYER
2013–15

The 1975–76 season began against Chicago. Ontario lieutenant-governor Pauline McGibbon stepped out onto the red carpet to drop the ceremonial faceoff at Maple Leaf Gardens. The new captain scored just 38 seconds into the campaign and the Leafs won, 2–1.

The Leafs experienced a couple of heartbreaking skids during the season. During a stretch that began in mid-November, the team won just one game in 11 starts. Later, in mid-January, the Leafs managed only one win in eight attempts. And once again, the outspoken owner made the situation worse. Ballard insulted his captain on February 6 by telling the *Toronto Star* that his team was looking for a "sensational centre" to play with wingers Lanny McDonald and Errol Thompson. "We'd set off a time bomb if we had a hell of a centre in there," Ballard churlishly avowed. Sittler, like Keon before him, had been undermined by the owner. The very next night, though, Darryl Sittler got his revenge.

The Maple Leafs were hosting the red-hot Boston Bruins. Boston had just signed Gerry Cheevers after the goaltender secured his release from the Cleveland Crusaders of the WHA, but he was not quite ready to play. In addition, Gilles Gilbert, the Bruins' number-one netminder, was injured. This meant that Boston coach Don Cherry had to go with Dave Reece in goal. The 27-year-old Reece had seven wins in thirteen games with the Bruins and had recorded two shutouts in the process. But he was about to play his last game in the NHL.

Earlier that day, Darryl Sittler's usual game-day routine had been altered.

"I was rushing around, doing errands, and my wife, Wendy, was out shopping, so I had to make my own pregame meal, but I was late, so I spontaneously drove into Swiss Chalet and ordered Swiss Chalet chicken and french fries and gravy. I remember eating it in the front seat of my car on my way home because I wanted to wolf it down so I could have a little bit of a nap before I went back down to the rink."

His day got even more confused. Ian Turnbull, who was going to drive Sittler to the rink that night, was late.

"I was late picking him up," Turnbull confessed, "and he was pissed. He said he was never going to talk to me again. Sitt was one of those guys that wanted to get down to the rink a few hours before the game and think things through, and I was of the school that I'd like to just show up, get dressed, and let's get out there and go."

It was in this foul mood, digesting his hastily gobbled meal and stewing over his teammate's poor timekeeping, that Darryl Sittler dressed for the game of his life.

Sittler collected two assists in the first period – already a fine night's work by anyone's standard. But in the middle frame, Sittler scored three goals and added two more assists. The centre now had seven points, with 20 minutes still to be played. During the intermission, Stan Obodiac, the Leafs' public relations man, went down to the dressing room and spoke to the captain: "Darryl, I don't know if you know it, but Rocket Richard had eight points in a game. If you get another point, you'll tie Rocket Richard." Now the whole team knew that it was a very special night.

Sittler, however, didn't just tie the record. He crushed it. The captain, in front of an ecstatic Maple Leaf Gardens crowd, implausibly scored another three goals in the third period. With six goals and four assists, Sittler's ten-point night on February 7, 1976, remains the greatest single-game performance in NHL history.

"I don't know why it happened," Sittler marvelled. "I always thought that someday Wayne Gretzky or Mario Lemieux might break it, but everything fell into place. Lanny and I had chemistry. Sometimes, you just find a player that's on the same wavelength. Errol Thompson played on our line that night too. He had a lot of skills, but he never got the recognition. The three of us had a lot of chemistry together."

After the game, Sittler addressed Harold Ballard's snipe of the day before: "Undoubtedly Mr. Ballard will figure his little blast inspired me to set the record, but it just isn't that way." For his part, Ballard offered something of a détente when he declared that Sittler's record-setting game was "a greater thing than what Paul Henderson did in Moscow." Ballard later arranged for an antique tea service, engraved to commemorate the achievement, to be presented to Sittler. The gift was presented to Darryl and Wendy Sittler by NHL president Clarence Campbell prior to a playoff game against the Philadelphia Flyers.

Meanwhile, the Leafs were still trying to find ways to ready their lineup for a postseason run. The team knew that any playoff path would eventually have to go through Philadelphia. With this in mind, the Leafs decided they needed to toughen up. Jim Gregory summoned Kurt Walker, who had earned 184 penalty minutes with the Oklahoma City Blazers, to join the parent team.

Walker knew the task that had been laid out before him. He had been determined since his first day at training camp:

> I had a few fights to establish myself. As camp was getting ready to break, Jim Gregory asked me to go with him to Ballard's office. They said they liked my style of

play and would I be interested in signing with the Leafs? You have no idea of the thrill and what went through my mind as I sat down and signed a four-year deal. I thought it was a dream. I called my dad and told him the news, and he said he'd be there for Saturday night's game. I didn't want to leave the Gardens, but I had to prepare for the game that night, so I went back to the hotel and tried to nap, but I couldn't. When I walked into the dressing room and looked around, I saw Sittler, McDonald, Salming, McKenny, Williams. They were the Toronto Maple Leafs, and I was now one of them.

Walker secured his spot in only his second game, when the Leafs faced those foreboding Flyers:

In the first two minutes, I started a fight with Jack McIlhargey, and it turned into a bench-emptying brawl. I fought [Joe] Watson and [Don] Saleski as well, and got thrown out of the game. We had set a new precedent – the Leafs would no longer be pushed around. As we mulled around the bus, my dad with me, Ballard and Clancy came walking towards us. Ballard asked me, "Where's your stuff?" I told him it was in Oklahoma. He said, "Get it. You're here for good."

This young American enforcer – who, at 14 years of age vowed he would one day play for the Toronto Maple Leafs – had made his dream come true through equal measures of sweat, gumption, and fearlessness in what was a ruthless age of hockey.

As for the hockey, Darryl Sittler scored a second-period goal in the penultimate game of the Leafs' season, which ended in a 4–2 loss to Boston. This gave the captain 100 points for the season, a plateau no other Maple Leaf had previously attained. For the fourth season in a row, Sittler led his team in scoring, finishing with 41 goals and 59 assists (ninth-best in the league), and was also Toronto's Molson Cup winner. Lanny McDonald finally reached the heights expected of him, contributing 37 goals and 93 points. The third member of that line, Errol Thompson, had a team-best 43 goals to go along with his 80 points. Tiger Williams collected 299 penalty minutes, but also added 21 goals to the Leafs' total. Ian Turnbull bounced back from an injury-marred season the year before and scored 20 goals. Börje Salming, who had been superb all season, scored 16 times, and his point production leapt to 57. He was named to the NHL's Second All-Star Team. Wayne Thomas was a pleasant surprise in goal; he had been selected to play in the All-Star Game that season.

Coach Red Kelly led his team to a modest third-place finish in the Adams Division with 83 points. In the playoffs, their first-round opponents were the Pittsburgh Penguins. Game One of the best-of-three series was played at Maple Leaf Gardens. It featured outstanding goaltending from Thomas, and Toronto's fierce forechecking guided the Leafs to a 4–1 win.

The series moved to Pittsburgh for Game Two, where the Penguins earned a 2–0 victory, and then back to Toronto for Game Three. In the end, the Penguins were no match for the Leafs, who shut them out, 4–0. Toronto advanced to the quarter-finals against the Philadelphia Flyers.

The Flyers had finished atop the Patrick Division with 118 points, which was good for second-best in the NHL. They were a threat in so many ways, having scored more goals *and* collected more penalty minutes than any other club that year. Salming knew the challenge ahead would be a difficult one: "The Flyers were feared and renowned throughout the NHL. No team was tougher or more intimidating." Still, Darryl Sittler was confident that if his team played the disciplined hockey they had used against Pittsburgh, they'd surprise the Flyers: "Our team really believes now that we can accomplish a great deal by working together." It would, however, be hard to remain disciplined against a team considered by many to be the most aggressive ever to play the game.

The series opener in Philadelphia was a surprisingly clean, albeit muscular, game. The line of Bobby Clarke, Bill Barber, and Reggie Leach neutralized the Sittler line, and the Flyers comfortably skated away with a 4–1 win. Darryl Sittler tried to explain the loss: "Maybe we were thinking too much about a roughhouse game and not enough about how well they play hockey minus the nonsense."

But the Flyers upped the nonsense quotient in Game Two. Philadelphia's ruffians challenged Börje Salming at every opportunity. Playing more of their usual style, the Flyers also won Game Two, 3–1. The Leafs, down two games to none, returned home for Game Three.

From the onset, the Flyers came out aggressively. Several players exchanged blows, including heavyweights Kurt Walker and Dave Schultz. The *Toronto Star* stated: "The Flyers were obviously out to destroy Salming's effectiveness by making him so wary he couldn't concentrate on playing the game. In that, they failed."

Flyers coach Fred Shero marvelled that "the Swede never gets tired – he can skate all night, we have to keep dumping the puck into his corner and forechecking aggressively. It's the only effective way to counter him."

The Toronto Maple Leafs were my favourite team growing up. I was a big fan of Darryl Sittler and Lanny McDonald. We watched *Hockey Night in Canada* every Saturday with my parents. I had the opportunity to join the team as an unrestricted free agent. Playing my first game with the Leafs gave me goosebumps. I was excited. I was nervous, too. It was an honour to play in Toronto for all those Leafs fans who stood behind the team for so many years.

Shayne Corson
PLAYER
2000–03

Rookie Mel Bridgman's elbow knocked Salming's helmet off behind the Leafs goal. Salming then delivered, by comparison, a very innocuous check on Bridgman, who then engaged Salming in the first true fight of his career. Although he was outmatched, Salming did not back away.

Toronto beat Philadelphia, 5–4, that evening. "The best part of the night was the fact that we beat the Flyers," said Salming, who was celebrating his 25th birthday. "It was the first win over them in the three seasons I've been with the team." The defenceman, however, was going to exact even more revenge for the beatings he'd been receiving.

Far from broken, Salming played the game of his life in Game Four. He was on the ice for more than 35 minutes, blocked shots, earned an assist, and then, on a feed from Sittler, cut through the middle of the ice and found himself all alone in front of Bernie Parent. Firing a shot high, on Parent's glove side, Salming beat the Flyers goalie. The Toronto faithful stood and rewarded Salming with a two-minute standing ovation as they chanted: "B.J.! B.J.!" Salming still recalls the moment: "The feelings went up and down my body. Shivers!" Led by Salming's finesse, Toronto had tied the series with the 4–3 victory.

There was the small matter, though, that Toronto hadn't won a game at the Spectrum in Philadelphia since December 19, 1971. The team rolled into the City of Brotherly Love to try to break that drought in Game Five. The Flyers, however, enlisted their secret weapon: Kate Smith, who belted out "God Bless America" as only she could. This good-luck talisman was pulled out whenever the Flyers really needed a win. And in the second period, when Philadelphia was ahead, 1–0, the dam burst wide open. Within 93 seconds, the Flyers were up 4–1. Wayne Thomas was mercifully pulled during the third period and relieved by backup Gord McRae. The Leafs, nevertheless, went down to a 7–1 defeat.

Looking to end the series, the Flyers travelled back to Toronto for Game Six. Meanwhile, Red Kelly looked for something – anything – to aid his club. The coach's daughter had been introduced to the healing power of pyramids when suffering from severe migraines. She had been given several small pyramids to place under her pillow, and she attributed her feeling better to their power. Kelly senior borrowed the idea for his team, and had a large plastic pyramid hung in the dressing room, telling the team that they could draw energy from it. Several smaller ones were also placed under the Leafs bench. A pyramid-power craze had hit Leafs Nation.

The captain of the team embraced the idea. The Leafs needed something to put their faith in, and Sittler was ready to lead the way.

"This was a do-or-die game for us, so we used the power of the pyramid," he said. "I took the six sticks I was going to use in the game and put them under the pyramid. Then, I stood under the pyramid. A lot of guys on our team saw what I was doing and soon each guy was standing under the pyramid."

Sittler, who had been enjoying a career season, had been held without a goal through eight playoff games, but that all changed in explosive fashion. Channelling the good vibrations, Sittler scored five goals and added an assist in a decisive 8–5 Toronto win. Only a couple of months after his incredible ten-point night, Sittler added another entry to the record books: Darryl's five-goal performance equalled the playoff record set by Maurice Richard in 1944, while his six-point game matched a record shared by both Dickie Moore and Phil Esposito.

But those weren't the only records set in the game. The teams collected 185 penalty minutes – 94 to the Leafs, while the Flyers collected 91. After a pair of second-period fights, the Flyers scored two goals in eight seconds to narrow the lead. Then, in the third, came the heavyweight bout, as Tiger Williams and Dave Schultz engaged in a spirited battle.

Pyramids aside, the Toronto coach was proud of his team. "They just don't frighten us in the least anymore," Kelly said of the Flyers. "We don't want to play that way, but if they start it, we can give it right back to them." Nevertheless, prior to Game Seven, Kelly had each of his players sit under a pyramid in the dressing room in Philadelphia. "Thank God I don't play for Philadelphia," Tiger Williams cracked. "I'd hate to have to sit under Kate Smith."

The Flyers once again trotted out Smith to rouse the crowd and bring good fortune to the team for Game Seven. It worked. Within 3:16 of the second period, Philadelphia had pumped four goals past a devastated Wayne Thomas. While the Leafs had pushed the Flyers to the limit, the dream came to an end. Philadelphia overcame the Leafs and their pyramid power for the 7–3 win. It was the second consecutive spring in which Toronto had succumbed to the Philadelphia Flyers.

Although the Leafs were out, the team could be buoyed by the fact that they had taken the Stanley Cup champions to seven games. The Flyers would make it to a third consecutive Stanley Cup final, where their brawn

was outclassed by the speed and finesse of the Montreal Canadiens. As for Toronto, the Leafs now had, for the first time in years, a real foundation to build upon.

DARRYL'S GOAL

The CN Tower officially opened to the public on June 26, 1976. Standing 1,815 feet high, the tower remains the tallest freestanding structure in the Western Hemisphere, and the fifth tallest in the world. Used primarily for communications and observation, the tower also became a popular tourist destination, one that forever punctuated – and made instantly recognizable to the rest of the world – Toronto's skyline. It was an engineering marvel that elevated the city's international profile.

Meanwhile, the Leafs were happy to have elevated their NHL profile in 1975–76 and were mostly satisfied with the team they had engineered. Toronto went into the June draft without a first-round selection, but did well by choosing Randy Carlyle in the second round.

Carlyle, however, had signed a letter of intent with the WHA's Cincinnati Stingers. It looked as though the dispute was heading to court and that the Leafs would lose another very promising young player through complacency. The issue was resolved in August 1976 when Toronto assumed former Leaf Mike Pelyk's contract with Cincinnati; in return, the Stingers dropped their claim on Carlyle's rights.

Before the NHL season kicked off, the hockey world was treated to a new international tournament. Inspired by the interest the 1972 Summit Series had generated, the 1976 Canada Cup featured those teams that were generally recognized as the world's hockey powers of the day: Canada, the United States, Czechoslovakia, Finland, Sweden, and the Soviet Union.

The series concluded with a memorable finale, played in the Montreal Forum, between Canada and Czechoslovakia. During the intermission between the third period and overtime, and with the score tied 4–4, Team Canada assistant coach Don Cherry informed the

Mike Palmateer quickly became a fan favourite for his daring, gymnastic-like moves for the Leafs. The confident goaltender was a key reason why Toronto ousted the New York Islanders during the 1978 playoffs.

team that he had noticed that Vladimír Dzurilla, the Czech goalie, had been coming well out his crease to cut down the angles, and that it therefore might be easy to deke him out.

After receiving a pass from Marcel Dionne, Darryl Sittler beat one Czech defender and then, brilliantly, faked a slap shot on Dzurilla. The goalie bought Darryl's fake pump and now, too far out of his goal for any recourse, was helplessly stranded. Sittler simply took a couple of strides to his left and drilled the puck into the yawning cage. Canada had won the Canada Cup.

Darryl's goal inspired a nationwide celebration. The man who, only a few months earlier, had scored ten points in a single game was now the toast of the country.

Less than three weeks after his most famous goal, Sittler was ready to lead his Leafs into a new 80-game campaign. The 1976–77 season opener took place in Denver against the Colorado Rockies – the relocated Kansas City Scouts. In the opposing goal stood Doug Favell, whom the Leafs had sold to the Rockies earlier that summer. Favell and his new team stunned Toronto, defeating the Leafs, 4–2, for Colorado's first-ever win.

The Maple Leafs returned home feeling low and took it out on the Boston Bruins with a decisive 7–5 victory in the home opener. Former Kid Line member and Leafs coach Joe Primeau dropped the puck for the ceremonial faceoff. It would, however, be the only highlight in the early part of the season.

Toronto won just one of its first nine games, and it seemed some of Wayne Thomas's magic had evaporated. The Leafs called up Mike Palmateer from the Dallas Black Hawks, their CHL farm team. When informed by the Leafs general manager, the cocksure Palmateer advised his new boss. "Your troubles are over, Mr. Gregory. When do you want me?"

Palmateer, who grew up in the Marlboros organization, had dreamed of being a Leaf for many years.

"I actually started practising in Maple Leaf Gardens after school, which made it that much more special to be drafted by the Leafs," he recalled. "The Marlie system started at peewee back then. We'd stick around after practice and get autographs from the Maple Leafs, all those cool guys in their trench coats and fedoras. It was awesome! Frank Mahovlich was the guy. He was my favourite, but I liked Johnny Bower as well."

As acrobatic as he was confident, the young goaltender played like a pro in his first game, on October 28. The Leafs enjoyed a 3–1 win over the Red Wings. Then, encouraged by the play of their plucky new netminder,

the Maple Leafs went on a roll: winning six, tying one, and losing just two in Palmateer's first string of games. In mid-November, Palmateer also managed back-to-back shutouts against Vancouver and Montreal.

Imbued with confidence, the team continued its winning ways into the new year. On February 2, Ian Turnbull, who hadn't scored a goal in his previous 30 games, scored on each of the five shots he took in a 9–1 win against Detroit. The five-goal game broke the team and league records for goals by a defenceman. A handful of NHL blueliners had scored four times in a game in the league's early days, including the Blueshirts' Harry Cameron, in a 7–5 win over the Canadiens on December 26, 1917. The Leafs' Hap Day was the most recent, in a 10–5 loss to the Pittsburgh Pirates on November 19, 1929.

"The Leafs needed the offence, so they pretty much let Börje and me do whatever we wanted to do," Turnbull recalled. "They weren't too worried about keeping the puck out of the net, although we did okay." To be sure, neither defenceman was shy about carrying the puck deep into an opponent's zone. Turnbull and Salming would end up with 79 and 78 points, respectively, during the 1976–77 campaign, a very laudable output for a defensive pair.

While there was no question that Turnbull was an excellent defenceman, Salming was just that extra bit more special. Gerry McNamara, the Leafs scout who found Salming, knew that "Börje was a once-in-a-lifetime find. Here is a player you can mention in the same sentence with Bobby Orr, Brad Park and Larry Robinson when you're talking about the great defencemen of the modern era." Salming was voted onto the First All-Star Team, and was also Toronto's Molson Cup recipient.

While Salming had already established himself as a special player, the 1976–77 campaign proved that the Leafs were right in giving Lanny McDonald a chance to prove his mettle. It had taken time for the young forward to develop, but once he did, McDonald became a bona fide NHL star. Lanny had earned a modest 30 points as a rookie, improved to 44 in his second season, and then exploded for 93 points in season three. He was now going to regularly feature as a top scorer in the league.

The humble McDonald reflected on his progress and the job that his coaches had done:

Red Kelly and Jim Gregory showed tremendous patience. They gave me a chance to really come into my own and develop the confidence I didn't have in the first couple years. In the middle of all that, I became friends with Darryl and Wendy [Sittler]. I played on the same line

My first game here, I practically had to tape my jaw closed because my mouth was hanging open, I was so much in awe.

Pat Quinn
PLAYER
1968–70
COACH, GENERAL MANAGER, PRESIDENT
1998–2006

with Darryl for the last four and a half years that I played with the Toronto Maple Leafs. That friendship still exists today. I call Darryl my best friend and we probably talk every three or four days. When you spend as much time together as we did, both on and off the ice, that friendship just blossomed into something that has lasted a lifetime.

It was these off-ice relationships that allowed the Leafs to transform – albeit briefly – into a powerful team that threatened to do something special in the late 1970s.

McDonald led the team in scoring with 46 goals and 90 points, good for eighth in the league, and he was also selected for the Second All-Star Team. Darryl Sittler also collected 90 points, including 38 goals, and finished ninth, just behind his best friend.

In what was becoming an annual occurrence, the Leafs finished third in the Adams Division, with 81 points. In the first round of the playoffs, they were again matched with the Pittsburgh Penguins. The Penguins, third in the Norris Division, had finished with an identical 81 points. The series began in Pittsburgh, where coach Red Kelly surprised many people by choosing Wayne Thomas to start in goal over Mike Palmateer, and Toronto stole the game, 4–2.

Game Two wasn't the only big game in town on April 7, 1977. Earlier in the day, the Toronto Blue Jays of baseball's American League had played their first-ever game. Borrowing a Leafs tradition, the Blue Jays enlisted the 48th Highlanders to perform "The Star-Spangled Banner." Then, Canada's favourite songstress, Anne Murray, performed "O Canada." The Jays did not disappoint, beating the Chicago White Sox, 9–5, on the snow-framed field of Exhibition Stadium.

Some of the baseball fans made the 20-minute drive up to Maple Leaf Gardens in plenty of time for the opening faceoff. Red Kelly had chosen to go with Thomas again for Game Two. While it looked like a good decision for a time, Pittsburgh battled back from a 4–1 deficit to tie the game at 7:52 of third. Toronto then surrendered two additional goals and let the game slip away. The Penguins outscored the hometown boys, 6–4.

Back in Pittsburgh for Game Three, the Maple Leafs enjoyed a convincing 5–2 win. Lanny McDonald was in on every one of the Leafs' goals, including a hat trick of his own. While delighted with the result, the Leafs were less joyous about their next task. For the third spring in a row, they would face the unforgiving Philadelphia Flyers in the quarter-final. The Flyers had earned a bye into the second round, so they were starting the series after an eight-day rest. Conversely, Toronto opened the series playing their fourth game in seven nights.

Despite the hectic schedule, Game One still went the Leafs' way. They scored three goals in the first nine minutes of the series opener at the Spectrum, and then held on for a 3–2 win. Palmateer started in goal, but had to leave late in the second period after suffering from dizziness and a sore back. Thomas took his spot in the crease.

Toronto could hardly believe its luck in Game Two. Palmateer returned and was sensational in goal. It was, however, the defence pairs that really shone for the Maple Leafs. Börje Salming and Ian Turnbull were cruising at their collective peak, while Randy Carlyle and Mike Pelyk escalated their game to match the top pairing. The *Toronto Star* believed that the rookie Carlyle was "showing the poise of a highly competent major league back-liner." The Leafs had, improbably, taken their second straight game in Philadelphia by a 4–1 score and now led the series, two games to none. The impossible dream seemed within reach.

The Flyers made a rather bold change in advance of Game Three at Maple Leaf Gardens, as Wayne Stephenson replaced Bernie Parent in the Philadelphia goal. For much of the contest, it seemed to make little difference, and Toronto was only 39 seconds away from winning its third straight. Then Rick MacLeish scored to tie the game at three, and at 2:55 of overtime, he victimized the Leafs again to give the Flyers the 4–3 win. Toronto had let Philly get up off of the mat.

Two nights later, McDonald scored four goals and Toronto was up 5–2 with seven minutes left to play, looking to restore a two-game lead in the series. That's when Bobby Clarke took hold of his team. Spurred on by their captain's tenacity, the Flyers had, by the end of 60 minutes, rebounded all the way to tie the game at 5–5. Philadelphia's Reggie Leach played the hero in overtime when he ripped a shot from 45 feet out that hit Pelyk's stick and flew past Palmateer for the 6–5 victory. The Flyers had tied the series.

Red Kelly couldn't believe the Flyers' comebacks. "With any kind of luck, the series would be over and we'd have won it four straight," he said. "We've had them beat but allowed them to get off the hook both times." The series, though, was all even and shifting back to Philadelphia for Game Five.

While Palmateer was brilliant in the Toronto goal, Stephenson was even better, and the Flyers won, 2–0, to take a three-games-to-two lead in the series. Game Five took the wind out of the Maple Leafs' sails. And while

Growing up in P.E.I., we watched *Hockey Night in Canada* on Wednesdays and Saturdays. It was always the Leafs or the Canadiens who were playing. As a child, you think, "Wow! If I could play for one of those two teams, it would be amazing!" To wear the Maple Leaf on the front of the sweater for that length of time was pretty amazing. An Original Six team; a historic franchise. Sometimes you had to pinch yourself because you didn't know whether it was real or not.

Rick Vaive
PLAYER
1980–87

Game Six was close, the Flyers brought the Leafs' season to an end – for the third straight year – with a 4–3 win.

Nevertheless, there had been some excellent individual postseason performances. Salming had nine points and Turnbull eight. It was, however, the line of Darryl Sittler, Lanny McDonald, and Tiger Williams that was the real story. Sittler had 21 points in nine playoff games, McDonald 17, and Williams 9. And therein lay the problem: the other lines had contributed a grand total of six goals.

The rest of the NHL began to see the Achilles heel of the mid-1970s Toronto Maple Leafs: it was a one-line team. While the Leafs would come tantalizingly close in the following season with much the same team, it would, in retrospect, be hard to argue with the prevailing league-wide evaluation of the Blue and White.

As for the third consecutive dismissal at the hands of the hated Flyers, Sittler was dumbfounded. "I'll think back over the season and shake my head when it hits me about what might have happened if we'd just been a little sharper a little longer in those two games."

Many questioned whether this was as far as Red Kelly could take the Leafs. Harold Ballard assured everyone that "Red Kelly's job is as secure as mine, and I'm not going to get fired."

Eight weeks later, Harold fired Kelly.

LANNY'S GOAL

Some players felt that Red Kelly had simply been too nice. Others felt that his stubbornness had hastened his departure. Tiger Williams knew the end was nigh for his coach. "You had to suspect that Red Kelly was a goner when we blew a two-game lead in the series with Philly," he said. "That was the kind of thing that Harold Ballard just couldn't stomach." Still, several of the players had enjoyed some of their strongest seasons under Kelly's direction.

The shortlist to replace Kelly consisted of George Armstrong, Bob Pulford, and a relative newcomer, Roger Neilson. After years of sending well-trained juniors from the Peterborough Petes to the NHL, Neilson had been hired to coach the Dallas Black Hawks, a CHL team shared by the Chicago Black Hawks and Toronto Maple Leafs. Neilson had impressed Leafs management enough in his one professional season that they hired him as the new coach.

In his introduction to the media, Neilson stated that his top priority was to improve the Leafs' defensive game.

He would insist on defensive responsibility from his forwards. Yet Neilson would introduce some new tactics that differentiated him from just about every other NHL coach at the time. The Leafs' new coach would also record faceoffs won and lost, scoring chances for and against, and giveaways and hits. There was more, as Neilson explained to the gathering of reporters: "I'll be using video systems, lectures, and I intend to have one-on-one sessions with players to get things across." It was music to the ears of some of the hometown media. As the *Toronto Star* insisted, Neilson's ideas and approaches showed forward thinking, away from the dull old notions: "A decade ago, he would have been regarded as a hockey heretic." The new coach would spend hours poring over footage illustrating patterns and areas that could be improved upon. These innovations were, as it turned out, the birth pangs of hockey analytics.

At the 1977 draft, the Maple Leafs picked up three players who would become important components of the team for several years to come. With two first-round selections, the Leafs chose forward John Anderson and defenceman Trevor Johansen, both from the Toronto Marlboros, and in the second round, forward Rocky Saganiuk.

Johansen already had a connection to the Blue and White: his father, Bill Johnson – his professional name during a less-enlightened era – had played a single game for the Maple Leafs during the 1949–50 season. Johansen made the Leafs straight out of junior; Anderson joined the big club later in the season. Toronto also picked up hardworking Jimmy Jones, but lost goaltender Wayne Thomas on waivers to the New York Rangers.

After a two-year hiatus, Ron Ellis returned to the Maple Leafs for the 1977–78 campaign. The path back to his hockey home was a curious one. Ellis had heard that Canada was sending a team to the IIHF World Championship for the first time since 1969, and professionals from the NHL and WHA would be allowed to take part. Ellis was invited to try out, and then made the team. Although Canada finished fourth and went without a medal, he had a good series, collecting five goals and four assists in the ten-game tournament. After the series, Jim Gregory invited Ellis back to the Maple Leafs.

Meanwhile, the Leafs' core, which seemed to be coming into its own, had to get used to the new coach's revolutionary approach.

"There were times, especially at the start, when we didn't understand Roger's coaching techniques," Lanny

Roger Neilson – nicknamed "Captain Video" – took his team to the third round of the playoffs in 1977–78 and to the second round in 1978–79. The innovative coach employed several creative strategies during his two seasons behind the bench with the Toronto Maple Leafs.

McDonald confessed, "but it didn't take us long to realize one thing: he was two or three steps ahead of the opposing coaches. The amazing thing about playing for Roger was that you never knew what he was going to do next."

Neilson appointed a committee of veteran players to make suggestions about everything from travel to practices to team concerns. The committee included Ron Ellis, Lanny McDonald, Börje Salming, Darryl Sittler, and Ian Turnbull.

Sittler, for one, was on board with the new coach. "Roger was ahead of the curve for most NHL coaches, but I liked that," he said. "[Neilson] made everybody within the organization feel that they were as important as the next guy." The importance of Neilson's methods might not have been fully understood at the time, but their impact would, in time, be felt far and wide. Bruce Boudreau, for instance, had led the Dallas Black Hawks in goal scoring during the 1976–77 season under Neilson, and would spend the next several seasons boomeranging between the NHL and CHL. For Boudreau, who has enjoyed success as an NHL coach, Roger Neilson "was a fundamental figure in my life. Roger invented video study for hockey. We watched it and watched it. I learned so much about how to play the game from Roger."

There were, of course, some detractors. Not everyone agreed with the coach's methods. "I always bumped heads with Roger," Ian Turnbull admitted. "We had philosophical differences between total defence and offence. His philosophy was kitty-bar-the-door; play it real tight to the vest and don't take chances and we'll see how it works out." It would be difficult for the offensive-minded Turnbull (and Salming, for that matter) to maintain production while observing the new directive from Coach Neilson.

The first game of the season showed just how much incongruence there was between the respective systems used by Kelly and Neilson. The Leafs began the 1977–78 campaign in Detroit against the Red Wings. Much to the frustration of the rookie coach, Toronto squandered a two-goal lead in the last five minutes of the game. The Leafs had to settle for a 3–3 tie.

Two nights later, it was the Leafs' home opener, and retired NHL president Clarence Campbell dropped the puck for the opening faceoff. The visiting Buffalo Sabres likewise dropped the hometown squad, 5–2. The learning curve, it seemed, was steep.

The lineup also underwent a few changes over the course of the season. The much-maligned Inge Hammarström, who Harold Ballard once famously suggested "could go into the corners with a half-dozen eggs

in his pocket and not break one of them," was dealt to the St. Louis Blues for forward Jerry Butler on November 1. Bob Neely was sold to the Colorado Rockies (although he was bought back after the season), and Claire Alexander was sold to the Vancouver Canucks. Finally, the Leafs sent Errol Thompson, along with a first-round selection in 1978, a second-round pick in 1979, and a discretionary first-round pick to the Wings for Dan Maloney and a second-round draft pick in 1980. Management considered Maloney's toughness to be indispensable if Toronto was to make a proper run at the Cup. Given Thompson's output in recent years, the controversial trade would be debated in Leafs Nation for years to come. For now, though, Maloney was placed on a line with Sittler and McDonald, while Tiger Williams was moved onto a line with Ron Ellis.

Disappointingly, a strong season began to tail off towards the end of the 1977–78 campaign. The Leafs lost 10 of their last 12 games, finishing third in the Adams Division with 92 points. The team won 41 games, tying the franchise record set in 1950–51, and had embraced Neilson's defence-first philosophy: while scoring 30 fewer goals than the previous season, they reduced their goals against by 48, from 285 to 237.

Darryl Sittler led the team in scoring, and his 117 points was third-highest in the NHL. Lanny McDonald was tenth in scoring, with 87 points, including a team-best 47 goals, one shy of the club record established by Frank Mahovlich in 1960–61. Ron Ellis added 26 goals in his return to the Leafs. Sittler and Börje Salming were both named to the NHL's Second All-Star Team, and the latter won the team's Molson Cup. Crucially, the Maple Leafs knew that they had the tools to contend. It would, however, take all-out efforts from every member of the team to make it happen.

In the preliminary round of that spring's playoffs, the Maple Leafs faced the Los Angeles Kings. The Kings had finished third in the Norris Division with 77 points and were led by talented forward Marcel Dionne, with Rogie Vachon, certainly no longer considered Junior B material, in goal.

In the hard-hitting opener, the Leafs' George Ferguson shone with a hat trick and Toronto came out convincingly on top, 7–3. The teams made the transcontinental flight to L.A. for Game Two of the best-of-three series, and Toronto played another muscular game, with an opportunistic offence that scored three goals in the first period alone. Palmateer slammed the door on the Los Angeles forwards, and the Leafs shut out the Kings, 4–0, to win the series.

The New York Islanders, in the quarter-finals, posed the next challenge. New York had finished atop the Patrick Division with 111 points, which was good for third overall in the NHL. The up-and-coming Islanders were considered to be the season's team of destiny. Certainly, unseating the Montreal Canadiens as Stanley Cup champions was going to take a special group, and the Islanders had been the only team to win a playoff game against Montreal during the past two years (the Habs were a combined 24–3 in 1976 and 1977; all three losses came against the Isles). Since then, the Islanders had added the supremely talented Mike Bossy, who scored 53 goals as a rookie. And they were well rested, having had a week off thanks to a bye into the second round. The Maple Leafs were clear underdogs.

That fact became even clearer in Game One, when the Islanders drew first blood with a 4–1 victory at home. Game Two was much tighter. The teams took a 2–2 tie into overtime before New York's Bossy scored the winner at 2:50 of the first extra frame. The winning goal was not pretty, and looked, as the *Toronto Star* suggested, like "men trying to kill a snake with a stick." Bryan Trottier took a couple of stabs at the puck in Palmateer's crease before Bossy poked it in as Dan Maloney sent him flying. Toronto protested, claiming that Trottier had used his hand to move the puck in the crease, to no avail. The goal stood, and the Islanders now had a two-games-to-none lead.

The Leafs were, however, able to build some momentum through their good play. Game Three, played at Maple Leaf Gardens, was scoreless past the midway point before Ron Ellis tallied against Chico Resch. Shortly afterwards, Börje Salming was clipped close to his eye by Lorne Henning's stick and had to be hospitalized for several days. While Salming's vision would be fine, the Leafs had nevertheless lost their most talented defenceman. In the same game, Lanny McDonald broke his nose for the second time in a month. He insisted that it wouldn't stop him from playing – and it didn't. The Leafs' perseverance paid off with a 2–0 win.

Roger Neilson dressed Randy Carlyle to take Salming's spot on the blueline for Game Four. Happily for Leafs Nation, Toronto came out on top, 3–1. The Leafs had tied the series at two games apiece.

The teams returned to Long Island for a tight and aggressive Game Five. The score was knotted at one goal apiece at the end of 60 minutes. But at 8:02 of extra time, the Islanders' Bob Nystrom made it New York's when he picked up a loose puck in the neutral zone, tucked it

through Brian Glennie's legs, and beat Mike Palmateer with a 20-foot shot to the short side.

Fortunately for Toronto, Game Six back at the Gardens would have a very different ending. The Leafs scored four goals by the 13-minute mark of the first period, which chased Resch from the Islanders goal. Resch's replacement was the belligerent Billy Smith, and it didn't take long before Battling Billy and Tiger Williams were engaged in a fight (after the game, Smith would swing his large goal stick at some young hecklers). Smith did not help his team's cause; while he allowed only a single goal, he incurred nine minutes of penalty time. When the buzzer sounded, the Leafs had won 5–2, which pushed the series to a seventh and deciding game. Tiger Williams exclaimed, "Them Islanders is worse than done like dinner; they're burnt toast!"

The Islanders returned Chico Resch to the crease for Game Seven on Long Island. It was a long, defence-oriented contest. In fact, the only goals scored during regulation were by defencemen: Denis Potvin scored for New York, while Ian Turnbull replied for Toronto.

The Islanders were not, as it turned out, "burnt toast." Had it not been for the play of the Leafs' goaltender, the game would have long been decided.

"The Islanders were outplaying us terribly; killing us is a better way of putting it," Lanny McDonald recalled. "One play in particular sent us a message that it was our night. Trottier was in front of our net with the puck and Palmateer was out of the goal. Trottier let go what looked like a sure goal, and Palmateer, sprawling, stuck out his stick and deflected the puck. The guys knew then that it was meant to be."

The Leafs, however, rarely did things the easy way. In the third period, Tiger Williams picked up a double minor. It was a dreadful situation to be in, as Williams explained: "Those four minutes in the penalty box seemed like four years. Leaving the penalty box with the game still tied was like leaving a death cell." Still, regulation time ended with the game in a 1–1 tie.

For the third time in the series, overtime would be required to determine a winner, and in this case, to see who would be heading to the semifinals. Early on, it seemed as though the Islanders would surely end the game, but Mike Palmateer turned away every attempt.

Then, at 4:13 of overtime, Ian Turnbull carried the puck up the ice. Lanny McDonald, nursing a broken nose *and* a broken bone in his wrist, refused to quit.

"I cut into the middle to spread the defence," McDonald recounted. "[Turnbull] flipped a high pass to

It was impossible to believe that I would one day put on that jersey and skate on the same sheet of ice as my heroes and in front of the famous Leafs fans. Being drafted to the Toronto Maple Leafs was a surreal experience. Imagine your first game, standing in front of your family and friends at the Gardens; the crowd proudly singing the Canadian national anthem. I knew that this accomplishment was not just mine, but that of all of the people who helped me get to this special place. My parents, friends, coaches, and teammates were all a special part of this accomplishment, and I was just thrilled to share it with all of them by playing for the Toronto Maple Leafs.

Darryl Shannon
PLAYER
1988–93

me, which hit an Islander, hit me and dropped at my feet. All of a sudden, there was nobody between me and Resch. I needed an instant to realize that I was in the clear. Chico came out to cut down the angle and I let the shot go. I had to get the puck over his glove. I didn't get a hard shot away, but somehow, a fluttering shot became the winning goal."

The underdog Maple Leafs had upset the heavily favoured Islanders in what was a sensational series.

Lanny's goal became a defining moment for the Toronto Maple Leafs of the 1970s. With this victory over the Islanders, older members of Leafs Nation began to feel that the ship had been righted. And for the younger contingent of Leafs fans, it was a singular, bright moment.

The Leafs poured over the boards to congratulate their hero. The city was alive with Leaf mania. The Blue and White had completed the upset and were now, for the first time in 11 years, heading to the Stanley Cup semifinals.

When they got there, though, the Leafs faced the herculean task of beating the Montreal Canadiens. Led by the always-threatening Guy Lafleur, Jacques Lemaire, and Steve Shutt up front, the superb trio of Guy Lapointe, Larry Robinson, and Serge Savard on defence, and the brilliant goaltending of Ken Dryden, this particular Canadiens team was marvellous. Even by the team's incomparable standards, it had had an extraordinary season, finishing first overall with a staggering 129 points and losing only ten games all season (having lost only eight the year before). As if all this weren't enough to intimidate any foe, Montreal was coming off back-to-back Stanley Cup championships. Defeating them would be a very tall order indeed.

Game One proved how difficult the challenge really was. The Canadiens manhandled the Leafs and comfortably took the opener, 5–2. In fact, the Leafs didn't get a shot on Dryden from the time of Ian Turnbull's goal at 8:27 of the second period until 10:13 of the third, and even then, it was a slow sliding puck that Dryden stopped easily. Mike Palmateer kept Montreal from running away with the game completely.

The Leafs came out aggressively in Game Two, but quickly learned that Montreal could hit too. Only seconds in, Larry Robinson sent Tiger Williams sprawling with a big-time check. In the second period, Williams was sent from the game with a knee injury after being hit by Savard. Neilson shuffled the lines and moved Ian Turnbull up to the wing along with Lanny McDonald and Darryl Sittler. While Turnbull responded with a goal and an assist, Toronto still lost, 3–2.

The series moved to Toronto for Game Three. In spite of the energy of the crowd, the Canadiens pushed the Maple Leafs to the edge of elimination with a dominating 6–1 win. While Game Four was a better showing for the Blue and White, the Leafs weren't able to score a single goal, and the Habs won 2–0. A season that had seen the Leafs roar back to form ended with a whimper as Montreal swept Toronto in four straight games.

There was little shame in the outcome. Of all the great Canadiens teams, this was surely one of the best. "No one likes to lose, but if we had to do it, it was better to lose to the best," said Coach Neilson. "The Canadiens are a great team – well coached, no weaknesses, an ideal blend of scorers and checkers and tough when they want to be. As close to perfect as a team can be."

The sentiment was shared by Harold Ballard. Although the Toronto Maple Leafs didn't fully complete their Stanley Cup quest, he treated them to a champagne celebration and gave each player two tickets anywhere a major airline flew.

The 1977–78 season had been an immensely satisfying one for the team and for Leafs Nation at large. With a solid 41–29–10 record (sixth-best in the NHL) and a trip to the semifinal, Toronto was on an upswing. The team had a couple of the best forwards in the league in Sittler and McDonald, one of the most gifted defencemen in Salming and another very capable one in Turnbull. There was toughness with Williams, and excellent netminding from the always-entertaining Mike Palmateer. Hopes remained high for this particular incarnation of the Toronto Maple Leafs, though it would prove to be a long time before the club got even this close to a Stanley Cup championship.

LAST CHANCE

Entering the 1978–79 season, most everyone would have agreed that the Leafs were just a step or two away from becoming a legitimate contender. And the team retained its core, choosing only to tinkering with the supporting cast. The Leafs acquired goaltender Paul Harrison to support Palmateer, and sent Scott Garland, Brian Glennie, Kurt Walker and a draft pick to Los Angeles for Lorne Stamler and the tough Dave Hutchison. In another exchange, Toronto received Dave Burrows from Pittsburgh, but it cost them George Ferguson and Randy Carlyle. Just three years after the trade, Carlyle would win the Norris Trophy as the league's best defenceman.

Burrows would be back with the Pens by then. Just prior to the season opener, the Leafs also grabbed veteran Walt McKechnie from Minnesota and reacquired Garry Monahan from Vancouver. In the NHL Amateur Draft, Toronto chose Windsor Spitfires captain Joel Quenneville with their first pick, a second-round selection.

Harold Ballard's predilection for impulsive behaviour was becoming increasingly more evident to those inside the Leafs organization. Former Leafs captain Bob Davidson, who had served the franchise since 1934 as a player and later as head scout, was forced to retire. Davidson had contributed significantly to building both the 1960s dynasty and the current competitive squad of the mid–1970s. In August 1978, however, he was astonished to discover that his salary had been cut by almost two-thirds. While Davidson found work with the NHL's Central Scouting Bureau, Ballard's mercilessness was coming into clearer focus for those who had been labouring under any misapprehensions.

Meanwhile, Toronto started the season with a win on the road in Pittsburgh, where they edged the Penguins, 3–2. Sittler scored two goals, McDonald earned two assists, Palmateer was spectacular, and Salming was the best player on the ice. The *Toronto Star* confirmed that "the club's established workers did their number to demonstrate once again that Leafs' frontliners are among the best." It was a positive start for the Blue and White.

Toronto played its home opener against the New York Islanders. Despite Denis Potvin's three goals in just 3:21 of the second period, Toronto outscored and outmuscled the visitors from Long Island. Darryl Sittler exploded with seven points – a hat trick plus four assists – while Salming added five assists of his own in the 10–7 Leafs victory. Former wrestling great and humanitarian Whipper Billy Watson had performed the ceremonial opening faceoff prior to the contest.

Generally, the season started out well for the Leafs. Sittler, McDonald, and Salming were skating into the peaks of their respective careers, and Mike Palmateer's goaltending was outstanding. Harrison had proven that he was more than capable of stepping in to give Palmateer a rest from time to time. It was a talented, hardworking team that had claimed a spot among the NHL's top tier.

The Leafs' biggest problem, however, lay in the behaviour of Harold Ballard. By March 1, 1979, Toronto had dropped five games in a row. In a postgame interview with Dick Beddoes of television station CHCH, Ballard dropped the bombshell that he was going to fire the team's much-loved coach, Roger Neilson. Leafs Nation was thrown into a panic, and Neilson could scarcely believe the implausible scenario he was now embroiled in.

"I asked our GM, Jim Gregory, and he said, 'Yeah, you're done,'" Neilson remembered. "The next morning in Toronto, I went down to the Gardens to clear out my stuff, and all the players were there, plus about a million reporters, but not one person from the Leafs management was there. I told the reporters we'd have a press conference at noon. I assumed somebody would be there by that time. By noon, there still wasn't anybody there from the front office, so I had to announce my own firing. It was a bizarre situation!"

The Leafs wanted Ed Johnston, the coach of the New Brunswick Hawks, an AHL farm team the Leafs shared with the Chicago Black Hawks. But Chicago had hired Johnston and had designs on promoting him to the NHL one day, so they refused to release him to Toronto. Leafs scout Gerry McNamara was offered the job and declined, as did former coach Johnny McLellan.

Toronto was scheduled to play the still-formidable Philadelphia Flyers on March 3. To a man, the Leafs players knew that if they were going to go anywhere in the playoffs, they needed Neilson. That day, the players, led by Darryl Sittler, implored Ballard to reinstate him. Desperate, and with no alternative coach at hand, Ballard acquiesced.

"That night, I was still hanging around the dressing room and Ballard came in," Neilson recalled. "He said to me, 'What are you doing this weekend?' I told him I didn't have any plans. He said, 'Don't go away. We may need you here.' That was his way of saying I was back in."

But Ballard couldn't resist the urge to have some fun with the affair. Because speculation had run rampant on who would be hired to coach the Leafs, the owner decided he would have Neilson come out with a paper bag over his head, in the style of the Unknown Comic, a performer on TV's *The Gong Show*. Ballard's vision was that Neilson would remove the bag and reveal the identity of the Maple Leafs' coach, and the fans would go wild.

GM Jim Gregory called Neilson and relayed the scenario to him. Neilson begrudgingly agreed, but upon reflection, he realized how ludicrous the idea really was. He told both Gregory and Ballard that he would *not* be wearing a paper bag.

On game night, during "O Canada" (Ballard only allowed the Canadian anthem to be performed; eventually the NHL insisted that the American anthem also

I was the third broadcaster for the radio broadcasts following the father and son combination of Foster and Bill Hewitt. Foster, of course, was a true legend starting with the first-ever hockey broadcast from the Mutual Street Arena and continuing for fifty years. He simply was the best! Bill followed in his footsteps with the same excitement and phrasing, as if by osmosis listening to his famed father. I started doing the intermission interviews travelling with them and then added some colour commentary, until one night in Montreal with Foster listening at home and Bill doing the play-by-play. At the end of the first period and after my interview with Toe Blake, Bill introduced me for the second period, stood up, and walked away! I did every game and every period after that, and what a time it was. It was the time of my life.

Ron Hewat
BROADCASTER
1966–82

be played before games involving U.S.–based teams), there was no coach behind the Toronto bench. After the anthem, scout Gerry McNamara walked behind the bench to tease the crowd, followed mere steps behind by an unmasked Roger Neilson. The crowd, realizing that Neilson was returning to coach the Leafs, gave him a prolonged ovation that continued even as Darryl Sittler and Bobby Clarke prepared for the opening faceoff. To his credit, Clarke refused to move into position until the cheers subsided, and referee Wally Harris stepped back to let Neilson bask in the applause. Toronto edged Philadelphia, 4–3, that evening to end the five-game losing skid. They would go on to win their next four.

Despite the off-ice distractions, the Maple Leafs still managed to post a winning record of 34–33–13 and secure a spot in the playoffs. Along the way, they added scoring depth, gaining Paul Gardner (son of former Leaf Cal) from Colorado for Trevor Johansen and Don Ashby.

For the fifth year in a row, Toronto finished third in the Adams Division, with 81 points. And for the fifth time in six seasons, Darryl Sittler led the team, with 87 points, including 36 goals, and was Toronto's Molson Cup honouree. Lanny McDonald had a team-best 43 goals and finished with 85 points. Börje Salming continued his supreme play and was selected to the NHL's Second All-Star Team.

Toronto's postseason opened in Atlanta, where the Flames provided the opposition for a best-of-three preliminary-round series. Walt McKechnie, playing in the first playoff game of his 11-year career, scored two goals within a three-minute period in the second period. It was all the offence the Leafs would need. Palmateer was brilliant, and Toronto won Game One by a 2–1 score. With 51 seconds remaining in the second period, nine players – five Flames, as well as Dave Burrows, Dave Hutchison, Darryl Sittler, and Ian Turnbull – were ejected from the game following a wild brawl. Once the dust settled, the Leafs and Flames had together set a record for most combined penalty minutes in a single playoff game: 222. With Toronto down to just three defencemen, Salming played an exhausting 16 of the 20 minutes in the third period.

The Leafs continued to attack in Game Two, while adding another entry to the playoff record book. In just a 23-second span in the first period, Toronto scored three times (two by Sittler and one by Ellis) to set a NHL record for the fastest three goals by one team in a playoff game. The Leafs pounded the Flames, 7–4, to win the series.

Unfortunately for Leafs Nation, Toronto once again drew the Montreal Canadiens in the next round of the playoffs. The Leafs, however, had far more confidence than the previous spring. In the first game of the quarter-final in Montreal, Toronto took a 2–0 lead into the second period, banging and crashing at every opportunity. It was here that the Canadiens – who had won three consecutive Stanley Cups and were on their way to a fourth – woke up. Montreal scored five unanswered goals to take Game One, 5–2.

Game Two was equally disastrous for the Leafs. The Habs were seemingly invincible and led 5–0 before Lanny McDonald ruined Ken Dryden's shutout in the final minute of play. The Leafs lost the game, 5–1, and goaltender Mike Palmateer, who was forced to leave during the second period after colliding with Steve Shutt. Still, Roger Neilson remained positive: "We're disappointed but not down."

The Maple Leafs played much better in front of their hometown fans in Games Three and Four. Palmateer was given the go-ahead to play and was brilliant in Game Three, facing 48 shots. At the end of 60 minutes, the game was knotted at three. But during the first overtime, Palmateer was again injured after he banged into Mark Napier. Although he stayed in the game, it might have been better if he had been replaced. The Habs' Cam Connor – who hadn't seen any ice time during regulation and who had scored just one goal during the season – skated in on the Leafs goalie early in the second overtime period. Palmateer slid out to block the unlikely Canadiens hero, and it appeared that Connor had lost the handle on the puck. The shot, however, trickled under the Toronto netminder and into the net at 5:25 to give Montreal the 4–3 win and an unassailable three-games-to-none lead in the series.

Palmateer's injury proved to be worse than originally thought and would require surgery, so Paul Harrison started in his place for Game Four. At first, it appeared that the Leafs had just rolled over: the Canadiens were up 4–0 early in the second. Three unanswered Toronto goals made a game of it. Then, Guy Lapointe deflected a puck into his own net and the game was tied. In the dying seconds of regulation, Jacques Lemaire fired a shot that was a sure goal, but Harrison stoned him with what Scotty Bowman called "the best save I've ever seen."

The drama continued to unfold during overtime. At 2:38 of extra time, referee Bob Myers called Tiger Williams for high-sticking Larry Robinson. Neilson and

the Leafs were apoplectic. They believed it was a questionable call at a pivotal time of the game and voiced their disagreement vehemently. On the ensuing power play, Robinson let go a slap shot from the blueline that found the back of the net through a maze of players. The Canadiens had won, 5–4, to eliminate the Leafs.

Williams was beyond livid and tried to get at the referee. "I wanted to kill [him]," he later admitted. Dan Maloney had to tackle his own teammate in order to prevent Tiger from doing anything he would later regret. At this point, and while he was celebrating with his own much happier teammates, Larry Robinson glanced over and saw what was transpiring: "I skated over to Tiger and grabbed him and told him to forget it – that it was a crappy call but it was over, and he shouldn't do anything stupid. I think I even told him I'd take him fishing that summer. It seemed to calm him right down."

While promises of casting off with Robinson may have placated Williams, the Leafs had already gone fishing. Their season was over. But so was an era; it would be seven long years before the Leafs won another play-off round.

Leafs owner Harold Ballard (right) and his great friend King Clancy (left) were familiar sights in the "bunker" they occupied in the northeast corner of Maple Leaf Gardens.

PUNCH BACK
1979-80 TO 1980-81

BEDLAM

On November 1, 1979, Bob Marley and the Wailers made a return appearance at Maple Leaf Gardens. That night, the multicultural crowd was spellbound by Marley's "Positive Vibration." Meanwhile, the Gardens' usual occupants had embarked on their 1979–80 campaign, and many would regard the vibrations as anything but positive. The season would come to be viewed as a turning point in the history of the Toronto Maple Leafs.

To begin with, Roger Neilson had been fired – for good this time – after Toronto lost to Montreal in the 1979 playoffs. It seemed that this was a foregone conclusion, given the events of the previous season. If not for the intervention by the players, and if not for the absence of a suitable substitute, Neilson would have been jobless after Ballard fired him the first time, in March 1979.

General manager Jim Gregory was fired too. During his tenure, Gregory had made many positive changes to the way the franchise operated. He was, for instance, the first NHL manager to truly recognize Europe as a bona fide talent pool for the NHL to draw on. His record was a fair one: the Maple Leafs won 334, lost 324, and tied 130, and made the playoffs in eight of his ten seasons.

The way Gregory's firing was handled was unorthodox, to say the least.

"After the series [against the Habs], Ballard saw me in the parking garage and said, 'Perk up,'" Gregory related. "I said, 'Every day I read in the paper that I'm getting fired.' He said, 'Oh, don't worry about that. You're too valuable around here. You're going to be here forever. Go off and enjoy your vacation.'

"I went to my cottage and got a call from Brian O'Neill [executive vice-president of the NHL]. He said, 'John Ziegler wants to talk to you about a job.' I said, 'What kind of a job?' He said, 'You're not working for the Leafs anymore, are you?' That's how I found out I'd been fired!"

Gregory drove straight to Maple Leaf Gardens. To his astonishment, Punch Imlach had been hired in his place,

and was sitting in Gregory's office.

Imlach was hired by Ballard on July 4, 1979. Imlach, of course, had served the Maple Leafs from June 1958 to April 1969. After he was fired by Stafford Smythe, he had accepted the role of coach and general manager with the expansion Buffalo Sabres in 1970. However, Imlach, who had health issues dating back to his first term with the Leafs, suffered a heart attack in January 1972. He resigned as the Sabres' coach but stayed on as GM.

Imlach was subdued at the media conference held to announce his new appointment with the Maple Leafs. There was no abrasiveness, no promise of instant success. Punch did, however, lay down the gauntlet and rankle some members of his new team when he stated that the Leafs "have five or six good hockey players, but the remainder of the talent on the team needs to be improved." This was not the positive vibration that the club sorely needed.

With a new GM secured, the Leafs went in search of a coach. Both Don Cherry and Mike Nykoluk were courted, but neither accepted. Then Imlach reached out to Floyd Smith, a former Maple Leaf player who had coached the Sabres from 1974 until 1977.

The new management team was unsettling for the Leafs players. "I had a lot of respect for Punch Imlach for winning the Stanley Cups and for being a successful hockey man," Darryl Sittler later said, "but I knew when he came back in 1979 that things weren't going to be the same." The captain's concern was well founded.

First, Imlach harboured a not-so-veiled hatred for the NHLPA. Punch simply despised Alan Eagleson, the association's executive director, who as an agent also happened to represent many individual Leafs.

One early dispute between Imlach and the players involved a *Hockey Night in Canada* feature called "Showdown." It was a skills competition involving many of the top stars from around the league. Imlach refused to allow any Leafs to take part. Conversely, Darryl Sittler insisted that it was his right to participate. Imlach was adamant that he would decide whether or not Sittler would

Much to the astonishment of most, Punch Imlach was rehired in July 1979 to coach the Maple Leafs. His second term will be remembered mostly for butting heads with Darryl Sittler. Heart attacks finally ended his second tenure in September 1981, but his records shows 365 wins with Toronto – the best in franchise history.

take part, and Ballard backed his GM: "If Sittler thinks he's going to run this hockey club, he's got another thing coming." The line in the sand had been drawn, and the Leafs captain had come down on the opposite side of management. As it happened, NHL president John Ziegler fined the Maple Leafs over the fallout from the "Showdown" affair.

It became apparent to those on the inside that Imlach wanted to rid himself of Sittler, the player who had been the Leafs' top scorer every year since 1973. He was, however, hamstrung by the captain's no-trade clause.

It was in this edgy environment that the Maple Leafs began the second Imlach era. It did not start out as hoped. Despite the appearance on opening night of Cardinal Gerald Emmett Carter, the Archbishop of Toronto, the Leafs dropped their home opener, 6–3, to the New York Rangers.

Tensions between Imlach and his captain boiled over in November. Imlach had criticized Sittler and goaltender Mike Palmateer in the press, so Sittler gave a candid interview to the *Globe and Mail*, which was printed under the headline DARRYL DROPS THE GLOVES. Imlach believed the captain had crossed a line.

Through December, the team held its own. But on December 19, there was a loud confrontation between Imlach and the team. The issue this time centred on the Leafs' participation in a charity game against the Canadian Olympic team. Imlach wanted none of it, and let his players know that he wouldn't allow it. The next night, the Leafs were humiliated by the Boston Bruins, 10–0. While Imlach couldn't touch Sittler, he began to dismantle the team.

On December 24, the Leafs sent Pat Boutette to the Hartford Whalers for Bob Stephenson. It came as a complete shock to Boutette, who said, "It was a blessing in disguise. I went on to play with players who I idolized growing up – Gordie Howe, Dave Keon, and Bobby Hull. Plus, I had the best playing days of my career." Boutette would play over 400 more games in the NHL with Hartford and Pittsburgh. Bob Stephenson, on the other hand, would play just 14 games for the Maple Leafs, the last of his NHL career.

Galling as the Boutette trade might have been to some, no one could have predicted what Punch would do next. On December 28, he traded Lanny McDonald and Joel Quenneville to the Colorado Rockies for Pat Hickey and Wilf Paiement. In 477 regular-season games with the Leafs, McDonald had managed 459 points.

"A part of me died the day the Maple Leafs traded me," McDonald stated. "I still believe I was traded out of spite. I think Punch really wanted to show who was boss. It didn't matter how much he hurt the hockey club or tore

it apart, he only wanted to make sure everyone knew who was running the team. Ardell was two weeks away from giving birth to our second child, and we had been traded."

Leafs Nation was livid. Toronto was set to meet the Winnipeg Jets the night after the trade. Before the game, hundreds protested outside Maple Leaf Gardens with signs bearing slogans such as BAD PUNCH SPOILS A PARTY and A KICK IN THE FANNY FOR TRADING LANNY. Others wore walrus-like moustaches and chanted slogans in support of McDonald.

Before the game that evening, Darryl Sittler held his own protest. He removed the *C* from his jersey and emotionally explained the reason to his teammates: "They couldn't get me, so they traded my best friend." That night, the Leafs beat the Jets, 6–1. Sittler registered an assist.

Despite the win, the team continued to twist in the wind. The Leafs were still getting good production from various players, including star defenceman Börje Salming, who was approached about wearing the *C* but turned it down. The Leafs would remain without a captain for the rest of the season.

While the fans were reeling, there was little doubt as to how the Leaf players felt about Imlach's regime. Reporters respected the anonymity of various players, but still managed to retrieve some incendiary comments. One anonymous Leaf growled, "It has become a madhouse. I guess Imlach is succeeding in doing what he set out to do from the start – tear the team to pieces."

The boss wasn't done. On January 10, Imlach shuffled Dave Hutchison off to Chicago for Pat Ribble. The latter played just 13 games with the Leafs before he, too, was traded to Washington for Mike Kaszycki. Hutchison, like Boutette, had been a London Knight with Sittler during the 1969–70 season. Hutchison would not remain silent on the state of affairs in Toronto. "Imlach's campaign against Sittler is just ridiculous," he fumed. "It seems that if he can't get rid of Sittler, then Imlach will get at him by trading away all his friends on the team."

Imlach had not yet finished his deconstruction of the team. On February 18, Tiger Williams was packaged with Jerry Butler and sent to Vancouver for Rick Vaive and Bill Derlago. Williams, who was also close with Sittler, was deeply upset. "I never wanted to leave Toronto. I like this city. I like the fans." Jerry Butler was informed of the trade by Tiger and wasn't sure whether or not he was joking. He wasn't.

As it turned out, this particular trade was actually good for the Leafs. Derlago, who owned a powerful wrist shot, was only 21 years old, and 20-year-old Vaive would one day become the first Leaf to score 50 goals in a season – a feat he would accomplish three times with Toronto. Still, Vaive's initial response to the trade was one of disappointment.

"You work so hard to get there, and then all of a sudden in your first season, you're traded," Vaive said. "You're thinking, 'This is happening *already*?!' But once I got to Toronto, Punch Imlach said, 'You're going to get an opportunity to play a lot here.' And that was all you wanted to hear. Everything just took off from there."

Still more trades were in the offing. On March 3, the Leafs shipped Walt McKechnie to Colorado for a draft pick. McKechnie had originally been drafted by the Maple Leafs in the first-ever NHL Amateur Draft in 1963, and was now going to his eighth NHL team. McKechnie had played with Sittler in London during the 1967–68 season. By now, it was apparent to everyone that Imlach's modus operandi was not to better the team, but to rid it of Sittler's caucus. The general manager – with the tacit approval of the owner – had systematically removed Sittler's closest friends in McDonald and Williams, as well as his former junior teammates in Boutette, Hutchinson, and McKechnie. Even the *Toronto Star* felt compelled to comment: "Somehow, Sittler has managed to maintain his dignity and class while being strung out to dry for all to see."

Throughout all of this shedding, the Leafs had made a bizarre addition to the lineup earlier in the season. Carl Brewer had last played professional hockey with the WHA's Toronto Toros in 1974. A sportswriter, after watching him play in an old-timers' game, suggested that Brewer could suit up again in the NHL, and that put a bug in the former Leaf's ear. He contacted his old adversary, Punch Imlach, and the two men decided to give the idea serious consideration. Brewer briefly went to Germany to play himself back into shape.

"I went up on December 13 at 5:00 P.M.," Brewer recalled. "The Leafs were playing that night, and Imlach had been looking for me. I hadn't even made up my mind, but Imlach had already made up a press release indicating that I would be starting back with the Leafs the next day."

Instead, Brewer suggested that he go to Moncton to play with the Leafs' AHL farm team to get a few games under his belt. But after three games with the New Brunswick team, the 41-year-old Brewer – who hadn't played an NHL game in over seven years – was a Maple Leaf.

The Leaf players, understandably, were suspicious. Unlikely as it was, given the history between Brewer and Imlach, many on the team suspected that Brewer was serving as a spy for the GM. So they distanced themselves from him. In fact, in Brewer's first game, on December 26,

he was partnered with Börje Salming, who refused to pass him the puck. Even the coach had to walk a tight-rope with the new-old Leaf, as Brewer explained: "As for Floyd Smith, on several occasions, he said he didn't want to play me 'now' because 'those guys won't even talk to you, let alone pass you the puck. They won't come back when you're on the ice, either.'" Carl Brewer's comeback consisted of just 20 frustrating games.

Meanwhile, on March 14, 1980, Floyd Smith was involved in a tragic car crash near St. Catharines, Ontario. Smith was hospitalized with lacerations and bruises to his head and a broken left kneecap. Unable to continue coaching that season, Smith was assigned to scout, a role he continued in for several years. Dick Duff, who was scouting for the Leafs and had played for Imlach in Buffalo, took over behind the bench for the games on March 15 and 17. Joe Crozier was then parachuted in from the New Brunswick Hawks to observe and assist. Then, for the final ten games of the regular season, Crozier became the unofficial coach behind the Leafs bench, although Imlach remained the de facto coach on paper.

In spite of the many distractions, the 1979–80 Toronto Maple Leafs did modestly well, finishing fourth in the Adams Division with 75 points, and eleventh in the 21-team NHL. Despite the trades, goal scoring was not a problem. In fact, the Leafs scored a franchise-record 304 goals, seventh-best in the league that season. As a testament to his professionalism, Darryl Sittler again led the team in scoring, with 40 goals and 97 points. His point total was ninth-best in the league.

On the blueline, Börje Salming continued to excel, scoring a career-best 19 goals, and was rewarded by being named to the Second All-Star Team. The defenceman also won Toronto's Molson Cup. Despite his success, Salming confessed that he had lost his spirit: "When Imlach cut out the heart of the team, he bled me of my enthusiasm. I did my job, but I didn't have the same spark."

While they could score, the run-and-gun Leafs left their defensive inefficiencies exposed. The team had slipped from allowing the fourth-fewest goals under Roger Neilson in 1978–79 to the league's worst under the combination of Smith, Duff, Crozier, and Imlach in 1979–80. Toronto surrendered 327 goals and juggled goaltenders. While Mike Palmateer and Paul Harrison got most of the work, the Leafs also used 1979 draft pick Vincent Tremblay, Curt Ridley (who came over in a trade from the Canucks), and Czechoslovakian Jiří Crha, the first netminder to defect from an Eastern Bloc country and play in the NHL.

The Maple Leafs showed
patience with young winger
Lanny McDonald, and it paid
off. In his third season, he scored
37 goals, and he connected
43 times in 1976–77. By
December 1979, as part of the
coach's feud with Darryl Sittler,
McDonald was traded with
Joel Quenneville to the
Colorado Rockies for Pat Hickey
and Wilf Paiement.

The defensive deficiencies did not bode well for the Leafs' first-round series with the offensively powerful Minnesota North Stars. "Because consistently strong defensive hockey and Leafs were infrequent bedfellows this season, it means a sudden change in approach or a quick trip to the sidelines," the *Toronto Star* observed.

Much to the displeasure of Mike Palmateer, it was Jiří Crha who won the start in Game One. After facing 61 shots in a 6–3 loss, Crha said that he was "too tired to know I am tired."

Palmateer got the start in the second game, but the North Stars managed to fire 43 shots at the Leafs net and cruise to a 7–2 victory.

Crha was back in goal for Game Three at Maple Leaf Gardens. Riding the energy of the Leafs faithful, Toronto played a much better game. The game was tied 4–4 at the end of regulation. Just 32 seconds into the extra period, however, Al MacAdam scored to end Toronto's season.

At the beginning of the 1978–79 season, the Leafs had been a piece or two away from Cup contention. By the spring of 1980, however, it had all came undone. Burrows, Ellis, Maloney, Palmateer, Salming, Sittler, Anderson, Saganiuk, and Turnbull were the only regulars remaining from the previous season. And even this small group of survivors would be further cut before the end of the next campaign.

"I had never been through anything like that in my life," Ron Ellis reflected. "I had been so proud to be a Toronto Maple Leaf . . . all I could do was shake my head and wonder what was going on with the franchise."

THE CAPTAIN AND THE FOX

After losing a leg to cancer, Terry Fox – a native of Port Coquitlam, British Columbia – was inspired to run across Canada to raise awareness and funds for cancer research. Fox trained for 14 months; then, on April 12, 1980, he dipped his prosthetic right leg into the Atlantic Ocean near St. John's, Newfoundland, and began his Marathon of Hope.

While attention to his quest was scarce at first, by the time Fox crossed into Ontario, momentum had increased substantially and a nationwide audience was following Terry's incredible journey. He was running approximately 26 miles every day on a prosthetic leg, but also meeting dignitaries and attending fundraising functions at most stops.

On July 11, Fox was scheduled for a day in Toronto. He had already run 13 miles before taking a brief hiatus for a reception at City Hall. On the way, Fox and his crew stopped at the Four Seasons Hotel in Toronto's chic Yorkville neighbourhood. There, he was surprised to meet one of his idols: Darryl Sittler. "He had no idea I was coming," the Leafs captain explained. "I was in my shorts and T-shirt. I walked into the room and said, 'Would anyone like to go for a run?'"

The two of them ran down University Avenue towards Nathan Phillips Square. There, a crowd of more than 10,000 greeted Fox, cheering wildly as he and Sittler came into view.

"I was thinking, 'What could I do as a Canadian to show my appreciation for what Terry has done?'" Sittler said later. "I went home and got my [1980] All-Star sweater. I didn't play in a lot of All-Star games, so that sweater was pretty precious. So I had it with me at City Hall. I gave it to Terry and he put it on. I'll remember that day for the rest of my life."

The Canadian Cancer Society, the recipient of funds raised through the Marathon of Hope, estimates that $100,000 in donations was collected that day alone. By the time Terry was forced to abandon his venture near Thunder Bay, Ontario, due to a recurrence of his cancer, Terry Fox's extraordinary effort had raised a staggering $1.7 million. By the time the marathon concluded on September 1, 1980, Fox had run 3,339 miles (5,373 kilometres) over 143 days. Fox succumbed to his cancer on June 28, 1981.

SCHOOLYARD SCUFFLE

At the start of the 1980–81 seaon, goaltender Mike Palmateer was looking for a substantial raise and a multi-year deal. He rejected the Leafs' offer, and was traded to the Washington Capitals in June for defenceman Robert Picard, forward Tim Coulis, and a draft pick. His words hinted at the fractious atmosphere of the franchise: "My only regret is leaving Toronto and all the people who have been so good to me. I love the city and the people. I haven't left Toronto, I've left the Leaf organization." Palmateer's parting shot was not lost on his teammates.

While Imlach – under Ballard's watchful eye – had managed to alienate Sittler by trading away his closest friends, the no-trade clause in the centreman's contract made it impossible for management to realize its ultimate goal: to get rid of Darryl Sittler. Still, Harold Ballard publicly vowed that Sittler would not be allowed to attend training camp. For Ballard and Imlach, Sittler had challenged management, and the owner was not prepared to tolerate it. It was, according to the *Toronto Star*, the "longest-running soap opera in hockey history."

Darryl Sittler's tumultuous term under Punch Imlach came to an end when Sittler left the team in January 1982, forcing Toronto to finalize a trade. On January 20, the captain was dealt to the Philadelphia Flyers. Sittler left the Leafs having collected 916 points, including 389 goals, in 844 regular-season games in blue and white.

While Ballard declared that the former captain would "never wear a Toronto Maple Leaf uniform again," Sittler assured the press, "I'm going to training camp with the Leafs. That's why I have a no-trade clause in my contract."

A month later, Punch Imlach was hospitalized after suffering a heart attack. Ballard then sought a personal meeting with Sittler. The owner hoped to "resolve this thing" himself. For his part, Sittler asked his agent, Alan Eagleson, to stand down and let him meet with Ballard face to face. It was a wise move. Ballard returned the captaincy to Sittler and announced that he had made peace with the star centre. The city breathed a collective sigh of relief.

In a moment of candour, Ballard later admitted, "All our differences really were created by me, Punch, and Eagleson like kids in a schoolyard, and Darryl was caught in the middle." This moment of self-awareness, however, was soon interrupted by Ballard's pronouncement that "all those things I said about Sittler – that he was a cancer on the team and a traitor – I was only kidding, but it sure got everyone excited and kept hockey on the front pages all summer!"

When Ballard was asked about Imlach's health and his status as the team's GM, the owner went on the record: "The job's his, depending on what the doctors say. Sure, I want him back, but I don't want to be the one to put him in a box. I'm going to be the one in control of things, and if the players want to argue instead of playing hockey, they'll get an earful from me."

In the meantime, Joe Crozier's interim role as head coach was made more permanent. Among the targets Crozier set was to reduce the team's goals against by 75. To achieve this, Crozier hoped to combine veteran defencemen such as Dave Farrish, Börje Salming, and Ian Turnbull with newer blueliners such as Slava Ďuriš, Robert Picard, and Dave Shand. The coach also named Jiří Crha as his number-one goaltender.

For the season opener, with former police chief Harold Adamson dropping the first puck of 1980–81, Crha was in net as Crozier's Maple Leafs were trounced, 8–3, by the New York Rangers. To his credit, Crozier was able to turn the team around for a spell early on, and Toronto won its next six starts. Darryl Sittler was more than prepared to give Crozier his due. "We're playing more disciplined hockey all the time," the captain said. "Joe has the system he wants us to play and that's what he drills us in every day."

On November 18, the Leafs sent Dave Burrows back to Pittsburgh along with Paul Gardner and then picked up Barry Melrose off of waivers. Neither these small tweaks nor the early good luck held. Toronto won just three times in November, against two ties and six losses. It was clear

that Crha was not ready to assume the heavy workload required of a Leafs starting goalie.

Crha needed time to develop, but in the meantime, Toronto was anxious for a replacement goaltender. The Leafs knew they couldn't afford to trade another first-round draft pick (something they had done in three of the previous drafts), so they sent centre Mark Kirton to Detroit for Jim Rutherford.

While there was concern about the netminding position, there was another, perhaps more worrisome storyline beginning to develop. Although he still led all forwards in scoring, Darryl Sittler was in a slump. The team's overall performance did not help the situation, and in the weeks leading up to Christmas, Crozier told the media that all he wanted from Santa Claus was a team leader. It seemed as though Sittler was back in the same position he had been in when Imlach was in charge.

Unfortunately, the first game of the new year brought little cheer. The Leafs were humiliated, 8–2, by the last-place Winnipeg Jets. During the game, Toronto's young goaltender Vincent Tremblay was booed by the home crowd. Fans filed out of the Gardens in droves after the second period. Those who remained chanted for a new coach: "We want Cherry!"

Two days later, Joe Crozier was fired. "Joe was a good man, but he wasn't right for the Leafs at that time," Ron Ellis recalled. "There was a lot of turmoil." Sadly, no coach had been hired to replace Crozier. Darryl Sittler was left to run the morning practice on January 10. Afterwards, he met with the reporters and explained that being a part of the Toronto Maple Leafs was a great honour, but that honour came with unique demands:

> This city is the centre of hockey in North America. People expect a winner, and it's been a long time since they've had a contending team. Look at the players who go elsewhere and excel. There are not the same pressures in Pittsburgh and Colorado and places like that. Here, the game is always there.

That afternoon, three hours before their opening faceoff against the Philadelphia Flyers, Harold Ballard signed Mike Nykoluk as the new coach of the Toronto Maple Leafs.

Nykoluk had played half a season with the Leafs in 1956–57. Over his career, he had become a well-respected hockey man, serving as an assistant coach with the Flyers and New York Rangers. More recently, Nykoluk had been providing analysis of Leafs games on the radio. In his debut,

Toronto rose to the occasion and managed to tie Philadelphia, 4–4.

Still, the ever-shifting sands at Maple Leaf Gardens continued to scatter. When Ellis showed up at the Gardens in advance of a game, the longtime Leaf found his stick rack empty and his sweater missing. Trainer Joe Sgro told Ellis that Punch Imlach wanted to see him. Prior to the season, Imlach had assured Ellis that the Leafs had plans for him. In the ensuing months, however, the forward had been relegated to a penalty-killing role and saw only occasional fourth-line duty. On his way to meet Imlach, Ellis had already guessed, correctly, that he had played his last game as a Maple Leaf.

In his memoir, Imlach blithely wrote about his meeting with Ellis that night: "I told him he could call the shot – either retire with a lump sum payment or go to the minors. In this era of 18-year-old hockey players, there is no great demand for a 36-year-old with two goals in 27 games." As Ellis had made the leap from the junior Marlboros to the NHL without ever playing a game in the minors, there was – at least in his mind – really no decision to be made. He retired – for good this time.

Meanwhile, the Leafs were still looking for greater stability in goal. In Montreal, goaltender Michel "Bunny" Larocque had asked the Canadiens for a trade. He played in the shadow of Ken Dryden for five very successful seasons, sharing the Vézina Trophy with him on three occasions. When Dryden retired, Larocque was certain that he would be named the starting netminder, but was surprised when the Canadiens brought in Denis Herron *and* Richard Sévigny to platoon with him.

Toronto thought Larocque could be the goaltender they had been lacking since Palmateer's departure. They traded defenceman Robert Picard to the Habs for him. Jiří Crha was pencilled in as the backup, and the team could call up Vincent Tremblay from the minors when occasion demanded. This meant that Jim Rutherford was expendable, so he was dealt to Los Angeles. In just two seasons, the Leafs had used seven different goalies: Palmateer, Crha, Harrison, Ridley, Tremblay, Rutherford, and now Larocque.

Despite the merry-go-round in the crease, the struggling Maple Leafs still had a chance to assure themselves of a playoff spot with a win against the Nordiques in Toronto in the penultimate game of the season. With less than two minutes to play, though, Quebec scored to tie the game, 5–5. The next night, the Leafs faced the Nordiques in their rink. There, Toronto doubled Quebec, 4–2. The two points gave the Leafs 71, one more than Washington for the 16th and final playoff berth.

For the first time in nine years, Darryl Sittler neither led nor tied for the lead in Leafs scoring. In 1981, that honour went to Wilf Paiement, who got 40 goals and collected 97 points. Sittler was just one point behind, but was the team leader in goals, with 43. Goals were reasonably plentiful – the Leafs were eighth in the NHL. But far from meeting Crozier's target of shaving the team's goals against by 75, the Maple Leafs allowed 367 – which was actually 40 *more* than the year before and was the third-worst in the NHL.

While the Leafs made the playoffs, it was a brief visit. Toronto met the first-place New York Islanders in the opening round. The Islanders had won the Stanley Cup the previous season and were now on their way to their second of four consecutive championships.

Game One of the best-of-five series exposed the talent gap that existed between the two teams. While Toronto kept close to the Islanders for the first 25 minutes, New York went on to demolish the Leafs, 9–2. Crha was replaced after the second period, having surrendered six goals. The line of Mike Bossy, Bryan Trottier, and Bob Bourne combined for a dozen points.

Larocque started Game Two on Long Island and didn't fare much better. He left the game with a rib injury after being bowled over by Garry Howatt, and was replaced by Crha. It made little difference, as the Islanders once again mauled the Leafs, 5–1.

Still, the Maple Leafs were sure that a hometown crowd would change the momentum in Game Three. They were wrong. With Larocque injured, Toronto brought up Paul Harrison from Dallas in case anything happened to Crha. It did: the Islanders scored five goals in the first period. Nykoluk summoned Crha to the bench and tried his luck with Harrison. The backup was solid, but it was too little, too late, and the Maple Leafs' season ended with a 6–1 thumping.

The Islanders had outscored the Leafs, 20–4, over the course of the three games. The New York team was in the early stages of a dynasty, while the Leafs – and their city's hopes – had been methodically bulldozed.

In September 1981, Punch Imlach suffered a second heart attack and underwent triple-bypass surgery. While recuperating, he read with interest a quote from Harold Ballard in a local newspaper: "I'm not going to have Punch back as my general manager."

Harold then suggested that Punch retire; he refused. Ballard offered him a consulting role. That, too, was declined, and Punch Imlach's final chapter with the team came to an end. The damage, however, had already been done.

It was a tremendous honour to put on a Leafs jersey and play in front of the fans. They expect you to play hard, and if you give all your effort, they respect you. Leafs Nation was incredible to me after my accident. There were so many letters and cards that came in with their prayers and good wishes, it was amazing. You can really see what a hockey town – what a sports town – Toronto is. It's just a great city, and a great place to play hockey.

Bryan Berard
PLAYER
1999–2000

RUN AND GUN
1981-82 TO 1984-85

O CAPTAIN! MY CAPTAIN!

Before the 1981–82 season began, the adjective *interim* was removed from Mike Nykoluk's job title and he officially took on the role of head coach. With Imlach's unceremonious departure, Harold Ballard elevated Gerry McNamara to interim GM. McNamara had played seven games in goal for the Maple Leafs, and had replaced Bob Davidson as the team's chief scout. By December, his status was also made permanent.

It was no secret that the Leafs were, at least in recent times, defensively challenged. A number of Toronto blueliners from the previous season therefore found themselves toiling in the minors. Remaining with the big club were stalwarts Börje Salming and Ian Turnbull, as well as Barry Melrose and the recently acquired Bob Manno. Joining this foursome on defence was a trio of young teenage draft picks: Fred Boimistruck, Bob McGill, and the Leafs' first-round pick in 1981, Jim Benning.

The ongoing Sittler saga, however, had yet to fully play itself out. It was clear that Harold Ballard wanted him gone, but the captain did not want to abandon ship, at least not at the beginning of the season. It was into such murky waters that Toronto sailed into its new campaign. With young Vincent Tremblay in goal, the Maple Leafs took the 1981–82 season opener in Winnipeg, beating the Jets, 6–1.

After a 3–3 draw with Minnesota, the team returned to Toronto for the home opener. In what better resembled a baseball score, the Leafs beat the Chicago Black Hawks, 9–8. Salming, who picked up a hat trick, expressed the view that the injection of youth had given his team more spirit.

Unfortunately, while the young blueliners were adding excitement, veteran Ian Turnbull was regularly being booed. While they are, on the whole, a hockey-savvy group, some elements of Leafs Nation have historically been uncharitable to those players who, rightly or wrongly, they have identified as the team's scapegoats. Just as it

had been for Gord Drillon, Frank Mahovlich, and others before him, Ian Turnbull had now become that goat.

After several admittedly poor performances, the incessant booing from the crowds made the situation untenable for the defenceman. On November 5, he was dropped from the roster. "Turnbull will not play for the Leafs again," Nykoluk announced. "I was afraid his lack of motivation might rub off on our younger players." Turnbull had a different perspective.

"No one likes to get booed, but that's the price you pay for being in the public eye," he conceded. "I didn't have that motivation, but nothing was ever done about it. At training camp, I was a little disappointed that I was still a Leaf. Mike Nykoluk is a super guy and we got along tremendously. He made the right decision [to drop Turnbull from the lineup]. After nine seasons with the Leafs, what I need is a change of scene. If I felt I'd become a brutal hockey player, I'd pack it in, but I feel I've got more good years."

After the 1978 playoffs, Roger Neilson had tried to convince the team to trade Turnbull while his value was at his highest. Ballard had balked. "It's a hell of a lot easier to find a coach than it is to find another defenceman like Turnbull," he roared. "If you can't get along with Turnbull, we'll get rid of you!" Now, both Neilson and Turnbull were gone. Toronto swung a deal on November 11 that sent the defenceman to the Los Angeles Kings for John Gibson and Billy Harris, who was the second Leaf to bear that name.

Turnbull wasn't the only one who wanted out early that season. On October 26, after having played just one game, Pat Hickey was traded to the New York Rangers.

With Turnbull and Hickey dispatched, the Leafs captain felt that he, too, had had enough. Sittler finally asked to be traded in November. Because of the no-trade clause in his contract, Sittler was able to name the teams he was willing to be traded to. He chose the Minnesota North Stars and Philadelphia Flyers. Both teams relished the idea of adding Sittler to their respective lineups, and both were equally aware that they held the upper hand in terms of a bargaining position. The suitors lowballed the

The Maple Leafs employed a teenaged defence in 1981–82: 19-year-olds Fred Boimistruck and Bob McGill were joined by 18-year-old Jim Benning (pictured). Boimistruck stuck for parts of two seasons, McGill for parts of seven (in two different terms), and Benning wore the blue and white for parts of six seasons.

Leafs, offering packages that weren't at all attractive to GM Gerry McNamara.

The stalemate lasted until the new year, when Sittler – unhappy with the Leafs' failure to make a deal – forced the team's hand. Toronto was scheduled to fly into Minnesota for a game on January 6. While his equipment made the flight, the captain did not. Sittler insisted that he would stay in shape but wouldn't play again until he was traded.

Finally, on January 20, 1982, McNamara pulled the trigger on a trade that sent Sittler to the Flyers for prospects Rich Costello, Ken Strong, and a second-round draft pick. Only two years earlier, Punch Imlach had rejected a deal with those same Flyers that would have landed André Dupont and Rick MacLeish. Costello would play a total of 12 games with Toronto, while Strong would manage 15. More promising was the draft pick, which was used to select Peter Ihnačák, a forward who enjoyed a solid eight-season career with the Maple Leafs. Meanwhile, the Leafs' all-time leading scorer (a distinction he held until eclipsed by Mats Sundin in 2007), who had amassed 916 points in 844 regular-season games as a Maple Leaf, was on his way to Philadelphia. By the time he finished his career in Detroit in 1985, Sittler would register 1,121 points in 1,096 regular-season games.

With Sittler gone, Rick Vaive became the captain of the Toronto Maple Leafs. Vaive recalls the equal measures of pride and pressure that he felt:

> It was a great honour to be the captain of an Original Six team and especially the Toronto Maple Leafs. Not too many people get the opportunity to do that. Harold Ballard told me that I was the captain. I was a little bit hesitant because I wasn't sure if I was ready for that obligation. We had an older team and it wasn't always easy to be the captain at 22 years old, trying to get guys that were ten years older than you on the same page.

The young captain was destined to serve as a consistent bright spot on a team that would seem to be perennially rebuilding over the course of the next few years.

Toronto made several trades in early March, picking up tough winger Jim Korn from Detroit for a couple of draft picks. That same day, Laurie Boschman was dealt to the Edmonton Oilers for Walt Poddubny and a prospect. Boschman was philosophical about his trade: "There seemed to be quite a few distractions. I don't want to dwell on them because they're in the past for me now. I'm very thankful to the Leafs for giving me the chance I had."

The next day, Wilf Paiement was sent to the Quebec Nordiques for little-known winger Miroslav Fryčer and a late draft pick. Paiement had scored 40 goals the previous season, but at the time of the trade had stumbled to a mere 18 in 69 games. It was a positive sign when Fryčer, facing the Nordiques for the first time since the trade, picked up three goals in a 6–3 win at Maple Leaf Gardens on March 18.

Despite the largely disappointing season, the Maple Leafs witnessed a franchise first courtesy of their new captain. On March 22, in a game against Tony Esposito and the Chicago Black Hawks, Vaive scored four goals to break the Leafs' single-season record of 48, held by Frank Mahovlich. That gave him 49 as the Leafs met the St. Louis Blues on March 24 at Maple Leaf Gardens.

In the first period, and with the Blues shorthanded, Jim Benning picked up the puck and headmanned the puck to Bill Derlago, who had been waiting in the middle of the ice. From there, as Vaive recalled, Derlago "came down the middle and went over to the right side. I just got open, found the seam and he threaded a perfect backhand pass right across to me. All I had to do was let a good one-timer go." At 14:57 of the opening period, the young captain hit the corner of the net before Mike Liut could move, becoming the first player in Maple Leafs history to score 50 goals in a season.

Later in that same game, with only 12 seconds separating the Leafs from being eliminated from the playoffs, Vaive set up Fryčer for the winning goal. It was a memorable 4–3 victory. And Vaive could afford to celebrate, since the Leafs' playoff hopes had, at least for the night, stayed alive with the win.

Three nights later, the Detroit Red Wings halted their 14-game winless streak with a 2–1 win over Toronto. It was over. The *Toronto Star* called the season "the long journey into naught." The regular season ended on April 4 in Philadelphia, where Sittler and his new team destroyed Toronto, 7–1. It could have been a lot worse if not for the play of goalie Bunny Larocque: the Flyers outshot the Leafs, 59–18.

The Leafs finished fifth in the Norris Division, 16 points behind the fourth-place Black Hawks; Toronto's 56 points were 15 fewer than they had collected in 1980–81. It was the first time the Toronto Maple Leafs missed the playoffs in almost a decade. Their .350 points percentage was the team's worst since 1957–58.

The dissension within the ranks, the lack of stable management, and a combination of inexperience on the blueline and injuries through the season had made the

Rick Vaive was the first Maple Leaf to hit the 50-goal plateau in a season, accomplishing the feat three times: 54 in 1981–82, 51 in 1982–83, and 52 in 1983–84. He was named captain of the team in 1982–83.

1981–82 campaign a challenging one for the team and for Leafs Nation. There were several embarrassing games that haunted Leafs fans: losses of 11–2 to Washington, 9–2 to Minnesota, 8–2 to Calgary, 9–5 and 10–1 to the New York Islanders, and a 10–2 thrashing at the hands of the Winnipeg Jets. Between January 21 and March 13, the Leafs went through a 24-game stretch where they won only twice.

There were, of course, a few redeeming features of the Leafs that season. Rick Vaive led the team in goals (54) and points (89), and Darryl Sittler managed 38 points in his 38 games with the Leafs that season.

Toronto had the league's worst goals-against total. In spite of valiant efforts by Michel Larocque, Vincent Tremblay, and Bob Parent, the team surrendered 380 goals. Perhaps it was with a hint of irony that Bunny Larocque was awarded the Molson Cup Trophy for his three-star selections. In four seasons, the Leafs had fallen from near-Cup contender to third from the bottom of a 21-team league. The grim reality was hard for Leafs Nation to reconcile with the possibility of what might have been.

BEHIND THE IRON CURTAIN

And then there were three.

By the time the 1982–83 season kicked off, Börje Salming, Rocky Saganiuk, and John Anderson were the only holdovers from the roster that existed before Imlach's return. Without much of a foundation, the Leafs set themselves to the task of rebuilding. With the third-overall pick in the June 1982 NHL Entry Draft, the Leafs chose Gary Nylund. Although he would miss the first three months of the season while recovering from knee surgery, the young defenceman promised to add depth to the Leafs blueline.

The team's second choice was Gary Leeman, who had impressed Leafs scouts as a defenceman. With the very next pick (the one obtained in the Sittler trade), Toronto picked up Peter Ihnačák, who had defected from Czechoslovakia in April. Goalie Ken Wregget and forward Leigh Verstraete were others among the 15 Leaf selections who would wear the blue and white, as was Ihnačák's brother Miroslav.

The Slovak brothers' journey had not been an easy one. Despite the grave deterrents that Czechoslovakia's communist government had put in place to prevent athletes from escaping to the West, several, like Peter, were compelled to make the bold move to freedom. Three siblings had already made it out from behind the Iron Curtain. Sister Magdalena had left the country just prior to the Soviet invasion of 1968; brother John likewise fled

to West Germany; and sister Maria managed to make it to the United States.

In Czechoslovakia, Peter began to establish himself as a rare hockey talent. Despite his obvious skill, the authorities would not – considering his siblings' departure – let Peter play outside of the Soviet bloc. Canadians, however, were able to catch a glimpse of the forward at the 1977 IIHF World Junior Championship held in Prague. Despite his good play, Ihnačák was considered a high flight risk and was therefore not able to join his team for a tournament in Switzerland – nor, more disappointingly, for the 1980 Winter Olympics in Lake Placid. As Peter explained to the National Post years later, he was dropped from the Czechoslovak team just before the 1981 Canada Cup, was denied a tourist visa, and subsequently had his passport confiscated. Peter Ihnačák was an "enemy of the state." He had to plead with authorities for months before his passport was returned to him. When it finally was, Ihnačák began to seriously consider defecting. He began to collect as much Western currency as he was able to source on Czechoslovakia's black market and waited for a moment to arise.

Perhaps at the urging of the national team's coach, Peter Ihnačák was in the Czechoslovakian lineup for the 1982 world championship in Finland. His opportunity had come. Peter sought his older brother's help, and John Ihnačák flew to Finland for the tournament. Serendipitously, John happened to meet Leafs coach Mike Nykoluk and GM Gerry McNamara, who were on their way to scout the tournament. John discreetly inquired whether they'd be interested in having Peter play for the Leafs. They were.

Unbeknown to Peter, several of his Czechoslovakian teammates were doubling as KGB informants; a slip of the tongue around any of these players and Peter might have been on his way to prison. It was in this frightening environment that John Ihnačák made contact with his brother. The message was brief: "Meet me behind the hotel on Thursday at 5 P.M." After practice the next day, Peter snuck out of the hotel to meet John, and the two made their way by car to the harbour, where they safely boarded a boat for Sweden.

Miroslav was still in Czechoslovakia, and now the government was more wary than ever of the younger Ihnačák. The secret police seized his passport and banned him from travelling anywhere. Miroslav would try to leave Czechoslovakia legally several times, but was repeatedly denied. It would be over three years before Miroslav Ihnačák joined his brother Peter in the Maple Leafs lineup.

It took great effort to secure Peter Ihnačák for the Maple Leafs, but the diligence paid off. Born in Czechoslovakia and drafted in 1982, he set a Leafs rookie record with 66 points in 1982–83, and spent eight productive seasons in Toronto.

Back in Toronto, the Leafs tried to address their goaltending needs by reaching out to a familiar face. Mike Palmateer had been sidelined with a knee injury through much of the previous season in Washington, and, pending approval from team doctors, the Leafs purchased his contract from the Capitals in September 1982. Palmateer was elated. Coach Mike Nykoluk was likewise delighted to have one of Toronto's favourite players back on the roster: "Palmateer doesn't play textbook goal, but he is awfully quick, has great hands and a wonderful sense of anticipation."

Still, Palmateer hadn't played an NHL game since November 11, 1981. The goaltender asked management if he could get into shape by playing a few games with the AHL affiliate, which had relocated to St. Catharines as the Saints. As a result, the season started with Michel Larocque tending goal in the season opener, a 3–3 tie with the Black Hawks in Chicago.

Five games into the new season, though, the Leafs were still winless. Then, on October 16, Palmateer played his first NHL game in almost a year. He performed well, but the Leafs still lost to the Hawks, 3–2.

The lineup just didn't have the necessary depth to compete night after night. While there were occasional glimpses of a competitive team, the Maple Leafs struggled terribly, winning only six games before the end of the year (against twenty-one losses and seven ties), including two in December. It was, as the *Toronto Star* attested, "a dreadful team from the very outset."

There were some additions that helped shore up the lineup. Toronto plucked Greg Terrion, a defensive centre, from the Los Angeles Kings in exchange for a draft pick. Also, the Leafs' first-round draft pick, Gary Nylund, finally returned from surgery to repair ligament damage in his left knee. His physical play added a spirited edge to the team. To add depth, Toronto made a rare swap with the Montreal Canadiens, sending draft choices to the Habs for Dan Daoust and Gaston Gingras.

After ringing in the new year with a five-game unbeaten streak, the Leafs made a stab at improving their goaltending further, sending Michel Larocque to Philadelphia on January 10 for Rick St. Croix, who was pegged to serve as Palmateer's backup.

With these tweaks, the Leafs became far more competitive – in February, they won six in a row. In fact, of the 46 games they played in 1983, the Leafs won 22, lost 19, and tied 5. With a blistering shot from the top of the faceoff circle on March 30, 1983, team captain Rick Vaive beat Red Wings netminder Gilles Gilbert for his 50th goal of the season, giving him back-to-back 50-goal seasons.

With 68 points, the Maple Leafs finished third in the Norris Division despite their losing record of 28–40–12. With 51 goals, there was little doubt that Rick Vaive should be Toronto's Molson Cup winner, though his 79 total points trailed linemate John Anderson by one. Peter Ihnačák scored 28 times, establishing a franchise mark for goals in a season by a rookie.

The Leafs faced the powerful Minnesota North Stars in the Norris Division semifinal. The first two games of the best-of-five series, played in Bloomington, were tight. Game One went the home team's way, 5–4, in regulation time, while Toronto tied the second match, 4–4, late in the third period. Bobby Smith lifted the puck over a prone Palmateer at 5:03 of overtime to give the North Stars a two-games-to-none lead in the series.

The Leafs gave their hometown fans something to cheer about with a decisive 6–3 victory in Game Three. Palmateer earned the kudos of his teammates after facing 49 shots. Unfortunately, it was all for naught, as Game Four finished with Minnesota on the winning side of a familiar 5–4 score in overtime. During the extra frame, the North Stars' Dino Ciccarelli fired a shot that a lunging Palmateer was unable to stop.

The season was over. Truthfully, the Maple Leafs were always going to be hard pressed to beat the North Stars, but the sense was the Leafs had redeemed themselves with a relatively strong finish after such a dreadful beginning to the season.

50 × THREE

The young defencemen on whom the Toronto Maple Leafs had pinned so much hope in 1982–83 had not delivered. In truth, the players had been hurried into the NHL far earlier than they should have been. While Jim Benning stuck with the team in 1983–84, Fred Boimistruck and Bob McGill were both sent to start the season with the St. Catharines Saints of the AHL. Gary Nylund was still suffering with his knee issue, and so Börje Salming, Dave Farrish, and Gaston Gingras were the Leafs' steadiest forces on the blueline. Toronto lost free agents Barry Melrose and Bob Manno to the Detroit Red Wings, but picked up veteran Bill Stewart to supplement the defence corps.

In net, Mike Palmateer and Rick St. Croix were acknowledged as the Leafs' starting tandem, while Bruce Dowie, Ken Wregget, and the Leafs' third-round choice in the 1983 draft, Allan Bester, would all see action for the Blue and White. In the 1983 NHL Entry Draft, Toronto chose

Russ Courtnall with their first pick, seventh overall. Rocky Saganiuk was traded to Pittsburgh, while the undrafted Steve Thomas, a Toronto Marlboro alum, was signed.

The Leafs were in Edmonton to open the 1983–84 season. While Toronto led, 2–0, in the first period, the home team rallied and took the game, 5–4. With a 1–2–1 record by mid-month, the Leafs were involved in a historic game on October 15, beating Chicago by an implausible 10–8 score. Two speed records were set that night: fastest four goals by two teams (53 seconds) and fastest five goals by two teams (84 seconds).

Early in the season, the Leafs picked up Dale McCourt, George Armstrong's nephew, from the Buffalo Sabres. McCourt had had a couple of good seasons with the Sabres and would provide the Leafs with another scoring threat. Toronto also signed Dave Hutchison for his second term as a Leaf. Hutchison hadn't even been skating for a few months, but decided to lend his tough approach to a team that was trying to improve in every area.

On January 8, Mike Palmateer came down with a cold bad enough that he couldn't dress for a game against St. Louis. Rick St. Croix was given the start, and GM Gerry McNamara called up Allan Bester from the junior Brantford Alexanders to serve as backup. When St. Croix surrendered five goals, Coach Nykoluk decided to pull St. Croix in favour of the younger goalie. Bester held off the Blues for the remaining 23 minutes and 20 seconds of the game, and while Toronto lost, 5–2, the game was a good indicator that Toronto's netminding future was solid. In fact, Bester's play was so steady that he went on to play in 32 games for the Leafs that season. As he recalled, "It was a real baptism by fire. The team was going nowhere. I went into every game just wanting to play the best that I could. I had nothing to lose."

The Maple Leafs were in third place in the Norris Division at the beginning of January, but they lost 11 games in that nightmarish month, winning just one and tying another. They slipped too far back to fully recover.

Other playoff-bound teams began to circle Toronto like vultures, hoping to pick off one or two of the players before the trade deadline. The most appealing asset was Börje Salming. Harold Ballard, however, knew what he had in his starring defenceman and rejected an offer from the Quebec Nordiques. Ballard's response was succinct: "There's no way I'd trade Salming; not for the entire Quebec team." Unfortunately, Salming's season ended prematurely when he cracked his kneecap in an 8–7 overtime loss to Winnipeg on March 12.

With no real chance of making the playoffs, Leafs Nation focused its attention on the team's captain. Going into the March 14 game against Minnesota, Rick Vaive needed just two goals to hit 50 for a third consecutive season. It took just nine minutes for him to reach the milestone. Vaive was particularly pleased: "A lot of people thought it was a fluke when I scored 54 goals, and there were still some that thought my second 50-goal season was a fluke. I hope this will end that kind of talk."

Toronto was put out of its misery on March 28 with a 4–2 loss to Detroit, officially eliminating them from post-season play. The Leafs finished last in their division, with 61 points, and surrendered a disconcerting 387 goals. Only the woeful, 21st-place Pittsburgh Penguins gave up more (390). Rick Vaive finished as the team leader in goals (52) and points (93) and received the Molson Cup.

Harold Ballard was furious. "It was the most disappointing year I've ever had in hockey, and I've been in hockey for 60 years," he snarled. "I'll be following the playoffs. I have to get some players, not this rubbish." Ballard handed McNamara a list of players he did not want to see back with the team in September.

The first casualty was the coach. Ballard had already stated that Mike Nykoluk was, in his opinion, "too nice a guy to coach." In saying goodbye, the deposed coach didn't stray from his trademark congeniality: "Harold Ballard never interfered with the way I did the job, never told me how to use players, and never second-guessed anything I did." Under Nykoluk, the Leafs' record was 89–144–47.

"YOU NEEDED ME"

During his 11-season career, Dan Maloney had been feared as a player. Upon retiring from the Leafs in 1982, he was immediately hired as an assistant coach under Mike Nykoluk. With Nykoluk's firing, Maloney was promoted to head coach on May 26, 1984. It was, at least for Maloney, a logical transition: "I've been in the city awhile and I know the players, the strengths, the weaknesses, the city and the overall situation. A lot of people would like this job; I was in the right place at the right time." Maloney and GM Gerry McNamara added the hard-nosed John Brophy to the coaching staff, and the three men identified several immediate needs for the Leafs. After finishing 18th in a 21-team league, the needs were many.

Number one was to better the team defensively. The second priority was to toughen up the lineup. To address these issues, the Leafs chose Al Iafrate in the first round of the draft, and added Todd Gill and Jeff Reese with

His style behind the bench differed little from his efforts on the ice: tough, spirited, and persistent. Dan Maloney was a Maple Leaf forward from 1977–78 to 1981–82, and returned as head coach for 1984–85 and 1985–86, taking Toronto to the division final in his last season with the Maple Leafs.

later picks. Toronto also added free agents Bill Kitchen and Wes Jarvis. In the waiver draft, the Leafs lost Terry Martin, but added tough winger Jeff Brubaker. Another tough winger, Kevin Maguire, was signed as an undrafted free agent, while Bill Root was added from the Canadiens through a trade.

Mike Palmateer had a strong training camp, but his relationship with the new coach soured when he asked if he could rest his damaged knees by skipping practices on days after games. Maloney turned him down without discussion. He went further, making it clear that he intended to start the season with youngsters Allan Bester and Ken Wregget in goal. Rick St. Croix was sent to St. Catharines, which meant there was no spot for Mike Palmateer. He was left unprotected in the waiver draft, but teams were wary of gambling on Palmateer and his questionable knees. (When all was said and done, he had had 14 knee operations.) The goaltender remained philosophical about the end of his career: "I managed to squeeze a couple of years out before my knees finally gave out."

Bester earned a 1–0 shutout in the opener against the North Stars in Minnesota – the Leafs' first shutout since Vincent Tremblay blanked the Flyers on November 14, 1981. The season continued to look promising when

Toronto edged Buffalo, 4–3, in overtime in the home opener on October 13. Then the bottom fell out – and the Leafs fell to the bottom. For the remainder of the calendar year, the Leafs added just four more wins.

The goaltending experiment with the kids simply didn't work. Ken Wregget, for instance, faced 53 shots in a 12–3 annihilation at the hands of the Quebec Nordiques on October 20. The season crawled miserably along for Toronto and Leafs Nation from that point forward.

While the team's play had become bleak, an interesting machination was taking place off the ice. On January 10, 1985, Canadian songstress Anne Murray was involved in making a bid to purchase the Toronto Maple Leafs. As Murray later explained, "Lyman MacInnis from my office was behind it. I couldn't afford to buy the team, but Lyman put a consortium of investors together with my name on it."

MacInnis had assumed responsibility for Murray's business and financial affairs in 1971, when she was just becoming one of the most successful recording and touring artists on the planet. Now, MacInnis was looking to diversify her investments.

"I got the idea that Anne Murray would be a perfect owner of the franchise. She was a fierce hockey fan, a

Toronto resident, and a universally loved and respected Canadian international superstar," MacInnis explained. "Harold Ballard, who held the controlling interest in the public company that owned the Leafs, was, on the other hand, despised by most Leaf fans and seemed to care only about making money rather than having a winning team. I floated the idea at one of the meetings that Anne, her manager, Leonard Rambeau, and I regularly held. Although they were skeptical that we could raise the money to pull it off, Anne loved the idea."

Murray did adore sports, especially hockey, but purchasing the Maple Leafs was going to be expensive. In spite of the dismal on-ice record of recent years, it was estimated that the franchise was worth upwards of $18 million. The offer prepared by Lyman MacInnis was reportedly $40 million for Maple Leaf Gardens, the Toronto Maple Leafs, and Ballard's other sports property, the Canadian Football League's Hamilton Tiger-Cats. MacInnis laid out his plan.

"My proposal was that [Ballard] would stay on as a special consultant on all non-hockey operations, which would mean he would manage the building, which would allow his son Bill to keep the inside track for his concert promotion business. This would keep Harold involved in the company and allow him to maintain his office, bunker, and apartment at the Gardens, but he would have nothing to do with the hockey team. I also knew that he was a big Anne Murray fan."

Ballard and MacInnis met three times to discuss a possible purchase, before "Harold finally confessed to me that because of an intricate web of borrowing covenants involving the TD Bank and Molson Breweries, he was unable to sell his shares to anyone without their approval. Because Molson knew that I was an advisor to archrival Labatt, there was no way they would ever approve a sale to a group of which I would be CEO and chairman. So that was that."

MacInnis, Murray, and company spread their wings and flew away.

Meanwhile, the Leafs' free fall to the bottom continued. They were eliminated from the playoffs for the third time in four years, and by the time the season was over, they had lost 52 games. With just 48 points, Toronto finished dead last in the National Hockey League.

The line of Rick Vaive, Bill Derlago, and John Anderson was a rare bright spot for the Blue and White. While Vaive's 35 goals and 68 points led the team, both figures were down significantly from recent years. Anderson, who set a team record for consecutive games with a goal

(14 goals in a 10-game period), had 32 goals and 63 points, while Derlago had 31 goals and 62 points and was awarded the team's Molson Cup.

Despite Vaive's excellent scoring record, Harold Ballard suggested that it might be a good idea if he and John Anderson were traded in the off-season. The *Toronto Star* and most fans felt that blame for this horrific season fell at the feet of one man. "The Leafs have earned residence in hockey's Siberia, and as long as the current czar remains in power, they won't likely move to a warmer climate."

Ballard's behaviour was erratic, his decisions often ill thought out and occasionally outrageous. He had once told reporters that Laurie Boschman's faith was hurting his play. He made several sexist comments on public radio, and his rehiring of Punch Imlach – only to undermine him while the manager was in his sick bed – had been irresponsible. The Neilson-led Leafs had reached the semifinals just a few seasons prior with a lineup that was a piece or two away from real contention. Now, Ballard's Toronto Maple Leafs had tumbled to the NHL cellar.

Yet Börje Salming enjoyed a special relationship with the owner.

"A lot of people worked at the Gardens. It was like a big family," the All-Star defenceman recalled. "Harold was the boss and everybody would say, 'Good morning, Mr. Ballard.' But I'd say, 'Hey, Chief.' He liked that. I was always late getting out of the dressing room after practice. He'd come in and we'd talk for hours about everything. We were friends. He really treated me well. If you got to know him really well, then he was such a nice guy."

But even Salming could not deny Ballard's eccentricities.

I can recall one time after practice, we came in the dressing room and the reporters came in the dressing room after us. They had the right to come in the dressing room. He came in and said, 'Get out, you guys! You're not supposed to be here!' He kicked them right out of Maple Leaf Gardens! Somebody must have written something bad about the Maple Leafs, but when he came in the dressing room and I asked what happened, he said, 'Oh, nothing. I was just sick and tired of them.' He sat down, opened a Coke, and laughed. He was so crazy sometimes.

Still, the team's legion of fans desperately needed something to hope for – something to believe in. Toronto was about to import that something from Kelvington, Saskatchewan.

CAPTAIN CRUNCH
1985–86 TO 1987–88

NUMBER 17

While a last-place finish opened up the franchise to the indignities of an annoyed fan base, it did give the Toronto Maple Leafs the first-overall selection in the 1985 NHL Entry Draft. Most pundits believed Craig Simpson would be the first selection. The London, Ontario–born winger had starred at Michigan State University and, according to a *Globe and Mail* article a month earlier, the Maple Leafs had "just about decided" to make Simpson their selection. But a week before the draft, word filtered back that a meeting between GM Gerry McNamara, coach Dan Maloney, and the Simpson family had not gone well. While a second appointment went much more smoothly, many still wondered whether Simpson would, if drafted, say yes or no to joining the Leafs.

There was also Dana Murzyn, a highly touted defenceman from the Western Hockey League's Calgary Wranglers, and while the Leafs needed help everywhere, improving their defence was paramount. Therefore, for most people trying to guess the Leafs' intentions, an "if not Simpson, then Murzyn" scenario seemed most likely.

On June 15, 1985, more than 7,000 fans attended the draft at the Metropolitan Toronto Convention Centre. It was a warm summer day, and the building was filled with hundreds of young hopefuls, all mostly uncomfortable in new suits and sporting fresh haircuts, accompanied by family and friends. The crowd hushed as the roaming mic was taken over to the Maple Leafs' table, where Gerry McNamara announced the team's number-one pick: "The Toronto Maple Leafs are very happy to select Wendel Clark from Saskatoon."

While Clark was certainly not an unknown, his selection with the top pick in the draft came as a surprise to most of hockey's intelligentsia. And no one was more surprised – or indeed, delighted – than the Saskatoon Blades defenceman himself: "I really had no idea that I was going to go number one until draft day. It didn't matter where I

was drafted as long as I had a chance to play at the highest level at the time."

Wendel Clark had enjoyed a sensational season with the Blades in 1984–85. He was named the Western league's top defenceman after scoring 32 goals and 87 points, while accumulating 253 minutes in penalties. Clark had also starred for Team Canada at the IIHF World Junior Championship. It appeared that the Leafs had filled a huge void on the blueline with a rugged, rushing defenceman.

Only they hadn't. Clark wasn't going to play defence. In a move that recalled the acquisition of Red Kelly in 1960, the Leafs wanted to convert the dominant blueliner to left wing. Clark took the change in stride: "I didn't really know until I got to training camp and I read my name as a forward. That's how I found out. My whole life I played defence, although they probably got the idea from that year in the World Juniors." Clark had played half of the tournament as a defenceman and the other half as a forward.

Whichever position Clark was pegged for, most everyone concurred that he was going to be an impact player. But he was only one player, and the Leafs needed more. Gerry McNamara had often been derided for his lack of trades and acquisitions. But during this particular off-season, the GM rolled up his sleeves and went to work.

First, he picked up veteran goaltender Don Edwards from Calgary to help solve the team's recurring netminding issue. Then he worked hard to stabilize what was a very green defence corps. Apart from veterans Börje Salming and Bill Root, the Leafs blueline featured 23-year-old Bob McGill, 22-year-old Jim Benning, 21-year-old Gary Nylund, and 19-year-olds Todd Gill and Al Iafrate. With this in mind, the GM shipped John Anderson to the Quebec Nordiques for the experienced Brad Maxwell, while Stew Gavin was sent to Hartford for defenceman Chris Kotsopoulos. Blake Wesley, another veteran defenceman, was picked up as a free agent, as was right winger Brad Smith. While the Leafs planned on

The first-overall selection in the 1985 NHL Entry Draft, Wendel Clark was converted from a defenceman to a winger as he stepped onto the ice with the Toronto Maple Leafs.

Wendel Clark (right),
Russ Courtnall (centre), and
Gary Leeman (left) were united
on the exciting Hound Line
in 1985–86. All three had
played Midget AAA with
the Notre Dame Hounds.
Leeman was there in 1980–81,
Courtnall in 1981–82, and
Clark in 1982–83.

sending Smith to their AHL farm team, the St. Catharines Saints, injuries opened a spot for him on the big club and Motor City Smitty soon became a fan favourite. All told, the Leafs had added an incredible influx of new bodies to a beleaguered lineup. Leafs Nation had been afforded renewed hope.

Unfortunately, the opening game – a 3–1 loss to the Bruins in Boston – looked eerily similar to what fans had witnessed in the previous campaign. The very next day, Bill Derlago was traded to Boston for Tom Fergus. It was a curious move: the Leafs, who had scored the fewest goals in the NHL the year before (253), had now traded away two-thirds of their top line. The question remained: How were the Leafs going to replace Derlago and Anderson's combined 63 goals? This point was hammered home during the home opener against the Quebec Nordiques, when Anderson opened the scoring for his new team just over four minutes into the game as Quebec soundly beat Toronto, 4–0.

The Leafs bounced back in the third game of the season. Maloney started Tim Bernhardt in goal against Chicago, and Toronto reacted with a 5–1 victory. The Leafs, however, followed this up with an abysmal stretch. In the course of the next 19 games, the Leafs recorded

just 3 wins and 3 ties against 13 losses. The pattern was all too familiar; the Toronto Maple Leafs once again found themselves mired in last place.

It didn't help that injuries were plaguing the lineup. Salming's season was effectively cut in half due to back spasms, a throat infection, and a knee injury. Bill Root broke his ankle, returned, then rebroke it, and played just 27 games. Rick Vaive sat out a number of games with a broken hand. As a result, there was a constant stream of traffic between St. Catharines and Toronto, and youngsters such as Todd Gill, Dan Hodgson, Jeff Jackson, Gary Leeman, Craig Muni, Steve Thomas, and Ken Wregget all got a chance to play with the big club.

In the meantime, Gerry McNamara flew to Vienna in early January in a bid to speed up the process of securing landed-immigrant status for Miroslav Ihnačák, Peter's young brother. The Leafs, who hoped to reunite the brothers, were now trying to secure a minister's permit to let Miroslav travel to Toronto immediately on the grounds that living in Austria posed a risk to his safety, close as it was to communist Czechoslovakia. While the Leafs were able to bring Miroslav to North America, the youngest Ihnačák would play only 55 games over three seasons, toiling mostly in the AHL, before he was sent to the Detroit Red Wings organization in advance of the 1988–89 season.

The Leafs' number-one problem in 1985–86 continued to be goals against. The speedy young team had no problem scoring goals – but it was ill suited to preventing them. In the first eight games of calendar year 1986, Toronto surrendered 51 goals. Meanwhile, there was no better example of the team's freewheeling style than a game against Edmonton on January 8, when the Leafs took on the defending Stanley Cup champion Oilers, featuring Wayne Gretzky, Mark Messier, Glenn Anderson, Jari Kurri, and Paul Coffey, and beat them at their own game. On the strength of four goals from Miroslav Fryčer, Toronto upset Edmonton, 11–9. The game set a franchise record for highest combined score.

This success, perhaps unsurprisingly, was short-lived. On January 15, with Vaive and Salming out with injuries, the Leafs endured what the *Toronto Star* called "one of the all-time stinkeroos" as the St. Louis Blues walloped Toronto, 10–1. Don Edwards was in net for seven of the Blues tallies and Tim Bernhardt was responsible for three. "It was almost cruel to watch the Leafs manhandled the way they were," the *Star* observed. By mid-February, the Edwards–Bernhardt tandem had crashed and burned. Ken Wregget was proclaimed the team's number-one goalie.

Still more problems arose. On February 23, captain Rick Vaive slept in and missed an early-morning practice in Minnesota. Vaive was stripped of his captaincy.

The timing couldn't have been worse. The team was just beginning to improve its overall mental state. For the former captain's part, Vaive fell on his sword and addressed the situation with his teammates before that afternoon's game against the North Stars: "I just said that I was sorry and I told them I would do all I could to help the team win because that was the only thing that mattered." Playing without a letter on his chest, Vaive scored in a 4–3 loss to Minnesota. The line of Vaive, Tom Fergus, and Steve Thomas proved that it could battle and score. This gave Maple Leafs fans something to get excited about for the first time in a long while. So, too, did the emergence of the team's number-one draft choice.

Wendel Clark was bulldozing his way through the NHL. The young winger combined a lethal wrist shot with lightning-quick fists to make his mark on the league. Comparatively, Wendel wasn't very big, but he was fearless. The young prairie boy also had a deep sense of humility that made him that much more attractive to fans and Toronto's media. In essence, Wendel had restored something intangible that had been missing on the team, in the city, and throughout Leafs Nation. In just 66 games, Wendel Clark had brought back hope.

The season concluded with the Maple Leafs finishing a distant fourth in the Norris Division with 57 points. Despite their losing record, and despite the fact that no fewer than three teams that missed the playoffs had accumulated more points, the Toronto Maple Leafs had made it into the postseason – because the last-place Detroit Red Wings collected just 40 points.

The Leafs got solid contributions from a number of players. Miroslav Fryčer led the team with 74 points. Seven players scored at least 20 goals, including Clark, whose team-leading 34 set a team record for goals by a rookie. Clark would be the runner-up, to Calgary's Gary Suter, for the Calder Trophy as rookie of the year.

In the division semifinal, the offensively minded Leafs faced off against the heavily favoured Chicago Black Hawks. Ken Wregget, who had had been awarded Toronto's Molson Cup, was given the goaltending duties for the series. To the astonishment of all, Wregget manhandled a club that had finished a cool 29 points ahead of the Leafs in the regular season. The Leafs took Games One and Two in Chicago, 5–3 and 6–4, respectively. Then Toronto obliterated Chicago, 7–2, in Game Three at Maple Leaf Gardens. Implausible as it seemed to most, Toronto had swept the Black Hawks.

The sense of hope that had sprung up around the city in late winter had, by now, flowered into a joyous celebration. The *Toronto Star* reported that fans "clapped their hands for a change, yelled themselves hoarse, threw brooms and pumped up a young team which believed and a young goaltender who was almost unbelievable. They beat them on the boards, in the corners, in the faceoff circle, on the bench, in the nets, on the fight judges' scorecards and everywhere else you'd care to mention."

Forward Gary Leeman revelled in the enthusiasm that the city had been showing for his team: "The town's alive right now and everybody's pulling for us. It's going to help us." It had been a long time coming.

Roaring into St. Louis on an unexpected high, the Leafs faced the Blues in the Norris Division final. Game One, however, quickly sent the Leafs back down to earth, as they lost, 6–1. Game Two would prove more pleasing to Leafs Nation. Toronto returned to the basics and blanked the Blues, 3–0. Ken Wregget earned his first NHL shutout in the effort.

The Leafs kept up the momentum by dumping St. Louis, 5–2, in Game Three at Maple Leaf Gardens.

Wendel Clark scored the winner on a wraparound shot that beat goaltender Rick Wamsley. The Blues, though, came back in Game Four with a 7–4 win.

The temperature in St. Louis on April 26 hovered near 92 degrees Fahrenheit (33 Celsius) as the teams faced off for Game Five. Despite the fact that the outside heat had slowed down the ice, the play was spirited. In the end, the Blues eked out a 4–3 overtime win to take a one-game lead in the series.

Back in Toronto, the Leafs found that they would have to play Game Six without the injured Rick Vaive. Brad Smith, who had scored five regular-season goals to Vaive's 33, was inserted into the latter's place on the first line. The Leafs nevertheless came out on top, 5–3. Walt Poddubny scored the game-winning goal.

Unfortunately for Leafs Nation, Game Seven in St. Louis would be the last stop on the Blue and White's postseason train. While Motor City Smitty scored a goal, the Blues managed two. The loss ended an improbable run for Toronto. Still, the playoffs had been a revelation. There was the emergence of Steve Thomas, who racked up a team-best 14 points in the ten postseason games. Gary Leeman contributed 12 points and Russ Courtnall added 9, while Gary Nylund came into his own on the blueline. Börje Salming spoke to the new energy on the team: "We never gave up. We kept digging all the time. This is a real team, 20 or so guys, who give all they have to win. There was a great deal of heart on this team and it showed right to the end." A single, low-scoring game had separated the Leafs from a return to the Stanley Cup semifinals, where they hadn't been since 1978. It was a vast improvement, and Leafs fans everywhere were hopeful that what they were seeing was a true return to form, and not simply a flash in the pan.

THE FEDORA RETURNS

The new and improved Toronto Maple Leafs went into the off-season feeling optimistic for the first time in years. Coach Dan Maloney was so optimistic that he asked for a raise and a two-year contract. Unfortunately, the general sense of enthusiasm didn't extend quite that far; the team countered with a one-year offer that Maloney rejected. Two days later, he signed a contract to coach the Winnipeg Jets. As of June 21, 1986, the Maple Leafs were without a coach.

Looked to replace Maloney from within, management turned to John Brophy, who had begun 1985–86 as an assistant coach in Toronto but had been sent to St. Catharines to take over as head coach, replacing ex-Leaf Claire Alexander. When the AHL farm team was moved to Newmarket, Ontario, Brophy was slated to be the Saints' general manager until he got the call from the big-league club.

For Brophy, becoming the coach of the Maple Leafs was a dream come true. "It's the only thing I've ever wanted to do, and a hell of a lot of time went by before I got the chance," he said. "I'm going to enjoy every minute of it. The actual coaching isn't much different here than at any other level, except that more people are watching. No matter where you are, winning is fun. Lose up here and it's tougher because much more is at stake."

Given the surprise playoff run of the previous season, the stakes were even higher for the new coach.

Overall, the Leafs felt positive about the team's 1986–87 lineup. Vincent Damphousse, the Leafs' first pick in the 1986 NHL Entry Draft, looked as though he would step directly from the junior Laval Titan to the Blue and White. While Damphousse was in, Walt Poddubny was on his way to the New York Rangers in a trade for Mike Allison. Following an arbitration hearing, the Leafs also picked up Jérôme Dupont, Ken Yaremchuk, and a fourth-round draft pick from Chicago for Gary Nylund, who had received a more attractive contract offer from the Blackhawks (the team had recently altered the spelling of its nickname).

In goal, the Leafs chose to go with the tandem of youngsters Allan Bester and Ken Wregget. The pair would, for the foreseeable future, be considered the Leafs' final line of defence.

Toronto opened the season at home against the Montreal Canadiens, but the Habs left town with a 7–4 victory. Tom Fergus picked up a hat trick in the losing cause. The Leafs, however, had a good October: they went 5–2–3 and picked up 13 points. What followed was an emotional rough patch. On November 5, Börje Salming suffered an eye injury in a 6–4 win over St. Louis. The defenceman had suffered a similar injury during the previous season and been instructed to wear a visor, but he had quickly discarded it, saying that he found the eye shield "bothersome."

That same night, King Clancy – assistant general manager, Toronto icon, and bunker-mate to Harold Ballard – became seriously ill. Ballard knew it had been coming: "He'd been complaining of an upset stomach, but the little bastard wouldn't go to the hospital. Everyone hates hospitals, but there's a time when you have to be sensible." Clancy had his gall bladder removed, but went into septic shock and died on November 8. A distraught

Ballard remembered his best friend fondly: "Like most leprechauns, he never won a fight on or off the ice. In more than 50 years on the Toronto scene, he has been a player, a referee, a coach, and, most important, a friend of anyone he has ever met."

Those friends came out in droves to remember the beloved hockey icon. Conn Smythe, who had paid the then-unbelievable sum of $35,000 to claim Clancy's contract from Ottawa in 1930, once asked King to describe his duties with the Toronto Maple Leafs. Clancy chirped, "I don't do a damn thing, Conn," to which Smythe replied, "Keep right on doing it, because you're doing one hell of a job."

Out of respect for the memory of Clancy, Ballard announced that he would close the bunker, the nook at the northeast corner of Maple Leaf Gardens from which he and Clancy had watched almost every home game for 15 years. With this simple move, the owner had done the unthinkable: he had shown the public another side to Harold Ballard. Even the most cynical among the Gardens faithful were genuinely moved by the gesture Ballard had made for his dear, departed friend.

Meanwhile, John Brophy was taking a page from Imlach and Maloney's playbook. With a surplus of defencemen, Brophy made a proposal to Gary Leeman. The coach wanted to get the defenceman's obvious speed and skill up onto a forward line.

"When I did stick in Toronto, I didn't play much," Leeman recalled. "I sat on the bench for about two and a half years and played maybe one or two shifts a game. They felt I wasn't developing, so they sent me for stints in the minors, where I got some playing time. And then finally, John Brophy took me aside in training camp and said, 'I'll make you a right winger. Can you score me 20 goals this year?' And I said, 'If you play me I will.'"

Brophy put Leeman on a line with Russ Courtnall at centre, and another defenceman-cum-winger, Wendel Clark. It wasn't a wholly random strategy. The three had all attended the same private school in Wilcox, Saskatchewan: Notre Dame College, a legendary school with a legendary hockey team. The Notre Dame Hounds sent over 100 players to the NHL during the tenure of Père Athol Murray, the school's long-serving teacher and

Drafted by Toronto in 1985, Vincent Damphousse responded with 21 goals during 1986–87, his rookie campaign. He reached the 20-goal plateau in four of his five seasons with the Leafs.

coach. Leeman, the oldest of the trio, had played with the Hounds in 1980–81, Courtnall in 1981–82, and Clark in 1982–83. The trio were dubbed, logically enough, the Hound Line.

"Wendel was one of the toughest guys in the league at the time, and there was an expectation that he was going to hit somebody, fight somebody, or score," Russ Courtnall explained. "I was in the middle, trying to get them the puck. We enjoyed playing together, and having the Notre Dame connection was really special to us because we loved the school and we wanted to make the school proud of us. We were young. We were just so happy to be in the NHL. As excited as the fans were, we were just as excited to get on the ice and go out and play."

Clark very quickly made a name for himself as a skilled player who wasn't afraid of dropping his gloves with anyone. This pugilistic attitude was encouraged by John Brophy, who very much wanted a tough team that wouldn't even consider being pushed around.

And Clark wasn't the only combatant in town. Brophy was likewise nurturing a young American player who played four games for the Leafs that year. Val James was, according to Brophy, "one of the toughest guys in hockey." James's first game with Toronto was on November 24, 1986. While the Bruins won, 3–2, James became the first black player to skate for the Maple Leafs.

During a 3–1 victory for the Leafs in Detroit on November 26, Gerard Gallant was knocked over by Börje Salming during a goalmouth scramble. Gallant's skate blade cut Salming, starting above his right eye, continuing deep into his nose and then along the side of his face. Salming described the freak encounter: "It's odd, but there was no more pain than cutting your finger with a sharp knife. The cut was so fast and clean, it didn't hurt."

Salming tried to skate off the ice under his own power, but he collapsed by the time he reached the bench. Guy Kinnear, the Leafs' trainer, tried to stop the gushing blood with towels. Salming was taken to the infirmary, where a doctor insisted he be rushed to a Detroit ophthalmic hospital. Although there was no permanent injury to his eye, the skate had carved Salming's features for a grisly 250 stitches. It took over three hours to pull his face together. This was the third eye-area injury Salming had suffered in his 13-year career with the Leafs. The defenceman finally chose to wear a visor, something he did for the remainder of his career. Salming even became an advocate for facial protection: "I would love to see everyone wear one, and no one would have to go through what I have."

Toronto paired Ken Wregget (top) with Allan Bester (bottom) in 1983–84. The goaltending tandem was often spectacular, with Bester playing eight seasons for the Leafs, and Wregget six seasons.

By the end of January, the Leafs were an ailing team: Dan Daoust, Tom Fergus, Miroslav Fryčer, Chris Kotsopoulos, Bob McGill, Brad Smith, and Ken Yaremchuk had all joined Salming on the injured list. And while the Leafs had made some tweaks, such as adding tough guy Kevin Maguire and veteran defenceman Rick Lanz, the team was in a bit of a free fall.

There was a particularly bad game right in the middle of a six-game losing streak. On January 26, the Leafs scored five goals against the Calgary Flames in the first period and held that 5–0 lead into the third period, only to let Calgary come all the way back to tie the game in regulation time. The Flames then scored in overtime and took home an unbelievable 6–5 victory.

After flirting with first place in the early months of the season, the Maple Leafs dropped precipitously. By February, they were in the Norris Division basement. Tensions were running high, and fans, players, and owners were disappointed that the momentum from the previous year had not translated into a better season.

The Leafs were faced with a lack of goal production and the very real possibility that they would miss the playoffs. In an effort to effect some positive change, Toronto traded forward Jeff Jackson and a draft pick to the New York Rangers for Mark Osborne in early March. The trade paid an immediate dividend: in his first game in blue and white, Osborne scored in a 7–2 win over Pittsburgh at Maple Leaf Gardens. The Leafs followed two days later with an identical score over the New York Islanders, also at home.

And there was the problem: at home, the Maple Leafs had a record of 19 wins, 12 losses, and 4 ties. But the team struggled badly on the road, where they had just 7 wins, 22 losses, and 2 ties – the worst road record in the NHL. Ballard demanded that his general manager, Gerry McNamara, scour the league for players who might improve the hockey club. With his trademark stridency, Ballard explained his directive to the media: "I told Gerry to stay on the phone all night if necessary. You have to get on him once in a while. He gets a little sleepy but, if we don't make a deal this time, it won't be from lack of trying."

At the same time, McNamara was also fending off rival teams who thought the Leafs might be sellers. There were rumours circulating about interest in various players, but McNamara held fast – he did not believe he had been offered any deal that would improve the club.

The team did not do its general manager any favours. In a road game against Washington, the Leafs were bombed by the Capitals, 10–2. Coach Brophy was apoplectic. "This is

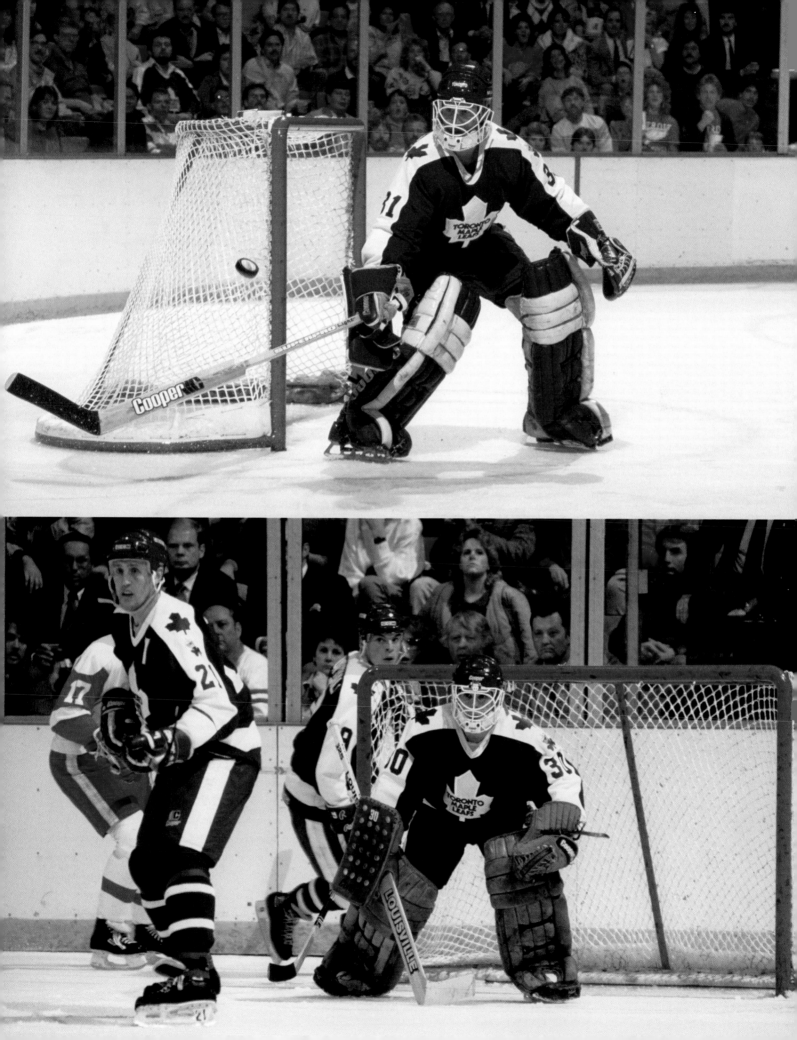

the first time this team's been in a stretch run for some time," he said. "It's a new experience. They don't seem to realize that you have to come every night to play. They lack the experience of having to play 60 full minutes." Despite the blowout, the inconsistent Maple Leafs somehow managed to sneak into the playoffs by winning three of their final five games. In the woeful Norris Division. As such, 70 points, on the strength of a 32–42–6 record, was enough for Toronto to claim the last playoff berth in the division.

Russ Courtnall led the team in scoring with 73 points, including 29 goals. Three players scored 30 goals or more: Wendel Clark (37), Steve Thomas (35), and Rick Vaive (32). Clark collected 271 minutes in penalties, and Vaive was awarded the Molson Cup for his three-star appearances.

Toronto faced the first-place St. Louis Blues in the first round of the playoffs. Coach Brophy, resplendent in a black fedora that became his signature that spring, stepped behind the bench in St. Louis for the opening game of the series, a 3–1 Blues victory.

Toronto evened the series with a 3–2 overtime win in Game Two. Peter Ihnačák won a faceoff, pulling the puck back to defenceman Rick Lanz, who crossed the St. Louis blueline, stepped around a defenceman, and fired a low shot that decided the game.

The Leafs lost a heartbreaking 5–3 decision to the Blues in Game Three in Toronto. Gino Cavallini's winning goal caromed off Steve Thomas and past Wregget. The Leafs bounced back in Game Four with a 2–1 victory, a feat they duplicated two nights later, back in St. Louis. The Leafs were now up three games to two in the best-of-seven series.

Brad Smith opened the scoring in Game Six. Fed a pass by Wendel Clark, he made a great move to elude an attempted poke check by sprawling St. Louis goalie Greg Millen, and then fired the puck into the open goal. As the self-deprecating Smith attested, "It's the only move I have. I go to my backhand, then pull it to my forehand. Our goalies are used to it. They stop me every time in practice." Motor City Smitty's goal would stand as the winner. John Brophy didn't play Smith in the third, despite the crowd's chants of "We want Smith!" During a break in the action, Brophy tapped Smith on the shoulder. The big winger skated out and embraced Ken Wregget in the Leafs goal, and the crowd went wild. Wregget earned the 4–0 shutout as the Leafs eliminated the Blues. Toronto was once again on its way to the second round of the playoffs, where the Detroit Red Wings awaited.

While the Maple Leafs exuded confidence in the series opener, the Red Wings looked rusty. Toronto was also riding hot goaltender Ken Wregget. The result was 4–2 in the Leafs' favour.

Game Two was even more convincing. Toronto shocked the crowd at Joe Louis Arena with a 7–2 win. "The Leafs dominated us," Detroit coach Jacques Demers conceded. "Maybe they're a better team than we thought. Maybe we underestimated them."

With the series shifting to Toronto, the Red Wings desperately needed a win in Game Three to stop the Maple Leafs' momentum. They got it, and took the third game, 4–2. Yet the Leafs rebounded well in Game Four. Mike Allison scored at 9:31 of overtime to give the Leafs a 3–2 win. The Toronto Maple Leafs were now up three games to one, and were just one game away from heading to the Campbell Conference final. Red Wings goalie Glen Hanlon was not ready to roll over just yet. He came up big in Game Five, stoning the Leafs, 3–0, to pull Detroit back into the series.

During Game Six at Maple Leaf Gardens, Börje Salming fed a blind pass to the centre of the ice. Wings forward Steve Yzerman picked off the puck and fed it to Gerard Gallant in the corner, who then fed a pass to Bob Probert, who fired it past Wregget for the Wings' third goal. It proved to be the winner, as the Red Wings went on to tie the series with a 4–2 win.

Back in Detroit, the Red Wings made no mistake in Game Seven, scoring two goals within just 71 seconds in the second period to ice the victory. Hanlon posted another shutout in Detroit's 3–0 win, which eliminated the Toronto Maple Leafs.

It had been a season of terrible inconsistency, once again punctuated by a solid, if unexpected run in the playoffs. On some nights, the Leafs had looked like world beaters; on others, a very confused club. There was still, however, a great deal of hope: Wregget had assumed the role of number-one netminder; Todd Gill and Al Iafrate were poised to lead the Leafs blueline for years to come; and the Hound Line, with fan favourite Wendel Clark, was bringing fans to their feet. Rookie coach John Brophy had demonstrated the ability to draw more than could be expected out of his squad. The question remained whether Leafs Nation could expect anything more.

CRASH ON CARLTON

In the June 1987 NHL Entry Draft, Toronto chose defenceman Luke Richardson seventh overall, followed by Daniel Marois, John McIntyre, Joe Sacco, Mike Eastwood, and

A truculent player in the Eastern Hockey League, John Brophy holds the league's career penalty-minute record. Brophy brought his tough-edged style to coaching the Maple Leafs when he joined Toronto for the 1986–87 season.

goaltender Damian Rhodes. All six would find their way into the club's lineup within the next few seasons.

And on September 3, Toronto pulled the trigger on a blockbuster trade that sent snipers Rick Vaive and Steve Thomas, along with hard-rock blueliner Bob McGill, to the Chicago Blackhawks for Ed Olczyk and Al Secord.

Toronto had coveted Olczyk since the ill-fated Gary Nylund arbitration settlement in 1986. Now, the Leafs had finally secured the young forward, who scored 29 goals in 1986–87. Al Secord was also a positive offensive addition. Secord had scored at least 40 goals three times with the Hawks, including a 50-goal season in 1982–83. He also brought toughness, having recorded 303 penalty minutes along with a 44-goal season in 1981–82.

Much to Coach Brophy's delight, the Leafs also secured another tough guy in Dave Semenko, acquired from Hartford for Bill Root. Semenko had played on two Stanley Cup–winning teams in Edmonton. What he might have lacked in offensive skill was compensated for by the fear he instilled in the opposition.

Still, while the Leafs were adding some muscle, they lost some. In October, Buffalo claimed Kevin Maguire off

the waiver wire. Brad Smith was also left unprotected, and when no one rescued him from waivers, Motor City Smitty's career was over.

The team elected to continue without a captain after the departure of Rick Vaive. "We've got some experienced people now," Gerry McNamara explained, "people who have had leadership roles with other teams."

After the major trade between Toronto and Chicago, it seemed fitting that the two should face each other in the opening contest of the 1987–88 season. The Leafs beat the Blackhawks, 7–5, in Chicago. They followed this up two nights later with a 5–2 win against the New Jersey Devils in the home opener at Maple Leaf Gardens.

Brophy chose Ken Wregget to start the season in goal, but following substantial losses to Montreal (10–3) and Minnesota (7–4), he handed the reins to Allan Bester. Fortunately, Bester came up with a strong performance in his first start of the season as the Leafs beat the Islanders, 5–2. Bester and company followed that game with a 4–0 shutout victory over the Penguins the very next night.

While the goaltending change had helped, injuries began to take a toll on the lineup: Secord injured his chest in a fight, Clark injured his back and had his season limited to just 28 games, and Todd Gill fractured his ankle. With part of the roster in sick bay and the rest of the squad playing less-than-spirited hockey, the Leafs dropped consecutive games to St. Louis, Montreal, and Boston in November.

Meanwhile, 69-year-old Punch Imlach, who had had a heart condition that stretched back to his first go-around with the Leafs in the late 1950s, suffered a heart attack on November 29 and died two days later. A cross-section of players who had worked and admired Imlach were among the pallbearers at his funeral, including Jean Béliveau (Quebec Aces), Johnny Bower and Allan Stanley (Toronto Maple Leafs), Don Edwards and Gilbert Perreault (Buffalo Sabres), and Doug Carpenter (coach of the Leafs' AHL farm teams, the New Brunswick Hawks and St. Catharines Saints).

More of the beleaguered Leafs sustained injuries. The defence corps was hit particularly hard, with Todd Gill, Al Iafrate, Chris Kotsopoulos, Rick Lanz, and Börje Salming all out of the lineup, leaving just Dale Degray and Luke Richardson. Gary Leeman, who had played defence in junior, was moved back to the blueline, and Mike Stothers was picked up from Philadelphia – he'd been playing for their AHL affiliate in Hershey.

More happily, Börje Salming returned to the squad and played his 1,000th NHL game on January 4 against the Vancouver Canucks. Salming had played all 1,000 games with the Maple Leafs. Only George Armstrong, Ron Ellis, Tim Horton, and Dave Keon had played as many games with the Blue and White. At the time, however, Harold Ballard was vacationing in Miami at his friend Steve Stavro's place. The team therefore agreed to delay any celebration of Salming's achievement until Ballard returned. Bob Stellick, the team's public relations director, explained that Ballard "wants to be part of it. Börje is special to him." As such, the game – a 7–7 tie – was played without any additional pomp or ceremony. An official celebration was held prior to a game against the St. Louis Blues on February 27. That night, Salming's parents, brother, and sister were all flown into Toronto from Sweden. Inge Hammarström was also on hand as Börje was presented with several gifts to honour his achievement, including a silver serving tray and a diamond ring from his Toronto teammates.

While in Miami, Ballard had suffered chest pains. He went to hospital, where doctors confirmed that the Leafs owner had suffered a heart attack. When the press got wind of this, the ramifications were astonishing. Shares in Maple Leaf Gardens sharply increased by $3.50, closing at $34. While Pal Hal rested comfortably in Florida, his personal wealth grew by over $10 million.

His team was not faring nearly as well. While December had been arduous for the Leafs, January was much worse. Toronto was winless in 15 games in a streak that started on December 26. There was controversy too: late in the second period of a game against Minnesota at the Gardens on January 6, 1988, Luke Richardson cross-checked Dino Ciccarelli into the boards. The feisty North Stars winger came back with a stick swung at Richardson's head. The Leafs defenceman retaliated with a punch to the face, and Ciccarelli took two more vicious swings with his stick. Richardson was assessed two minor penalties (for slashing and roughing), while Ciccarelli received a double major (high-sticking and intent to injure). Toronto police investigated the incident, and the file was turned over to Ontario attorney-general Ian Scott. In August 1988, a judge in Ontario Provincial Court sentenced Ciccarelli to one day in jail and a fine of $1,000.

The winless stretch for the Leafs culminated in a brutal 11–3 shellacking at the hands of the Calgary Flames on January 25. The convalescing Ballard was outraged: "I'm absolutely disgusted with the whole shooting match. [Things are going to change] when I return, and it'll be starting with the manager." Gerry McNamara had had warning shots fired across his bow before. This time, though, he saw the writing on the wall. Ballard's latest rant also caused a massive rift between the GM and Coach Brophy.

Likely smelling blood, many teams became very interested in some of the Leafs' assets. McNamara tried to address his detractors, saying, "The confidence level is really low, and somehow or another, we have to find a way to build up their confidence. The last thing I should do now is start talking about moving players out. I don't think a deal is the answer." The coach, however, was discernibly exasperated: "Don't ask me why this club takes months off at a time! I don't know. Everything's gone sideways. Seems to be a trend here every year!" Something was bound to give.

The team, with young Jeff Reese in goal, finally won on January 27, beating Los Angeles, 5–2. But the end had come for McNamara. On February 7, Ballard relieved the GM of his duties.

"I didn't want to embarrass Gerry," the owner said, "so I called him . . . and said, 'Gerry, I've been trying to get hold of you and tell you to resign on account of I'm going to make a change. You could say you don't want to work for that old son of a bitch Ballard any longer. A lot of people would give you credit for that.'"

Confronted by the media, McNamara was resolute: "[Ballard] did suggest I resign, but I refused. I never quit on anything in my life."

With McNamara gone, Ballard appointed a trio to handle the general manager's portfolio for the remainder of the season: coach John Brophy; Dick Duff, who was scouting for the Leafs at the time; and assistant general manager Gord Stellick. Ballard, who insisted on being involved in all decisions, punctuated this announcement with another: "There's going to be a housecleaning. There are a lot of guys on this club that shouldn't be wearing skates."

Predictably, the unsettled atmosphere did little to help the team, which continued to struggle. After a loss in Minnesota on February 22, Brophy lashed out publicly. When asked about moving players out and bringing others in, he simply shrugged: "Who wants to trade with us the way we're playing?"

March was a particularly horrible month for the Leafs, with just one win in 13 tries. But despite finishing 20th overall with just 52 points, the Maple Leafs edged out Minnesota by a single point to claim fourth place in the Norris Division and a playoff berth. This provoked much astonishment among the Leafs faithful, and much disdain among teams such as the New York Rangers (82 points), Pittsburgh (81), Quebec (69), and Vancouver (59), all of whom failed to qualify. In fact, the Leafs earned the ignominious distinction of being the team with the fewest points to make the playoffs since the NHL went to a 70-game schedule in 1949–50.

For Gary Leeman, the outcome was a relief: "It was a long season. I can't believe a team did worse than us, but it's nice to be in the playoffs."

The season hadn't been a total bust. As usual, there were some good individual performances. In his first season as a Maple Leaf, Ed Olczyk led the team in goals (40) and points (75). Leeman scored 30 times, Russ Courtnall and Mark Osborne both had 23, and Al Iafrate tied a Leaf record for goals by a defenceman with 22, the same number scored by Ian Turnbull in 1976–77. Ken Wregget was awarded the Molson Cup for his three-star selections.

Not surprisingly, the Maple Leafs had the cards stacked again them in the spring of 1988. Still, in hockey-crazy Toronto, fans lined up, some for as long as 24 hours, to buy playoff tickets. The Leafs, meanwhile, were preparing to meet the formidable Detroit Red Wings. That the Wings had finished 41 points ahead of Toronto in the regular season provided little reason for optimism.

Remarkably, with Allan Bester in goal and veteran Börje Salming rekindling some of his old magic, the Leafs dumped the Wings, 6–2, in Detroit in the series opener. Game Two, however, was closer to what pundits expected as the Wings cruised to a 6–2 victory. When Detroit scored their second goal of the game within the first four minutes of the first period, Brophy pulled Bester in favour of Wregget.

The same sort of beginning was awaiting the teams after they travelled to Toronto for Game Three. In fact, the game was over almost before it started. The Wings pounced, scoring two goals in the first ten minutes, and went on to win, 6–3. Hoping to rebound with extra effort in Game Four, the Leafs horrified their fans with a feeble 8–0 loss. Maple Leaf jerseys were knotted and tossed onto the ice, and the crowd returned wayward pucks to the playing surface. Ken Wregget was jeered every time he made even the easiest of saves. The ice had to be cleared of debris on a regular basis – among the trash were the "Brophy's Boys" black straw fedoras that were being sold outside Maple Leaf Gardens, imitations of the one the coach wore during the playoffs. The *Toronto Star* aptly observed that on this night, "20 years of frustration came to a head."

Unbelievably, the Leafs came back with a solid effort in Game Five and pulled out a 6–5 overtime win that left Detroit fans stunned. At the 34-second mark of the extra frame, Salming kept the puck in at the Wings blueline and fired a shot at Greg Stefan in the Detroit goal. Olczyk, in the faceoff circle to the right of the goaltender, spun and smacked the puck, and it found the back of the goal for the Toronto victory.

The teams returned to Maple Leaf Gardens for Game Six, but Detroit eliminated Toronto with a 5–3 win. Miroslav Frycer could not contain his candour about the team or its coach after the game. For him, the season had been "a nightmare for this team, this city, myself, and my family. There's no way I'll ever play for Brophy again. My days with the Maple Leafs are over! You just can't scream at guys all the time."

There were wounds that would not heal until changes were made: players who didn't respond well to the coach, players who didn't like each other, and the mercurial owner's often-disruptive nature. But while the era is often remembered for its disruptions and challenges, the Maple Leafs still – despite the odds – appeared in five playoff rounds over three seasons.

I was a young boy in the late 1940s the first time I walked through the doors of the Gardens to watch the Leafs. My family had held season tickets since the day the Gardens opened. I have vivid memories of sitting with my mother or father watching star players like Ted "Teeder" Kennedy, Tod Sloan, Max Bentley, Sid Smith, Harry Watson, Turk Broda, and Harry Lumley, and other memorable Leafs greats. I was a wide-eyed kid in awe of those hockey stars . . . The Conacher family had a long and varied history with the Gardens, from its first day to its last.

Brian Conacher
PLAYER
1965–68

CHANGE ON CHURCH AND CARLTON
1988–89 TO 1989–90

STELLICKTRICITY

Not surprisingly, the three-headed committee managing the Maple Leafs after Gerry McNamara's dismissal did not work particularly well. Simply put, the three men – Gord Stellick, John Brophy, and Dick Duff – had divergent ideas about how the team should be constructed. "Though we liked each other personally, the three months of our triumvirate were a disaster," Stellick said. "Brophy and Duff were old school. I wasn't. We couldn't get on the same page to work a consensus to make any trades."

As a result of this stalemate, Harold Ballard made his own move. On April 28, 1988, the Leafs owner gave the position of general manager solely to Gord Stellick. At 30 years of age, he was far and away the youngest GM in the league. He had, however, worked his way up through the Maple Leafs hierarchy and was familiar with most aspects of the organization. Stellick had earned respect by, as he put it, "keeping my mouth shut and my ears open."

Stellick was settled in as GM in time for the 1988 NHL Entry Draft, which saw the Maple Leafs pick up Scott Pearson with their first-round selection, sixth overall. In the next two rounds, they took Tie Domi and goaltender Peter Ing. Stellick added George Armstrong to the scouting staff after he was released from a scouting job with the Quebec Nordiques, traded Mike Stothers to Philadelphia in a deal that returned Bill Root to Toronto, and picked up free agents Craig Laughlin and Dave Reid. And, having called out the rest of his team and the coach, Miroslav Frycer was sent to Detroit for Darren Veitch.

While Stellick was busy adding and subtracting, the team's owner was once again hospitalized with heart problems. One week later, Harold Ballard underwent quintuple-bypass surgery. Before going under, Pal Hal vowed, "I won't die till the Leafs win the Stanley Cup!" As before, the market immediately reacted to the owner's predicament. Share prices jumped $2.50, to $42, and Ballard again saw the value of his investment swell, this time by more than $7 million, while he rested in hospital.

Meanwhile, just three days before the season opener, the Leafs picked up Brad Marsh off the waiver wire. A ten-season veteran, Marsh was a tough, stay-at-home defenceman who brought leadership to a team that had been without a captain in 1987–88. Despite the team's long-standing woes, Marsh was delighted with the news.

"It was very special to be picked up by the Leafs," he enthused. "I grew up in London, and back then, there were two teams in Canada. You cheered for one and hated the other. We were Leaf fans in the Marsh household. I've got a picture of me about seven or eight years old wearing the Leafs sweater and with Leafs pants, the Leafs socks, and Leafs hockey gloves."

While the Leafs dropped the season opener to Boston by a 2–1 margin, Marsh stood out.

The Leafs played their home opener two nights later. Hap Day, who had his name engraved on the Stanley Cup seven times with Toronto, performed the ceremonial opening faceoff. That night, Toronto mauled the Blackhawks, 7–4. Ed Olczyk had a four-point night, with two goals and two assists. Still, there was discontent within the Leafs core. Just three games into the season, Brophy made Russ Courtnall a healthy scratch. To be fair, the Leafs were deep at centre, with Olczyk, Vincent Damphousse, and Tom Fergus. Courtnall was therefore – though perhaps not justly – relegated to the fourth line. While skilled and fast, Courtnall was not particularly physical, and was therefore not the coach's kind of player.

Courtnall was unhappy being on the sidelines and, when he did play, with being given minimal ice time. Conversely, Brophy was looking to add yet more toughness to the team. He found it in Montreal's John Kordic, who was, in Brophy's mind, the top heavyweight in the league and exactly what the Leafs needed. He implored Stellick to try to make a move to secure Kordic.

On November 7, the Maple Leafs sent Courtnall, who had four 20-goal seasons with the Leafs (and would reach this plateau another six times in his career) to Montreal for Kordic, who had scored seven goals in his NHL career,

On November 7, 1988, 15 games into the turbulent 1988–89 season, rookie general manager Gord Stellick was convinced by coach John Brophy that the Leafs needed toughness. In response, he dealt Russ Courtnall (pictured) and a sixth-round draft pick to the Montreal Canadiens for John Kordic.

as well as a late draft pick. While Stellick was confident it was a good trade, he knew he'd have to defend his choice: "Heat? I'm expecting it on this one, but I can handle it. You've got to stand up and do what you think is necessary. [Kordic] gives us a presence we don't have."

But the Leafs had done more than just add toughness to the team. In an 8–2 loss to Edmonton on December 14, Kordic showed signs that the Leafs had a liability on their hands. Infuriated over what he believed to have been a transgression against him during the game, Kordic mugged Keith Acton from behind and broke his nose. It was Kordic's third major stick infraction of the season and he was handed a ten-game suspension.

After an 8–3–1 start, the team as a whole started to fade. Ken Wregget, who had been the key to that early success, began to struggle in goal. Likewise, rookie Daniel Marois, who had been red hot, suddenly became ice cold. When the team hit a ten-game winless streak, Harold Ballard cut short his vacation in the Cayman Islands and returned to Toronto. After conferring with his general manager, they both agreed that a change was essential. On December 19, Gord Stellick relieved John Brophy of his coaching position. As Stellick saw it, Brophy was no quitter, but the GM believed that the Leafs had done the former coach a favour, as "it lifted a burden off his shoulders."

Scout and assistant general manager George Armstrong was asked to coach the team for the remainder of the season, and he reluctantly agreed. "I'll do it as a favour to you and Mr. Ballard, but only for the rest of this season," Armstrong cautioned Stellick. "I don't want to do it. I'm no damn coach." In actuality, Armstrong had been a coach, and a good one at that. The former Leaf captain had not, however, coached since he was behind the bench for the Toronto Marlboros in the 1970s, taking the Marlies to Memorial Cup championships in 1973 and 1975.

Armstrong's debut as coach of the Leafs on December 21, 1988, was a success as Toronto broke its winless streak by beating St. Louis, 4–3. Eddie Olczyk spoke to the immediate positive effect Armstrong had had: "There was a better atmosphere around here all of a sudden. It was just so pleasant to come in for work knowing you wouldn't be yelled at if you were caught smiling."

Sadly, Armstrong's positivity was not a cure-all. Steadily, the Leafs tumbled from the top of the Norris Division standings and out of contention. Stellick was at a loss: "No one knows what happened after our great start, but it seemed that as hard as everyone tried to forget the turmoil surrounding the team last year, it started coming back again."

January was particularly difficult. The Leafs went 2–7–4 and collected only eight points. Al Iafrate was absent from the team and would miss several games. And Wendel Clark, who had yet to play that season because of a back injury, was shockingly called out by Harold Ballard in the press for what he perceived as malingering: "I sometimes think Wendel is swinging the lead. I think it's time Wendel tested the water."

Clark defended himself from the public barb, explaining, "There's a definite improvement, but it hurts the whole time in practice. I can live with that. But what happens in a game when the clutching, twisting, and hitting enter the picture? I'd say I'm about 70 per cent right now. I don't want to play until I'm convinced there'll be no chance of another serious injury."

The tenacious forward did push himself to return, however, and his back would pay the price. Clark returned against the New York Rangers on March 1. In a 7–4 loss, Clark bumped and banged from his first shift, and early in the game took three stitches near his eye from a high stick. When asked how his back felt after the game, he said, "It's not too bad. It hurts the same now as it did before the game."

With their fireplug back in the lineup, the Leafs made the choice to stick with Allan Bester and Jeff Reese in goal. This meant that Ken Wregget, one of the few players on the roster who could generate a substantial return, was now available on the trade market. On March 6, he was sent to Philadelphia for two first-round draft picks. The goaltender was deeply saddened to hear the news: "I've spent five years here and been through a lot of ups and downs. I definitely wanted to stay here."

Through the last days of the season, Toronto chased Chicago for the final playoff spot in the Norris Division. Each team lost its penultimate game, setting up a winner-take-all contest to determine whose season would continue. The Leafs, with 62 points, trailed the Blackhawks by two, but had won 28 games to Chicago's 26. So, by winning the final game, Toronto would tie the Blackhawks in total points and then win the tiebreaker for fourth place.

In that final game, the Maple Leafs came out strong, leading, 3–1, after two periods. Chicago scored twice in 91 seconds in the third, forcing the game into overtime. The next goal would decide which team made the playoffs. Sadly, it ended very quickly for the Leafs. The Hawks' Troy Murray broke in alone on Bester, drilling a shot over the goalie's left shoulder only 48 seconds into overtime.

Playing for the Toronto Maple Leafs was a dream come true. As someone who grew up in Toronto, I have many fond memories of heading down on the subway from Etobicoke and watching the Leafs at Maple Leaf Gardens. I recall receiving my first Leafs jersey as a nine-year-old – it was a Pete Stemkowski one. As teenagers, we all pretended to be Darryl Sittler and we would imitate him in our road hockey games. It was an amazing and surreal feeling putting on that jersey in the spring of 1987 when I was traded to the Leafs, and I would score in my first-ever game at Maple Leaf Gardens while wearing the home white jersey in front of the bright lights, and my family and childhood friends, who were also mesmerized.

Mark Osborne
PLAYER
1987–90; 1992–94

The Toronto Maple Leafs had made some noteworthy improvements from the previous year. The team increased its point total by ten. Ed Olczyk collected a team-best 38 goals and 90 points. In spite of missing 19 games, Gary Leeman, the team's Molson Cup winner, scored 32 goals. Rookie Daniel Marois was a pleasant surprise, contributing 31 goals. And through his back pain, Wendel Clark battled to score seven in the 15 games he was able to play.

These incremental moves towards respectability may have placated much of Leafs Nation, but they did little for the team's owner. As far as Harold Ballard was concerned, "You can bet the farm that there'll be a lot of changes here next season."

One player beat Ballard to the punch. Börje Salming's contract had expired, and although the Maple Leafs made him a solid offer, he chose to explore other opportunities. As the defenceman confessed, "Losing takes a toll on you." On June 12, 1989, he signed with the Detroit Red Wings. Ballard had the audacity to claim that there was "no loyalty" in Salming. This was a rather different tune to the one he had played prior to Salming's departure, when he said, "[Salming]'s given enough to Canada and the Maple Leafs over the years. I would like to trade him to a team that has a shot at winning the Stanley Cup. To be able to do that would please me no end." At that time, Salming had responded, "If I do get to play on a [Stanley Cup] winner, I want it to be in Toronto."

Salming had in fact been unfailingly loyal, but after 16 superb seasons, his career with the Maple Leafs had come to an end. The Swede left holding several team marks: most career assists by a Maple Leaf; most career goals by a Leaf defenceman, and most career points by a Leafs defenceman. He ranked third in franchise history in games played (behind only George Armstrong and Tim Horton) and career points (trailing Darryl Sittler and Dave Keon).

Salming played one year with the Red Wings before he returned to Sweden. At the time, he was the highest-scoring Swedish player of all time. His success in the NHL had an immense impact on the game in his home country. Mats Sundin, a Leaf from 1994 through 2008, later spoke about the "Salming effect": "All of us who came after Börje have a lot to thank him for. He really paved the way for all Swedish players and opened the eyes of NHL managers that Swedes can play in the NHL, do well, and be effective leaders."

The Leafs, however, were focused on the future, and Gord Stellick didn't see the Leaf icon as part of that future: "If we're going to be any better two years from now, it's not going to be with Börje Salming. It's going to be with Al Iafrate, Luke Richardson, and Darryl Shannon."

As it happened, Stellick would not be around in two years to see whether or not Iafrate, Richardson, and Shannon would deliver the goods. During the off-season, Stellick was stunned to read an article in the *Toronto Star* in which Harold Ballard stated, "I'm afraid Stellick is too young and still has too much to learn. He was the youngest general manager in the history of the National Hockey League when we appointed him, and we may have expected too much too soon." After digesting those words, Stellick made the decision that he no longer wanted to work for Ballard and his Leafs. At 9:00 A.M. on August 11, 1989, Stellick marched into Ballard's office and handed him his letter of resignation.

"It looked like it was going to be inevitable," Stellick told the press. "It's been building for eight or nine months. I was getting squeezed pretty good. I still think he's a great man. I hope he starts considering what's good for hockey again, not just what's right for Harold Ballard. Today, I can walk out with my pride and my dignity."

Gord Stellick had proven to be a very fair general manager, whom the players genuinely liked.

GOODBYE PAL HAL

Before Stellick left, he oversaw Toronto's table at the NHL Entry Draft in June 1989. Expectations were high, as the team held three first-round picks in that draft. As it happened, all three were used to select players from the Belleville Bulls of the Ontario Hockey League (OHL). The Leafs' first choice, at number three overall, was Scott Thornton, followed by Rob Pearson (12th) and Steve Bancroft (21st). Stellick also upgraded the team in June by acquiring defenceman Rob Ramage from Calgary for a second-round selection.

In search of a new GM, Harold Ballard actually approached Alan Eagleson, who was still executive director of the NHLPA, about the job. He declined. Ballard then offered the job to Frank Bonello, who had served as GM of the Toronto Marlboros team that won the Memorial Cup in 1975, but the deal fell through after Ballard lowballed the salary offer. On August 15 – just one day after the Bonello offer fell through – Ballard announced that head scout and former Leafs coach Floyd Smith had agreed to become the team's new general manager.

Smith then made his recommendation for coach, and on August 24 the Leafs hired Doug Carpenter to replace George Armstrong. Carpenter had been coaching the Halifax Citadels in the AHL and had NHL experience as head coach of the New Jersey Devils. Doug was also well liked within the Leafs organization from his days coaching Toronto's AHL team, the St. Catharines Saints.

To complete the overhaul in the chain of command, the Leafs appointed a new captain. Before he had ever played a game for Toronto, the Maple Leafs named the newly acquired Rob Ramage, who added a veteran presence to the young team and had just won the Stanley Cup with Calgary. As there was still some residue of division within the dressing room, it perhaps made sense that the Leafs awarded the captaincy to an absolute newcomer. Still, it was a privileged role, one that had been left vacant for three years and was fraught with challenges. No one knew this better than Ramage himself, who was understandably wary: "I'm looking at things with guarded optimism. We've got a new coach, new players, but let's face it – this team's in the infant stage. We've got to learn to crawl before we can walk."

Coach Carpenter decided that Allan Bester would be his primary goaltender, backed by Jeff Reese. The season opener took the team to California, where they faced the Los Angeles Kings. Early on, the Leafs looked good, but during the second period, there was a four-minute lapse in which the Kings scored three goals in the space of 3:53, burying any chance of victory, and the home team prevailed, 4–2.

The home opener, though, would be much worse. Retired wrestler Whipper Billy Watson, who had raised millions for the Easter Seals campaign throughout his life, accompanied Harold Ballard to centre ice to drop the puck for the opening faceoff against Buffalo. This was, for Leafs fans, the highlight of the night. The Sabres embarrassed the Leafs, 7–1, and the Gardens faithful booed the team unmercifully throughout the game. Then there was the 9–6 spanking at the hands of the Hawks on October 12, after which Jeff Reese was shipped to the Newmarket Saints and Mark LaForest was brought up to back Bester. Toronto was off to a terrible start, losing four of its first five games and surrending 30 goals in the process.

In an attempt to strengthen the team's defence, Floyd Smith swung a surprising deal, landing Tom Kurvers from New Jersey for a future first-round selection. Being traded to Toronto caught Kurvers off guard. Stunned, he refused to report at first, but acquiesced and played his first game on October 21, an 8–4 win over Washington. Toronto fans

have never taken kindly to players not wanting to play for their club, and they welcomed the defenceman with boos. Kurvers accepted the derision: "I can understand it because the fans want to see the team win and I wasn't helping things by not coming and playing." The new Leaf soon embraced the city and his role on a young and often exciting team.

While Coach Carpenter's run-and-gun offence was indeed rousing, the team's defence was porous. In fact, the Leafs had the league's worst goals-against average. Bester was sent to Newmarket to rediscover his confidence; Peter Ing, a young goaltender who had been signed a few weeks earlier and assigned to Newmarket, was called up to the big club in Bester's place. On November 15, Ing served as back up to LaForest. The very next night, he made his NHL debut against the New York Islanders. The Islanders scored four goals on seven shots in the first period. Carpenter pulled Ing for all of three minutes, then reinserted him for the rest of the game, and the rookie was tagged with a 6–2 loss. To be fair, he didn't get much help. According to the *Star*, Ing was "thrust into the leading role and then abandoned by his supporting cast."

There were other bad nights for the four goaltenders the Leafs would use throughout the season. On February 22, the Leafs rolled into Calgary, unaware of the carnage about to unfold. That night, Reese was pulled after the first five Flames goals beat him, and Calgary was up 9–0 before Toronto finally got on the scoreboard. In the end, Calgary beat Toronto, 12–2.

The Leafs took the highway up to Edmonton for a game the next night, and it seemed as though they were headed for another blowout after the Oilers pulled ahead, 5–2. The Leafs, however, battled back and won the game, 6–5. Teammates surrounded winning goalie Allan Bester and celebrated as if they had won the Stanley Cup. It was the first Toronto win in Edmonton since November 11, 1979.

Tie Domi was called up to replace John Kordic. On March 3, Floyd Smith informed Kordic that the Leafs would try to trade him, but it turned out that his reputation preceded him and Smith was unable to swing a trade. By late March, Kordic was back in the lineup, but it was an untenable situation for everyone involved.

More off-ice storylines were unfolding in Leaf Land. Ballard had flown with his companion, Yolanda, to the Cayman Islands for his holiday vacation. While there, the Leafs owner went into kidney failure. He was flown to Miami Baptist Hospital on January 4.

Not well enough to return to Toronto, Ballard remained hospitalized in Florida. The Maple Leaf

After winning the Stanley Cup with the Calgary Flames in 1989, Rob Ramage joined the Maple Leafs prior to the 1989–90 season. He was named captain before he had played a game with Toronto, and his veteran presence aided the team during a tumultuous time.

Gardens board of directors assumed responsibility for the franchise while Ballard was incapacitated. Board chair Paul McNamara assured everyone that the move was a temporary one, but the battle for control of the Gardens and the hockey team had already begun. The lion's share of Gardens stock was controlled by a holding company, H.E. Ballard Ltd. (HEB), of which Ballard's three children – Bill, Harold Jr., and Mary Elizabeth – each held one-third. In January 1989 Ballard bought Mary Elizabeth's shares, and in June he added Harold Jr.'s. The latter move prompted Bill to sue his father, brother, and Gardens directors Donald Giffin and Donald Crump, claiming he had a right of first refusal on Harold Jr.'s shares in H.E. Ballard.

Meanwhile, in 1980, Ballard, feeling a financial pinch because of loans he had taken out to buy out Stafford Smythe and John Bassett nearly a decade earlier, had turned to Molson Companies for help. The brewery, which held the sponsorship rights at the Gardens, agreed to pay the interest on his debt in return for an option to buy 19.9 per cent of Maple Leaf Gardens. Still, there was speculation that a bidding war might break out between the brewery, which already owned the Montreal Canadiens, and its main competitor, Labatt's. Still others pondered the possibility that Ballard might have willed his Gardens stock to Yolanda. It was, in every sense, a mess that would take the executors of Ballard's will – Giffin, Crump, and Steve Stavro – years to sort out.

In March, with a judge having ruled that Ballard was in no condition to run the organization, Giffin was installed by the board as president of Maple Leaf Gardens. Despite Stavro's attempts to unseat him over the ensuing year, Giffin would receive the endorsement of the Gardens directors a year later.

On the ice, the Leafs were in search of a respite from the drama. On March 24, they got it. That night, Mark Osborne scored an overtime goal that gave the Leafs a 4–3 win over Quebec – and with it, a playoff berth.

Then, some more reason to cheer. On March 28, Gary Leeman fired a slap shot from the slot at 10:04 of the third period to notch his 50th goal of the season. It was a Maple Leaf milestone previously reached only by Rick Vaive, who had accomplished the feat on three occasions. Leeman wasn't even thinking about hitting the plateau until he was directed by the Leafs GM. As Leeman explained:

I was stuck at 42 goals that year and got into a fight with Adam Creighton. I hit his helmet and I messed my hand up. I got to the penalty box and looked at my hand, and every fourth or fifth time I squeezed it, the tendon that runs on top of your knuckle slid between my knuckles. I thought, "Oh my God, I'm done!" . . . After about six games in which I didn't score, I got pulled aside by our GM Floyd Smith . . . and he said, "We don't want you to be fighting. We want you to put the puck in the net. You've got a chance to do something not many guys get a chance to do." I actually said to him, "What do you mean?" He said, "You have a chance to score 50 goals!" And I appreciated that, but I also didn't because all of a sudden, it was about that!

Leeman shared Smith's directive with his linemates, Mark Osborne and Ed Olczyk. Together, they helped Gary hit the 50-goal target.

The final game of the regular season saw the Maple Leafs host the Blackhawks. To the astonishment of everyone, Wendel Clark returned after missing 29 games because of knee surgery. Predictably, Number 17 was anything but tentative. Placed on the top line with Leeman and Olczyk, Clark picked up two assists and was in on a scrap as Toronto beat Chicago, 6–4.

In the end, the Leafs had enjoyed something of a revival under Coach Carpenter. The team finished with 38 wins, 38 losses, and 4 ties – good for a third-place Norris Division finish. It was the first non-losing season for the Maple Leafs since 1978–79.

The Leafs' top line was terrific. Leeman ended up with 51 goals, while linemates Olczyk and Osborne chipped in 32 and 23, respectively. The second unit added extra firepower to the team, with Daniel Marois, Vincent Damphousse, and Tom Fergus collecting 39, 33, and 19 goals, respectively. In fact, Toronto was third in the NHL in goal scoring, with 337. All-Star Al Iafrate added 21 goals and 42 assists from the blueline. Iafrate also participated in the inaugural NHL Skills Competition, where he recorded the hardest shot at 96 miles per hour.

Furthermore, the team had not been pushed around: the Leafs were the second most-penalized team, with 2,419 minutes. Brian Curran led the way with 301 minutes in penalties, followed by John Kordic, with 252, and captain Rob Ramage, with 202.

The '89–'90 Leafs were as weak defensively as they were a potent offensive force. Only the woeful Quebec Nordiques (407) and Pittsburgh Penguins (359) exceeded Toronto's 358 goals against. It was, without a doubt, the most worrisome aspect of the team's play. Carpenter earned the nickname Captain Hook, having pulled his starting netminder in 13 games during the season.

Drafted as a defenceman in 1982, the Maple Leafs converted Gary Leeman (left) to a forward, and in the 1989–90 season, he collected 95 points. The total included 51 goals, making him just the second Leaf to reach the 50-goal mark in a season.

That said, with all of the drama surrounding Ballard's failing health, the ownership conjecture, the John Kordic saga, and the introduction of a new general manager, new coach, and a new captain, the Leafs had done surprisingly well in 1989–90.

In the first round of the playoffs, the Leafs were matched with St. Louis. The Blues had finished second in the Norris, just three points ahead of Toronto. By all accounts, it was a winnable series for the Leafs. The series opened in St. Louis on April 4. Earlier that day, the team had been informed that Harold Ballard was in critical condition. The owner was now on life support.

Doug Carpenter announced that Allan Bester would be his starter for the playoffs. Meanwhile, the Blues had a surprise starter in goal for Game One: rookie Curtis Joseph started ahead of Vincent Riendeau and back-stopped the Blues to a 4–2 win. St. Louis had played a very aggressive game; in response, Carpenter dressed Curran, Kordic, and John McIntyre for Game Two. It mattered little, as the Leafs tumbled again to the Blues, 4–2.

Game Three, hosted at Maple Leaf Gardens, saw Toronto battle back from a 5–3 deficit in the third period to tie the contest. At 6:04 of overtime, however, Sergio Momesso's 60-foot slap shot slipped between Bester's pads to give St. Louis a 6–5 win and a suffocating three-games-to-none lead in the series.

Bester, who had been sensational in the first two games, was devastated. The goaltender battled back tears in a postgame interview. Then, in Game Four, Jeff Reese performed admirably as Toronto fended off St. Louis with a 4–2 victory. The series was headed back to Missouri.

The next day, April 11, 1990, Harold Ballard died. He was 86. Earlier in the day, the controversial owner had spent time with his three children and Yolanda, but when the end came, he was alone with his longtime friend, former Toronto mayor Allan Lamport, who remembered those final moments: "I squeezed his hand and asked him to squeeze my hand if he understood, and he did."

The next night, the black armband–wearing Toronto Maple Leafs were eliminated by the St. Louis Blues, 4–3.

UNDER NEW OWNERSHIP
1990–91 TO 1997–98

BRAND NEW DAY

There was a nervous energy surrounding the team in the days immediately following Harold Ballard's death. Fans and players alike were anxious to see how bigger-picture events would unfold for the franchise. In the short term, there were more routine matters to deal with, beginning with the 1990 NHL Entry Draft. In the first round, the Leafs took a gamble on Drake Berehowsky, a talented but injured defenceman who had played only nine games in junior in 1989–90. In the second round, the Leafs hoped to address the team's goaltending. While the team had some degree of confidence in its current netminders, the Leafs never-theless chose Félix Potvin with their second selection. GM Floyd Smith and Doug Carpenter, however, had already decided to go into the new campaign with Allan Bester and Jeff Reese as their goaltending tandem. By the end of training camp, three rookies had cracked the lineup: Berehowsky, Rob Pearson, and Scott Thornton. This young trio complemented a side that was riding high on the modest success of the previous season and was looking forward to positive change in the wake of Ballard's passing.

It was this confident Leaf team that rolled into Winnipeg for the opening night of the 1990–91 season. It left with its tail between its legs after being thrashed by the Jets, 7–1. The next two matches didn't go much better, as the Leafs dropped games to Calgary and Edmonton.

After three losses on the road, the Maple Leafs returned to Toronto for the home opener against the Quebec Nordiques. That night, four heroes of the Leafs' first Stanley Cup championship performed the ceremo-nial faceoff: Ace Bailey, Harold Darragh, Frank Finnigan, and Red Horner. Horner, who had been the NHL's penalty leader for eight consecutive seasons, said, "I just don't want to get carried away when I see those enemy sweaters. I might feel like dropping the man instead of the puck!" It was hoped that rubbing elbows with the 1932 champions might change the team's luck a little. It didn't – Quebec beat Toronto, 8–5.

To say it was an inauspicious start was an understate-ment; Toronto had won just once and tied one other in the first ten games. Floyd Smith had seen enough: "It's an embarrassment. These are supposedly professionals, so they have to act like professionals and perform." But, as is so often the case, the first to fall was the team's coach. On October 25, Doug Carpenter was relieved of his duties. In his place, Tom Watt stepped in as the Leafs' interim coach, and the three executives who succeeded Ballard – Donald Crump, Don Giffin, and Steve Stavro – called Floyd Smith to discuss what could be done to turn the team around. Yet the losses continued to mount. The Leafs went winless in their first six games in November.

And then the changes commenced. In early November, the Leafs returned Drake Berehowsky to junior (he would be named Canadian major junior defenceman of the year in 1992) and traded John McIntyre to Los Angeles for Mike Krushelnyski. Joe Sacco and Doug Shedden were summoned from Newmarket, and a day later, while in the delivery room waiting for his wife to give birth, Ed Olczyk learned that he and Mark Osborne were headed to Winnipeg for Dave Ellett and Paul Fenton. While the Leafs would miss Olczyk and Osborne's production, they had added a strong defence-man with puck-moving skill in Ellett and a defensive forward in Fenton.

On November 17, Scott Pearson and two draft picks were sent to the Nordiques for Aaron Broten, Lucien DeBlois, and Michel Petit. With Ellett and Petit, the Maple Leafs now had two proven NHL defencemen to shore up the blueline. Smith pulled off another trade, sending Lou Franceschetti and Brian Curran to Buffalo on December 17 for Mike Foligno and a late draft pick. In time, Foligno would prove to be a fireplug for the Leafs and, given his inimitable goal celebration – the so-called Foligno Leap – the forward became a fan favourite. Finally, Allan Bester was sent down to Newmarket and would later be dealt to Detroit for a sixth-round draft pick.

Peter Ing (pictured) debuted in goal with the Toronto Maple Leafs in 1989–90. The team struggled in front of Ing in 1990–91, yet he was the team's Molson Cup recipient for his three-star selections. In September 1991, Ing was part of a package that sent Vincent Damphousse, Luke Richardson, and Scott Thornton to Edmonton for Glenn Anderson, Craig Berube, and Grant Fuhr.

The changes helped to reverse the trend of the previous two months. In December, Toronto won seven, lost five, and tied one. Despite the improvement, however, the team often looked disorganized. And, once again, off-ice disorder shadowed the team's performance.

Al Iafrate was struggling. Along with a serious knee injury, he and new coach Tom Watt simply didn't get along. Iafrate didn't hide his chagrin in a *Sports Illustrated* interview: "They wanted me to get the puck and flip it out to the forwards. Man, you want somebody to flip it out, get some guy who's happy just to be in the league. I've got too much to offer." Everyone agreed, including Iafrate, that a change of scenery would be mutually beneficial. On January 16, Iafrate was sent to the Washington Capitals in return for Bob Rouse and Peter Zezel.

While Iafrate was happy to be getting out of town, Toronto native Zezel was delighted to be coming home: "It's really been in the back of my mind that I'd like to play at home. I'm glad I'm finally going to get the chance." The Leafs now had an expert faceoff man in Zezel and a solid defenceman in Bob Rouse. And Washington also became the new home for John Kordic. On January 24, they shipped him and Paul Fenton to the Capitals in return for a fifth-round pick.

While these additions were certainly positive, January was very much a negative month for Toronto. During this dreariest of months, the Leafs recorded only one win against six losses and four ties. In fact, that solitary win didn't come until January 28, when goalie Peter Ing recorded a 4–0 shutout win over the North Stars. It was the first Leaf shutout in two years.

With all of the changes, some players were now expendable. Brad Marsh, for instance, had appeared in just two of the previous 32 games. On February 4, he was dealt to Detroit. Marsh was devastated. "From the first day I came to Toronto, I've enjoyed every minute of my time here," he said through tears.

With the many adjustments, the Maple Leafs were now a vastly different-looking team. Yet, while their record had slowly improved under Tom Watt, the end of the season could not arrive quickly enough for many of the players and the fans. The post-Ballard team had actually dropped from a promising 80-point season in 1989–90 to a dismal 57-point finish in 1990–91 – last place in the Norris Division and second-worst in the league.

The team's goal scoring had evaporated. Only Vincent Damphousse (26) and Daniel Marois (21) surpassed the 20-goal plateau. The injured Gary Leeman's production dropped from 51 goals to 17. Goaltending was likewise inconsistent; the Leafs had the second-highest goals-against total in the NHL. While Carpenter was sure of the Bester–Reese tandem at the beginning of the season, the team had called upon 21-year-old rookie Peter Ing more often than not. For his sweat, Ing was named the season's Molson Cup winner for his three-star selections.

It had, in the end, been a season of transition. Question marks surrounding the ownership of the team, the coaching change, off-ice distractions, and ten trades involving 24 players (not including draft choices) had made success implausible. Forty-seven different players – including four different goalies – played at least one game for the Blue and White. As the *Toronto Star* eulogized: "This year, more than any other, the sacred covenant between team and fans was broken. The rot at the top made riveting drama but lousy hockey."

Despite the "rot at the top," the Leafs now possessed a core of players who would feature in the team's post-Ballard renaissance. But one player would not be part of the revival of fortunes.

In 1990, the owners of the Minnesota North Stars had sought to move their team to the San Francisco Bay Area. The league offered a counter-proposal: they would sell the financially troubled Stars and receive a California-based expansion team, the San Jose Sharks. The Sharks would then be entitled to take some of Minnesota's players with them, and to round out both rosters, the two teams took part in an expansion draft on May 30, 1991. The Leafs left team captain Rob Ramage unprotected in the draft, and the Minnesota North Stars scooped him up.

THE SILVER FOX

The battle over who would own Maple Leaf Gardens Ltd. heated up in 1991. The triumvirate of executors had been tasked with finding a party to purchase the legendary franchise. Meanwhile, the board of directors had mandated Don Giffin to hire someone to head the organization. There were, predictably, vastly different ideas about how the franchise should proceed. Giffin, for instance, wanted to keep Floyd Smith as the general manager and add a veteran to oversee the hockey operation. Steve Stavro, on the other hand, was eager to remove Smith and bring in an experienced businessperson to run the Gardens and a hockey person to run the team. For the former role, he nominated Lyman MacInnis, president of the John Labatt Entertainment Group, which oversaw the Toronto Blue Jays baseball team, the cable sports channel TSN, and a stake in a concert promotions business, among

other properties. He had also been the force behind Anne Murray's earlier bid to buy the Maple Leafs.

Meanwhile, Floyd Smith put forward the name of Cliff Fletcher. The incumbent GM was under no illusions as to what that meant for his own job: "I knew it would probably cost me my job, but I recommended very strongly that they hire Cliff Fletcher to run the show. I felt that, for the good of the organization, it was important that Cliff join us."

MacInnis was quoted as saying that, while he thought Fletcher would make a fine general manager, he lacked the experience to run a publicly traded corporation. But the idea appealed to the board of directors. With Steve Stavro casting the lone dissenting vote, Fletcher was signed to a five-year contract as chief operating officer and president of Maple Leaf Gardens, and general manager of the Leafs. Smith was shuffled back to the scouting department. Giffin stepped aside as president and became chair of the Gardens board.

Fletcher carried a sterling resumé. He had scouted for the Montreal Canadiens in the 1950s and joined the

expansion St. Louis Blues as a scout in 1966, working his way up to the office of assistant GM. The Blues advanced to the Stanley Cup final in each of their first three years. In 1972, Fletcher was hired by the expansion Atlanta Flames to be their general manager, and he moved with the franchise to Calgary in 1980. Through the next decade, Fletcher oversaw the Flames as they claimed two Smythe Division titles, twice led the NHL in points, and won a Stanley Cup in 1989.

Fletcher's first order of business was to announce that Tom Watt had been retained as head coach, assisted by Mike Murphy. He also began to repair the relationship between the franchise and the Maple Leafs alumni, which had been severely damaged during the Ballard era. To start, Fletcher contacted former Leafs captain Darryl Sittler and offered him a position as a special consultant to the Maple Leafs. Sittler agreed.

"I'd been out of hockey for a bit," he said. "I would love to have finished my career in Toronto, but obviously it didn't work, but Cliff's call was a very meaningful moment for me."

In 1991, Toronto acquired veteran Glenn Anderson from the Oilers, where he had been a key part of five Stanley Cup championships. Anderson marked back-to-back 20-goal seasons before he was dealt to the New York Rangers at the trade deadline in 1993–94.

Sittler has been with the organization ever since.

Preparations for the 1991–92 season began almost immediately in what would prove to be a busy summer. In the NHL Entry Draft, the Leafs picked up forward Yanic Perreault in the third round and defenceman Dmitri Mironov in the eighth. With Ramage gone, the Maple Leafs needed to anoint a new on-ice leader, and the choice surprised virtually no one: from his rookie season, it seemed almost preordained that Wendel Clark would one day captain the Toronto Maple Leafs.

Fletcher realized that the team needed to address the seemingly intractable issue of goaltending. After Grant Fuhr played in just 13 games for the Oilers in 1990–91, Fletcher believed that he could wrangle the veteran goalie out of Edmonton. Talks with Oilers general manager Glen Sather continued throughout the summer, and finally, on September 19, a seven-player deal was announced that saw Fuhr and fellow Oilers Glenn Anderson and Craig Berube brought to Toronto in exchange for Peter Ing, Vincent Damphousse, Luke Richardson, and Scott Thornton. Fletcher believed the team now had a cornerstone in goal.

While Fletcher rolled up his sleeves and renovated the roster, the protracted power struggle for ownership of the club reached a conclusion.

Ballard's death had triggered a flurry of boardroom and courtroom machinations. The owner's oldest child, Bill, had been fighting for control of the shares in HEB Ltd. that Harold had bought from his other son, Harold Jr. By September 1991, Bill had given up pursuing his case and agreed to sell his own HEB shares to the Ballard estate for $21 million. But Bill, a successful concert promoter who held a law degree from Osgoode Hall in Toronto, was engaged in a legal battle with Steve Stavro on another front.

To acquire control of HEB, and thus consolidate his control over the Gardens, Harold Ballard had borrowed $20 million from Molson's in 1989. And in November 1990, Molson exercised its option to buy 19.9 per cent of the Gardens, giving the company an ownership stake in two NHL franchises – putting them afoul of league bylaws. Molson wasn't particularly interested in owning the team; it aimed to protect its sponsorship rights and prevent the team from being sold to a rival such as Labatt's. The brewery wanted to sell its shares to a "friendly third party," while having its loan repaid.

Stavro came forward with an offer to pay off the Molson loan. Bill charged that Stavro – who was both an executor of Harold's estate and a Gardens board member – was in a conflict of interest when he voted on his own proposal. A judge found there was no conflict, a ruling supported by an appeal court. Stavro paid off the Molson loan, in return for which he received an option to buy the 60 per cent of Maple Leaf Gardens controlled by Ballard's estate. He also negotiated a deal with Molson's, giving him until April 1994 to acquire the brewery's stock.

Many legal hurdles remained to be cleared before Stavro, with the financial support of the Toronto Dominion Bank and the Ontario Teachers' Pension Plan, actually purchased Maple Leaf Gardens, but for the time being he had established his control over the operation. In October, he was named chief executive office and chair of the board of Maple Leaf Gardens.

Finally, it was time to raise the curtain on a new season. The Leafs were edged, 4–3, by the Canadiens in the season opener at the Montreal Forum, before returning to the Gardens to battled Detroit in the home opener. While the Leafs lost, 8–5, the new captain scored three goals and added two assists. Coach Tom Watt's defensive system was hardly in evidence: Grant Fuhr faced 50 shots in the loss. However, he bounced back in the next game as the Leafs shut out the St. Louis Blues, 3–0. The Leafs' joy was tempered by the fact that Wendel Clark collided with Ron Sutter, injuring his knee. The captain was out of action for ten games.

The Leafs then dropped seven games in a row. During that stretch, Todd Gill broke his hand against the Flames. No sooner had Clark returned than he reinjured his knee. Grant Fuhr was also injured, and his backup, Jeff Reese, had the flu, so the Leafs parachuted in unproven Félix Potvin from the St. John's Maple Leafs, Toronto's AHL affiliate. The Leafs lost to Chicago, 4–0, on November 14, but the *Toronto Star* remarked that Potvin had shown an "impressive stand-up style, quick feet and a Venus flytrap for a catching hand."

Still, the injuries mounted, thwarting any momentum the team was trying to develop. Energetic Mike Foligno, for example, was lost to the team for the season after breaking his leg in two places in a game against Winnipeg on December 23. While there were moments of solid play, the Leafs plodded along through the end of the calendar year.

The situation became dire when the Pittsburgh Penguins embarrassed the Leafs on Boxing Day by a 12–1 score, the largest margin of defeat in the history of the Toronto franchise. Tom Watt grieved, "All I could think of was Murphy's Law. Everything that could go wrong did go wrong." They had truly bottomed out.

Meanwhile, in western Canada, another drama was unfolding. On New Year's Day, Doug Gilmour walked out on the Calgary Flames in protest over his contract.

Félix "The Cat" Potvin joined the Maple Leafs full-time in 1992–93, and his 2.56 goals-against average was the best in the NHL as he backstopped the team to the conference final. He enjoyed a career-best season in 1993–94 with 34 wins, and again took the Leafs to the conference final.

On December 9, he had asked for a trade, but Doug Risebrough, Calgary's general manager, dragged his feet. Gilmour, who had collected 38 points in 38 games with the Flames, decided to force his hand by leaving the team. The move hastened a trade for a player who would change the trajectory of two franchises.

On January 2, 1992, in the largest NHL trade ever made, the Calgary Flames sent Gilmour, Jamie Macoun, Kent Manderville, Ric Nattress, and Rick Wamsley to Toronto for Gary Leeman, Craig Berube, Alex Godynyuk, Michel Petit, and Jeff Reese. New Leaf Macoun found out in dramatic fashion:

> I was in the hospital with my wife. We had just given birth to our first child and I had shown up to take her home. The nurse said, "You're to call the Flames office." This was 7:30 in the morning. I got it figured out right away; no one's in the office at that time unless there's something up. An hour later, the nurse came in again and said, "You're supposed to call the Flames office." I said, "I got it." She was confused, and I had to explain to her that I had just been traded somewhere. She said, "They would not do that. You just had a child!" It wasn't until 9:00 A.M. when Doug Gilmour's wife, Robyne, called me at the hospital and was screaming, "We're all traded! We're all going to Toronto!" I asked, "Who's 'we?' What's going on?" I couldn't believe it!

The Maple Leafs' top brass was, of course, quite familiar with the players headed Toronto's way. As the former GM of the Flames and mentor to Doug Risebrough, Cliff Fletcher knew exactly the quality of players that the Leafs had just acquired. Likewise, Toronto coach Tom Watt had been an assistant coach with the Flames in 1989 before joining the Maple Leafs, and was himself aware of what the team had just scored. And, as history would prove, it really was a score.

Only two weeks after the trade, the team really began to gel. Gilmour was at the height of his career and everyone at Maple Leaf Gardens could see how special he was. There was other on-ice excitement, too. On February 8, with the score tied, 2–2, early in the third against Montreal, Guy Larose scored his second goal of the game and the Leafs went on to win, 6–4. Toronto had found a new fan favourite. The winger hustled and hit, and when he showed his exuberance, the fans chanted "Guy! Guy!" as though he was the reincarnation of Lafleur. In a 4–3 win over Detroit on February 22, he scored two more goals, and again, the hometown crowd chanted his name.

The Leafs were energized. Still, Cliff Fletcher continued to make trades to improve his team. He reacquired Mark Osborne from Winnipeg for Lucien DeBlois, picked up Ken Baumgartner and Dave McLlwain from the New York Islanders for Clause Loiselle and Daniel Marois, and inserted Dmitri Mironov from Krylya Sovetov into the lineup to finish the season.

The Maple Leafs chased a playoff berth through the last half of the season, but during the final stretch, the league shut down for a strike initiated by the National Hockey League Players' Association against the NHL's owners. The strike began on April 1 and lasted ten days. The settlement saw the players earn an increase in playoff bonuses, increased control over the licensing of their likenesses, and changes to the free-agency system. Games lost to the strike were rescheduled, and in the first of these, the Maple Leafs were eliminated from the playoffs after a 6–2 loss to the Islanders. In the final game played at home, a 4–2 win over the Rangers, the Leafs received a standing ovation from the fans at Maple Leaf Gardens. It had, in the end, been a losing season, but Leafs Nation had seen the franchise turn a corner and they began – for the first time in a long time – to consider the possibility of "winning" anew.

Before the Gilmour trade, the Leafs had a record of 10 wins, 25 losses, and 5 ties and had scored just 103 goals. The massive trade breathed new life into the team: it won 20, lost 18, and tied 2, scoring 139 times. Unfortunately, there was no recovering from the miserable start to the season: the Leafs finished last in the Norris Division. Unlike in recent times, though, the city was alive with optimism for its team.

The Leafs were confident with future Hall of Famer Grant Fuhr in goal. Dave Ellett, Todd Gill, Jamie Macoun, and Bob Rouse provided the Leafs with a stable defence. Glenn Anderson led the team in scoring with 24 goals and 57 points; Wendel Clark, in an injury-abbreviated season, scored 19 goals and 40 points in 43 games; and Doug Gilmour lit up the offence with 49 points in his 40 games with Toronto. Cliff Fletcher, the Silver Fox, had given the team and its legion of fans a sense of direction. Even the most cynical observers were now wondering whether the Maple Leafs might only be a player or two away from making a run at the Stanley Cup.

KILLER

In the space of less than three years, the Toronto Maple Leafs organization had changed its ownership, its general manager, and its coach. Only three players remained from that pre-Fletcher era: Wendel Clark, Todd Gill, and the little-used Darryl Shannon. Fletcher's additions had helped the Leafs attain a degree of respectability after a decade of struggle, and he followed this command performance by pulling yet another rabbit out of his hat: he somehow managed to score arguably the best coach in hockey when Pat Burns resigned as coach of the Montreal Canadiens to accept the same position with the Toronto Maple Leafs. With the Habs, Burns had enjoyed four winning seasons, a Stanley Cup final appearance, and the Jack Adams Trophy as the league's best coach in 1989.

Yet the GM wasn't finished tinkering with his team. The Leafs brought back Bob McGill from Tampa and added defenceman Sylvain Lefebvre from the Canadiens. Lefebvre was well versed in Pat Burns's system. The Leafs also added Nikolai Borschevsky, who had nine seasons of elite-level Russian experience under his belt by the time he arrived in Toronto. All of these players would add important elements to the new mix.

The Leafs were at home to the Capitals for the 1992–93 season opener. Olympic gold medalists Marnie McBean and Mark McKoy were on hand to drop the puck for the ceremonial opening faceoff. With Grant Fuhr in goal, Toronto was edged, 6–5, by Washington.

It did not take long before the team felt the wrath of their new coach. After another loss, Burns tore a strip off of the players. It was a highly animated scenario that the boys would witness on several occasions throughout the campaign. "Pat was almost like an actor," Gilmour remembered. "He had played all these different roles in his own life. He'd been a cop, and he had a certain intuition about people. He could be the tough guy and the funny guy and the serious guy and the emotional guy." Burns would use various methods to get his point across.

"Burns had a stare he reserved for players that weren't playing up to standard," Todd Gill recalled. "When you were sitting on the bench, you knew if he was looking at you. You could feel it. He stared right at you until you turned your head away. Sometimes, there was no need for words."

Whichever method he chose, Burns affected change on the Leafs roster. But so, too, did injuries. Grant Fuhr sprained his knee in a late-October practice, and Rick Wamsley suffered a leg injury during the preseason. So with little recourse, Burns inserted Félix Potvin into the crease. Leafs management would have preferred to see Potvin spend another season in the minors, but when he stepped into the net for Toronto, the youngster was terrific. Nicknamed "The Cat," Félix thrived in the role of number-one goalie.

The Leafs plodded along at a pace just under .500. In an attempt to add some offence, Cliff Fletcher picked up John Cullen from the Hartford Whalers in November. Cullen, whose father Barry and uncle Brian had played with Toronto in the 1950s, had been a 30-goal scorer in Pittsburgh, but Hartford fans never warmed to him because he had arrived from the Penguins in a trade for Ron Francis, one of the most popular Whalers of all time. The GM also acquired Bill Berg on waivers from the New York Islanders on December 3. Although Burns famously quipped that he wouldn't know Berg if he ran over him with his truck, the winger would add important dimension to the Leafs squad.

And then, in the new year, Fletcher pulled off another blockbuster. When Grant Fuhr returned, Félix Potvin was reassigned to St. John's of the AHL. He would not be in Newfoundland long – a Chris Chelios shot to Fuhr's collarbone in a game against the Blackhawks on January 19 knocked the veteran out of action again. Potvin's play convinced Fletcher and Burns that they could rely on his solid goaltending for the rest of the season. On the strength of this conviction, Fuhr was sent to the Buffalo Sabres for Dave Andreychuk, Daren Puppa, and a draft choice on February 2, 1993. Given that the Leafs were deep in goal and in need of more scoring, it was a prudent trade. As the GM admitted, "It was very hard to trade Grant, who I believe is still the best goalie in the world. It was a case between a 31-year-old and a 21-year-old, and it was a tough decision to make."

Andreychuk, a big, dominant force who was all but immovable once he planted himself on the lip of a crease, had already scored 29 goals as a Sabre that season. The Leafs had found someone to play with Gilmour. Andreychuk paid immediate dividends, scoring 12 goals in his first 13 games as a Leaf.

February 13 was a particularly good night. Gilmour assisted on all six goals in a 6–1 victory over the Minnesota North Stars, tying a franchise record set by Babe Pratt during the 1943–44 season. It was just the first of several club records Gilmour would equal or break that season. Nine days later, he broke Darryl Sittler's franchise record for assists in a season when he contributed three helpers in an 8–1 humiliation of the Vancouver Canucks. The Andreychuk–Gilmour combination was proving to be unrelenting against opponents.

In that very same game, Glenn Anderson picked up a goal and two assists, which meant he had reached the 1,000-point plateau. Anderson recalled:

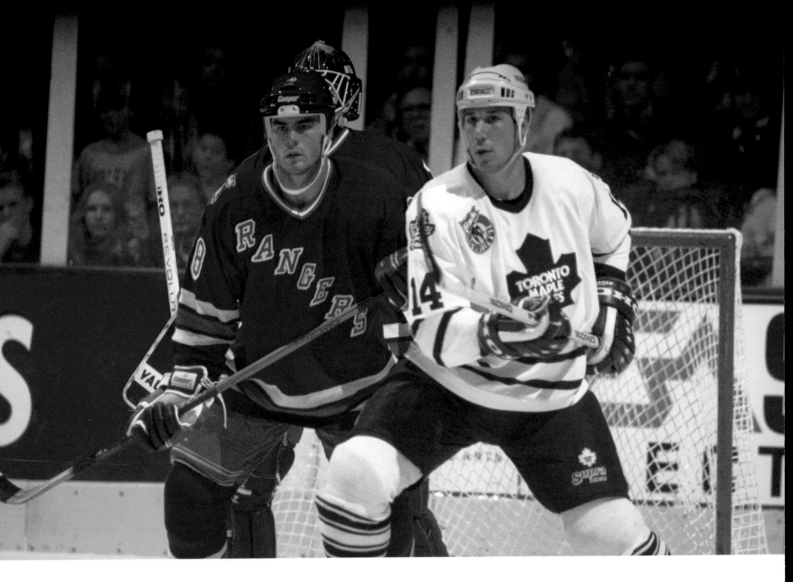

Part of a trade that saw Grant Fuhr move to Buffalo, Dave Andreychuk (pictured here in 1993, playing in the two-game French's Cup exhibition series at Wembley Arena, London, UK) joined the Maple Leafs in 1992–93, and completed the season with 54 goals. He scored 53 in 1993–94, his first full season with Toronto.

It was late in the third period when I ended up scoring my goal. I had two assists earlier, so it was my 1,000th point. The guys came onto the ice to congratulate me, and Denis Morel, the ref, ended up giving the team a penalty for delay of game! When Gretz got his goal against Edmonton [for his record-breaking 1,851st point], they rolled out the red carpet, the family came out to congratulate him, and the game was stopped for 20 minutes. But when I got my 1,000th point, we got a delay-of-game penalty and I ended up serving the penalty!

Anderson was just the second player to reach the 1,000-point plateau in a Leaf uniform, although most of his points had been collected as a member of the Edmonton Oilers.

Apart from all of the notable individual performances, the team had made an incredible stride forward, finishing with 99 points; a stunning 32-point increase from the previous season. With 44 wins (a club record), 29 losses, and 11 ties, the Leafs finished third in the Norris Division.

The turnaround had been the result of a full team effort, including behind the bench – Burns was awarded his second Jack Adams Trophy as coach of the year. On the ice, the best players led the pack but were supported by strong secondary scoring, outstanding goaltending, and a very effective checking line of Bill Berg, Mark Osborne, and Peter Zezel that hounded opponents to distraction. Félix Potvin had the league's best goals-against average (2.50) and finished third in Calder Trophy voting as rookie of the year and fourth in Vézina as the NHL's best goaltender. Nikolai Borschevsky led the Leafs in goals with 34, while Dave Andreychuk had 25 as a Leaf (54 when combined with the goals he scored as a Sabre).

And then there was Killer. With 127 points, Doug Gilmour had bested Darryl Sittler's 1977–78 mark of 117, setting a new record for points in a single season by a Toronto Maple Leaf. Gilmour was the league's eighth-highest scorer, while his 95 assists stood second only to Adam Oates's 97. So sterling was Gilmour's two-way play that he was awarded the Frank Selke Trophy as the NHL's best defensive forward, and would be runner-up to Mario Lemieux for the Hart Trophy as the league's most valuable player. With a team led by Gilmour, Leafs Nation was able to forget the challenges experienced by the team in the 1980s.

The Leafs faced the Detroit Red Wings in the opening round of the playoffs. Detroit had finished four points ahead of Toronto in the Norris Division. Toronto looked nervous and pensive in Game One. This was reflected on the scoreboard as the Red Wings, with a four-goal second period, hammered the Leafs, 6–3. Toronto also lost Borschevsky after the forward suffered a fractured orbital bone below his right eye in the third period.

The Red Wings dominated again in Game Two, blasting the Leafs, 6–2. Cliff Fletcher met with the media and admitted, "Detroit is a very talented team, and the way to beat talented teams is to outwork them. That didn't happen for us in the first two games." It seemed that the quasi-fairy-tale season was going to end abruptly.

The Red Wings' strategy had been simple: Sergei Fedorov blanketed Gilmour, while the fans at the Joe tried to neutralize Wendel Clark with never-ending derisive chants of "Wendy! Wendy!" As Nick Kypreos explained, "You can watch it from the outside as a kid growing up or you can live it every day as a fan, but until you're in that fishbowl, you'll never understand how truly difficult at times it can be on you."

Game Three at Maple Leaf Gardens provided just the tonic the team needed. The Leafs showed great self-restraint and did not allow Dino Ciccarelli and Bob Probert to distract them. This, coupled with superb goaltending from Potvin, allowed Toronto to bounce back with a 4–2 win. Appropriately, Wendel Clark scored the winner when he jabbed a loose puck under Detroit goaltender Tim Cheveldae.

Game Four was a tight affair. The teams got two goals each in the second period, but the lone goal of the third, by Dave Andreychuk, proved to be the winner.

To this point, the home team had taken all four of the games. This did not bode well for Toronto, who now headed to Detroit for Game Five. In fact, the Leafs were down 4–1 midway through the second period, but fought all the way back to tie it at four and send the game into overtime. Then, at 2:05 of extra time, Mike Foligno's wrist shot found the net behind Cheveldae for the game winner. The forward's trademark leap signified that the Leafs had taken the lead in the best-of-seven series.

The Red Wings, however, refused to roll over. They returned to Toronto looking for vengeance in Game Six and got it, scoring five goals in the second period – three

power-play tallies and two shorthanded goals – before Burns yanked Potvin and inserted Daren Puppa to finish the game. The final result was a 7–3 pummelling.

The medical staff surprised the Maple Leafs by giving Nikolai Borschevsky the green light to return to action for Game Seven in Detroit after he suffered what many feared was a season-ending facial injury earlier.

The game was, in every sense, a nail-biter. The teams exchanged goals in the first period before Bob Rouse gave the Leafs the lead in the second. Detroit responded with two of their own to take a 3–2 lead. Wendel Clark, with less than three minutes left in the third, fed a pass to Doug Gilmour, who made no mistake, putting the puck past Cheveldae to tie the game at 3–3. The suspense was impossibly high.

And then there was overtime. At 2:35 of the extra frame, Bob Rouse fired a shot from the point that was redirected past Cheveldae by Borschevsky. With his goal, the unlikely hero had eliminated the Red Wings and given Leafs Nation its happiest moment in 15 years. Borschevsky – to the best of his ability – recalled the moment: "Good play by Rouse. Very good. I score. Big goal. Big for team. Happy."

On the bench, equipment manager Brian Papineau sprayed a water bottle in celebration when he saw Borschevsky's tip-in ignite the goal light:

You're the underdog again, in some ways, and that was probably a good spot for us to be in . . . Guys like Zezel, Osborne, and Berg were hitting everything in sight, wearing down their defence. You could see the momentum change going into the third period. We were playing well and luckily tied the game. We almost won it late in the third period. The puck was sitting on the goal line. Then, it was just that magical moment of Borschevsky scoring, and the rest is history.

While the Maple Leafs celebrated wildly at the Joe, back in Toronto, Yonge Street between Lake Shore Boulevard and Bloor Street was brought to a standstill by a parade of cars filled with Leafs fans growing hoarse through screaming. The scene echoed one a few months earlier, when the Blue Jays won their first World Series. Toronto was once again electrified. The *Globe and Mail* headline put it succinctly: WINNING GOAL LIFTED SHADOW OF BALLARD ERA.

Next up was a series against the St. Louis Blues, who had finished fourth in the Norris, 14 points behind the Leafs, so Coach Burns could no longer play the underdog card. But in truth, St. Louis was not to be taken lightly. Curtis Joseph – "Cujo" – had been outstanding in goal, and Brett Hull and Brendan Shanahan had both scored more than 50 goals that season.

Toronto was warm in early May 1993, and within Maple Leaf Gardens it was sweltering. No one sweated more than Doug Gilmour and Curtis Joseph. The Leafs would fire 64 shots at the Blues goal in Game One, yet remarkably, the game was tied, 1–1, at the end of 60 minutes. The first overtime period solved nothing. In the second, Gilmour found himself behind the St. Louis net with the puck, while Dave Andreychuk and Nik Borschevsky positioned themselves in front, jostled by three Blues. Gilmour flitted back and forth behind the net, manoeuvring, desperately trying to find an opportunity. In reality, no more than five seconds passed, but it felt like an eternity for Leafs fans. Gilmour started to come out one side, then reversed to go out the other. Finally, the opportunity came. With Joseph pinned to the far post, Gilmour darted back again and stuffed the puck inside the post behind Joseph. The Leafs had taken Game One. The celebration was long and loud. The hero, as he had been so many times before, was Number 93.

Gilmour had played an exhausting 41 minutes in the 2–1 victory. Though gaunt with blackened eyes, the Leaf simply never seemed to tire. The forward shared his secret: "It's emotion that keeps you going at this time of year. The adrenaline is flowing; everyone is excited. You don't think about being tired. I just want to be an impact player. That's what I'm thriving on right now. I didn't get that chance in Calgary, but I am here. It's exciting! It's rejuvenated my career."

Killer and the Leafs were riding high.

Toronto blitzed Joseph again in Game Two, launching 58 shots. But this time it was the Blues who capitalized in double overtime. At 3:03 of the second extra frame, Potvin blocked a first shot, but Jeff Brown pounced on the rebound and fired it high into the Leafs goal for the win.

In front of the hometown fans, the Blues' Garth Butcher scored the goal that captured a 4–3 victory in Game Three. Despite the dizzy heights the Leafs had recently scaled with the dramatic Borschevsky and Gilmour goals, St. Louis was now leading the series by a game.

The gutsy Leafs fought back with a 4–1 win in Game Four, and were able to take that momentum home for Game Five. Back at Maple Leaf Gardens, the Leafs took a three-games-to-two lead on the strength of a 5–1 win. Now, the Leafs were one win away from reaching the Campbell Conference final.

While Dave Andreychuk struck early in Game Six, Curtis Joseph stymied Toronto the rest of the way. Behind a strong checking game, the Blues emerged with a 2–1 win to knot the series at three games apiece. For the second series in a row, the Leafs were headed to a Game Seven.

There would, however, be little to worry about back in Toronto. It was a cakewalk. In fact, the party began before the second period had concluded. The Maple Leafs blanked the Blues, 6–0. For the first time in 15 years, Toronto was set to appear in the third round of the playoffs.

The conference final against the Los Angeles Kings offered a number of storylines. Wayne Gretzky, now in his fifth season on the West Coast after a trade from Edmonton that rocked a nation, was being heralded as the saviour of Californian hockey. Wendel Clark and ex-Leaf Barry Melrose, who was now coaching the Kings, were cousins who had played hockey together as kids growing up in Kelvington, Saskatchewan.

Doug Gilmour enjoyed another spectacular outing in the opener, played at Maple Leaf Gardens. Double-shifted throughout the game, he singlehandedly dismantled the Kings with two goals and two assists, and for good measure laid a huge hit on Alexei Zhitnik. With Toronto leading, 4–1, in the third – outshooting Los Angeles, 22–1, in the period, and with the Kings shorthanded – all hell broke loose. Gilmour dropped a pass as he cut across the Kings blueline and was sent sprawling by an elbow from Marty McSorley. To Gilmour's rescue came Wendel Clark, who saw his teammate on the ice and immediately engaged McSorley in battle. As Kings coach Barry Melrose recalled, "Maple Leaf Gardens went crazy, like it was the days of the Roman gladiators."

A slightly dazed Gilmour staggered to his feet and went straight to the opposing bench, challenging all comers. Meanwhile, Pat Burns shook his finger at the cocky Kings coach, who infuriated him. "Pat was a little chunky, so I looked at him and inflated my cheeks like a blowfish," Melrose revealed. "He went really crazy after that!" Burns tried to reach the Kings coach and had to be restrained. The rising tempers set the tone for the rest of the series.

It seemed as though the Maple Leafs had lost their fight in Game Two. Los Angeles scored the winning goal with less than eight minutes to play. Burns was furious with the way his team played during the 3–2 Kings win: "We all seemed to sit back and wait for the Doug Gilmour Show. Just too many guys riding the bus tonight."

In Game Three, with a crowd of Hollywood stars looking on, the Kings prevailed. Two shorthanded goals by the home team sank the Leafs, 4–2. The score was identical in Game Four, except that it was Toronto who came out on top to tie the series.

Back in Toronto, the Kings dominated the Leafs for most of Game Five. Somehow, though, the Leafs forced overtime. Glenn Anderson became the hero, batting a bouncing puck past Kings goalie Kelly Hrudey to give his team a 3–2 victory. "I didn't know whether to take it and control it or just shoot," Anderson said. "My final thought was to just shoot it. There wasn't much time left and anything can happen." With the Leafs up three games to two, the teams once again made the long trip back to California.

Little separated the two teams in Game Six. The game, tied at 4–4, was heading to overtime when "it" happened: one of the most controversial moments in franchise history. With just 13 seconds remaining in regulation time, referee Kerry Fraser called Leafs winger Glenn Anderson for boarding. It was a fair call. What happened next – or perhaps, what *didn't* happen – was not. Anderson's penalty meant that the Kings were on the power play to start the extra frame. Just 39 seconds into overtime, Wayne Gretzky's stick caught Doug Gilmour under the chin, opening a wound that would require eight stitches to close. Leafs Nation expected Fraser to call a penalty. The referee conferred with his linesmen, and after a protracted debate, he decided that none of the officials could definitively say it had been Gretzky's stick that cut Gilmour. When no penalty was called, Leafs fans were outraged.

Fraser later expressed regret over the affair: "I worked 2,165 NHL games and that probably was my worst moment. I was blocked out and didn't see the play." Regardless, approximately one minute later, Gretzky scored to give Los Angeles a 5–4 victory. The win forced Game Seven to be held two nights later in Toronto.

The Maple Leafs simply had to find a way to move past the heartbreak of Game Six. They were, after all, just one game away from a first Stanley Cup final appearance in 26 years. Additionally, the Montreal Canadiens had defeated the New York Islanders in the Wales Conference final. If the Leafs won, it could be 1967 all over again.

Game Seven was an accurate representation of the series, in that the teams were very evenly matched. Late in the third period, Toronto and Los Angeles were deadlocked, 3–3. Wendel Clark had been sensational for the Leafs, scoring twice. Hopes were high in Leafs Nation. And then the bottom fell out. The Kings scored two goals within 37 seconds, the second of which caromed off of Dave Ellett's skate and into the net behind Potvin. The defenceman made restitution, bringing the Leafs

to within a goal with 1:07 to go. Yet despite a flurry of chances, the Kings were able to hold on for the 5–4 win.

There would be no Leafs–Habs Stanley Cup final rematch. Wayne Gretzky had killed the fairy tale. Gretzky's hat trick, plus an assist, ended the Maple Leafs' fantastic postseason run. Despite the countless brilliant games the Great One played in, Game Seven against the Leafs stood out for him: "I've taken the roses and I've taken the heat, but tonight, I stood up and answered the bell. [It's] the greatest game I ever played."

Leafs Nation was gutted. Still, the franchise had enjoyed its brightest hour in years, generating a sense of euphoria while it lasted. The mood was not lost on Cliff Fletcher: "That was the most electric I've seen any city in my long NHL career. The team came a long way in its development. The commitment was there from the start. I'm just so proud of them. We've restored credibility and pride to the franchise. We can build on this."

The 1993 playoffs rekindled the interest of an older generation of Leafs fans, while winning over a completely new one. More important, the team itself had found its own spirit. When he reflected on the accomplishments of his team that season, Pat Burns was duly gratified: "They loved each other on this team. Everybody was family. It was amazing. I've never been prouder of a team in my career!"

ENCORE

Leafs Nation had a summer of asking, "What if?" What if Fraser had made the call on Gretzky? What if the Leafs had gone on to meet the Canadiens – would they have fared better than the Kings, who bowed out to Montreal in five games? These were compelling questions, but perhaps the most compelling question was "What now?"

The Maple Leafs had two first-round selections in the NHL Entry Draft, with which they selected Kenny Jonsson and Landon Wilson. There was, otherwise, very little tweaking up and down the roster, and it was with roughly the same team that the Leafs began their 1993–94 season at home against Dallas. And it was as if the team's stars simply picked up where they had left off in May: Dave Andreychuk scored twice, Doug Gilmour collected three assists, Wendel Clark banged into everything in sight, and Félix Potvin played a strong, confident game. The Leafs dropped the Stars, 6–3. Opening night was followed up with wins against the Blackhawks at home and the Flyers in Philadelphia.

On October 13, 1993, the Maple Leafs paused to honour two of their most beloved alumni.

I remember watching Davey Keon, Lanny [McDonald] and Sit [Darryl Sittler], Börje [Salming], and all the guys on *Hockey Night in Canada* on Saturday nights. It was exciting when they became teammates of mine not long afterwards.

Joel Quenneville
PLAYER
1978–79

Toronto had been the first NHL team to retire a player's number, honouring Ace Bailey and his number 6 on Valentine's Day 1934, and later retiring Bill Barilko's number 5. Both players' careers had ended abruptly – and, in the case of Barilko, tragically.

These remain the only two numbers the franchise has officially retired. But the 1990s ushered in a new era for the relationship between the Toronto Maple Leafs and their alumni, as the franchise embraced its former players in a manner never dreamed of during the Ballard years. The time had come to recognize the greats upon whose shoulders all later players stood.

Team management decided that, while no further numbers would be retired, exceptional alumni would be commemorated with the raising to the rafters of banners bearing their images and numbers. The first two were former captains Syl Apps and Ted Kennedy. The latter openly wept when he saw his number 9 alongside his hero Apps's 10, raised to the rafters of Maple Leaf Gardens together. It was, for Kennedy, "the proudest moment of my life. To share that honour with Syl Apps, a superb player and perfect gentleman, was a great moment." On the night the two former Leaf captains were hailed, the current captain scored twice, added an assist, and played his usual hard-hitting game as Toronto blasted Washington, 7–1.

On October 23, the Leafs set an NHL record with their ninth straight win to open the season, blanking Tampa 2–0. Coach Pat Burns had the team playing exceptional hockey, but cautioned that "satisfaction is poison in sport. Figuring you've got it made is asking for trouble." The record-setting streak would even extend to a tenth game, in Chicago, where the Leafs beat the Blackhawks, 4–2.

But back on the night of the Leafs' ninth win, another Toronto team was also enjoying success. In Game Six of the World Series, the Toronto Blue Jays were facing the Philadelphia Phillies. With his team clinging to a 6–5 lead in the ninth, Phillies reliever Mitch Williams leaned in to concentrate on the batter, Joe Carter, while Rickey Henderson leaned off second base and Paul Molitor stood on first. On a count of two balls and two strikes, Carter muscled the next pitch over the left-field wall for a three-run homer to win the game and the World Series for the Blue Jays. "Touch 'em all, Joe!" cried announcer Tom Cheek. "You'll never hit a bigger home run in your life."

The NHL had scheduled the Maple Leafs to play back-to-back exhibition games against the New York Rangers at Wembley Arena in London, England. The games, played September 11 and 12, were for the French's Cup – named after the mustard company that sponsored the contests.

Coach Pat Burns argued with Cliff Fletcher all through the summer that the idea was awful and would guarantee a slow start to the season. The season-opening winning streak gave Fletcher opportunity to tease Burns. "Burnsie, you were right!" Fletcher would say. "We're never going to leave Toronto for training camp again!" The GM would chuckle, but Burns would just glare. Incidentally, the trip to jolly old England didn't have dire consequences for the Rangers, either. That season, they ended a 54-year drought by winning the Stanley Cup.

It took a 5–2 loss to the Canadiens in Montreal in the 11th game of the year – a game Burns dearly wanted to win – to bring the streak to an end. The team had nevertheless banked 20 points that helped carry them through the rest of the season.

However, after sitting atop the NHL in mid-December, the team began to tumble in the standings. The Leafs went into the new year winless in four, and started off 1994 with two losses and a tie. By mid-January, though, Toronto had righted its ship and the team was back in first place overall. Between January 6 and February 1, the Leafs went on another tear, going unbeaten in 11 games. Included in the upswing was a 3–0 Potvin shutout of Boston on January 10 – the first Toronto shutout in Boston since Johnny Bower blanked the Bruins on March 12, 1961. The current streak ended with a 4–3 loss to Detroit on February 5.

While there was great reason for optimism, Burns and Fletcher were concerned that there was little in the way of secondary scoring. Though the powerful trio of Gilmour between Andreychuk and Clark was producing as usual, other players were not. By March, this dearth of support began to affect the team's position in the standings. Fletcher responded by sending Glenn Anderson, a prospect, and a draft pick to the New York Rangers at the trade deadline to grab Mike Gartner for the stretch run. Gartner, still one of the fastest skaters in the league, had just moved into fifth place on the NHL's all-time goal-scoring list with his 611th goal. Gartner was thrilled with the news: "If I could have written a script for my career, I would have wanted to finish it up in Toronto."

In a 6–3 win over Quebec on March 26, Gartner picked up two goals to reach the 30-goal plateau for an unprecedented 15th time. Two nights earlier, Dave Andreychuk scored his 50th goal of the season in a 2–1 loss to the San Jose Sharks. Andreychuk joined Rick Vaive and Gary Leeman as the only Maple Leafs to reach that hallowed plateau.

One of the all-time favourites of Leafs Nation, Wendel Clark enjoyed three terms with the Leafs: 1985–86 to 1993–94; 1996–97 to 1997–98; and 2000. Wendel served as captain of the Blue and White from 1991–92 to 1993–94.

With Gartner on board, the Leafs finished the season second in the newly organized Central Division. With 98 points, Toronto was two behind first-place Detroit and one point ahead of the Dallas Stars. Chicago, which had finished fifth in the Central Division with 87 points, would be Toronto's first-round opponent in the playoffs.

Doug Gilmour finished fourth in NHL scoring with 111 points, and his 84 assists were second only to Gretzky's 92. He was the Leafs' Molson Cup winner for a second season and runner-up for the Selke Trophy as best defensive forward. Dave Andreychuk finished ninth in NHL scoring with 99 points, including a club-best 53 goals. Wendel Clark fired 46 goals and Mike Gartner had 34, although only six were scored as a Leaf. Earlier in the season, Félix Potvin, Gilmour, Andreychuk, and Clark had all been selected to play in the NHL All-Star Game, although Wendel was unable to participate because of an injured ankle.

But while several Leafs enjoyed an outstanding season, a few fell short of expectations. Borschevsky, for example, had fallen back from 34 goals in the previous campaign to 14, although much of this was attributable to his serious injury. Similarly, Glenn Anderson dropped from 22 to 17; Rob Pearson tumbled from 23 to 12; and Mike Krushelnyski fell from 19 to just 5.

Burns knew, however, that luck was needed in equal proportion to skill and preparation. As the coach observed, "It's all about catching a wave and staying on it."

Toronto seemed to catch that wave very early on in Game One against Chicago at Maple Leaf Gardens. Just 2:33 from the opening faceoff, Wendel Clark scored on a 70-foot shot that eluded Ed Belfour. The goal set the tone for the evening, and Toronto cruised to a 5–1 win.

Game Two was scoreless at the end of regulation, on the strength of exceptional play from both goaltenders. In the end, Todd Gill let a low blast go from the point to give Leafs the 1–0 win at 2:15 of extra time.

Toronto was well on its way, but Chicago wasn't done yet. Tony Amonte made certain of that, scoring four goals for the Blackhawks in Game Three in Chicago. The Hawks were up 3–0 within the first eight minutes of the contest. And while the Leafs certainly made a game of it, they weren't able to recover. The Blackhawks went on to a 5–4 victory to get back into the series.

Game Four proved to be another tight affair. The Leafs were up 3–2 when the Hawks capitalized on a power play late in the third period to tie the game. In overtime, Jeremy Roenick scored the winning goal at 1:23.

In Game Five in Toronto, Potvin and Belfour were once again terrific in goal. The latter would allow only one goal against the Leafs, but Mike Eastwood's marker was enough, as Félix Potvin turned away all 17 shots he faced in a 1–0 win.

Game Six, in Chicago, ended in an identical score. A Mike Gartner deflection that eluded Belfour would stand as the only goal of the game. With yet another 1–0 win, the Leafs had eliminated the Blackhawks. It was the Cat's third shutout of the series – the last Leafs goalie to accomplish the feat was Frank McCool, in 1945.

In the next round, the Leafs faced the San Jose Sharks. In just their third NHL season, the Sharks had improved by a staggering 58 points in the standings over the previous year and featured the ever-dangerous OV Line: Johan Garpenlov, Igor Larionov, and Sergei Makarov.

The Sharks came out strong in Game One and beat the Leafs, 3–2. Regrettably, the Gardens crowd booed the hometown team off the ice. Toronto – the team and its fans – fared much better in Game Two. The Leafs' checking line of Berg, Osborne, and Zezel faced the Sharks' top line all night and completely neutralized them. Toronto earned a decisive 5–1 win. This time, the fans sent their team off the ice with an ovation.

In a bid to reduce travel costs and fatigue, the league introduced a "2–3–2" format for the best-of-seven series instead of the traditional "2–2–1–1–1" format. This meant that the Leafs and the Sharks would play the next three games in San Jose. Game Three was something of a calamity for Toronto. The Sharks scored three soft goals on Potvin on their way to a 5–2 win. In Game Four, Gilmour, playing on an injured ankle, lifted the team onto his back and collected five points, all assists, in an 8–3 Leafs victory. Wendel Clark, who hit every Shark who crossed his path, added a goal in the win.

With Berg, Osborne, and Zezel doing their job, the OV Line had been held scoreless in the series to that point. Unfortunately, the Sharks' potent forward unit broke out with three goals in Game Five. With the 5–2 win, San Jose took a three-games-to-two lead in the series.

Game Six went into overtime. Fortunately for the Gardens faithful, it was Mike Gartner who decided it. At 8:53 of the extra frame, he scored to deliver a 3–2 win and tie the series.

The Leafs were generally more convincing in the seventh and deciding game at Maple Leaf Gardens. Wendel Clark took the reins, bounced Sharks all night, and scored twice and set up another in the Leafs' 4–2 win. With that, Toronto eliminated San Jose and moved on to their second consecutive conference final appearance.

Next up were the explosive Vancouver Canucks, a team that had finished second in the Pacific Division with 85 points. The Canucks' top line of Greg Adams, Pavel Bure, and Trevor Linden had troubled opponents all season. Pat Burns once again assigned his checking line to hold them back. As Toronto retained home-ice advantage, the series began at Maple Leaf Gardens. Berg, Osborne, and Zezel did not disappoint their coach. Not only did the Leafs' formidable checking line largely stifle Bure and company, but Peter Zezel also added two goals, including the overtime winner. As Zezel admitted, "That is the biggest goal I've ever scored."

The Canucks bounced back with a solid effort in Game Two. Jamie Macoun had been called late in the game for dumping Cliff Ronning. On the power play, Jyrki Lumme spun around and fired a shot that beat Potvin for the winning tally. Vancouver left Toronto with a 4–3 win and a split in the series.

In Game Three on the West Coast, Canucks goalkeeper Kirk McLean slammed the door shut. With the 4–0 win, Vancouver took a 2–1 lead in the series. Zezel, who had assumed something of a leadership position, spoke for his teammates: "We gave them the game. We just didn't play the way we're capable of playing."

It was apparent to most that the series was slipping away from the Leafs. Frustration bubbled up in Game Four when, despite Vancouver getting just seven shots in the first period and four shots in the second, Toronto was unable to capitalize. Once again, McLean was rock solid. Finally, with just over two minutes left in regulation, Ronning scored, and Bure added another into an empty net.

The Leafs came out much stronger in Game Five, keeping pace with the host Canucks throughout the game. At the end of 60 minutes, the match was tied, 3–3. Twenty additional minutes solved nothing. Then, at the 14-second mark of the second overtime, Potvin blocked a shot by Dave Babych, but the puck tumbled to the ice and Greg Adams shovelled it into the Toronto goal. The Leafs' season was over.

Twice the Toronto Maple Leafs had made it through to the final four, and twice the team had been halted. Yet, the team had found itself, as Gilmour remembered: "We had a good start and put a good run together. People forget that we went to the conference finals again. It was so close again, and yet so far away."

Félix Potvin was similarly enthused with the back-to-back runs: "When we hit Vancouver, we might have run out of gas. We played a lot of games those two years. We had a great team in the room and guys wanted to win, wanted to sacrifice themselves for each other. Pat was a big part of that team. He was a tough coach, but the guys felt that he respected us and we respected him."

Those two seasons reignited the passion of Leafs Nation. Fans fortunate enough to secure tickets could fully expect a win every time they entered the rink. And more often than not, the team delivered. But the question remained whether the Toronto Maple Leafs had gone as far as they were going to get.

SUNDIN'S ARRIVAL

Pat Burns knew in his heart that, as much as he loved his team, changes were necessary if the Leafs were going to take it to the championship level: "We've been there twice. It's time to do a bit of an overhaul." Cliff Fletcher shared the assessment. "It was clear that without extensive changes, we'd be in danger of missing the playoffs," he said.

At the NHL Entry Draft, the GM sent Rob Pearson and a first-round draft choice to the Washington Capitals for Mike Ridley and their first-round pick. And an hour before the draft was to commence, Fletcher made a controversial move that shook Leafs Nation to its core, sending Wendel Clark, Sylvain Lefebvre, prospect Landon Wilson, and a draft pick to the Quebec Nordiques for Mats Sundin, Garth Butcher, prospect Todd Warriner, and a first-round draft choice.

For many die-hard fans, it was an unconscionable move. Wendel, after all, had tattooed himself on the hearts of Leafs Nation by playing like a player much larger than he was. But Clark knew only one way to play, and this rambunctious approach had taken a significant toll on his body. Chronic back pain had caused Clark to miss 52 games in his third NHL season, 65 in his fourth, and 42 in his fifth. When he *was* healthy, Clark contributed goals, bodychecks, and excitement. Fletcher acknowledged his pain in trading away Number 17: "It was extremely hard. Wendel is Wendel. I just love the guy."

For his part, Clark was visibly disheartened, though he tried to see the silver lining: "I never wanted to leave Toronto, but in today's game, moving around is a big part of it. You always want to play for one team. It's a change in life for me, but everything will work out for the best. I'll miss Toronto, the fans, my friends. I've loved it but things will work out."

Later, a public goodbye was held at North York's Mel Lastman Square. Wendel was presented with the key to

If you were to ask, "What was the thing that stands out the most?" it was the fact that when we were going on those runs [in the spring of 1993 and 1994] and we'd won the game and beat someone out and were in Toronto, you couldn't go home! There was so much excitement within the city. There were so many people that jammed onto Yonge Street or onto Bay, you were literally not going anywhere for an hour! To realize that you were a part of that group that caused that euphoria within Toronto was incredible.

Jamie Macoun
PLAYER
1992–96

the city by Toronto mayor Mel Lastman. Wendel told the thousands of fans in attendance, "You're the number-one reason why everybody loves playing hockey in Toronto."

Conversely, Mats Sundin said that the trade was the best thing that had ever happened to him. Former Leaf Börje Salming advised Leafs Nation on their new acquisition: "The fans in Toronto are going to love Mats. He's spectacular!" It would take a little convincing, but year after year of solid production allowed the Swede to slowly penetrate the hearts of Leafs fans.

Several veterans found work elsewhere. The Leafs signed restricted free agent Mike Craig from Dallas, but had to surrender players from their own roster as compensation. An arbitrator ruled in favour of the Leafs' offer of Peter Zezel and prospect Grant Marshall.

In the end, the 1994–95 roster was the result of a substantial overhaul. Still, Toronto was confident that it had the ingredients to compete again for the Stanley Cup.

Wendel's departure raised the need for a new captain. On August 18, to no one's surprise, Doug Gilmour was named captain of the Toronto Maple Leafs. Red Horner, the Leafs' captain from 1938 to 1940, handed Gilmour the jersey with the C on its left breast and instructed the new captain to "be an example, not only to the rest of the players but also to the youth of the country."

In truth, Doug Gilmour owned Toronto. He was a media darling, and with Clark now in Quebec, Gilmour was the uncontested heart and soul of the franchise. Killer was thrilled with his new appointment: "When you try to get to the NHL, your expectations are just to go out and compete, and once you get there, try to stay there," he said. "To sit back and go, 'Okay, I want to be the captain of the Toronto Maple Leafs' is not realistic. But it happened, and I was in awe."

The awestruck captain was anxious to lead his team into the new season. The only trouble was that there was no season to lead anyone into. On October 1, the National Hockey League locked out its players after talks between the league and players' association had failed to deliver a new collective bargaining agreement in time for the 1994–95 season. The principal sticking point was a tax on payrolls beyond a certain limit, a feature the NHLPA viewed as a salary cap in disguise. A deal was not agreed to and ratified until the new year, leaving time for only an abbreviated 48-game schedule that began on January 20, 1995. To prepare, NHL teams held brief training camps before starting the season. For a squad like the Maple Leafs, with a great number of new faces in the lineup, there was little chance to develop any sort of chemistry.

The Leafs started the season on the road in California. In the opener in Los Angeles, both the Kings and the Leafs seemed jittery and sloppy in a 3–3 tie. Toronto then dropped its second game of the year, in San Jose, before flying home for the Gardens opener. That night, the Leafs rewarded their fans for their patience with a decisive 6–2 victory against the Vancouver Canucks. Sundin quickly began to endear himself to Leafs Nation with a goal and an assist.

The Leafs, however, soon suffered a rash of injuries: Mike Gartner was out for a few games with a collapsed lung in February; Ken Baumgartner required shoulder surgery that same month and was out for the season; Dave Ellett broke his foot in March; and Dmitri Mironov was also out of the lineup at the same time. More than this, though, the different pieces weren't fitting into place. Burns put Gilmour and Sundin together and tried various wingers with them – Mike Craig, Terry Yake, Nikolai Borschevsky – but no one fit the bill. The team's top guns were not producing, the defence was making errors, goaltending was good but not great, and the power play was abysmal. The entire team was frustrated.

Late in the shortened season, Fletcher decided to revamp his team, adding some grit with Warren Rychel from Washington, Rich Sutter from the Tampa Bay Lightning, and Dixon Ward from the Kings. With the end of the season – and the trade deadline – looming, the GM completed five trades within 24 hours. Fletcher sent goaltender Éric Fichaud to the New York Islanders for scoring winger Benoît Hogue and two draft picks. The Leafs added centre Paul DiPietro from the Canadiens for draft choices. Nikolai Borschevsky was sent to the Calgary Flames for a late draft pick. Grant Jennings, a stay-at-home defenceman, arrived from Pittsburgh for Drake Berehowsky. And tough winger and soon-to-be fan favourite Tie Domi returned to the Leafs from Winnipeg in exchange for Mike Eastwood and picks.

Prior to a game against the Blackhawks on March 11, 1995, the Maple Leafs honoured two of the franchise's great netminders. Turk Broda and Johnny Bower had both backstopped their teams during Stanley Cup dynasty eras. It wouldn't be a banner night for the Leafs, however, who skated to a 2–2 tie with Chicago that evening.

With this even-newer-look team, the Leafs finished a season that had felt more like a sprint than a marathon. Toronto completed the regular season in fourth place in the Central Division, sporting a record of 21 wins, 19 losses, and 8 ties. Mats Sundin, the team's Molson Cup winner for the season, was the club's leader with 23 goals and 47 points.

Two of the most well-known captains in Maple Leafs history. Doug Gilmour (left) broke franchise records for assists (95) and points (127) in 1992–93, and added 35 points that postseason. Mats Sundin (right) led Toronto in scoring in 12 of his 13 seasons in blue and white.

Still, Pat Burns believed he could ready his troops for the playoffs. While Félix Potvin had struggled at times (rookie Damian Rhodes had been inserted more frequently than the team would have liked), the coach made it clear that he was sticking with the Cat for the playoffs. And although Potvin pinched a nerve in his lower back during a practice, he was still ready to start Game One against the Blackhawks. The Leafs dumped Chicago in the Windy City by a 5–3 score. Ed Belfour, usually so reliable for the Hawks, was pulled after surrendering two soft goals, and Jeff Hackett finished the game.

The Leafs took just 17 shots on Belfour in Game Two, and only three in the third period, but in front of Potvin's shutout goaltending, Toronto blanked Chicago, 3–0, to gain a two-game advantage in the series. Feeling confident, the Leafs flew home for Game Three. They opened the scoring at Maple Leaf Gardens, but then allowed the Hawks to fight back. With a gallingly ineffective power play, Toronto lost, 3–2.

As the series progressed, it was apparent that the Leafs were simply unable to penetrate the Hawks' defence. When Toronto did manage to get by Chris Chelios, Gary Suter, or Steve Smith, Eddie "The Eagle" Belfour was waiting for them in goal. Chicago tied the series in Game Four with a 3–1 win.

The Leafs fell behind by two in Game Five, but through determination fought back to tie the game. But Chicago capitalized on penalties and defensive lapses to pot two, and ended up with a 4–2 victory. Still, the Leafs' Todd Gill nevertheless promised Toronto supporters, "We're going to fight tooth and nail until the final nail is in the coffin."

Back at Maple Leaf Gardens, Toronto looked like a sure bet to even up the series when the team went up 4–1 in Game Six. But in the third period, the Blackhawks fought all the way back to tie the game at 4–4. Sundin, however, got his team off the hook. The lithe Swede held the puck behind Belfour's net and, after a failed wraparound, the puck came out to Randy Wood, who slid it under the Chicago netminder to win the game and tie the series at three games apiece. That night, Doug Gilmour picked up two assists, which allowed him to surpass Dave Keon for the Leafs' career record for playoff points, with 68.

The teams travelled back to Chicago for the seventh and deciding game. The Blackhawks cruised to a 5–2 victory, which ended a frustrating season for the Toronto Maple Leafs.

Personnel changes and a shortened season had wreaked havoc on the Leafs' game. As Pat Burns aptly observed, "We lost something during the lockout. We never recovered." The chemistry that had existed for the previous two seasons was no longer present, and few of the many roster changes worked in the Leafs' favour. It simply was *not* the same team that had been to back-to-back conference finals.

"In my whole career, this has probably been the most frustrating year," a perplexed Cliff Fletcher told the *Toronto Star*. "There were seasons where a team has been very good, and seasons where a team has been very ineffective. But this is the one that will stick out in my memory as being the most frustrating."

It would be incumbent upon the GM to fix a team that, only one year previous, hadn't seemed all that broken to begin with.

TURNOVER

Cliff Fletcher wasted little time in trying to address the needs of his team. He sent Mike Ridley to Vancouver for Sergio Momesso, and made substantial strides in solidifying the blueline by picking up Dmitri Yushkevich and Rob Zettler from the Flyers for draft picks. In a huge swap, he landed top-class defenceman Larry Murphy from the Penguins for Dmitri Mironov and a pick. Then, in the draft, Fletcher and the Leafs added highly touted defenceman Jeff Ware with the team's first-round pick, although their most successful choice that summer would actually come in the ninth round, with Danny Markov.

Despite the additions, the Maple Leafs were hardly convincing in the 1995–96 season opener. That night, the Penguins crushed the Leafs 8–3 in Pittsburgh. Mario Lemieux returned from a 17-month absence and looked as though he hadn't missed a step. Pat Burns couldn't hide his bitter disappointment: "Maybe now we won't think we're as good as we think we are."

The Leafs' home opener was against the New York Islanders. It was the first game back at Maple Leaf Gardens for former Leaf Wendel Clark, who had been dealt from the Nordiques (now the Colorado Avalanche) to the Islanders in the off-season. The fans greeted Wendel with a standing ovation. It was the player Clark was traded for, however, who figured in the scoring; Mats Sundin scored twice in the Leafs' 7–3 win.

This was also the night that Carlton the Bear made his regular-season debut after getting a few exhibition games and several community appearances under his belt. The lovable team mascot takes his name and his number, 60, from the address of his original home, Maple Leaf Gardens, which still sits at 60 Carlton Street. Carlton is near the top of the Maple Leafs' all-time list of game appearances; at the time of the centennial, he has been seen at over 1,000 exhibition, regular-season, and playoff games, both at home and on the road, in addition to making more than 4,000 appearances in the community.

Since 1979, the J.P. Bickell Memorial Award, for personnel who contribute significantly to the Maple Leafs franchise, had been handed out just once – to Doug Gilmour in 1993. On October 24, it was presented to Bob Davidson, the captain of the 1945 Stanley Cup championship team. Davidson had served as the team's chief scout for four decades – in fact, he was the team's lone scout when he replaced Squib Walker in 1951. Davidson's greatest successes were seeing youngsters he signed in the 1950s – such as Bob Baun, Carl Brewer, Dick Duff, Billy Harris, Dave Keon, Frank Mahovlich, and Bob Pulford – lead the Maple Leafs to the Stanley Cup wins in the 1960s.

Toronto honoured two more greats, posthumously, on November 21, 1995, when King Clancy and Tim Horton had banners raised to the rafters. The two defencemen, both of whom wore number 7, would have enjoyed the ensuing game, in which Toronto dumped St. Louis, 5–2.

In November, the Leafs sat atop their division, but injuries, including Bill Berg's broken leg, Matt Martin's broken ankle, Dave Andreychuk's injured thumb, and Kenny Jonsson's separated shoulder, soon exposed Toronto's lack of depth, and the team dropped in the standings.

Fletcher and company entertained several possible acquisitions in the new year. On January 23, the GM completed a three-way deal involving the New York Islanders and Ottawa Senators. Toronto received Kirk Muller from Long Island and goalkeeper Don Beaupre from Ottawa. The Islanders received Ottawa's number-one draft pick, Bryan Berard, as well as Martin Straka, and Ottawa received Wade Redden from the Islanders and Damian Rhodes from Toronto.

The GM had yet more deals to make. Benoît Hogue and Randy Wood were sent to the Dallas Stars for Dave Gagner and a draft pick. Toronto also acquired hard-shooting defenceman Jamie Heward. The team, however, continued to tumble.

In December, the Leafs had still been challenging for the division lead; by February, they were clinging to fourth place. "We're no longer thinking about how we might do in the playoffs; we're just trying to make them!" said a frustrated Pat Burns. "I've tried yelling at them, I've run the crap out of them. I've tried reasoning with them. I don't know what more we could possibly do."

In fact, the team had not won a game in nine efforts and had scored just 18 goals during that skid. Some began to question whether or not the coach had lost his dressing room.

In late February, Fletcher made yet more swaps, sending Bill Berg and Sergio Momesso to the New York Rangers in return for Nick Kypreos and Wayne Presley. There was little change. As such, on March 4, 1996, the Maple Leafs fired Pat Burns. The coach had been loved by players, fans, and management alike, but something had to give, especially given the Leafs' recent abysmal record. Since the All-Star Game, the Maple Leafs had won just three games against sixteen losses and three ties.

With Burns gone, Nick Beverley was handed the head coaching job on an interim basis. Beverley had more or less backed into the position, as he remembered:

In all honesty, it was a situation where Cliff had some ideas of people that he would have liked to assume the role and he kept getting refusals. I was sitting in a room with Bill Watters, who was the assistant GM, and I just blurted out, "What the heck. I'll do it, to help." And lo and behold, the next thing I know, I'm on the plane coming back to Toronto, scribbling notes furiously and thinking, "What have I done?"

Beverley's style was the antithesis of Burns's. While the former policeman had been something of a disciplinarian, Beverley was more of a cheerleader. With the change, the team began to respond. In Beverley's first game behind the bench, the Leafs tied New Jersey, 2–2, breaking a streak of eight consecutive losses.

In the meantime, Fletcher continued to shift players about. On March 13, the GM sent Kenny Jonsson, Sean Haggerty, Darby Hendrickson, and a first-round pick to the Islanders for Mathieu Schneider, D.J. Smith, and returning prodigal son Wendel Clark. Fletcher then dealt Dave Andreychuk to the New Jersey Devils for a second- and a third-round draft pick. These were gambles, and many questioned the transactions at the time.

In the early going, though, he looked like a genius. Clark scored a goal and an assist in his return to Toronto as the Leafs blanked Dallas, 3–0. Clark accumulated six goals in his first seven games back in blue and white. Yet, there were other travails that offset Number 17's second time around with the Leafs. Doug Gilmour injured his hip and was out, and the overall team performance was still inconsistent. In a 4–0 loss to the Flyers, for example, the Leafs managed just 13 shots.

Cliff Fletcher joined Toronto as chief operating officer, president, and general manager in 1991, and was largely responsible for turning the franchise's fortunes around. Among his best moves was orchestrating the trade with Calgary that brought Doug Gilmour to Toronto, as well as hiring Pat Burns as head coach. The Maple Leafs went to the conference final in 1993 and in 1994.

More happily, on March 27, Larry Murphy picked up his 1,000th NHL point. Murphy was just the fourth player to reach that plateau in a Maple Leafs uniform. Toronto fans, however, did not give Murphy an easy time. The talented defenceman's salary made him the highest-paid member of the team, above Mike Gartner, Doug Gilmour, Félix Potvin, and Mats Sundin. As a result, expectations were exceedingly high.

The fairy tale of returning home to play for the legendary Blue and White had, in short order, turned into a nightmare for the defenceman. Murphy was booed every time he touched the puck. In the minds of many Leafs fans, he was the epitome of an overpaid and underachieving athlete. Others had suffered a similar fate, but the fans' disdain for Murphy was particularly cruel. He was in fact chosen for the All-Star Game that year, and would collect 100 points in his 151 games with Toronto.

Meanwhile, the Leafs would not book their ticket to the playoffs until the final game of the regular season. That night, Toronto doubled Edmonton, 6–3. The win concluded a decent season-ending stretch of nine wins,

six losses, and two ties. In the end, the Leafs finished third in the Central Division with 80 points, two games under .500, but good enough for a playoff berth.

Mats Sundin led the team in scoring with 33 goals and 50 assists for 83 points. Mike Gartner was the top goal scorer for Toronto, collecting 35, while Doug Gilmour had 32. Félix Potvin was awarded the Molson Cup for leading his teammates in three-star selections.

The first playoff series matched Toronto with St. Louis, a team that also finished with 80 points, although Toronto received home-ice advantage by having won two more games than the Blues.

St. Louis now featured former Leafs Glenn Anderson, Grant Fuhr, and Peter Zezel. The Blues lineup also boasted Wayne Gretzky. In the opening game, St. Louis dumped Toronto 3–1. While Gilmour did a commendable job of checking Gretzky, the Great One still managed to assist on all three of the Blues' goals.

In Game Two, the Blues again started Fuhr in goal. But when Chris Pronger pushed Nick Kypreos in a goalmouth scramble, the latter fell on Fuhr. The collision damaged Fuhr's knee and the Blues were forced to bring in backup goaltender Jon Casey. "It's a strategy the Maple Leafs decided to use, and the result is one of the greatest goaltenders in the history of the NHL is out of the playoffs," St. Louis coach Mike Keenan raged after the game.

The teams battled to a 4–4 tie at the end of 60 minutes. At 4:02 of the extra period, Gilmour held the puck behind the St. Louis net, spotted Sundin in front, and fed the Swede, who fired the puck. While it appeared that net-minder Casey had it, the disc actually trickled in. With the 5–4 win, Toronto had tied the series at one game apiece.

In Game Three, former Leaf Glenn Anderson was the difference maker, redirecting a Shayne Corson pass past Potvin at 1:24 of extra time to give St. Louis a 3–2 win. The games so far had been close, but the Blues won Game Five easily, 5–1. The Leafs were now one game from elimination.

Toronto did rebound in Game Five, with Mike Gartner's overtime winner – which completed a hat trick – giving the Leafs the 5–4 victory. Unfortunately, it would be the Leafs' final success of the season. In St. Louis on April 27, the Blues ended the Leafs' playoff run with a 2–1 victory.

The year had been an unqualified disappointment for the Toronto Maple Leafs. The immense turnover in personnel had made it difficult for talented players to find a rhythm with one another. The conference-final appearances in 1993 and 1994 were fading into the rearview mirror. The *Toronto Star* was particularly uncharitable in its summary of the 1995–96 Leafs, calling them "a throng of coddled, mentally flabby, sensationally overpaid players who submarined the organization with a lack of commitment."

MURPHY'S LAW

The Toronto Maple Leafs, so recently considered one of the league's top teams, had become also-rans. In trying to address the team's deficiencies, Fletcher and company had been quick to spend to add talent, and in the process had given up future stars such as Kenny Jonsson. The young Swede would become a standout NHL defenceman and future captain with the New York Islanders. While the Leafs may have undervalued the likes of Jonsson, they were also guilty of overvaluing several of the players they had acquired. Now, with owner Steve Stavro tightening the purse strings, Fletcher had to dump some of the team's more expensive assets.

The Leafs began to pare down the lineup in June. Todd Gill was sent to San Jose for Jamie Baker and a late draft pick; Dave Gagner left for Calgary in return for the Flames' third-round pick; Mike Gartner was sent to Phoenix for a fourth-round pick.

At the same time, the Leafs GM was working on securing Wayne Gretzky. The free agent, who had grown up in nearby Brantford, Ontario, had finished his term with the St. Louis Blues and was very interested in becoming a Maple Leaf. As Gretzky explained, "Toronto was my first choice. It was really where I wanted to go. I grew up a huge Toronto Maple Leafs fan."

Cliff Fletcher discussed the deal with Gretzky's agent and thought he had an agreement. Then he took the proposal to Stavro for the owner's blessing. He didn't get it. As Gretzky recalled:

Cliff came back and said he had taken it to the owner, and the owner nixed it. Timing is everything, and unfortunately at that time, [the Leafs] were trying to raise money to move out of Maple Leaf Gardens and move into a new arena, a new facility, and the ownership just felt at that time they needed to concentrate and put more of their resources into building an arena than to sign me. That's business and that's what happens, but I thought I was close to signing in Toronto.

While the Leafs had been tantalizingly close to signing the Great One, Fletcher had to move on and address several other holes on his team.

One of the holes was behind the bench. After the Game Six loss, Nick Beverley had been removed as interim coach and returned to his role as director of player personnel. On July 3, Mike Murphy, a former assistant coach in Toronto who most recently had served in the same capacity with the New York Rangers, was hired. "Any time you step into the shoes of the likes of Conn Smythe, Punch Imlach, Pat Burns or Joe Primeau, it really is a dream situation," Murphy said.

That fall, the Leafs broke camp with big hopes pinned on new additions Sergei Berezin, Fredrik Modin, and junior Jeff Ware.

The 1996–97 season began at home against Anaheim. The opening ceremony included 28 members of Canada's summer Olympic team, who looked on as the Maple Leafs handed the Mighty Ducks a 4–1 loss. Félix Potvin was especially sharp, and Mike Murphy was pleased with his team's overall effort.

Doug Gilmour and Mats Sundin had been carrying the bulk of the Leafs' scoring in the early going; the team needed someone else to step up. Wendel Clark answered the call. On November 9, in a 7–3 win over the Oilers, Clark banged in four goals and an assist. While it was a welcome change, the team was still struggling to garner some momentum.

There was one memorable night on November 10 in Philadelphia, during a particularly rocky patch for the Blue and White. The Leafs played well, but the Flyers took the game, 3–1. At the buzzer, the Flyers' Daniel Lacroix ran at Larry Murphy, and Félix Potvin broke his goal stick swinging at Lacroix. This prompted Flyers netminder Ron Hextall to leave his own goal and storm down the ice to take on Potvin. Had he known what was in store, Hextall might have reconsidered. The two goaltenders circled one another, then pulled off each other's masks and began trading punches. Potvin stood in and landed the more serious blows, cutting Hextall's forehead. The Leafs goalie emerged unscathed. As Potvin explained, "I saw Hexie coming, so I was ready. I had not been in any kind of fight since my first year of junior. I was just sticking up for my teammate."

On November 16, Doug Gilmour played his 1,000th NHL game. It was a 3–2 loss in Phoenix against the Coyotes. Killer was gracious after reaching the impressive milestone: "I'm very proud of that, but I realize I've been fortunate. I've never had a major injury and had the chance to play on good teams with great players." The trouble was, Gilmour would be a free agent at the end of the 1996–97 season, and the talented veteran was looking for an extension. For their part, the Leafs were reluctant to expend the same salary – or better – on a player who was still leading the team, but whose production had diminished. Gilmour could not contain his annoyance: "If they don't have any intention of signing me, they have to get something for me. They can't let me get away for nothing. I want to stay here and I want to play here, but I understand if something happens. It's part of the game." To many, that part of the game seemed imminent for the captain.

In the meantime, the season was quickly slipping away. As the *Toronto Star* observed, with the "split between aging players and inexperienced ones, the Leafs are going nowhere." Coach Murphy was deeply frustrated: "I haven't seen a lot of pride."

To be fair, the Leafs simply didn't have the talent. By mid-January, and after a fifth consecutive loss, Toronto was in last place in the NHL. Gilmour continued to work hard in a losing cause, but suggestions were being raised that the club should abandon hope for this season and start looking to the future.

And then the inevitable happened. On February 25, Toronto traded Doug Gilmour, Dave Ellett, and a third-round draft pick to the New Jersey Devils for defenceman Jason Smith, speedy Steve Sullivan, and prospect Alyn McCauley. It was a bold move that Fletcher felt needed some justification: "By taking one step backwards, we're taking two steps forward." Gilmour, who had been the heart and soul of the team since his arrival from Calgary, cautioned his now-former teammates: "I hope that my being traded is a wake-up call back there."

The Leafs were mathematically eliminated from the playoffs on March 12 after a 3–2 loss to Chicago. With nearly a week before the trading deadline, it was back to the drawing board for Cliff Fletcher. He signed Mike Johnson, a much sought-after prospect who had been starring with Bowling Green University. On March 18, he sent Kirk Muller to the Florida Panthers for prospect Jason Podollan. Then, mercifully, the Toronto Maple Leafs sent the much-maligned Larry Murphy to Detroit. Murphy, who had become a target of frustrated Leafs fans and suffered as the Gardens goat, went on to win the Stanley Cup with the Detroit Red Wings that spring.

All told, the Maple Leafs used no fewer than 44 players over the course of the season, including 20 rookies and 16 defencemen. No one, however, was able to fill the skates of players such as Dave Andreychuk or Mike Gartner, who had been so crucial to the Leafs' earlier successes. Toronto finished last in the Central Division with 30 wins, 44 losses, and 18 ties for 68 points – 12 miserable points worse than their total from the disappointing 1995–96 season.

Mats Sundin led the team in scoring, and was seventh in the league with 94 points, including a team-best 41 goals. Wendel Clark reached the 30-goal plateau despite a broken thumb, and rookie Sergei Berezin impressed with 25 goals. Doug Gilmour had contributed 15 goals and 60 points before leaving for New Jersey. In the end, no one needed to tell the GM that his team needed a redesign.

A NEW PRESIDENT

Cliff Fletcher did not try to sugarcoat the season that had been: "We did our best, and this past season was just bad hockey. Everything went wrong." Many agreed with the GM's candour, including his boss. Owner Steve Stavro asked the GM to relinquish day-to-day duties with the Maple Leafs, and on May 24, 1997, Cliff Fletcher resigned.

In a surprising announcement, the Maple Leafs hired Hall of Fame netminder Ken Dryden as the team's new president on May 30. While he had earned a law degree while starring with the Montreal Canadiens, Dryden had never served in the executive suite of a hockey franchise. Still, the new president appeared confident in front of the media: "I've been given the authority to have the right people in place both on the ice and off. I have been given the resources to build a Stanley Cup team. I wouldn't have taken that job without those assurances."

Dryden had his work cut out for him. His first job was to hire a general manager. Dryden outlined the person he was after: "We want someone the fans and the players can imagine carrying the Stanley Cup. If we can't imagine that, then it's not the right person." The team badly needed a facelift, and the incoming GM, whoever it was going to be, would have to hit the ground running.

While Dryden perused a field of possible candidates, Bill Watters served as the assistant general manager. But the NHL Entry Draft was conducted without a GM in place. As the Leafs had dealt away some of their higher picks, the yield was meagre. The free-agent pool proved far more beneficial. Toronto picked up Kevyn Adams from the International Hockey League, Glenn Healy from the New York Rangers, Derek King from Hartford, Kris King from Phoenix, and Igor Korolev from the Coyotes, all of whom would, to varying degrees, contribute to the Leafs as the team moved forward.

On August 20, after spending three months interviewing a number of experienced executives, Dryden decided on the new general manager of the Toronto Maple Leafs: himself. Dryden also hired former Winnipeg Jets GM Mike Smith to be the team's associate general manager.

There was also, with Gilmour's departure, the matter of the captaincy. On September 29, 1997, Mats Sundin was introduced as the new captain of the Toronto Maple Leafs. Right after the announcement, Sundin expressed his pleasure: "Even though I'm from Europe, I know what being captain of the Toronto Maple Leafs means. It's a big honour and responsibility. It feels great because it shows that people accept you for the way you are as a player and as a person. It's a sign of respect, especially when you know the players are also behind you. This is such a thrill."

The revised lineup, replete with free agents, rookies Mike Johnson and Danny Markov, and a new captain, began the season at Maple Leaf Gardens against Washington. Don Cherry and Ken Dryden faced off the first puck of the season. It was a tough opening night. Félix Potvin allowed four goals on the nine shots taken in the first period. The home crowd booed the team off the ice following the 4–1 loss to the Capitals.

Many players struggled out of the gate. Wendel Clark, the darling of the fans, was not the same player as the one who had broken in with Toronto in 1985. The fans begged him to hit somebody every time he stepped onto the ice, but his body simply wouldn't let him. His boisterous play contributed to a groin tear that saw him miss 35 games.

Two former captains had their banners raised on February 28: Charlie Conacher and George Armstrong. Following the ceremony, Potvin shut out the Montreal Canadiens, 4–0.

Despite all of the changes, the team found itself mired in last place in the Central Division for the better part of the season. At the trade deadline in March 1998, Toronto revamped the roster once again. And most everyone realized that the Leafs had become sellers. Jeff Brown's short-lived tenure in Toronto, which began with a January 2 trade with Carolina that saw the Leafs surrender a draft pick, ended less than three months later, when he was swapped for the Capitals' Sylvain Côté. Jamie Macoun was dealt to Detroit for a draft pick, and Mike Kennedy was sent to Dallas for a late pick. It was a clear message: the Toronto Maple Leafs had forsaken the 1997–98 season and were again looking to the future.

Sundin, however, never gave up. Despite the doomsayers surrounding the team, Sundin promised, "We'll do everything we can to win as many games as we can and we'll see after the last game where we are." But where the Leafs ended up was out of the playoffs. Toronto finished last in the Central again with 69 points on 30 wins, 43 losses, and 9 ties – an improvement of a single point over the previous season. Sundin took little comfort in his team-best 33 goals and 74 points. For his part, Tie Domi set a team single-season penalty record in a fight with Chicago's Cam Russell on April 15. The 17 penalty minutes he was assessed for the scrap gave Domi a total of 358 minutes in penalties, eclipsing Tiger Williams's 351 in 1977–78. Tie finished the season with 365. Félix Potvin earned the Molson Cup for three-star selections.

By any measure, it was a bad season. Ken Dryden's debut had not been a success. The president confessed: "We weren't good enough. We have to get better. We have to fill holes." Associate general manager Mike Smith tried to assure Leafs Nation that the team was not spiralling out of control: "This year was as much a process of identifying what we had and where we have to go."

As most fans saw it, there was only one way to go: up.

> The first eight years when we made the playoffs, the energy in the building and in the city was amazing. My dream to play for the Blue and White came true. The city literally bleeds those colours. Such loyal fans through thick and thin gave me energy to want to push through. The organization was really good to me and my family throughout my 12½ seasons there. Toronto takes up a big place in my heart.
>
> **Tomáš Kaberle**
> PLAYER
> 1998–2011

LUCK OF THE IRISH
1998–99 TO 2005–06

NEW DIGS

It was simple: changes had to be made in order for the franchise to turn around the misfortune of the previous two seasons. The first change occurred behind the bench. The Leafs began to actively speak with potential coaching hires at the conclusion of the 1997–98 campaign, leaving the beleaguered Mike Murphy in limbo. Finally, he was released on June 23, 1998. It came as a great relief. "I'm almost glad it's over," he said. "I'm not going to pass the buck and say they didn't get me the players. I didn't get it done. I'm a kid from this city. I dreamed at times about being the guy who would make a difference in getting that trophy back to this city."

The Leafs, as it happened, would reel from one Irishman to another.

Three days later, Pat Quinn was hired as the new coach of the Maple Leafs. Quinn had been fired as the Canucks' president and general manager earlier in 1998. The former Leaf defenceman had been named the NHL's coach of the year twice – once with Philadelphia and once with Vancouver. Toronto added assistant coaches Alpo Suhonen and Rick Ley, another former Leaf blueliner.

The Leafs went off the board at the NHL Entry Draft by selecting Nik Antropov with their first pick, and followed up by selecting Alexei Ponikarovsky in the fourth round. A handful of players were allowed to sign elsewhere for the new season, including Wendel Clark, Marcel Cousineau, Mike Craig, and Matt Martin. At the same time, Toronto assembled a collection of free agents who added value to the roster: Garry Valk, for example, joined the team, and after 11 seasons away from Toronto, Steve Thomas returned to the fold.

In goal, the Leafs decided that Félix Potvin was *not* the netminder who would carry them to the Promised Land. When the free-agent period opened on July 1, they hunted for a new number-one goaltender. As the story goes, Ken Dryden and his son were in line at a grocery store and encountered agents Don Meehan and Wade Arnott in the same shop. Meehan represented Curtis Joseph, and as

Dryden and Meehan waited in line, they concluded a deal that would see Joseph join the Toronto Maple Leafs.

Toronto looked good on defence going into the 1998–99 season. Sylvain Côte, a late addition during the previous campaign, was ready to step up. Joining him was a strong, young group that included Danny Markov, Jason Smith, Dmitri Yushkevich, and a rookie named Tomáš Kaberle, who had been impressive enough in training camp to make the team. For the first time in a long time, the Leafs looked much improved on paper.

Perhaps the most important move would come with the team's change of address. By 1998–99, theirs was the last of the arenas remaining from the NHL's Original Six era. But after 67 years, the Leafs were leaving Maple Leaf Gardens for a new home.

By the early 1990s, Maple Leaf Gardens had really begun to show its age. More and more, the Gardens became a relic of an earlier time: its scoreboard was unable to show replays, it had a limited number of suites, and it lacked air conditioning. It seated just over 16,000 fans, and the new arenas held thousands more. Cliff Fletcher had championed the idea of a new building, which Steve Stavro initially balked at, believing that the historic Gardens could remain the proud home of his team. The owner sank millions of dollars into renovations, but even these did not eliminate most of the deficiencies, and in the spring of 1996, Stavro and his partners finally agreed to seek out a site for a new arena. Several were considered, including the Canadian National Exhibition grounds, but the partners soon focused on a complex built on top of the soon-to-be renovated Union Station. At the same time, John Bitove Jr. and Allan Slaight, who had secured a National Basketball Association franchise for Toronto, were aiming to transform the long-vacant Postal Delivery Building at Bay Street and Lake Shore Boulevard in downtown Toronto into a basketball arena. This meant that there would be, in effect, two new arenas within a block of one another. A common-sense solution suggested itself: Why not

As a player, Pat Quinn spent 1968–69 and 1969–70 as a hardnosed blueliner with the Leafs. He returned to Toronto as head coach in 1998–99, and took the team to the conference final in his first season behind the bench. The Maple Leafs reached the playoffs in six of seven seasons with Quinn as coach, which included three 100-point seasons.

share one arena? But the stubborn Stavro insisted that the Maple Leafs would never be anyone's tenant.

Fortune, however, would shine on Stavro. The partnership agreement between Bitove and Slaight for the NBA team included a shotgun clause that, if exercised by one partner, would force the other to buy him out or agree to be bought out. Slaight invoked the clause, and in November 1996, when Bitove was unable to secure funding, Slaight bought out his former partner for an estimated $65 million, giving him 79 per cent control of the team and the proposed arena. Two years later, Steve Stavro and his partners in MLG Ventures, which controlled the Leafs and the Gardens, offered to buy the Toronto Raptors basketball team and the arena that would come to be known as Air Canada Centre. The bid was accepted by Slaight. What in due course would be known as Maple Leaf Sports and Entertainment (MLSE) had acquired the Raptors for a reported $179 million and the arena for a reported $288 million.

With a change of arenas and coaches came a switch from the Western Conference to the Eastern Conference. The Leafs were added to the Northeast Division, where they would renew rivalries with the Boston Bruins, Montreal Canadiens, and Buffalo Sabres, and establish a new one with the Ottawa Senators.

In anticipation of the move to Air Canada Centre, the Leafs began to celebrate their time on Carlton Street. The ceremonial puck drop prior to the 1998–99 season opener was performed by four men with ties to the early days of Maple Leaf Gardens: Tommy Smythe, Conn's grandson and Stafford's son; Jim Thomson-Boulton, whose grandfather's company had constructed Maple Leaf Gardens in 1931; Brian Young, whose grandfather was the Maple Leafs' first season-ticket holder; and Bernie Fournier, who joined the Gardens staff in 1952 and represented Maple Leaf Gardens employees through the years. It was a classy move, and the 2–1 victory over the Detroit Red Wings was a good omen of things to follow.

In the early going, Leafs fans soon noticed the obvious and rapid transition that had occurred on the ice. Pat Quinn had converted the Leafs from a plodding, checking team to a high-tempo, scoring team. The change in direction paid substantial dividends. Derek King repaid the Leafs for having confidence in him with terrific play. Steve Thomas got a new lease on life wearing the blue and white once again. And Curtis Joseph's sensational play gave teammates confidence that they could gamble, knowing that he was back there to bail them out. By mid-November, the Leafs were first overall and led the league in goals scored.

Unhappy in his role backing Joseph, Félix Potvin forced a trade by leaving the team in early December. "I told them I just couldn't handle it anymore," he recalled. "It was very difficult to go to the rink every day when you don't feel like you're part of the team." To replace Potvin, Glenn Healy was summoned from the IHL.

Finally, on January 9, Leafs associate GM Mike Smith finalized a trade that saw Potvin dealt to the New York Islanders for defenceman Bryan Berard, a former first-overall draft pick and the Calder Trophy winner in 1997. Berard was an exceptional puck-rushing defenceman whose defensive liabilities had put him at odds with GM Mike Milbury. Berard would add to an already solid blueline, but could also contribute to the Leafs power play, which had been suffering.

"[The Islanders] were just starting a road trip and I got wind that the trade was going down. I actually went to Mike Milbury's room to intercept the trade. I was still young and I really didn't want to be traded. As I got to his door, he opened it and said, 'It's too late.' After the initial shock, I was excited about going to Toronto to start a new chapter."

Meanwhile, everyone was preparing to say goodbye to Maple Leaf Gardens. Throughout the season, pilgrims had returned for one last service of hockey in the weathered yellow-brick cathedral on Carlton Street. More than 40,000 fans made their way to an open house to say goodbye on February 6 and 7. The Gardens had opened on November 12, 1931, with a contest between the Maple Leafs and the visiting Chicago Black Hawks. In a fitting epilogue, 67 years and 24,522 nights later, the same team returned for the Leafs' final game at Maple Leaf Gardens, on February 13, 1999.

Former Maple Leaf players were invited to return to the site of their most memorable hockey-playing exploits, and seven decades' worth of alumni made their plans to attend the bittersweet evening. Paul Morris, the voice of Maple Leaf Gardens since 1961, introduced the celebrants for the ceremonial faceoff. Representing Toronto was Red Horner, and for Chicago, Harold "Mush" March, both of whom had played in that first game at the Gardens. Morris called upon Leafs captain Mats Sundin and Doug Gilmour, now a Hawk, to take the ceremonial faceoff. Horner and March, using the same puck with which March had scored the first-ever goal at the Gardens, leaned over and collaboratively dropped the puck between Sundin and Gilmour. Michael Burgess sang the American national anthem and was joined by a choir to perform the Canadian national anthem.

With a final game on February 13, 1999, Maple Leaf Gardens came to the end of its 67 years as home to the Toronto Maple Leafs. Here, Red Horner (right), the oldest surviving captain at the time, passes the symbolic flag to Mats Sundin, the then Leafs captain.

While the evening was an emotional one for Leafs Nation, the game itself was anticlimactic: Chicago dumped Toronto, 6–2. Reid Simpson, who hadn't scored to that point in the season, got two goals and assisted on the final NHL goal scored in Maple Leaf Gardens, a tally by Bob Probert at 11:05 of the third period. Derek King scored what would be the final Maple Leaf goal at the Gardens at 8:15 of the second period. With just under a minute to play, and despite the score, the capacity crowd rose to its feet in unison to send the Maple Leafs off the ice. The Gardens era concluded with Toronto winning 1,208 games, losing 783, and tying 333.

While the current Leafs showered and dressed, the ice surface was prepared for the closing ceremonies. Stompin' Tom Connors emerged and performed "The Hockey Song." Paul Morris stepped out to centre ice to introduce the master of ceremonies for the postgame formalities, *Hockey Night in Canada* host Ron MacLean. MacLean paid tribute to Morris and his late father, Doug, who had served as the head electrician at Maple Leaf Gardens since its opening.

Next, the 48th Highlanders marched onto the ice, just as they have at every single home opener for the Maple Leafs since 1931. MacLean then introduced over

a hundred individual Maple Leafs alumni, grouped by decade, starting with the 1990s and tracing back through history to the 1930s and that decade's lone representative, Red Horner. After them came the former Maple Leafs who had been inducted into the Hockey Hall of Fame. While they stood at centre ice, several long-tenured employees were introduced, representing the thousands who had worked in one capacity or another since the building's opening. The remaining players from the Leafs' Cup-winning teams were then introduced. This was all followed by youngsters from Toronto-area minor hockey programs, carrying individual banners to represent the 11 Stanley Cup championships won during the Gardens era, one standing at each of the 11 points of the massive Maple Leaf at centre ice. The final banner read MEMORIES AND DREAMS, the theme of the year-long celebration.

The oldest and most recent captains were brought into the spotlight. In a particularly poignant moment, Horner handed Sundin the MEMORIES AND DREAMS banner and instructed hin, "Take this flag to our new home, but always remember us." Canada's songbird, Anne Murray, adorned in a white Leafs jersey, then sung – appropriately – "The Maple Leaf Forever."

The Toronto Maple Leafs hosted the Montreal Canadiens in the first game played at Air Canada Centre. Todd Warriner scored the first goal in the Maple Leafs' new home, and Toronto went on to edge Montreal, 3–2, in overtime.

It was, of course, a bittersweet night. Paul Morris surmised that it was "a sad night in some ways, but it almost feels like a celebration. We're leaving our home, the home we've been in our whole lives, and I think the rest of Canada feels the same way. Even if they didn't live here like I did, they did so in their dreams." After the ceremony, the Maple Leafs went on a short road trip, tying New Jersey and beating Buffalo before returning to Toronto to their new home and a new chapter.

The team staged a parade from Maple Leaf Gardens to Air Canada Centre on February 19. During the midday celebration, thousands of fans lined the route, which was just less than two and a half kilometres long. Former players sat in groups of three along with current players in open convertibles that made the trip down Yonge Street, turning west onto Front Street at the Hockey Hall of Fame, and then along Front to Bay Street and their destination.

Toronto mayor Mel Lastman sat with Pat Quinn and Leafs radio broadcaster Joe Bowen. Longtime season-ticket holder Tom Gaston, who had watched Leafs games dating back to the Arena Gardens, was on a float with organist Jimmy Holmstrom. Also included in the celebration were the 48th Highlanders – with guest piper Glenn Healy – the Queen's University marching band, and the Burlington Top Hat Marching Orchestra. The Stanley Cup

and Conn Smythe Trophy were given a place of pride in the procession, too. The parade concluded with a dedication ceremony at Air Canada Centre, where Ken Dryden winked and said, "Let's just hope at some point that there is another real nice parade in Toronto."

The next night, February 20, 1999, the Montreal Canadiens visited to face the Leafs and inaugurate the new arena. A special ceremony saw new banners raised for the Maple Leafs' Stanley Cup–winning teams and those players whose number had either been retired or honoured. Youngsters playing minor hockey in the Toronto area had been randomly selected to drop the first puck.

Todd Warriner scored the first goal in Air Canada Centre at 6:04 of the first period. "Scoring the first goal has taken on a life of its own, but at the time, I didn't think too much about it," admitted Warriner. "It was a nice thing to happen to a fourth-liner like myself, and it is now one of my proudest memories as a player and as a Leaf."

The game concluded with Steve Thomas receiving a perfect cross-ice pass from Ladislav Kohn, which he backhanded past Canadiens netminder Jeff Hackett for the winning goal at 3:48 of overtime to give Toronto a 3–2 victory. "It's an incredible feeling to score the game-winning goal, especially in the first game in the building," Thomas beamed. "I was just lucky to be that guy tonight."

On March 4, the Leafs were involved in a bizarre game against the Washington Capitals. Toronto won the game, 4–0, while firing just nine shots on goal, the fewest the team had ever taken in a victory. Still, the Leafs were a steady team throughout much of the season. After a 5–1 win over the Oilers on April 1, combined with Florida's loss to Washington that same evening, the Maple Leafs clinched their first playoff spot in three seasons. Toronto finished second in the Northeast Division with 97 points, a huge 28-point improvement on the previous outing. The team's 45 wins set a franchise record.

Mats Sundin led the team in scoring with 83 points, including 31 goals, and Sergei Berezin had a team-best 37 goals. Bearing testament to the team's strategic shift, the Leafs' 268 goals led the NHL. Curtis Joseph exceeded expectations and was the team's Molson Cup recipient for the most three-star selections through the season, as well as a finalist for the Vézina Trophy. Meanwhile, Pat Quinn was a finalist for the Adams Award as the NHL's best coach.

The opening playoff series saw Toronto face the Philadelphia Flyers, a team that finished four points behind them in the conference. Philadelphia was without high-scoring centre Eric Lindros, who had been sidelined with an injury. The presence of former Leafs coach Roger Neilson, now head coach of the Flyers, added an intriguing note.

Toronto tried to play a physical game against one of the biggest teams in the NHL. In this way, the Leafs abandoned the offensive focus that had taken them to the playoffs in the first place. Sitting Kaberle and Warriner, Coach Quinn instead dressed Chris McAllister and Kris King in their place. The strategy backfired in Game One at Air Canada Centre, and John Vanbiesbrouck and the Flyers shut out Toronto, 3–0. With less than two minutes to play in Game Two, and the home team down 1–0, fans began booing the Leafs. This quickly stopped when Steve Thomas tied the game. A minute later, there was wild cheering as Mats Sundin scored to put the Leafs in front for good with a 2–1 win.

Curtis Joseph was spectacular in fending off the Flyers' attack in Game Three, and Thomas once again came up with a crucial goal to give Toronto another 2–1 victory, this one on the road. The Flyers were not, however, prepared to roll over just yet. John LeClair was dominant, flattening everything in his path. The big forward parked himself in front of Cujo and scored twice as the Flyers evened the series with a 5–2 win.

Back in Toronto for Game Five, the teams were knotted at one apiece at the end of regulation. In overtime, Yanic

Perreault scored to restore the Leafs' lead in the series. In Game Six, Sergei Berezin became the Leafs' hero when he scored the game's only goal in the very last minute of the third period. Toronto had won, but it was a peculiar victory. The Leafs, who had led the league in goals scored, had seen their offence dry up – in the six games, they managed only nine goals. Still, it was the first time the Leafs had defeated the Flyers in four postseason attempts.

Toronto was not quite done with the Commonwealth of Pennsylvania. The Leafs now faced the Pittsburgh Penguins, a team that had finished seven points back of Toronto in the Eastern Conference. Yet the Leafs delivered an uninspired performance in Game One as the Penguins blanked Toronto, 2–0.

Game Two was a different matter. Mats Sundin put the team on his back and delivered a classic performance. On the strength of the captain's two goals and two assists, the Leafs drew even in the series with a 4–2 win.

The teams split the two games in Pittsburgh: the Penguins edged the Leafs, 4–3, in Game Three, but Toronto rebounded with a 3–2 overtime win in Game Four. Sergei Berezin, who tapped in another winning goal at 2:18 of overtime, confessed, "My son could have scored that goal. It was a dream come true."

The Leafs put in a strong defensive effort in Game Five in front of the home crowd and allowed just 16 shots. Pat Quinn shuffled his roster and added Kevyn Adams, Lonny Bohonos, and Adam Mair for speed in place of Tie Domi, Fredrik Modin, and Todd Warriner. As far as Quinn was concerned, "The young kids did a great job. They gave us some jump. It means we can change our look depending on what lies in front of us and still hope to be successful." The Leafs took Game Five by a convincing 4–1 score.

The teams returned to Pittsburgh for a nail-biting Game Six. The score was tied, 3–3, at the end of 60 minutes, and for the second time in the series, overtime was required. At 1:57 of the extra frame, Sergei Berezin fired a shot that Tom Barrasso blocked, but the rebound fell into the crease. Garry Valk dove in and swept the puck past the Penguins goalie. "I saw the red light go on and I was on my stomach," Valk remembered. "When you're playing street hockey, you want to score a big goal in the Stanley Cup playoffs. All those years of hard work really paid off. Just to be a big part of a big game is every kid's dream."

Valk's dramatic goal eliminated the Penguins from the playoffs. Back in Toronto, the city erupted. Music blared, horns honked, and Leafs Nation waved flags on Lake Shore Boulevard and high-fived each other while hanging out of the thousands of cars that cruised up and down Yonge Street. It was an outpouring of joy that confirmed that the Maple Leafs had once again recaptured the heart of their city.

Toronto was on its way to the Eastern Conference final against the Buffalo Sabres. While the Sabres had, like Philadelphia and Pittsburgh, finished behind the Maple Leafs during the regular season, they were still a very formidable foe, especially with Dominik Hašek in goal.

To everyone's surprise, when the Leafs skated out for the opening faceoff of Game One and glanced at the far end of the ice, it wasn't Hašek that they saw in the Sabres crease, but backup Dwayne Roloson. Hašek, as it happened, was out with a groin injury. It was a gift that the Leafs wanted to take advantage of. And Toronto appeared to be in command of Game One, with Mats Sundin shaking off Mike Peca's tight checking to score twice. But Buffalo pumped in two third-period goals and took the opener, 5–4. "We expected Hašek and all of a sudden, one of the best goalies in the world isn't there," Dmitri Yushkevich explained. "We were sure we could win easily, but it worked the wrong way for us."

Fortunately, the Leafs rebounded convincingly. Toronto scored two goals 18 seconds apart in the first period and went on to double the Sabres, 6–3, in Game Two.

Hašek was in goal for the Sabres for Game Three, in Buffalo. While the Leafs took a 1–0 lead, the Sabres scored three goals in the first eight minutes of the second period and went on to win, 4–2. The story was much the same in Game Four: Buffalo raced out of the chute and held a 5–0 lead after two periods. Mats Sundin scored on a penalty shot to break Hašek's shutout bid, but Toronto could only manage one other goal, dropping a 5–2 decision.

The Sabres were up three games to one and poised to advance to the Stanley Cup final for the first time since 1975. A desperate Maple Leafs squad battled hard in Game Five, but Buffalo was too strong, eliminating the Leafs with a 4–2 victory. It was the first time since late October that the Maple Leafs had lost three consecutive games. In the final moments of the game, and in full knowledge that the writing was on the wall, the Air Canada Centre crowd rose to salute their Leafs for what had been a season of great promise.

"It was a heartbreaking game," the Leafs captain conceded. "I thought we deserved a better destiny tonight. No doubt Buffalo was the better team in the series, but we've learned from this and we'll be back."

Pat Quinn said, "Maybe we weren't realistic, but we thought we had a chance to come out of this. I'm sure they'll remember this all their lives." The season of surprises had revealed hidden depth in the lineup. No fewer than 12 players had made their playoff debuts for Toronto in the spring of 1999. Everyone was hoping for – and on some level expected – a repeat performance.

THE MIGHTY QUINN

Coming off a strong season with Pat Quinn behind the bench, the Leafs appeared solid. The team had made a substantial leap with a 28-point gain on the previous season, finishing with a franchise record for wins in a season. While there was every reason for optimism on the ice, there was turmoil in the head office. There was friction between Ken Dryden and associate GM Mike Smith, and in June 1999, just before the NHL Entry Draft, Smith was fired.

Dryden temporarily assumed the GM's position in addition to the presidency. Many suggested that Bob Gainey, who had just won the Stanley Cup as GM with the Dallas Stars, was in discussion with his former Canadiens teammate about the role in Toronto. Pat Quinn, apparently concerned about who he would eventually have to report to, made a pre-emptive strike. When Dryden inquired about Quinn's possible interest in assuming the dual role of GM and coach, he replied, "I may have to do it out of self–preservation." As such, on July 14, 1999, Quinn was named coach and general manager of the Toronto Maple Leafs, becoming the only man in the NHL with the dual role. But then, Quinn had always exceeded expectations. As journalist Mike Ulmer wrote, Quinn "made himself a player when it would have paid as much to be a goon. He made himself a lawyer when it would have been enough to have been an ex-player. He made himself a coach when it might have paid better to be a lawyer and a GM when it would have been easier just to be a coach."

In short, Quinn had *not* chosen the easy route.

The NHL added a 28th team for the 1999–2000 season, returning to Atlanta for another go-round. In the resulting expansion draft, the Maple Leafs lost Yannick Tremblay to the Atlanta Thrashers. During the off-season, the team picked up free agents Jonas Höglund, Bryan Fogarty, and Syl Apps III. The well-travelled Fogarty split the season between the Leafs' farm team in St. John's, Newfoundland, and Knoxville of the United Hockey League, never playing with Toronto. Apps, grandson of the former Leaf great, likewise did not play for the parent club. His sister, Gillian, would win gold medals with the Canadian Olympic women's team in 2006, 2010, and 2014.

Netminder Jeff Reese was dealt to Tampa Bay for a draft pick, and then, on the eve of the season opener, Fredrik Modin was also traded to the Lightning, for Cory Cross and a draft pick. Cross was broken up:

Tampa was home to me. I had lots of friends, a great house, and good memories of an organization giving me the chance they did. As soon as I flew off to meet the [Maple Leafs] in Montreal, I got this huge smile on my face and it sunk in: I am a member of the Toronto Maple Leafs, the team my dad listened to growing up and had shared stories with me [about]. The excitement I had was incredible, and the next day I was playing on *Hockey Night in Canada* versus the Montreal Canadiens – every boy's dream!

That game in Montreal saw new Leaf winger Jonas Höglund face his former team. He was paired successfully with fellow Swede Mats Sundin on Toronto's top line. Olympian Bruny Surin dropped the first puck of the season, and the Leafs sprinted out of the gates by dumping the Habs, 4–1.

Two nights later, the Maple Leafs were welcomed by a new voice resonating over the public-address system at Air Canada Centre for the home opener. Andy Frost had been hired to replace the ubiquitous Paul Morris, who had been behind the microphone for 38 years and 1,585 consecutive home games, stretching back to the home opener of the 1961–62 season. That night, Toronto blanked Boston, 4–0. Through the first 14 games of the season, Curtis Joseph was spectacular and was credited with four shutouts as the team won ten, lost just three, and tied one.

The season, of course, was not without its trials. In a loss to Ottawa on October 9, Sundin broke his ankle. The initial prognosis was a six-week recovery; remarkably, the captain healed much more quickly than expected and was back in action in just four weeks.

There were also some minor roster moves in the early going. Toronto sent Sylvain Côté to the Blackhawks for a draft pick. The Hawks also plucked Steve Sullivan from the waiver wire. The Leafs sent Derek King to St. Louis for a prospect, while Dmitri Khristich was picked up in a trade with Boston. And in late November, Todd Warriner was sent to Tampa Bay for a draft pick.

The city had been chosen to host the 2000 NHL All-Star Game on February 6 – the first time the league's showcase had taken place in Toronto since 1968. With a

very competitive team, the Maple Leafs were well represented. The game boasted a "North America vs. the World" format; Pat Quinn was behind the bench for Team North America, while Curtis Joseph was one of its netminders. Sundin and Dmitri Yushkevich skated for the World team.

The team underwent something of a slide in February, and called on a familiar face to lend a hand. Wendel Clark had played nine seasons with the Leafs before he was traded to the Quebec Nordiques in 1994, and had returned to the Leafs in March 1996, but in the summer of 1998 he was signed as a free agent by the Tampa Bay Lightning. As a member of the Chicago Blackhawks, Clark had been placed on waivers in mid-November 1999. Toronto rolled the dice and brought him home for a third time on January 9, 2000. "I'm just going to try to slide in and not interrupt anything going on," Clark suggested. "I think I can help this hockey team. That's my goal." Clark's return took place in a 3–2 overtime win over the Oilers on January 14. Curtis Joseph said, "With Wendel out there banging bodies, it was an inspiration for us."

Another strategic deal was made on February 9, when Darcy Tucker and two draft selections were acquired from the Lightning, with Toronto surrendering Mike Johnson, Marek Posmyk, and three picks. Tucker explained how he got the news:

I was sitting in a restaurant with Mike Sillinger, and back then, the cell phones were big and bulky so I left mine in the vehicle, but Mike happened to have his. Rick Dudley [the GM of the Lightning] called him and said that he wanted to talk to me. We were leaving on a flight, so I had to go to the plane to get my bag. All the boys were at the airport when I got there, so it was a different kind of feeling. I was excited, though, because my wife is from Barrie, so it was a bit of a homecoming for me.

Quinn was pleased with this acquisition: "He's a great competitor who will sacrifice his body. You need those kinds in your group." The *Toronto Star* was a little more candid, calling Tucker a "mondo-sized, fingernails-down-the-blackboard, mosquito-buzzing, in-your-face ball of hate." Tucker agreed with their assessment: "I love going into a rink and being the most hated guy in the rink."

A game in Ottawa on March 11 was marred by a horrific incident. In the second period, Marián Hossa swung around to fire a shot at the Leafs net, but his stick caught Leaf defenceman Bryan Berard in the eye. Berard crumpled to his knees with his forehead on the ice as blood

From the first time I put my skates on in our backyard rink in Windsor, Ontario, I wanted to be a Toronto Maple Leafs player. It's every kid's dream! My young life revolved around *Hockey Night in Canada*, reading about Leaf stars, and idolizing the goalies of the past. Playing junior hockey in both Windsor and Kitchener offered the opportunity to play at Maple Leaf Gardens. Draft day, a call from Johnny Bower welcoming me to the Leafs, my first training camp, the executive offices, signing my first contract, and, although a long, tough road to get to the NHL, my first game was a dream that came true.

Bob Parent
PLAYER
1982–83

pooled around him. Curtis Joseph immediately summoned help, and trainer Chris Broadhurst ran onto the ice to assist the fallen defenceman. Berard instantly knew he was in trouble: "I got to the training room. They started with the eye wash in my eye. I knew my eye was cut pretty good. Anxiety set in. I knew something was definitely wrong."

Berard had suffered a 20 millimetre (one-inch) cut across the eyeball, a detached retina, and other injuries to the eye. The defenceman spent over six hours in surgery that night. Doctors discussed the possibility of removing Berard's eyeball in the event that they could not stop the bleeding. It was a frightful situation.

Once the eye had become somewhat stabilized, doctors in New York were able to reattach Berard's retina. Berard and his parents flew home to Woonsocket, Rhode Island. It was a difficult period for the young player:

> All of a sudden, my career came to a halt. It was just a freak accident, but it was definitely a life-changer for me. I'm very thankful for all of the doctors in Ottawa who spent the time, the guys at the rink, the Toronto

team doctors and the Toronto trainers. They all responded pretty damn quickly to get me to the right place, the right hospital, the right trauma centre and thankfully, they were able to save my eye.

Fortunately, after missing the rest of the schedule and all of 2000–01, Berard was able to play another six years in the NHL.

Meanwhile, the Maple Leafs went on to finish first in the Northeast Division and fourth overall in the NHL. Their 100-point season was a first for the franchise. To no one's surprise, Mats Sundin again led the team in scoring, as he had done every year since 1994–95. He collected 32 goals and 41 assists for 73 points. Curtis Joseph had a terrific season, finishing with a .915 save percentage and four shutouts, and was awarded the Molson Cup for his three-star selections. Joseph was also awarded the King Clancy Memorial Trophy, given to the player who best exemplifies leadership qualities on and off the ice and who has made a noteworthy humanitarian contribution in his community.

The opening round of the playoffs provided the first modern instalment of the Battle of Ontario. The Ottawa Senators had finished second to the Maple Leafs in the Northeast Division, and there was no love lost between the rivals. In fact, the Leafs lineup had been badly compromised by the Senators throughout the season: Mats Sundin broke his ankle during a game against the Sens, Yanic Perreault's arm had been broken by Ottawa goalie Tom Barrasso, Danny Markov had injured his foot badly during a game against Ottawa, and there was the horrific Berard eye injury. There was, then, plenty of ill feeling to fuel the rivalry.

The Leafs got off to a good start in Game One at Air Canada Centre. Curtis Joseph was brilliant in goal as the Leafs blanked the Senators, 2–0. But the tension between the two teams reached a fever pitch during the game. Perreault suffered a knee injury after a hit by Jason York late in the third period. Coach Quinn called it a "cheap shot," while Senators coach Jacques Martin questioned whether Perreault was actually hurt. The incident set the tone for the rest of the series.

Toronto came out even stronger in Game Two and cruised to a decisive 5–1 win. Steve Thomas, who scored two of the Leafs' goals that night, believed that this "was one of the best games we've played all year."

The return home suited the Senators well, and they tied the series by winning both matches: 4–3 in Game Three and 2–1 in Game Four. When the teams returned to Toronto for Game Five, Ottawa seemed to pick up where it had left off, dominating the play for much of the contest. But with 4:30 remaining, Thomas tied it up. The game went into overtime, and at 14:43, Sergei Berezin carried the puck into the Senators end on a two-on-one. Barrasso expected the shot, but Berezin feathered a perfect pass to Thomas, who backhanded the puck into the net to secure the victory.

Game Six featured thrilling end-to-end action. The Senators went up 2–0 and appeared certain to win again on home ice. The Maple Leafs, however, rebounded with four goals in the second period. In the end, Toronto was able to close out the series with a 4–2 victory that eliminated Ottawa. The final goal of the game was also the last of Wendel Clark's career. While the players celebrated in the nation's capital, flag-bearing fans poured out onto Yonge Street to celebrate.

Next up was New Jersey. The Devils had finished second in the Atlantic Division with 103 points, three more than the Leafs, but as a division champion, Toronto retained home-ice advantage. As such, the series began

at Air Canada Centre, where the Leafs drew first blood in Game One. Toronto's defence greatly aided netminder Joseph, with Alexander Karpovtsev and Danny Markov particularly effective at blocking shots. As a result, the Leafs beat the Devils, 2–1.

Bryan Berard arrived to inspire his team in Game Two. When he was shown on the videoboard, wearing dark sunglasses and seated in one of the boxes, the crowd gave him a long, loud ovation. The Leafs, however, dropped the second game to the Devils, 5–3. "We're not going to win this series playing the way we did in the first two games," Mats Sundin admitted.

Toronto was solid in the first period of Game Three, but the Devils scored three times in the second on their way to a 5–1 win. The visiting Leafs' play was so uninspired in the third period that New Jersey fans mocked the team by chanting, "1967."

While the Leafs were badly outplayed in Game Four, the score was nevertheless tied, 2–2, late in the game. With 1:35 left in the third period, Tomáš Kaberle fired a slap shot from the point that beat goalie Martin Brodeur and allowed Toronto to steal a 3–2 victory and even up the series.

Returning to home ice, the Leafs played particularly well in Game Five, but the Devils twice erased Toronto leads. In the end, New Jersey emerged on the winning end of a 4–3 score. Sundin spoke to the team's frustration: "I think we played our best game of the series, but it still wasn't enough."

Game Six would prove even more frustrating. The Devils held the Leafs to a measly six shots during the entire game – the fewest a Leafs team had ever registered in a playoff game. And the team's futility was evident in other ways. The Leafs, for instance, had failed to score in 20 power-play chances against the Devils, and had scored only twice in 43 power-play attempts throughout the course of the playoffs.

With the 3–0 win, New Jersey ended Toronto's 1999–2000 season. Coach Quinn was understandably disappointed: "I anticipated we would be able to go on further. We'll have to really look at this year. We thought more of ourselves." The question remained whether or not the Leafs, upon self-reflection, had the necessary pieces to take the next step.

PROGRESS

Toronto embarked on the 2000–01 campaign without the player who had long served as the archetypal

Maple Leaf. Game Four of the New Jersey playoff series was Wendel Clark's last. On June 29, Clark announced his retirement from hockey. For several years after he broke into the league, he had been the only bright spot on an otherwise moribund team. Though he had made brief stops with the Quebec Nordiques, New York Islanders, Tampa Bay Lightning, Detroit Red Wings, and Chicago Blackhawks, Clark played the vast majority of his career – albeit in three separate tenures – with the Toronto Maple Leafs. Later, Clark confessed that he had been happy with his lot:

> I got drafted as a Toronto Maple Leaf, I spent my first nine years as a Toronto Maple Leaf and basically the next six years getting traded in and out of Toronto, coming back two more times throughout those six years while playing in other cities, but the team that always felt like home was Toronto. At the end of my career in 2000, with my body pretty much worn out, I was very fortunate to be able to retire a Leaf, where I started.

Certainly, few other players had endeared themselves more to Leafs Nation.

Meanwhile, the Leafs believed they were just a player or two away from being able to go to the Stanley Cup final, and on July 4 they believed they had found those players. That day, Toronto signed free agents Gary Roberts from the Carolina Hurricanes and Shayne Corson from the Montreal Canadiens. "The Leafs were looking to sign a couple of guys to add that sandpaper element to the team," Darcy Tucker, who married Corson's sister Shannon, recalled. "Shayne was becoming an unrestricted [free] agent. I tried to talk him into coming here because I thought it would be a great situation for the two of us to play together."

Corson was given sweater number 27, which had belonged to his childhood hero, Darryl Sittler. Roberts wore number 7, once worn in Toronto by Lanny McDonald, who mentored Roberts in Calgary with the Flames. Both players were 34 years of age, so while they wouldn't replicate the exploits of Sittler and McDonald in their prime, they would battle opponents for puck possession and space, attributes the Leafs had lacked in 1999–2000.

The team added more grit with the signing of free agent Dave Manson, and just prior to the beginning of the season, Toronto packaged Alexander Karpovtsev and a draft choice to Chicago in return for defenceman Bryan McCabe. The roster had undergone a large makeover:

only 13 players on the 2000–01 roster had been with the Leafs at the beginning of the previous season.

Pat Quinn built the team around Curtis Joseph in goal, a defensive quartet of veterans Dmitri Yushkevich and Bryan McCabe with youngsters Tomáš Kaberle and Danny Markov, and forwards Sergei Berezin and Mats Sundin. It was this youthful team that took on the Montreal Canadiens on the opening night of the new campaign. After a pregame tribute to Wendel Clark, the game got underway. The Leafs were solid, and Cujo was once again spectacular. Toronto blanked Montreal, 2–0. It was the second straight season opener in which Curtis Joseph had earned a shutout.

Still, the Maple Leafs' identity hadn't quite coalesced; it was unclear whether or not this incarnation of the Blue and White was a team that would rely on skill or one that would grind out wins. Amidst such uncertainty, the Leafs staggered out of the gate. In a 5–2 loss to the Canucks on October 17, for instance, Toronto managed just 15 shots. Coach Pat Quinn was candid in his assessment: "At this point, scoring is not a big concern. We need to clean up a lot of things before we get chances. Defence creates a lot of opportunities and we've been trying to correct that first. Our defence hasn't been good, but our defence is also tied into forwards."

Toronto continued to stumble at times in the early going. On November 29, Toronto was up 5–0 against the Blues with 15 minutes to play and ended up losing, 6–5, in overtime. It was an epic collapse, reminding many of a game against Calgary on January 26, 1987 – when Toronto had been up 5–0 at 6:02 of the third and ended up losing, 6–5, in extra time.

Fortunately for Leafs Nation, things got better. The team began to gel, and Toronto went six games without a loss to start December. Later that month, Cujo marked his 300th NHL win in a 5–2 romp over Montreal. But the Leafs were hastily brought down to earth on a visit to Pittsburgh on December 27, when Mario Lemieux returned to action after missing a remarkable 1,336 days. Injuries had forced Super Mario to retire prematurely on April 26, 1997. Some three and a half years later, Leafs fans wished he had stayed retired. Lemieux led the Penguins charge with a goal and two assists as Pittsburgh dumped Toronto, 5–0.

The inconsistent play carried over into 2001. During the slide, Pat Quinn summoned each player to his office for a one-on-one chat. The talks seemed to rally the troops. The team also benefited from the veteran leadership Roberts provided. But there were still struggles, especially

It means a lot to have played for the Maple Leafs. Growing up in Toronto, I played minor hockey with C.B. Parsons [Junior High School] and I went to high school at Bathurst Heights. I can remember coming home one day after talking to one of the scouts. I signed a C-Form, and with the signing came a hundred-dollar cheque. I was talking to my dad and I said, "Oh, by the way, I've got a hundred dollars in my pocket." And he said, "What! Where'd you get that?" "Oh," I said. "I signed some kind of a form with the Toronto Maple Leafs that says they own me." My dad was probably making about fifty bucks a week at the time, so it was kind of a neat thing to do.

Bob Nevin
PLAYER
1957–64

on the defensive side. To address this issue, Toronto supplemented its roster by picking up Wade Belak on waivers from Calgary. What Belak lacked in skill, he compensated for with toughness and desire. And while predominantly a defenceman, he could also play wing. A little later, in March, the Leafs also acquired defenceman Aki Berg from the Los Angeles Kings in return for Adam Mair.

The team began to play with more deliberation and grit. During a game in Philadelphia on March 29, Tie Domi and the Flyers' Luke Richardson were called for unsportsmanlike conduct. While Domi sat in the penalty box, Flyers fans began to heckle him from behind the Plexiglas. Domi jawed with them, and when the razzing showed no sign of abating, he stood and squirted the hecklers with his water bottle. One of them leapt over the top of the partition, but the glass gave way and he landed in the penalty box with Domi. Startled, Domi pulled the man's jacket over his head. When the penalty-box attendant tried to subdue the fan, he pushed the attendant away to get at Domi. Tie wrangled with the fan to defend himself. Finally, a linesman jumped into the penalty box and was able to bring the altercation to an end. "It was like watching somebody fall into the lion's den," Cujo chuckled. "In this game, you expect the unexpected." Tie won the scrap, and the Leafs won the game, 2–1.

Still, Toronto's playoff hopes were hanging by a thread in March – a disappointing situation for a team that, at the beginning of season, believed it was of championship calibre. There were individual disappointments, too. Steve Thomas, for instance, missed 22 games with a knee injury and another three with an infected hand, and his scoring fell precipitously from 26 goals in the previous campaign to eight.

The Maple Leafs nevertheless clinched a playoff berth in the team's penultimate game of the season with a 1–0 win over Chicago. Toronto finished third in the Northeast Division with 90 points. Mats Sundin led the team in scoring with 74 points, including 28 goals. Curtis Joseph won the Molson Cup, and sported a terrific .915 save percentage, along with six shutouts.

Despite any sense of disappointment the team might have had with the regular season, the playoffs represented a clean sheet of ice for the Leafs. Dmitri Yushkevich knew it and was brimming with confidence: "The greatest thing about the playoffs is no one cares about their own statistics, their ice time, their points or their goals," the defenceman said. "Everybody understands that on the Stanley Cup, there won't be room to inscribe how many goals you scored in the playoffs."

The question remained whether this confidence would be enough to carry the Leafs further along their quest.

The opening round once more saw Toronto facing Ottawa. The Senators had dominated the Leafs throughout the regular season, winning all five meetings – including the last game of the season, in which the Senators, playing with only 15 skaters (three fewer than the usual complement), beat the Leafs, 5–3.

The adversaries were scoreless after 60 minutes of play in the opener in Ottawa. The Leafs blocked shots, took the body, and enjoyed sensational goaltending from Cujo. Toronto kept Senators sniper Alexei Yashin at bay by employing Corson to, as the *Toronto Star* described it, "nip at Yashin's ankles as he pursued him around the Corel Centre ice surface."

During the overtime period, Mats Sundin was in need of a change after having been on the ice for a long shift. Exhausted, he hollered, "Change! Change!" as he skated towards the Toronto bench. But in the meantime, Steve Thomas had knocked the puck down, and it landed at the feet of the Leafs captain. Sundin took it and leaned into a slap shot that blistered past Patrick Lalime for the deciding goal at 10:49 of extra time.

Game Two produced yet another display of outstanding positional play by the Maple Leafs. Toronto kept emotions in check, worked exceptionally hard, and again rode brilliant goaltending to a victory, this time a 3–0 shutout.

The third game appeared to be going very much Toronto's way, as the Leafs led 2–0 in the third. Ottawa managed to roar back with a pair of goals late in the period, including Daniel Alfredsson's marker with only 36 seconds remaining. Once again, overtime would be required, and once again, it was the Leafs who took advantage. Defenceman Cory Cross proved to be the hero when he scored at 2:16 to give his team a stranglehold on the series.

For Ottawa, there was no coming back. Led by two goals from Yanic Perreault, Toronto locked up the series with a 3–1 win in Game Four to sweep the Senators. It was the first sweep in a seven-game series for the Maple Leafs since 1949.

The Leafs had hardly been the favourite in the series, and they wouldn't be in the next series either, when they again faced a tough Devils team in New Jersey. Still, Toronto pounced quickly in Game One, winning, 2–0. Steve Thomas explained what he thought was working for the Blue and White: "Every guy is willing to sacrifice, block shots, and battle in the corners. That's what wins hockey games in the playoffs."

When I played my first game in Maple Leaf Gardens [on November 16, 1955], I was really nervous, but I got lucky. There was a scramble in front of the net and I scored my first goal against Jacques Plante. I will never forget that day for the rest of my life!

Ron Hurst
PLAYER
1955–57

The Devils, however, were not about to roll over just yet. While Toronto rebounded from a 5–2 deficit in Game Two to force overtime, the Devils scored in extra time to earn a 6–5 win.

Game Three would also require overtime. Seven minutes in, the Devils' Brian Rafalski banked a shot off Cory Cross's skate and behind Joseph to break the hearts of the Leafs and their fans.

While the Leafs played well and won Game Four, 3–1, the match will be better remembered for an incident that occurred with only seconds to play. Tie Domi had been playing well on the Leafs checking line alongside Corson and Tucker. His solid play, however, was overshadowed by a poor decision. With 21 seconds to play, Domi levelled an elbow to the head of Scott Niedermayer. The Devils star lay unconscious on the ice, and Domi was given a match penalty for deliberate intent to injure. When Niedermayer was later diagnosed with a concussion, Domi was suspended for the remainder of the playoffs, should the Leafs advance past New Jersey. If, however, the Leafs were eliminated, Domi would miss the first eight games of the

2001–02 season. It was the longest penalty ever assessed in the history of the NHL playoffs.

Still, the Leafs pressed on. In Game Five, Tomáš Kaberle scored with 30 seconds to play in the game. The goal was disputed by the Devils, who believed that Corson had interfered with Brodeur on the goal. But the officials ruled that New Jersey's Colin White had pushed the Leafs winger into Brodeur while Kaberle's shot flew high above a tangle of players. The defenceman's goal stood as the winner, and with the 3–2 victory, Toronto was now ahead in the series, three games to two.

Unfortunately for Leafs Nation, that was as close to the conference final as their beloved team was going to get. New Jersey fought back and outplayed the Maple Leafs in Game Six, with a 4–2 win that tied the series at three games each. The seventh and deciding game in New Jersey was a colossal disappointment for Toronto and its team. The Devils simply pasted the Leafs, 5–1, to end their season. "It's hard to stomach," a dejected Steve Thomas admitted. "We had an opportunity to really make a name for ourselves and we dropped the ball."

Coach Quinn took heart: "We made progress, especially mentally. You have to learn how to win in the playoffs, when every man plays harder." Indeed, despite the exit from the postseason, there was much to look forward to. Toronto had a strong and youthful lineup, the team's stars were arguably at the peak of their careers, and most pundits pegged the Leafs as a playoff certainty. It was, however, uncertain just how far this team could go.

A NEW WORLD

It was a glorious, sunny late-summer morning in the city of Toronto on September 11, 2001, and equally beautiful in New York City. But on this day, the entire world changed when terrorists hijacked four passenger airliners. Two of the planes, American Airlines Flight 11 and United Airlines Flight 175, were steered into the World Trade Center's two towers. Within less than two hours, both 110-storey buildings had collapsed. Another plane, American Airlines Flight 77, was flown into the western flank of the Pentagon in Arlington County, Virginia. A fourth plane, United Airlines Flight 93, was prevented from hitting the hijackers' initial target of Washington, D.C., after passengers overpowered them. This plane instead crashed into a field near Shanksville, Pennsylvania. A total of 2,996 people perished in the attacks.

The Leafs were busy preparing for a trip to St. John's, Newfoundland. A team of employees of Maple Leaf Sports and Entertainment was already there, laying the groundwork for what was to be the biggest training camp in the franchise's history. A week of events had been planned, including the grand opening of Mile One Stadium, the new home of the AHL's St. John's Maple Leafs. The new rink was scheduled to host the annual Blue and White Game as well as an exhibition match between the Maple Leafs and Montreal Canadiens.

The morning of September 11 changed everyone's plans – particularly for the people of Newfoundland. While the world was reeling, all air traffic was grounded. All westbound flights still flying over the Atlantic were immediately diverted to Newfoundland, where the closest North American international airports could be found. Several thousand confused and anxious passengers were about to set foot on "The Rock." Most of these accidental tourists had never been to Canada, and some had never even heard of Newfoundland.

In all, 4,400 passengers and 400 crew members landed in St. John's. Once on the ground, the travellers were transported to Mile One Stadium. While it had not yet hosted a single event, the arena had been commandeered by the Canadian Red Cross. Mile One Stadium was now essentially a crisis centre.

Staff members from both the Toronto and St. John's Maple Leafs were enlisted to help the Red Cross, serving as front-line workers in charge of processing all of the travellers. While the world knew the basic facts about what had happened in New York, Pennsylvania, and Washington, few knew why it happened or who was responsible. "I was stationed at a desk and the first passengers to arrive at our table were an elderly couple from the Netherlands," MLSE employee Mike Ferriman recalled. "They were frightened. The gentleman handed me his and his wife's passports, and as he did, he asked me, 'Is this World War III?' My reply was 'I don't know.'"

It was, for everyone, a dark moment. Fortunately, Newfoundlanders quickly lived up to their reputation for congeniality and hospitality as they tackled the logistical challenges posed by the sudden arrival of so many unexpected visitors. There was food for everyone, and – with some expert improvisation – the residents of St. John's found everyone a place to sleep, pressing motels, hotel ballrooms, and even spare (and not so spare) bedrooms in people's homes into service.

Air traffic remained grounded for days. And every day, weary travellers sat in the seats of the arena under signs that denoted their respective flight numbers, waiting and watching as the St. John's Maple Leafs practised below.

Happily, the stranded were able to return home. Meanwhile, the Blue and White Game was a huge success and turned out to be something of a reward for all the Newfoundlanders who had helped out in the aftermath of 9/11. With this game, as well as the match against the Habs the next night, the Maple Leafs were the first North American pro sports team to return to action after that horrible Tuesday in September.

Canada was profoundly affected by the 9/11 attacks. Still, just as it had done during the Second World War, hockey – and all sports, for that matter – served as a much-needed distraction from the grim times. Everyone shared the irrefutable fact that hockey was, after all, just a game.

Despite the horrors of 9/11, Leafs Nation had reason to be hopeful as their team readied for the season ahead. With Curtis Joseph in goal, Mats Sundin, Shayne Corson, and Gary Roberts up front, and Tomáš Kaberle, Bryan McCabe, and Dmitri Yushkevich manning the blueline, the Leafs appeared to have a strong foundation. Pat Quinn nevertheless went to market and, through trades and free-agent signings, pieced together what now looked like a legitimate championship squad.

In June, the GM picked up two proven NHL players: Czech Robert Reichel and Swede Mikael Renberg were acquired from Phoenix in return for Danny Markov and Sergei Berezin, respectively, in two separate transactions. Toronto also picked up Travis Green from the Coyotes. With Sundin as the centre on the first line, Reichel would centre the second line and Green the third.

The Maple Leafs then acquired the highly sought-after free agent Alexander Mogilny. While the winger had been a 43-goal scorer with New Jersey in 2000–01, he was also a premier two-way player. Mogilny's signing, however, left local favourite Steve Thomas on the outside looking in. "Stumpy" would subsequently sign with Chicago.

Meanwhile, Bryan Berard, who had undergone seven operations on his eye, now met the league's minimum vision requirement of 20/400 with the help of a contact lens. The defenceman announced his imminent return. But first, he had to find a team. Toronto, of course, was interested in his services – Pat Quinn believed the Leafs should be the team to give him a chance to get back in the league. Berard, however, felt that he needed a new start away from the media frenzy of Toronto. "I really wanted to get away from the injury. I knew in Toronto the pressure would have been a lot more," Berard explained. "I loved Toronto. I loved being a Leaf. There's nothing you can do about an eye injury. I wish things would have worked out differently, and [that] I could have been a Leaf for a long time."

Berard instead opted to sign with the New York Rangers. In so doing, Berard surrendered the $6.5 million insurance settlement he had received.

The Leafs faced the Senators in the home opener at Air Canada Centre. Prior to the game, the Maple Leafs raised Frank Mahovlich's number 27 to the rafters, honouring his tremendous accomplishments while playing for Toronto. The Leafs' other great Number 27, Darryl Sittler, was also scheduled to be honoured that night. Unfortunately, Sittler's wife was too ill at the time, so his ceremony was postponed. Wendy Sittler passed away shortly afterwards.

As for the game itself, the Leafs did not convince. The defence was sloppy – an unfortunate but recurring trait throughout the upcoming season. To be fair, the Leafs were missing some important pieces. Kaberle was still in contract negotiations, and Tie Domi was serving the eight-game suspension he had received during the playoff

series against New Jersey. The silver lining was Mogilny, who, in his first game in blue and white, collected a pair of goals. But it wasn't enough, as Ottawa skated away with a 5–4 victory.

Despite inconsistent defensive play, the Leafs enjoyed a very strong season. Still, it was a season disrupted by a series of bizarre incidents. Yushkevich was diagnosed with a blood clot in his right leg on February 5 and would miss most of the rest of the season. Renberg, who in mid-March was trying to work through a groin injury, found that he had, in actuality, a broken pelvis. Gary Roberts missed ten games with a rib injury. In the third period of a 4–1 win over the Carolina Hurricanes on February 26, Curtis Joseph got his left hand caught up in the mesh of his net. X-rays confirmed the diagnosis: a middle metacarpal bone in Cujo's left hand was broken.

The loss of Cujo – a finalist for the Vézina Trophy in 1999 and 2000 – was a massive blow to the Maple Leafs' fortunes. Corey Schwab became the de facto number-one goalie in Toronto, while Pat Quinn picked up Tom Barrasso from the Hurricanes for additional help in goal. Schwab, who had spent the 2000–01 season in the International Hockey League, fared well and helped to save Toronto's season.

The Leafs held a pregame ceremony on March 2 to celebrate the 75th anniversary of the team being renamed the Maple Leafs. To mark the occasion, the Maple Leafs wore the green-and-white sweaters of the Toronto St. Patricks, and the franchise honoured its top 25 players of all time. The players were seated on the Leafs bench and were introduced individually by public-address announcer Andy Frost. After being announced, each honouree walked out to centre ice to the roar of the Air Canada Centre crowd. That was, of course, until 78-year-old Art Jackson, the nephew of 1930s star Harvey "Busher" Jackson, stood up for his turn. Art had been chosen to represent his late uncle. Although Busher was one of the greatest players of his time, he had been blacklisted from the Hockey Hall of Fame by his former boss, Conn Smythe. Jackson was finally inducted into the Hall five years after his death.

Art Jackson stood on the Leafs bench, set to walk out and accept the honour on behalf of his uncle. As Andy Frost was making his introduction, however, Jackson collapsed. Team physician Michael Clarfield worked furiously to revive him under the hushed gaze of the Air Canada Centre crowd, but it was futile. Jackson died on the Toronto Maple Leafs bench. Forty-five minutes later, the Leafs and the Sabres skated to a 3–3 tie.

The final regular-season game was against the Senators. Former Leafs coach Roger Neilson, now an assistant coach with Ottawa, was battling cancer. Senators head coach Jacques Martin stepped aside for the final two games of the regular season, allowing Neilson, who had just over a year to live, to reach his milestone 1,000th game as a head coach in the NHL. The Leafs prevailed, 5–2, finishing the season on a four-game winning streak.

In spite of some setbacks, Toronto completed the 2001–02 season in second place in the Northeast Division with 100 points, just one point behind the Boston Bruins. It was just the second time that the Leafs had reached the century mark. And the Leafs' record found them in third place overall – only Detroit, with 116, had more points than Toronto and Boston. Mats Sundin led the team in goals and points; his 41 goals tied him for second in the league, while his 80 points were fourth-best. Sundin also won the Molson Cup and was selected to the NHL's Second All-Star Team.

The first round of the playoffs matched Toronto with the New York Islanders, who finished second in the Atlantic Division with 96 points. Tie Domi was the hero in Game One when he scored the winner in the 3–1 Leafs victory. The win, however, was overshadowed by a significant injury when Michael Peca slashed Mats Sundin's hand late in the first period. Although Sundin would play in Games Two and Three, he was diagnosed with a broken wrist and would sit out the remainder of the series.

Fortunately, and in front of some spectacular goaltending by Curtis Joseph, Toronto won Game Two, 2–0. Alyn McCauley, who had stepped up to centre the first line in the absence of Sundin, scored the winner in the third period.

The Islanders lashed back in Game Three and chased Joseph from the net early in the third after the Toronto goaltender allowed his sixth goal. Schwab replaced his shaky partner, but the damage was done and the Islanders beat the Leafs, 6–1. And in Game Four, the Islanders picked up where they had left off. New York's Shawn Bates scored on a penalty shot with just 2:30 remaining in the game to give the Islanders a 4–3 victory.

Curtis Joseph was signed by Toronto for the 1998–99 season, and ended it as runner-up for the Vézina Trophy as the league's top goaltender and a finalist for the Pearson Award as the NHL's most valuable player. By the time he signed with Detroit in 2002, he had compiled three seasons with 30 or more wins as a Leaf. Joseph ended his NHL career with one final season with the Leafs in 2008–09.

Game Five began with an unfortunate gaffe by Pat Quinn that could easily have hampered his team for the entire contest. While drafting his lineup, Quinn listed Renberg as one of his scratches, but inadvertently put down Reichel's number, 21, rather than Renberg's number, 19. Renberg was indeed a scratch, but Quinn's mistake meant that Reichel was also dismissed from the game. It didn't matter. The Leafs played a physical game that stifled the Islanders and resulted in a 6–3 win, including a pair of goals from Bryan McCabe.

The Islanders came back in Game Six on home ice. There, New York was able to draw even in the series with a 5–3 win. Back at Air Canada Centre, Leafs Nation was ready for Game Seven. Once again, Curtis Joseph was brilliant in net and Mogilny provided a pair of goals in a 4–2 victory that concluded a bitter and hard-fought series.

The victory set up yet another meeting with the Leafs' rival of recent times, the Ottawa Senators. Domi, speaking for his teammates, expected a rough and ready instalment in the Battle of Ontario. "If people don't like tough hockey," he warned, "they'd better not watch it." Yet the Senators had finished their series against Philadelphia in five games, and were well rested by the time the puck was ready to be dropped for the conference semifinal series. The time off had served Ottawa well, and the Senators shut out the Leafs, 5–0, in Game One. Sens goalie Patrick Lalime counted his fourth shutout in only six playoff games.

The Leafs were somewhat better in Game Two. After 60 minutes, the teams were tied 2–2. In fact, the teams were still tied after two overtime periods. Finally, at 4:30 of the third extra frame, Gary Roberts fired the puck through Lalime's legs for the decisive tally.

The Leafs were pleased to see Cory Cross and Mikael Renberg return to action in Game Three. Cross had missed 19 games with a hip injury, but came back and played well; Renberg quickly realized that he couldn't be effective and left the game, and missed the remainder of the playoffs. The Leafs ended up on the short end of a 3–2 final score.

The teams then traded wins at one another's home rink. In Game Four, Toronto beat the Senators, 2–1, in Ottawa, while the Senators once again pulled ahead in the series by dumping the Leafs, 4–2, in Game Five at Air Canada Centre. Toronto now faced an uphill battle and needed to win two games in a row to stay alive in the playoffs. The task was made even harder after the loss of Darcy Tucker, who suffered a separated shoulder after a hit by Daniel Alfredsson.

Still, Toronto came out strong in Game Six. For his part, Alfredsson was booed every time he touched the puck by the thousands of Toronto fans in attendance at the Corel Centre. Fortunately, Gary Roberts once again played like a man possessed and scored twice. Alex Mogilny, who had been unusually quiet through the playoffs to that point, scored the winner. With the 4–3 win, the Leafs had drawn even in the series and forced a Game Seven.

Gary Roberts's approach was rubbing off on the team as a whole, and Pat Quinn was awed at his play: "We hear about how athletes raise their game at playoff time, but he seems to have found another gear, even though we all thought he played at high gear all the time." Several sportswriters noticed that various Leafs had the initials GRH written on their undershirts. It was revealed that the players, motivated by the diligent work of their teammate, wanted to play "Gary Roberts Hockey." In Game Seven, they did just that, and Toronto finished Ottawa off with a 3–0 win.

With the series win, the Leafs effectively became Canada's team. It was a group of "ragamuffins," as the *Toronto Star* wrote with pride, "that played with the precision of a surgeon and the heart of a lion with absolutely no regard for their personal welfare." The ragamuffins were off to the Eastern Conference final for the first time since 1994.

Waiting for them in Raleigh, North Carolina, were the Carolina Hurricanes. The Leafs were outshot, 32–14, in Game One and found themselves getting into penalty trouble. Despite this, Toronto found a way to win and took the opener, 2–1. After the game, Quinn found himself gasping for breath and went to hospital, where doctors discovered that he had an erratic heartbeat. Quinn convinced doctors to release him, and the big Irishman was behind the bench for Game Two. While the score was identical, it was the Hurricanes who skated away with the overtime win to tie the series.

Quinn's health challenges continued, and when the team returned to Toronto, the coach was admitted to hospital. Rick Ley was behind the Leafs bench for Game Three. Once again, the teams required overtime to decide a winner, and once again, it was Carolina that took advantage. The Hurricanes' Jeff O'Neill roofed the winner at 6:01 of the overtime period for yet another 2–1 score.

Having convinced the medical staff at Toronto General Hospital to issue him a pass, Pat Quinn was back in his usual spot for Game Four. The coach made a dramatic entrance as Leafs organist Jimmy Holmstrom played

Manfred Mann's "The Mighty Quinn." Carolina net-minder Artūrs Irbe, however, ruined the surprise return by stoning the Leafs, 3–0.

Quinn did not accompany the team to Raleigh for Game Five, but his team delivered the best "feel better soon" present in the form of a 1–0 victory. Bryan McCabe's shot struck a skate, bounced off Darcy Tucker's stick, and eluded Irbe for the game's lone goal.

Game Six saw the teams return to Toronto and Pat Quinn to his regular rinkside post. It truly was anybody's game. Carolina led 1–0 and it appeared as though they were about to wrap up the game and the series. But with Curtis Joseph on the bench in favour of an extra attacker, Mats Sundin – still recovering from a broken wrist in the first round – scored with 22 seconds left to tie the contest. For the third time in the series, the Hurricanes and Leafs would need overtime. At 8:05 of the extra period, the heart of Leafs Nation was broken. Martin Gélinas scored to give the Hurricanes the win and a berth in the Stanley Cup final. The Leafs' season was over.

It had been a thrilling spring. Unfortunately, Curtis Joseph and Gary Roberts could carry the team only so far. "I've never figured out a way to deal with losing," the stoic but disappointed Pat Quinn confessed. The coach, however, would have to find a way to deal with his lifestyle. Doctors informed Quinn that he simply had to eat better, lose weight, and abandon his habit of smoking cigars. He followed their orders, knowing that he had little choice.

EDDIE THE EAGLE

During the off-season, the Maple Leafs made a substantial offer to Curtis Joseph in order to re-sign him before his contract expired on July 1. The offer would have made Cujo the highest-paid goaltender in the National Hockey League. But Joseph wanted a four-year deal, and the Leafs refused to offer more than three years. "We've made a significant offer and we hope he stays with us," Quinn said. "But we're not going to get caught shorthanded." Still, many wondered how sincere the Leafs and Cujo were about wanting to continue their relationship. Joseph had been sensational for most of his four seasons in Toronto but had, at times, given the media the sense that he would have preferred to join a team closer to winning the Stanley Cup. And then there was an apparent snub: Quinn, when serving as Team Canada's coach at the Salt Lake City Olympic Games earlier that year, chose to start Martin Brodeur in goal after Cujo and Canada dropped a 5–2 decision to Sweden in the opening game of the

tournament. It was, as far as some were concerned, a slap in the face of the Leafs' number-one netminder.

Perhaps not surprisingly, the day after free agency commenced, Curtis Joseph became a Detroit Red Wing. In short order, the Maple Leafs announced the acquisition of Ed Belfour. Two years older than Joseph, Belfour carried an impressive resumé to Toronto. A Calder Trophy winner, he had been to the Stanley Cup final on three occasions, including a championship with Dallas in 1999. Belfour had also been awarded the Vézina Trophy in 1991 and 1993, and the Jennings Trophy, presented to goaltenders on the team giving up the fewest goals, on four occasions. The All-Star goaltender was ecstatic to join the Leafs: "I can't tell you how excited I am to be playing in Toronto. I am happy to have the opportunity to get a fresh start on a team that is gearing up to mount a run at the Stanley Cup."

Belfour was not the only new addition. The Leafs picked up Róbert Švehla from the Florida Panthers for Dmitri Yushkevich, and added free agents Tom Fitzgerald and Trevor Kidd from Florida. At the same time, Toronto lost Tom Barrasso, Cory Cross, Nathan Dempsey, and Corey Schwab to free agency, but added some terrific prospects in the NHL Entry Draft. Alex Steen was the team's first-round pick. Although raised in Sweden, Steen was born in Canada while his father, Thomas, was playing with the first incarnation of the Winnipeg Jets. Toronto also selected Matt Stajan, Ian White, and Staffan Kronwall.

And then there was the "new" coach. When training camp opened, Pat Quinn was fit, trim, and tanned. His health scare had shocked him into transforming his lifestyle, and he appeared all the better for it. Quinn's Maple Leafs, however, got off to a rocky start. After dumping Pittsburgh, 6–0, in the season opener, they stumbled through October, recording three wins, six losses, and two ties. But then Ed Belfour returned to his Vézina form. His coach saw how the transformation affected the whole team: "I think our guys finally realized that this guy can play, and started to get better in front of him."

After a strong December, Mikael Renberg suffered a freakish injury that only added to his accumulated woes (the forward had also had a boating accident during the summer). This time, while tying his skates playing in Edmonton on December 28, Renberg aggravated a blister on his hand. The hand became infected, and by the time the team landed in Vancouver for a game on New Year's Eve, he was battling a fever of 104 degrees Fahrenheit (40 Celsius) and was rushed to hospital. Renberg's left hand had become so infected that doctors considered amputating in order to save the player's life. Fortunately, the doctors got the infection under control and Renberg would be all right.

On February 8, 2003, the Maple Leafs were finally able to honour Darryl Sittler by raising a banner with his number, 27, to the rafters of Air Canada Centre. While Darryl and his family watched the banner being raised, there was one person who was noticeable by her absence: Darryl's wife, Wendy, who succumbed to cancer on October 6, 2001.

Darryl wanted to honour his wife and everything she meant to him. During a visit to Ken Dryden's office to review the artist's rendering of the banner, Darryl approached Ken with an idea:

> I said, "Ken, what would really mean a lot to me is if I could put Wendy's name on the banner." That caught him off guard, as that had never been done before. Wendy and I met when I was playing junior hockey, and we got married after my first year of pro. We had three kids. Wendy was a significant part of my Leaf career. It wasn't always easy to be the wife of the captain and going through the ups and the downs that go with that while being married and raising kids. I said, "I'll leave it with you, but to me, Wendy's been a huge part of my life and my success."

The night of the ceremony, Sittler stood at centre ice with his three children: Ryan, Meaghan, and Ashley. He mentioned Wendy during his speech and the fact that her name was on the lower corner of the banner: "I know that her big, warm, beautiful smile is shining down on us." Darryl later shared the importance of having his wife's name on the banner.

"I'm happy that the Leafs accepted my idea and I'm proud that Wendy's name is up there," he said. "Scott Morrison wrote a book asking different individuals their greatest moment in hockey [*My Greatest Day*, published in 2008]. The story of the banner was my contribution. You can talk about the ten points, or the Canada Cup win, both of which were great, but the banner was the pinnacle for me. It's there forever, and that, to me, was so meaningful."

And it was meaningful to Leafs Nation; there wasn't a dry eye in Air Canada Centre or among those watching on television the night Sittler's banner was raised.

Back on the ice, the Leafs were trying to combine skill with toughness. In a 4–1 loss to Ottawa on March 4, Toronto collected 111 penalty minutes. A third-period brawl saw Darcy Tucker challenge the entire Senators bench, earning him a five-game suspension. And Tie Domi was slapped with a three-game suspension for chasing Magnus Arvedson around the rink and knocking him to the ice with a punch to the face.

In truth, the Leafs needed to make some adjustments while they still could. Quinn realized that if his team was to progress through the playoffs, the time had come to bolster the defence and add more offence. On March 5, he landed Owen Nolan from the San Jose Sharks. Some considered the cost – Alyn McCauley, prospect Brad Boyes, and a first-round draft pick – too high. Nolan quickly silenced his detractors when he scored two goals in his first game in blue and white in a 3–3 tie with the Canucks on March 8.

While Nolan added some scoring power, the team's defence corps still needed attention. As Quinn observed, "From a depth standpoint, you just never have enough defencemen. Teams that think they have a chance to go a ways in the playoffs are looking for that kind of depth." To make it happen, the coach added Glen Wesley from the Carolina Hurricanes for a second-round selection, and Phil Housley from the Blackhawks for two picks.

Then, in a deal co-orchestrated by the player, Quinn brought back one of Leafs Nation's favourites. Doug Gilmour was added from the Montreal Canadiens for a sixth-round draft choice, and was thrilled to be returning to a city that simply adored him: "It's a dream come true. This team has been successful without me. I'm just going to try and add to their success and contribute the best way I can." With the addition of Dougie, the man known as Stand Pat had belied his nickname by adding veteran presence, goal-scoring potential, and defensive strength. The Leafs, thanks to Quinn, were now built for a deep playoff run.

Still, Toronto first had to finish up the regular season, which was not uneventful. On March 10, Mats Sundin scored the game-winner at 14:12 of the third period in a 3–2 win over the Edmonton Oilers. The point gave Sundin 1,000 in his career, making him the first Swedish-born and -trained player in NHL history to reach that plateau. He was the fifth player to reach the milestone while playing with the Maple Leafs.

Then, on March 28, an entirely different and unwelcome storyline emerged. Just over four minutes into his first game after returning to the Maple Leafs, Doug Gilmour collided with Dave Lowry of the Calgary Flames. The collision looked innocuous enough, but Gilmour was forced to crawl to the bench. Soon afterwards, team doctors confirmed the worst: Gilmour had torn the medial

collateral and anterior cruciate ligaments in his left knee. There would be no more hockey for Doug Gilmour that night – or any other night, for that matter. In the blink of an eye, Dougie's career was over.

At the same time, the Leafs roster was riddled with other injuries. Shayne Corson's colitis had flared up, Travis Green was out with bruised ribs, Phil Housley had a broken foot, Owen Nolan was suffering from back spasms and a bruised face, Karel Pilař was out with a heart condition, Mikael Renberg's recurring hamstring injury had him out of the lineup, Gary Roberts had a torn groin muscle, and Glen Wesley had a broken foot. It was a pitiable scenario.

The season ended with the Maple Leafs second in their division with 98 points, although this was well behind the Ottawa Senators' league-leading 113. There were, nevertheless, some impressive individual performances. In the penultimate game of the 2002–03 season, Eddie Belfour was spectacular. The netminder backstopped the Leafs to a 2–1 win over the Minnesota Wild. The victory, Belfour's 37th of the season, eclipsed Curtis Joseph's record for wins in a season by a Leafs goaltender. Belfour was also the

team's Molson Cup winner and finished with a .922 save percentage. While Mats Sundin led the team in goals with 37, the Leafs' overall scoring leader was Alexander Mogilny, with 79 points, including 33 goals. Mogilny also received the Lady Byng Trophy as the league's most gentlemanly player. The Leafs as a whole, however, were not that gentlemanly – Toronto led the league in penalty minutes. Wade Belak topped the list with 196 penalty minutes, followed by Tie Domi (171), Bryan McCabe (135), Nik Antropov (124), and Darcy Tucker (119).

The Leafs met an old foe in the Eastern Conference quarter-final – the Philadelphia Flyers, second-place finishers in the Atlantic Division. There were striking similarities: both teams boasted a freewheeling, physical style, as well as payrolls that were among the highest in the league.

Opening in Philadelphia, Toronto drew first blood with a 5–3 win. Alex Mogilny picked up a hat trick, but the team added Nik Antropov to the injured list with a cracked bone in his foot. The Flyers, however, evened the series with a 4–1 win in Game Two. It was, as the Leafs coach suggested, "a good, old-fashioned whupping."

Gary Roberts was secured by Toronto in the 2000–01 season, and the veteran reacted by leading the Leafs with 29 goals. Roberts's immense contributions were most evident during the playoffs in 2001–02, when the hard-working forward contributed 19 points in 19 games.

It took double overtime to settle the wildly entertaining third game of the series, played at Air Canada Centre. Tomáš Kaberle pinched in from the point and fired the puck over Roman Čechmánek at 7:20 of the second extra frame for the 4–3 Leafs win. It was Kaberle's second goal of the night.

Already tired from the five-period marathon of the third game, the teams would get no relief in Game Four, which required three overtime periods to reach a conclusion. Finally, at 13:54 of the third extra frame, Mark Recchi scored to give the Flyers a 3–2 victory. Despite stopping 72 of the 75 shots fired at him, Ed Belfour was on the wrong side of the result.

The Flyers forechecked relentlessly in Game Five, grinding down the veteran Leafs, who subsequently committed errors in their own end. The strategy paid off, and with little offence from Toronto's forwards, Philadelphia earned a 4–1 victory and took a three-games-to-two lead.

The Maple Leafs recovered and battled hard in Game Six. Once again, overtime was required to decide a winner between the evenly matched squads. At 10:51 of the second extra frame, Travis Green picked up a rebound and backhanded the puck past Čechmánek to pick up a 2–1 win and tie the series.

With everything now down to a single game, both teams prepared – and were expected – to leave everything on the ice. Yet, inexplicably, the Leafs didn't show up. The Flyers completely dominated from the opening faceoff, and blasted Toronto, 6–1. It was a devastating conclusion to a season in which Toronto believed they had the team and chemistry to carry them to the Stanley Cup. Instead, the Leafs simply fizzled out in the opening round.

In truth, the trade-deadline acquisitions had not added to the Toronto Maple Leafs in any appreciable way. While Owen Nolan had 12 points in his 14 regular-season games, he had been unable to score in the playoffs. Then there was Doug Gilmour's career-ending injury on the first shift of his Maple Leaf return. Phil Housley would, in the end, play only one regular-season game and three playoff games in his brief sojourn in Toronto. Similarly, Glen Wesley played seven regular-season games and five playoff contests before he too ended his time with Toronto.

JFJ

The Maple Leafs announced in June 2003 that Pat Quinn would no longer carry both the coach's mantle and the general manager's portfolio. Quinn would continue to coach, but the team would search for a general manager.

Many names were discussed and several candidates interviewed, but Ken Dryden ultimately hired John Ferguson Jr. At just 36, Ferguson already possessed a long resumé. A one-time American Hockey League player who, after earning a law degree, had worked as an agent, Ferguson had also been a scout and spent two summers in the hockey operations and legal departments of the NHL's New York headquarters before he was hired as the St. Louis Blues' assistant general manager. He had extensive knowledge in contracts and the collective bargaining agreement. John Ferguson Jr. was, at least as far as Dryden was concerned, an obvious choice.

At the same time, majority owner Steve Stavro was bought out by the Ontario Teachers' Pension Plan and stepped down as chairman in favour of Larry Tanenbaum. And Ken Dryden's position as team president was eliminated; instead, the general managers of both the Leafs and Raptors would report directly to Maple Leaf Sports and Entertainment president and CEO Richard Peddie. Dryden was given the title of vice-chairman and a seat on MLSE's board of directors. He remained with MLSE until 2004, when he left to pursue a career in politics.

The team acknowledged that mortgaging the future to obtain veterans in order to contend for the Stanley Cup was not the most prudent move Quinn and the Leafs had made. Acquiring Owen Nolan, at the cost of Alyn McCauley, Brad Boyes, and a first-round pick, had not worked in Toronto's favour. Quinn himself admitted, "I made the deal and gave away three young pieces, and it didn't pay out in the sense of winning [the Stanley Cup]. I'm not sure, if I put my manager's hat on, whether I would do it again." Conversely, John Ferguson would preach a doctrine of youth.

In the entry draft, the Leafs selected John Mitchell in the fifth round, but the draft cupboard had been stripped bare as a result of previous transactions. And while there was hope that young players such as defenceman Carlo Colaiacovo might finally crack the lineup, the team turned to veterans to fill the holes. The Leafs signed defencemen Bryan Marchment and Ken Klee, as well as centre Joe Nieuwendyk, a free agent from the New Jersey Devils. Even with a desire to grow younger, Toronto was forced to ice one of the oldest rosters in the league: 13 Leafs were over the age of 30, including the team's number-one goaltender, 39-year-old Ed Belfour.

The Leafs lost Travis Green, Jonas Höglund, and Glen Wesley to free agency. And Doug Gilmour, although he had hoped to make a comeback, decided instead to retire on September 8, 2003. Gilmour explained his decision

Smooth-skating Tomáš Kaberle played 878 games as a Leaf defenceman, collecting 520 points through 12 seasons.

during a media conference: "I've always felt I would not play if I was at a level I was unhappy with. My body is telling me the time has come."

Gilmour had been revered in the city; his six years leading the Leafs into battle in the early '90s yielded some of the most cherished memories for a generation of fans. Few other athletes could hope to command the attention that Leafs Nation and the city at large afforded the tenacious forward. The fans would continue to speak of Dougie's near-mythical achievements with teary eyes and a whispered reverence.

Toronto opened the 2003–04 season at home with a 4–0 loss to the Montreal Canadiens. In fact, it took just 30 minutes for the crowd to begin booing their team. Leafs Nation had begun to despair.

As the season progressed, however, the team's record improved. Beginning with a 5–3 win over Vancouver in November, the Maple Leafs won eight in a row before they were edged, 3–2, in overtime by St. Louis. By Christmas, Toronto had a very strong 20–6–3 record.

The Maple Leafs received one additional Christmas gift in New York City on December 26. That night, Mats Sundin beat Mike Dunham in overtime to give the Leafs a 6–5 win over the Rangers. It was Sundin's 13th overtime winner, breaking the NHL record of 12 held by Steve Thomas. More importantly, it was the 16th straight game in which Toronto had earned at least a point, which was also a franchise record.

On January 8, 2004, in a game against Nashville, Sundin was poised to take a shot when his stick broke. Frustrated, the captain threw the broken stick aside, but it hit the glass and went into the crowd. The NHL suspended Sundin for one game for his uncharacteristic recklessness. Later, Ottawa captain Daniel Alfredsson likewise broke his stick and sardonically mocked Sundin when he feigned throwing the stick into the crowd. He didn't, but his mimicking earned him the eternal scorn of Leafs Nation.

Still, the Leafs were having a very good season. By March, Toronto had already won 35 games and appeared poised for a solid playoff run. Undaunted by the previous season's result, John Ferguson Jr. chose to make some moves that he thought would end his team's Stanley Cup drought. On March 3, he landed New York Rangers defenceman and captain Brian Leetch, surrendering two prospects and two draft picks. With Leetch, Ferguson had added a premier NHL defenceman and a Stanley Cup winner.

Less than a week later, Ferguson pulled off another shocker, this time acquiring Ron Francis, a favourite son

in Carolina with the Hurricanes. The future Hall of Famer would, at career's end, sit in fifth place on the list of all-time scoring leaders. But in 2004, Francis was simply delighted to be heading north. The same day he joined the fold, the Leafs also signed free agent Calle Johansson and claimed Chad Kilger on waivers from Montreal. Without surrendering a single player off their roster, the Leafs had acquired character players with playoff experience. These moves left absolutely no doubt that Toronto was gunning for the Stanley Cup.

In the end, the Leafs finished second in the Northeast Division with 103 points, one point back of Boston. Toronto's 45 wins led the division. Mats Sundin led the team in scoring with 75 points, including 31 goals. Bryan McCabe earned a spot on the NHL's Second All-Star Team, where he was joined by Sundin. The late-season pickups of Leetch and Francis had provided the desired result: Leetch added 15 points in 15 games with the Blue and White, while Francis collected 10 in his 12-game appearance. Eddie Belfour was exceptionally strong in goal with a 2.13 goals-against average and a .918 save percentage. Belfour earned ten shutouts on the year and was awarded Toronto's Molson Cup for the second year in a row.

The first-round playoff matchup had a very familiar ring to it. For the fourth time in five years, the Battle of Ontario was re-engaged. In the six games in which Toronto faced Ottawa during the regular season, the Leafs had won four, lost one, and tied one. Yet, prior to the opening faceoff, Ottawa captain Daniel Alfredsson guaranteed that the Senators would win the Stanley Cup. He looked like a soothsayer after Game One, in which the Senators earned a 4–2 win.

The Leafs came back with a much better effort in Game Two. Gary Roberts tallied twice to give Toronto the 2–0 win. Toronto won Game Three by an identical score. Belfour continued to have a hot hand, and had now played more than 138 minutes of shutout hockey. His shutout streak ended, though, when Alfredsson scored late in the first period of Game Four en route to a 4–1 Senators win. And Toronto fans held their breath during the game when Mats Sundin left the game with an injured ankle. The captain missed Game Five, but Belfour again stood on his head. While they were confounded at times by the Senators (recording just six shots in the first two periods), the Leafs managed to persevere and hold on for yet another 2–0 victory.

Despite an incredible display of netminding by Belfour in Game Six, Toronto dropped a 2–1 decision to the host

Senators in double overtime. Ottawa's Mike Fisher scored at 1:47 of the second extra period. The Eagle had recorded 116 minutes and 55 seconds without surrendering a goal before Ottawa broke his latest streak.

Back in Toronto, the Leafs were able to restore order. Joe Nieuwendyk scored twice in the Leafs' 4–1 victory in Game Seven. Much to the chagrin of Ottawa fans, Toronto had once again taken the Battle of Ontario.

The Leafs moved on to the Eastern Conference semifinals against the Philadelphia Flyers, a team structured much like the Leafs: tough, with strong goaltending and the ability to score. But there was no love lost between the two teams. "When we knew we'd be playing Toronto, we didn't have to build up a lot of hate because it's already there," said Flyers captain Keith Primeau. Head to head in the regular season, the Flyers had won three of four games against Toronto.

The Maple Leafs were outplayed throughout Game One, which they lost, 3–1. In Game Two, there was renewed hope for Toronto as Sundin returned from his injury. But the Leafs lost Nieuwendyk, who was out with an aggravated back injury. In the end, and despite being held to a single shot in the second period, Philadelphia scored two power-play goals, which was good enough for a 2–1 victory.

In Game Three, the towering APB Line – Nik Antropov (six feet, six inches), Alexei Ponikarovsky (six foot four), and Wade Belak (six foot five) – faced off primarily against the Flyers' Primeau line and proved to be quite effective. In fact, Toronto battled back with a 4–1 victory, and then tied the series with a 3–1 win in Game Four.

The Leafs confidently skated out for Game Five with fire in their bellies. The flames, however, were promptly extinguished by the Flyers, who won in a 7–2 romp. Primeau had been able to skate outside the shadow cast by the APB Line to score three times. The Leafs went more than 19 minutes without a shot.

There was a far more convincing effort in Game Six. While the Leafs were down 2–0 to start the third period, they rebounded to tie the game with only five minutes to play. In overtime, however, Jeremy Roenick broke the hearts of Leafs fans everywhere when he wired a shot over Belfour's catching glove at 7:39 of the extra frame. The 2003–04 season was over.

While Leafs Nation was understandably disappointed, there was reason to be hopeful. After all, JFJ had collected some key pieces before the trade deadline. And while the roster might have been a little long in the tooth, many Leaf stars still appeared to be, more or less, at or near the peak of their careers. How cruel, then, that despite such promise and expectation, Leafs Nation was about to enter the longest playoff drought in franchise history.

From 1926 until 1928, the St. Patricks-turned-Leafs had been kept out of the playoffs for three consecutive years. Who could have guessed that the current edition of the Leafs would not return to the playoffs for nine long and unforgiving years?

As it happened, no team would be going to the playoffs in the spring of 2005, as fans everywhere would have to endure a full year without NHL hockey.

THE GAME RETURNS

After nearly two years of negotiations, the National Hockey League and its players were still nowhere near shaking hands on a collective-bargaining agreement as the 2004–05 season drew near. And once again, as in 1994–95, the owners would be the ones to force the issue by locking out the players. A day after the existing collective-bargaining agreement expired on September 15, 2004, the lockout began. It would last ten months and cause the entire 2004–05 season to be cancelled. And for the first time since 1919 – when the Spanish influenza pandemic raged through the final series between the Montreal Canadiens and Seattle Metropolitans – the Stanley Cup would not be awarded.

Without a first- or second-round selection in the 2004 NHL Entry Draft, Toronto had chosen goaltender Justin Pogge in the third round, 90th overall. In 2005, they had a first-round pick, but the loss of the 2004–05 season meant there were no standings on which to base the draft order for the 2005 NHL Entry Draft. The league's solution was to hold a lottery in which a team's chance of picking first overall was weighted according to their performance in recent years. Teams that had missed the playoffs in the past three seasons *and* had not drafted first overall in the previous four years stood the best chance at the number-one pick. The Pittsburgh Penguins won the lottery and selected superstar-in-waiting Sidney Crosby. Toronto's picks included netminder Tuukka Rask in the first round and Anton Stralman in the seventh.

By training camp in September, Toronto's team had changed drastically since its last game on May 4, 2004. Robert Reichel had returned to the Czech Republic, and Mikael Renberg went home to Sweden. Childhood friends Joe Nieuwendyk and Gary Roberts signed with the Florida Panthers. Alexander Mogilny signed with the New Jersey Devils, and Bryan Marchment left for Calgary.

When Curtis Joseph exercised his free-agent status and signed with the Red Wings in the summer of 2002, Toronto reacted by signing Ed Belfour (pictured). In the 2002–03 season, the Eagle set a franchise record with 37 wins. In 2003–04, he backstopped Toronto to 34 wins, including 10 shutouts.

Brian Leetch, ever so briefly a Leaf, signed with the Boston Bruins.

To fill the holes, Toronto picked up several free agents. Jason Allison was signed from Los Angeles, despite not having played an NHL game since 2003. Goalie Jean-Sébastien Aubin arrived from Pittsburgh, right winger Mariusz Czerkawski from the Islanders (though he lasted just 19 games), defenceman Alex Khavanov from St. Louis, and right winger Jeff O'Neill from Carolina. And after years of courting, the Leafs finally landed Eric Lindros after his stint with the New York Rangers.

Although Pat Quinn had a reputation for favouring veterans over rookies, several first-year players cracked the Leafs lineup throughout the season, including Carlo Colaiacovo, Staffan Kronwall, Alex Steen, Kyle Wellwood, and Ian White. All were Toronto draft picks, developed within the Leafs system.

The season opened at home against the Ottawa Senators. Seven minutes in, a deflected puck caught Mats Sundin in the face. He was taken to hospital, where doctors confirmed that there was no damage to the eye, but the captain nevertheless missed 12 games with a broken orbital bone. As far as the game was concerned, Toronto squandered a late lead and finished regulation time tied at two with the Senators. Then, after overtime settled nothing, Daniel Alfredsson beat Ed Belfour to give Ottawa the win in the NHL's first-ever shootout.

The Leafs had a fairly strong first half to the season. The line of Jason Allison, Jeff O'Neill, and Darcy Tucker worked well together and singlehandedly thrashed the Atlanta Thrashers on October 14, scoring five and collecting 12 points in the 9–1 victory in the Georgia capital. It was the most goals the Maple Leafs had scored in a single game since they dumped Chicago, 10–3, on

November 12, 1998. Toronto then earned its first-ever shootout victory on October 24, when Eric Lindros beat Andrew Raycroft to give the Leafs a 5–4 win over the Bruins. Lindros was proving to be a sound addition, scoring seven goals in Toronto's first eight games.

After a 2–1 win over Florida on November 28, Ed Belfour tied Terry Sawchuk for the second-most wins by an NHL goaltender. While it took him five tries, Belfour finally surpassed Sawchuk on December 19, when the Leafs beat the Islanders, 9–6. It was Belfour's 448th win. Belfour ended his career with 484 wins. At the time of writing, only Martin Brodeur and Patrick Roy have more.

By January 7, the Toronto Maple Leafs had won 24, lost 15 in regulation time, and lost 3 more in overtime or shootouts and seemed playoff-bound. A precipitous free fall, however, soon dashed those hopes. Between January 10 and February 11 (the last game before the Winter Olympics break), the Leafs won three, lost ten in regulation, and lost one each in overtime and via a shootout. It was a spectacular fall from grace.

Not long after the NHL resumed its season following the Olympics, the Leafs lost Eric Lindros, who had enjoyed such a strong start to the 2005–06 campaign. In a 4–2 loss to the Senators on March 4, he reinjured a wrist he had hurt in a 2–1 win over Dallas on December 10. This time, surgery was required, ending the season for the Big E. In fact, it was the end for Lindros in Toronto. During his time with the Leafs, Lindros scored 11 goals and accumulated 22 points over 33 games.

Still, March was a better month for Toronto, fuelled in part by Sundin. The captain had struggled through his eye injury at the start of the season and scored just 13 times in his first 49 games. But in the final 21 games of the schedule, he contributed 18 goals and assisted on 13 others. In one game against Florida, on April 11, Mats bulldozed his way to a win when he scored four goals and added two assists in the 6–5 overtime victory.

Eddie Belfour suffered a season-ending back injury in March, which opened the door for backup Mikael Tellqvist. But when the latter dropped back-to-back games against Montreal (5–1 and 6–2, respectively), Toronto summoned Jean-Sébastien Aubin from the Toronto Marlies of the AHL. Aubin had NHL experience with Pittsburgh, but in Toronto had been playing in the minors. Aubin nevertheless became an unlikely hero, giving the Leafs a late-season surge. With him in goal, the Leafs lost just once in regulation during April, winning seven and losing twice in overtime. Yet, the team's

playoff hopes were hanging by a thread. While Aubin and the Leafs dumped Ottawa, 5–1, on April 15, it wasn't enough – Tampa Bay won its final game of the season and snuck into the eighth and final playoff spot in the Eastern Conference, with 92 points. The Leafs, with 90 points, finished ninth.

Mats Sundin was the team's Molson Cup winner, collecting a team-best 78 points, including 31 goals, in 70 games. Despite his eye injury, Mats had reached the 30-goal plateau for the fourth consecutive season and the 12th time during his career. The Leafs blueline had also contributed offensively. In particular, Tomáš Kaberle and Bryan McCabe had career seasons, with Kaberle collecting 67 points (including 58 assists), while McCabe scored 19 times and had 68 points. The duo comprised the most feared power-play tandem in the league that season, and Toronto led the league with 107 power-play goals. But it was generally believed that the Leafs had taken a step backwards since the previous NHL season.

On April 20, only two days after the conclusion of the Leafs' season, John Ferguson Jr. fired coach Pat Quinn and assistant coach Rick Ley. While 2005–06 marked the first time Toronto had failed to make the playoffs with Quinn as coach, the firing seemed to be borne more from philosophical differences between Quinn and Ferguson. Quinn had not wanted to relinquish the job of general manager, but was forced to under Ken Dryden. The coach had also lobbied to have others hired instead of John Ferguson Jr. As a coach, Quinn preferred to ride the veterans during the season and was perhaps too cautious about infusing younger players into the roster. Ferguson had a different vision.

At the time of his firing, Pat Quinn was the winningest active coach in the NHL and was fourth on the all-time list. During Quinn's seven seasons coaching the Maple Leafs, the team had finished with three 100-point seasons and made the playoffs in six of the seven seasons, twice progressing to the conference final. For Ferguson, announcing Quinn's dismissal was an opportunity to put his own indelible stamp on the Toronto Maple Leafs. It was absolutely JFJ's team now. The team's success or failure, in the end, would lie squarely at his feet.

TENACITY IN THE
BLUE AND WHITE CITY
2006–07 TO 2014–15

BY A SLIVER

On May 12, 2006, the Toronto Maple Leafs appointed Paul Maurice to fill Pat Quinn's shoes. Although he was only 39 years old, the personable Maurice had been an NHL coach for nine years – in fact, he had guided the Carolina Hurricanes past the Leafs and into the Stanley Cup final in 2002. The Leafs had hired him to coach the AHL Toronto Marlies in 2005, and the promotion to the parent club meant Maurice would now oversee many of the young players he had helped to develop in the minors. It was, for everyone, a comfortable fit.

Meanwhile, general manager John Ferguson Jr. worked diligently during the off-season to further impress his own fingerprints on the Maple Leafs roster. For starters, several players were now finished with the team. Eric Lindros was signed by Dallas. Luke Richardson's second foray in Toronto was short-lived, and the defenceman moved on to play for the Tampa Bay Lightning. Ferguson bought out the final season on Tie Domi's contract, and, when the popular tough guy hadn't found a team by September 19, he announced his retirement. Jason Allison retired, and Aki Berg returned to Finland. The turnover, it seemed, was going to be substantial.

One of the more important changes came in goal. Thirty-nine-year-old Eddie Belfour was released and picked up by the Florida Panthers. Although they had Mikael Tellqvist and Jean-Sébastien Aubin, the Leafs were now in need of a top-flight netminder. So, on June 24, Ferguson sent junior netminding prospect Tuukka Rask to Boston for 2004 Calder Trophy winner Andrew Raycroft. It was a curious trade. While the Leafs had Rask pencilled in as one of their future goaltenders, Raycroft had struggled with the Bruins and sat out much of the 2005–06 season as a healthy scratch while Tim Thomas and Hannu Toivonen carried the load. Rask would go on to win a successful trip to the Stanley Cup final in 2013.

Still, JFJ made a number of prudent signings, adding veteran defencemen Hal Gill from the Bruins and Pavel Kubina from the Lightning. Ferguson also picked up forwards Boyd Devereaux from the Coyotes and Michael Peca from the Oilers. At the draft, Toronto chose Jiří Tlustý in the first round, Nikolai Kulemin in the second, James Reimer and Korbinian Holzer in the fourth, and Viktor Stalberg and Leo Komarov in the sixth round. It was, by all measuring sticks, a significant makeover.

The opener saw Toronto welcome Ottawa to Air Canada Centre. Prior to the ceremonial puck drop, Hap Day, Red Kelly, and Börje Salming had their numbers honoured and raised to the rafters. Hap Day was represented by his son Kerry, who as a youngster had served as team mascot while his father was coach. Leafs Nation chuckled when Red Kelly said, "I never ever dreamed that I'd be hung from the top of the building." Salming admitted that "it was amazing to have my banner up there with all the great Toronto Maple Leafs." But the current Leafs were unable to honour the gentlemen with a win. Mats Sundin scored Toronto's only goal in the 4–1 loss, on a penalty shot. The teams then travelled up Highway 401 to Ottawa for the rematch, and Raycroft answered his detractors with a 6–0 shutout.

The Leafs were competitive through the first two months of the season, but then hit a seven-game losing skid. As far as Coach Maurice was concerned, only a handful of players were contributing in a meaningful way: "You can see on their faces and you can see on the bench. They perform." It didn't help that the Leafs lost defensive bulldog and team leader Michael Peca in a game against the Blackhawks on December 22. Peca was lugging the puck out of his zone when a knee-on-knee hit sent him spinning, and the doctors later confirmed that he had suffered a torn medial collateral ligament and fractured his tibia. It would be Peca's final game in his hometown. He missed the remainder of the season and signed with Columbus in the off-season.

The Leafs had a positive start to 2007. In a home-and-home series with Boston, Raycroft came up big against his former club, leading the team to a 5–1 win in Toronto

Although he was selected seventh overall by the Maple Leafs in the 2009 NHL Entry Draft, it took several seasons for Nazem Kadri to earn a full-time position with Toronto. He scored 18 goals and collected 44 points in 48 games in 2012–13, and by the next season had established himself as part of the franchise's future with 20 goals and 50 points.

and a 10–2 victory in Boston. It was the first time the Leafs had scored ten in a game since they blasted Chicago, 10–3, on November 12, 1988. Later, on April 3, Raycroft would tie Eddie Belfour's franchise record for most wins by a goaltender in the regular season. Raycroft notched his 37th in a 3–2 overtime victory against Philadelphia.

Despite this impressive individual milestone, the Leafs were struggling to secure a playoff spot, and the season concluded with a heart-stopping, heart-breaking weekend.

The Maple Leafs needed a win against Montreal – and some help from the New Jersey Devils – to earn the eighth and final playoff spot in the Eastern Conference. It was a thrilling contest against the Canadiens on April 7. With the score tied 3–3 in the second, Paul Maurice pulled Andrew Raycroft in favour of Jean-Sébastien Aubin. Montreal went up 5–3, but the momentum shifted and the Leafs battled back to tie the game in the third. "The crowd came out for us in the third period," the Leafs' coach later said. Later in the period, Tomáš Kaberle fired a shot that Kyle Wellwood deflected past Habs goaltender Cristobal Huet for the 6–5 winner.

The two points gave Toronto 91 – one more than the Canadiens, eliminating Montreal from playoff contention. But now the Blue and White had to hold their collective breath. Their postseason fate rested on a game between the New Jersey Devils and New York Islanders. The Islanders had 90 points, and a win would trump the Leafs' total.

The Devils rested netminder Martin Brodeur, inserting Scott Clemmensen, starting just his fourth game of the season, in his place. Wade Dubielewicz, a 28-year-old rookie playing in his 17th NHL game, was in the crease for New York.

The Islanders went into the third period up 2–0, but John Madden of New Jersey scored twice in the final five minutes of regulation, his second goal knotting the score with just a second remaining on the clock. The teams went into overtime and, despite great chances at both ends, the extra period elapsed with the score still tied, forcing a shootout. With the first two Islanders shooters beating Clemmensen, the Devils had to come out big – but Dubielewicz came out even bigger, foiling Brian Gionta and Sergei Brylin on poke checks to claim the 3–2 victory for the Islanders, and in doing so, eliminating Toronto's last-gasp attempt to make the 2006–07 postseason.

Toronto finished ninth in the Eastern Conference with a record of 40 wins, 31 losses, and 11 overtime/shootout losses for 91 points, a single point behind the eighth-place Islanders. Sixteen of Toronto's losses were by a single goal, and five of those were in regulation. The Leafs could score, ranking ninth in the league in goals, led again by Mats Sundin's 27 markers and his team-high 76 points. Missing the playoffs in this fashion was a bitter pill to swallow: a single win, even in a shootout or overtime, was all that separated the Toronto Maple Leafs from the play-offs. Unfortunately, the team was not trending upwards.

LOYALTY

Despite Andrew Raycroft's impressive win total, John Ferguson Jr. felt that he needed to strengthen the team's goaltending. When he discovered that the San Jose Sharks were going to make Vesa Toskala available, JFJ pounced, sending three draft picks to San Jose for Toskala and forward Mark Bell. Toskala had shared the Sharks goal crease with Evgeni Nabokov for two seasons, and in 2006–07 he posted a 26–10–1 record with a 2.35 goals-against average and a .908 save percentage. Mark Bell, on the other hand, had been a 25-goal scorer with Chicago in 2005–06 but had fallen back in San Jose.

JFJ also secured Jason Blake, a speedy forward who had scored 40 goals for the New York Islanders during the previous campaign. Just days before the season commenced, however, Blake sat in the dressing room with his teammates and revealed that he had been diagnosed with chronic myelogenous leukemia, a treatable blood cancer. Blake was confident: "I can play hockey and live a normal life, so I feel the lucky one." Remarkably, although Blake would undergo treatments during the season, the resilient forward didn't miss a single game in 2007–08.

Opening night brought Ottawa to town for the third consecutive year. Raycroft was in goal as the Leafs earned a 4–3 overtime win. Toskala made his first appearance for the Blue and White the next night in Ottawa, but the Leafs fell 3–2 to the Senators. During that game, Sundin scored his 389th goal as a Maple Leaf, which tied him with Darryl Sittler for the team record. A week later, on October 11, the Leafs hammered the New York Islanders, 8–1. In the second period, Sundin was awarded an assist on Tomáš Kaberle's goal. This gave the captain 917 points with Toronto, which was one more than Sittler's team record in that category. The game operations crew ran a video of Sundin's career highlights on the scoreboard and Leafs Nation gave their captain a standing ovation. There was one problem: Sundin hadn't touched the puck on Kaberle's goal. In order to remedy the situation, Sundin went out and scored a goal in the third period, which officially gave him the team records in both goals and points. At the end of the game, with the fans chanting Sundin's name, public-address announcer Andy Frost announced the Leafs captain as the first, second, and third stars of the game. Captain Mats would break one more record that season: in a 4–2 win over the Penguins on December 1, Sundin broke Babe Dye's 83-year-old Toronto record when he extended his home-game point streak to 15 games.

There wasn't much else for fans to cheer about this season, as the Maple Leafs fell out of contention early on. Toronto's inept play really began with a loss to Montreal on December 15 and carried through until January 12, 2008. During that stretch, the Leafs won just two and lost 11, including five games in a row. As the team continued to struggle, the board of directors met privately and decided that a change had to be made in the front office. On January 22, John Ferguson Jr. was relieved of his duties and Cliff Fletcher was hired as interim GM until a replacement could be found.

Fletcher had, of course, managed the Leafs from 1991 until he was fired in 1997. Through prudent acquisitions, Fletcher had taken the club to the conference final in 1993 and 1994. He was quick to protect his new/old team: "In this room, we all know there's only one way to turn this around and that's to stay positive, stick together, and support each other and just battle through it." In the meantime, Richard Peddie and Toronto sports lawyer Gord Kirke would search for a permanent general manager.

As the Leafs fell further out of playoff contention, Sundin dominated the discussion about hockey, and trade rumours began to surface. With his contract set to expire, management asked Mats to waive his no-trade clause so that the team might deal him for prospects or draft picks to improve the future of the franchise. Sundin refused and provided a passionate rationale:

> I never believed in rent-a-player [trades] to start with. If you want to be a part of a team that has a chance to win a Stanley Cup, or a team that is going far in the playoffs, my opinion has always been that you want to be there from training camp, be there the whole season and part of the group. I have to do what feels right in my heart. I just don't want to play for another team.

On trade-deadline day, Cliff Fletcher executed several moves, none of which included his star centre. Instead, Fletcher sent Wade Belak and Chad Kilger to the Florida Panthers for draft picks, and Hal Gill was traded to the Pittsburgh Penguins for two selections.

After a 4–2 loss to the Bruins on March 27, the Maple Leafs were once again mathematically eliminated from the playoffs. At season's end, they had finished last in the Northeast Division, collecting 83 points on 36 wins, 35 losses, and 11 overtime losses. Having remained with the Blue and White, Mats Sundin led the team in scoring for the fourth straight year and for the 12th of his 13 seasons with Toronto. The captain scored 32 goals and finished with 78 points. Tomáš Kaberle was the top point-producing defenceman with 53 points. Jason Blake, while undergoing cancer treatment, contributed 15 goals and 52 points. While these were laudable performances, the Leafs were mired in mediocrity.

TRUCULENCE

The search for a general manager to right the Good Ship Maple Leaf continued through the summer of 2008. But on top of that human-resources issue, the Leafs also now needed to find a coach: on May 7, interim GM Cliff Fletcher fired Paul Maurice. At the same time, Fletcher assured that he would *not* be the GM when the season began. Fletcher admitted to favouring Brian Burke, the architect of the Anaheim Ducks' Stanley Cup championship in 2007, for the job. The problem was, he had a year remaining on his contract, and when approached, Ducks owner Henry Samueli denied Toronto permission to talk to his GM.

To replace Maurice, the Maple Leafs hired Ron Wilson, who had been released by San Jose in May 2008. Prior to his time with the Sharks, Wilson had coached in Washington and Anaheim. As a player, he had spent parts of three seasons as a Leaf, between 1977 and 1980. Ron's father, Larry, had also played in the NHL, with Detroit and Chicago, while his uncle Johnny Wilson – known for an iron-man streak that saw him play 580 consecutive games between 1951 and 1960 – played parts of two seasons with the Maple Leafs. As a tribute to his hockey pedigree, Ron carried a 1949–50 hockey card of his father in his pocket.

The NHL Entry Draft proceeded in June, with Fletcher at the table, flanked by a battery of Leafs scouts. In order to assure themselves of the fifth-overall pick and the opportunity to select defenceman Luke Schenn, the Maple Leafs sent the New York Islanders their seventh-overall pick and two conditional selections. The Leafs got their man.

The general rebuild would continue throughout the summer of 2008, but the biggest news came on July 1, when Mats Sundin became a free agent. Though he received offers, Sundin chose to demur while he contemplated retirement back home in Sweden. After missing the start of the NHL season, Sundin finally announced that he would return to the NHL . . . with Vancouver. On December 18, the Canucks announced his signing.

It was, for many, a difficult scenario to reconcile. Many irate fans raised the fact that Sundin had been unwilling to waive his no-trade clause just a few months earlier. Now, with Sundin a free agent, the Leafs were entitled to nothing in return as they watched their former ace move to British Columbia. Eventually, though, Leafs Nation would forgive their longtime captain. After all, Mats Sundin had played 13 seasons with the Maple Leafs and led Toronto in scoring every year but one. He remains the Toronto Maple Leafs' all-time leader in goals with 420 and in points with 984.

Sundin wasn't the only one leaving Toronto. Andrew Raycroft had struggled in 2007–08, winning just two of the 19 games he played for Toronto, and his contract was bought out. The Leafs also bought out the contracts of Darcy Tucker and Kyle Wellwood.

Added to the Leafs roster were Jeff Finger, Mikhail Grabovski, Niklas Hagman, Ryan Hollweg, and Jamal Mayers. Bryan McCabe was sent to the Florida Panthers with a draft pick for Mike Van Ryn. Tyler Bozak and Christian Hanson were signed as free agents out of their respective American colleges. And to replace Raycroft in goal, veteran Curtis Joseph was signed from the Calgary Flames for a second tour of duty in Toronto.

Once the season began, and in what would be his last significant move as interim general manager, Cliff Fletcher sacrificed youth for a proven scorer when he dealt promising young defenceman Carlo Colaiacovo and Alex Steen, a player often discussed as a potential future captain, to St. Louis for Lee Stempniak. The latter had been a 27-goal scorer with the Blues back in 2006–07. Not surprisingly, Leafs fans were very unsure as to what sort of team they had in the post-Sundin era.

Toronto travelled to Detroit for the first game of the season and edged the Red Wings, 3–2. The result was less festive at the home opener two nights later, when the Canadiens routed Toronto, 6–1.

With fans sporting stick-on moustaches, the Maple Leafs raised Wendel Clark's banner to the rafters on November 22, 2008. The winger, who had played every game in blue and white with reckless abandon, commented, "I was hoping when I played that I would always be known as someone who battled every game, whether it was getting a goal or doing something physical." (Though sweater number 17 has not been formally retired, no Leaf has worn it since Clark's career ended in 2000.) Reflecting the former captain's style of play, the Leafs battled hard that evening, but an overtime goal by future Leaf Dave Bolland swung the game in favour of the Blackhawks, 5–4.

The search for a general manager concluded on November 29, when the Maple Leafs hired the man they had been targeting all along. A couple of weeks earlier, Brian Burke had declined the offer of a contract extension from Anaheim. When he opted to step down from his position with the Ducks on November 12, the Leafs were free to court him. Burke signed a lucrative contract as president and general manager of the Toronto Maple Leafs. It was a serendipitous acquisition for the coach – Ron Wilson and Brian Burke had been roommates while playing hockey under Lou Lamoriello at Providence College. The message to the fans – and to the rest of the league, for that matter – was clear: with Burke's signing, the Leafs meant business.

Soon afterwards, Burke hired a lieutenant in Dave Nonis, who joined Toronto as senior vice-president and director of hockey operations. This was the third time Burke and Nonis had worked together, having partnered in similar working arrangements in both Anaheim and Vancouver.

In his version of a State of the Union address, Brian Burke outlined the vision he had for the Toronto Maple Leafs:

> We require, as a team, proper levels of pugnacity, testosterone, truculence, and belligerence. That's how our teams play. I make no apologies for that. Our teams play a North American game. We're throwbacks. It's black-and-blue hockey. It's going to be more physical hockey here than people are used to. The first thing, and probably the easiest thing to change on your team, is the amount of the snarl, the amount of the bite. That's an important part of how my teams play. I don't care where players are born. I don't care where they come from. I don't care what colour their passport is. But they've either got to be a contributing offensive player in our top six forwards or they've got to be a hard-hat guy in our bottom six. If they can't fill a role, regardless of what their passport says, then they're not going to be here.

The new GM made good copy – and fans and commentators alike would react to his use of such multisyllabic words as *pugnacity* and *belligerence* when his predecessors had touted *grit* and *toughness*. But nobody needed convincing about Burke's sincerity.

Wilson, for example, understood well what his new boss craved. He also knew that the type of team Burke desired was not going to be created overnight: "Just because we hired Brian today doesn't mean we're going to play like the Philadelphia Flyers from 1975. We just don't have that right now." To be sure, there were several Leafs in the lineup who simply did not fit the Burke mould. Matt Stajan, not particularly known for his "truculence," spoke on behalf of his teammates: "There has been a lot of changes. There's going to continue to be changes. We can't worry about that. It's out of our control. Brian will be making all the decisions now."

An indication of the type of player that Burke envisioned wearing the blue and white arrived in Toronto on January 7, when the Leafs acquired Brad May from the Ducks in return for a late draft pick. At the trade deadline, Nik Antropov was sent to the New York Rangers for draft picks, and Dominic Moore, a feisty forward, came home to Toronto in a deal with Buffalo involving draft picks. Slowly, Burke began to assemble his ideal squad.

Meanwhile, preceding a 5-4 win over Pittsburgh on January 31, 2009, the Maple Leafs honoured one of their most beloved players: Doug Gilmour. All intensity and heart, "Killer" had carried the team to the conference finals in 1993 and 1994, carving his name into the record books as he led Toronto through one of the most exciting periods in recent franchise history. No other athlete had captured the imagination of Toronto's sports fans quite like Dougie. "Thanks to the fans," he said prior to the banner raising. "You inspired our hockey club to make us that much better, so keep cheering."

As far as the season was concerned, however, the Maple Leafs fell out of the playoff race quite early. In January, the Leafs won four, lost seven, and lost two overtime games. February and March saw modest improvement. In a most improbable series of events, beginning on February 19, Toronto played in seven consecutive overtime games, winning four and dropping three. One of these, against the Vancouver Canucks on February 21, marked the return of Mats Sundin to Toronto. A video tribute during a break in play in the first period afforded the former captain a prolonged standing ovation from his adoring fans. Leafs centre Matt Stajan took his time setting up for the ensuing faceoff. "It was his moment," he later explained. "I wasn't going into the faceoff circle before he did." After being deadlocked at 2–2, the game went to a shootout. It was almost poetic justice that Sundin scored the winner on Vesa Toskala, bringing the Toronto crowd to its feet for

the longest ovation in ACC history. Mats was named the game's first star.

"A lot of feelings came to mind on the ice – all the battles and everything we've gone through over the last 13 years, so many ups and downs and disappointments and happiness," Sundin reflected. "The ovation from the fans was very special. I'll remember that the rest of my life."

A former teammate of Sundin's would receive a hearty salute of his own from the Air Canada Centre faithful in a game against the Washington Capitals on March 24. With less than a minute to play, the Leafs' starting netminder, Martin Gerber, fired the puck vaguely towards referee Mike Leggo to protest a late goal by Washington, knotting the score at two. For his action, Gerber was tossed from the game. Curtis Joseph took the ice in his place. On one particular play, Cujo stoned Washington sniper Alexander Ovechkin. Joseph was similarly brilliant throughout the overtime period, and in the shootout he stopped Nicklas Bäckström, Alexander Semin, and Ovechkin. Toronto took the game, 3–2. The ecstatic crowd chanted, "Cujo! Cujo!" and the netminder was awarded the game's first star.

Coveted by the Toronto Maple Leafs, Brian Burke was hired by the franchise in November 2008. He proceeded to fashion the team with "proper levels of pugnacity, testosterone, truculence, and belligerence." Among his most memorable moves were trades for Phil Kessel in 2009, Dion Phaneuf in 2010, Jake Gardiner and Joffrey Lupul in 2011, and James van Riemsdyk in 2012.

While the appearance harked back to the brilliance the goaltender had shown around the turn of the 21st century, Joseph, who was nearing the end of his career, tied an ignominious record in his final NHL game just a few days later. On April 8, the Maple Leafs lost to the Buffalo Sabres, 3–1. It was the 352nd loss of Joseph's NHL career, which tied him with Gump Worsley for most career losses. To be sure, the record speaks more to longevity than ineptitude: Cujo also sat fourth all-time in career wins, with 454. Still, while Cujo showed occasional glimpses of the brilliance he had once displayed in front of Toronto fans, his best days were now behind him. In January 2010, having not signed a contract for the new season, Curtis Joseph announced his retirement.

The Maple Leafs were mathematically eliminated from the playoffs on March 31, 2009. Goaltending and defence had been the team's Achilles heel. The team's 293 goals against were the worst in the NHL. Vesa Toskala, the team's principal goalie, won 22, lost 17, and suffered 11 overtime losses, and his save percentage was just .891. Martin Gerber and Justin Pogge had also played a handful of games each, while Curtis Joseph appeared 21 times. As far as the other end of the rink was concerned, the Maple Leafs proved they could score – their 250-goal output ranked 11th in the league. Jason Blake led Toronto in goals and points, with 25 and 63, respectively.

While Leafs Nation was cautiously optimistic about the direction in which GM Burke was taking the team, there was also an undertone of concern about the fact that Toronto had now missed the playoffs in four consecutive seasons – one more than the previous franchise record set by the St. Patricks/Leafs between 1926 and 1928.

MONSTERS AND SNIPERS

Beyond the fact that the Toronto Maple Leafs were not playoff contenders, it seemed that the club – notwithstanding Burke's vision – lacked an identity. No one, especially in GM Brian Burke's eyes, was fit to wear the captain's C. Certainly, there were some good players, but there was no single player around whom Burke felt he could build a team. He set his sights on remedying that state of affairs.

With the seventh-overall selection at the 2009 NHL Entry Draft, the Maple Leafs chose Nazem Kadri from the London Knights. It was a good start. Then, once the free-agency period began, Burke picked up Mike Komisarek from the Montreal Canadiens and enforcer Colton Orr from the New York Rangers. Burke signed another tough

forward, Jay Rosehill – whom the Marlies had acquired in March from Tampa Bay's AHL affiliate. François Beauchemin, a veteran defenceman, was signed from Anaheim to add some leadership and a bit of offence.

In a bid to upgrade their goaltending, the Leafs won a bidding war for the right to sign Jonas Gustavsson, a highly touted free agent from Sweden. The goalie known as the Monster was ready to compete for the number-one job, as he told the *Toronto Sun*: "I'm going to try to steal as many games from Vesa Toskala as I can. I know the best goalie gets the ice time and if I play good, I'm going to get the chance. We will be good teammates and try to push ourselves, but my goal is to be the number-one goalie." Eager as he might have been, Gustavsson encountered a setback on his first day of training camp, when an irregular heartbeat required him to undergo a cardiac ablation – the insertion of a catheter into his heart. Remarkably, the Monster recovered quickly from the process and started the Leafs' season opener.

Burke dealt Pavel Kubina and Tim Stapleton to Atlanta for Garnet Exelby, while Anton Stralman, Colin Stuart, and a draft pick were packaged and sent to Calgary for Wayne Primeau. But a trade consummated just before the season opened would have the greatest impact on the fortunes of the Blue and White.

Brian Burke was looking for star power, a player to serve as a franchise cornerstone. And he believed he had found that player in Phil Kessel. The American was just about to turn 22 and had already been with the Boston Bruins for three seasons. Conquering testicular cancer in his rookie campaign, Kessel was the recipient of the Bill Masterton Trophy for perseverance. In 2008–09, his third season with the Bruins, he exploded for 36 goals. Now, in 2009, Kessel was a restricted free agent and looking for a large contract. The Bruins lacked space under the salary cap to meet his asking price, but the Maple Leafs had room. The teams discussed the trade throughout the summer, and in the end it resulted in the Leafs landing Kessel in return for a first- and a second-round draft pick in 2010 and a first-round selection in 2011.

It was, of course, a steep price to pay. But the Leafs GM had every confidence that Kessel would make a significant difference to the Maple Leafs' attack. "Our view is that he's already accomplished quite a bit for a young man his age," Burke said. "We think the 36 goals from a year ago is really a platform, not a peak, as far as what he can accomplish. He's gotten dramatically better each year. Does it push us closer to our goal of making the playoffs? Absolutely."

Like Burke, Wilson knew Kessel from the U.S. National Team and was equally excited about the new addition: "He's going to add some speed. He's a sniper."

It was this new and seemingly improved team that Burke and Wilson led into the 2009–10 season. The Leafs' opening game was at Air Canada Centre, and ended in a 4–3 overtime loss to the Canadiens. It was a harbinger of things to come.

In fact, the team endured its worst-ever start, winning just one of its first 13 games. The hole in which the Maple Leafs found themselves was almost impossible to climb out of. By the end of January 2010, Toronto had dropped into last place in the Eastern Conference. At this point, Burke pulled the trigger on a blockbuster deal with Calgary, sending Niklas Hagman, Jamal Mayers, Matt Stajan, and Ian White to the Flames in return for Dion Phaneuf, Keith Aulie, and Fredrik Sjöström. Phaneuf was

a physical defenceman with a cannon for a shot who had scored 20 goals as a rookie and been a Norris Trophy finalist and First Team All-Star in 2008. Phaneuf was surprised by the trade, but liked what Brian Burke told him about the future of the team.

"When the trade happens, it shocks you, but as soon as I got the call from Burkie to welcome me to the Toronto Maple Leafs, I was extremely excited to get here," Phaneuf said. "And then, when I landed here and I was driving downtown that night, I could feel the passion of the fans right from when I landed."

As far as Burke was concerned, Phaneuf was "a warrior. He plays the game hard. He's a big open-ice hitter and he's a quality person."

Burke wasn't done. He further changed the complexion of the Maple Leafs by trading Jason Blake and

Brian Burke rolled the dice and came up with Phil Kessel in the summer of 2009, surrendering first- and second-round draft picks in 2010 and a first-round selection in 2011. Kessel led the Leafs in points in each of his six seasons, and contributed 30 goals or more in four of those seasons.

Vesa Toskala to Anaheim for goalie Jean-Sébastien Giguère. J-S had won the Conn Smythe Trophy in a losing cause in 2003 before winning the Stanley Cup with Anaheim in 2007. Giguère made an auspicious debut with Toronto on February 2 by shutting out the New Jersey Devils. In his next game, a tilt against Ottawa on February 6, he earned another shutout in a 5–0 Toronto win. In so doing, Giguère became the first goaltender ever to record shutouts in his first two games as a Leaf.

Still, the acquisitions came too late to have any meaningful impact on what was another disappointing season. The team staggered to the finish line and was eliminated from postseason play after a 3–2 loss to the Thrashers on March 30. Toronto finished last in the Northeast Division, well back of the pack with 74 points on 30 wins, 38 losses, and 14 overtime losses. In fact, the Maple Leafs finished in 29th place in the 30-team NHL.

The team's 267 goals against were just one fewer than the conference-worst New York Islanders. Among the goalies, only Gustavsson achieved double digits in victories, with a record of 16 wins, 15 losses, and 9 overtime losses. Up front, and to no one's surprise, Phil Kessel led the team in scoring in his first season as a Leaf with 30 goals and 55 points. Tomáš Kaberle led the team with 42 assists. In general, goals were hard to come by – the Leafs' 214 goals scored ranked 26th in the league.

The painful rebuild was still, it seemed, far from complete. While Burke had been able to jettison players who had no future with his Maple Leafs, the 29th-place finish was shocking. The insult to injury was that, because of the Kessel trade, the Leafs were without a first-round draft pick in 2010. Instead, the team would have to rely on the talent of existing players such as Tyler Bozak, Jonas Gustavsson, Nazem Kadri, Nikolai Kulemin, Luke Schenn, and, of course, Dion Phaneuf and Phil Kessel. Still, Leafs Nation was now becoming increasingly more aware of the calendar: for the fifth straight season, the Toronto Maple Leafs would not be playing hockey in mid-April.

A MATTER OF PRIDE

Ideas about masculinity have continued to evolve during the 21st century, and Toronto's team has featured many male archetypes. There were the "survivors," in the mould of Charlie Conacher, Red Horner, Wendel Clark, and Tie Domi – when backed against the wall, they had to fight just to survive. There were also the "soldiers," those men who were simply "doing their duty" – players such as Syl Apps and Ted Kennedy, who stoically

undertook the sometimes-difficult task of doing the right thing. Later, there came the "contemplative" ones who challenged the status quo – clever players such as Carl Brewer and Ron Ellis, who exposed to the rest of us the mental and emotional costs of a life in hockey. But over time, conceptions of manhood have become a little more pliable in the hockey world, and it may be argued that the bravest steps in this direction were taken by the team's president and general manager at the end of the first decade of the 21st century.

In June 2009, Brian Burke attended Toronto's Pride Parade with his son Brendan. The parade is the marquee event of a week-long festival that celebrates the region's LGBT (lesbian, gay, bisexual, and trans) communities. Toronto's is one of the largest events of its kind in the world. Brendan had told his father and the rest of his family that he was gay only a couple of years earlier. Brian, who had a no-nonsense approach and a reputation for preferring tough guys on his team, immediately and unconditionally accepted his son's announcement. As the *Toronto Star* reported, "When news that Brendan was gay hit the media last November, the Burke family became pioneers for acceptance in a sport that has never had an openly gay athlete."

Only a few months later, however, in February 2010, Brendan Burke died in a car crash in Indiana during a winter storm. He was only 21. The following summer, Brian Burke not only attended Toronto's Pride Parade, but took part in it. The GM marched with the local chapter of PFLAG (Parents, Family, and Friends of Lesbians and Gays), a support group for the families and friends of LGBT youth. As Burke explained, "I promised my son I'd march with him, and he's not here. He would have wanted us to do this."

While Burke was recognized as a hero for his open support of his son and the Pride celebration, the Leafs' top gun played down the accolades: "There's nothing heroic about loving your child. I didn't do anything that a parent who loved their child wouldn't do." Still, Burke has continued to support the LGBT community and has since attended and marched in several different Pride parades and celebrations. His actions have served as a call to those in the hockey world who cling to one rigid idea about masculinity to consider the diversity of what it means to be a man in the 21st century.

THE CAPTAIN

After playing without a captain for the two seasons that followed Mats Sundin's departure from Toronto, the

Dion Phaneuf joined the Toronto Maple Leafs from the Calgary Flames on January 31, 2010. By the following June, Phaneuf's presence convinced management to award the captaincy to the veteran with the booming shot and the bruising bodychecks.

Maple Leafs named Dion Phaneuf as their new on-ice leader on June 14, 2010.

"There's such history when you look back at the captains that they've had here," Phaneuf acknowledged, "and I've had the opportunity to talk with a lot of the previous captains and try to learn as much as I can from them. It was a huge honour when I was named captain of the Toronto Maple Leafs."

To bolster the new captain's supporting cast, the Maple Leafs loaded up on veteran free agents, including Colby Armstrong, Joey Crabb, Clarke MacArthur, and Brett Lebda. Toronto also picked up goaltenders Jussi Rynnas and Ben Scrivens, and forward Mike Zigomanis. In terms of muscle, the Leafs added fast-skating Mike Brown from Anaheim and 20-goal scorer Kris Versteeg from the Stanley Cup champion Chicago Blackhawks.

The season began on the right note as Toronto defeated the Montreal Canadiens in the home opener by a 3–2 score. It was the first home opener the Leafs had won since the year 2000. Going on to win their first four games, the team was off to its best start since 1993–94.

On January 11, 2011, Ron Wilson celebrated his 600th NHL win as a coach when the Leafs dumped the San Jose Sharks, 4–2. The victory was even sweeter for Wilson because the Sharks were a team he had previously coached. At the time of writing, Wilson ranks tenth on the NHL's list of winningest coaches of all time.

On February 9, the Maple Leafs sent François Beauchemin back to Anaheim in return for the talented but oft-injured Joffrey Lupul, defence prospect Jake Gardiner, and a conditional draft pick. Lupul made an immediate impact on the lineup, while Gardiner showed a great deal of promise as he honed his skills with the Toronto Marlies.

After a promising start, the Leafs faded and missed the playoffs for the sixth consecutive spring, finishing fourth in the Northeast Division and tenth in the Eastern Conference with 85 points on 37 wins, 34 losses, and 11 overtime/shootout losses. For the second year in a row, the team was in the bottom ten in goals for *and* against. Fans could be excused for wondering how the Leafs managed to be shut out a staggering 11 times, given that they had players capable of putting the puck in the net. Phil Kessel led the team with 32 goals as well as 64 points, while the surprise of the season was the Blue and White's second line of Nikolai Kulemin, Mikhail Grabovski, and Clarke MacArthur, who combined for 80 goals and 177 points. Tomáš Kaberle led Leaf defencemen with 38 points before

he was sent to Boston on February 18, with Toronto receiving a first- and a second-round draft pick as well as prospect Joe Colborne. With the Bruins, Kaberle enjoyed his sole Stanley Cup championship, while his former teammates were once again idle in the postseason.

In goal, the Leafs were pleasantly surprised by the play of James Reimer, who had been selected by the Maple Leafs in the fourth round of the 2006 NHL Entry Draft but had bounced around the AHL and ECHL before eventually getting a legitimate look from the Leafs. Between injuries and poor play, the Maple Leafs were disgruntled with the goalkeeping of both Jean-Sébastien Giguère and Jonas Gustavsson, and therefore summoned Reimer to the big club. He made the most of the opening. In his first start, on January 1, Reimer backstopped the Leafs to a 5–1 victory over the Senators. As the rookie shone, the fans tagged him "Optimus Reim," a reference to Optimus Prime, the protagonist in the *Transformers* films, animated TV series, and comic books.

Reimer was in goal for 28 of the last 33 games down the stretch, in which the Leafs picked up 42 of their 85 total points. The numbers told the tale: Giguère went 11–11–4, with a 2.87 goals-against average and a save percentage of .900; Gustavsson was 6–13–2, with a goals-against average of 3.29 and a save percentage of .890; Reimer bested both with a record of 20–10–5, a 2.60 GAA, and a scintillating .921 save percentage.

The Leafs were, nevertheless, on the outside looking in for a frustrating sixth consecutive postseason. Burke had made some progress, and the team was more competitive than it had been of late, but the GM wasn't satisfied: "Overall, it's a failure," he told the *Toronto Star*. "You don't make the playoffs, it's a failure . . . We intend to be active in free agency and we intend to explore trades." Leafs Nation, ever patient, had some reason to hope as they waited for Burke to make the next moves.

COLOSSAL COLLAPSES

Expectations were high for the 2011–12 edition of the Toronto Maple Leafs. It seemed that for the first time in a long time, the team had a core of good, young players that was developing wonderfully. Burke targeted Tyler Biggs, a big winger in the U.S. National Team Development Program, as the junior he wanted most in the Entry Draft. To ensure that he could select Biggs, Burke traded up to get the 22nd pick overall. Later, with the 25th pick in the first round, the Maple Leafs added Stuart Percy, while Josh Leivo was chosen in the third round.

The team plucked free agents Tim Connolly and Philippe Dupuis and sent Brett Lebda and a prospect to Nashville for hard-shooting defenceman Cody Franson and speedy Matthew Lombardi. Toronto picked up David Steckel from New Jersey in exchange for a draft pick, and John-Michael Liles from the Colorado Avalanche for a second-round selection.

James Reimer was proving to be the strong netminder that the team had long yearned for, while Jonas Gustavsson served as a very capable backup. For insurance, the team had access to goaltenders Ben Scrivens and Jussi Rynnas, who were playing with the Marlies. The defence was a nice combination of size (Keith Aulie, Cody Franson, Mike Komisarek, Dion Phaneuf, and Luke Schenn) and skill (John-Michael Liles, Jake Gardiner, and Carl Gunnarsson).

Toronto looked as though it would be able to put the puck in the net, too. With Connolly, Toronto seemed to have found the much-needed centre who could feed Phil Kessel. There was also the second line of Grabovski, Kulemin, and MacArthur, which had really clicked in the previous season. And youngsters Matt Frattin and Nazem Kadri looked as though they could contribute significantly now that they had had a taste of NHL life.

It was with this lineup that the Maple Leafs began their new campaign. Toronto opened the season with Reimer in goal, and the young man blanked Montreal, 2–0. The Leafs won the next two games, and would, through the month of October, win seven of their first 11. By month's end, the Leafs were first in the Northeast and second in the conference.

There were, however, some concerns. During the team's seventh game of the season – a 5–4 overtime win in Montreal – Reimer was injured. Early in the first period, he was run into in the crease by the Canadiens' Brian Gionta. The netminder's mask flew off and it took a few moments for him to regain his equilibrium. Reimer finished the period, but Gustavsson was in goal to start the second. Ben Scrivens was called up, and he and the Monster shared the crease duties until Reimer was able to return on December 3.

In December, Brian Burke drew criticism after quietly extending the contract of coach Ron Wilson. The extension was made public by way of social media when Wilson tweeted, "This Xmas could be better if Santa stuffs a certain piece of paper in my stocking." This was followed by "He came! He came! I got a new Red Ryder BB gun and a contract extension!" Burke then replied, "Congratulations to Ron Wilson on his contract extension! Merry Christmas Ron!" The GM defended the move, stating that despite three straight losing seasons with Wilson behind the bench, "This is a coach who's earned this extension." Unfortunately, the good cheer and glad tidings would not last.

The season, which started out on such a high note, turned into a debacle. Beginning with a 2–1 loss to Winnipeg on February 7, Toronto would win just one of its next ten games. There was a rare bright spot on February 11, however, when Mats Sundin's banner was raised in Air Canada Centre. There are few things as wonderful as the broad smile exhibited by Mats when he scored, and on that day 18,000 fans grinned along with him. "The number one thing that I miss, being retired and not living in Toronto, is the people of Toronto," Sundin said. "There is no one more loyal, passionate, and committed about their team than you Leaf fans."

However, in 2012 those fans were having to watch their team fall further and further away from a playoff berth, and Leafs Nation's audible cries for Wilson's head grew louder and longer with each game. Finally, on March 2, the patience of the team and its fans had been exhausted. Only two months after granting him an extension, Burke fired Wilson. It was not an easy decision, given the history between the two men, who had been teammates in collegiate hockey and had been manager and coach of the silver medal–winning United States hockey team at the Winter Olympic Games in 2010. As the GM explained, "Every coach has a shelf life. After the last home game [a 5–3 loss to Florida], it would be cruel and unusual punishment to let Ron coach another game in the Air Canada Centre."

Burke immediately replaced Wilson with Randy Carlyle, with whom Burke had won the Stanley Cup in Anaheim in 2007. Like Wilson, Carlyle had also once been a player with the Toronto Maple Leafs. Still, it was going to be a tall order for Carlyle and the Leafs to get back into a playoff position. To this end, Burke made some deals at the trade deadline, picking up Carter Ashton from Tampa Bay in exchange for Keith Aulie, as well as Mark Fraser from Anaheim in return for Dale Mitchell. The moves were little help. After a win in his first game as coach of the Leafs, Randy Carlyle completed the season with a record of six wins, nine losses, and three overtime losses. Just before the end of the season, Burke confessed, "I've never had a team fall off a cliff like this before. I've had dips, slumps, rough patches, but this is akin to an 18-wheeler going right off a cliff. I don't know what happened." The Maple Leafs finished fourth in the Northeastern Division with 80 points, and 13th in the Eastern Conference, comfortably out of the playoffs – for the seventh consecutive season.

Striking a penitent tone, MLSE chairman Larry Tanenbaum told fans, "We are disappointed with the results of this season. We have fallen short of everyone's expectations and for that, we are sorry. We take full responsibility for how this team performs on the ice, and we make no excuses. The way the year ended was unacceptable."

Burke echoed his boss's sentiments: "On behalf of the coaching staff, management and the players, I want to echo Mr. Tanenbaum's apology for our failure to deliver this year. We had a good first half, but we didn't deliver at the end. We have the best fans in the National Hockey League and all of pro sports, and that loyalty needs to be rewarded."

The "best fans," though, were growing weary. As disappointing as the season had been, Leafs Nation was more confused than anything else. On paper, it looked as though the team had the goods. Unfortunately, it just hadn't panned out. Tim Connolly, for instance, didn't turn out to be the centre who would spur Kessel to new goal-scoring heights. And then there was the mystery of Nikolai Kulemin, who had been a 30-goal scorer the season before, but managed only seven this time around.

There were, of course, some bright spots. Phil Kessel had the sixth-best point production in the NHL, with 82 points, including a team-best 37 goals. Joffrey Lupul scored 25 goals, and had been one of the more dangerous forwards in the league until he was injured on March 6 against Boston. Perhaps the most encouraging sign for the future was the emergence of the speedy American defenceman, Jake Gardiner. A first-round pick by Anaheim in 2008, Gardiner made an almost immediate impact on the blueline, and at season's end was chosen for the NHL's All-Rookie Team. It was these precious few bright spots that Leafs Nation would have to meditate on through yet another early-arriving and lengthy off-season.

A DIFFERENT VOICE AND AN IMPROBABLE FINISH

On August 22, 2012, the Ontario Teachers' Pension Plan sold its 75 per cent stake in Maple Leafs Sports and Entertainment to a partnership between Bell Canada Enterprises (BCE) and Rogers Communications. As a result, BCE and Rogers each held 37½ per cent of MLSE, while Kilmer Sports, headed by Larry Tanenbaum, owned the remaining 25 per cent. Canada's Competition Bureau, the Canadian Radio-Television and Telecommunications Commission, and the NHL Board of Governors all gave their approval to the valid, if curious, transaction (curious

because Bell and Rogers are usually in direct competition in the telecommunications business).

Meanwhile, the collective bargaining agreement between the NHL and NHLPA – which had been in place since the 2004–05 lockout – expired on September 16, 2012. As commissioner Gary Bettman warned, if the league and players were unable to come to terms on a new pact before the current one expired, the owners would once again resort to a lockout. Unlike in 2004–05, an agreement was reached in early January, and the league was at least able to play a 48-game season that began on January 19, 2013. Fans just wanted to have their game back. When the deal was announced, most were pleased that, in the dark days of winter, big-time hockey had returned.

In the end, the labour dispute resulted in the cancellation of 510 games; of these, the most notable and regrettable was the 2013 Winter Classic, to be played at the massive Michigan Stadium in Ann Arbor. Beginning in 2008, the NHL schedule had included an outdoor game on New Year's Day, played in football or baseball venues and broadcast over the full NBC television network in the United States. In short order, it became an eagerly anticipated marquee event for the league, and a serious rival to the Stanley Cup final in terms of fan interest. The 2013 game at the University of Michigan's "Big House" was expected to draw more than 100,000 fans, and TV audiences of millions on both sides of the border – not least because the scheduled combatants were the Detroit Red Wings and Toronto Maple Leafs, a pair of high-profile Original Six franchises. The matchup was subsequently rescheduled for New Year's Day 2014.

While he waited for the season to start, Brian Burke continued with his renovation of the Leafs roster. In the 2012 NHL Entry Draft, Toronto selected Morgan Rielly with its first choice, fifth overall. The Leafs also added depth players, signing free agents Mike Kostka, Jay McClement, and Frazer McLaren. Perhaps the most impactful acquisition, however, was one that had been fodder for the rumour mill for some time. On June 23, the Leafs dealt Luke Schenn to the Philadelphia Flyers and received forward James van Riemsdyk in return. Schenn would join his brother Brayden in Philly, while the Leafs were getting a proven sniper in the player known simply as JVR.

The biggest change was yet to come. On January 9, 2013, just ten days before the team opened its shortened season, MLSE president Tom Anselmi opened a media conference by stating that the team had decided it needed

Although Toronto had both Jean-Sébastien Giguère and Jonas Gustavsson ahead of him on the goaltending depth chart, James Reimer (pictured) stepped into the crease on December 20, 2010, and wrestled a spot from the regulars. Through six seasons, Reimer supplied strong goaltending to the Maple Leafs, and won the hearts of Leafs Nation.

a "different voice" in its leadership, and that Brian Burke had been fired from his role as president and general manager of the Toronto Maple Leafs. Leafs Nation was stunned by the announcement, but no one was more shocked than Burke, who commented, "This was like a two-by-four upside the head to me."

Burke had fashioned his team around the tenets he most admired: "pugnacity, testosterone, truculence, and belligerence." The only trouble was that the team had failed to make the playoffs during his term. In fact, the Leafs were the only team in the NHL that hadn't made the playoffs since the 2004–05 lockout.

While he – and many others – questioned the timing of the decision, Burke understood the reason. He was replaced on an interim basis by his assistant, Dave Nonis.

Ten days later, the Maple Leafs beat the Canadiens, 2–1, in Montreal. An identical 2–1 score was the result in the Leafs' home opener, although this time it was a loss at the hands of the Buffalo Sabres. "I think our effort was there," Randy Carlyle said. "I don't think our execution was at the level required to get points."

Prior to the contest, the ceremonial faceoff was out of this world . . . literally. While appearing on the video-board from the International Space Station, orbiting the planet at 27,600 kilometres (17,100 miles) per hour, Commander Chris Hadfield, a Leafs fan, dropped the puck. Or rather, he released the puck and it floated in the zero-gravity environment. So he gave it a nudge in the direction of Earth. Fans then saw former goalie Félix Potvin, stationed outside the arena, catch the puck in his glove and then drop it down a hatch to Darcy Tucker. Tucker took an elevator to ice level and handed the puck to Darryl Sittler, who ran through the kitchen of Air Canada Centre, puck in hand, and emerged at rinkside, where he was greeted by an explosion of cheering from Leafs Nation. Sittler then handed the puck to Hall of Famer Johnny Bower, who took it to centre ice for the faceoff.

From the space station, Hadfield stated, "I just want to say how proud I am to be the first member of Leafs Nation in space, and how exciting it is to take part in tonight's ceremonial puck drop."

The Leafs were a competitive team in the shortened season. James Reimer carried most of the goaltending load, winning nineteen games, losing eight in regulation, and another five in either overtime or a shootout. Reimer's save percentage was a sparkling .924. At the same time, Ben Scrivens was a very capable backup, posting back-to-back 3–0 shutouts in the middle of February.

With a 4–1 win over Ottawa on April 20, Toronto earned a playoff berth, their first in nine years.

The Maple Leafs finished third in the Northeast Division and fifth in the Eastern Conference with 26 wins, 17 losses, and 5 overtime losses, good for 57 points. Phil Kessel finished eighth in scoring with 20 goals and 32 assists for 52 points. His linemates, James van Riemsdyk and Tyler Bozak, made the line extremely dangerous by adding 18 and 12 goals, respectively. Nazem Kadri was impressive in his first full, albeit shortened, NHL season and recorded 18 goals and 44 points. There was also improvement in team play, including on special teams: Toronto had given up the fewest power-play goals (19) and had the best penalty-killing percentage (88.2 per cent). It was this much-improved team that would face the Boston Bruins in the first round of the playoffs.

The two teams were ancient rivals, and their recent pasts had been no different. Boston, with Tyler Seguin, Tomáš Kaberle, and Tuukka Rask in their lineup, all of whom had arrived through transactions with the Maple Leafs, had won the Stanley Cup in 2011. The Bruins still had 17 players from their Cup-winning team in the current lineup. Toronto, meanwhile, hoped that enthusiasm and exuberance would trump experience.

The Leafs proved early on in Game One that there was reason to hope. They scored first, but the home-town Bruins answered back . . . four times. By the third period, Boston fans were taunting the Leafs with chants of "Thank you, Kessel!" The 4–1 victory gave Boston the early lead in the series.

Phil Kessel answered back in Game Two, and his goal gave Toronto a 3–1 lead. It would prove to be the winner. Toronto had evened the series with the 4–2 win. It was a victory that, according to Coach Carlyle, "eliminated that doubt that we could go out there and compete with them."

The tradition of watching games in Maple Leaf Square was born when almost 10,000 fans showed up to watch Game Three on a massive outdoor screen. The Leafs played with determination, firing 47 shots at Tuukka Rask, but the Bruins netminder was up to the task. Boston regained the series lead with the 5–2 win. It was much the same in Game Four: the Leafs fired shot after shot at the Bruins net – 48 this time – but Rask was there, responding with save after spectacular save. And although the Leafs were up, 2–0, they could not hold on to the lead. In a portent of what was to come later on in the series, Boston came back with three unanswered goals. Toronto nevertheless tied the game; in overtime, Dion Phaneuf tried to lay a hit on Nathan Horton, but in the process, the puck squirted out to David Krejci and Milan Lucic. The duo went on a two-on-one rush with only the Leafs' Ryan O'Byrne back. Krejci completed his hat trick by beating Reimer at 13:06 of overtime.

The Bruins were up three games to one, but the Maple Leafs were not quite ready to concede. Tyler Bozak scored a shorthanded goal in the second period of Game Five in Boston, while Clarke MacArthur added a goal early in the third. The Bruins worked hard to try to equalize. Boston picked up a goal from Zdeno Chára, and then, with just 11 seconds to play, Jaromír Jágr fired what looked like the game-tying goal, but Reimer made a miraculous save that left Jágr just shaking his head. Toronto held on for a 2–1 win.

The teams returned to Toronto for Game Six. Both goalies were equally terrific. It was another low-scoring affair, but fortunately for Leafs Nation, Toronto came out on the right side of another 2–1 victory. The Leafs had, implausibly, tied the series at three games apiece.

The thrill of playoff hockey had returned to the city, and Torontonians were awakening to the possibility of another round. The *Toronto Star* captured the excitement: "This is how it should be in a hockey-mad capital in the springtime, with heightened anxieties and hearts thumping in the chest. Even if the Leafs win not another in 2013, they've already reclaimed their self-respect and earned the enduring affections of a city."

For those of a certain vintage, the Leafs had once again stirred the soul and elicited memories of an earlier time – perhaps with Dougie, or possibly Sittler, or Keon, or heroes of an even earlier era. For younger or recently arrived Torontonians, this was the first time they had been stricken by the highly contagious playoff fever that only the Maple Leafs can spread. Toronto and its Leafs marched into Boston with hope, which made Game Seven all the more devastating.

When Nazem Kadri put the Leafs up 4–1 at 5:29 of the third period, it all seemed just a little too easy. Leafs Nation began to try to figure out which team the Blue and White would meet in the next round. Shoulders were relaxed, blood pressure dropped, and there was lightness in the air in the living rooms and sports bars wherever Leafs fans gathered. After nine years, it seemed as though the Leafs hadn't just made the playoffs, but were actually going to go on a bit of a run. And then, like a cruel joke, it happened. And this joke stung like no other.

At 9:18 of the third, Nathan Horton scored to cut the Leafs' lead to 4–2. Still, the Leafs and their fans held *some* comfort in the two-goal lead with only half

a period left. As the clock ticked down to less than 90 seconds to play, it appeared that it would be next to impossible for Boston to come back. But the Leafs were now playing scared. The Bruins knew it and poured on the pressure. With 82 seconds left, and the Bruins net empty for the extra attacker, Lucic banged a rebound past Reimer to reduce the Toronto lead to a single goal. Shoulders tensed up, blood pressure rose uncontrollably, a gripping silence returned to the rooms and sports bars wherever Leafs fans gathered. Leafs Nation held its collective breath.

Unsurprisingly, the Bruins left Rask on the bench for the extra skater. Thirty seconds later, at 19:09 of the third period, Patrice Bergeron stabbed a knife into the hearts of the Maple Leafs and their fans. The game was tied at four.

Though it scarcely needs saying, the momentum shifted dramatically in Boston's favour. Even the most hopeful Leafs fans must have known in their hearts that there was simply no coming back from the crushing change in fortunes. Blowing a three-goal lead with only ten minutes left in the third period of a deciding game was one of the NHL's all-time spectacular playoff collapses, and certainly the worst in the history of the Toronto Maple Leafs. Then, just six minutes into extra time, the Bruins hemmed the Leafs into their end and Bergeron swooped in from the faceoff circle to fire the final dagger past James Reimer.

It was, as poor Reimer explained, "An empty feeling . . . It's over, and there's nothing you can do about it."

Oscar Wilde could easily have been referring to the Leafs' infamous collapse when he wrote, "Man can believe the impossible, but man can never believe the improbable."

A DAY TO REMEMBER

On June 30, 2013, Tim Leiweke was named president and CEO of MLSE. Leiweke had served as president and CEO of Anschutz Entertainment Group, owners of, among other teams and properties, the Los Angeles Kings.

With question marks surrounding James Reimer's ability to raise his game, GM Dave Nonis sent goalie Ben Scrivens, forward Matt Frattin, and a draft pick to the Los Angeles Kings for Jonathan Bernier. Bernier had served as Jonathan Quick's backup for three seasons and had demonstrated he was worthy of a crack at a number-one position somewhere in the league.

Nonis also landed David Clarkson, a Toronto native who had scored 30 goals with the Devils in 2011–12 and

I was very happy with my career. I thought I was a pretty decent player. It was something I grew up wanting to do. Truth be known, I felt if I played ten years, I'd be happy and then I'd be out of the game, and that's exactly what happened. The Maple Leaf isn't tattooed on me, but I have lots of fond, fond memories.

Ian Turnbull
PLAYER
1973–81

led New Jersey in goals and penalty minutes in 2012–13. Upon signing with the Leafs, Clarkson confessed, "It's something that I dreamed of as a little boy, one day playing in the NHL and being lucky enough to wear this jersey."

The Leafs also picked up Dave Bolland from the Chicago Blackhawks. Bolland had scored the Stanley Cup–winning goal just a few months earlier. The acquisition cost Toronto three draft picks.

In the 2013 NHL Entry Draft, the Leafs selected highly touted forward Frédérik Gauthier with their first-round pick. Meanwhile, the team's first-round draft pick from the previous year was proving a very pleasant surprise. Nineteen-year-old Morgan Rielly had a strong camp in September 2013 and not only made a compelling case for full-time employment in the NHL, but cracked the opening-night roster. The Leafs now had a ten-game window to make a decision on whether to keep him in Toronto for the full season, or return him to junior. Toronto kept him.

Making the team was the proverbial dream come true for Rielly:

My dad was born in Hamilton. His parents were both homegrown in Hamilton and they were always Leaf fans. I have a lot of aunts and uncles who live close to Toronto, and they're all Leafs fans. Growing up in Canada, you're always watching the Leafs on TV and my dad always cheered for them. When I got drafted to the Leafs, that was a pretty special experience for the people close to me.

While Rielly had made the team, others were on their way out. The Maple Leafs freed up salary-cap space by releasing Mikhail Grabovski, Mike Komisarek, Mike Kostka, and Clarke MacArthur, who all found work elsewhere in the NHL.

An incident in a preseason game against Buffalo on September 22, 2013, would shape the Leafs' season – particularly for one of the team's recent acquisitions. Buffalo's John Scott, who at the time had scored one goal in 179 NHL games, lined up for a faceoff directly across from Phil Kessel, who had scored 185 goals in 504 NHL games. In a move that recalled something out of the Broad Street Bullies' playbook, the six-foot, eight-inch, 270-pound Scott tried to engage the six-foot, 200-pound Kessel in a fight. Naturally, Kessel backed away, but not before swiping his stick at Scott. That's all the latter needed. Then, from the bench, David Clarkson bolted over the boards to protect Kessel. As noble as the gesture was, it earned Clarkson a ten-game suspension for leaving the bench. It was an inauspicious start to his Leafs tenure. Meanwhile, goaltenders Ryan Miller of

Buffalo and Toronto's Jonathan Bernier engaged in a spirited bout, trading punches in their bulky gear.

When the regular season finally kicked off, the Maple Leafs looked strong, winning their first three games – dropping the Canadiens, 4–3, in Montreal; the Flyers, 3–1, in Philadelphia; and the Senators, 5–4, in a shootout win in the Leafs' home opener. A competition in goal was also emerging between Reimer and Bernier. Reimer played in the season opener, and he and Bernier split the goaltending duties at first, but as the season progressed, Bernier assumed the starter's role. Overall, the team looked great through October, with a 10–4 record. Then the team's pace slowed considerably, and by the end of the calendar year, the Leafs had a middling 20–16–5 record.

On New Year's Day 2014, the Leafs and the Red Wings were finally able to meet in the Winter Classic, and 105,491 fans jammed into the Big House in Ann Arbor. Both teams had 45 points going into the contest. Many denizens of Leafs Nation made the five-hour drive west along Highway 401 to cheer on their boys and celebrate the special occasion, and the stands at Michigan Stadium seemed to contain equal shares of Red Wings red and Maple Leafs blue. With snow falling steadily throughout the terrifically entertaining game, the teams concluded regulation time tied at two. Overtime solved nothing, and after considerable backing and forthing in the shootout, Tyler Bozak decided the outcome and Toronto took the Winter Classic by a 3–2 score.

The Maple Leafs seemed to have a tight grip on a playoff spot through most of the season, but a familiar and ugly trend once more began to play out. On March 13, during an extended road trip, the Leafs edged the Los Angeles Kings, 3–2, in what many consider to be the team's finest performance of the season. With the win, the Leafs had amassed a respectable 36–24–8 record. That night, however, Bernier was forced to leave the game after the first period with a hernia. While Reimer was strong in relief, the team stumbled badly after that game, losing the next eight in a row and 12 of their final 14. It was Brian Burke's 18-wheeler all over again.

Still, Toronto clung to hopes of making the playoffs until the third-to-last game of the season, a 3–0 loss to the Tampa Bay Lightning on April 8.

In the end, Toronto finished fifth in the reconstituted Atlantic Division, with 84 points and a final record of 38–36–8. Phil Kessel led the team in scoring for the fifth consecutive season. His 80 points, which included a team-best 37 goals, placed him sixth in the NHL.

An astonishing 105,491 spectators attended the Winter Classic contest between Toronto and Detroit at Michigan Stadium in Ann Arbor, on January 1, 2014. The stands in "The Big House" included a large percentage of Leafs Nation in their loyal blue and white, who watched the Maple Leafs edge the Red Wings, 3–2, in a shootout.

David Clarkson, who had been signed to a seven-year deal by Toronto, struggled badly after serving his ten-game suspension and finished the season with just 5 goals and 11 points in 60 games. While the season didn't end with the sort of blood-curdling Game Seven collapse of the previous spring, the Toronto Maple Leafs had disappointed Leafs Nation once again.

THE SHANAHAN ERA

On April 14, 2014, MLSE head Tim Leiweke introduced Brendan Shanahan as the new president of the Toronto Maple Leafs. Shanahan was a natural fit for Leafs Nation. As the *Toronto Star* wrote, "[Shanahan as a player] had a knack for both scoring in bunches and bleeding in the penalty box." He is the only NHL player to have scored more than 600 goals – he finished his 21-season career with 656 – while also recording over 2,000 penalty minutes (he retired with 2,488). Shanahan's record as a competitor speaks for itself: three Stanley Cup championships with the Detroit Red Wings, a gold medal at the 2002 Olympics, and a world championship with Team Canada in 1994. In November 2013, Shanahan was inducted into the Hockey Hall of Fame for his extraordinary career.

Shanahan had long been pegged by many as management material. As a player, he had served as a conciliatory voice during the 2004–05 lockout and organized a two-day conference that included both players and coaches in order to discuss improvements to the game. After retiring as a player, Shanahan served as the NHL's vice-president of hockey and business development. Later, he became the NHL's senior vice-president responsible for player safety and hockey operations. The Hall of Famer had built a staggeringly impressive resumé.

While he never wore the blue and white, part of Shanahan's heart was always dedicated to the Toronto Maple Leafs. "I always dreamed about playing for the Leafs," the native of Mimico, in Toronto's southwestern corner, told *Sportsnet* magazine. "Darryl Sittler was my favourite player." As an 18-year-old rookie with the New Jersey Devils in 1987, his second NHL game was played in Toronto: "Most of my friends were at the game. Somehow, somewhere, they were able to scrounge up tickets because I had gone over the allotment I was allowed to buy."

Shanahan took an equally reverential tone at the media conference held to announce his hiring: "Having grown up here, I knew the importance of what this team means to the people here and their fans. There are lessons you learn along the way. I've taken a little bit from everything throughout my life. You value people who sacrifice, people who pull for others to succeed."

Studious and methodical, Brendan Shanahan did not attempt the sorts of quick fixes that had compromised the future of the Toronto Maple Leafs so many times in the past. Instead, he built a management team. First, Kyle Dubas was hired as the assistant general manager. Dubas had been the general manager of the Ontario Hockey League's Sault Ste. Marie Greyhounds, where he made deft use of statistical analysis to improve the team. To bring focus to the draft and the players in the system, Shanahan hired Mark Hunter as director of player personnel. As the former general manager of the OHL's London Knights, Hunter brought an unparalleled knowledge of the best teenaged players in the world.

While Shanahan was observing his team and strategizing the future of the Toronto Maple Leafs, David Nonis began making some moves. Over the summer of 2014, Toronto sent reliable Carl Gunnarsson and a draft pick to St. Louis for a more physical blueliner in Roman Polák, and welcomed back Matt Frattin, who arrived from Columbus. They picked up free agents David Booth and Mike Santorelli from Vancouver, and Stéphane Robidas and Daniel Winnik from Anaheim. Tim Erixon and Richard Pánik were also picked up on waivers. The Leafs brought back Leo Komarov, who had been playing in the KHL. And finally, with their first pick in the 2014 NHL Entry Draft, eighth overall, the Leafs selected talented William Nylander. The future was beginning to look much brighter.

LEGENDS ROW

For several years, the Toronto Maple Leafs had raised banners to honour the team's greats, but the idea of immortalizing the franchise's greatest players with statues began in earnest in 2012. Maple Leafs president Brendan Shanahan said, "In addition to our focus on building a winning team for today and the future, there is an important responsibility to celebrate our team's history, and to create opportunities for a strong connection between our fans and that tradition. Legends Row will be a fitting tribute that honours many of the greatest players to ever wear the Maple Leaf while giving our fans the chance to feel a part of that history."

There were several decisions that required answers: Who would be selected to be cast in bronze? How many statues would be included? Where would they be located?

When I was a young lad growing up not too far from Toronto, the Leafs were in their heyday and on national television. We'd have our noses, as kids, pressed to the window of the local TV shops. And then to be able to play with the [junior] Marlies and be looking to play for the Leafs. I was fortunate to play a couple of games for the Leafs the last time they won the Cup in '67, and it was a great thrill. As a kid, you wanted to play in the National Hockey League, and what better place to play than in Toronto?

Wayne Carleton
PLAYER
1966–69

One idea gained immediate traction: placing a row of statues around a representation of a player's bench. The greatest teams in Leafs history had always been more about the team than about any individual. Legends Row would, therefore, be a snapshot of a team, composed of the franchise's greatest players from across the generations, standing together.

Erike Blome, a sculptor based in Crystal Lake, Illinois, was selected to bring the Maple Leafs legends to life in the way that MLSE envisioned. "I am so proud to be creating a part of Leafs history," he stated. "The Maple Leafs occupy a special place in NHL hockey as one of the six original storied teams. The players are terrific characters that make great subjects for dynamic and interesting artwork."

The first three – Johnny Bower, Ted Kennedy, and Darryl Sittler – were unveiled on September 6, 2014, on Legends Row, in Maple Leaf Square just outside Air Canada Centre. Bower remarked, "I'm very, very proud of it. I'll never forget this as long as I live." Teeder Kennedy, who died in 2009, was represented by his son Mark, who said, "I know that the idea of being immortalized in his number 9 Maple Leafs sweater alongside some of the best players to ever play for this great franchise would bring a tear to his eye." Darryl Sittler was no less emotional: "I'm very humbled and truly honoured to be part of this tradition."

The fourth and fifth legends to be honoured were Börje Salming and Mats Sundin. At the ceremony on September 12, 2015, Salming was astounded by the fan support: "Toronto has been treating me like this from day one until now, and I haven't been playing hockey for 30 years now, so this is fantastic." Sundin also offered his appreciation to Leafs Nation: "As a player, you never have the time to take it all in, but these great Leafs fans, supporting this franchise over the years, and all these legends, and now myself – it's a huge honour."

Two months later, on November 8, 2015, Syl Apps and George Armstrong became the next to be commemorated on Legends Row. Syl Apps Jr., speaking on behalf of his father, who passed away in December 1998, underscored the humility of his legendary dad when he said, "I think I might have been seven before I even knew he played hockey. He just didn't talk much about it. He wasn't one to live on his past laurels." No less humble, George Armstrong later said, "I don't deserve to be where I'm at, but if I do, it's because of my teammates, having played with a lot of great players."

In January 2016, Turk Broda, Tim Horton, and David Keon were the next to be selected for Legends Row. Broda died in 1972, but his daughter, Barbara Tushingham, expressed the joy the family felt at the announcement: "My dad would have loved this. He loved the Leafs and the fans." George Armstrong described Tim Horton, who died in 1974, by stating, "No finer person, teammate, or hockey player has ever lived." Dave Keon, who played with Horton and Armstrong on the Stanley Cup champion teams of the 1960s, stated, "I am very happy to have been selected with Turk Broda and Tim Horton to Legends Row."

The legacy of those greats on Legends Row, now permanently captured in bronze, celebrates the greats upon whose shoulders each successive Maple Leafs squad is built, and gives Leafs Nation the opportunity to visit the statues and take pictures with their heroes.

THE LONG, COLD WINTER

The club opened the 2014–15 season at home to Montreal with a 4–3 loss. It did not take long for fans to show their displeasure. In fact, it took two games. After Pittsburgh dumped Toronto, 5–2, the second loss in as many games, a Maple Leafs jersey was tossed onto the ice just before the final buzzer. Even Penguins captain Sidney Crosby felt bad for Toronto: "You feel for the other guys. It doesn't make it easy when that happens. It doesn't help, but fans make their opinions known. They let you know what they're thinking." Coach Randy Carlyle made sure that everyone knew the fans weren't the only disgruntled people in the building: "They're frustrated. We're frustrated!"

The Leafs were scheduled to face the Senators in Ottawa on October 23, but tragedy struck the national capital the day before. At about 10 A.M, Corporal Nathan Cirillo, a Canadian soldier guarding the Canadian National War Memorial, was killed by a gunman who then ran into the Parliament Buildings, where he was killed by security personnel. The NHL postponed the game.

The War Memorial could actually be seen from the hotel where the Maple Leafs were staying, and a number of players crowded into Nazem Kadri's room to watch the aftermath of the terrible event. The players were instructed to remain in their hotel, away from the windows. Late in the afternoon, the team left the hotel through a rear exit and headed to the airport to return to Toronto.

Beginning on November 20, the Leafs appeared to have turned things around, embarking on a terrific sequence of ten wins against just one loss in regulation time and a shootout loss. The Leafs collected 21 of 24 possible points during the run and outscored their opponents, 51–27.

As I walked to the Gardens [the night of my first game], a million thoughts ran through my head. These were the Toronto Maple Leafs, and I was now one of them! As I walked out to the ice surface with the team, I saw my dad standing in the runway with a big smile on his face. He leaned over to me and said, "You made it! I love you!" I told my dad that I loved him, too. When I stepped onto the ice, I looked around at the banners from the Stanley Cups that had been won over the years, and glanced at the fans cheering, getting ready for the game to start. There I was, about to play in Maple Leaf Gardens! . . . I have so many great memories of my days with the Leafs – memories that no one can ever take away from me.

Kurt Walker
PLAYER
1976–78

Perhaps the brightest spot on the newish-look Leafs was the play of two young blueliners who were coming into their own: Morgan Rielly and Jake Gardiner. The Leafs regarded the two, both of whom are great skaters and creative puck handlers, as major components in the franchise's future success. Rielly, however, stressed the importance of focusing on the present moment:

Me and Jake, we're not too worried about what's going to happen in eight years. We're just worried about playing well now and helping this team win. We want to make the playoffs. I think we have a bright future, and me and Jake understand that we're a big part of the future, but I think we both enjoy that, and we're using that to motivate each other to be better.

The man behind the Leafs bench was far less certain about the future. And after a 5–1 loss in Winnipeg on January 3, there was the distinct sense that his time with Toronto was over. While the Leafs' 21–16–3 record might have seemed respectable, the team had won just two of its last nine games. After serving as head coach since March 2012, Randy Carlyle was fired on January 6, 2015. Assistant coach Peter Horachek was promoted to head coach on an interim basis.

The change did little for the team's fortunes. In fact, after Carlyle was fired, the bottom fell out. The Maple Leafs registered one lonely win in January, and had just three points to show for the month.

In February, Toronto was still in sixth place in the Eastern Conference, just two points out of fourth, but the team was trending in the altogether wrong direction. The Leafs transformed from a team that had led the NHL in goal scoring to one that had difficulty finding the net. In February, Toronto was winless in 11 games. Horachek pulled no punches with the media, believing that there had to be more commitment: "When things are going the way they are going, we have to find a way to rally around each other. We have to smarten up and play with passion; play like men. We don't have that right now." While there were *some* modest improvements after Horachek's comment, most everyone realized that the 2014–15 season was a lost cause. At the trade deadline, the Maple Leafs were definitely sellers.

Hardworking Daniel Winnik was traded to Pittsburgh for a prospect and draft picks. Cody Franson and Mike Santorelli joined Nashville in exchange for Olli Jokinen, a prospect, and a first-round draft pick. Two weeks later, Jokinen, a six-game veteran of the team, was sent to St. Louis for Joakim Lindström and a draft pick. Korbinian Holzer was delivered to the Anaheim Ducks for veteran blueliner Eric Brewer and a draft pick.

And then there was the most intriguing deal of the lot, one that was, to many, almost miraculous. The Maple Leafs sent David Clarkson, who had a contract that made him seem untradable, to the Columbus Blue Jackets for winger Nathan Horton. Clarkson's $5.25 million cap hit for five more seasons was entirely unattractive to most teams. Yet Columbus saw the opportunity to move Horton – a player with a similar salary and term, but one whose back issues may keep him out of the NHL forever – for a player who could at least play. For their part, the Leafs created some cap space.

The Leafs were officially eliminated from playoff action on March 17, when Boston earned a point in a shootout loss to Buffalo. It was the earliest Toronto had been excluded from postseason play since 1972–73, when they had been eliminated on March 11. It put an exclamation mark on a very poor season.

The regular season ended on April 11 with a 4–3 shootout loss to the Canadiens. Toronto finished 27th overall with a record of 30 wins, 44 losses, and 8 overtime losses for 68 points, seventh in the Atlantic Division – 23 points behind sixth-place Florida – saved from further disgrace only by the even more woeful Buffalo Sabres. Excluding lockout-shortened seasons, the 68 points were the fewest the Maple Leafs had earned in a season since 1996–97.

Throughout the season, the spotlight had shone directly on Phil Kessel. Critics began suggesting that he wasn't giving an all-out effort in each game. Kessel countered, "I'm going out there and playing hard for the guys every night, giving my all. I'm out there giving 100 per cent of what I have, and some nights are better than others." In his defence, Kessel led the Leafs in scoring once again, with 61 points on 25 goals and 36 assists.

Within 24 hours of the final game, Brendan Shanahan relieved general manager David Nonis and interim head coach Peter Horachek of their positions. It had been a crippling season for the team and the fans, and the Leafs had been booed off the ice by the team's faithful on several occasions.

Brendan Shanahan had watched all of this from a distance with a critical eye. Now he was about to put his imprint on the Toronto Maple Leafs.

Acquired from Anaheim in February 2011, Jake Gardiner joined the Maple Leafs fulltime in 2011–12. His deft stickhandling and strong skating made Gardiner a selection to the NHL's All-Rookie Team that spring.

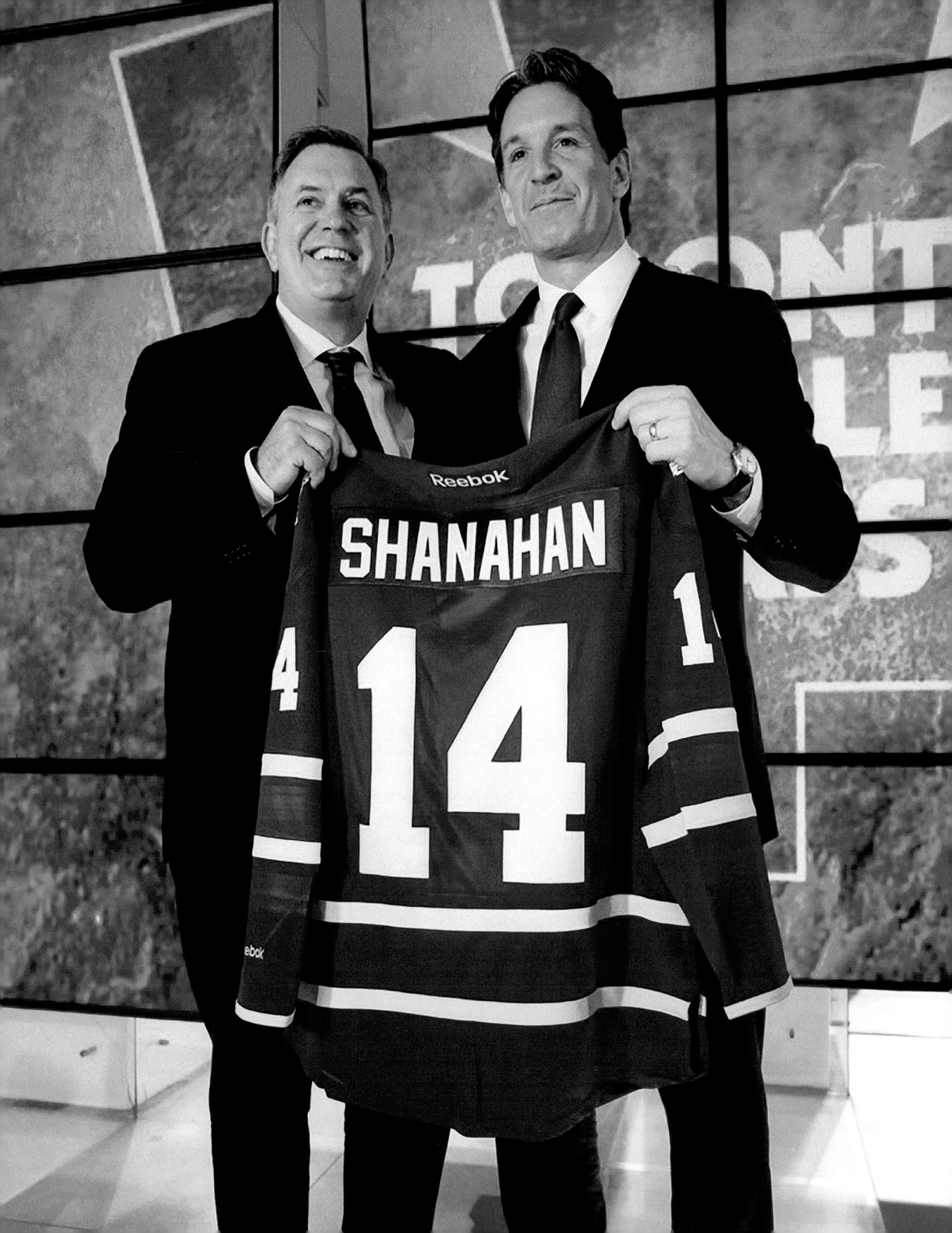
Reebok
SHANAHAN
14

HOPE
2015—16 AND BEYOND

THE SHANA-PLAN

Brendan Shanahan began his evaluation of the Toronto Maple Leafs the moment he arrived, but rather than act immediately, he chose to hang back, spending his first season observing where his team stood and what the franchise would need to move forward. And when he did make changes, it became apparent they would be done methodically. On May 20, 2015, he hired Mike Babcock – the biggest name on the coaching market – to a long-term deal.

Babcock had coached the Detroit Red Wings for ten years and led them to a Stanley Cup championship in 2008. He had also made two other trips to the Stanley Cup final – one with the Wings in 2009, and one as coach of the Anaheim Ducks in 2003.

The acquisition of Babcock represented a seismic shift in the Maple Leafs organization, and it sent a message to Leafs Nation that the group steering the ship meant business. To be sure, the Leafs would be in building mode for some time, but at least the fans knew that the organization was going to be doing it the right way.

The outgoing CEO of MLSE, Tim Leiweke, said of the signing:

> This is really Brendan. It was an outstanding effort on his behalf, an outstanding vision. Our president became a great president today, and I'm proud of him . . . And we were very comfortable he was going to turn it into a great organization. This is a step toward that vision and that goal. I can't say enough good things about Brendan and the way he handled this, and obviously everyone here should be pretty excited about getting Mike to come here as our coach.

Leiweke then looked straight at the television cameras and added one final thought: "If I'm a Leafs fan today, I'm feeling awfully good about the leadership of this organization." For his part, Mike Babcock was thrilled:

"I have a big picture in mind. So does Shanny. So does Larry [Tanenbaum]. So do the people on our staff and that is where we are going. But if you think there is no pain coming . . . there is pain coming."

There would be no quick fixes, and the new management team wanted to impress upon Leafs Nation that the evolution of the Toronto Maple Leafs into a championship-calibre franchise would be slow and systematic. The management team was not yet complete, however: Shanahan had one more surprise up his sleeve. On July 23, he announced that Lou Lamoriello had resigned from the New Jersey Devils and accepted a position as general manager of the Toronto Maple Leafs. Shanahan explained that Lamoriello, who had been the Devils' GM since 1987 and had built three Stanley Cup championship teams, was exactly the sort of person he wanted for this vital position: "I do think we were lacking in some experience, so if I could map out a description of the type of person we wanted [as general manager], it would be Lou. I was happy when the Devils gave me the opportunity to talk to him, and I was happy when he was interested."

Later in the summer, Jacques Lemaire, a two-time winner of the Jack Adams Award as NHL coach of the year, was hired as a special assignment coach. As such, the management and coaching teams now included three members of the Hockey Hall of Fame: Lamoriello in the Builders' category, and Jacques Lemaire and Brendan Shanahan, who are in the Hall because of their playing careers.

At a fan-oriented town hall, Shanahan, Lamoriello, and Babcock were all singing from the same song sheet. The tune promised a rocky road ahead. This is what a real and meaningful build would be all about. Hockey-savvy Leafs Nation knew that the short-term pain would be necessary for long-term gain. The team was expected to lose, and likely lose a great deal, while prospects were nurtured and the team evolved.

A Hall of Famer as a player, Brendan Shanahan (right, with MLSE CEO Tim Leiweke at the media conference announcing his hiring) translated his considerable skills to the front office when he became president of the Toronto Maple Leafs on April 14, 2014. After a season observing the team, he put his "Shana-plan" into place, remaking the front office. He and his management team then set in motion their ambitious plan for the on-ice roster.

When he joined Toronto as head coach on May 20, 2015, Mike Babcock's NHL resumé included a Stanley Cup championship with Detroit in 2008, and visits to the Cup final with Anaheim in 2003 and Detroit in 2009. His insistence on speed, puck possession, and defensive responsibility made the 2015–16 squad exciting for Leafs Nation to watch, and gave fans a glimpse into the Maple Leafs' future.

The team would be evolving without Phil Kessel, however. The winger the *Toronto Star* had described as "mercurial" was traded to Pittsburgh, along with prospect Tyler Biggs and a second-round draft pick, for Scott Harrington, Kasperi Kapanen, Nick Spaling, and a first-round draft choice. "Sometimes," Shanahan offered, "you have to give up some very talented players to get some assets and picks. It's our job now to turn these into things of value for this club." Toronto's reinvention could not proceed with Kessel on the roster. With the trade, the Maple Leafs had cleared the decks of a substantial long-term contract with a hefty salary-cap hit.

With nine picks scattered over seven rounds, the new management team approached the 2015 NHL Entry Draft with a hopeful eye towards expanding the core. Choosing fourth overall, their first pick was the highly skilled forward Mitch Marner. In July, the Maple Leafs fleshed out their roster with a number of players on short-term contracts, including defencemen Frank Corrado, Matt Hunwick, and Martin Marinčin, as well as forwards Mark Arcobello, Michael Grabner, Shawn Matthias, P. A. Parenteau, and returning Leafs Daniel Winnik and Brad Boyes.

There remained, of course, the very real issue of replacing Kessel's production. The gauntlet had now been thrown down for Nazem Kadri, James van Riemsdyk, and Tyler Bozak.

More generally, the 2014–15 season had bruised the psyche of the Toronto Maple Leafs. Professional hockey players are trained to win, and losing can wear on them, no matter how strong their resolve. The new coach understood this. "They feel like no one has their back," he said. "They're not as proud as they should be. We're going to build confidence and a way to play. We don't have to change the people; we just have to change how we do it."

The 2015–16 season opener saw Toronto drop a 3–1 decision to Montreal, and the rest of October was no better. In fact, the Maple Leafs lost nine of ten games during that opening month and managed one goal or less in six of those defeats. And then, hope. In November, the Leafs picked up 17 points and added 14 more in December. Leafs Nation began to ask if this might be a playoff team.

In truth, Mike Babcock had done an admirable job with the personnel he had to work with. On balance, the Leafs played a spirited, hardworking brand of hockey, and the team was competitive in nearly every game. There was, however, a dearth of top-end talent that put Toronto at a disadvantage against the bulk of the NHL. Players were being asked to punch well above their weight.

And while there were valiant efforts, the Leafs more often than not came up short.

Jonathan Bernier struggled in goal, going 0–6–3 before James Reimer took over the starting job in mid-November. Bernier was sent to the Toronto Marlies to regain his confidence in what Coach Babcock called a "conditioning opportunity." The netminder played sensationally for the Marlies, winning three games, all of them shutouts, before losing in his final start.

For his part, Reimer had played inspired hockey, going 6–2–3 and allowing two goals or fewer in the 11 games in which he played. During practice on November 25, however, Reimer's oft-injured groin was aggravated again. This kept him out of the lineup for a month. Babcock therefore called on Garret Sparks to make his NHL debut on November 30 against the Edmonton Oilers. Sparks, who was with the Marlies, recorded a 24-save, 3–0 shutout win in his debut. It was a sensational beginning to a young career. An emotional Sparks was informed that it was the first time in Maple Leafs history that a goaltender had recorded a shutout in his first game. Sparks would continue to surprise, winning three of his four games before the Leafs received Bernier back into the fold.

There were some surprises up front as well. Few would have expected "Uncle Leo" Komarov – nicknamed after a character from the 1990s sitcom *Seinfeld* – to step up as the team's leading scorer. In fact, Komarov surpassed his career highs in goals and points, and in January he was named Toronto's sole representative at the NHL All-Star Game in Nashville.

There would also be some aesthetic alterations. On February 2, the Toronto Maple Leafs unveiled the new logo they would wear during their centennial season. The 31 points on the outer perimeter of the leaf represent 1931, the year in which the team moved into Maple Leaf Gardens. Thirteen "veins" superimposed on the leaf symbolize the team's 13 Stanley Cup championships. There are another four veins under the team's name, bringing the total number of veins to 17 – honouring 1917, the year in which Toronto joined the National Hockey League. It was altogether a thoughtful and symbolic tip of the hat to past glories.

There would be a more concrete alteration to the lineup. On February 9, the Maple Leafs made the bold move of trading Dion Phaneuf to the Ottawa Senators. The captain was traded alongside four players who didn't figure into Toronto's future plans. In return, the Leafs received defenceman Jared Cowen, forward Colin Greening, prospect Tobias Lindberg, veteran

Milan Michálek, and a second-round draft pick. "This was a transaction that certainly wasn't for today," GM Lou Lamoriello commented. With the move, the Leafs freed up another sizable amount of salary-cap space and now had the opportunity to sign some of the young, promising prospects in their fold. Meanwhile, the Maple Leafs would play without a captain for the remainder of the campaign.

The "Shana-plan" was, it seemed, at full throttle. Over the course of a year, the Leafs had brought in a legendary general manager, a much sought-after coach, and a new scouting department. The team had also jettisoned three sizeable contracts by trading David Clarkson, Phil Kessel, and Dion Phaneuf. In so doing, the Leafs freed up over $20 million in cap space (they would continue to pay $1.2 million of Kessel's salary).

In the week leading up to the 2016 trade deadline, the Leafs were able to unload several players. Matthias, Polák, Spaling, Winnik, and goalie James Reimer were all moved for prospects and draft selections. Now, more than ever, the Leafs had to rely on still-developing youngsters to fill out the lineup. In a 3–2 loss to Nashville on February 23, the Leafs were without injured veterans Tyler Bozak, Matt Hunwick, Joffrey Lupul, and James van Riemsdyk, as well as suspended Leo Komarov. In their place, Toronto added the likes of Mark Arcobello, Rich Clune, Brendan Leipsic, Josh Leivo, Viktor Lööv, and Stuart Percy, all of whom had spent much of the season with the Toronto Marlies. As the *Toronto Star* pointed out, the AHL-heavy lineup wearing blue and white that night carried a cap hit of approximately $29.4 million. The salary floor for the 2015–16 season was $52.8 million.

When the dust had settled on trade-deadline day, the Toronto Maple Leafs had deliberately gotten much worse as a first step towards getting much better. By mid-March, 41 different players had worn the blue and white, 25 of whom were playing for the Maple Leafs for the first time. The Leafs were now armed with useful draft picks, attractive prospects, and much-needed salary-cap space in order to compete for hockey's greatest goal. The team rewarded many of those prospects starring with the Marlies with their first taste of NHL action. Connor Brown, Frédérik Gauthier, Zach Hyman, Kasperi Kapanen, Tobias Lindberg, Viktor Lööv, William Nylander, Nikita Soshnikov, and Rinat Valiev all made their NHL debuts and gave fans a glimpse into a future that promised speed, skill, and success.

The play of the youngsters was a bright spot in the season. Brendan Shanahan said, "Our fans have enjoyed watching them. Even our veteran players have enjoyed watching them come up." But their elevation to the big club was more than an olive branch to the fans. "We want these young players to get a bit of a taste of the NHL, whether it's five, ten, or twenty games, and give themselves a measuring tool to go back and prepare for just how hard it is to be successful at the NHL level."

Leafs Nation felt optimistic despite the last-place finish. There was hope on the horizon, and this feeling grew exponentially when the draft lottery was held, and the Toronto Maple Leafs drew the first-overall draft pick in the 2016 NHL Entry Draft, a milestone they hadn't enjoyed since 1985. Then, the Leafs brightened their future by selecting Wendel Clark. This time, Toronto chose 18-year-old Auston Matthews, a native of Scottsdale, Arizona.

HOPE

The Toronto Maple Leafs management has earned the patience of Leafs Nation. There is great optimism that, one day soon, promise will translate into deliverance.

All who share this hope, both on and off the ice, want to be delivered: delivered back to glory, back to the days of crystal sets, radios, and black-and-white televisions that trumpeted, "Toronto wins!" Back to Paul Morris's unaffected voice intoning, "Toronto goal scored by . . ." Back to honking horns and red lights along Bay Street on a crisp spring night. Back to hot cashews on Carlton Street or, for the dwindling few, a walk into deep winters past at "the Arena." Leafs Nation wants to be delivered back to playoff runs, overtime winners, and ticker-tape parades; back to Dye and Denneny, Broda and Bower, Sittler and Sundin, Kennedy, Apps, and Conacher too. As fans, we want to come home to our proud Leafs Nation – this place where we all belong, where the future promises new glories for our beloved Blue and White.

Much of the Toronto Maple Leafs' hope moving into the future revolves around the play of defenceman Morgan Rielly. A first-round, fifth-overall selection in the NHL Entry Draft, Rielly joined the NHL team as a 19-year-old in 2013–14, and quickly established himself as a smooth-skating blueliner, with strong offensive sensibilities married to defensive responsibility.

BIBLIOGRAPHY AND WORKS CITED

PRIMARY SOURCES

PERSONAL INTERVIEWS

Glenn Anderson
George Armstrong
Andy Bathgate
Bob Baun
Ken Belanger
Bryan Berard
Drake Berehowsky
Nick Beverley
Laurie Boschman
Pat Boutette
Johnny Bower
Darryl Boyce
Kurt Browning
Mike Bullard
Wayne Carleton
Ed Chadwick
Rob Cimetta
Wendel Clark
David Clarkson
Kitty Cohen
Brian Conacher
Pete Conacher
Bobby Copp
Shayne Corson
Jim Dorey
Dick Duff
Ron Ellis
Tom Fergus
Andy Frost
Paul Gardner
Mike Gartner
Tommy Gaston
Doug Gilmour
Gaston Gingras
Jim Gregory
Bob Haggert

Paul Harrison
Glenn Healy
Paul Henderson
Darby Hendrickson
Ron Hewat
Pat Hickey
Larry Hillman
Jimmy Holmstrom
Red Horner
Greg Hotham
Ron Hurst
Peter Ing
Jeff Jackson
Mike Johnson
Jimmy Jones
Red Kelly
Mike Kennedy
David Keon
Kris King
Mike Krushelnyski
Tom Kurvers
Gary Leeman
Joffrey Lupul
Jamie Macoun
Kevin Maguire
Frank Mahovlich
Danny Markov
Brad Marsh
Matt Martin
Brad May
Lanny McDonald
Brian McFarlane
Bob McGill
Walt McKechnie
Jim McKenny
Jack McLean
John Mitchell
Jim Morrison
Gus Mortson

Craig Muni
Mike Murphy
Anne Murray
Ric Nattress
Bob Neely
Bob Nevin
Ed Olczyk
Bert Olmstead
Mark Osborne
Mike Palmateer
Brian Papineau
Jim Pappin
Bob Parent
Pat Park
Mike Peca
Fred Perlini
Nathan Perrott
Dion Phaneuf
Félix Potvin
Marcel Pronovost
Joel Quenneville
Dave Reid
Curt Ridley
Morgan Rielly
Jim Rutherford
Börje Salming
Phil Samis
Eddie Shack
Darryl Shannon
Doug Shedden
Darryl Sittler
Tommy Smythe
Lorne Stamler
Allan Stanley
Bob Stellick
Gord Stellick
Peter Stemkowski
Mats Sundin
Greg Terrion

Alan Thicke
Steve Thomas
Darcy Tucker
Ian Turnbull
Garry Unger
Rick Vaive
Jack Valiquette
Garry Valk
Kurt Walker
Bob Warner
Tom Watt
Randy Wood
Mike Zigomanis

NEWSPAPERS AND PERIODICALS

Billboard
Boston Globe
Boston Record
Canadian Press
Chicago Tribune
Dorchester Review
Financial Post
Guardian
Hamilton Spectator
The Hockey News
Hush
International Journal of the History of Sport
Life
Los Angeles Times
Maclean's
Maple Leaf Annual
Mississauga News
Montreal Star
Montreal Gazette
Montreal Herald
National Post
New York Clipper

New York Post
New York Times
New York Evening Telegram
New York World-Telegram
Northern Miner (Cobalt, ON)
Ottawa Citizen
Ottawa Journal
Quebec Chronicle-Telegraph
Saturday Evening Post
Saturday Night
Star Weekly
Sport
Sporting Life
The Sporting News
Sports Illustrated
Time
Toronto Daily News
Toronto Globe
Toronto Globe and Mail
Toronto Mail and Empire
Toronto Star
Toronto Sun
Toronto Telegram
Toronto World
Timmins Daily Press
Vancouver Sun
Vancouver World
Weekend Magazine
Winnipeg Free Press
Winnipeg Tribune

ELECTRONIC MEDIA

CBC Archives
Hockey Hall of Fame
Society for International Hockey Research (SIHR)
Hockey Night in Canada
Leafs TV *Classic Games*
Canadian Heritage

MISCELLANEOUS

Arena Gardens. *Official Hockey Program*, November 1930. City of Toronto Archives.

Bower, Johnny, and Little John with The Rinky-Dinks. "Honky the Christmas Goose." Composed by Chip Young and Orville Hoover. Capitol 72318. Recorded 1965.

Clarke, James Paton. *Lays of the Maple Leaf, or Songs of Canada.* Toronto: A.S. Nordheimer, c.1853.

Hockey Night in Canada. Longines Symphonette Society HNIC 1. Released c.1971.

"Manuscript" [document placed in the cornerstone of Maple Leaf Gardens, September 21, 1931].

Maple Leaf Gardens. *Official Hockey Program.* Various editions. Authors' collections.

Marley, Bob, and the Wailers. "Positive Vibration." Credited to Vincent Ford. From *Babylon by Bus.* Island ISLD-11. Released 1978.

McMurtry, William R. *Investigation and Inquiry into Violence in Amateur Hockey.* Toronto: [Ontario] Ministry of Community and Social Services, 1974.

Muir, Alexander. "The Maple Leaf For Ever: A Canadian National Song!" Toronto: Published by the author, 1867.

Rankine, Douglas, with the Secrets. "Clear the Track, Here Comes Shack." Composed by Brian McFarlane and William McCauley. RCA Victor Canada International 57-3384. Released 1966.

Rheostatics. "The Ballad of Wendel Clark, Parts I and II." Composed by Dave Bidini, Dave Clark, Martin Tielli. From *Greatest Hits.* Green Sprouts Music Club GSMC-001. Released 1987.

The Tragically Hip. "Fifty Mission Cap." Composed by the Tragically Hip. From *Fully Completely.* MCA Records MCAD-10700. Released 1992.

Vallee, Rudy. "Brother Can You Spare a Dime?" Composed by E.Y. "Yip" Harburg and Jay Gorney. Columbia 2725-D. Released 1932.

Williams, Ozzie, and Your Favourite Music, featuring Betty Carr and Charles Baldour. "Sunday in Toronto." Composed by Ozzie Williams and Lige McKelvy. London 662. Released 1950.

———. "The Toronto Subway Song." Composed by Mel Hamill. London 662. Released 1950.

SECONDARY SOURCES

BOOKS

Bailey, Peter. *Leisure and Class in Victorian England: Rational Recreation and the Contest for Control, 1830–1855.* London: Routledge and Kegan Paul, 1978.

Barris, Ted. *Victory at Vimy: Canada Comes of Age: April 9–12, 1917.* Toronto: Thomas Allen, 2007.

Batten, Jack, *Hockey Dynasty.* Toronto: Pagurian Press, 1969.

———. *The Leafs: An Anecdotal History of the Toronto Maple Leafs.* Toronto: Key Porter, 1994.

Baun, Bobby. *Lowering the Boom: The Bobby Baun Story.* Toronto: Stoddart, 2000.

Benedict, Michael, ed. *Canada at War.* Toronto: Viking, 1997.

Berger, Howard. *Maple Leaf Moments.* Toronto: Warwick, 1994.

Blake, Jason. "Representations of Hockey Violence." In *Canadian Hockey Literature.* Toronto: University of Toronto Press, 2010.

Bowlsby, Craig. *Empire of Ice: The Rise and Fall of the Pacific Coast Hockey Association.* Vancouver: Knights of Winter, 2012.

Brewitt, Ross. *Clear the Track: The Eddie Shack Story.* Toronto: Stoddart, 1997.

Brignall, Richard. *Big Train: The Legendary Ironman of Sport, Lionel Conacher.* Toronto: Lorimer, 2009.

Bynum, Mike, ed. *Toronto Maple Leafs' 50 Unforgettable Moments in Hockey from the Sports Pages of the Toronto Star.* Birmingham, AL: Canada Hockey, 2005.

Cole, Stephen. *The Last Hurrah: A Celebration of Hockey's Greatest Season, '66–'67.* Toronto: Viking, 1995.

Coleman, Charles L., and National Hockey League. *The Trail of the Stanley Cup.* 3 vols. Montreal: National Hockey League, 1966.

Cook, Tim. *At the Sharp End: Canadians Fighting the Great War, 1914–1916.* Vol. I. Toronto: Viking, 2007.

———. *Shock Troops: Canadians Fighting the Great War, 1917–1918.* Vol. II. Toronto: Viking, 2008.

Conacher, Brian. *As the Puck Turns: A Personal Journey Through the World of Hockey.* Mississauga, ON: Wiley, 2007.

Conrad, Margaret, and Alvin Finkel. *History of the Canadian Peoples: 1867 to the Present.* Vol. II. 4th ed. Toronto: Pearson Longman, 2006.

Corelli, Rae. *The Toronto that Used to Be.* Toronto: Toronto Star Limited, 1964.

Cosentino, Frank. *The Renfrew Millionaires: The Valley Boys of Winter 1910.* Burnstown, ON: General Store Publishing House, 1990.

Cox, Damien, and Gord Stellick. *67.* Mississauga, ON: Wiley, 2004.

Diamond, Dan, ed. *Total Hockey: The Official Encyclopedia of the National Hockey League.* 2nd ed. Kingston, NY: Total Sports, 2000.

Harrison, Richard, and Jamie Dopp, eds. *Now is the Winter: Thinking about Hockey.* Hamilton, ON: Wolsak and Wynn, 2009.

Duff, Bob, with Johnny Bower. *The China Wall: The Timeless Legend of Johnny Bower.* Wayne, MI: Immortal Investments, 2006.

Ellis, Ron, with Kevin Shea. *Over the Boards: The Ron Ellis Story.* Bolton, ON: Fenn, 2002.

Farris, Jason. *Hail Cesare!: Trail Through the NHL.* Vancouver: CircaNow Productions, 2006.

Fitkin, Ed. *Gentleman Joe Primeau, the Kid Line, and the Gashouse Gang of Hockey*. Toronto: Castle, 1953.

Foster, Susan, with Carl Brewer. *The Power of Two: Carl Brewer's Battle with Hockey's Power Brokers*. Toronto: Fenn, 2006.

Fuhr, Grant, with Bruce Dowbiggin. *Grant Fuhr: The Story of a Hockey Legend*. Toronto: Random House, 2014.

Fussel, Paul. *The Great War and Modern Memory*. Oxford, UK: Oxford University Press, 1975.

Garner, Hugh. *Cabbagetown*. Toronto: McGraw-Hill Ryerson, [1950] 1968.

Gaston, Tom, with Kevin Shea. *A Fan For All Seasons*. Bolton, ON: Fenn Publishing, 2001.

Gregoire, L. Waxy, David Dupuis, and Pierre Pilote. *Heart of the Blackhawks: The Pierre Pilote Story*. Toronto: ECW Press, 2013.

Gruneau, Richard and David Whitson, eds. *Artificial Ice: Hockey, Culture, and Commerce*. Toronto: University of Toronto Press, 2006.

———. *Hockey Night in Canada: Sports, Identities, and Cultural Politics*. Toronto: University of Toronto Press, 1994.

Harris, Billy. *The Glory Years*. Scarborough, ON: Prentice-Hall, 1989.

Hewitt, Foster. *Foster Hewitt: His Own Story*. Toronto: Ryerson Press, 1967.

Hodge, Charlie. *Golly Gee, It's Me: The Howie Meeker Story*. Toronto: Stoddart, 1996.

Hollett, Michael Lynn. *Flash's Hat Tricks*. Unpublished, 2013.

Holman, Andrew C., ed. *Canada's Game: Hockey and Identity*. Montreal: McGill-Queen's University Press, 2009.

Holzman, Morey, and Joseph Nieforth. *Deceptions and Doublecross: How the NHL Conquered Hockey*. Toronto: Dundurn, 2002.

Hornby, Lance. *The Story of Maple Leaf Gardens: 100 Memories at Church and Carlton*. Toronto: Toronto Sun, 1998.

Horton, Lori, and Tim Griggs. *In Loving Memory: A Tribute to Tim Horton*. Toronto: ECW Press, 1997.

Houston, William. *Inside Maple Leaf Gardens: The Rise and Fall of the Toronto Maple Leafs*. Toronto: McGraw-Hill Ryerson, 1989.

Howell, Colin D. *Blood, Sweat, and Cheers: Sport and the Making of Modern Canada*. Toronto: University of Toronto Press, 2001.

Hunter, Douglas. *War Games: Conn Smythe and Hockey's Fighting Men*. Toronto: Viking, 1996.

Hunter, Douglas. *Open Ice: The Tim Horton Story*. Toronto: Viking, 1994.

Imlach, George "Punch," with Scott Young. *Heaven and Hell in the NHL*. Toronto: McClelland and Stewart, 1982.

———. *Hockey Is a Battle*. Toronto: Macmillan, 1969.

James, Valmore, and John Gallagher. *Black Ice: The Val James Story*. Toronto: ECW Press, 2015.

Jenish, D'Arcy. *The NHL: A Centennial History*. Toronto: Random House, 2013.

Kamchen, Richard, and Greg Oliver. *The Goaltenders' Union*. Toronto: ECW Press, 2014.

Kendall, Brian. *Shutout: The Legend of Terry Sawchuk*. Toronto: Penguin, 1996.

Kidd, Bruce. *The Struggle for Canadian Sport*. Toronto: University of Toronto Press, 1996.

Kluckner, Michael. *Toronto: The Way it Was*. Toronto: Whitecap, 1988.

Leonetti, Mike. *Defining Moments – Toronto Maple Leafs*. Markham, ON: Red Deer Press, 2014.

Leonetti, Mike, and Paul Patskou. *100 Things Maple Leafs Fans Should Know & Do Before They Die*. Chicago: Triumph Books, 2014.

Lemon, James. *Toronto Since 1918*. Toronto: Lorimer, 1985.

Lewicki, Danny. *From the Coal Docks to the NHL: A Hockey Life*. Toronto: Accent Printing & Graphics, 2006.

Logan, Anne M. *Rare Jewel for a King: A Tribute to King Clancy*. Erin, ON: Boston Mills Press, 1986.

Lorinc, John, Michael McClelland, Ellen Scheinberg, and Tatum Taylor, eds. *The Ward: The Life and Loss of Toronto's First Immigrant Neighbourhood*. Toronto: Coach House Press, 2015.

Mahovlich, Ted. *The Big M: The Frank Mahovlich Story*. Toronto: HarperCollins, 1999.

Maple Leaf Sports and Entertainment. *Maple Leaf Gardens: Memories and Dreams, 1931–1999*. Toronto: Dan Diamond and Associates, 1999.

Mason, Mary Willan. *The Well-Tempered Listener: Growing Up with Musical Parents*. Toronto: Words Indeed, 2010.

McDonald, Lanny, with Steve Simmons. *Lanny*. Toronto: McGraw-Hill Ryerson Limited, 1987.

McFarlane, Brian. *Clancy: The King's Story*. Toronto: ECW Press, 1997.

McKinley, Michael. *Putting a Roof on Winter: Hockey's Rise from Sport to Spectacle*. Vancouver: Greystone Books, 2000.

McParland, Kelly. *The Lives of Conn Smythe: From the Battlefield to Maple Leaf Gardens*. Toronto: Fenn/McClelland and Stewart, 2012.

Meeker, Howie, with Charlie Hodge. *Stop It There, Back It Up!* Toronto: Stoddart, 1999.

Melrose, Barry, with Roger Vaughan. *Dropping the Gloves: Inside the Fiercely Combative World of Professional Hockey*. Toronto: Fenn/McClelland and Stewart, 2012.

Metcalfe, Alan. *Canada Learns to Play: The Emergence of Organized Sport, 1807–1914*. Toronto: McClelland and Stewart, 1987.

Miller, Ian Hugh MacLean. *Our Glory and Our Grief: Torontonians and the Great War*. Toronto: University of Toronto Press, 2002.

Morrison, John, and Doug McClatchy. *Toronto Blue Shirts a.k.a. The Torontos*. Stouffville, ON: The Hockey Information Service, 1996.

Moss, Mark. *Manliness and Militarism: Educating Young Boys in Ontario for War.* Don Mills, ON: Oxford University Press, 2001.

Myers, Jay. *The Fitzhenry and Whiteside Book of Canadian Facts and Dates.* Revised and updated by Larry Hoffman and Fraser Sutherland. Richmond Hill, ON: Fitzhenry and Whiteside, 1991.

Obodiac, Stan. *Maple Leaf Gardens: Fifty Years of History.* Toronto: Van Nostrand Reinhold, 1981.

Obodiac, Stan, ed. *The Leafs: The First 50 Years.* Toronto: McClelland and Stewart, 1977.

Oliver, Greg. *Written in Blue and White.* Toronto: ECW Press, 2014.

O'Malley, Martin. *Gross Misconduct: The Life of Spinner Spencer.* Markham, ON: Penguin, 1988.

Opp, James, and John C. Walsh, eds. *Placing Memory and Remembering Place in Canada.* Vancouver: UBC Press, 2010.

Podnieks, Andrew. *Lord Stanley's Cup.* Bolton, ON: Fenn, 2004.

———. *The Blue and White Book.* Toronto: ECW Press, 1996.

Pronovost, Marcel, with Bob Duff. *Marcel Pronovost: A Life in Hockey.* Windsor: Biblioasis, 2012.

Reed, Thomas. *The Blue and White: A Record of Fifty Years of Athletic Endeavour at the University of Toronto.* Toronto: University of Toronto Press, 1944.

Salming, Börje, and Gerhard Karlsson. *Borje Salming: Blood, Sweat, and Hockey.* Toronto: HarperCollins, 1991.

Sandor, Steven. *Illustrated Guide to Hockey Sites and History: Toronto.* Surrey, BC: Heritage House, 2007.

Scanlan, Wayne. *Roger's World: The Life and Unusual Times of Roger Neilson.* Toronto: McClelland & Stewart, 2004.

Seglins, David. *Just Part of the Game: Violence, Hockey, and Masculinity in Central Canada, 1890–1910.* Kingston, ON: Queen's University Press, 1995.

Selke, Frank, with Gordon Green. *Behind the Cheering.* Toronto: McClelland and Stewart, 1962.

Semenko, Dave, with Larry Tucker. *Looking Out for Number One.* Toronto: Stoddart, 1989.

Shea, Kevin. *Barilko: Without a Trace.* Bolton, ON: Fenn, 2010.

Shea, Kevin, with Paul Patskou, Roly Harris, and Paul Bruno. *Toronto Maple Leafs: Diary of a Dynasty, 1957–1967.* Richmond Hill, ON: Firefly, 2010.

Shea, Kevin, with Larry Colle and Paul Patskou. *St. Michael's College: 100 Years of Pucks and Prayers.* Bolton, ON: Fenn, 2008.

Sittler, Darryl, and Chrys Goyens with Allan Turowetz. *Sittler.* Toronto: Macmillan, 1991.

Smith, Ron. *Kid Dynamite: The Gerry James Story.* Fernie, BC: Oolichan, 2011.

Smythe, Thomas, and Kevin Shea. *Centre Ice: The Smythe Family, the Gardens, and the Toronto Maple Leaf Hockey Club.* Bolton, ON: Fenn Publishing, 2000.

Smythe, Conn, with Scott Young. *Conn Smythe: If You Can't Beat 'Em in the Alley.* Toronto: McClelland and Stewart, 1981.

Stellick, Gord. *Stellicktricity: Stories, Highlights, and Other Hockey Juice from a Life Plugged Into the Game.* Mississauga, ON: Wiley, 2011.

Stellick, Gord, and Jim O'Leary, *Hockey, Heartaches, and Hal.* Toronto: Prentice-Hall, 1990.

Walden, Keith. *Becoming Modern in Toronto: The Industrial Exhibition and the Shaping of a Late Victorian Culture.* Toronto: University of Toronto Press, 1997.

Wilson, Jason. *Soldiers of Song: The Dumbells and Other Canadian Concert Parties of the First World War.* Waterloo, ON: Wilfrid Laurier University Press, 2012.

Wong, John Chi-Kit, ed. *Coast to Coast: Hockey in Canada to the Second World War.* Toronto: University of Toronto Press, 2009.

———. *Lords of the Rinks: The Emergence of the National Hockey League, 1875–1936.* Toronto: University of Toronto Press, 2005.

Young, Scott. *The Leafs I Knew.* Toronto: Ryerson Press, 1966.

———. *A Boy at Leafs Camp.* Toronto: Little, Brown, 1963.

Zwolinski, Mark. *The John Kordic Story: The Fight of His Life.* Toronto: Macmillan, 1995.

ARTICLES, JOURNALS, BOOK CHAPTERS

Ammirante, Julian. "Globalization in Professional Sport: Comparisons and Contrasts Between Hockey and European Football." In *Artificial Ice: Hockey, Culture, and Commerce,* edited by Richard S. Gruneau and David Whitson. Toronto: University of Toronto Press, 2006.

———. "Manufacturing Players and Controlling Sports: An Interpretation of the Political Economy of Hockey and the 2004 NHL Lockout." In *Canada's Game: Hockey and Identity,* edited by Andrew C. Holman. Montreal: McGill-Queen's University Press, 2009.

Barlow, John Matthew. "Scientific Aggression: Commercialization, Class, Irishness, and Manliness in the Shamrock Hockey Club of Montreal, 1895–1901. In *Coast to Coast: Hockey in Canada to the Second World War,* edited by John Chi-Kit Wong. Toronto: University of Toronto Press, 2009.

Bellamy, Robert, and Kelly Shultz. "Hockey Night in the United States? The NHL, Major League Sports, and the Evolving Television/Media Marketplace." In *Artificial Ice: Hockey, Culture, and Commerce,* edited by Richard S. Gruneau and David Whitson. Toronto: University of Toronto Press, 2006.

Blake, Jason. "'Just Part of the Game': Depictions of Violence in Hockey Prose." In *Canada's Game: Hockey and Identity*, edited by Andrew C. Holman. Montreal: McGill-Queen's University Press, 2009.

Cantelon, Hart. "Have Skates, Will Travel: Canada, International Hockey, and the Changing Hockey Labour Market." In *Artificial Ice: Hockey, Culture, and Commerce*, edited by Richard S. Gruneau and David Whitson. Toronto: University of Toronto Press, 2006.

Clarke, Nic. "'The Greater and Grimmer Game': Sport as an Arbiter of Military Fitness in the British Empire – The Case of 'One-Eyed' Frank McGee." *International Journal of the History of Sport* 28 (March 2011): 3–4.

Dopp, Jamie. "Win Orr Lose: Searching for the Good Canadian Kid in Canadian Hockey Fiction." In *Canada's Game: Hockey and Identity*, edited by Andrew C. Holman. Montreal: McGill-Queen's University Press, 2009.

Field, Russell. "Constructing the Preferred Spectator: Arena Design and Operation and the Consumption of Hockey in 1930s Toronto," *International Journal of the History of Sport*, 25 (May 2008): 6.

———. "'There's More People Here Tonight Than at a First Night of the Metropolitan': Professional Hockey Spectatorship in the 1920s and 1930s in New York and Toronto." In *Canada's Game: Hockey and Identity*, edited by Andrew C. Holman. Montreal: McGill-Queen's University Press, 2009.

Harrison, Richard. "Stanley Cup/Superman. In *Now Is the Winter: Thinking about Hockey*, edited by Jamie Dopp and Richard Harrison. Hamilton, ON: Wolsak and Wynn, 2009.

Holman, Andrew. "Frank Merriwell on Skates: Heroes, Villains, Canadians, and Other *Others* in American Juvenile Sporting Fiction, 1890–1940." In *Now Is the Winter: Thinking about Hockey*, edited by Jamie Dopp and Richard Harrison. Hamilton, ON: Wolsak and Wynn, 2009.

Hyatt, Craig and Julie Stevens. "Are Americans Really Hockey Villains? A New Perspective on the American Influence on Canada's National Game." In *Canada's Game: Hockey and Identity*, edited by Andrew C. Holman. Montreal: McGill-Queen's University Press, 2009.

Kossuth, Robert S. "Chinook Country Hockey: The Emergence of Hockey in Pre–World War II Southern Alberta." In *Coast to Coast: Hockey in Canada to the Second World War*, edited by John Chi-Kit Wong. Toronto: University of Toronto Press, 2009.

Mills, David. "The Blue Line and the Bottom Line: Entrepreneurs and the Business of Hockey in Canada, 1927–1990." *The Business of Professional Sports*, edited by Paul Staudohar and James A. Mangan. Urbana, IL: University of Illinois Press, 1991.

Wilson, Brian. "Selective Memory in a Global Culture: Reconsidering Links Between Youth, Hockey, and Canadian Identity." In *Artificial Ice: Hockey, Culture, and Commerce*, edited by Richard S. Gruneau and David Whitson. Toronto: University of Toronto Press, 2006.

Wilson, John Jason. "Skating to Armageddon: Of Canada, Hockey, and the First World War." *International Journal of the History of Sport* 22 (May 2005): 3.

IMAGE CREDITS

HOCKEY HALL OF FAME

Copyright Page (Graphic Artists); Introduction (top) (Imperial Oil–Turofksy); 3 (Michael Burns Sr.); 4 (Hockey Hall of Fame); 6 (Hockey Hall of Fame); 9, 12 (Hockey Hall of Fame); 14 (Imperial Oil–Turofksy); 17 (Le Studio du Hockey); 20 (Hockey Hall of Fame); 28, 31, 34 (Imperial Oil–Turofksy); 39 (Le Studio du Hockey); 40 (Imperial Oil–Turofksy); 44 (bottom), 49 (Hockey Hall of Fame); 50–51 (Imperial Oil–Turofksy); 54 (Le Studio du Hockey); 58 (Imperial Oil–Turofksy); 61 (Hockey Hall of Fame); 62 (Imperial Oil–Turofksy); 64 (Imperial Oil–Turofksy); 68 (Hockey Hall of Fame); 69 (Le Studio du Hockey); 71, 74–75, 76, 81–82, 85–86, 90, 93, 95–96, 98, 101–102, 105, 109–110, 113–114, 118 (Imperial Oil–Turofksy); 120–121 (Michael Burns Sr.); 122, 124, 127, 129–130, 134, 137 (Imperial Oil–Turofksy); 138, 142 (Graphic Artists); 145 (Hockey Hall of Fame); 146, 151 (Imperial Oil–Turofksy), 152 (Graphic Artists); 155 (Imperial Oil–Turofksy); 156 (Graphic Artists); 159–160 (Imperial Oil–Turofksy); 163, 170 (Graphic Artists); 173 (Imperial Oil–Turofksy); 176–177, 179–180 (Graphic Artists); 184 (Frank Prazak); 189 (Imperial Oil–Turofksy); 190 (Graphic Artists); 195 (Frank Prazak); 197, 198, 201, 203 (Graphic Artists); 206 (Portnoy); 209, 211, 214 (Graphic Artists); 216 (Portnoy); 218 (Graphic Artists); 225 (DiMaggio-Kalish); 228, 235 (Robert Shaver); 236 (Frank Prazak), 240-241 (Frank Prazak); 243 (Hockey Hall of Fame); 246, 249 (O-Pee-Chee); 250 (Miles Nadal); 254 (Hockey Hall of Fame); 256, 261, 263 (Paul Bereswill); 265 (Robert Shaver); 268 (O-Pee-Chee); 272 (Paul Bereswill); 275 (Doug MacLellan); 276 (Paul Bereswill); 279 (Chris Relke); 284 (Doug MacLellan); 289, 292 (Chris Relke); 300 (Dave Sandford); 312 (Matthew Manor); 315, 319–320, 326 (Dave Sandford); 331 (Steve Poirier); 334 (Dave Sandford); 339 (Graig Abel)

GETTY IMAGES

258 (Bruce Bennet/NHL); 296 (Colin McConnell/Toronto Star); 308 (Dave Abel/Stringer); 342 (Jamie Sabau/Stringer); 346 (Graig Abel)

GRAIG ABEL

281, 303, 304, 324; 333, 350, 353 (Graig Abel/Toronto Maple Leafs)

CITY OF TORONTO ARCHIVES

24–25 (Globe and Mail fonds, Fonds 1266, Item 9946); 44 (top) (Fonds 1266, Item 5561); 46 (John L. Brower, Fonds 1646)

OTHER

vi (bottom) "Captains Row" courtesy of Derek Shapton; 24–25 colour by Mark Truelove/Canadian Colour; 56 courtesy of Kevin Shea; 348 courtesy of the Toronto Maple Leafs

ACKNOWLEDGEMENTS

KEVIN SHEA

I am honoured beyond belief to have been selected to write *The Toronto Maple Leafs Hockey Club: Official Centennial Publication*. It is no exaggeration to state that the research and writing of this tome was absolutely the highlight of my professional life – a true labour of love that, in many ways, was a lifetime in creating.

There are so many to thank for their support and assistance in crafting this epic 100-year history of the greatest franchise in sports.

First, my writing partner, Jason Wilson – an amazing researcher and writer, and wonderful friend. This was our third book together. The outstanding team at Maple Leaf Sports and Entertainment helped us frame this project, and provided encouragement throughout. Special thanks to Mike Ferriman for his excellent suggestions and support, Steve Keogh for helping set up interviews, and the watchful eye of Brendan Shanahan, who also provided a passionate foreword. Major thank yous, too, to the editorial team that held our hands through the creation of this publication: Kimberlee Hesas and Doug Pepper at McLelland and Stewart/Random House, as well as Gemma Wain and Lloyd Davis. Immense thanks to Jordan Fenn for his vision.

So many assisted in research, and my appreciation goes to Jim Amodeo, Rick Cole, Jan Frolic and Dianne McFeeters, David Keon Jr., Jennifer Mabee, Paul Patskou, Skip Stanowski, and Eric Zweig. I must also thank Mayor John Tory for providing his foreword.

I can never properly thank Andrea Orlick, who transcribed virtually every interview that you read within this book – a tireless job and one that is largely thankless, but certainly not from me. And her ongoing encouragement was always more than welcomed.

Finally, I send my love and eternal appreciation to the greatest supporters a writer could ever hope for. My dear mother, Margaret (as big a Maple Leafs fan as anyone I know; it must run in our DNA), as well as my stepfather, Gerry England, are my biggest fans and, without official designation, my best publicists. My brother Dale and I were weaned on hockey, sitting side-by-side on Saturday evenings to watch *Hockey Night in Canada* with a glass of ginger ale and a salad bowl of potato chips to last us through the three stars. My thanks and love to you, Dale. While I lost my father in 1991, I know that no one would be more proud. My wonderful pals have also been there every step of the way since the publishing of my very first book in 2000, offering unconditional support. I thank Tim Burgess, Kim Cooke, and Steve Waxman for their friendship and for tolerating my anecdotes through the years. Finally, to my patient partner, Nancy Niklas, I send my love and thanks for enduring my long absences while locked away in front of a computer. Coffees and snacks magically appeared with great regularity, fueling my endeavour, and knowing you'd be there when I crossed the last *t* and dotted the final *i* made it all worthwhile.

JASON WILSON

I would first like to thank Elizabeth Thomson for the diligence and sound judgment she demonstrated while fixing that which needed fixing (and there certainly was an awful lot of "that"). I would like to also thank Jessica Dee Humphreys for the supreme care she took in helping to correct the more egregious of my awkward passages. I would not be blessed with the opportunity to "thank" anyone if it wasn't for Kevin Shea, who afforded me the great privilege of working on a book of such cultural importance to, well, almost everyone I know! Finally, I'd like to thank Dad for taking me to see my first Leafs game at Maple Leaf Gardens (2–1 win v. Buffalo, September 24, 1977); Mom, for believing in the Blue and White perhaps, astounding as it may seem, even more than I do; and my wife, Alana, for falling in love with the team after relocating to Ontario from her native Saskatchewan, although I confess that this is likely more a product of Carlton's irresistible charm than it is my blind faith.

AUTHOR BIOGRAPHIES

KEVIN SHEA

An accomplished hockey historian, Kevin Shea is the author of 14 books about hockey, including *Barilko: Without a Trace* (2004), *Lord Stanley: The Man Behind the Cup* (2006), *Toronto Maple Leafs: Diary of a Dynasty, 1957–1967* (2010), and Derek Sanderson's autobiography, *Crossing the Line: The Outrageous Story of a Hockey Original* (2012). In 2010, he was awarded the Society of North American Historians and Researchers Heritage Award for Outstanding Sports Writing, and in 2012, the Society for International Hockey Research presented him with the Brian McFarlane Award for Excellence in Hockey Research and Writing.

He has also contributed to the books of many others, including former prime minister Stephen Harper's *A Great Game* (2013). Shea is also the editor of publications and online features for the Hockey Hall of Fame and teaches a hockey history course at a Toronto college. His writing credits span North America, and he is a frequent contributor to television and radio shows discussing hockey. Kevin and his wife, Nancy, live in Ajax, Ontario.

JASON WILSON

Dr. Jason Wilson is a two-time Juno Awards–nominated musician and a celebrated Scottish-Canadian historian from Downsview, Ontario. An adjunct professor of history at the Universities of Guleph and Guelph-Humber, Wilson has six books to his name and has been widely published on a variety of topics including music, Canada and the First World War, and hockey. In musical terms, Wilson has released seven studio albums and has performed and recorded with, among others: UB40, Alanis Morissette, Sly & Robbie, Ron Sexsmith, Dave Swarbrick, Jackie Mittoo, and Pee Wee Ellis. Dr. Wilson and his wife, Alana, reside in Musselman's Lake, Ontario, with a variety of furry friends, wild and otherwise.

INDEX

Library and Archives Canada Cataloguing in Publication is available upon request

Published simultaneously in the United States of America by McClelland & Stewart,
a division of Penguin Random House LLC, a Penguin Random House Company

Library of Congress Control Number is available upon request

ISBN: 978-0-7710-7929-0
ebook ISBN: 978-0-7710-7931-3

Edited by Gemma Wain
Book design by Five Seventeen
Typeset in Whitman by M&S, Toronto
Printed and bound in the USA

McClelland & Stewart,
a division of Penguin Random House Canada Limited,
a Penguin Random House Company
www.penguinrandomhouse.ca

1   2   3   4   5   20   19   18   17   16